FRANKLIN'S INDIANS

Irish Motorcycle Racer Charles B Franklin
Designer of the Indian Scout & Chief

*Harry V Sucher, Tim Pickering,
Liam Diamond, Harry Havelin*

Panther Publishing

Published by Panther Publishing Ltd in 2011

Panther Publishing Ltd
10 Lime Avenue
High Wycombe
Buckinghamshire HP11 1DP
www.panther-publishing.com
info@panther-publishing.com

© Harry V Sucher, Tim Pickering, Liam Diamond, Harry Havelin

The rights of the authors have been asserted in accordance with the Copyright Designs and Patents Act 1988

If you want to provide the authors with any comments or feedback about this book, or offer additional information about Charles B. Franklin's life and achievements, or tell us where there's an old Indian motorcycle sitting in a barn that we can have for $50, then please do not hesitate to send an email to charles_b_franklin@yahoo.com or contact the authors through the publisher if you prefer.

All rights reserved, no part of this publication may be reproduced, stored in a retrieval system or transmitted, in any form or by any means, electronic or mechanical, including photocopying, digital copying, and recording without the prior permission of the publisher and/or the copyright owner.

ISBN 978-0-9564975-5-0

*When we say that he is the man who designed the Indian Scout,
that means more to Indian Riders than pages could explain.*

(Photo courtesy of the National Library of Ireland)

Dedication

To all those who toiled during the production era to achieve greatness for the Indian marque, especially George Hendee, Oscar Hedstrom, Frank Weschler, Charles Gustafson Snr and Charles Franklin, and to the present-day enthusiasts who keep the name 'Indian' alive in the public consciousness through their ownership, restoration and riding of these magnificent motorcycles.

Contents

Acknowledgements	*vii*
Foreword	*ix*
Why a book about Charlie Franklin?	*xi*

The First Great Irish Motorcycling Competitor — 1

Prologue: In the beginning	3
Birth, ancestry, and upbringing	5
Ireland in Franklin's day	8
First motorcycle	10
In competition at the dawn of motoring	16
From International Cup to Isle of Man Tourist Trophy	24
Indian gets noticed in Britain	46
Brooklands track	65
1911 – an Indian Summer	73
Charles Franklin - Indian's man in Dublin	94
Franklin goes to America	116
Franklin's competition career summary	121

American Motorcycle Designer — 129

Springfield in 1916	131
Settling in at Indian	133
Powerplus and Light Twin	144
US motorcycle competition up to 1919	153
Indian Scout – the marvel of motorcycle engineering	158
Harley vs Indian Wars 1919-22	178
Side-valve Genius	192
Chief Engineer	208
Out on a high note – Indian in British competition 1920 - 1923	211
Indian Chief – a heavy-duty plugger	232
Overhead-valve racer experimentation	240

Contents (cont.)

Indian Prince - the personal motor	252
Scout Forty-Five and the overhead-valve hill-climb motors	267
Weird scenes at the Wigwam	279
The immortal 101 Scout	289
Modernisation for the 'thirties	297
Illness and death	307
Franklin's motorcycling legacy	311
Appendix: The search for Charlie Franklin	319
Epilogue: Why any of this still matters	328
Bibliography	331
Notes	332
Index	335

Acknowledgments

We are greatly indebted to many people in several countries who were generous with their time, their knowledge, and their access to information, who made it possible to bring together the various pieces of this story about Franklin and his Indians, and who helped to improve its quality. These people include:

Northern Ireland	Patricia Buller, Jimmy Mc Dermott, Liam Mc Afee, Mittley Mc Fadden, Roisin Diamond, Tom Diamond, Kate Diamond, John Loughlin, Michael Boyle.
Irish Republic	Charlie Somerville, Paul Gorry, Joe Walsh, Ann Tuohy, Noel Ross, Rev. Denis McCarthy, Catherine FitzMaurice, Carole Mahon, Niamh D'Arcy, Ann Miller, Jonathan Bewley, Harry Lindsay, Bob Montgomery (Royal Irish Automobile Club archive), staff of the National Library of Ireland.
England	Rick Howard, Andrew Franklin, Angela Davies, Ann Nesbitt, Roger Knights, Kirsten Duffield, Maureen Hunt, Richard Rosenthal, Nick Jeffery, Tim Raindle, the late George Hendee Wells.
France	Frederic Dufrene.
Australia	Finbarr Diamond, Beverly Kropp, Marilen Hamilton, Mick Atkins, Lindsay Urquhart, Darryl Woodhouse, Valma Woodhouse, David and Marilyn Wells, Jim Parker, Leon Mitchell.
New Zealand	Malcolm Brown.
USA	Stephen Harmison, Margie Ellis, Joe Buggy, Tina Peters, David Allen Lambert, Alice Allen, Christine Hoffman, Jerry Hatfield, Daniel Statnekov, George Yarocki, Margaret Humberston, Frederick Johansen (aka RedFred), Margery Sucher, Carol Northern, Tim Graber, Richard Doherty, Timothy K Nenninger, Paul d'Orleans, Jared Zaugg.
Canada	Peter Gagan.

Photographs and Illustrations

We are very grateful to the many people and organisations who were kind enough to let us make use of their photographs. In some cases and in spite of making every effort to find the rights holders, the passage of time has made this impossible. The photographers are identified on the individual photos but some have been abbreviated to avoid too much repetition. Abbreviations used are as follows:

EMIMA	Esta Manthos Indian Motocycle Archives, Lyman and Merrie Wood Museum of Springfield History, Springfield, Massachusetts
NLI	National Library of Ireland
HH	Harry Havelin
TP	Tim Pickering
RHC	Rick Howard Collection
MMG	Mortons Media Group Archive

Foreword

My name is GEORGE HENDEE WELLS. I must tell you how I got this illustrious name. My father was Billy Wells and he was born in Maine, USA. He became a great friend of George Hendee when they were both young men through their common interest in bicycle racing, first on high wheelers and of course then on the so-called 'safety bicycles'. It followed quite naturally that when motors were added to the bicycles that MOTORCYCYLING followed. From the beginning the targets were 'speed' and 'reliability'. And so racing and trials were the main competitive arenas.

Billy was in England at the turn of the 20th century, competing with and selling Vindec motorcycles. He could not resist entering for the first Tourist Trophy (TT) race in the Isle of Man in 1907. To his ever lasting regret he was leading the field when he got three punctures in the last lap and could only claim second. But he had got the racing bug.

On his return to the USA in 1908 he contacted his old buddy Hendee who promptly said 'You are the chap to open up a branch of the HENDEE MANUFACTURING COMPANY in Great Britain'. And so it was.

The company's products proved very successful in Britain and INDIAN MOTOCYCLES gained a great reputation for 'speed' and 'reliability'. Charles Franklin of Dublin was recruited into the Tribe by my father, and soon became synonymous with Indian as a renowned racer and tuner. He ultimately became the Hendee Mfg. Co.'s design engineer, responsible for the constant stream of technical improvements. The Great Day for my father, Franklin and other Indian associates was the 1911 TT Senior Race when Indians came first, second and third. They were successful in many other events of the period.

During all this expansion of the UK Indian business I was born, and although my mother had a list of possible names my father was adamant that I should be named after his great friend.

There are always a great number of fans for successful marques, and Indian in its day was no exception. It is interesting that this band of fans is still enthusiastic although Indian Motocycles have not been made for many years. In 1995 I was invited to a convention of Indian Owners in Scotland. It was a large gathering and Indian Motocycles of all ages and types had brought their owners safely over long distances. It was an emotional time for me. That evening I was asked to give a short talk. At the end they wheeled onto the stage an Indian motorcycle and said 'This is the actual machine your father rode from London to Edinburgh in the 1,000 Mile Reliability Trial and won a Silver Medal'. It looked perfect, but the original saddle did look its age.

Then they kicked it over, and it started first go. Great!

George Hendee Wells
London, 2009

Why a book about Charlie Franklin?

Is there room in the world for another book about Indian motorcycles?

Absolutely.

Indian's motorcycle design engineer, Charles Franklin, is an enigmatic character to whom the label of 'genius' has been applied. He was a central figure in the fortunes of the Indian Motorcycle Company for many years, credited with saving the factory from early demise in the 1920s. A comprehensive account of his life and achievements has not been available, until now. It's high time he was given his due for his contributions to the sport of motorcycling.

Four of us collaborated to write this book, three of whom have been owners of Indian motorcycles. It was primarily from our standpoint as riders of these antique machines that we first approached the subject of motorcycle history.

It was from riding our Indians that we came to appreciate just how good these motorcycles really were back then, in the production era. In their day, Indian 'motocycles' were among the best available. Comparison with the contemporary models of other marques shows that, of the post-Hedstrom era Indians, the early 1920's Chiefs and Scouts in particular were design leaders of their time. Even arch-rival Harley-Davidson had to follow the trends that they set.

Nowadays in the New Millennium, sixty years after motorcycle production at the Wigwam in Springfield MA ceased, Indian Scouts and Indian Chiefs are iconic models remembered and appreciated by knowledgeable motorcyclists everywhere. This sentiment is captured in the slogan 'Old Indians never die'.

Buried in the fine-print of the glossy books so far published about Indian motorcycles, you'll find the Scout and Chief models attributed to the talents of a Charles B. Franklin. But there will not be much in the way of details. Published information about Franklin is very scanty.

Not only that, the books about Indian will only tell half of the story about Franklin. Before his emigration to the USA to join the Indian factory as a design engineer, Irishman 'Charlie' Franklin (as he was known to his friends and colleagues) had a whole other life and career as a sportsman. He was one of the foremost British motorcycle racers and speed record-breakers of the pre-WWI era.

This is the reason why the fourth collaborator in this book (HH) developed an interest in Charles Franklin, and it was sparked by a conversation he'd had with the legendary Irish road racer, Stanley

Woods. More than 20 years ago, Woods declared to HH that as much information as possible should be collected together about Franklin's racing career, 'because Franklin was the first great Irish motorcycle competitor, but this is now completely forgotten'.

Awareness about Franklin's contribution toward the shaping of motorcycling history has for the past eighty-odd years been both restricted to, and divided up between, two fairly small groups of people. The first is those people who fondly appreciate Indian motorcycles. Though staunch, they are but a small minority within the already-minority pastime of motorcycling. The second is those people who perpetuate memories of British racing at Brooklands track and the Isle of Man in the era before the First World War. Such people are nowadays a very precious few indeed, and restricted mainly to the membership of the Brooklands Society.

Add to this the fact that Franklin's greatest achievements came at a time when Indian's star position in global motorcycling was waning due to protectionist international trade politics, and the picture that emerges is one of Franklin being very much an unsung hero of motorcycling.

And yet, there is a very interesting story here. The more we dug into the Charlie Franklin story, the more strongly we felt that it ought to be shared with a wider audience. Interest in, and the prices paid for, antique American motorcycles have never been greater. The recent centenaries of the inauguration of the Isle of Man Tourist Trophy Races and the Brooklands Track have similarly sparked a resurgence of interest in the very early days of motorcycling history. The beginning of a new century and a New Millennium is the perfect time to look back upon the motoring achievements of the century and millennium just ended.

Efforts to keep the Indian name alive in connection with a new two-wheeler are still on-going, for better or worse. With genuine Indian history again in danger of being pilfered and misrepresented to lend credence to yet another ersatz product, what better time to further highlight and clarify the long-ago events that made the Indian name so illustrious in the first place?

Franklin's story is even bigger than Indian, however. His influence was felt industry-wide. Design elements he popularised were adopted by other manufacturers, in particular Harley-Davidson. Jointly with Harley-Davidson and Excelsior, he helped developed a 'look' and style of American motorcycle that persists through to the present day, echoed in a raft of 'metric cruisers' originating from the Far East.

But the full impact of Franklin's contributions to motorcycle sports and manufacturing can only be seen if the various scattered historical threads and scraps of evidence are consolidated and interpreted within a single volume. This is the task we set ourselves to do, and it's what you'll find presented here in this book.

As an historical figure in motorcycling, we can demonstrate that Charles B. Franklin is both significant and fascinating. It's been well worth writing a book about him.

If you're a person whose pulse quickens at the off-beat rumble of a big vee-twin motorcycle, or you're simply interested in the story of a genuine Irish-American hero, then this book is for you.

Harry V Sucher, Tim Pickering, Liam Diamond and Harry Havelin

The First Great Irish Motorcycle Competitor

Prologue

In The Beginning

Wind rushing past his ears, anxious that his tightly pulled-down flat-cap might fly off and be lost in the dust cloud of his wake, he hung on to the long handlebars grimly. But he didn't slow down, though. Not even for an instant. The chuffing of the engine, whose power pulses in normal use were distinct enough to be counted, now merged into a steady bubbling roar. On the other side of the dry-stone wall, sheep went careering away in panic.

This device could be tricky to manage around corners, when the dreaded 'side-slip' tendency of its tall, heavy frame threatened to fetch you off. He'd seen it happen a couple of times, and knew that if ever a machine like this fell on its side then petrol spilling from the swirl box of its 'surface carburettor' onto the hot engine could see the whole plot go up in flames. Fortunately his machine now had one of the first of the spray-type carburettors – a vast improvement.

But right now a straight road beckoned. He thumbed the tank-side lever to admit even more fuel into the carburettor, then re-adjusted its companion lever to control the amount of air, playing with the mixture until through the seat of his pants he could judge that the amount of 'pull' from the engine was strongest. While he was at it, he gave the engine another squirt of oil with the hand plunger. At this speed it would need about one squirt every two miles, and he'd forget it at his peril.

There was no instrument yet available to indicate one's speed, but a week ago on the hard beach sand of Portmarnock his younger brother had timed him with a stop-watch over a measured mile. Together they'd calculated a figure of 48 mph. Incredible! It was still widely thought the human body could not withstand prolonged exposure to such velocities.

The road surface here was a lot bumpier than the beach, and all this hopping and bucking would surely be costing him speed. Still, he must be doing at least 40. Now, he was nearing the end of the straight section. Thumbing back the throttle lever brought on a braking effect caused by the engine's own internal friction, and this got him down to a steady 'chuff-chuff-chuff' once more that would get him around the corners safely. No use operating the brake handle, it never did much more than make a few squealing noises. He again had to adjust the air lever to suit the new fuel setting. Then another squirt of the hand-oiler. One's hands were kept very busy tending to the engine-room of this beast!

Negotiating the bends in this winding stretch of roadway at a moderate pace, the rider looked for a place to turn and re-trace his route. This machine couldn't be stopped without stalling it, because the leather drive belt acted directly from the engine pulley to the rear wheel. A feet-up turn needed a lot of space because the machine was quite top-heavy, even with an engine perched as low in the frame as this one, whose front down-tube was thoughtfully divided in two to go around it. If you went too slowly so as not to capsize, the engine simply juddered to a stop.

Then the rider spied a side lane leading up a small hill. That'll do nicely! Turning gently up the slope, the engine immediately struggled and steadily lost power until it died completely. Leaping down athletically from his high leather saddle, the rider pointed the machine back downhill. Standing on one pedal whilst holding the exhaust-valve lifter forward (another of the tank-side levers), he got it rolling to a speed where he could fling his free leg over, get astride, and draw the lever back again. The sucking of the cylinder became a chuffing, and once more he was under power. Taking the corner with ease, he was back on the main thoroughfare and headed back towards town. The same long straight section awaited, and the rider anticipated another intoxicating dose of sheer speed.

But the engine gave a cough, and missed a couple of beats. It caught again, then surged and hesitated for a good several yards. His mind raced feverishly to solve the problem before a strength-sapping push re-start on the flat became necessary. Fumbling at the tank-mounted levers, he tried to find a happier air lever setting. But there was more to it this time. The pauses got longer, the chuffing got less, and then ... no sound but the crunch of gravel as he leapt off just before forward motion ceased completely.

Was there petrol? Check. Carburettor clean of dirt? It passes inspection.. Spark plug insulation? The ceramic could be extremely fragile, but such was not the answer this time. Accumulator? No acid could be seen leaking, and the wires were all intact. That only left the battery-and-coil ignition system itself, the various components of which took up several locations about the bike and engine. Trembler-coil? It could still be persuaded to give its characteristic 'buzz'. Getting out a screw-driver, he removed the cover on the end of the camshaft to reveal the timing ring. Aha! A large fragment of brass-embedded fibre material lay loose in the housing. The timing contact had broken free of its insulating ring. The rider rummaged in his over-loaded coat pockets. He had almost enough spare parts about his person to build a second motor bicycle, but of replacement timing rings he had none.

That was it. There'd be no more riding that day. Fortunately his precautionary approach to route-planning meant that the nearest railway station was only about three miles away. No use trying to pedal this thing like a normal bicycle though, because it was geared way too high. The pedals were really only there for spinning the engine to get it started from cold, while sitting stationary with the bike's rear supported by a cast-iron stand. Nope, there was nothing for it now but to push.

Which gave him time to contemplate this new addiction of his. For addiction it must surely be, to gladly suffer the danger of falling, these annoyingly frequent breakdowns, the verbal abuse and threats of physical violence from irate horse owners, and pitying looks from uncomprehending friends and loved ones as he once more returned, hours late, oily, sweaty and dishevelled, from another 'joy ride'.

Expert opinion in the motoring press of the day held that three- or four-wheeled motorised vehicles might someday have a future as practical transport, once a few of the rough edges had been designed out of them. Motor-bicycles, on the other hand, were gimmicks. The playthings of iconoclasts, who'd clearly made some kind of Faustian pact if they could stay aboard for more than five minutes without falling off or breaking down. Any product that appealed mainly to lunatics with a death-wish would fizzle out in next-to-no-time, surely?

The rider's steps as he pushed were necessarily slow and measured, and his chest heaved, but his mind was whirring. Yes, these machines did have their faults. But when they were running well, the grin-factor was immense. Practical transport be damned! This was pure sport. More exhilarating than any other he'd ever tried.

Yes, these motor bicycles are as fascinating as they are impractical. They can only get better, and faster, from here. He had a few ideas of his own about them that he'd someday like to try ....

Birth, Ancestry, And Upbringing

CHARLES BAYLY FRANKLIN was born on the 1st of October 1880 at 1 St Patrick's Villas, Whitworth Road, Drumcondra, Dublin, to Lorenzo Bruce Clutterbuck Franklin, 'shipwright', and his wife Annie Honor Wrixon Bayly.[1]

Charles was born into tragic family circumstances. Lorenzo and Annie lost four of their children to scarlatina (scarlet fever) in the space of less than a year, between December 1879 and October 1880. Jane Maude (age 12) and William Bayly (4) were both buried on the same day, 22nd December 1879, in Mount Jerome Cemetery. Five days later, on 27th December, they were joined by Robert aged 6. Lastly, Florence Annie (age 9) was buried there on 5th October 1880, only four days after the birth of Charles Bayly.[2]

Scarlet fever is a throat infection caused by streptococcal bacteria of a type that exude toxins, causing a range of symptoms including a strawberry-coloured tongue. Common complications are rheumatic fever and pneumonia. It became easily treatable after the 20th Century discovery of penicillin but, prior to the advent of modern medicine, scarlet fever was a common cause of death, or of illness needing long convalescence, and in Ireland was second only to influenza.

Despite saying 'shipwright' on his son Charles' birth certificate, during the 1890s Lorenzo Franklin's occupation was the related trade of 'iron merchant'. His 'L.C. Franklin Iron & Metal Stores' business address up until 1891 was 33 Mecklenburgh Street Lower, Dublin (this street was re-named Tyrone Street in 1887). From 1891 until his death in 1902, Lorenzo's business address was 34 Talbot Street.

Charles Franklin's ancestors included Cromwellian settlers who came to Ireland from England in the mid to late seventeenth century. His paternal grandfather Robert Franklin's wife, Jane, was the daughter of Lorenzo Clutterbuck, and Eliza Clutterbuck *née* Lane. The name Clutterbuck originated in the Low Countries. They were a family of skilled weavers who were originally invited into England by Edward III in the fourteenth century to help develop the woollen trade.[3] Other histories have stated they came to England to escape religious persecution in their native land.

The Clutterbucks first came to Ireland when Richard Clutterbuck, a 'merchant adventurer' and a member of the Mercers Company of London, was one of the Names that helped finance Oliver Cromwell's conquest of Ireland after the 1641 Rebellion. After the defeat of the Irish, huge tracts of land were taken over and given to the sponsors of the campaign. Amongst these was Richard Clutterbuck who obtained thousands of acres at Fethard in County Tipperary and at Kilrea in County Derry.[4]

Charles Franklin's grandmother, Jane Clutterbuck, was descended from this line, however her mother Eliza's maiden name was Lane. The Lanes were another prominent Plantation settler family from England with an interesting history. Again we have to go back in time to the mid seventeenth century and the aftermath of the English Civil War. After the execution of King Charles I by

Parliament, the army of his son Charles the Prince of Wales (who in normal circumstances would have automatically succeeded his father as King) were defeated by Oliver Cromwell's New Model Army at the battle of Worcester in 1651. The Prince of Wales escaped from the battlefield with parliamentarian troops in pursuit. He made his way to a 'safe house' at Bentley Hall in Staffordshire. This was the home of the Lane family, where the Prince of Wales was disguised as a servant and then, riding behind Mistress Jane Lane on a horse, he managed to get to Bristol where he escaped on a ship to France.

After the Restoration in 1661, the newly-crowned King Charles II didn't forget the loyalty shown him by the Lane family. He granted them one of the highest honours in heraldry, in the form of the Three Lions of England added as a canton (the 'Canton of England') to the Lane family coat of arms.[5] In addition, the Lanes were given one thousand acres of land at Ballygrenny in Co. Tipperary - this was subsequently renamed Lanespark. Jane Lane's brother, William came over from England to live in this newly acquired estate until his death in 1672. It is from William that Eliza Lane, Charles Franklin's great grandmother, is descended.[6]

Franklin's birthplace, No. 1 St Patrick's Villas, is a red-brick house on the corner of St Patrick's Road and Whitworth Road, at the Drumcondra Road end of Whitworth Road. It nowadays equates to 18 Whitworth Road, after a re-numbering of houses in this neighbourhood in about 1883 or 1884.[7] The house in which Charles B. Franklin was born is still standing and is in good order (see colour photo 1).

From 1887 the Franklins are listed as being at 2 Carlisle Terrace, Malahide, Co. Dublin, until 1891. After 1891 Lorenzo is not listed as having a residence in Dublin. It is possible that he moved elsewhere in Ireland, but maintained his business in Dublin. One possibility is that he moved to Clonaleenan, Co. Louth, where his recently widowed sister Mary Bailie was now sole owner of Clonaleenaghan House, situated on a 233 acre property comprising two large farms.[8]

When in his early teens, Charles reputedly contracted pneumonia and nearly succumbed to the infection, recovering only after a long period. It is possible that his pneumonia may have been a complication from his own bout of scarlet fever from which, unlike his older brothers and sisters, he nevertheless recovered and reached adulthood.[9] Besides Charles, there were two younger brothers who also reached adulthood - Lorenzo Bruce Franklin Jnr, and Rupert Fairfax Franklin.

Lorenzo Franklin Snr was sufficiently prosperous that he could send his son to a private, fee-paying school, where Charles took science and mathematics subjects. On the 13th September 1894 he was enrolled at St Andrews College, St Stephen's Green, Dublin (this college is now located in Blackrock, Co. Dublin). St Andrews was a new college and Charles was one of a small number of students who enrolled in the first year.

During his time at this school he resided at the home of his grandfather Robert Franklin, at No.8 Appian Way, Leeson Park, Dublin 4. Robert was listed with the school as Charles' 'parent/guardian', which further hints that Charles' father Lorenzo was not resident in Dublin at that time. The *Dublin Directory* shows that Wilton, 8 Appian Way was the home of Robert Franklin from 1894 until his death in 1903 aged 95. This building still stands – it is a large and impressive red-brick dwelling that is now in use as offices, located in an exclusive and expensive area of Dublin.

Charles left college on the 31st March 1898 having studied French, Chemistry, Drawing, Physics and, as was called at the time, 'General'. It isn't known how well he did in his final exams, but his results must have been good because he was accepted into the Civil Service where he began training as an Electrical Engineer. The field of electrical engineering was becoming prominent in industrial applications as well as residential, because many municipalities were at that time converting from gas illumination to electric. Charles would have completed his training and become qualified by about 1901.

Charles' mother, Annie, died at Richmond Hospital in 1898 of heart disease, at the age of 52. When signing her death certificate, husband Lorenzo now put his home address as 8 Appian Way, Leeson Park, Dublin. The death record for Lorenzo C. Franklin shows that he passed away on the 13th of May 1902 at 8 Appian Way, a widower aged 62 years, and a merchant. It also shows that Charles, by now 21 years old, still resided there. In his will, Lorenzo Snr left a total estate of £1,231-3s-9d (note this is one thousand two hundred and thirty one pounds, three shillings and nine pence in the UK currency of the time. There were 12 pennies in a shilling and twenty shillings in a pound). The Franklins were listed as being of the Church of Ireland.

Grandfather Robert outlived his son Lorenzo Snr and died on 29th December 1903 in Co. Louth leaving a considerably larger estate of £10,014-7s-0d. This decent-sized legacy, combined with Robert's stated occupation of 'gentleman' in various vital documents, indicates that he was quite well-off, either by virtue of descent from a family of 'independent means' (that is, with enough money and property that he did not need to have an 'occupation' as such) or as a result of having married well (that is, to a Clutterbuck). This was an era when, upon marriage, a woman's independent wealth and property became her husband's.

With his education and training completed, Charles gained the post of engineer at the Rathmines electrical power station in Dublin. The Rathmines Electricity Works, opened on 31st August 1900, was owned and operated by the Rathmines Urban District Council. Consisting at that time of an engine, boiler, and two sets of generating plant, the Electricity Works was located behind and slightly to the north of the Rathmines Town Hall.[10] The old buildings that used to house the Works can still be seen today at the top of Gulistan Terrace, inside a Dublin City Council recycling centre. We do not know exactly when Charles Franklin took up his post here, however the reminiscences of motorcycling contemporary Noel Drury state that by 1904 Franklin's place of work was the 'Rathmines Township Electric Power Station'.[11]

This building in Dublin was formerly the Rathmines Electric Power Station, where Charles Franklin worked as an electrical engineer until 1910. (Photo HH)

Ireland In Franklin's Day

The city of Dublin is surrounded by the beautiful Dublin mountains, and is drained largely by the Liffey and Tolka rivers of which Dubliners are very proud. By 1880 the city had greatly expanded as the better-off went out to the suburbs. Much of the old city's road surfaces were unsuitable for the new motor cars, so the cycle, be it pedalled or powered, was preferred as it was also cheaper. Working class people now occupied large swathes of the city centre. The contrasts in living conditions were huge, for example the slums in the Liberties district compared with Merrion Square. Dublin is an old settled capital city, once a Viking settlement and the most important urban centre in Ireland by the time of the 'Anglo' Norman invasion of 1170. By 1880, the year of Charles Franklin's birth, it had long been seen as central to political, social and economic life in Ireland, but it was a city of many contrasts.

Charles Bayly Franklin was born to a Protestant family in Dublin in 1880 and remained in Ireland until 1916. His life in Ireland was co-terminous with arguably the most eventful period of change that the nation had ever experienced.

Since 1869 the Anglican Church had been disestablished and the Protestant ruling elite, who had long dominated political and social life, were now under threat from the more numerous Catholic majority. The new demand for Home Rule would have served to further their insecurities and Franklin was one of their number. This would not have been evident from the lifestyles of the Protestant Ascendency, who continued to live in large houses with servants in Merrion Square or the suburbs of Sandymount or Rathfarnham. There was an active, even hectic social life of theatre, balls and various sports like rugby and cricket enthusiastically pursued, but this stood in marked contrast to life for the poor. While Dublin retained its broad streets and fine buildings and, by the turn of the 20th century, was just starting to move from gaslight to the electric era, it also contained far more destitutes, beggars, unemployed and possibly unemployable people than one would have thought possible in a modern capital city.

For while some Dubliners might claim their city as the second most important in the British Empire, in fact Dublin had still not recovered from the Irish Famine of 1845-49 which had brought thousands of people flocking to the city to find work or even the workhouse. Indeed, while the famine had caused a dramatic drop in Ireland's population, the number of people living in Dublin increased by nine percent. By the end of the 19th century the population of Dublin was approaching half a million, but twenty three percent of them were illiterate, they had the highest infant mortality rate in western Europe and huge numbers of people lived in overcrowded and unsanitary tenement rooms.

The backstreets of Dublin then stood in marked contrast to the middle and upper class areas, and new forces for political and social change were starting to emerge simultaneously with the technological developments which made the late Victorian Age so remarkable. Ireland's relationship with Britain was being questioned forcefully and new political forces such as the Home Rule Party, the Land League, the Gaelic Revival and Ulster Unionism were to interact in a manner that dominated political life at the time.

Undoubtedly, Charles Franklin would have at least taken notice of the revolutionary changes that were taking place, especially as he was a native of Dublin. In that most loquacious of cities he would have met those who remembered, or possibly have been affected by the Great Irish Famine of the late 1840s. Shortly before he was born, the Land League was formed to make a New Departure alliance of militant republicans and democratic Irish members of Parliament whose stated aim was to give Irish farmers ownership of the land. A chain of events followed which led to the 1916 Easter Rising and what is sometimes called the 'Irish Revolution'. The Land League's tactics of mass protest and boycott gave them limited success but only at a cost. Atrocity and murder became common in the countryside as landlords and their agents faced the anger of their tenants. Even in Dublin, the Chief Secretary of Ireland and his assistant were murdered in Phoenix Park, in May 1881.

The Irish Ascendancy class, to which Charles belonged was coming under increased pressure as the nineteenth century merged into the twentieth. Advocates for and against Home Rule took increasingly polarized positions and it is probable that only the intervention of the Great War in 1914 prevented a Civil War in Ireland itself.

Charles, then, grew up in a period of discord in Irish life which remains a passionate interest for professional historians and laymen alike. What makes his story remarkable is the way in which he was able to transcend these events. Charles Franklin represents another facet of life at that period for he embraced technology rather than revolution or counter revolution. The revolutions that most claimed his attention were those of a motorcycle engine running at full throttle.

The fact is that the sheer scale of political and social change during the period 1880-1916 obscures the technological progress in Ireland at the same time. The period was extraordinarily stimulating to anyone with a good technical mind. Although bicycles of different kinds had been in use before Charles Franklin's birth, it was only after 1887 that John Boyd Dunlop developed the pneumatic tyre (ironically in a desire to stop his son getting headaches while riding his pushbike). The new invention revolutionised travel as it made the already affordable bicycle comfortable as well. Cycle clubs flourished very quickly. By 1894 Annie Cohan, a young American girl, was able to set out to cycle around the world.

The bicycle had a massive social impact on Irish life long before the invention of the motorcar. Whereas working class life in the early nineteenth century had been characterised by a stultifying parochialism, by the later part of the century the bicycle had made it possible to travel much further for work, to explore new regions at will, and had helped to break down old social barriers between classes and genders. Developments in the motorcycle soon followed. Daimler and Maybach built what is arguably the first motorcycle in 1885, and by 1894 Hildebrand and Wolfmuller made the first series of motorbikes 'the Motorrad'.

Up until the outbreak of World War One in 1914, the world's leading producer of motorcycles was Indian in the USA. 1916 is usually remembered by Irish people as the year of the Battle of the Somme and the Easter Rising in Dublin. The titanic struggles on the Western Front and the start of a revolutionary movement between advanced Irish Nationalism and the British Government have tended to overshadow other very significant events of that year. Among these was the departure from Ireland of a young engineer who had already made a significant contribution to the quality of Irish life generally and was soon to have an influence on the world stage. In 1916 Charles Franklin left Ireland to take up a post at the Indian factory.

It is for this contribution to technology that Charles Bayly Franklin is justifiably remembered. While he may have lived through interesting times in Ireland, his legacy is not related to Ireland's politics but to the universal progress of transport and the sport of motorcycle racing. It is a legacy which has been too long downplayed.[12]

First Motorcycle

The earliest available evidence that the young Charles Franklin had become seriously involved with motorcycles dates from 1903, and can be found in a magazine called *Irish Cyclist*. This magazine first appeared in 1885, later evolved into *The Irish Cyclist & Motor Cyclist* with the advent of motor-bicycles, and continued to be published until 1931. In September 1903 it reported that a C.B. Franklin, riding an FN machine with forecarriage, gained 8th place in the Motor Cycle Union of Ireland (Dublin Centre) Reliability Trial from Dublin to Maryborough (Portlaoise) and back. This is the first time that Franklin's name appears in the magazine. This event was the first Reliability Trial for motorcycles ever held in the Dublin area (the first one in all Ireland took place in Ulster on the 22nd of August 1903). Charles Franklin was just nearing his 23rd birthday at this time. The full results of this and other subsequent competition events in Franklin's racing career are set out on page 121.

FN motorcycles were the products of a Belgian firm which was chiefly an armaments manufacturer. Located at Herstal (near Liege), the company's full title was the Fabrique Nationale d'Armes de Guerre. The company was known in Britain as the 'BSA' or 'Woolwich Arsenal' of Belgium. Manufacture of the motor-bicycles that came to be affectionately known as 'Herstalliones', commenced in December 1901. There had first been a prototype bicycle with 'clip-on' engine rated at about 1 hp, but the model put into production for 1902 was a 133cc model (engine dimensions of 50 x 68 mm) rated at 1¼ hp This was soon improved and expanded to 188cc (57 x 74 mm) and 2 hp for early 1903, then further updated during 1903 to 2¾ hp (70 x 80 mm, 300cc).

The engine-frame layout of the early FN singles gave them a comparatively modern look. The frame front down-tube was split to allow the engine to sit in a central and upright position, rather than forward and inclined in an under-slung position as on most other contemporary motor bicycles. Initially battery-and-coil ignition was fitted, which meant that one's ride lasted only until the battery went flat because there was no charging system. From 1904, magneto ignition was also available as an option. The FN 2¾ hp single-cylinder model remained available through 1904 to 1907, when around this time the singles became 224cc (64 x 70 mm) and 2¼ hp.

FN's interests in the United Kingdom were at that time handled by W.R. McTaggart of Dublin, the 'sole UK representative' according to period advertising. McTaggart's business was mainly as agents for Arrol-Johnston and Argyll cars. Scottish marque Argyll was at that time the most popular automobile in Ireland, with Daimler a close second. McTaggart's premises were at 102 Grafton Street, Dublin, next door to jewellers West & Son. FN motorcycles were then all single-cylinder models, but in 1905 were joined by the famous four-cylinder FN model. They were the first manufacturer in the world to offer a four-cylinder motorcycle.[13]

Irish Cyclist next reported that Franklin entered the Motor Cycle Union of Ireland (Ulster Centre) Belfast to Dublin Reliability Trial for the Canning Cup, which took place on Saturday, 10th of October, 1903 and this time he came second with a perfect score, losing no marks whatsoever. The Canning Cup was presented to the Ulster Centre by Leopold Canning, later Lord Garvagh.

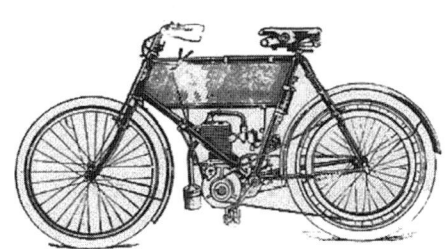

A period advertisement for the 1903 FN that Charles Franklin purchased as his first motorcycle. (Source unknown)

This was followed by another item in the *Irish Cyclist* of 28th of October, 1903, that:

C.B. Franklin, who has ridden prominently in the competitions of the Motor Cycle Union of Ireland during the past season, and who tied for first place in the Belfast to Dublin Reliability Run, made an attempt last week to beat Oswald-Sealy's recently made record from Mizen Head, in south-west Ireland to Fair Head in the north-east. He did not get beyond Mitchelstown, Co. Cork, the roads being almost unrideable in places.

An attempt on the Irish End-to-End Record in those days was not a trifling matter. As a feat of endurance, reliability and logistics it could perhaps not be placed in quite the same league as riding coast-to-coast across the USA, but even so it involved almost a day and a half of near-continuous riding on primitive roads, in Irish weather, with no assistance whatsoever for breakdowns. Even obtaining petrol en route could be a drama, because in 1903 petrol was a very scarce commodity. By choosing an End-to-End record as his target so soon after first taking up the sport of motorcycling, Franklin showed that his aim was already high.

A retrospective article on Franklin's racing career in Ireland published in *The Irish Cyclist & Motor Cyclist* on 9th June 1915 confirms that he'd bought the FN, his first machine, in 1903. For his first competition, he entered it in a hill climb held at a place called Glenamuck. The article states that this event was stopped by the police. Presumably this was because riders had breached the speed limit of 12 mph then prevailing on all public roads of the United Kingdom. A small measure of legislative relief was not long off, however. The 12 mph limit was raised by the *Motor Car Act* 1903 to 20 mph for the open road (10 mph in built-up areas) and here it stayed, viciously enforced, until 1930 in Britain and 1933 in the Irish Free State.

1903 was a huge year for motoring in the British Isles as a whole, and particularly for Ireland, because it was in this year that the Gordon Bennett Motor Cup Race for motor cars came to Ireland. It was run on a course marked out over public roads in counties Laois, Carlow and Kildare. The Gordon Bennett Cup race series was the world's premier motoring event from 1900 until 1905, at which time James Gordon Bennett, an indolent yet filthy-rich man who'd inherited the *New York Herald* newspaper, lost interest and withdrew his sponsorship. Its position in the car racing world was replaced by the Grand Prix events organised by the Automobile Club de France from this time onwards.

The 1902 Gordon Bennett Race from Paris to Innsbruck had been famously and unexpectedly won by an English motorist, S.F. Edge. The rules of the event stipulated that the winner's home nation had the right to host next year's race. This posed a major problem for organisers of the 1903 race because, unlike on the Continent, officialdom in Britain frowned upon the very idea of motor cars. The maximum speed limit throughout the British Isles was only 12 mph, and it was illegal to use public roads for the purpose of motor racing.

The problem was solved by bringing the race to Ireland, where local authorities, the general populace, and (crucially) Earl Dudley, Lord Lieutenant of Ireland, all enthusiastically recognised the benefits to the local economy of such a draw-card event for tourists. It still required a special Act of Parliament at Westminster, duly introduced by motoring enthusiast the Hon. John Scott-Montagu MP (father of the present Lord Montagu of Beaulieu) to enable closure of selected public roads in Ireland for use as a motor racing course, and to exempt motor cars driving around the prescribed course from application of the national speed limit on the day of the race. This was supported unanimously by all of Ireland's political parties. When the *Light Locomotives (Ireland) Bill* came to the House of Lords for debate, Lord Spencer commented that this was the first occasion on which all members of both Houses of Parliament had ever been in harmony on anything to do with Ireland.

The race was duly run on 2nd July 1903 and was a huge success for all concerned, except maybe for Selwyn Edge, for the race was won not by him but by Mercedes-driving Camille Jenatzy. Thousands of visitors came to Ireland for the race, many bringing over their own private motor cars to tour the Irish countryside afterwards. Ireland only had 300 motor cars in total at that time, but this number swelled to 1,500 during the race period.

Other motoring events were organised all over Ireland during the two-week period surrounding the main race, known officially as 'Automobile fortnight in Ireland'. These events made the most of the opportunity to promote motor sport, and to provide more attractions for visitors. They brought in entries by top competitors from outside of Ireland. One such event was a Speed Trial, for both motor cars and motorcycles, held in Dublin's Phoenix Park over a measured standing-start mile followed by a flying-start kilometre on the long straight road from Mountjoy Corner, past the Phoenix Monument to the Gough Monument. During this Trial, a new world Land Speed Record for the kilometre was set at 84 mph Another event that also included motorcycles in the programme was a hill-climb at Castlewellan, Co. Down.

The timing is such that Charles Franklin's new-found interest in motoring competition can most likely be attributed to the huge publicity generated in Ireland by the Gordon Bennett Fortnight's momentous motoring events. If Charles Franklin had already 'ridden prominently' in competition 'during the past season' of 1903, as reported by *Irish Cyclist* at the end of October, then it's likely that he acquired his first motorcycle, and his taste for winning, at least by the middle of that year, if not sooner. On the other hand, he is not listed among the entries of motorcyclists for the Phoenix Park Speed Trials. This implies that he either did not yet own a machine or he couldn't yet ride it properly, because otherwise he would surely have wanted to take part.

Another factor leading to him taking up motorcycling at this time may have been his commencement of paid employment at the completion of his engineering studies in 1901. By 1903 Franklin had already been working for a year or more, and possibly had just gained a promotion, or at least more secure employment, by leaving the service of a private-sector electrical contractor to join a local authority electrical power generation facility as a civil servant. This would presumably have provided him with the means to indulge in the expensive and somewhat 'wacky' new pastime of motor-bicycling. His wherewithal in this regard was further increased upon the passing of his father Lorenzo Snr in 1902 and his grandfather Robert in 1903, from whom Charles received legacies amounting to around £1,000 each.[14]

To get a feel for the impact that indulging in motorcycling might have on one's social status during those early days of motoring, we can turn to that *doyen* of the early motorcycle journalists 'Ixion' (revealed in later life to be a clergyman, Canon Basil Davies) who, under this pen-name, wrote a regular and influential column in *The MotorCycle*. In 1920 and 1927 he wrote a two-volume set of books entitled *Motor Cycle Reminiscences* which remains one of a very few first-hand accounts of pioneer motorcycling in existence, and the only one where the author's scope was far wider than merely technical. Ixion's books provide us with a social commentary of those times, and have merit as works of literature, in addition to being very informative about the early motorcycles. He offers us the following summary about what motorcycling was like in the pioneer era, and why on earth anybody would want to indulge in such a mad-cap pursuit:

> Our weird hobby seemed to be without excuse or justification: it veneered us with a permanent grime which exceeded every known form of filth alike in squalor and in adhesiveness. The uncertainty of being able to start on a journey was only exceeded by the improbability of our ever reaching our destination in the saddle. We were unquestionably doomed to spend long hours by the roadside, under conditions that ranged from grilling sun to a frosty night, from desperate solitude to a seething mob.
>
> Such times of penance were usually devoted to the identification of some mystic ailment which afflicted our machines. The odds in the first place were heavily against our being able to trace the trouble; in the second place the betting was equally strong against our being able to remedy it, if found.
>
> There were no garages; the longest push could only bring us to the door of some ambitious cycle repairer, more ignorant and less cautious than ourselves.
>
> When it rained, we side-slipped and got drenched, for our machines were woefully top-heavy, and the modern dreadnought clothing was not dreamt of. In winter we suffered from frostbite. In summer our engines over-heated. Our belts slipped and broke and pulled through without partiality under all conditions; the slip which they developed in wet weather was not more habitual than the glaze from which their leather suffered when roads were dry and dusty. Most of us were ex-cyclists; but such a hideous past was no palliation of our folly. We could not claim that motorcycles were faster than pushbikes; we often covered a few miles at a speed which was then regarded as suicidal - say 24 miles an hour or so; but from beginning to end of a cross-country journey the prehistoric motorcycle was generally slower than a scissors-grinder's handcart. We could not claim that we preferred the motorcycle for hill work; for the main difference between it and the pushbike where gradients were concerned, was that the latter was very distinctly easier to push. Economy could be no factor in our inexplicable conduct. A new machine might easily cost £75 to buy. Its repair bill was long enough to stagger a munition magnate, and it was out-of-date soon after it had been delivered.
>
> But the bother we used to cause! Pedestrians twisted round in their tracks when we were half a mile away. People ran to their windows to stare. Only a very Prussian foreman could keep his hands at work when the unaccustomed *'tuttatutta'* in slow time was audible in the road. Presently the public decided, as it always does, that a new noise was an intolerable nuisance. Jeers or scowls became our portion. We knew what it was to have an elderly stranger shake his fist at us in front of an empurpled and twitching countenance. Even our nearest and dearest could furnish up no sort of defence for us. As far as was possible they hushed up our delinquencies, and spoke of our insane hobby behind closed doors and with bated breath, much as if we had cheated at cards or made an unsuitable marriage.
>
> The uplift beneath motorcycling in those early days must have been equivalent to a religion, or we should never have borne its manifold disagreeables as we did. It was derived from three motives. Some of us were engineers; we may hardly have believed in the ultimate road possibilities of a featherweight high-speed engine, but even if we privately regarded the machine as a product of Bedlam, it was certainly an amusing little

toy. Others gambled on its commercial possibilities. Others, again, were adventurers, pure and simple. When there is no war on, no filibustering in South America, no uncharted islands to explore, this land of policemen and accurate maps and black coats on Sundays is apt to bore a certain type of temperament. The purchase of a motorcycle imported a spice of risk and uncertainty and Bohemianism into such a life.

So we were not quite as mad as we seemed, though we were unquestionably odd. The proof of the pudding is in the eating. Somehow or other we stuck to our job or our hobby during the years which motorcycling spent in the 'teething stage.' We have reaped our several rewards. The men who came in because of technical interests have travelled farther than their dreams - many of them are leading lights in aviation nowadays. The cycle agent who hoped to double his annual turnover very probably owns acres of garages ere this. The sporting youngster has a cabinet full of medals, and what is worth more than ten sideboards full of cups - a memory richly packed with reminiscences of effort, peril and fun, which may serve to keep his heart young when his limbs are stiff with age and rheumatism. So I pass on to some assorted memories, linking the dim age of the pioneer motorcyclists to these times in which the machine threatens to become disgustingly utilitarian.

Because so few of Franklin's own words have been recorded for posterity, we are often forced to indulge in speculation when we search for reasons about why he did many of the things he did. In this instance however, we do have a direct quote. The 17th of October 1906 issue of *The Motor Cycle* carried a feature article entitled 'Autobiographies of Motorcyclists', in which a certain C.B. Franklin had this to say:

> I became a motorcyclist, as I recognized the possibility of obtaining a great deal of exciting sport out of the motor cycle, as well as deriving a lot of pleasure studying its details and trying to get the most out of the engine, so satisfying my engineering tastes.
>
> I am a member of the Auto Cycle Club, and a vice-president of the Motor Cycle Union of Ireland. My successes include twenty-five first prizes, six second, and three third. My favourite touring ground is undoubtedly the South and West of Ireland, both on account of the scenery and the hospitality of the people. Unfortunately, the roads are not all one could desire, but the above compensates for their roughness.
>
> At present I ride a twin-cylinder JAP machine, 85 x 85, and do not find it difficult to manage in traffic. Also a 3 hp Triumph, which latter machine is certainly the most comfortable touring machine I have yet ridden, but I like more power. I am no believer in the ultra light weight pedal-assisted motor bicycle.

Although brief, this statement is quite revealing. In terms of the three possible motives provided to us by Ixion, Franklin scores solidly in two of them. He was an engineer who found the workings of motorcycles fascinating. And he was an 'adventurer', or 'sporting youngster'. Although he uses a gentlemanly turn of phrase - 'I recognized the possibility of obtaining a great deal of exciting sport' - in modern-day slang we'd simply say that he was a speed freak, or a petrol-head. Hence, 'I like more power'.

In other words, Franklin enjoyed riding. He enjoyed riding fast. And he liked to cross the finish line first. Mild-mannered off the track, one can well imagine him getting a steely glint to his eye each time he rolled his machine up to a start line alongside other motorcycling competitors. 'Ixion' elaborates upon this 'adventurer' motive, and chooses words which, to this day, perfectly express the reasons why anyone would put up with the inconvenience and approbation of being a motorcyclist.

Pleasures of Motorcycling: Recreation Combined with Health
The motorcycle never fails to blow the cobwebs out of a stuffy brain. An hour in the saddle, and the week's work simply ceases to exist, whilst the entire body is oxygenated more entirely than a week at Brighton could do it. As a healthy distraction for busy men past their first youth, the motorcycle has no equal …

Nor should its independence be forgotten. Gloomy deans do not lie when they emphasize the slavery of life in an overcrowded democracy. The stoker may call himself a wage-slave. He is rather less of a slave than the millionaire with delicate interests in six continents and a dozen industries, less of a slave than the rising young doctor with four children to educate and an ambitious wife. On the road our intrinsic slavery is forgotten. We may go where we will, and - except in Surrey - we may go as fast as we please. The willing machine between our knees is our slave, and we are its king. Nobody except a policeman can command our obedience, and even police authority does not extend beyond the next corner unless fate should have placed a second bobby there. During these brief hours in the saddle we be free men; and we like the taste of it.

That pretty much works for us. How about you?

A beautifully restored 1903 FN (Photo courtesy of Leon Mitchell)

In Competition At The Dawn Of Motoring

There was not a whole lot of motorcycle 'racing' going on in the British Isles in the period up until 1905. The main focus of competition was on reliability, and fuel economy. Only when the machines of the day could show themselves capable of actually making it to the finish line did speed-oriented events become more predominant. Racing on roads was in any case illegal in Britain. Racing on tracks was not conducted by motorcycles so much as by bicycles, which had been a boom industry over the previous two decades so racing was well supported. Much could be gained by bicycle manufacturers from the publicity of race wins and record speeds. The main role of motorcycles in track racing was therefore as pacers – mobile windbreaks that preceded the pedalling cyclist around the track, enabling them to 'slip-stream' and reach even higher speeds.

There was a wooden board track for bicycle racing at Canning Town in London: Crystal Palace was another venue. Paris had its Parc des Princes track, where huge V-twin motorcycles were evolved with over 2,000cc capacity and rated at 20 hp. In London there were sometimes special races held for the pacers in between cycle events. Two men in particular, Harry and Charlie Collier, stood out in these early competitions. They were the sons of the owner of the company making 'Matchless' machines in Plumstead, London, and they were self-taught engineers who could also ride.

Meanwhile, slightly earlier (1899) in New York City, another young bicycle competitor and self-taught engineer had built his own pacer machine. He felt it necessary to improve upon the De Dion models imported in late 1898 to assist in competition at bicycle tracks like Madison Square Gardens and Springfield Coliseum. His name was Oscar Hedstrom, and his device impressed a bicycle manufacturer and former competitor from Massachussetts named George Hendee. This will later become very relevant to our plot.

After the Irish Gordon-Bennett race for cars in 1903 and the ensuing car and motorcycle speed trials in Phoenix Park, awareness about the good publicity generated by race results, and the first stirrings of the motto 'racing improves the breed', began to filter through to British manufacturers. But at the time it was left mainly to a few enthusiasts to try, as private citizens, to promote racing in the face of a hostile Establishment.

Ireland has apparently never been short of such enthusiasts. A group of them gathered in Dublin's Hotel Metropole on 7th March 1902 with the relatively modest aim of forming a local motorcycle club. Two weeks later they adopted a far more ambitious plan, and established instead the Motor Cycle Union of Ireland. First paid-up member was William McTaggart, the motor and cycle dealer who in the following year sold Charlie Franklin his first motor bicycle. The first President of the MCUI was one John Boyd Dunlop, inventor of the pneumatic tyre that had enabled the whole bicycle craze to get going in the first place. The first MCUI Captain was Richard

Mecredy, publisher of *Irish Cyclist*, the magazine in which vital snippets about Charles Franklin's early motorcycling career came to be documented.

Competition events organised by the MCUI in these early days were usually either timed hill-climbs, such as at Glenamuck in South County Dublin, or social runs where the object was simply to get somewhere and then get back again. Word soon spread, and it was not long before an Ulster Centre was established by MCUI's Belfast members.

MCUI then got into a fight with the Irish Cyclists Association (ICA), who controlled bicycle competitions in Ireland and naturally viewed the motor-bicycle as another species of the same genus. This turf war was finally resolved in MCUI's favour in early 1903.

The next high point for MCUI came when it was invited to help out with the organisation of the 1903 Gordon Bennett race. Richard Mecredy, through his car interests (he was also publisher of *The Motor News*) had, among other things, been instrumental in helping to find a suitable course over which to stage the race in Ireland. MCUI members were given roles as race marshalls and as despatch riders. No doubt they also entered the Phoenix Park Speed Trial organised two days later by the Irish Automobile Club (IAC), and pitted their mounts against those of visiting English riders.

In September 1903 the Dublin Centre of MCUI ran its first Reliability Trial. It is in connection with this event that the name 'C.B. Franklin' first appears among the published results of a motorcycle competition (he came 8th). For a full summary of Franklin's competition career see page 121.

Reliability trials took place on public roads, and competition rules strongly discouraged riders from breaking the 20 mph speed limit. Riders needed to maintain a set average speed over a course, and pass by several check points where their arrival times were recorded. Participants lost marks for arriving too early or too late. To win, one had to ride consistently rather than quickly. Success entailed careful machine preparation to avoid losing time through breakdowns or punctures. The competitor who achieved the lowest petrol consumption while maintaining an average speed of 20 mph (in other words, while riding as fast as legally possible) received an additional prize. Perhaps viewed as somewhat tame nowadays, but at the time a reliability trial could be a severe test of the capabilities of both rider and machine.

In early 1904 the Irish Automobile Club, mindful of the huge success of the Speed Trials held at Phoenix Park in July 1903, sought permission from the authorities to close the same road again and hold another, similar event in 1904. This was firmly declined. *The Light Locomotives (Ireland) Act* 1903, the only piece of legislation in the entire nation which provided a mechanism to legally close public roads for racing, had been a definite one-off. It contained a clause of 'self-repeal' in which the Act was deemed to remain in force only until the end of 1903.

Doubtless still intoxicated by the heady 40 mph plus speeds achieved by motorcycles in the 1903 event, the MCUI were not inclined to take this refusal lying down. A Mr R.W. Stevens suggested a speed trial be held on the Silver Strand at Portmarnock. On Saturday the 23rd of April 1904 a group of MCUI members rode out to Portmarnock, a seaside village about eight miles from Dublin, where a long wide beach runs from there back down the coast toward Howth Head. This beach is popularly known as the Silver Strand, or 'Velvet Strand' for the soft powdery quality of its sand. Upon arrival the MCUI group assessed the suitability of the Strand as a venue for speed trials, by the simple expedient of whizzing up and down it several times. Among the 20 riders who took part was C.B. Franklin. *Irish Cyclist* reported that 'a number of trials were indulged in to test the suitability of the venue. C.B. Franklin, on a new FN, travelled remarkably fast'. A consensus was quickly reached that, in both practical and legal terms, the Velvet Strand at Portmarnock would make an excellent venue for speed events.

Portmarnock beach racing in 1904. Franklin (2¾ hp FN) is in the centre, with number 46 visible on his back. Nearest the camera is Oswald Sealy, who was also a champion bicyclist. (Photo courtesy Jonathan Bewley Collection)

The Dublin Centre of MCUI held its annual general meeting on 29th April 1904 at the Dolphin Hotel. Three new members were elected to the committee - J.G. (Jack) Drury, C.A. Summers and C.B. Franklin - 'all enthusiastic motorcyclists who have consistently supported the Union in all its competitions'.

The first motorcycle speed trials on Portmarnock Strand, organised by the Dublin Centre of the MCUI, took place on Saturday 14th May 1904. This event was a first in motoring history, being the first occasion upon which motor racing had taken place on sand in the British Isles. The timed trials were held over a distance of one mile, from a standing start.

In later life one of the competitors, Noel Drury (brother of Jack), wrote out by hand a set of notes that described his recollections of Irish motorcycle competition in these early times, and these were published in a VMCC newsletter in 1980. Even after the passage of some sixty-odd years, Drury was able to recall the names of most of the runners in the racing held at the Strand on that very first day of competition. This who's-who of Irish speedsters in 1904 is listed on page 122.

Drury added the comment that Oswald-Sealy, who was a well-known racing bicyclist, used a very high pedalling gear and was thus able to help his engine for almost the whole of each lap. *Irish Cyclist* on 25th May 1904 reported that:

C.B. Franklin, who rode so successfully in the speed trials of the Motor Cycle Union of Ireland at Portmarnock on Saturday week, is one of the cleverest manipulators of a motor bicycle in Dublin. An electrical engineer by profession, he takes the keenest interest in his machine, and he invariably has it at 'concert pitch'. Last year he went through the Belfast to Dublin trial without a stop, and he did creditably in the Dublin to Maryborough and back event. He made an attempt on Oswald-Sealy's end-to-end record in October last, but the weather stopped him. He still has ambitions in that direction.

Copies of the *Irish Cyclist* held by the National Library of Ireland in Dublin provide a record of other MCUI-organized events in 1904 (and subsequently), such as the MCUI Reliability Trial for the Canning Cup held from Dublin to Belfast on Saturday 4th June 1904. Billed as the 'Inter-branch Contest: Ulster v. Dublin Centre', the event was run over 96 miles starting from Tolka Bridge, Drumcondra, at 1.00 pm The route headed north through Swords, Balbriggan, Drogheda, Dunleer, Dundalk, Newry, Loughbrickland, Banbridge, Dromore, Hillsborough, Lisburn and Belfast. The finish was at Finaghy Schoolhouse Bridge, the southern terminus of the Belfast City tramlines. The following description of road conditions was given to contestants on their route card:

> Characteristics of the road: Telegraph and telephone wires run along the road all the way from Dublin to Belfast. Those who do not know the road will find the wires a good guide outside the towns. The first 12 miles from the start are bad, and mostly uphill. The road improves towards Balbriggan, and is better still towards Drogheda. There is a long hill (Tullyesker) between Drogheda and Dunleer. The road is undulating between Dunleer and Castlebellingham; flat from the latter town to Dundalk. From Drogheda to Dundalk the surface is good. From Dundalk to Newry it is also good. There is a steady rise out of Dundalk and a steep drop into Newry. From Newry to Hillsborough the road is excellent, mostly steam-rolled. From Hillsborough to the finish it is very bad.

C.B. Franklin, on his FN, was one of the 11 members of the Dublin Centre team, who rode Singer, Triumph, Quadrant, Riley, Brown, Bowden, James and FN machines. Dublin beat the 8-person Ulster Centre team to win the Canning Cup, and their top performers were T. W. Murphy (Singer), A. Summers (Triumph), H. A. Evans (Singer), and C.B. Franklin (FN), who did non-stop runs and each scored a perfect 100 marks. For Ulster, Hamilton (Ormonde), Denby (Riley) and Holden (Rover) each scored 100 marks.

The first Canning Cup event, named for MCUI Ulster Centre president Leopold Canning, had been run from Belfast to Dublin on 10th October 1903 and on that occasion was won by the Ulster team. Even so, Charles Franklin had tied for 1st place in this inaugural Trial. Dublin won the event again in 1905 and, by winning two times in a row, became perpetual holders of the Canning Cup.

Franklin continued to be among the front-runners in speed trials held at Portmarnock on the 11th June and 23rd of July 1904, as detailed on page 122. From the initials R.F. Franklin among the place-getters, it appears that Charles had allowed his teenaged brother Rupert Fairfax to have a go on his cherished FN. There was an incident at the start of Intermediate weight Class A when A. Summers fell, almost bringing down R.F. Franklin who was starting with him.

Noel Drury's notes describe something of the atmosphere of the sand-racing events held at Portmarnock.

> In these early days of motor cycling we had various forms of competition nearly every week-end. Every Saturday during the summer when the tide was at full ebb we had races on the sands at Portmarnock. One mile was measured out with a surveyor's chain, and a large blue flag fixed to a post driven down into the sand at each end. One of the first effects noticed when racing at sea level was that a larger jet was required owing to the denser air. The air inlet to the carburettors had no sort of filter, so something had to be contrived to keep out the sand which was driven along by the wind. A rough system of handicapping was

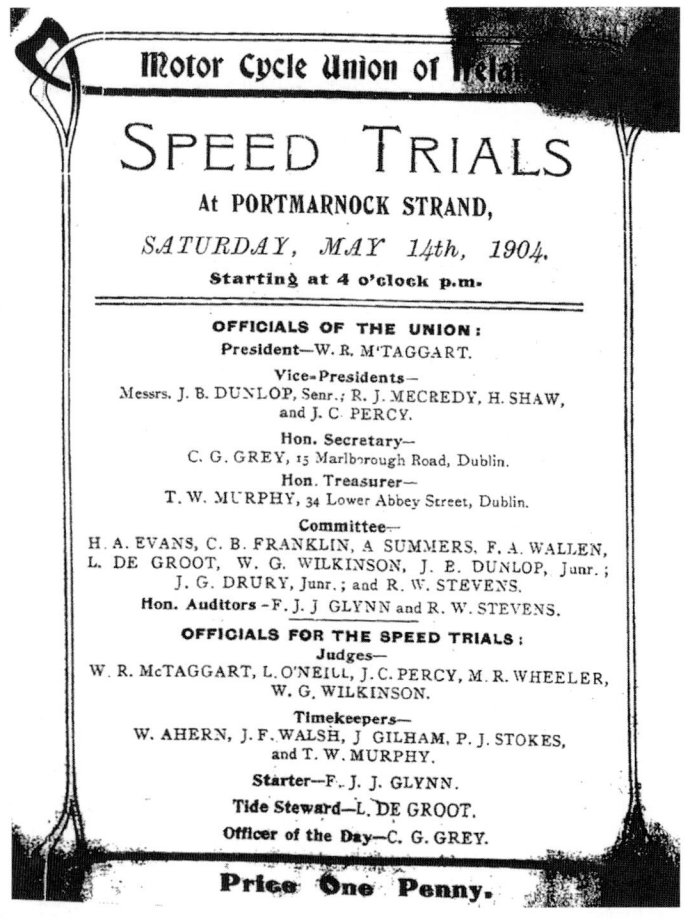

Portmarnock race programme, 1904. (Courtesy Jonathan Bewley Collection)

gradually evolved, mainly by T. W. Murphy, the time-keeper, and great fun was always had. Among those who seemed to get the best results from any machine he happened to have was Charles B. Franklin, who was one of the staff of the Rathmines Township Electric Power Station. The speed which he got from a 2¾ hp FN was astonishing. Hampden Shaw, the architect, rode a fine 3 hp Excelsior with considerable success.

Sometimes trade men used to come over from England to race and we considered this a great compliment to our organisation. I remember J. F. Crundall bringing over a very fast Humber and in his first race over 20 miles he worked out a considerable lead, so he thought it would make a spectacular finish if he slowed down a bit. He kept switching off and on with his handlebar switch until suddenly it stopped working and he was left stranded two miles from the finish, and had to push home! Frank Hulbert of the Triumph Cycle Co., Coventry, came over once or twice and he was a charming fellow.

The only way down on to the sand was a rough track between the Martello tower and Mr. W. G. Jameson's place, and it was usually blocked with about two feet of soft sand so that getting the machines up on to the road after the racing was over took three or four men to push each machine. In those days the road stopped at this point, and there was a footpath round the coast to Malahide, no cycles being permitted to use it.

The cleaning of the machines after an afternoon's races on the sand was quite a big job, for the sea water and sand got into every crevice and if left there serious corrosion soon set in. Sometimes we were driving almost through the incoming tide if any delay occurred in starting the races. The V-belt drive in use then was wont to slip badly if wet got on it, and one always hoped that centrifugal force would throw off the wet before it got on to the side gripping surface. After much trial it was found that an angle of 28° for the driving pulley was the best compromise between a wedging-in of the belt coupled with loss of power pulling it out again, and a more open angle which liberated the belt easily on the slack side, but did not transmit the power well.'

On Tuesday 2nd August the MCUI held a Dublin-Waterford Reliability Trial over a distance of 200 miles from the Custom House in Dublin to Waterford and back to a finish point at Inchicore, in which both Charles Franklin and brother Rupert obtained perfect scores.

Only three days later, on Friday 5th August 1904, C.B. Franklin made another attempt on the Irish end-to-end record. This time, he succeeded in breaking it. He started in the wee hours of Friday morning and rode throughout that day, and for most of the following night, to set a new time of 31 hours 30 mins. The record had been held by Oswald-Sealy since the previous year, at 32 hours 49 mins. Franklin's achievement was reported in the *Irish Cyclist* of 10th August 1904.

Franklin had set off on his FN from Rock Island, Mizen Head, Co. Cork, at 1 am on early Friday morning. His departure was timed by an officer at the Coastguard Station. He arrived in Skibbereen at 2.10 am At Drimoleague, rocks on the road damaged his front wheel rim and he lost half an hour making the machine road-worthy again. Arriving in Bandon at 3.30 am, he found his spare petrol tin had burst and all had leaked out. He was unable to get a supply in Bandon, however he got some paraffin which got the machine to Cork city. He made it to Cork at 6.30 am, and lost a further half-hour there looking around for petrol. He made Fermoy at 8.30 am and Mitchelstown at 9.10 am A tyre burst at Lyttleton and he lost another hour repairing it. He arrived at Maryborough (now called Portlaoise) at 2.15 pm, then a spark plug flew out at Monasterevin. Next was Dublin at 4.40 pm and Drogheda at 7.05 pm, whereupon a tyre burst again and he lost half-an-hour repairing it. Dundalk 8.20 pm, and Newry 9 pm, then the heavens opened and heavy rain fell from there until the end of the journey. Franklin reached Lisburn at 11 pm and Glenavy, Co. Antrim, at midnight. Here the floods were very bad and the rain fell in torrents. Franklin failed to get into any of the houses or the hotel in the village, but Rev. Mr Clarke, the Methodist minister, invited him in and he stayed there from 1.45 am until 5.00 am He then left for Antrim, losing his way for a while but arriving at 6.45 am. After Antrim finally came Ballycastle at 8.30 am. His overall time was 31 hours 30 mins, beating the 1903 record set by Oswald-Sealy by 1 hour and 19 minutes.

Motor cars came to the Silver Strand at Portmarnock on Tuesday 6th and Wednesday 7th September 1904, when the Irish Automobile Club decided to join in the fun and organise an event combining car and motorcycle speed trials. Quality entries were attracted from other parts of the British Isles, and there was a good turnout of around 10,000 spectators. Motoring historian Bob Montgomery described the racing thus:[15]

> The course was a measured mile with several cars racing abreast and a further quarter mile allowed for the cars to stop after crossing the finishing line. The greatest interest was in the contest for the IAC Challenge Cup for racing cars weighing not more than 19 cwt. In the first heat Arthur Rawlinson drove his Darracq to a win over the mis-firing Mors of CS Rolls (later of Rolls-Royce fame).
>
> Algy Lee Guinness, making his debut in what was to prove a most distinguished motor sport career, took the second heat, again in a Darracq, beating the Napier of Mark Mayhew. The third heat fell to a Napier driven by Arthur MacDonald (in the absence of SF Edge), who beat Maurice Egerton's Panhard, one of the cars which had competed so well in the Gordon Bennett Race the previous year. Rolls, Lee Guinness and MacDonald lined up for the final and this time the winner by some 15 yards was the Napier of MacDonald, with Rolls claiming second and Lee Guinness third.

After the official events, several 'match' races were held over a flying kilometre. This time it was Arthur Rawlinson's Darracq which ran out the winner over the similar car of Algy Lee Guinness. Rawlinson had the fastest speed of the meeting - an average 77.62 mph.

Over the following years Portmarnock was used several times by the motor cycle fraternity but 1904 remained the only occasion on which cars raced there apart from two poorly supported events in 1930 and 1931.

The motorcycle classes of the Portmarnock Speed Trials (Irish Automobile Club) of 6/7 September 1904 produced results that were now becoming increasingly familiar: Class A (Wheatley Challenge Bowl) - 1st C.B. Franklin (FN); Class B - 1st C.B. Franklin (FN). Class C - 1st C.B. Franklin (FN). Class D - 1st C.B. Franklin (FN). The *Irish Cyclist* report of this event went as follows:

> Franklin's performances on the 2.75 hp FN were a remarkable display. He got away well, knew how to place his pedalling with best effect, and attained a speed unapproached by the other competitors. The unique feature of his performance was that he repeated his successes to the end, and thoroughly deserved the credit of a splendid all-round exhibition.

We do not have available to us any description of what Charles Franklin's 2¾ hp FN motorcycle was like to ride. If he ever wrote any memoirs or recollections of his early days in motorcycling, they have not survived. All we are left with are tantalizing but brief 'sound bites' published in the motorcycling press such as *Irish Cyclist* or the English magazines *The Motor Cycle* and *MotorCycling*. This makes Noel Drury's scribblings even more valuable. Although he rode an early Triumph rather than an FN, Drury's description of operating it while in motion cannot be too far removed from what Franklin himself experienced.

> The first machine which I owned was a secondhand Triumph with a two horsepower Minerva engine (a Belgian make) having a 'surface' carburettor. This system of carburetting the air was a very economical one, although quite unknown to present day motorists. The motor cycle tank of those days fitted the diamond of the cycle frame and consisted of four sections. On the top level of the tank were the main petrol supply and a place for the battery, or accumulator, as it was usually called. Under this were two other spaces, one with a quantity of petrol, and the other with a supply of engine oil. The lower petrol compartment was kept approximately half full by the driver letting down from time to time a 'topping up' supply from the top tank, the level being indicated by a cork float attached to a wire running up a tube through the upper tank.
>
> There was a pipe from the inlet valve of the engine up the outside of the tank to a barrel throttle on the tank top and thence down to the bottom. When the engine was revolved air was sucked down a pipe into the lower tank where it collected a very concentrated amount of petrol gas when this reached the tank-top throttle. There was an air inlet controlled by a lever, this air corrected the over-rich gas, and the correct mixture then flowed down to the engine. Sometimes the down coming air was brought below the surface of the petrol and allowed to bubble up through it. These throttle and air lines on the tank top required constant handling, as each change of speed or gradient needed throttle movement, and this in turn required air adjustment. One's hands were kept busy! One was compelled to ride at a very steady speed owing to this slow method of engine control, but the result was extreme economy in petrol consumption.

During this period from 1903 through to 1907, it can be seen that motorcycle competition in Ireland was a relative hive of activity. The Irish Gordon Bennett Cup race in 1903 had given the local motoring scene a lot of impetus, not just in Ireland but throughout the British Isles. The Lord Lieutenant of Ireland's innovative Vice-Regal Tour of Connemara in 1902 aboard two Panhard automobiles and a Mors was similarly seen as a historical motoring milestone, because it was the first occasion on which the newly fangled and much-resented motor car was seen as receiving any kind of official blessing from an otherwise fanatically horsey Establishment. These events meant that, in motoring terms, Ireland was by no means a provincial backwater.

Continental countries like France and Belgium were at that time the dominant force both in motorcycle manufacture and in racing. This was mainly because road racing was allowed in those countries. Motoring historians from the days of Ixion to the present have been unanimous in their view that the stresses and strains of racing, especially road racing, provide the quickest way to expose and rectify any weaknesses in a motoring product. In Britain, the motor industry's development was lagging behind that on the Continent or in the USA. A major factor in this was that there was hardly anywhere to race without running foul of the law.

Charles Franklin and his happy band of fellow MCUI members in Ireland, on the other hand, were able to go down to the Silver Strand almost every Saturday and run with their throttles open wide. This must have made them the envy of many enthusiasts on the other side of the Irish Sea.

Franklin was by now widely acknowledged as the first big star of Irish motorcycle competition. He'd been consistently winning right from the start of his competition career in 1903, and had become the most successful Irish motorcyclist of his time.

This success could be attributed both to his skills as a rider, and to his mechanical abilities. Of his qualities as a motorcyclist, an *Irish Cyclist and Motor Cyclist* retrospective article of 1915 had this to say.

> Originally trained as an electrical engineer, to which profession he devoted his attention until he entered the motor cycle industry, Franklin was much sought after in the early days of the pastime by his friends who possessed motor bicycles. Those were the days when electrical knowledge was of the greatest value. The ignition was the part of the machine that called for constant attention, and as most of us knew very little of the mysteries of primary and secondary circuits, condensers, coils, etc., we took our troubles to Franklin in the sure and certain hope that he would be able to find the cause of the trouble that mystified us. Nor did we go in vain. Many of Franklin's friends consulted him in this way in the early days, and he got a good deal of riding on crocks that the owners could not make go.

The same article also described his performances in competition on the Silver Strand at Portmarnock, his main stamping ground in this early phase of his career.

> Franklin was amongst the competitors (of the first event in 1904), and bringing his machine to the post in the perfect tune that we have since come to regard as a matter of course, he made an impression that is remembered today. Since then Franklin has been a regular competitor at the races on the sands, and it is rarely, indeed, that he does not win one or more events. In fact, his persistent successes at one time looked like killing all interest in the racing at Portmarnock. If one were to be asked for the cause of his consistent success the answer would be in his painstaking attention to detail. He invariably brings his machine to the post in apple-pie order, and if he fails to finish in a race one may safely bet, without making enquiries, that the cause was due to something beyond his control.
>
> Franklin's successes at Portmarnock are literally without number. Perhaps his biggest score at that venue was at the two-day meeting of the Irish Automobile Club in 1904, when he won each of the two races on both days. He must have ridden many thousands of miles on the Velvet Strand, and yet we cannot recall his ever having fallen at the turns that bring so many to grief. Caution is his motto, and in cornering he plays for safety rather than for spectacular effect. Of his successes in reliability trials and hill climbs it is superfluous to write. A list of them would fill a volume.

From International Cup to Isle of Man Tourist Trophy

As motorcycles continued to be developed, their reliability improved to the point where completing a journey without breakdown was becoming routine rather than a pleasant surprise. In order to gain the attention of prospective customers, manufacturers now had to place more emphasis upon power and speed. To win recognition for their products and gain an edge in the marketplace over rival manufacturers, it became increasingly important to win speed competitions. Off-road speed meant hill climbs, but there were not going to be any on-road speed contests in Britain for as long as the *Motor Car Act 1903* remained in force. For this reason, it was road races held over on the Continent that next drew the attention of British manufacturers and enthusiasts.

In 1904 the Motor Cycle Club of France announced a 'Gordon Bennett' type event for motorcycles, the Coupe Internationale (International Cup). Ixion noted that the organizers somewhat un-sportingly gave other nations only eight weeks notice of the event, which gave nobody any chance to prepare, however he observed that France would probably have won in any case. Three British firms, JAP, Lagonda and Quadrant hurriedly scraped together entries, which on 26th September 1904 duly circulated the 34 mile course near Dourdan. All three British entries failed to complete the required five laps, owing to repeated punctures. Where all those nails on the roadway came from, nobody seemed to know. Or if they did, then they weren't telling. The race was won by Frenchman Demester, riding a Griffon machine fitted (as were all the French machines) with *arrache clous* or nail catchers – a metal bracket in close proximity to each tyre to sweep off sharp objects picked up by the outer cover before they had a chance to perforate the inner tube. The rules placed a weight limit of 108.5 lbs for the riders' mounts, and many found it difficult to comply.

Meanwhile, Charles Franklin was competing in his own first 'overseas' event. The particular sea he crossed was the Irish Sea however, and the event was the Auto Cycle Club annual race meeting held on the cycling board track at Crystal Palace, London, on Saturday 24th September 1904. In the racing for the Motor Car Journal Challenge Cup, Heat One of five heats was won by C.B. Franklin (FN). The final was won by C. Collier (Matchless), with Franklin in 3rd place. This was Franklin's first track race. In its report of the Crystal Palace event, *Irish Cyclist* quoted a contemporary of C.B. Franklin as saying: 'With a little more practice he will develop into a first-class rider'.

Back in Dublin, Franklin competed in the MCUI (Dublin Centre) Reliability Trial for two-seated vehicles on Saturday 8th October 1904 from Dublin to Maryborough and back. Five competitors had clear runs and shared the cup: C.G. Lewis (FN forecar), H.A. Evans (Singer Tandem Tricycle), C.B. Franklin (FN forecar), T.W. Murphy (Singer with trailer), and A. J. Fenton (Peugeot forecar). At the MCUI (Dublin Centre) annual general meeting held in the Dolphin Hotel on Friday 27th January 1905, C.B. Franklin was elected as a vice-president.

At the Portmarnock Strand Speed Trials on Saturday 29th April 1905, Franklin and his FN came 1st in the One Mile Open event for machines under 150 lbs. and 3.5 hp, and 1st in the One Mile Standing-start Open event for engines less than 3.5 hp of unlimited weight. *Irish Cyclist* reported that:

> 'C.B. Franklin won both of the open events on an FN of last year's make, and seemed to score with his customary ease. His best performance was in the final heat of the first race, in which he covered a mile from a standing start in 1 min 29 secs, a speed of over 40 mph The best performance at Portmarnock is Ireton's 1 min 28 secs at the Irish Automobile Club's meeting last September'.

Irish Cyclist next reported on 10th May 1905 that, up until that time, the machines ridden by C.B. Franklin were 2¾ hp Royal Progress, Humber, and 2 and 2¾ hp FNs. It was at about this time, however, that Franklin, in company with fellow MCUI member Noel Drury, began trying out the products of John Alfred Prestwich. His company, JAP Ltd. of Tottenham in London, had been making proprietary power units for a range of British marques beginning with Triumph in 1903 (Triumph used Belgian Minerva engines on their first 1902 model).[16]

That first 1903 JAP motor must have been somewhat awful because, within only a very few months it was dropped by Triumph's Managing Director, the exacting Maurice Schulte, in favour of Fafnir (another Belgian product) while he set to work on an engine design of his own. But John Prestwich stuck at it and by 1905 JAP, along with Triumph, was at the forefront of efforts to produce a thoroughly decent all-British motorcycle. In particular, JAP was among the very first firms to develop an overhead-valve motor for racing.

The new 70 x 95 mm 6 hp V-twin JAP motor introduced in 1905 was particularly fascinating to both Franklin and Drury. In *The Motor Cycle* of October 1906 Franklin stated that he had a twin-cylinder JAP 85 x 85 mm of his very own, and did 'not find it difficult to manage in traffic' (in case *The Motor Cycle's* readers were wondering). Drury, for his part, stuck with riding thumping great JAP V-twins for the remainder of his serious competition career.

In 1905 Britain gave itself plenty of time to select the best possible three-rider team of motorcyclists to enter the next International Cup competition. From 1904 the Automobile Club of Great Britain started using a system of selection trials to choose the British team for each Gordon Bennett Motor Cup, and for this they went over to the Isle of Man. Uniquely in the British Isles, the Isle of Man is self-governing and has its own legislature, the Tynwald from its Norse heritage. As keen as the Irish to foster a tourism industry, the Manx government responded positively to the idea of enacting legislation to allow motor racing events on their roads. One may wonder why the Gordon Bennett trials were not taken back to Ireland, which after all had hosted the Race itself in 1903. Apparently the Irish venue was not popular with drivers and besides, as already mentioned, Ireland was subject to rule by the British Parliament at Westminster which had both banned racing on public roads and set a maximum speed limit of 20 mph.

For the International Cup (aka 'Little Gordon-Bennett') the Auto Cycle Club piggy-backed onto the car arrangements, running a selection trial of their own which used the same opportunity for roads on the Isle of Man to be legally available for racing. The ACC's trial took place on the 29th of May 1905 with an entry of nineteen motorcycles, run over a 25-mile triangle linking Douglas, Castletown and Ballacraine (the total distance run was 125 miles). The motorcycles could not use the same course as the cars, which ran up and over the shoulder of Snaefell ('the Mountain'), because in those days cars already had gearboxes whereas motor bicycles did not. Amongst other reasons, they got in the way of the pedals. For this reason, the easier Castletown course was used.

Charles Franklin's privately-entered bike was one of seven JAP powered machines in the race, his being fitted with a 6 hp 76 x 95 mm V-twin engine. This machine was described in detail in an article entitled 'Ireland's representative in the Little Gordon-Bennett' that appeared in *Irish Cyclist* on 10th May 1905:

The coming eliminating motor trials in the Isle of Man should have a special degree of interest for Irishmen, inasmuch that the country is able to find a champion of no mean prowess in the person of Mr C.B. Franklin, whose photo, together with that of his specially built racing cycle, is here presented.

Mr Franklin is an electrical engineer by profession, and some 24 years old. He has been identified with motor cycling for three years, and is, in the real sense of the term, an expert in the mechanical and electrical features of the high-speed motor; in fact, almost all his success in competitive events on the track and in reliability trials has been due to this practical knowledge, which it is but fair to add, has been very largely self-taught. The element of chance has counted for little in most of these events so far as he was concerned, and many of the events have been largely the reward of mechanical study and practical effort. It is chiefly because of' this fact that his friends have little doubt of his being a formidable competitor in the coming event, which will have an historic importance second only to the greater one of which it will be the reflex in miniature.

The machines handled and owned by Mr Franklin have been a 2¾ hp Royal Progress, one of the first fitted with the Simms engine and the Simms-Bosch l.t. magneto ignition, a Humber, and 2 hp and two 2¾ hp FN machines. His racing and other events have been all won on one of these popular mounts, the 2¾ hp model being the one used for the last and present seasons. He has competed in almost every event held by the Motor Cycle Union of Ireland (Dublin Centre), though his first competition was for the Canning Cup, from Belfast to Dublin, in which, however, his team did not score. His Portmarnock and road successes are fresh in the reader's mind, and it is only necessary to say that his record has been consistently and phenomenally good. He has twice accomplished the end-to-end tour of Ireland, and held the record until Mr L.R. Oswald-Sealy's successful *coup* last autumn, on the 3½ hp Brown machine, when an hour was knocked off Mr Franklin's record. He has also once competed at the Crystal Palace track, and made a plucky show in competition with other cracks of long experience of that track, though it was his first experience of a banked track when in a greasy condition. His decision to incur the expense – and it is no light one – in entering for the little Gordon-Bennett event is a worthy tribute to his ambition and sportsmanlike qualities. He has had many difficulties to surmount, both as regards the designing of the machine, and in respect of testing the quality of its all British workmanship.

The frame has been specially built by the Chater-Lea Company, and strengthened at integral points, notably at the steering head and lower tube stay. It is furnished with Palmer tyres, and has a wheel base of 4 feet 4 inches. A circular brass tank is strapped to the top horizontal tube, the tank being moulded to fit up under and flush with the tube, so that the bands are free from any 'set' which might tend to their becoming slack. The back wheel is built up with 40 spokes of No.12 gauge, and the belt rim has been drilled for lightness.

The engine is the work of Messrs. J.A. Prestwich, and is practically a combination of two of their famed JAP motors, with the cylinders arranged V-wise with the connecting rod ends, driving on to a common crank pin. The ignition is on the h.t. system, with a positive make and break, Prested accumulator, and a pair of special Fuller non-trembler coils. These are neatly fitted in a wood case, which will be noted below the saddle and between the pillar tube and back stays. The accumulator is carried in a metal case below the coil. The carburetter is a B.B., fitted with the maker's twin valve adjustment, for extra air and throttling, and both movements are by short levers attached to the twin valve box. An exhaust lifter, which acts on one cylinder slightly in advance of the other, is worked from the handle-bar by a Bowden wire and lever. Similar mechanism is used for the two pull-up brakes, but the advance ignition lever is fitted at the side of the tank. The inlet valves are atmospherically opened, and a trunk vapour pipe of large diameter connects the carburetter with the combustion chambers. Flexible metallic oil piping is used for the petrol feed pipe to the carburetter, and from the pump to the base chamber. The drive is by a long V-belt, and the speed ratio of the engine shaft pulley and the one on the rear wheel is approximately 2¾ to 1. The engine is rated at 6 hp, and the weight is well under the limit, 110 lbs.

The writer of the article makes clear that Franklin built his machine and travelled to the Island for the Cup Trials at his own expense, and takes this as indicative of Franklin's confidence and determination as a sportsman and motorcycle competitor.

The writer also suggests that Franklin had the major role in both the designing and the testing of his machine, with JAP and Chater-Lea building it up in accordance with his instructions. Chater-Lea were originally bicycle makers, who as a side-line would also supply bicycle parts and fittings for do-it-yourselfers to construct their own home-built 'specials'. This practice continued when they moved into motorcycle manufacture. The bike that in 1908 won the first-ever organised race at Brooklands, the Peugeot-powered NLG ('North London Garages') ridden by Will Cook, is another famous example of a racing 'special' built from Chater-Lea lugs and fittings.

It would be nice to report that JAP built this engine for Franklin *gratis* as a way of lending factory support to his racing efforts but, typical of the parsimony of British motorcycle manufacturers

Charles Franklin in front of the Rathmines Electric Power Station, and the JAP powered special with which he was a private entrant in the 1905 International Cup British team selection trials on the Isle of Man, and subsequently rode in the race itself at Dourdon in France. (NLI)

Charles Franklin and his JAP special (in the archway), photographed at Quiggan's Yard in Douglas, Isle of Man, with other entrants for the 1905 International Cup British Team selection trials. (NLI)

throughout their entire history, added to the fact that in 1905 they were experiencing a slump in sales attributable to the overall pitiful standard of their products at that time, it appears that Franklin ordered and paid-for the engines from his own pocket, and spent much of his own time on further fettling to get them running right.

Indeed, a telling remark in this narrative is the comment that one of the difficulties Franklin faced was the quality of his machine's 'all British workmanship'. This is consistent with the year 1905 being within the period when French and Belgian motorcycle brands were the world leaders, while all-British contemporaries were still inferior products. Noel Drury similarly experienced problems with race engines he commissioned from JAP

Once underway, only two machines (J.S. Campbell's Ariel and H.A. Collier's Matchless) completed all five laps of the trial before time was up and the roads had to be opened again. Franklin had been in the lead from Lap 2 to Lap 5, then a gudgeon pin came adrift and he had to retire. Despite this, he had impressed the selectors with his fast and consistent running so he too was selected for the team. Fellow JAP rider H. Rignold was taken along as a reserve.

In its report of the event, *Irish Cyclist* stated that 'C.B. Franklin is a busy man, whose avocation as an electrical engineer calls for a daily and punctual attendance to his duties. He rode like a practised jockey, was cool throughout, and though he had two punctures, one in the fourth and the other in the fifth laps, was as collected at the end of each as his Portmarnock friends had hitherto found him'.

Back at Portmarnock for the MCUI (Dublin Centre) Speed Trials on Saturday, 3rd June 1905, *Irish Cyclist* in its report of the event announced,

'The success of the handicaps at Saturday's meeting of the MCUI gives, we venture to think, a new lease of life to these contests. There is no disguising the fact that the manner in which C.B. Franklin scored time after time was making the less clever men and those with slower machines lose interest.'

Franklin and his FN won two of the three events - the One Mile scratch (weight unlimited, hp restricted to 3.5) in 1 min 31.4 secs, and the Two Miles out and home race (starting from scratch) in 3 min 16 secs. In the One Mile handicap final, he finished 5th.

In the 1905 International Cup held in France on 25th June 1905, the British again struggled and none of their team finished. After experiencing both tyre and plug problems, Franklin retired in the first ten miles owing to an inlet valve failure. Campbell had ignition and other problems, while Collier could not keep his tyres inflated. This race was as controversial as the 1904 event, with many protests lodged afterward and the race results considered fairly meaningless. Technically the race was 'won' for Austria-Hungary by Vaclav Vondrich riding a Laurin & Klement.

On 5th July 1905 *Irish Cyclist* caught up with Franklin back on the job at his electricity works, and published the following report based upon a personal interview with him:

The International Motor Cycle Race. C.B. Franklin Interviewed.
C.B. Franklin has no cause to regret his recent and first experience as a racing motor cyclist in competition with the crack riders of France, Germany, and Austria. He has profited no little by what he saw and heard, and, with that quiet resolve characteristic of the man, much of the experience will yet bear fruit, even for the benefit of his home friends in Ireland.

In the limits of a brief interview kindly afforded our representative when busily engaged in his duties as an electrical and mechanical engineer, only a brief outline of his adventures was possible, and of that we append a summary. The British team was awkwardly placed at the outset. It arrived on the course to find neither petrol nor lubricating oil in evidence, though in other respects, thanks to the untiring zeal of the Marquis St. Maur, who had kindly agreed to act in lieu of his friend and relative the Hon. L. Canning, the members were looked after and almost nursed with the prodigality of the genuine enthusiast. The French 'essence,' however, proved singularly good, being free from both grit and water, and this standard was maintained at all the controls.

As regards the route, Franklin remarked that none better could have been selected, there being but about a 20 kilometre stretch which could be regarded as loose, but amply compensated by miles of long straight stretches, with a billiard table-like surface.

As regards the competition, there would seem to be little to choose in the personnel, the British showing on the whole well as riders, and possessed of the necessary skill, but somewhat lacking in experience. Vondrich's victory was well deserved; he rode a fine race, and was equally fortunate with both machine and his Continental tyres. The machine, according to Franklin, was a beautifully made piece of work. The carburettor was of the surface type, but had a species of mixing chamber. The ignition was by the low tension magneto (not h.t. as stated in our report), the whole outfit weighing only 5 lbs and there was not the slightest trouble with any portion of the mechanism for the make and break in the combustion chambers.

Thanks to the assiduity of the Marquis St. Maur much attention was paid by the British contingent to familiarising themselves with the course, and with the one very bad bend, Franklin repeatedly practising at that point, and altogether touring the course some eight times. One of the crack French riders failed at the above point in one lap, and in another instance a competitor is reported to have faced it by walking the machine. Though Demester was afterwards disqualified he made the fastest time in the flying kilom., his speed being at the rate of 56.6 miles per hour. In a subsequent issue we will give more particulars as regards the machines, but now pass on to:

Franklin's personal experience.

As it unfortunately turned out, on the advice of friends to guard against punctures, a change was made at the eleventh hour in the air tubes on his machine, and non-puncturing ones were substituted for the Clinchers previously in use. The former stood up alright on the front wheel, but the rear one could not stand the heat and pull on the wheel. It split up in three places, and was finally replaced after a delay of some twenty-five minutes by the Clincher, which successfully withstood the test up to the time the rider finished. The Palmer covers behaved excellently, and were much admired.

Overheating at the engine was, however, the chief cause of delay. The heat engendered proved so great that no less than five sparking plugs - four of them of the Prested make, a really well made article - fused at the central pole. It speaks well for the little Fuller coils that they were found able to spark across the cavity of about $3/16$th inch, so formed by the fusing. Of the accumulators, three were used, broken bridge-pieces being the cause of failure. The B. and B. carburetter gave no trouble, and the Watawata belt was not touched throughout the entire French trials. The only actual mechanical disablement Franklin suffered was one due to an inlet valve cotter coming out, which caused some delay in discovering its whereabouts. The over-heating of the engine entirely accounted for his failure to score, as, so far as tyre troubles are concerned, he was by no means alone. Pressed on the former point, in view of his not having experienced similar troubles in the I.O.M., he pointed out that the Manx trials commenced early, and were held over a mountain course, often bathed in dew, whereas the Dourdan course is comparatively flat, and the day was an exceptionally hot one; besides, the starting hour was at 10 o'clock, as against 3.30 am in the Manx event. The frame of the machine stood the trials well, and looks nothing the worse. The same applies to the minor fittings, tank, Bowden exhaust lifter, and brake mechanism. The latter point the critics highly commended.

It may be of interest to add that the course was over an open road, no attempt to close any portion having been made, and in consequence at points, more particularly in the neighbourhood of controls, the throng proved very aggressive, limiting the competitors to hardly the proverbial elbow room. The greatest courtesy was shown by all to the visitors, and not a few of the competitors - more especially the French and Austrian - were able to converse in English. The number of quads, and the comparatively few tricars, mostly of a discarded type - according to British notions - struck the visitors. The feature of the display in this respect was, however, the two Puch side cars, attached by a simple method to 6 h.p, twin cylinder Puch bicycles. The ease with which these machines were handled, not to say wheeled round in the most scribed circle, astonished everyone. Herr Puch has made quite a speciality of the make, and seemed to score as big an advertisement by its performance as by the actual race itself.

The weight limit of 110 lb for any motorcycle entered in the International Cup was resulting in entries far removed from rugged standard road models, and tending toward very lightweight and highly-specialized 'freaks'. Machines were being reduced in weight at the expense of safety, and manufacturers and public alike could be forgiven for wondering what the relevance was to standard production models. Similar sentiments were being expressed within the Automobile Club about the monster racers evolved for the Gordon Bennett Cup races, and by way of a backlash they started running on the Isle of Man each year a 'Tourist Trophy' race for automobiles which were meant to at least resemble production touring cars.

Though seriously flawed as a race, the 1905 International Cup was nevertheless a significant event for Ireland in that, by being selected for the British team, Charles Franklin became the first Irishman ever to compete in an international motorcycle competition. His selection for the Cup race from among the cream of the British riders of the day, including the famous Collier brothers, now placed him at the pinnacle of his chosen sport not just in Ireland, but throughout the British Isles. At this point, he had been riding and competing for not quite three years.

Back in Dublin, JAP-racing Franklin had not yet completely given up on his FN. The results reported for the MCUI (Dublin Centre) Hill-climb at Glendhu on Saturday 8th July 1905 show that he was beaten into second place by A. Summers (Triumph) with 3 min 22 secs to which his FN replied with 3 min 23.2 secs, however in the handicap event Franklin beat Summers.

But clearly he was experimenting with other marques, as indicated by the results for the Portmarnock Strand Speed Trials on Saturday 29th July 1905 in which he rode an Ariel to 3rd place in the One Mile Members Handicap, but still kept his FN handy to gain 2nd in the 10 Mile Members Handicap.

Then Franklin unveiled his 6 hp JAP in Irish competition. Its first reported Irish outing was the MCUI Inter-Centre (Dublin-Belfast) Reliability Trial on Saturday 9th September 1905. During the trial Franklin had two side slips, and scored 90 marks. There were 15 members in the Dublin team and 10 members in the Ulster team. *Irish Cyclist* in its report of the event stated that 'Franklin's brother would have been on the Dublin team but for an accident'. The team from Dublin Centre was victorious on this occasion. One can't help thinking that a V-twin JAP was total overkill for this event, it being a Reliability Trial where one was not supposed to exceed 20 mph.

The FN was still getting a regular airing however, as demonstrated by results for the MCUI (Dublin Centre) Hill-climb at Stepaside, Saturday 23rd September 1905. The reason for continued use of Franklin's FN appears related to competition rules for some events, as indicated by this report of the MCUI Speed Trials at Portmarnock Strand on Saturday 30th September 1905:

> In winning the Wheatley trophy, C.B. Franklin (6 hp JAP) covered the mile from a standing start in 1m. 17.4 secs. (an Irish record) despite the fact that for the first quarter of a mile only one of his cylinders was firing. This was the only occasion he had been able to use the 6 hp machine as it is barred by MCUI rules which have a limit of 3.5 hp on machines competing in speed trials.

At the MCUI (Dublin Centre) annual general meeting held in Gresham Hotel on Friday 16th February 1906, C.B. Franklin was re-elected a vice-president.

Charles Franklin's younger brother, Rupert Fairfax, followed in Charles' footsteps and became qualified in a profession related to generation of electricity. In 1906 he started work with the (then) Midlands Electricity Corporation, and lodged with a family named Thompson in the Bilston area of Staffordshire, England. Rupert (known in the family as 'Kipper') married Mary Ann Thompson in 1913, and their first child Rupert Jnr was born in 1915. They had three other sons, Ernest, Robert, and George.[17] In 1924 Rupert Snr inherited the 233 acre estate at Clonaleenaghan, Co. Louth, and £1,280 from his aunt Mary Bailie, although later this farm was compulsorily acquired from him by the Irish government during a program of agrarian land reforms in the Irish State. In the same will, Rupert's two brothers Charles and Lorenzo Jnr received just £10 each.

Irish Cyclist, 7th March, 1906: 'Mr. C.B. Franklin has offered the committee of the Motor Cycle Union of Ireland (Dublin Centre) a gold medal as a prize for one of the events at Portmarnock this season' At the Portmarnock Speed Trials on April 21, 1906, this gold medal was the prize for the winner of the 10 Miles Handicap event. Franklin attended the event, but did not take part – he acted as starter.

> In the 10 Miles Handicap for the C.B. Franklin gold medal, H. Quinn, who was in receipt of 5 minutes, the limit, was never overhauled, and was first past the post, but was disqualified for pedalling beyond the mark on the completion of the first mile, and first place was awarded to C.G. H. Lewis, who had finished second. However, as the time limit had been exceeded, the result did not justify an award being made, and the event has been declared void. Mr. Franklin's prize will therefore have to be competed for again.'

For the 1906 International Cup in Austria, Franklin commissioned JAP to build him this 90-degree 85 x 85mm V-twin race motor which he installed in a frame of Chater-Lea components. He is on record as saying that he 'did not find it difficult to manage in traffic'. (NLI)

The 1906 International Cup race was going to be run in Austria-Hungary, by virtue of Vondrich's victory the previous year. The trials to select the British team attracted five entries representing four manufacturers, however it did not look as though any course would be available for them anywhere in England, owing to the restrictive motoring legislation mentioned earlier. Then Lord Derby came to the rescue and offered the use of a roughly five-mile course within his private estate, Knowsley Park, in Derbyshire.

Franklin commissioned engine-maker JAP to design and build a special racing engine, a 90° V-twin with square dimensions of 85 x 85 mm and rated at 8 hp. This engine layout has perfect primary balance which renders it very smooth, though there is some vibration caused by secondary imbalance. Nowadays, it is a layout used by both Ducati and Moto Guzzi (transversley).

Irish Cyclist on 23rd May 1906, in its Preview of the Selection Trials for the International Cup race, reported:

> These trials should be of particular interest to Irish motorcyclists as Mr. C.B. Franklin is entered to ride, although his machine has not yet been delivered from the makers, giving him very little time in which to tune up and run it in.

And then, on June 6 1906, they continued:

> The Selection Trials take place today Wednesday… C.B. Franklin is amongst the competitors, but as he only received his machine last week his chances of repeating his success of last year are not of the rosiest. He will carry with him the best wishes of Irish motorcyclists.

On Wednesday 6th June 1906 the trials started at 9.40 am and constituted 27 laps of a 4.5 mile course of private roads. There were only five competitors – C.R. Collier, H.A. Collier, R. Morewood, C.B. Franklin and Tom Silver. *Irish Cyclist* of June 13, reported that:

> C.B. Franklin rode well, but it was evident his machine was not in perfect order. It had only recently been delivered (7 hp, 2 cyl. JAP) and he had had little opportunity of getting it properly tuned up. Added to this, his racing gear had not arrived, and he was compelled to ride with the gear he had been using on the road.'

Great! Thanks, JAP, for going right down to the wire on delivery of a racer which, if successful, would surely lift the profile not only of themselves but of Great Britain as a whole. No wonder these Sceptered Isles were yet to be taken seriously as engine makers!

The outcome of the selection trial was that Charlie Collier and his Matchless twin came 1st after completing 27 laps at an average speed of 40 mph, and a best lap of 6 min 26.4 secs. His brother Harry came 2nd, and Franklin was 3rd, despite coming to a halt after 24 laps. His best lap was 7min 19 secs. After the event, lunch was provided by Lord Derby at the Boat House. There then followed one-mile speed trials for each of the three placed men, C.R. Collier, H.A. Collier and C.B. Franklin. C.R. Collier did not run because his machine was not running right. H.A. Collier did three runs, at 1 min 7.8 secs, 1 min 6.8 secs, 1 min 4.4 secs. Franklin's machine was misfiring and he made only one attempt in a time of 1 min 14.8 secs. As a result of these trials, the British team for 1906 comprised the two Collier brothers and Charlie Franklin, with the Marquis de Mouzilly de St Mars, an aristocratic motoring enthusiast resident in London, acting as a team manager.

Both Franklin and Drury became regular patrons of the JAP factory from about 1905 onward. In Noel Drury's own reminiscences, he almost casually lets slip the fact that he used to design his own race engines which JAP then built-up on his instructions. It does not appear JAP gave any official support to either rider or did anything to help them out of the goodness of their hearts, nor could JAP even be bothered to deliver engines on time or in fit state for competition work. The two men were private owners whose race entries were funded entirely from their own pockets. Both were thus sporting gentlemen who competed as 'amateurs', in the sense of the philosophy eloquently described by pioneer racing motorist Charles Jarrott in his famous book *Ten Years of Motors and Motor Racing*, to wit; 'Competitive effort for any reward except the gain of money is exhilarating and ennobling to the individual character'.

When the 1906 International Cup race was run at Pacov in Bohemia on 15th July, Harry Collier secured 3rd place, half an hour after E. Nikodem crossed the finish line on the winning Puch. Franklin was stopped by engine trouble during his 24th lap. The fastest lap of the event was by C. R. Collier at 6 min 26.4 secs (Franklin's best lap was 7 min 19 secs). Continuing the traditions set by the previous two events, there was much chicanery on the part of the organising host nation. As Ixion put it, with considerable understatement; 'It was rather a free-and-easy race, for though the rules stipulated that only competing machines were allowed on the course, the Austrian riders were assisted by racing sidecars full of spare parts and tyres! Our protest was naturally turned down.'

The extremely fed-up British team of Franklin and the Collier brothers, their manager the Marquis de Mouzilly de St Mars, and the Auto Cycle Club's Freddie Straight certainly had much to talk about during their long train journey back from Austria. The germ of an idea was hatched. One thing led to another and sure enough, at the annual dinner of the ACC in London a few months later, plans were announced to run an alternative international race, the Tourist Trophy, on the Isle of Man. Like the automobile Tourist Trophy, by now being organized annually by the Automobile Club, the stated aim of the motorcycle Tourist Trophy was to foster the development and efficiency of production touring machines, not 'freak' racers.

The rest, as they say, is history. Over 100 years later, the TT races are still being run on the Isle of Man each year. Ireland's Charlie Franklin was there at the outset, as one of the people who helped to make it happen.

Meanwhile back in Dublin, the MCUI (Dublin Centre) organised a Hill-climb on 21st July 1906 in which 11 riders took part, and all were weighed before the start. C.B. Franklin's weight was given as 10 stone 13 lbs. In the Pedalling class, J. G. Drury won on his 3 hp Triumph while Charles Franklin, also on a 3 hp Triumph, took third place. First in the Non-pedalling class was Franklin, again on a Triumph. *Irish Cyclist* reported the event as follows:

> Franklin was unlucky not to win both classes as he went so fast in the pedalling class that he was unable to take the corner at the top of the hill. He had to choose between a wall and the road, and selected the latter. He remounted, and despite the loss of several valuable seconds, he was only beaten for second place by .6 of a second. His performance is at once a tribute to his skill as a motor cyclist, and to the Triumph, as he only borrowed the machine a few days before the competition.'

Next was the MCUI (Dublin Centre) Speed Trials at Portmarnock Strand on 18th August 1906. In the 10 Miles Handicap for the Shaw Cup, Franklin was 3rd on a Triumph. In the One Mile Handicap for the Wheatley Bowl, he was 1st on an 8 hp JAP. *Irish Cyclist* reported:

> The Wheatley Bowl was generally looked on as a gift for Franklin, and so it proved. He rode the 8 hp JAP which he had used in the International Race, and although he was slow in starting he soon pulled in the others and won easily. In crossing the last of the gullies he buckled his back rim and his tyre came off, but as he had a comfortable lead the accident did not affect the result. He covered the mile in 1m. 18.8 secs., and by his third successive victory made the Wheatley Bowl his own property.

The Speed Trials held at the same venue on Saturday 29th September 1906 featured a 10 Miles Handicap race, in which Franklin came 2nd, again on a Triumph.

These race reports demonstrate that Franklin had by now acquired a Triumph. By this one simple gesture he demonstrates both taste and discernment. Throughout his racing career, Charlie Franklin consistently showed he had a good nose for quality machinery. He was quick to spot trends, and could recognise the worth of new industry developments as they emerged, rather than later on when popular opinion had passed judgement with the benefit of hindsight. He rode an FN when this machine was at the forefront of design and could beat the British machines hollow. He switched to JAP the instant they became ascendant. He rapidly adopted the Simms-Bosch magneto for his single-cylinder machines, instead of the then customary, but fickle, battery and coil ignition system.

And he invested in a Triumph, at the very time they released the model widely credited with wresting the sport of motorcycling from its pioneering period, 'when rich young men regarded mechanical defects as personal challenges to be overcome through strength of leg, wallet or character' (in the words of Dave Minton), to a period where the average person could use one as credible, dependable transport. Or, as that fine gentleman and sportsman Ixion put it, motorcycles became 'disgustingly utilitarian'.

Franklin would probably have sided with Ixion. His own assessment of the 3 hp Triumph, the first real machine for the masses produced by any British factory, damns it with faint praise. Asked to list his hardware for the October 1906 interview with *The Motor Cycle*, he first mentions the 8 hp JAP and then goes on to say, almost as an after-thought:

> Also a 3 hp Triumph, which latter machine is certainly the most comfortable touring machine I have yet ridden, but I like more power. I am no believer in the ultra light weight pedal-assisted motor bicycle.

For a long time now the general consensus among historians and enthusiasts has been that Triumph's first own-brand engine saved the British motorcycle industry and gave it a future. Following the euphoria of the pioneering days of motorcycling, a sales slump had set in from 1904 to about 1907. It was becoming clear that motorcycle manufacturers were not going to sell very many machines if custom remained limited to men strong in leg, wallet or character. To expand the market, and thereby beat the emerging trend for many of the bright, hopeful new motorcycle manufacturers to either go to the wall or revert to making bicycles, motorcycling would need to appeal to an 'average person' looking not for sport but for personal transport. Unfortunately, many average people had tried the motor-bicycle products on offer and quickly found that they did not live up to the claims in the advertisements. Writing in 1950, Ixion recalled that:

> Magnates associated with rival firms have often frankly confessed that (Triumph engineer) Schulte saved the industry from possible extinction in the early days, when a limited body of customers were growing somewhat weary of roadside trouble, weak climbing and the marketing of so many inadequately tested designs.

In his memoirs Ixion reveals that he was on first-name terms with Triumph's Maurice Schulte, and from time to time he and his riding friends were given various experimental and hush-hush two-wheeled devices to discreetly test and report back on. When Schulte let Ixion loose on the impressively simple, solid and attractive 3 hp Triumph to rack up some serious miles, to their mutual horror he soon found that its promise faded very quickly. He wrote:

> They will forgive my saying after all these years that the first engine of their make that I owned was uncommonly bad. Delightful when new, it rapidly weakened down to the power of a cat and a half. Its soft valves pitted and scaled and warped with incredible rapidity. After 500 miles the compression became a minus quantity, and you could hardly get enough suck on the carburetter to start the engine up. But the firm realised these defects, and set their metallurgists to work. Year by year they have eliminated every possible cause for criticism, and today they enjoy such public confidence as few firms in any industry can command.

So the real turn-around for the British industry came with the improved 3½ hp Triumph in 1907, described by Ixion as 'probably the first really excellent motorcycle ever built'. The 'Trusty Triumph' became an industry standard for the next two decades, and formed everybody's ideal of what a 'motor' cycle (as opposed to motor-bicycle) should look and go like. The 1920 edition of a popular annual book *Motorcycling Manual: All about the Motorcycle in Simple Language*, written by the staff of *Motor Cycling*, opined that 'the Triumph was the original successful single-cylinder machine', and that 'ten or twelve years ago', that is, in 1908 – 1910, 'most newcomers to the motorcycling industry, and many of those already in existence, slavishly copied the Triumph design, on which they thought they could not improve'.

Noel Drury's scribbled notes provide us with his own assessment of the new Triumph models, and also an account of personal dealings with Schulte during a visit to the Triumph factory.

Triumph 3½ (photo courtesy VMCC)

The Triumph Co. of Coventry made, I think, the best finished machine of that period. When they started they used in succession the 2 hp Minerva, the 2½ hp JAP (John A. Prestwich & Co. of Edmonton, London N., makers - 1904 2½ hp JAP machine £36), the 3 hp Belgian Kelecom engine, and then in 1905 they brought out their own make of engine with mechanically opened inlet valves and ball bearings on the pulley or drive side. A Bosch magneto was also fitted. They were fine machines and a great advance on everything else on the market at that time. The only snag was the design of spring forks that altered the trail angle at every movement and caused serious trouble when cornering fast. One of the most reliable and well built machines of the early days was the Triumph and when they brought out their first all-Triumph machine both I and my brother Jack got them. The engines were much given to knocking on hills but I devised an adjustable jet which I could increase slightly in size to make the mixture richer while riding. All machines of this period suffered more or less from this trouble. Jack and I went for a tour in England and decided to call at the Triumph works to have the machines checked over. We were received like royalty by Mr. M. J. Schulte, the Managing Director, and Frank Herbert, the Works Manager. My engine was entirely replaced by a new one as they said the original was not up to standard. Both machines were gone over, wheel and head bearings adjusted and lubricated, Jack's engine stripped. After a final run by Frank Herbert the machines were handed over next morning, the bikes being marked 'NO CHARGE'! One can't imagine this being done now, 55 or more years later.

Most of the books available these days about Triumph motorcycles divide the history of Triumph into two Eras of Greatness; that of Edward Turner's twins (1936 - 1984), and the Hinckley era (1990-). Presumably such books were written for the younger generation, that is, for people less than seventy years old. It's almost beyond living memory now, but Triumph has altogether had three Eras of Greatness, the first being 1905-1925 when the Bettemann-Schulte flat-tank singles were the British industry standard and the benchmark for sturdiness and reliability. The only recent Triumph history to adequately cover all three eras in a single volume is *The Triumph Story* by David Minton (Haynes).

Besides the appearance of the 'trusty Triumph', writers like Ixion and James Sheldon who, like Drury, were actually there at the time, do mention two other factors that also helped motorcycles to break through into general acceptance throughout Britain and her Dominions. One was the advent of the Bosch high-tension magneto in 1906 which, reports Ixion, immediately halved the occurrence of ignition failures (the cause of 90 per cent of all engine breakdowns). The other was the emergence of motorcycle magazines like *The Motor Cycle*, *MotorCycling* and Ireland's own *Irish Cyclist and Motor Cyclist*, all of which did much to promote the sport, increase levels of mechanical sensitivity among novices, and engender a feeling that motorcyclists are a tight-knit band of adventurers and sportsmen.

The MCUI (Dublin Centre) held its annual general meeting at the Central Hotel on 21st February 1907. C.B. Franklin presided over the meeting. He was re-elected a vice-president of the centre. Then on 16th March there was a conference between representatives of the MCUI (Dublin Centre) and Ulster Centre at Williams' Hotel, Dundalk. *Irish Cyclist* listed the Ulster representatives as: J. Holden, A.W. Hamilton, E.B. Waring, and the Dublin Centre representatives: C.B. Franklin, L.B. Franklin, T.W. Murphy. The meeting discussed relations with the Auto Cycle Club, the International Federation of Motorcyclists and the *Irish Cyclists Association*. The decision was taken that the MCUI should have complete control of motorcycle sport in Ireland. The meeting is interesting in providing us with evidence that Charles Franklin's other brother Lorenzo Jnr was also interested in motorcycle competition, at least to the point of wishing to be a member of the Motor Cycle Union of Ireland.

While the Gordon Bennett race of 1903 was the first huge milestone in British motoring competition, the next two major milestones both occurred in 1907. First the inaugural Isle of Man Tourist Trophy race for motorcycles and then, two weeks later, the Brooklands track in Surrey (south of London) was opened.

The first TT event for motorcycles had to be run 'on the smell of an oily rag' budget-wise, for industry magnates were still in the process of deciding whether speed competition really was good for business, and consequently they were too tight to open their wallets in support of what was still an unknown quantity as a promotional event for their products. It was left to the enthusiasm of amateurs through the ACC to organise and grub-stake the event. The Marquis de Mouzilly de St. Mars fronted up with a magnificent trophy, but a public subscription had to be opened to come up with the other prizes. Maurice Schulte contributed medals, and ultimately enough cash was raised from donations to award £25 to the winner, £15 for second, £10 for third, and some extra small prizes like £5 for the best private owner.

But there was bad news concerning the participation of Charles Franklin, as reported in the *Irish Cyclist and Motor Cyclist* on 15th May 1907:

> THE TT RACE - FRANKLIN WITHDRAWS
> Our readers will be sorry to learn that C.B. Franklin has been compelled, owing to pressure of business, to withdraw his entry for the Tourist Trophy race. He was looking forward with considerable pleasure to taking part in the event and had taken no small amount of trouble with the building and timing up of his machine.

The first Auto-Cycle Club Tourist Trophy Race was held in the Isle of Man on a cold and windy Tuesday 28th May 1907. It was run on a special 15-mile course known as the 'St John's course' that avoided any really steep hills. This was essential, for motorcycles did not yet have variable gears so could not cope with the automobile Tourist Trophy course which climbed Snaefell (the 'Mountain Course'). As with the Tourist Trophy for cars, there was a fuel consumption limit that had to be complied with.

Single-cylinder machines were allowed one gallon per 90 miles, and twins one gallon per 75 miles. Seventeen singles and eight twins started in pairs a minute apart, owing to the narrowness of the roadway. Once the staggered starts were completed and everybody was underway, all entries were then circulating the course at the same time. But to all intents and purposes there were two races being run, for the twins had their own Hele-Shaw Trophy and their own prize money allocation.

Less than half of the entrants finished the race, thus giving all manufacturers pause for thought about the high visibility conferred by road racing upon the quality, or otherwise, of their product. Charlie Collier won the single-cylinder race on his Matchless-JAP at 38.5 mph, and got to take home the Marquis de Mouzilly de St. Mars Tourist Trophy. The Triumph of Jack Marshall was the second single home. The winner of the twin-cylinder race was Rembrandt Fowler, riding a Peugeot-engined Norton, but he didn't get to take home anything at all because the organisers hadn't quite got around to procuring an actual, in-the-metal, Hele-Shaw Trophy just yet. The second twin to finish was that of an American residing in London named William H. (Billy) Wells. He rode a German-made Vindec Special, for which marque he was the British importer and dealer. During the last lap Wells had been leading by 15 minutes, but suffered three punctures in quick succession and it was while repairing the third that he was overtaken by Fowler. He spent the rest of his life regretting that he did not win the multi-class of the inaugural Isle of Man TT race.

Overall the event was judged a complete success, and inspired many manufacturers to immediately begin dreaming up improvements to their designs in order to make them perform better next year. In other words, the hopes of those far-sighted enthusiast organisers that speed competition would jerk the motorcycle industry out of its lethargy were straightaway being realised. It was this race more than any other, more so even than the Brooklands track events, that would be the proving ground and cradle of development for British motorcycles, which would see them outstrip the early and rapid achievements of the Continent and USA, and become for several decades of the 20th Century the very best motorcycles in the world. These same TT races are still held being each year on 'The Island', one hundred years later.

Charles Franklin had been one of the first people to submit an entry for the inaugural Isle of Man TT, as you'd expect, since he was himself one of those far-sighted enthusiasts; on the train back from Austria he'd been a party to the very first discussions that led to the establishment of this event. He'd entered a 3½ hp JAP powered special made from off-the-shelf Chater-Lea components but, as reported above, withdrew due to work commitments.

Work was not the only commitment for Franklin in 1907. On 10th of July, in a marriage solemnised at Christchurch, Leeson Park, Diocese of Dublin, Charles wed Annie 'Nancye' Wilson Kerr (b. 29th July 1883) of Ashgrove Villa, Palmerston Park, Dublin, at Ashgrove Villa 'according to the rites and ceremonies of the Church of Ireland by Special Licence'. One of the witnesses was Lorenzo Jnr., whose grand-daughter in America still possesses his wedding invitation card. Charles's address at the time was 62 Ranelagh Road, and his father's occupation was given as 'merchant'. The bride's father was George A. Kerr, civil servant (a postal clerk).

We'll now pause for a moment to introduce a character into this story who was later to have a momentous influence upon Charles Franklin's career, both as a racer and as an engineer. The gentleman in question is Billy Wells, the American rider placed second among the twins in the 1907 TT. A businessman first and foremost, and destined to become one of the magnates on the retail side of the motorcycle trade in Britain as Indian's concessionaire, he was at that time noted for being a fierce competitor in English hill-climbs.

William Huntingdon Wells was born in Winthrop, Maine, USA, on 28 March 1868 and died in Harrow, Middlesex, England on 15 January 1954.[18] As a young man he was a keen cycling competitor,

William H. ('Billy') Wells, with a Vindec Special competition model. He was the British concessionaire for this German marque from 1903 until early 1909, and a fierce hill-climb competitor.(EMIMA)

initially on 'high-wheel' or 'penny-farthing' cycles and then on the new 'safety' bicycles. Wells started working as a bicycle builder in 1884. He had been married with two children in the USA but apparently divorced, and came to England in late 1902 to advance the interests of the Prescott Steam Company, makers of the steam-powered automobile known as the Stanley Steamer. This was not a commercial success, and Wells switched to importing German-made Allright/Lito motorcycles through an entity called the South British Trading Co. These were marketed in Britain as the 'Vindec Special'. This annoyed Brown Bros. who had their own motorcycle which was being sold as a 'Vindec'.

After about five years of activity South British Trading went into liquidation, owing money to the Southern Draw Steel Co. of America. The German end of the operation persuaded Wells to resurrect their UK interests by establishing a new entity, which he did from November 1908. Meanwhile Brown Bros. had seized this opportunity to secure the 'Vindec Special' name in Britain. Although they never used this name, it meant that Wells' machines thereafter had to be dubbed the 'VS'. But dissatisfaction with the new business arrangements soon led to Wells' departure, and he was replaced by NSU man Martin Geiger. With no immediate prospects in England, Wells returned to the USA in March 1909.

There he met up with an old friend and associate from his cycle competition days, a fellow named George Hendee, who was nowadays engaged in the manufacture of motor bicycles under the brand name of 'Indian'. There will be more on this subject later.

Wells was clearly an early believer in two motorcycling philosophies that decades hence have come to be seen as very typically American, namely, 'Race on Sunday, sell on Monday', and 'There ain't no substitoot for cubes'. Or, as Ixion put it in his *Reminiscences*, written some fifteen years later:

> Meanwhile various earnest men were trying to provide us with better hill-climbing. W. H. Wells, now of Indian fame, launched a most taking machine. His motto was that hill-climbing required horsepower. So he bought some 5 hp Peugeot twin-cylinder engines of the V type, and mounted them in excellent frames. He fitted a French spring fork, the Truffault, which if ugly was smoother than many, which survive to this day. Incidentally he reduced the belt troubles, because the big engine could stand a big pulley, and a big pulley gave a better grip. This machine was a regular roarer for those days. With a frenzied rush it could get up almost any main road hill. Its chief weakness was the automatic action of the inlet valves. When we learnt that they must both have equal springs of a certain strength, and open exactly $^3/_{32}$ in. we were able to enjoy life. Speaking from memory, this very fast mount can hardly have weighed more than 170 lbs.

Noel Drury has his own recollections of the products sold by Wells' motorcycle import and retail business.

> About 1908 I bought a 'Vindec Special', sold by the South British Trading Co., of Finsbury Square, London. It had a 5 hp twin cylinder Minerva engine, and had 'Truffault' spring forks, controlled by friction pads running up and down a heavy tube fitted in front of the frame head tube. The hinged side members of this contraption were made of flat steel strip about ½ in wide by $^3/_{16}$ in thick. This used to spring sideways and put the front wheel out of line, making the machine nearly impossible to ride safely if the roads were at all greasy. I had a tour in Scotland with Lewis, I rode the Vindec and he an NSU. I soon got rid of this machine and bought another Vindec with a short wheelbase, light frame and a Peugeot 5 hp twin engine. This was a splendid machine, and I won a number of hill climbs and races with it. I had it enamelled cream with fine light blue lines on the tank and frame, and was very proud of it!

Present-day VMCC member Rick Howard has owned a Vindec Special. His ride-impression of it, in comparison with other veteran machines he's experienced is (and we quote); 'Frightening! A killer to start. Very powerful at 1000cc, with non-existent braking ability'.

It is not known precisely when Charles Franklin and Billy Wells first made each other's acquaintance. It is possible that Franklin was introduced to Wells at about this point of the story (in 1907 or 1908), owing both to Wells' being a dealer of rip-snorting Vindecs (for example, he sold one to Franklin's friend Drury) and to Wells' own prominent participation in early British motorcycle competition.

It is very possible that Franklin and Wells had met even sooner than this. The evidence is circumstantial and relies upon the scanty information provided in some FN and Vindec advertisements that appeared in the motorcycling press of 1903 and 1904. For example, Dublin's W.R. McTaggart advertised in 1903 that he was the UK 'sole representative' for FN, and mentioned that he had an agent, R.V. Asbury, located in Bayswater in London's West End. Advertisements for Vindec Specials from 1903 and 1904 show that they were at that time fitted with FN 2¾ hp engines, which may well have been sourced from FN's 'sole UK representative' in Dublin. A 1904 Vindec advertisement mentions that South British Trading Co. also had an agent in the West End, and it was none other than this same R.V. Asbury of Bayswater. To complete the picture, add the fact that Charles Franklin began his motorcycling career on 2 hp and 2¾ hp FNs, which he almost certainly purchased in

Billy Wells seated upon a touring Vindec fitted with French-made Truffault forks (later developed as Earles forks). (RHC)

Dublin from W.R. McTaggart. How could two competitors as nationally prominent as Franklin and Wells, both engaged in constructing and racing the same brand of engine sourced from the same UK concessionaire, not know each other, or at least, not know about each other?

It is not known for sure whether Franklin himself ever owned a Vindec, but he certainly would have been interested in any type of machine that promised 'more power'. He must surely have taken his club-mate Drury's own Vindec out for a spin, just to try it.

What is certainly known is that Charles Franklin had a JAP V-twin, and what's also certain is that he was using it to good effect in Irish competition, as shown by his competition results for 1907 (see page 123).

The Dublin and District Motor Cycle Club (D&DMCC) was formed at a meeting in Dublin in November 1907, and Charles Franklin became one of its first office-bearers (a vice-president). The exact date of the inauguration meeting is unknown, because the Club's original Minutes book was lost many years ago. Then on 17th February 1908 at the MCUI (Dublin Centre) annual general meeting held in Wynn's Hotel, Lower Abbey Street, Franklin was re-elected as a vice-president.

The first events run by the D&DMCC took place over the Easter weekend in 1908, beginning on Good Friday with a Run to Blessington and Baltinglass, Co. Wicklow, followed on Easter Saturday by a Tour to Waterford, and on Easter Monday by a Run to Navan and Kells, Co. Meath. The first competition event they organised was a Hill-climb on 23rd May 1908 at Sugarloaf Mountain, Co. Wicklow. The winner of the event was R. H. Taaffe (Triumph). Charlie Franklin did not take part in this event.

Subsequently the Dublin & District MCC became the most active motorcycle club in Ireland, organising competitions for every branch of motorcycle sport. The club has been at the forefront of the sport in Ireland since its formation. It is the second oldest motorcycle club in Ireland, the oldest being the Belfast and District Club, formed in 1906.

A further milestone in British motoring was the running of the first organized motorcycle race on Brooklands track, which occurred on 20th April 1908. A private match race between two Oxford undergraduates had already been run on 25th February that same year. This one-lap duel between W. Gordon McMinnies on a TT Triumph and Oscar L. Bickford on a Vindec Special (the Triumph won at 53 mph) had caught the eye of Clerk of the Course, Mr De Rodakowski. Looking to increase gate takings for the new track by diversifying the range of activities being held there, he wondered about the prospects for regular motorcycle events at Brooklands. In late March 1908, as an experiment, he invited three people whom he considered by reputation to be the foremost motorcycle racers of the period to come, circulate Brooklands and demonstrate what they could do. The chosen three were Harry Collier who brought along a Matchless, and G. Reynolds and Billy Wells who both rode Vindec Specials.[19]

De Rodakowski was suitably impressed, and in due course twenty-one machines lined up for the first such event on 20th April, organized under the auspices of the Brooklands Automobile Racing Club (BARC). It was run as a 'scratch' race, that is, all entrants were started off at the same time. This resulted in Will Cook's big 9 hp NLG-Peugeot V-twin winning convincingly at 63 mph over a very mixed field of singles, V-twins, and even a four-cylinder FN. Billy Wells on his Vindec Special came

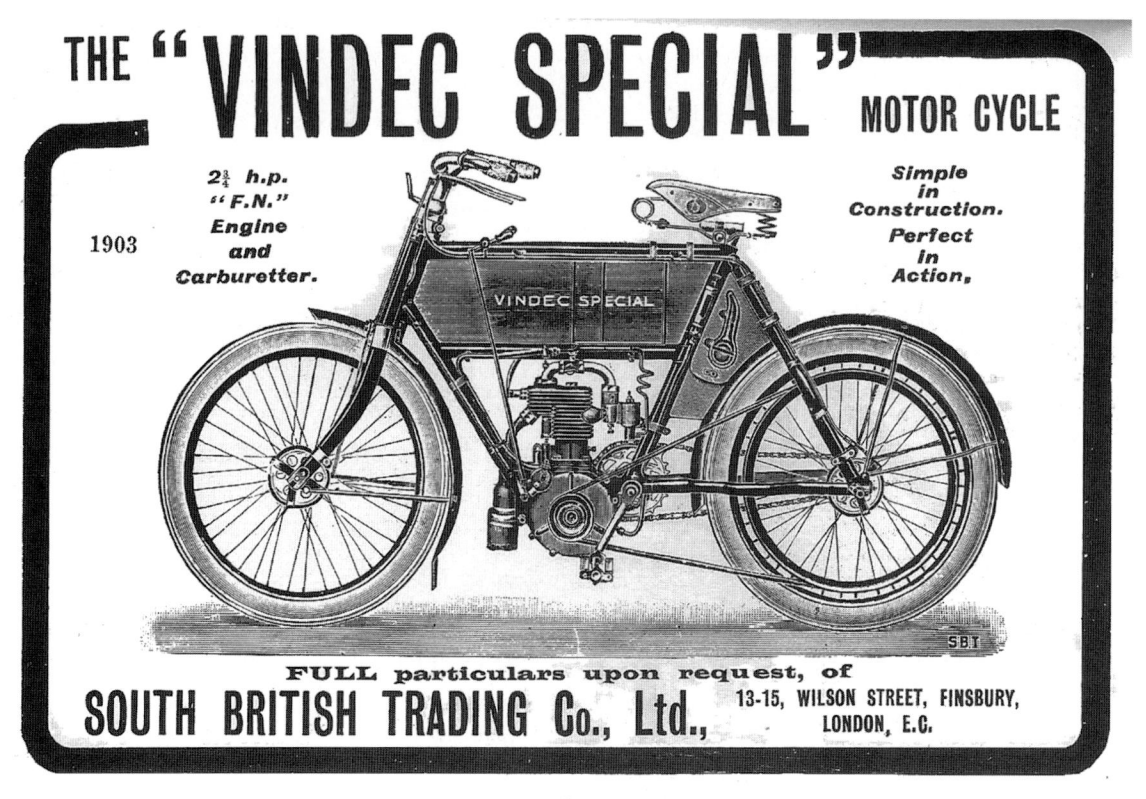

An early Vindec advertisement dating from 1903, when they used 2¾ hp FN engines. (RHC)

in at 5th place. Both Collier brothers competed, and Charlie placed 3rd on the same Matchless-JAP he'd taken to Austria for the 1906 International Cup.

To avoid such mismatches in future, motorcycle races were mainly run on a handicap basis from May 1908 onwards. Official starter and time-keeper E.V. 'Ebby' Ebblewhite, destined to become an institution at Brooklands, devised a handicap system of starting slower runners off sooner, with the amount of head-start calculated from their recent race performances. In the jargon of Brooklands habitués, the first riders away came to be known as the 'limit' men while the fastest riders who started last were the 'scratch' men. In theory this meant that all race entrants should cross the finish line at the same time, which ought to make for exciting finishes from a spectator's point of view. In practice, any recent improvements in an entrant's riding skill or tuning ability would see them finish ahead of the field.

A draw-back of this type of racing is that it's difficult for race spectators to know who is winning a race until it has actually finished. Riders also got frustrated because the harder they tried and the better they got, the more they were handicapped out of the running. Given the sheer diversity and fairly restricted numbers of motorcycles that raced at Brooklands throughout its thirty-two year history, historians generally agree that it's difficult to see how a handicap system could have been avoided.

Franklin was again very successful at Portmarnock on 22nd August 1908, moving *Irish Cyclist & Motor Cyclist* to comment as follows:

> Noel E. Drury and C.B. Franklin rode the machines they plan to ride in next month's TT race in the Isle of Man. Drury's is a two-cylinder JAP but it was not running right. Franklin's was a 3.5 hp single-cylinder JAP, which was, as usual, timed to perfection, and he did some very fine work on it during the afternoon. Franklin had an easy win in the 4 miles Dublin & District MCC members' handicap. In the 20 miles handicap he gave a grand exhibition of speed. The race was run over an out and home course, involving a turn at the end of each mile, and as Franklin's time for the full distance works out at 41.7 mph, he must have been travelling at close to 45 mph in the middle of the course.

On Thursday 17th September 1908, Charles Franklin became a father. His wife Annie Wilson Franklin gave birth at home (31 Hollybank Avenue) to a baby girl who they named Phyllis Enid. Then Charles promptly packed his bags, his tools, and his home-built JAP 'special', took his leave of new mother and baby, and went over to the Isle of Man to compete in his first Tourist Trophy race. Never mind work commitments - even the arrival of his first-born was not going to get in the way of him competing this time.

The 1908 Isle of Man TT race was held on Tuesday 22nd September. Main changes in the event since the inaugural race were that the allowable fuel consumption limits were reduced to one gallon per 100 miles for singles and 80 miles for twins, and (amusing to relate) any pedalling of one's machine was outlawed because this was deemed to confer an unfair advantage. Motorcycles did not have speedometers in those days, yet the fuel limit required tactics of riding at a set speed and not exceeding it, lest the allotted fuel be all used up before the finish. Fortunately, speeds in some parts of the course (like the climb up Creg Willey's Hill) were so low that support crew could simply trot alongside a rider's puffing mount, and give their man a full discourse about his current lap time, the progress of others in the race, or indeed any other subject that he cared to know about.

Despite the TT event being rather a hit with the public in the previous year, the motorcycle trade had still not seen fit to rally to the cause with financial support. Prizes remained small and were the result of donations raised by public subscription. Thirty six machines started, comprising 21 'twins' (which included two FN Fours) and 15 singles, all belt-drive single-speeders except for the shaft-drive FNs. They set off in pairs of one single and one twin each until all the singles had started. First away were 1907 winners Charlie Collier and Rem Fowler. Spectator interest was mainly on Collier (Matchless single) and Triumph-single mounted Jack Marshall, owing to a media war between these two firms the previous year about whether using foot-pedals (which Triumph had eschewed) was cheating or not. Marshall took an early lead, but was passed later on when he broke an exhaust valve and had to spend 10 minutes to unscrew the valve-cap, fish out the fragments, and drop in a new one. He then made up time to re-pass Collier, winning the Marquis de Mouzilly de St Mars Tourist Trophy at an average speed of 40.4 mph and by so doing he evened-up the score in what had come to be a Matchless-Triumph grudge match. Triumph riders overall did well, filling five of the first seven places. Harry Reed on a Dot-Peugeot finished first of the twin-cylinder entries at 37 mph.

We have no accounts of Franklin's 1908 TT campaign available to us in his own words. Apart from the dry statistics of his placing, time and speed, we have only the testimony of Noel Drury, who makes it clear that he and Franklin were both in this enterprise together:

> Charlie Franklin and I were greatly interested in the accounts of the first race in 1907 and we decided to get suitable machines, which we would enter for the 1908 race. He picked on a single cylinder JAP engine 85 x 85 in a frame which he built of Chater-Lea fittings. I got Johnnie Prestwich to make me a twin cylinder engine 85 x 60 with overhead valves and an included angle between the cylinders of 90°. In this way a perfect mechanical balance was obtained, provided that each piston and rod were exactly the same weight and that a counterweight equal to one of them was arranged opposite them, dividing the 270° angle. Battery ignition was used and a separate contact breaker and coil for each cylinder. The conditions laid down provided for two classes, one for single cylinder machines and the other for twin cylinder machines. There was no limit to the size of engine which could be used but each class had a limited petrol allowance. I believed that a big engine driving a high gear and using light throttle opening would be more successful than a smaller single cylindered machine. Franklin supported the latter opinion.
>
> In practice round the course in the Isle of Man we all found that if we used the full speed possible we couldn't get near the petrol consumption, so we had to do slower and slower laps till we got down to the petrol allowance. I managed to finish fourth in spite of having several punctures and I had about 8 or 10 ounces of petrol left after averaging about 39 mph. Charlie Franklin calculated wrongly and finished away down the list, 16th or 18th I think, and had enough petrol left in his tank for another 20 miles or more!

In writing the above account sixty years later, it appears that Noel Drury's memory has failed him perhaps just a little. History records that Franklin in fact came 6th in the singles race with a time of 4 hours, 40 minutes and 38 seconds and an average speed of 33.81 mph. Drury himself was also 6th (but amongst the twins) in a time of 4 hours, 35 minutes and 56 seconds, and an average speed of 34.38 mph It was Billy Wells who was 4th in the twins race, on a Vindec, with a time of 4 hours, 25 minutes and 15 seconds, and a speed of 35.77 mph.

To get some idea of the running conditions experienced by Franklin and other TT participants during these early years on the relatively flat St John's TT course, we have the testimony of Jack Marshall, winner of the 1908 single-cylinder class:

> The course was plain macadam roads (earth and stones rolled together), very dusty in dry weather, mud-covered and slippery in the wet, pretty badly churned up on the stretch from Ballacraine to Kirk Michael, which, of course, the cars were using in their race over today's Mountain circuit, and plenty of loose stones on corners. In an attempt to keep down dust, the officials sprayed the course with an acid solution which was supposed to keep things moist. The acid got onto our clothes and in a couple of

days they looked as if the rats had been at them! Those who had pedals pedalled fit to bust themselves. Those who hadn't frequently jumped off and ran. Creg Willey's Hill was the worst of all, of course. A lot of chaps conked right out on that, and, being unable to re-start single-gear machines on the gradient, had to go back to the bottom. There was not much danger in going back the wrong way, you had to pick your time but everyone was pedalling or running anyway. Our main troubles were punctures, broken or slipping belts, broken or stretched exhaust valves, seized engines – and crashes. We found our compulsory toolkits very useful, I can tell you! Also we carried spare belts wound round our waists and at least one spare butt-ended inner-tube. The brakes weren't much good and the roads, of course, were shocking. The Ballacraine and Kirk Michael corners were about worst of all, but a good many of us fell off quite regularly on the Devil's Elbow hairpin, which, with its downhill approach, was the 'Governor's Bridge' of those days. In Peel there was an 'S' bend with a lamp-post at each side of it. The authorities took the lamp-posts down in advance. I suppose they knew we should knock them down in any case and taking them down saved many a chap from hurting himself! What did we wear? Why, just ordinary motor cycle clothing. Some of the chaps wore long leather coats or raincoats, others even had rubber ponchos. I was one of the first to adopt a leather waistcoat, breeches and knee-boots, which for many years after that were called 'TT boots'. Pit signals? There weren't any, for there weren't any pits. We started from the pub yard at St Johns and pulled in there for refreshments at half-time. But I did have a chap timing for me at Creg Willey's and he used to tell me my position each lap. There wasn't any need for signals. As I came up Creg Willey's, my chap ran alongside me and just shouted. It was easy for him – I was running anyway, and I had a machine to push, too!

Noel Drury knew Franklin well. From 1905 to 1910 both men competed with JAP powered specials, like this overhead-valve example photographed at Enniskerry on St. Patrick's Day of 1909

Drury was sixth-in-line on the very first day that motor vehicle registration plates were issued in Ireland. (NLI)

Lieut. Noel E. Drury, Royal Dublin Fusiliers.

Indian Gets Noticed In Britain

It was another noteworthy motorcycling event held in 1907 that drew increased attention in Britain to the products of the American firm Hendee Mfg. Co. Ltd, sold under the brand name of 'Indian'. The premier reliability events in England in those days were the Reliability Trials organized by the ACC from 1903 onwards, which challenged competitors to cover 100 miles per day over ten days, with a two-day break after the fifth day to give their 'l.p.a.' ('light pedal assistance') leg muscles a chance to recover. This type of event came to be called the Thousand Mile Reliability Trial. It was run over fewer and fewer days as designs improved and the need for pedalling got less, and ultimately evolved into the International Six Days Trial.

For the 1907 Thousand Mile Trial an American named T.K. (Teddy) Hastings came over from New York to take part and brought with him his Indian motor bicycle, one of the early 'camel-back' models. These had been in production as single-cylinder machines from 1902 onwards, however Hastings' example was one of the new V-twin variants that first became available in 1906. Hastings' score in the Trial was a very creditable 994 out of a possible 1000 points. The Oscar Hedstrom designed engine proved very reliable, and enabled the type of consistent running necessary to do well in reliability trials. In these events one had to adhere to a set time schedule, or else lose points.

This was by no means the first occasion on which an Indian 'motocycle' was entered in a British competition. For example, *The Motor Cycle* of 19th February 1906 reported on a hill-climb organised by the Lewisham Automobile Club in which 'H. Mogridge entered a 2 hp chain-driven Indian, a much boomed American motorcycle.' However Hasting's excellent result in the 1907 Thousand Mile Trial made quite a splash in the English motorcycling press, and it raised the profile of Indian motorcycles in Britain.

Indian motorcycles were being made in Springfield, Mass., by the Hendee Mfg. Co. Ltd, a firm incorporated in 1897 as bicycle makers and founded by George M. Hendee who'd himself been a champion cyclist in the high-wheel ('penny farthing') era. On retirement from competition and after a spell in bicycle retailing in NYC he returned to Springfield, which was his home town, and there set up as a manufacturer of bicycles. These were marketed using model names like Silver King, Silver Queen … and Indian. Use of the name 'Indian' by Hendee Mfg. Co. thus pre-dated motorcycle manufacture.

The precise reason why 'Indian' was chosen as the trade name for Hendee's bicycles, and subsequently for his motorcycles, has long been a mystery and a matter for conjecture. It is only recently that an authentic explanation in Hendee's own words has been discovered. Quite by accident we stumbled upon a newspaper story in *The Syracuse Herald* of 22nd February 1914, which settles this matter once and for all.

Why Indian is a good name for a motorcycle (By the Big Chief George M Hendee)
The Indian motorcycle was named three years before it was even thought of, in 1897. The Hendee Manufacturing Company was building Silver King and Silver Queen bicycles, gentlemens and ladies models respectively, in Springfield. Its business was pretty healthy for that time, its annual output being in the neighbourhood of 4,000 machines. Incidentally, it did considerable export business through New York commission houses, these shipments consisting of what were termed 'nameplate' bicycles. When a commission firm placed an order with us, which usually consisted of 100 bicycles or so, he specified the name by which that particular lot of machines were to be known, and we attached name plates accordingly.

In the course of time, naturally, a large number of our machines went abroad under all sorts of names. Practically all of these bicycles were identical except for the name, and sometimes the color. Finally we realised that this practice would have to be stopped, and I made a special trip to New York to take this matter up with the commission houses. "Look here", I said to the manager of the first place I called, "why not discontinue this indiscriminate branding of our goods, and send them all out under one name hereafter. For instance, the name 'American Indian' is a pretty good bet, for the American Indian is known round the world, and a bicycle of that name would become equally well known".

My suggestion instantly appealed to them and those concerned with production. Fortunately I had little difficulty in persuading our other brokerage customers to fall in line. Thereafter, all of our export bicycles were known as the 'American Indian', but at the factory we always referred to them simply as the 'Indian'.

Soon I realised that in the name 'Indian' we had a winner for bicycles, and we just discontinued our other brands then and there, and built Indian bicycles exclusively. When the motorcycles came along, a year or so later, it simply was out of the question to think of calling it anything but Indian. This name suited the motorcycle even better than it did the bicycle, and before many moons passed, this new warrior had deposed the old chief altogether from the wigwam. That is why there is an Indian motorcycle today.

In partnership with the president of the Springfield Baseball Association, Charles T. Shean, and with his former cycle racing trainer Jack Prince installed as Track Manager, Hendee financed the building of a cycling and bicycle pacing board track, the Springfield Coliseum, which opened on 30th June 1900.[20] From the outset a major draw was race events with motorized tandem pacer machines, in which the cyclists 'slip-streamed' behind the pacers to obtain the very fastest possible track times. A New York duo, Charles S. Henshaw and Carl Oscar Hedstrom, routinely appeared at the Coliseum and at other East Coast tracks throughout 1900 in a pace-making role. They used a pacer machine which they'd designed and built themselves during 1899, and had been operating in public since at least the beginning of 1900.

Reliability was definitely an issue with the early motor-tandem pacers, as evidenced by the number of contemporary sports-page cycling reports which noted that this or that competitor had 'lost their pace' during an event. It was in regard to its above-average reliability that the device of Henshaw and Hedstrom now attracted the particular attention of Coliseum track president George Hendee.

Hendee would have already heard of, and probably met, these two men even before they got involved with internal combustion engines. As members of the Greenwich Wheelmen club from downtown Manhattan, both Henshaw and Hedstrom were top-flight cycle racers in Class A amateur competition. They were good enough, both individually in solo race events and as a duo in tandem events and world record attempts, to have their names regularly appear in the sports-pages of major eastern-seaboard newspapers from 1891 onwards.

Swedish-born Hedstrom hailed from Brooklyn N.Y. and for his livelihood was engaged in bespoke bicycle manufacture, specializing in competition cycles. A qualified tradesman with machining and pattern-making skills, he had close ties with the Worcester Cycle Manufacturing Co.'s workshops in Middletown, CN. Hedstrom had seen the de Dion powered pacers brought to New York by Henri Fournier in 1898 and, though intrigued, felt that they needed improvement. By 1900 he and Henshaw had built and were jointly operating their own de Dion inspired 'Hedstrom & Henshaw' gasoline-powered tandem pacing machines. Posterity has been left in no doubt as to which of the two men brought this motor tandem into being, for in a rare photograph it can be seen that it bore on its side the sign-written legend 'Built by O. Hedstrom, New York N.Y.'. In connection with this powered tandem, the 'News for Wheelmen' column of the *Boston Globe* on 21st June 1900 (just one week before the opening of the Springfield Coliseum) had reported:

> Arrangements are being made between Oscar Hedstrom and Charles Henshaw to race their fast motor tandem against the fastest train on a well known railroad. The idea is similar somewhat to the ride of Murphy, except that instead of riding behind the train they will race alongside of it on a specially built board track. It is claimed that the tandem can go 1m 15s for a mile on a track and on a straightaway, it will be able to cover the distance in 45s.

It appears that several examples of the Hedstrom & Henshaw pacer were built, giving their creator valuable early experience in gasoline engine construction and operation. Period newspapers show that the duo's pacers were routinely operational in support of bicycle competition during the 1900 and 1901 seasons. They also entered the pacer-only competition events now being staged as bonus features during 1900 bicycle race programmes. The subject of one press report was match-race challenges issued by Henshaw to the pacers of other cycle competitors like Jimmy Michael, in which the expected protocol was that money be staked in advance by each protagonist with independent third-party A.G. Batchelder, chairman of the NCA board of control. When famous pioneer English racing tricyclist Charles Jarrott brought his Ariel machine over to the US with him in 1900, in case he got bored and needed some sport during his auto-industry business trip, Henshaw was reportedly very anxious to meet up with him. For evidence that there was indeed more than one H&H pacer, we can quote the *Boston Globe* 'News for Wheelmen' column of 11th May 1901 which reported (and note the reporter's use of the plural term 'tandems have', not the singular 'tandem has'):

> The Springfield Coliseum will have one of the largest pacing outfits of any track in the country. The Henshaw and Hedstrom tandems have been merged with those of Hausman and Rutz, and Hausman will be manager of the outfit.

At the beginning of 1901 Hendee proposed to Hedstrom that he develop a powered bicycle for offer to the public as a new form of personal transport. This was by no means an original idea, for there were already one or two such devices like the Marsh and the Orient being built and sold in the US. It was nevertheless a far-sighted idea, for it was by no means clear at this time that powered two-wheelers had any kind of a future. In fact, noted expert Charles Jarrott was decidedly pessimistic about motor-bicycles when he reviewed his experiences of two-, three- and four-wheelers in his 1906 memoir *Ten Years of Motors and Motor Racing*. George Hendee was taking a bit of a gamble here, in accordance with the time-honoured American tradition of keeping an eye for the main chance.

Hedstrom duly completed a prototype motor-bicycle at Worcester Cycle Mfg. Co. in May 1901, and built at least two others in that same year. On 29th October 1901 he signed a two-and-a-half year contract with effect from 1st January 1902 to transfer his inventions and patents in said motor-bicycle (these patents had been applied-for on 28th October) to Hendee in return for a salary of $1500 (about $40,000 in today's dollars) and one dollar in every five as royalties. During 1902 Hedstrom worked to organise commercial production of the motor-bicycle in a loft built above the bicycle portion of Hendee's Springfield factory. Indian thus preceded Belgium's FN (1902), England's Triumph (1902), and USA's Harley-Davidson (1905)[21] into the motorised bicycle business.

The first powered Indian model made by the Hendee Mfg. Co. used an original-design 213cc single-cylinder inlet-over-exhaust-valve ('F-head') engine which neatly took the place of the seat-tube in a heavier-than-usual bicycle-style frame. The overhead inlet valve was of automatic (atmospheric) actuation in accordance with de Dion practice. Ignition was by coil, using current supplied by dry-cell batteries held in a cylinder attached to the front frame down-tube. The hump-shaped gas/oil tank sat over the rear wheel, leading to the name 'camel-back' for these first Indians. The bike sold for $200, and would travel at up to 25mph.

Very unusual for those times, Indian motor bicycles transmitted power to the rear wheel by chain rather than belt, a feature of distinct advantage in hilly country. Belt drive was almost universal in those days because belts were cheap, light, silent, and had natural shock-absorbing properties that gave a smoother ride. They were difficult to gear low for hill work however, because the engine pulley then needed to be small in diameter and this resulted in belt slip.

Chains running on toothed sprockets did not suffer from slip, but they were a harsh and unyielding way of transmitting power in those days before transmission shock absorbers had been invented. Owing to the puny chain then available, the result could be frequent chain breakages. If the chain held, on the other hand, un-absorbed drive-train tremors would pass into the frame and running gear

An unrestored example of the early 'camel-back' Indian motor bicycles (Photo Jim Parker)

and this could simply shake the bike to pieces. In Britain, Ixion found this out the hard way when conducting his own private experiments with chain-driven variable-gear transmissions. It was perhaps no coincidence that, when the power of the early Indians got increased in 1905, they also came to be fitted with a 'compensation sprocket', which is American-industry parlance for a drive-train shock absorber. Apart from the pioneering Phelon and Rayner (later Phelon and Moore) with its chain drive and free-engine clutch, the British clung affectionately to the notion of belt drives for another two decades. One possible reason which has been advanced by some US commentators, for earlier adoption of chain drive by US manufacturers could be that American chain, such as that made by the Baldwin Chain Co. (est. 1896), was by 1901 generally stronger than British chain.

Also unusual, Hedstrom didn't bother with the then-typical, crude, but simple surface carburetor. Instead, he immediately developed his own design of spray carburetor. He soon added twist-grip for the throttle and ignition advance controls (an idea borrowed from regular Wigwam visitor Glenn Curtiss), rather than force riders to take their hands off the handlebars and fiddle around with throttle and advance levers mounted on the frame top-tube. Right from those first early days, when no clear pattern had yet crystallized as to what a 'motor-bicycle' ought to look like, the first Indian had gained features which would still be typical of motorcycles a hundred years hence.

In 1902 Indian built around 150 'motocycles' (so-called because legal issues surrounding use of the term 'motorcycle' were by no means clear) and this increased to 586 by 1904, 1,181 in 1905, and then 2,176 in 1907. As a comparison, the British industry sold about 8,000 machines of all makes in 1907, of which industry leader and biggest-seller Triumph was pleased to produce just over 1,000.

Once established in the US market and with sales expanding, Hedstrom began developing and improving his product, seeking to maintain its technological edge. By 1905, Hedstrom was already experimenting with fitment of two- and three-speed gearboxes and adjustable front suspension, and was personally entering motorcycle competition events mounted on a 'three horse-power double-cylinder' machine.[22] The first production Indian V-twin appeared in 1906 and was a 636cc 42-degree ioe (inlet over exhaust) machine capable of 45mph. This was the model that Teddy Hastings brought over to England in 1907.

Hastings returned to England in 1908 to again compete in the Thousand Miles Trial. This time he had factory sponsorship from Hendee Mfg. Co. president George Hendee, who'd been pleased with the publicity gained by Hastings' 1907 effort. Hastings again did well, and Indian garnered further publicity in Britain. One person who was clearly impressed by the Indian twin was Billy Wells, purveyor of Vindec Specials. He is pictured in a famous photo taken of the Indian during the Trial, and is looking admiringly at the machine while Hastings signs in to a check-point.

After declining to further serve the interests of Vindec in UK, Wells returned to the US in March 1909 and while there he looked up his old friend and fellow cycle competitor George Hendee. On learning that Wells was currently at a loose end, Hendee urged him to immediately return to England and set up an Indian marketing, sales and service organisation for all of Britain and her colonies, and for Europe. Hendee himself termed this entity a 'branch office' of the Hendee Mfg. Co. Ltd.

The Indian Depot in London was thus financed by the Indian factory, with Billy Wells appointed on salary as its manager. It opened for business in May 1909 at 178 Great Portland Street, in the West End close to fashionable Oxford Street. Two registration plates SJ80 and SJ81 were issued to Wells for 'trade purposes' on 13th May 1909 in Bute, Scotland. Wells launched an extensive sales campaign, and worked hard to set up a dealership network in Britain. Always a keen competition man, he began offering Indians as rides for top British racers to enter in motorcycle events at Brooklands and on the Isle of Man. In recognition of his efforts overall to boost Indian export sales, Wells was made a member of the Hendee Mfg. Co.'s Board of Directors in 1911, a position he held until the company was reorganized and renamed as the Indian Motocycle Company in November 1923. In his capacity as a Board member, during the sixteen-year period from 1909 to 1925 Billy Wells made in total approximately thirty trans-Atlantic crossings for US visits of about one month duration each.

Billy Wells married his secretary Clara at about this time and, her maiden name being Wilson, prevailing child-naming conventions dictated that their son (born in 1915) should have been christened William Wilson Wells. Billy managed to avoid saddling the poor lad with such an awkward tongue-twister by instead naming him George Hendee Wells, in honour of his friend who'd set him back up in business. In addition to writing the foreword of this book, Billy's son George has kindly provided his childhood recollections of the atmosphere and surroundings of Indian's new London depot.

> Great Portland Street runs from Euston Road in the North to Oxford Circus in the South and is very much typical of London's West End. There were shops and offices of varying age and, in the years before the 1914 - 1918 war, can be described as part Victorian and part early 20th century. There was a dental hospital and, importantly, a modern block of flats called Portland Court. I was born in one of these flats, and so this building is one of my earliest milestones.
>
> There was a lift from the entrance to four or five floors and at the back of the building was a metal fire escape. Our flat had three bedrooms, dining room, sitting room etc. Some of these looked out onto Great Portland Street and I suppose this street was my first glimpse of the big wide world.
>
> I remember some of the shops. There was a grocer where everything had to be weighed. None of today's packaging. Butter was sized from a big slab and knocked into a neat shape with a couple of paddles. Biscuits came from large tins and the nice man would give me one to try.
>
> Most memorable was the showroom by our entrance which was the motorcycle business of Godfreys (established by Oliver Godfrey and Frank Applebee, 1911 and 1912 TT winners respectively). There was the business of Gillette which had an enormous safety razor on display, a chemist and a restaurant called 'Paganis', plus several car showrooms. The only car I remember was a Renault because it had this

The London branch of Hendee Mfg. Co. in Great Portland Street, off Oxford Street, which opened in May 1909. (EMIMA)

strange shape front not like a radiator. Warren Street was one of the streets off Great Portland Street which became a venue for men selling and buying second hand cars. I was told in later years that all their business was done without offices!

One of my first memories of the road was the noise. It was a cobblestone surface and the horse and carts clattered along and the local urchins would often jump on the tail for a free ride. One time there was a lot of hay lying in the road and I was told that this was from Victorian times when if someone was ill the hay would make the road quieter.

One day I saw a repair being carried out on the road. It was a four man job!! One man held the chisel type thing with long tongs and the other three armed with sledge hammers hit the chisel in rhythmic sequence. The advent of mechanical drills was an obvious improvement.

Another day I saw a small cart like thing with a motor on it and a long flexible pipe going up the side of the building and in a window and I was told that this was one of the latest inventions for cleaning called a 'vacuum cleaner'. I suppose all inventions have to start somewhere.

I think I was always interested in motor vehicles. One day when I was out I heard a big bang and, on looking round, there was a taxi and on one of its tyres was a huge orange balloon about a foot in diameter. My father explained to me that this often happened in the early days of pneumatic tyres when the casing got a long cut in it, and the inner tube burst through it to produce the orange balloon.

The establishment of an Indian organization in Britain in 1909 coincided with the Indian motor bicycles themselves making a design leap to become fully-fledged *motor*cycles. In this regard, it has to be said that the Hendee Mfg. Co. were a little slow off the mark. Though preceding other famous brands like FN, Triumph or Harley-Davidson into the motor-bicycle business, the Indian motor-bicycle remained just that – a motor-bicycle – until the end of 1908. Triumph had released Britain's first recognizable and credible motorcycle, the 3 hp model, in 1905. In their second attempt at building a prototype in 1904, William Harley and the Davidsons avoided the diamond-frame-with-pedals bicycle type of machine altogether. When the first complete motorcycles to be produced by H-D became available to the public in mid-1905, they were a Merkel-inspired loop-frame model that straightaway gave pride of place to its substantial engine rather than to its foot pedals.

Hendee Mfg. Co., on the other hand, instead concentrated on expanding their factory facilities to ramp up production of the original-concept 'camel-back' Indian, in order to meet the rapidly increasing demand for it. Though both Hendee and Hedstrom were racing men at heart and had successful cycle racing careers behind them (Hedstrom himself remained active in cycle competition until at least 1904) they sensibly focused upon the Indian standard road model until its sales had built up satisfactorily. Only in 1908 did the 'camel-back' engine gain a mechanically-operated inlet valve, and then only as an optional extra.

Herbert Wagner's book *At the Creation: Myth, Reality, and the Origin of the Harley-Davidson motorcycle, 1901 – 1909* (Wisconsin Historical Society Press) provides evidence of an interesting debate within the blossoming US motorcycle industry from about 1904 onwards. Two schools of thought were evident. One held the view that motor-bicycles of all-up weight less than 110 lbs were the ideal to which all should aspire. These lightweight machines can be more easily pushed, dragged or lifted out of soft going by their riders with less need for 'wrath and profanity'. To encourage the industry in this direction, several captains of that industry (who tended to be from places adjacent to the eastern seaboard) felt that machines heavier than 110 lbs should be banned from racing. A certain G.M. Hendee of Springfield MA is on record as belonging to this school of thought. Perhaps coincidentally, his motorcycle products weighed just an ounce or two less than 110 lbs.

'Nonsense!' declared the other school of thought, made up mainly of gung-ho mid-westerners. The 'westerner' concept of motorcycling was to have something big enough and powerful enough that you wouldn't get stuck in soft going in the first place. Better to just power your way through! Naturally, 'can-do' types like Glenn Curtis, and William Harley with his associated trio of Davidsons (their first production effort being a whopping behemoth of 140 lbs) openly held to this view. And it was this view that steadily gained momentum in the US motorcycle market during the 'noughts. When Indian saw the light and dropped its lightweights in 1908, naturally H-D's advertising crowed that they'd done so in order to 'copy a Harley-Davidson'. Never mind that H-D themselves had copied a Merkel!

When Oscar Hedstrom did transform his motor bicycle into a big and hairy-chested 'westerner' type of road-burner, he did so with a vengeance. During 1908 he added two racing models to the line up, which retained the frame and layout of the motor bicycle but replaced the 'camel-back' fuel/oil tank with a torpedo-shaped tank clipped to the frame top rail in the now-customary motorcycle fuel tank position. The seat was moved back onto a special sub-frame to perch the rider over the rear wheel, leading to this machine being dubbed the 'monkey-on-a-stick' model. Going a step further, Hedstrom next made a one-off racing 'special' with a loop frame that dropped the engine down low in front of the pedal bracket, rather than above it as on the bicycle-type frame. The move to a loop frame gave this unique new Indian the look of a true 'motor' cycle.

Former bicycle racer and pacer driver Jake de Rosier, now a free-lance motorcyclist, was let loose upon this 'special' to have a summer of fun at the Paterson, New Jersey, velodrome. At this venue he ran demonstration laps, and challenged all-comers to match races. He set the first Federation of American Motorcyclist (FAM) recognized US board track speed records during this summer of 1908 at speeds of around 68 mph, thereby single-handedly ensuring that the very first opening pages of the inaugural US speed record book had the name 'Indian' written all over them.

Born in 1880, the same year as Charles Franklin, de Rosier was a French Canadian raised in Massachusetts. His competition career began at age 14 as an amateur cyclist at Fall River, Mass., but before long he was re-designated a professional and he kept this up for four years until 1898. Then he spied the two motor tandems brought across from France by Henri Fournier in November of that year. Immediately Jake wanted to have a go, and he took to it like a duck to water. De Rosier consequently had the honour of being steersman in the first motor-paced cycle event ever run in the US which took place at Waltham, Mass., at the end of 1898. The advent of motor pacing revolutionized cycle sport in the US, as it had already done in Europe.

Operating a motor tandem was not for the faint of heart. Because keeping an internal combustion engine alive and spinning was in those days a full-time occupation for a dedicated *mécanicien*, a separate person (the steersman) meanwhile had his own hands full with keeping the long and unwieldy device pointed in the right direction. According to a January 1900 commentary on the new technology, 'The experience of running a motor at 40 miles an hour is thrilling, and requires nerve, which is often found wanting if a 'chauffeur' should have ever experienced a fall'. Just because a person could ride a bicycle did not mean they could also drive a motor tandem. There were those who assumed it to be so, and in at least one case this was the result:

> Arthur Ross, the well known little middle distance rider, who claims distinction for being a human bubble-maker as well as a fast rider, tried last Wednesday to be an expert steersman of a motor tandem. It was at Brockton where Harry Caldwell was training. Caldwell's steersmen were not handy and little Ross climbed into the front saddle and with a man on the rear the tandem started off. Curves were then in order and up and down the bank the machine swung, traveling about as straight as a

Opening day at the Springfield Stadium board track in 1909, showing the spectacle and gala atmosphere typical of US motorcycle racing during the board-track era. (EMIMA)

Oscar Hedstrom and George Hendee, with Julia Hedstrom on the right, at the completion of the Springfield Stadium board track in 1909, showing the steepness of the banking on the turn (EMIMA)

> Brookline man walking from Roxbury late on a Saturday night. The rear man got scared and jumped without pulling the plug and within a few seconds it was Ross and the tandem in a heap inside the pole. He won't try again.

It was as a pacer-driver and a mechanic that de Rosier entered the employ of Hendee Mfg. Co. in 1901, but he left after a few months. De Rosier continued his career as a pacer steersman until 1905, when he switched instead to motorcycle racing which was now gaining ground as a sport in its own right. As a result of various mishaps and spectacular get-offs it is said that, toward the end of the new century's first decade, small and slightly-built de Rosier had not a patch of skin more than three inches square that had not yet been gouged, cut, bruised or torn. Of broken bones, multiple fractures and missing ribs there was now an extensive catalogue in his weighty medical file. His grit and determination to get to the top of this glamorous but dangerous new sport, and stay there, was very evident in his conduct, his competitive spirit, and his refusal to be deterred by the prospect of further physical agonies or months-long spells of enforced idleness in a hospital bed. In a contemporary (1910) feature article about de Rosier, a journalist for the *Indianapolis Star* put it this way:

> One would imagine that he had been slammed about enough to make him sour on the motorcycle game, but he cannot quit, for the same reason that Harriman only quit the railroad-building game because he

died. It is seldom that auto drivers, motor riders or aviators decide to retire until some barber is hired for $5 to shave them so they will look natural. De Rosier says he will not quit because he is not a quitter.[23]

In 1908 he was hired again by Indian, this time to be the official factory rider, on the strength of his feats on the prototype loop-frame Indian at the Paterson NJ track. De Rosier thus became the world's first professional salaried motorcycle racer. Not for him the ennobling spirit of amateurism in sport! He knew he was good at what he did, and he expected to be paid accordingly.

Jake de Rosier quickly repaid Hendee's investment in him, and then some. By 1910 he held the US records for all distances from one to one hundred miles in the name of Indian. He was firmly established as the major star of US motorcycle racing, among a coterie of riders whose gladiatorial feats had greatly popularized the new sport and of whom it was said 'They furnish excitement as thrilling as it is served in any form and cause one's blood to creep every minute they are in action'[24]. As a result, timber board tracks were now being established all over America by promoter Jack Prince. Racing speeds soon climbed up to the low nineties, undreamt of and widely doubted in Britain where the mid-eighties was the best that anyone could yet manage.

In 1909 the 'camel-back' models were dropped completely and all production Indians became loop-framed 2¾ hp singles or V-twins of either 5 hp (38 cu in) or 7 hp (61 cu in or 1,000cc). These were thoroughly modern, up-to-the-minute motorcycles which again gave Indian a big technological edge. They came with either coil ignition or Bosch magneto, had mechanically (pushrod) operated overhead inlet valves in an inlet-over-exhaust or F-head configuration, race-proven steering geometry, and (an Indian trademark from the beginning) all-chain drive. Billy Wells had picked exactly the right moment in which to begin promoting the Indian marque for British road use, and for racing.

The first appearance of this re-vamped Indian in a race in Britain was in a 2-lap event held at the Brooklands Track on Wednesday 19th May 1909. Billy Wells rode a 5 hp (638cc) twin in this event and another American, a young chap named Guy Lee Evans, was entered on a single-cylinder 2 ¾ hp (319cc)

Guy Lee Evans in the paddock at Brooklands with a Hedstrom ioe. twin. (Photo courtesy Indian Archives)

model. According to Brooklands historian Peter Hartley,[25] Wells flooded his carburetor on start-up so didn't get away well and ultimately finished fourth, however Lee Evans took second place. One should perhaps not read too much into these results, because this was the first time any Indian had ever been rolled out onto the bumpy cement of Brooklands. The official starter 'Ebbie' Ebblewhite would've had to just take a guess about how much to handicap them.

Even so, Wells' new Indians created much interest among technically-minded Brooklands habitués, for these machines sported Splitdorf magnetos, twist-grip throttle and spark controls operating through articulated rod linkages, and (like P&M) all-chain drive divided into primary and secondary stages, with power transmitted through a countershaft-mounted shock absorber and clutch mechanism that allowed a 'free' engine (that is, the engine could continue running when the bike was stationary).

This was pretty advanced stuff for motorcyclists in Britain, where progress in motorcycle design had by this time reached a plateau, or 'comfort zone'. Ixion has related how both manufacturers and customers alike seemed generally content with motorcycles that by now were reasonably reliable and reasonably powerful. Most people didn't seem to mind that British machines were, for the most part, still clutch-less, so needed pushing or pedalling to get them started and, once started, couldn't be brought to a stop without stalling the engine, which required one to then repeat the starting process in order to move off again. Further, British motorcycles were still single-speed and belt-driven. They therefore needed to be geared fairly tall to put up a decent average speed on the flat and to avoid belt slip from too-small an engine pulley, but this meant they soon ground to a halt on any decent hill. This is why the relatively-flat St John's course had been chosen for the motorcycling Tourist Trophy on the Isle of Man – the automobile TT course over the Mountain (Snaefell) would have been too stern a test.

Naturally, Noel Drury ultimately bought himself an Indian twin. How could he not, after being so closely associated with MCUI and D&DMCC club-mate Charlie Franklin during these exciting years spent racing? Here's how he summed up his own opinion of the 1909-onwards Hedstrom Indians.

> The first chain driven machine which I owned was a 5 hp twin cylinder Indian, with 45° included angle, side exhaust valves, overhead inlet mechanically opened. This engine was designed by Oscar Hedstrom and made by the Hendee Manufacturing Co., in USA. The drive was by primary chain to a countershaft embodying a slipping clutch and then a secondary chain to the back wheel. This machine was revolutionary in many ways. It had a pressure oiling system for the engine; the clutch was worked by a long flat metal lever lying alongside the tank with a friction device to hold it in any position. The clutch had a large surface and could be slipped quite a lot in traffic without harm.
>
> The controls on this machine were worked by twisting handlegrips which operated rods to the carburettor and spark advance. The front wheel was sprung very well and the machine was a delight to drive, being very comfortable and extremely silent. The carburettor acted without any air correction after the first few minutes. I bought this machine from W. H. Wells who ran the South British Trading Co. of Finsbury Pavement, London, who had the Indian agency. After some months I sold this machine, and bought a 7 hp Indian from Waite Brothers of Lemon Street, Dublin. This was generally similar to the 5 hp machine, but had a more powerful engine, a two-speed gear and foot operated clutch. This was a very fast and lovely machine, and I had it for a long time, eventually selling it to C.B. Franklin in the autumn of 1914 when I joined up.

In early 1909 neither Franklin nor Drury had yet discovered Indian motorcycles, however. At the end of 1908 Franklin was still wreaking havoc in Irish competition with his 6 hp JAP. For example, at the MCUI (Dublin Centre) Speed Trials, Portmarnock Strand on Saturday 10th October 1908, C.B. Franklin (JAP) won both the 2 miles and 20 miles Members' Handicaps.

Throughout the summer of 1909 Wells and Evans made the Indian marque fairly conspicuous in race results at Brooklands, placing consistently in handicap events and winning scratch races, like the 16th June 'Tourist Trophy Scratch Race' run to Isle of Man TT regulations as a part of build-up for the next event over on the Island. Lee Evans was particularly successful on a 5 hp Indian at the two-day (Saturday 31st July and Monday 1st August) Bank Holiday weekend race meeting, in which six motorcycle races were interspersed among a mainly automobile race programme. Despite the presence of the Collier brothers and their equally swift cousin, Bert Colver, on Matchless-JAP machines, Lee Evans won three out of the four motorcycle races he entered. He then ran against three of the cars in the 'August Winners Handicap', which he also won. His speeds were just over 60 mph Before Indian aficionados get too cocky, however, we must also let the record show that the one race won by Charlie Collier (admittedly on a 964cc machine) was at a speed of 69.25 mph

At the Dublin & District MCC annual general meeting at the Waverley Hotel in Sackville Street on 28th January 1909, C.B. Franklin was re-elected a vice-president. Similarly, at the MCUI (Dublin Centre) annual general meeting on Wednesday 17th February 1909 at Wynn's Hotel, C.B. Franklin was also re-elected as vice-president. At the AGM a sub-committee consisting of Messrs. J.A. Armstrong, C.B. Franklin and N. Quinn was appointed to draft new competition rules.

The Irish events documented on page 124 for the early part of the 1909 competition season show that Franklin had put away his JAP machinery and brought out a Triumph instead. This could be viewed as his preparation for the Isle of Man Tourist Trophy race. Sure enough, when Franklin lodged his entry for that race it showed that he intended to appear on a Triumph. It is likely that he was influenced in his choice of mount by the very strong showing of Triumph 3½ hp singles in the 1908 TT, and subsequently at Brooklands.

When the 1909 TT race was run on 23rd September, there was this time no petrol consumption limit. Riders could now go hell-for-leather with throttles wide open and dice with each other, rather than putt along sedately at fixed speeds calculated to let them finish within their petrol allowance. Singles and twins were now combined into one class competing for one trophy and one set of prizes, however singles could not exceed 500cc nor twins 750cc. This was not considered unfair to singles, since in those days they tended to do better in racing than twins by virtue of being more reliable and less likely to go so quickly out of tune. It was becoming apparent to some racers, however, that the future of truly fast motorcycling lay with multis.

The 1909 race was a thriller. Billy Wells and Lee Evans had both entered, and duly appeared at the start on 5 hp Indian twins. Lee Evans and the Collier brothers straightaway set out at a (for those days) blistering pace. Billy Wells, on the other hand, came a cropper and was officially listed as 'Did not finish'. The Colliers, who'd themselves just made the switch to twin-cylinder machinery (Matchless-JAP, newly fitted with Bosch magneto rather than battery-and-coil), were initially of the opinion that the fast pace of Lee Evans would soon see him break down and retire. Harry and Charlie were content to tag along after him, poised ready to take the lead when (as they hoped) the bright-red Indian inevitably ground to a halt. But this did not happen.

Then Charlie Collier, reputedly riding the faster of the two Matchless machines, was himself forced to retire fairly early in the race. His drive belt broke and tangled in the rear brake mechanism, causing damage that rendered him unable to continue. It was now up to Harry Collier to get into the lead, dig deep, and try every trick he knew to stay out in front of Evans' Indian. In this he succeeded, winning the race in 3 hours 13 min and 27.8 secs at an average speed of 49.01 mph and pipping Evans into second place at 3 hours, 17 min and 35.2 secs and 48.07 mph Among the singles, Jack Marshall on a Triumph tussled with Oliver Godfrey on a Rex and they both gave the twins a good run for their

The starting line-up of a typical handicap motorcycle race at Brooklands Track in 1910. Indian competitor Guy Lee Evans, starting from 'scratch' at the far end, is recognisable by his distinctive hooped sweater. Timekeeper 'Ebby' is about to start off the 'limit' men. This photo was taken by an American visitor named Oscar Hedstrom.

money. Marshall's Triumph then broke a valve on the eighth lap. Triumph rider Billy Newsome took over the pace-setting role to squeeze home just half a minute before Godfrey.

The race was a wake-up call for the British riders and manufacturers. The Indian menace had arrived, and had thrown down the gauntlet. Harry Collier's was a very popular victory with the British racing public for the thrilling way in which he had managed to hold out the foreign invader.

Charles Franklin on his Triumph took 5th place overall with a time of 3 hours 41 minutes and 10 seconds and a speed of 43.02 mph This effort was very creditable, and good enough to net him the Private Owner's Prize. What happened to Billy Wells in this race?

One version has it that, it being Wells' custom to mount from a running push-start with a dramatic high-flying leap into the saddle, on this occasion his hands slipped from the handlebars and he fell heavily, landing awkwardly on top of his machine with his chest. He sustained injuries from this mishap which not only put him out of this race but effectively ended his solo-machine racing career, though he did continue to compete at Brooklands in sidecar events.

Further light on this is shed by an old Isle of Man postcard in the Rick Howard Collection of veteran motorcycle memorabilia. Addressed to someone named Oscar Hedstrom c/o Hendee Mfg. Co., Springfield Mass., USA, it is signed off by what appears to be 'W.H. Wells' and is postmarked 'Douglas 4:15 24 Sep 09.' The writer lists the first three TT place-getters and their race times, then finishes with a cryptic comment; 'I had accident. Brake caused loss of race'. If Wells really did crash-out right at the start, this left only Lee Evans in contention for Indian. So rather than interpreting this comment as meaning a faulty brake caused Wells to crash, it could instead mean that Wells crashed (for reasons too embarrassing to specify) whereas it was a faulty brake on Evans' machine which prevented him from winning.

At the end of each season's racing programme at Brooklands, before the track was closed over winter for maintenance and repairs, it was customary to run speed record attempts. Apart from the fact that the track could more easily be booked exclusively for large blocks of time without hindrance by scheduled events, it just so happened that any new records set at this time of the year could immediately be used in factory promotions at the annual motorcycle industry trade show held at Olympia in London. And so it was that, on Saturday 15th November 1909, Guy Lee Evans and Billy Wells took a 497cc single-cylinder Indian down to the track where, with Evans on board, it set new records in the 50-mile, 100-mile and 2 hour categories at 55.58, 54.34 and 54.38 mph respectively.

Franklin had done moderately well in the 1909 TT race by choosing to ride a Triumph, a decision no doubt based upon the excellent record of wins and places by Triumphs from the very inception of the TT, which included 1st place in 1908. The deserved popularity of Triumph 3.5 hp singles at this time is a fact commented upon by *Irish Cyclist & Motor Cyclist* on 26th January 1910:

> TRIUMPHS IN THE ASCENDANT
> The phenomenal success of the Triumph motorcycle in Ireland continues in a very marked degree. The demand in Dublin for the new model promises to exceed even last year's record. Orders are not usually received before February, but already a considerable number have been booked by Mr. F. A. Wallen of Nassau Street, the Dublin agent of the famous Coventry firm, who for the past seven years has been mainly responsible for the placing of a very large number of Triumph motorcycles on Irish roads. Among the list of recent purchasers was C.B. Franklin.

Nevertheless, the leather saddle of Franklin's own Triumph TT model would have proved an excellent vantage point from which to witness the strong challenge mounted by the vermillion Indians of Wells and Evans. It was not very hard for Franklin to correctly read the tea leaves regarding the most likely outcome of the next TT in 1910. In due course, the following item appeared in *Irish Cyclist* on 16th March 1910:

> C.B. Franklin has taken delivery of the 5 hp two-cylinder Indian that he proposes to use in the Tourist Trophy next May. The very indifferent weather we have had during the past week, coupled with the fact that he has just recovered from a bout of influenza, has prevented Franklin from getting the machine on the road, but he hopes to do so in the next few days.

This was followed by another brief report on 30th March 1910 that 'The Dublin & District MCC opened their season on Friday last with a run to Wicklow. C.B. Franklin was out on his new twin-cylindered Indian which he is to use in the Tourist Trophy race.'

By 1910 the performances of the twins in TT races were starting to almost (but not quite yet) eclipse that of the single-cylinder machines. In fact, the race results of twins in Brooklands competitions over subsequent years shows that, even in the 1930s when big V-twins were certainly the fastest things around, their riders and tuners paid dearly for that extra 10 or so mph They paid for it in terms of high fuel consumption, heavy weight, unwieldy handling, rapid tyre wear, and hours of aggravation spent seeking that perfect state of tune when both cylinders would run in harmony, chasing that perfect moment when a good run could be achieved before the engine slipped out of tune again. Singles, by comparison, ran only slightly slower but they ran like trains, especially if the year was post-1925 and the label on the tank said 'Norton'.

The TT organizers in 1910 still felt a little sorry for the people who entered on twins, though not as sorry as previously because the maximum allowable engine capacity for a twin was now reduced to 680cc. Top riders could see that twins would ultimately prevail over singles and that, if the aggravation of tuning and riding a twin meant that one could finish first, the aggravation would be worth it. The

Franklin tries out his recently-acquired Indian 5 hp twin in an Irish competition event in 1910. The bike bears his Irish registration number IK40 (RHC)

Collier brothers had already eschewed singles in favour of twins for the 1909 TT race. Franklin made the same decision for 1910.

The 1910 Tourist Trophy Races, run on Thursday 26th May, should have been the occasion on which Indian cleaned-up at the Island. Indians twins were there in force, and carried some top riders of the day. A total of seven Indians appeared at the start, their riders and race numbers being Charlie Bennett (2), Guy Lee Evans (3), Dudley Clarke (4), Walter Bentley, later to be famous as 'W.O.' of Bentley cars, (6), Charles B. Franklin (10), Jimmy Alexander (26), and Arthur Moorhouse (32). Not only that, but the Great Medicine Man of Indian, Oscar Hedstrom himself, came over from the US to personally watch over the official Indian entries.[26]

Of the seven Indian entrants, only three were members of an 'official' Indian team – Evans, Bentley, and Bennett. They had been appearing together on 638cc (that is, TT-eligible) Indians in events at Brooklands since March of that year. For example, on 16th March they were photographed at Brooklands together with Wells after competing in a One-hour TT Race run under Tourist Trophy regulations, in which they packed out the top three places. This and other One-Hour and Two-Hour events held at Brooklands during the three-month run-up to the TT are all described in Hartley's book (see Bibliography page 331), and the Evans-Bentley-Bennett trio feature prominently in the results. The other four TT Indian riders Clarke, Franklin, Alexander and Moorhouse were private entrants riding their own machines. There was to have been an eighth Indian in the TT, but its rider, New Zealander Alan Woodman, crashed in practice and one of his legs had to be amputated.

There were twelve JAP-powered entries in the race, ridden by well-known competitors like Harry Martin, Noel Drury, Harold Bowen, Frank McNab, Harry Reed and, of course, the Matchless-JAP team of the two Collier brothers and Bert Colver. These latter three had also been using the recent Brooklands One- and Two-Hour 'TT style' events as practice for the Island. Overall the Indians were regarded as being the bikes to beat, and all eyes were upon the Collier Bros. as being the ones most likely to beat them.

In the event, the race was a let-down for those expecting a repeat of the excitement of 1909. The Indians dropped out one by one with tyre troubles. This left the two Colliers in the lead by the half-way mark, and from there they had a nice romp home with little in the way of serious challenge. Charlie was 1st, followed by Harry in 2nd place, comfortably ahead of the Triumphs that made up most of the other top places. The best Indian was Alexander in 14th place, and the only other Indian rider to finish was Lee Evans who came 21st. Clarke retired in the 4th lap after falling near Kirk Michael and his machine caught fire. Up till then his times for the first three laps had been 20.13 - 19.39 - 19.23, about a minute or so off the pace of the race's fastest lap at 18.17. Moorhouse retired in the 5th lap with tyre inner tube trouble. Bently retired in the 2nd lap after his rear tyre burst near the top of Creg Willey's Hill. Charlie Franklin had his back tyre burst at the Devil's Elbow section of the course (see colour photo 3). He was thrown with great force against the low wall and almost went over. His lap times up to that point had been 57.16 and 48.41, each being an absolute eternity which surely spells '*Tyre Trouble*'. Ixion reported in his 1920s *Reminiscences* that the Indian team had been let down by a faulty consignment of tyre inner tubes, and commented that 'the race as a whole lacked interest'.

Harry Collier (No. 1, Matchless) looks anxious at the start of the 1910 T.T. race, as well he might since he is surrounded by a sea of vermillion Indians at 2, 3, and 4 with other Indians starting further back (Franklin is at No. 10). But the Indians all had tyre problems, so Charlie and Harry Collier comfortably finished 1st and 2nd respectively. (EMIMA)

On the day after the 1910 TT race, a hill-climb was organised from Ramsey up to the top of Snaefell. This is Franklin rounding the Ramsey Hairpin. He came second in the Private Owners class. (Photo Carol Northern)

The next day, on Friday 27th May 1910, a hill-climb competition was held on the road from Ramsey to the top of Snaefell. Charles Franklin entered, even though he only had the use of one hand after his spill the day before. He nevertheless came second in the twin-cylinder class (private owners), beaten by P. Butler on a 5 hp DOT

For Noel Drury, 1910 was to be his last TT. Faithful to his JAP big twin, he'd been 6th in 1908 but had been forced to retire during the 1909 and 1910 races. Here, in his own words, is the story of another well known Irish motorcyclist's TT campaigns.

'I see by an old paper that the range of JAP engines offered for 1907 consisted of a 4 hp single cylinder 85 x 85 aiv (automatic inlet valve); 6 hp 45° twin 70 x 95 aiv; 8 hp 90° twin 85 ·x 85 mov (mechanically operated inlet valve); 9 hp 45⁰ twin 85 x 95 aiv These JAP engines were made by the firm of John A. Prestwich & Co., of Tottenham, who originally made all kinds of precision instruments, like the so-called magic lanterns, telescopic fittings, and their range of tools and machines was very fine but they were still capable of making the most awful mistakes. About 1909 I got a single cylinder ohv 85 x 85 engine from them, and worked a lot in the evenings fitting up the machine, making engine brackets, silencer, bending exhaust pipe, etc. At last I had the machine ready for its first run. Hardly had I gone a few miles when a tremendous hissing noise came from the engine. Inspection showed that there was a flaw in the cylinder casting and this had been plugged by driving in a piece of copper wire which blew out when the throttle was opened full for the first time.

Another instance of the weird things they did at Prestwich's at times is this. In conjunction with them in the autumn of 1907 I designed a twin cylinder engine, 85 x 60 overhead valves, cylinders set at 90° included angle to get perfect balance. This machine was entered for the 1908 TT race. I built up the machine at home during the winter and when I got it finished I took it out for the first run. It appeared to be firing altogether on one cylinder and the second one coming in very weakly. After a lot of examination and measurement I found that one cylinder casting was longer than the other and to avoid making new ones Prestwich made one connecting rod longer than the other, but when assembling the engine they put the long rod into the short cylinder and the short one into the long cylinder! Of course the whole engine had to be rushed back to them and a new one prepared. This was quite a special job and had ball bearing big ends and ball bearing main bearings and I entered it for the 1908 TT race in the Isle of Man. This eventually turned out to be a very fine engine and should have done very well in the Island, but I was dogged by punctures and only managed to get fourth in the twin-cylinder class. My average speed was between 39 and 40 miles per hour.

Later I had the stroke of this engine reduced to 54 mm to bring the engine within the new engine limit for the 1909 TT and its power and speed were quite unaffected. Again I was put out of the race by hitting a large boulder which fell out of a loose wall round a bend in Glen Helen and I came a 'purler', bending the forks and other damage.

I entered again for the 1910 TT race and decided to use the same engine but with the stroke reduced still further to comply with the new regulations. The engine was now 85 x 54 with cylinders at 45° included angle. It is extraordinary how the power and speed improved in spite of the very short stroke. I cannot now remember what valve overlap I eventually used, but I remember many hours work with a dentist's foot operated drill working on the cams before hardening them. I had a couple of very fast laps in this race and was feeling very hopeful when the saddle fastening broke off and left me in the ditch. My leg was hurt too much to get the machine going again (without a saddle) and I had to get a lift back into Douglas as soon as the roads were cleared. The winner was Charlie Collier, Matchless, 50.63 mph Fastest lap, H. A. Bowen on a Rex, 53.15 mph I decided to give up this racing as it was getting far too expensive for a mere amateur; all the firms entering had elaborate headquarters with spare engines and parts available.

The above passage represents Drury's own thoughts on the subject, penned sixty years later. His withdrawal from racing was considered newsworthy at the time, and was still being reported three years later, in *The Irish Cyclist and Motor Cyclist* of 4 June 1913 when firstly they commented in general:

The degree of importance that the trade attaches to the winning of the Tourist Trophy races is evident from the list of entries, but a week on the Island brings home to one even more forcibly the great pains the manufacturers take to secure a win. Some of the firms have what practically amounts to little factories, while few are without staffs of mechanics sufficiently large to man a repair works of considerable size. Most of the teams have managers as well, while Rudges have gone one better than the rest by securing the services of a trainer to look after the physical welfare of their riders, an exemplification of the fact that the race is a test of the endurance of the riders as well as of the machines. The thoroughness of these trade preparations makes one realise that the TT is becoming too highly specialised an affair for the private owner to take part in, unless he is prepared to become a member of a trade team and take all the assistance the manufacturers can give him. It has, in fact, become a business affair, though still not without its sporting side. One cannot help regretting this state of affairs. It was the fact that there were a sufficiently large number of private owners to keep alive the contest that made the trade bar of the event of practically no effect. The race has done an immensity of good to the British motor cycle industry and is capable of doing more. As long as the trade help is forthcoming all is well for the TT. But what will happen if the motorcycle manufacturers follow the lead of the car trade and put what amounts to a ban on all competitions? A few years of the present fierce trade rivalry will make the private owners an extinct class in competition work.

Quite a turnaround in attitude by manufacturers since the first two or three TT races, when they were still trying to decide whether motorcycle speed competition was going to be important or not. Specifically on Noel Drury's case, this same issue of *The Irish Cyclist and Motor Cyclist* had this to say:

> Noel E. Drury was amongst the Irish visitors to the Island. He has probably ridden in as many TT races as any Irishman, with the exception of Franklin, but has now given up the game, recognising it has become too highly specialised for the private owner to do himself or his mount justice. He was not, however, amongst the lookers-on. He went round each morning with the boys, and found as much sport in the practising as in the race.

Pioneer racing motorist and well-moneyed English gentleman Charles Jarrott used similar reasoning to explain his own withdrawal from competition in 1906, after ten years at the forefront of two-, three- and four-wheeled motor sport:

> Competitive effort for any reward except the gain of money is exhilarating and ennobling to the individual character. The curse of commercialism is the ruin of every sport, and the degeneracy of motor-racing as a sport is due to the financial issues now involved in each race – the immense value of victory and the commercial disaster of defeat. The same story has been told of other sports, where the gain of the victor can be made use of for commercial profit and value. The charm disappears, the sordid element is obtruded to the extinction of every other feature; and I can see in the near future, and before the racing of motor-cars dies the death which is yearly predicted for it, the sporting element obliterated altogether by the all-devouring monster of commercialism – the curse of the twentieth century.

Where did Charles Franklin stand in all of this? To borrow the words of *The Irish Cyclist and Motor Cyclist*, he very shortly showed himself 'prepared to become a member of a trade team, and take all the assistance the manufacturers can give him'.

Brooklands Track

The coterie of Indian riders being nurtured by Billy Wells were, to some extent, able to overcome their disappointment at the Island with some more excellent results at the Brooklands track over the rest of the summer of 1910. And now, for the first time, and as a member of this 'trade team', Charles Franklin came over from Dublin to compete at Brooklands.

Brooklands was the first ever track built especially for motor racing, and as such it ranks as one of the Seven Wonders of the World. A colossal civil-engineering undertaking, it had been built in only seven months at huge expense upon private land in Surrey by Hugh Fortescue Locke-King, and was opened in 1907. It was the only place in Britain apart from the Isle of Man where motor vehicles could be run at full throttle for hours on end without running foul of the 20 mph national speed limit. Unlike the Isle of Man, the track was handy to London and accessible from the Midlands motor industries' heartland, and could be used on practically any week of the year. For this reason, Brooklands was of immense value to the development of the British motor industry.

A contemporary of Charlie Franklin's in the pre-WWI era P.J. Wallace, and a mere sixteen-year-old at the time, has described in an oft quoted passage the experience of competing in a motorcycle race run at Brooklands during this pre-war period. The reference to the death of Arthur Moorhouse a month later makes the event identifiable as the BMCRC Hundred-Mile All-Comers Scratch Race held on 27th March 1912. The scene he describes can be taken as typical of the atmosphere surrounding motorcycle racing at Brooklands during the period in which Charles Franklin frequented the track.

> The number of starters in a Brooklands race might be as few as five or as many as 50; with the larger fields a simultaneous standing start provided an awe-inspiring spectacle to spectators and riders alike. Before 1914, clutches and gear-boxes were nearly unknown on motor-cycles, the rear wheel being driven directly by the engine through the medium of a rubber and canvas belt.
>
> It was this mechanical austerity which compelled the rider to push and run along-side the machine with the exhaust valve lifted from its seating in order to reduce resistance from cylinder compression. When sufficient speed had been attained, the exhaust control lever would be released and, with luck, the engine would burst into life. At this point, and not a moment later (otherwise the handle-bars might be wrenched from his grasp), the rider would leap into the air and vault into the saddle. Failure of the engine to fire could reduce the rider to a stage of physical exhaustion. High compression-ratio, big valve-overlaps and large-bore chokes all combined to make starting more difficult and uncertain; yet all three were required for maximum speed.
>
> In my first race I was positioned near the middle of some 30 or 40 competitors spaced across the whole 100ft width of the track at the Fork, and I tensely awaited the signal to start. Away to the left and in front stood A. V. Ebblewhite, chief-starter and time-keeper; his left-arm was extended horizontally and in his hand was a small flag; the dropping of this flag would be the signal to go.
>
> Although I had never been round the circuit before, the possibility of any surprises being in store

never occurred to me, so intensely had the situation been imagined. The correct technique was believed to be simple enough - to get away smartly and make a bee-line for the inner edge of the track; the closer one got, the shorter the distance to be covered. The present race was for a 100 miles, the equivalent of 37 laps.

At last the flag dropped and immediately the scene was transformed. Three dozen young men were heaving their heavy machines forward and running as fast as they could go. In a very few seconds there was bedlam; first a few, one after another, and then the whole mass of engines burst into life. As the riders leapt into their saddles, motor-cycles swerved dangerously close to one another and for a few moments a number of collisions seemed inevitable. As my own engine sprang into life the competitor on the right swerved in front, missing my wheel by inches as he made towards the inside.

For my own part, once safely in the saddle all thought of the inside line vanished into thin air; it was one thing to know the correct procedure, it was another to carry it out. Quite apart from the fact that everybody displayed the same intention, my machine bucked about in the most unexpected manner and every effort was required to keep it on a straight course.

The difficulties were accentuated by the need to juggle with the pair of levers which controlled the carburettor. It was not simply a matter of opening the throttle. Motor-cycle carburettors possessed both a throttle lever and another lever which controlled the strength of the petrol/air mixture. Then there was the ignition advance-and-retard lever, this one situated on the side of the petrol tank about which my knees were tightly gripped, otherwise it would have been impossible to remove one hand from the handlebars.

As we climbed the one in thirty incline towards the curve round the Members' Hill, most were doing about 50mph but varying our speeds sufficiently to space ourselves out: the inside edge was now becoming more accessible. Still much disconcerted to find the going so rough, I settled down to take things as they came. There was not long to wait. Sweeping round the long bend and under the Members' Bridge, all the time the way overshadowed by the high Members' Banking on the right and the hill on the left, I became aware of going downhill as the speed rose perceptibly.

Emerging from this wide ravine, there came into view the whole vast expanse of Brooklands, the Railway Straight commencing in the immediate foreground and stretching far ahead. It was an inspiring sight and a memorable moment; it was only a second later when it became yet more memorable but distinctly less inspiring. There came a sudden thrust from the left and in response the machine veered to the right, accompanied by a wobbling of the front wheel and handlebars. I was in a cold sweat, heightened by the attainment of maximum speed (about 65mph) as the bottom of the one in twenty-five incline was passed. Beginning the long straight beside the railway embankment the machine became stable and the bumps less troublesome.

The temporary deviation had been caused by sudden exposure to a southwest wind on emerging from the shelter of the Members' Hill. The strength of the wind that day was relatively light, its effect much exaggerated by my own stupidity. It was a requirement of regulations that motorcycles should carry on each side a circular disc of 12in diameter, painted black and bearing the competitors number in bold white figures. A man with a brush and bucket of whitewash was posted in the Paddock for this particular duty. In my inexperience I had bolted my number-plates to the front-forks, with the result that even a moderate wind-pressure had produced a marked turning-moment on the front wheel assembly.

It may be added that when a really strong southwest wind was blowing the sudden impact could be a considerable hazard no matter where the number-plates might be situated; to the unwary even a racing-car was not immune.

The journey down the Railway Straight was not marked by any similarly untoward event; which was just as well because there was plenty to contend with. The motorcycles of those days depended upon the timely operation of a hand-pump for their lubrication; failure in its proper operation could result in engine seizure, causing in turn a serious skid or even the propulsion of the rider over the handlebars. At touring speeds one pumpful every ten miles would normally be sufficient; at racing speeds, very much more because so much oil was thrown out of the exhaust pipe.

Without experience, which might be bought dearly, it was difficult to decide how many pumpfuls should be given during each lap; too little would mean seizure, too much would oil up the sparking-plug. It was a difficult decision to take for quite a different reason: operation of the pump meant taking one hand off the handlebars. It was not too bad when the pump was fitted with a non-return valve and the plunger returned under the action of a spring; one hand was required for only a few seconds in one single operation. The more common case of a simple pump, worked in conjunction with a hand-operated two-way cock and requiring four consecutive operations extending over 20 seconds, could be a veritable nightmare. Hitting a bad bump with one hand off the handlebars was a combination of events to be avoided.

After the Railway Straight came the long, almost semi-circular curve of the Byfleet Banking; it seemed almost interminable. Soon the aeroplane sheds and hangers were visible just beyond the inside edge. Then came the narrow bridge over the track which gave access to the flying-ground; after that had been passed the circuit was monotonous apart from the discomfort. At last, the banking came to an end and the Fork could be seen ahead. Its passing would register the end of the first lap. As all the asides will have tended to distortion of the time-scale, it should be mentioned that this lap had taken just less than three minutes.

Being in line and usually close to the inner edge, one saw little ahead beyond the man immediately in front except on the Byfleet Banking, where it was possible to see across to a few riders curving off to the left. During the first lap I was overtaken by one or two whose get-away had been even slower than my own; it was only after a few more laps that the really fast machines came by after completing one more lap than myself. The race included several classes of engine ranging from 250cc to 1,000cc twins.

At about the ninth or tenth lap, apart from feeling tired, I had really settled down, but without warning there came a stunning blow on my back, my machine went into a skid and stopped almost abruptly. The driving-belt had broken and become wedged between the belt rim and a rear tubular member of the frame - it was this jamming which had caused the skid and allowed the free end of the belt to hit me in the back.

Not only had the belt broken, but one half of the fastener had become stuck in the groove of the engine pulley; in consequence, the spare belt entwined about my middle was useless. There was nothing to be done except to walk, pushing the machine all the way to the Fork.

Far and away the fastest competitor was Arthur Moorhouse riding a 1,000cc Indian twin; with unfailing regularity he would pass about halfway up the banking although his speed was not more than about 75mph. In the course of this race he was to break the existing one-hour record. At the next meeting, the following month, he met his death along the Railway Straight by hitting a telegraph post in which remained the imprint made by the impact of his goggles. The cause was never established although it may be surmised: despite the fact that Indians were fitted with automatic mechanical lubrication of the engine, an automatic (single control) carburettor, its throttle operated (as in the case of ignition advance/ retard) by twist-grips instead of awkward levers, Moorhouse was in the habit of riding with only one hand on the handlebars while he fiddled with something or other on his engine.

By the time the Fork had been reached, I was in company with a number of other unfortunates pushing their machines. The pushers were an assorted lot, two professionals and the rest amateurs, one little older than myself, all of them inspired by the indomitable spirit of Brooklands, the determination to try again and do better next time.'

Peter Hartley's book *Bikes at Brooklands in the Pioneer Years* describes the race meeting in which Charles Franklin first competed at Brooklands. It was a major event, being the occasion of the first truly long race for motorcycles ever to be run at Brooklands. Held on 22nd June 1910, it was run under TT regulations and the distance was 60 laps (163 miles 103 yards). Franklin didn't travel over from Dublin alone however, for Noel Drury and his JAP were also present.

> For a long time it had been evident that the multi-cylinder machine was nowhere near as reliable in long-distance racing, as the single cylinder. Thus in the Isle of Man races the multi-cylinder class had always been given a higher capacity limit to make up for this deficiency. Moreover it was to help engine tuners working on multis, that the One-Hour TT events had been organised at Brooklands. Such events, however, proved inadequate as tests for the lengthier Island races.
>
> So it was, that a sixty-lap marathon was organised for the Fourth BMCRC Brooklands' meeting on Wednesday, June 22nd, 1910. A total distance of 163 miles 103 yd was involved.
>
> The event, which was run under 1910 IOM TT Race Regulations, had two classes: one for singles up to 500cc, the other for multis up to 670cc. The start and finish were at the Fork, where pit facilities had been set up for refuelling and repairs during the race.
>
> Although a heavy thunderstorm spoilt the morning, improving weather enabled the race to start on time at 4.00 pm. By then a considerable crowd of spectators had gathered at the Fork. In view of the historic nature of this, the first really long long-distance race to be staged at Brooklands, it is worth considering its entry list in detail:
>
> SINGLE-CYLINDER CLASS (up to 500cc).
> Will Cook and H. E. Parker (482 NLG-JAPs); Sam Wright and Bert Yates (499 Humbers); Lieut. Spencer Grey RN, Ray Abbott, E.Colrick-Herne, Jack Marshall, Billy Newsome, Billy Creyton, E. Gwynne, W. Dewar, Rex Mundy and F. Lister Goodacre (all on 499 Triumphs); Frank McNab, John Gibson and Angus Maitland (488 Trump-JAPs); G.E. Stanley (499 Premier); and J.H. Slaughter (498 Ariel).
>
> MULTI-CYLINDER CLASS (up to 670cc).
> Guy Lee Evans, Arthur Moorhouse, Charlie Franklin and Archie Fenn (639 Indians); D.R. Clarke (662 Indian); Harry and Bizzy Bashall, Sam Witham, and Harold Bowen (all on 666 BAT-JAPs); Martin Geiger and F.H. Arnott (662 Vindec-Specials); Vickers Jones and F. Savory (665 Premiers); E. C. W. FitzHerbert and R.O. Clark (448 FNs); Noel E. Drury (665 Chater-Lea-JAP); A.V. Deacock (666 Wanderer); and Harry Reed (658 DOT-JAP). All of the multis were twins, except for the FNs which had four cylinder engines.

Both classes were started simultaneously and within a quarter of a mile, the tailing out process had begun, with Sam Witham in the lead. For the first few laps the BAT-JAP riders were dominating the leading positions. Midfield struggles were developing between Moorhouse and Marshall, and between the two FN riders.

Bowen was the first to come into the pits, changing a defective sparking plug and getting away quickly. Harry Bashall had plenty of plug trouble in this race as well, due to central electrode breakages. In fact one piece the size of a pea, remained trapped inside a cylinder of his engine for the whole of the race, without being blown out of the exhaust or causing damage!

Four or five laps at the pace set by the leading BAT-JAPs were beginning to weed out the field, and a number of riders had disappeared from the scene on the Railway Straight, the fastest part of the circuit.

One of the first to go was Stanley, drenched with fuel due to his large and heavy filler cap having been shaken loose from his petrol tank and lost somewhere on the track.

Lee Evans was early in trouble. His engine was off form and needed excessive lubrication, so he was forced to stop for oil after only eight laps. Plug trouble caused him another pit stop a lap later. In contrast, the other Indians were going well as was also Sam Wright, on his new single cylinder ohv chain driven Humber. But his team mate Bert Yates had to retire after only two laps.

Of the Trump-JAPs, Angus Maitland's (pulling a 4-to-l gear and revving higher than most) was amongst the fastest single-cylinder machines. He soon had valve-lengthening troubles, but after a short spell in the pits and the use of a file he was soon away again.

Only one pit helper per rider was officially allowed, and the race officials at the Fork had their work cut out preventing extra unauthorised assistance from causing the disqualification of some competitors. Many riders suffered from valve-lengthening and had to come in to the pits to remedy it.

The Triumphs as a team had been going very rapidly and consistently, but unfortunately two of the best Triumph riders dropped out of the race early on. Billy Creyton like Colrick-Herne came to grief badly with a buckled wheel, in his case just beyond the Members' Bridge. A few laps later Billy Newsome was unlucky enough to run over Stanley's lost filler cap. His back wheel ended up in a similar condition.

Archie Fenn came in to his pit, changed his engine sprocket and was quickly away again. Then both Jack Marshall and Arthur Moorhouse came in to refuel. Their partnership of some fifteen laps was about to be dissolved, for Moorhouse seemed to have acquired a lot more 'steam'. He soon left the restarted and pursuing Marshall far behind.

At fifty miles Sam Witham (666 BAT-JAP) still led, having broken Bert Colver's Class D (750cc) record for the distance by averaging 65.56 mph. Scarcely had he accomplished this than he was put out of the race: on the Byfleet Banking his front mudguard came adrift, locking the wheel, bringing him off his machine at something in the region of 70 mph. Fortunately he escaped with but a few bruises. Bizzy Bashall then took over the lead with his brother, Harry, and Bowen close behind, so that BAT-JAPs still held the first three places.

Casualties now seemed to increase, valve troubles being the dominant cause. Harry Bashall stopped to clean oil off his driving belt, while his brother still led after fifty two laps with Moorhouse now in second place-having completed forty eight laps. Fate now caught up with Bizzy, when on the Byfleet Banking, a valve broke and its head dropped into the cylinder. This misfortune let Moorhouse (49 laps) and Franklin (46 laps) into first and second spots on their Indians. At this juncture Gwynne's front tyre burst and almost caused a mass pile up of riders and machines, but with great skill he managed to save the situation and pulled up safely. The race finished shortly after 7. 05 pm with Harold Bowen just scraping into second place despite his engine failure. Arthur Moorhouse rode in an easy winner 24 min 54 sec ahead of Bowen, to a highly popular victory. The single cylinder race resulted in yet another win for Frank McNab.

Clearly many lessons had been learnt from this event by competitors and officials alike. Snags to be avoided in the organisation of similar events, and the tuning requirements for high-speed reliability, were becoming clearer. Taken over all the event was judged a great success.

Noel Drury had this to say about competing at Brooklands, not in the above BMCRC race but in another long-distance event organized by the ACU

The Auto Cycle Union organised a 350 mile race at Brooklands track at Weybridge for TT type machines and I entered my machine. I asked the Dunlop Co. to fit a pair of new covers and tubes on the morning of the race. I brought my bike over to London by the night mail and had a really wonderful drive from

Euston to Surrey on this high geared belt driven machine. Although it was early in the morning (8.00 a.m.) there was a lot of traffic about, and tram lines to negotiate, but I got to Brooklands in good time and had some breakfast and then a few trial laps. I found the machine going great guns, keeping up between 75 and 80 mph without forcing it. I then handed the machine over to Dunlop and went off into Weybridge to get an early lunch as our race was to start at 1.00 pm

The machines were lined up for the start in two rows right across the finishing straight, and I was in the middle of the first. When there was only about two minutes to go a fellow behind me said he thought my back tyre looked very soft, so I pumped it up hurriedly, cursing Dunlops for being so careless. After two or three laps I felt the machine swerving about under me and I found both the front and back tyres only half pressure. I stopped and hurriedly pumped both tyres and set off, all-out to recover lost time. This same thing happened every three or four laps until I was so far behind and feeling completely exhausted with pumping and re-starting the machine that I had to chuck up and retire. Examination by Dunlop disclosed that the new tubes fitted that morning were completely porous! I put the machine on the afternoon train and brought it to a firm, The Motor Mart in the Strand, where I sold it after much haggling for £55, which they gave me in a bag of golden sovereigns! This was nearly double what the machine cost me to build.

On 10th August 1910 *Irish Cyclist and Motor Cyclist* announced a major career shift by Charles Franklin:

FRANKLIN ENTERS THE TRADE
Motorcyclists will be interested to learn that C.B. Franklin has resigned his position in the Rathmines Electricity Works to take up the post of Irish representative of the Hendee Manufacturing Co., the manufacturers of the well-known Indian motor bicycles. We have little doubt that Franklin will be very successful in his new role, and his long experience of the sport, coupled with his electrical and mechanical knowledge, should stand him in good stead. Pending the making of other arrangements, Mr. Franklin may be communicated with at his private address, 31 Hollybank Avenue, Ranelagh.

The first advertisement for Franklin's Indian agency appeared in the 15th February 1911 issue of *Irish Cyclist and Motor Cyclist*, and it highlighted the Free Engine Clutch feature of Indian motorcycles. The advertisement ran weekly and used the Hollybank address until 26th April 1911, after which the address became 8 Vernon Avenue, Frankfort Avenue, Rathmines, Dublin (an error; it should have read 'Vernon Terrace').

The house at Hollybank Avenue, where Franklin first opened his Indian agency and where his daughter was born just days before he departed for the 1908 Tourist Trophy race, is still standing today. The house at 8 Vernon Terrace, where he operated the agency from May 1911 to 1915, is gone and a Centra Mini-Market now occupies this site.

Franklin made the Indian free engine clutch his main selling point when he established his Indian agency in 1910. This advertisement ran in every single issue of Irish Cyclist & Motor Cyclist for many months.(NLI)

Giving up his 'day job' at the electricity works was most likely the deciding factor that henceforth gave Franklin the freedom to begin competing in races at Brooklands over in England. The timing is certainly significant in that Franklin did not ever compete at Brooklands until mid 1910, despite the fact that motorcycle races had been organised there regularly since early 1908. Getting himself and his machine over to Brooklands from Ireland for race meetings must have been a time and travel commitment too difficult to combine with his civil service responsibilities in Dublin.

The significance of these life events is simply that Franklin had now given up a secure civil service post, one that was effectively a job for life, in order to start up an Indian agency as his own small business, operating from his suburban home. A cautious and reserved man, he must surely have felt strong belief in the Indian product, and a confidence that enough of them could be sold in Ireland to provide him with an adequate living, if he now chose to turn his hobby into a career. Barely six months had elapsed from the moment when he bought his own first Indian, to the moment he took on the task of selling them to others as his sole livelihood. The energy and devotion with which Franklin now dedicated his life to racing, servicing and selling Indian motorcycles exclusively, has about it the air of a religious conversion.

1910 was a year in which the motorcycle reached its peak in the global marketplace as a popular form of motorised transportation. Motorcycles had matured from the spindly and erratic motor bicycles of the pioneer days to something longer, sleeker, lower and more substantial. They were now quite reliable. Completion of one's journey, or being able to re-start one's machine after stopping it somewhere, had become much more of a certainty. At this time the automobile, which had reached a similar state of refinement, was still far too expensive for the average person. Motorcycles were right then the most practical, affordable and accessible form of powered transport on the planet. These are sentiments captured by the opening paragraph of the 1907 edition of the popular book *Motorcycles & how to manage them* (Iliffe & Sons Ltd):

> The motor cycle in its many forms has taken so strong a hold upon a large section of the British public that the need of a thoroughly up-to-date work, which deals solely and entirely with a vehicle affording the cheapest means of transport yet known in the history of the universe, is only too apparent.
>
> If good in the first place and well looked after, its upkeep is infinitesimal, while the money to be laid out on a hundred miles ride is not much more than the price of a good cigar. It annihilates distance, brings far-off roads near to hand, enlightens the mind, soothes the tired brain, invigorates the feeble lungs, simply by enabling those who cannot afford a car to possess something which is within an ace of becoming an equivalent.

Indian leapt into the forefront of the popular-transport trend with the re-vamped model line-up it offered from 1909. In the United States, where the road network was scarcely developed, tough and rugged V-twins held up best under what the British makers euphemistically referred to as 'colonial conditions'. American motorcyclists had a lot of rough riding to do on surfaces like unpaved rutted tracks or sandy wastes. A decent amount of power was needed to keep the machine moving in soft going, and this dictated that American machines were going to be larger, heavier and more powerful than their European counterparts. American designer and manufacturer Glenn Curtiss (later a famous aviator) put it this way:

> No rider who has ridden the different classes of motorcycles can consistently say that a machine of the heavier weight is not much easier riding, and can be driven over much worse roads with more comfort and safety than machines of a lighter weight.

Riding in these conditions involved a lot of stop-start work as machines got bogged, so a 'free-engine' device (that is, a clutch) made life a lot easier. By 1910 all Indians were fitted with a clutch as standard. This feature was not common on British machines so was chosen by Franklin as the Indian's premier selling point, in his *Irish Cyclist* advertising campaign. In 1910 your brand-new Indian could also be supplied with a two-speed countershaft transmission as an optional extra.

Indian therefore had the right machines at the right time for a boom in personal powered transportation in an America that was then motorcycle-oriented, and which supported a profusion of new manufacturers. Indian was the leader in this expanding market, grabbing the biggest share of sales. Encouraged by this rapid success, the two founders invested heavily in enlarging their factory at the site they'd acquired at the junction of State Street and Wilbraham Road in Springfield, famous to this day as the location of 'The Wigwam'. They did this on the back of sales that by 1913 had soared to over 32,000 machines per year, making Indian the largest motorcycle factory in the world. Sales of road bikes and performances of their race bikes made these very good times to be associated with Indian. Charles Franklin must have loved every minute of it.

Expanding the factory proved Indian's undoing in the long run. It was now capable of building over 100,000 motorcycles per year, but Indian never again out-did the 32,000 of 1913. Meanwhile the company had way over-capitalized, on the assumption that motorcycles would always remain big sellers as personal transportation, while cars would remain the exclusive preserve of the well-to-do. A man named Henry Ford had other ideas. To finance Indian's rapid expansion, Hendee had issued stock. By 1912, he no longer held the controlling interest in his own company. The seeds of Indian's ultimate demise had already been sown.

While by 1910 motorcycling in America was at a high point and American factories were at the forefront of design, in Britain sales were steady but expectations about the designs on offer were not as great. Because a sizeable chunk of the British Isles is fairly flat and the going in those days was not as rough as in America, one could get by with direct belt drive, a single gear ratio, and no 'free-engine' clutch. People simply planned their routes to avoid any tough hills and, if you lived in hilly Scotland or Wales, well, that's just too bad. Even the ACC and its successor the ACU, organisers of the TT race, adopted this approach. The 'St. John's' course chosen for the motorcycle TT race had been selected for the mildness of its gradients, in contrast to the 'Mountain' course used for TT car events.

Ixion has described at length, in his 1950 book *Motorcycle Cavalcade*, the reasons for this apparent stagnation in British design. In preferring belt drive to chain for so long, the British were not completely stupid. Direct drive by belt was cheap, light, and smooth. Besides, if you rashly gave your customers an additional low-gear ratio to play with, they'd only wreck their engines through over-heating from all that slow-speed running at higher revs.

Ixion also described how, from 1906 onwards, he and a few other idealists nevertheless waged a persistent media campaign to prod their industry in the direction of variable gears and clutches. He asserts that the biggest wake-up call for British manufacturers, customers and patriotic race fans alike was the appearance of Oliver Godfrey, Charles Franklin, Arthur Moorhouse, Jimmy Alexander and Jake de Rosier at the 1911 TT Senior Race, mounted on Indians with two-speed countershaft gearboxes.

1911 – An Indian Summer

The year 1911 was to be a momentous one in British motorcycling. It was the achievements of Billy Well's Indian riders at Brooklands Track and on the Island that helped to make it so memorable. Indian so dominated in competition, and had such an influence on subsequent British motorcycle design, that Peter Hartley's chapter covering this particular year in *Bikes at Brooklands in the Pioneer Years* is entitled '1911 – An Indian Summer'.

The pattern set in 1909 and 1910 was repeated in 1911, whereby Brooklands was used as a proving ground for the machines of the top TT aspirants. Races were added to the programme that ran over much longer distances than the usual three laps, and they were organised under TT regulations. Peter Hartley's book describes one such race meeting at Brooklands, and his description helps to set the scene for the up-coming 1911 TT event. The name 'C.B. Franklin - the Irish Champion' features prominently. But kindly take note of the strong running by Charlie Collier on his own-brand Matchless machine. It was the Colliers who'd shut out Indian from winning the TT on the two previous occasions, and it was they who were expected to do the same thing again in 1911.

> Fine weather but a brisk breeze greeted competitors and spectators arriving at Brooklands for the Second Annual ACU Race Meeting on Saturday, June 10th.
>
> In the open scratch race for the Motor Car Journal Challenge Cup, Matchless machines did well. The event was over four laps, for any type of machine up to 1,000cc. Charlie Collier was riding a 986cc 90-bore twin-cylinder Matchless-JAP fitted with an oil pump controlled by Bowden cable from the handlebars. He led easily at the end of the first lap, keeping this position to the end of the race. In fact he led so easily, that he even had time to look behind him in the third lap to see if he was threatened. Charlie was followed in by Charlie Franklin (994 Indian) - the Irish Champion, A. J. Luce (733 BAT JAP) and A. J. Sproston (499 Rudge); he won by about 500 yd.
>
> OPEN SCRATCH RACE FOR THE 'MOTOR CAR JOURNAL' CHALLENGE CUP over 4 laps. Fork start and finish.
>
> | | |
> |---|---|
> | 1. C.R. Collier (986 Matchless-JAP) | 68.22mph |
> | 2. C.B. Franklin (994 Indian) | 65.83mph |
> | 3. A.J. Luce (733 BAT-JAP) | 57.30mph |
>
> For the first time in 1911, a passenger vehicle race was run and a scratch event at that. This was for machines up to 1,000cc over two laps. Trailers were banned. There were only three starters and all were sidecar outfits. The runners were: J. T. ('Bizzy') Bashall (964 BAT-JAP s/car), Billy Wells (994 Indian s/car) and E. Webster (976 Matchless-JAP s/car). Of these, the only single-geared outfit - Bizzy Bashall's - led at the end of the first lap, followed closely by that of Billy Wells, while Webster brought up the rear. The positions remained unchanged on lap two and Bizzy won by about a hundred yards.

SIDECAR SCRATCH RACE (up to 1,000cc s/car) over two laps. Fork start and finish.

    1. J.T. Bashall (964 BAT-JAP s/car)   48.44 mph
    2. W.H. Wells (994 Indian s/car)
    3. E. Webster (976 Matchless-JAP s/car)

Only three out of eight entries turned out for the International Open Scratch Race over 50 kilometres, despite the excellent prize money of £10 for a first, £3 for a second and £1 for a third. An unfortunate incident prior to this event put Oliver Godfrey (994 Indian) out of the race. Apparently, some ill-disposed person had sabotaged his engine by inserting a broken-off piece of workshop file into one of the auxiliary exhaust ports of his engine. This led to a broken piston on starting up.

The three starters: Charlie Franklin (994 Indian), Harry Collier (976 Matchless-JAP) and A. J. Sproston (499 Rudge), pushed off in the Railway Straight and finished at the Fork. At the end of the first lap the riders were in the previously mentioned order. In the next, Harry Collier led and Sproston withdrew. All that happened for the remainder of the race was that Harry gradually increased his lead. When at the end of the eleventh lap, he was over two miles ahead of Franklin.

INTERNATIONAL SCRATCH RACE (up to 1,000cc) over 50 km. Railway Straight start and Fork finish.

    H.A. Collier (976 Matchless-JAP) ENGLAND   67.92 mph
    C.B. Franklin (994 Indian)   IRELAND   63.54 mph

According to Oliver Godfrey, one of his team mates in the 1911 Isle of Man TT Race, it was Franklin who had inadvertently discovered the so-called 'squish' effect, whereby combustion turbulence is promoted, resulting in an increase in power. Apparently, in an attempt to raise the compression ratio of his ohiv (overhead inlet valve or ioe) engine, he had welded a lump of metal on to the underside of his cylinder head above the piston, and produced a pre-Ricardo 'Ricardo-type' combustion space. This antedated the pioneer work of Sir Harry Ricardo on the effects of combustion, by almost ten years.

A week prior to this race meeting Jake de Rosier had arrived from the United States with Oscar Hedstrom, the designer of Indian Motor Cycles for the Hendee Manufacturing Company. Hedstrom was over here to look after the Indian entries in the Isle of Man TT Races. Jake, who was due to ride in The Island, was a spectator at this meeting, and was down in the race programme to attempt the Class E (1,000cc) five-mile record. This announcement was apparently unauthorised as Jake had no machine of his own available. Instead, he gave a demonstration run on Franklin's Indian during the tea interval, covering a lap at 64 mph.

Yes, the Medicine Man had returned, to take matters in hand for the 1911 Indian TT campaign. Hedstrom brought along three Indian factory mechanics and one Jake de Rosier, Indian's salaried-professional factory rider and darling of the US board-track scene, now at the peak of his illustrious career. This was going to be a serious and all-out factory supported effort of the type so frowned upon by Charles Jarrott, Noel Drury, and other 'noble amateurs'. Billy Wells was to be the team manager, Hedstrom the 'technical advisor', and Wells was to augment Hedstrom's own personal choice of rider (Jake) by picking a team from the best available names in Britain. He picked Oliver Godfrey, Arthur Moorhouse, Jimmy Alexander and ... Charles Franklin.

Hedstrom had also approached another famous US rider about representing Indian at the 1911 TT, this other being Paul 'Daredevil' Derkum from Los Angeles. Letters had been written to both Derkum and de Rosier asking about their availability, but swearing them to secrecy. In the event it was de Rosier who was chosen, most likely based upon his spectacular race and record results on his 7 hp Indian 'No 21' at Playa del Rey board track in the early part of 1911.

An L.A. correspondent for the English magazine *MotorCycling* reported on 'De Rosier's Sensations at 90 miles per hour' in their 14th March 1911 issue:

> How does it feel to ride over 90 miles per hour?' said Jake de Rosier, repeating the question our correspondent had put to him. 'Well, it's just punishing. For the first few miles of that race here things went more than well. I went sweeping round the track like the world belonged to me – felt that way, anyway. But along about the 15th mile things began to go wrong. First my right goggle slipped a bit and my eyes began to fill with water. You know it's not so easy to keep the water out of your eyes when you're just strolling along the beach on a raw morning. Rush along through the wind at the rate of a mile-and-a-half a minute and your eyes turn to water. Before I'd ridden 40 miles I was riding in a mist thicker than a London fog. Then, to add to my troubles, I was riding without gauntlets, and had not put on any additional clothing, and the cold wind just cut through me. By and by, my head began to get woozy. The thump and jerk of the machine, and the tremendous speed I was making, had knocked me silly. I had an idea I'd forgotten to fill the lubricating tank. Just a fancy, of course, for I never start out for even a plain ride without filling it. But I thought it was empty and worked the pump vigorously. That got oil on my bare fingers and they almost froze together. Along about that time I got the idea that everybody in the world was dead but me, and I was just racing round and round through space. Blind as I was, I thought I could see dead faces topping dead bodies staring down at me from the seats around the track. I wanted to quit then, but I couldn't. I didn't stop till my gasoline gave out. And when I found out I'd almost made the century, I wished I'd started out with more of the stuff, even if I'd had to finish while I thought I was dead myself. No, I didn't start out to make the century, I just wanted to beat the Hour's record if I could. I had a fellow posted to wave a white flag at me when the hour was up, but he saw I was going along so well he just thought he'd see me make the hundred mile finish. I came within eight miles of it, and I'd have made it if I'd just had the gas.

After this and other record-breaking performances out West, 'No. 21' was sent by rail over to New York for independent dis-assembly and measurement to verify the records it had set. After that, it went back to The Wigwam in Springfield to be 'freshened up' by Oscar Hedstrom for use by de Rosier in any match races he could manage to arrange while in Britain.

Soon after arriving in London, de Rosier was interviewed by a journalist from *MotorCycling* for a report which appeared in the 20th May 1911 issue, entitled 'Jake de Rosier arrives. Here to do things.' The interview is interesting for the way de Rosier contrasts the motorcycling environments of the UK and the USA, both on the race track and in everyday road riding.

> We found Jake de Rosier at the Hendee depot in Great Portland Street the other day, and he kindly consented to give us a few of his experiences and observations.
> "Did you have a good crossing?" we asked him.
> "Yes, on the whole we did; but two days were very rough, and the ship was rolling very badly. We passed the *Iverais* just before she went on the rocks, and I didn't know she had gone aground till I opened a newspaper on this side."
> "What machine will you be using for the TT race?"
> "I shall ride one of the little twin Indians, but for everything else I shall use my 'seven'. I expect you know I am riding in a competition from London to Edinburgh? After that I shan't do anything till after the Tourist Trophy, where I will ride any of the boys for speed on Brooklands, Canning Town, the Crystal

Palace, or any other track, but I won't ride anything but my 'seven'".

"Have you been out on the roads yet?"

"Yes, I went in a side-car with Mr Wells to Hatfield this morning."

"Have you ever been in a side-car before?"

"No, but it is fine. Your roads have no bumps here. I don't know how they make roads that way. I have only seen a very few side-cars in the States. I saw one in California and two or three in New York, but the roads are too bad for them. With a motor-bicycle you can pick your track, but not if you have a side-car, as one or other must go over the bumps."

"What is the usual size of tracks in America?"

"One mile tracks in a perfect circle."

"What are they made of?"

"Dirt, cement, and wood."

"Which do you prefer?"

"I ride on anything; but the wood is two seconds to the mile faster than cement, which tires the machines just as it tires a man to walk on it. Wood has life in it, just like rubber, but cement is dead – stone dead."

"Hasn't there been some question about your records?"

"Yes; you see, the East and West in the States are like you English and Irish, and when some of the boys in 1849 went West with their families and found gold, they constituted themselves natives of the place, so that now the East have a grudge against the West. So you can bet that what I did there, there was no mistake about, as they had their own judges and officials, and they wouldn't 'low me anything, you can guess."

"Is there any tampering with machines?"

"Now, that's something I wouldn't say, but I keep a man to watch my 'seven' when I'm racing."

"Have you had many falls?"

"Yes, I reckon I've had more spills than anyone living. I've been at the game since 1898, when I used to pace Jimmy Michael, the great pedal cyclist. I have broken my ankle, collarbone, several ribs, my left arm and my nose, and my body is all covered with marks like this." Then de Rosier bared his left arm and showed us a member all battered and scarred as the result of numerous falls.

"Is there much jockeying to prevent you passing other riders?"

"Yes, they do anything to stop you getting past."

"Have you had any trouble with your machine going wrong on the track?"

"Well, I lost two races in Salt Lake City because some cotton waste had got into the mechanical oiler and prevented it working, but I fitted new rings, and it didn't do the engine any harm."

"Have you had any experience of belt drive?"

"I had the first Indian belt-driven machine, but the belt broke and fixed the back wheel. I like the chain best for with it the power of the engine gets right there."

"Do you like road racing better than the track?"

"Yes, road racing needs more experience than the path, and the best men have more chance."

"Do you think the TT course is too long?"

"No; it ought to be 300 miles, then the game man and machine would win; any learner ought to 'get' your Tourist Trophy course, but it needs the right man to ride 300 miles with his eyes full of dust after two or three falls."

"What do you expect to do on Brooklands?"

"Lookye, I've come over to do things. When I've done them I'll talk; not before."

"Do you notice anything particularly here?"

"Well, yes, your machines are very different to ours – and then the roads. It must be grand not to have to

push your machine through sand and over cart ruts, now in the States if you get in a rut you can't get out."
"What about road races in America?"
"We don't have many, but I won the great road race in 1906. My time was 24 miles in 29 minutes, and it was a straight six miles, and we had to turn around a barrel at each end, so that we were always passing one another in different directions, and had to be very careful at the corners. Glen Curtis also rode in this race."
"What about records?"
"It is a fact that every time I have been for a world's record I have got it."
"Will the twins beat the single cylinders in the TT, do you think?"
"Yes; certainly they will."
And then we bade him goodbye.

The TT race itself was going to be vastly different in nature for 1911. There'd at long last been a result from the long-running campaign by Ixion and other visionaries who, through the pages of *The Motor Cycle*, had been needling industry magnates and the controlling bodies of racing on the subject of variable gears and clutches for motorcycles. The motorcycle trade had thus far been quite happy with the 'St. John's' TT course, because its gentle gradients did not embarrass their products too much. Race organisers, hoping to gain more industry support for the fledgling TT event, had so far not felt inclined to rock the boat by setting any sterner test for man and machinery. In early 1911, however, a torrid ACU meeting produced the decision to abandon the 15-mile 'St. John's' course and switch instead to the 37 ½ mile 'Mountain' course that the motorcar TT races used, up and over Snaefell (a climb to an elevation of 1,400 feet).

Frank Applebee, winner of the 1912 Senior TT Race, in his later years described his recollections of racing on this new Mountain circuit in the pre-WWI years.

> As far as I can remember there was no tar on the roads at all, except perhaps in Douglas. Dust was our main problem, although, of course, we got plenty of mud, particularly under trees. In those days we got real TT weather and I don't remember a wet race until the Junior of 1912. By the way, the dust and general roughness of the course made the race a terrific strain for the competitors – I think it was a far greater physical endurance test, even at the comparatively slow speeds of the period, than it is now. At the end of a race many competitors had to be lifted from their machines and held up – nowadays a chap who has lapped the course at 90 can go along within a minute or two and talk to the crowds through the microphone. And he scarcely seems to be out of breath! Before the first war and even in the early 1920s, a rider was considered amazingly fresh if he could stand at all at the end of a race.
>
> When the course was first used for the TT in 1911, the Mountain road was a derelict moorland track, used principally by farm-carts and shepherds who plodded up it to tend their sheep at the Mountain top. These sheep, too, were a constant menace to the riders, for the fences were in several places either broken or non-existent, and particularly during practice early arrivals on the stretch had some hectic times avoiding them. The road was littered with stones of all sizes and it was no uncommon thing for a rider to crash on a straight after hitting a small boulder or getting into a steering wobble on the rutted surface. In spite of this, the climb up the Mountain was something in the nature of a rest. We recovered our breath after the Gooseneck, lay down on the tank and plodded slowly upward, often with clouds of blue smoke to witness the extra pumps of oil with which we were trying to ease our weary engines.
>
> Thirty-seven and a half miles of dusty, stony, rutted roads in the old days, 37 ¾ of first-class tarmac today. How many corners are there on it? Don't ask me! No-one has ever been able to answer this

question, for it all depends on what you call a corner. But at full bore on a racing motor cycle, there are very few places where the rider is not either banked over one side or the other, gear-changing, braking or accelerating.'

This fresh and unexpected challenge threw the British motorcycle manufacturers into consternation. It was obvious that variable gears would be needed to tackle such a course and win. They had only a very few months to get cracking and design something to suit, or else don't bother entering. There was no consensus in those days about what a change-gear system for motorcycles ought to be like, and a range of possibilities existed. From 1910 Triumph had been offering a free-engine clutch enclosed in the confined space of the rear-wheel hub, so they now crammed into this same space a three-speed Sturmey-Archer change-gear mechanism that was a scaled-up version of the hub-gear type used for pedal cycles. The Armstrong company came up with their own epicyclic-gear hub system for fitment to the lightweight machines used for the Junior TT. Matchless devised a variable pulley system for their belt-drive machines. Various other lash-ups were hurriedly pressed into service.

For Indian, finding an answer to the variable gears question was the easiest part of their TT campaign. Thanks to Oscar Hedstrom's progressive thinking, spurred by the harsher US motorcycling environment, standard production-model Indians had already been available since 1910 with two-speed countershaft transmissions, clutches, and all-chain drive split into primary and secondary stages. Of the profusion of devices now appearing, it was the power-train format already adopted by makers like Indian and P&M that ultimately became the global-industry standard. It worked so well that, decades hence, riders with long memories would pause to wonder why any other systems had ever been considered.

The TT race became 'races' plural in 1911, with two separate events now to be run – a 'Junior' TT for smaller capacity motorcycles and a 'Senior' for the larger ones. For the Senior event there was a field of 67 riders entered, competing on twenty different makes of machine. One third of the entrants rode single geared machines, and well over three-quarters had belt drive.

The Indian team consisted of five machines (see colour photo 4), with de Rosier billed as the leading rider. With flair for publicity as well as for aerodynamics, he rode in tennis shoes and black theatrical tights. He also covered his chin with heavy bandages to protect it from hitting the tank rail, when riding in a prone position.

With a personality described as 'magnetic', and a fearsome reputation preceding him to the UK in terms of races won and records held in the US, de Rosier was very quickly in a motorcycling media spotlight. In February 1911 it had been reported in the British motorcycling press that he had covered 84 miles 135 yards in the hour on an Indian motorcycle, but most British motorcyclists thought this to be another typical case of American brashness and exaggeration. Once in England, however, de Rosier soon won people over through his personality, and by suiting his actions to his words. He was well-liked by the time he left.

The 27th June 1911 issue of *Motor Cycling* contained a range of snippets about the practice sessions for the 1911 TT, and had this to say about de Rosier.

> Whenever Jake de Rosier stops on the course he is at once surrounded by a crowd of hero-worshippers, who are anxious to get a look at the much-boomed American. He has, however, been unlucky on corners, and only this morning had a fall owing to his front wheel hitting a stone and upsetting his steering. His hand is now bandaged up, and he feels rather disconsolate. By the way, his wonderful 7 hp racer 'Number 21' has just arrived from fresh victories in America, and it is said that he is to attempt to lower Cissac's record of 87 ½ miles an hour on the promenade next Tuesday. Unfortunately, there are rather rough cross sections on the track which will have to be levelled up if a record is to be made with any safety to rider or spectators.

THE INDIAN FREE ENGINE CLUTCH.

The clutch as fitted to INDIAN motocycles adds the one vital feature that is needed to produce an absolutely perfect system of transmission. With its aid, together with the INDIAN system of engine control, the rider is given the most absolute control of his mount under every possible condition. In the traffic of a city street the machine may be made to crawl along as slowly as its rider can balance it, or it may be stopped and started again without stopping the engine. On rough roads, in sand, and on awkward corners the speed may be checked as necessary, and by skilfully slipping the clutch the engine may be caused to run at its most effective speed whilst steadily pulling the machine over a difficult road. To a certain extent this clutch acts as a change speed gear—a gear with a thousand speeds—for so wide is its scope of action, and so sensitive is it in operation, that an infinite range of speeds may be obtained from the highest to the lowest balancing speed, and the clutch holds in any position in which it may be set without the aid of any stop or lock.

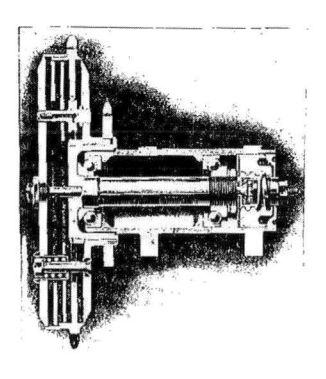

The Clutch is also ideal as a shock absorber, and the many hundreds of riders of INDIAN motocycles will testify to the fact that the chain transmission fitted to the INDIAN gives as steady a drive as any belt-driven machine on the market.

The description of the Clutch as fitted to the two-speed gear likewise applies to this Clutch, the operation of releasing being exactly the same.

The adjustment of the Clutch is extremely simple, requiring only a minute's time. Full instructions for this will be found in our booklet on the "Care, Starting and Operating of INDIAN Motocycles," which is sent out with each machine.

The INDIAN Two Speed Gear is operated exactly like an automobile transmisson. A small lever provided with a latch to hold it in the desired position is conveniently mounted on the top bar of the frame. Moving this lever forward or backward puts in the high or low speed as desired. In the central position the gear is in neutral. The clutch is operated by a conveniently placed hand lever which permits of most sensitive engagement, a feature which will be found to be particularly desirable for traffic riding or for negotiating hairpin bends on steep hills.

The whole system of the INDIAN Two Speed Gear is so perfectly operated that not the slightest sound can be heard when changing from high to low gear or *vice versa*.

All the gears and wearing surfaces are unusually large and heavy, which overcomes any tendency to wear.

Indian's two biggest advantages going into the 1911 TT on the new Mountain Course was the standard free-engine clutch (above) and optional two-speed countershaft transmission (below). Both features became industry standards taken for granted by 1920s-on, but for 1910 this was innovative, visionary, and downright revolutionary stuff.
(Indian Factory Archives)

It would be nice to say there was similar press coverage given to the deeds past and present of other Indian team members like Charles Franklin, and that these deeds were also adequately recorded in the pages of history. If only it were so, for then we would today have a lot more knowledge about these men than we do. It appears, however, that all eyes were upon Jake. If we want to know what events the other riders like Franklin experienced and how they fared at this time, our best clues are gained from the coverage given to de Rosier. For example, here is another news report of de Rosier, this time that of an eyewitness who saw him in practice at the Island.

The other morning, when all properly-minded people were in bed, I stood shivering at the top of Bray Hill, when, far away, I could hear the roar of a twin motor cycle. Closer and closer it came, until the machine came into my view from the Willaston corner. Like a flash, like a shot from a gun, the machine approached me, the rider lying behind the handle-bars, steering with one hand, with a look of perfect ease and contentment upon his face. He took the Bray Hill corner in such a perfect manner that to me, who had seen the pick of the English riders it appeared wonderful. He stopped further down the road and came slowly back. Then I noticed over the handlebars a tiny American flag, and I knew at once that this was Jake de Rosier, about whom I had been reading so much lately. My card was produced, we shook hands, and with the accustomed cigarette, we talked of the coming race… "Well," he said, "I think the course is an ideal one for testing a machine, and the man who wins deserves all he gets…" He then proceeded to tell me that he had already had three falls. He is using a 7-9 hp Indian, and he approached the well-known Sulby Bridge too fast and came off—as he expected to. He came off at the Hairpin—who has not—and he fell badly on the Waterworks corner on the mountain road, and was knocked unconscious and cut his arms badly. "No," said Rosier, "I am not taking any more risks. I think the practice mornings are more dangerous than the race. My advice to the boys is mind the turns."
Having finished the cigarette, he said that there was still time for another round, and, with an 'au revoir,' he was off, and I was left thinking of it all: the race that is coming and wondering if, in motorcycling, America is to best the Old Country, as she does in nearly every other sport.

Above, Jake De Rosier and 'Number 21' (Photo MMG)

Right, Arthur Moorhouse with habitual cigarette on his lip, ready for race day, 1911 TT (Photo courtesy of Indian Archives)

8   THE MOTOCYCLE NEWS

THE INDIAN TOURIST TROPHY TEAM
Moorhouse, Alexander, Franklin, DeRosier, Godfrey

The Indian team for the 1911 Senior TT, with Billy Wells and Julia Hedstrom. Where is Oscar Hedstrom? Behind the camera, taking the photo. (EMIMA)

It turned out, however, that Jake was much more comfortable as a track specialist than a road racer, for he found the going pretty tough in the 1911 TT. After a particularly hair-raising set of practice laps on his 'Seven', he was famously quoted as saying 'I tell ye what boys, I guess this ain't no tea party'.

After a promising start in the Senior race itself, he crashed (yet again) and was not able to stay in the hunt. It was the British Indian riders and Charlie Collier who snuck home ahead of the pack. For a detailed description of the 1911 Senior race run on Monday 3rd July, we defer to a report entitled 'The Great Race 1911', written by Arthur M. Ritz.

Oliver Godfrey on race day, 1911 TT (Indian Archives)

Franklin in action: he dabs a foot to help round a bend during the running of the 1911 Senior TT (RHC)

The greatest race in the motor cycle world, 'The International Tourist Trophy Race,' conducted by the Auto Cycle Union in the Isle of Man, was won by an Indian motocycle; and not only this, but two other Indian machines took the second and third places as well. Such a performance has never been equalled, not even in the races of previous years, where the distance was not only much shorter, but also over a far easier course than that traversed in the event of the present year. Think what it means to cover a distance of 187½ miles at an average speed of over 47 miles an hour! If the way were straight and level it would be sufficiently astounding; but when this long journey included a four mile climb up a mountain side, not once, but five times, with many other ordinarily trying grades, together with innumerable twists and turns where the speed must be suddenly checked, and the motor again required to accelerate, frequently right on a steep bank - under such unusual and exacting conditions the latest Indian performance is almost inconceivable.

To succeed in such an undertaking, a motor cycle must possess not one good quality alone, but every quality that can be asked of a motor cycle, under every conceivable condition. The motor must develop wonderful power, and continue to do so under most adverse conditions. A stop to cool down is impossible, and the machine must go on continually with undiminished speed. The endurance, not only of the motor, but of every part must be everlasting. The failure of a screw would be fatal. The control must be simple in the extreme, easy and certain in its operation, and instant in action. The doings of these Indians was a modern miracle, and a wonderful demonstration of cunning designing, clever combinations of materials, and precision of workmanship.

For this race motor cycle manufacturers spend a great amount of time and money, and take the utmost pains in preparing machines, for it is considered the greatest achievement they can accomplish.

Charles Franklin on race day, 1911 TT (RHC)

The object of the race, as officially stated, 'is intended to assist the development of an ideal touring motor cycle of the power required by the ordinary user, regardless of the number of cylinders. It is not intended for racing motor cycles, and is not necessarily a race between existing standard types.'

When the race was instituted in 1907, the winner was determined by the amount of petrol consumed, and two classes were recognized, the single and twin cylinders. This method of deciding the race proving unsatisfactory, in 1909 the system of piston displacement was adopted, the single cylinder class being limited to 500 cubic centimetres, while the multi-cylinder machines admitted anything under 750cc. The twin cylinder machines so far out ran the singles that in 1910 the limit of the twin cylinder machines was reduced to 670cc, the single cylinders remaining at 500. The speed of the twins was still considered too great for the course and for 1911 the limit of the twins was again cut down to 585cc. This is a smaller size than most manufacturers catalogue, and necessitated the building of special size engines for this race. As a matter of fact, most of the machines entered, whether single or twin cylinder, are special machines, for, as stated above, the race is considered a most important one, and every effort is put forth to win it.

Five twin cylinder Indians were entered for the race this year, which was held on July 3, these machines being exact duplicates of the regular twin machines except in the reduced size of the cylinders, and as the course was a very hilly one, they were fitted with the regular Indian two speed gear and free engine clutch.

The course for this year was the most severe that has ever been attempted, being a circuit of 37½ miles which included Snaefell Mountain, a very sizeable elevation, the length of which is in the neighbourhood of four miles. Besides the mountain, there were a number of lesser hills, but with trying grades, and as this circuit had to be made five times, the total length of the course was 187½ miles. Such a course is evidently a most severe test, not only of power, but of endurance and reliability, and the winner must make the entire distance with absolutely no stop except the regular ones for fuel.

For this race 59 machines started, and the severity of the test may be easily understood from the fact that only 28 machines, less than half of the starters, survived. Such a wiping out of machines especially prepared to meet known conditions is the best evidence of the test. The result of the race was a wonderful victory for the Indian, for the first man in was O. C. Godfrey, one of the leading Indian riders. The second to finish was C. R. Collier, on a Matchless, a rider who has competed in these events since their inception, and who has been twice a winner and finished once in the second place. Collier's long experience on the course, and special study of conditions have always given him and his machine a great advantage, and to beat Collier on a Matchless gives a man an enviable standing in England. The third man in was C.B. Franklin riding an Indian, and the fourth was A. J. Moorhouse, also mounted on an Indian, and he wins the honor of being the first private owner to finish. All of these men rode very carefully, and the regularity with which they made their circuits was highly commented on by the spectators as an indication of the splendid construction and reliability of their machines. Jake De Rosier, who had come to England to take part in this race came in twelfth, but he had encountered hard luck, and his performance was most creditable. During his practice riding on the course he had six severe falls, which did not leave him in any too good condition for the great trial. In the race he was leader of the first lap, but dropped back a little on the second, and on the third had a severe fall which nearly put him out of commission. He really was in a dazed condition, and it required great nerve to keep on riding as he did, and finish the entire course.

J.R. Alexander, the fifth Indian entered, was the twentieth man home, but was really the hero of the team. In rounding a bend in the road he came upon another rider falling directly in front of him. This brought Alexander down, and he stripped everything from one side of his machine and sustained a terrible cut on his knee. Notwithstanding this, he got on his machine and started again and completed the lap, with his leg dangling, before fitting his extra foot rests. In the meantime he had to hang on to his ignition connection with one hand, as it had been detached from the handle bar by his fall. Owing to his insecure position he sustained a second fall before the end of the lap, which broke his rear mud guard containing the nail catcher, and afterwards he had two punctures in his rear tyre. Even with all these mishaps and delays he was not the last man to finish, and he brought his machine home, making a clean score for the Indian team.

The road conditions, from an English point of view, are described as very bad, and even De Rosier, who knows something of American roads; remarked, 'This race ain't going to be no tea party.' The elimination and retirement of more than half of the machines fully corroborates De Rosier's opinion.

When the reports of the marshals came in, it was found that Collier had taken on petrol at unauthorized controls, and as this was in direct violation of the rules, protests were sustained, and Collier was disqualified.

De Rosier lost his bag containing all his tools and spare parts in the second round, and when he damaged his machine in his fall he had nothing to repair with, and one of his spark plugs was out of commission. He had to ride three miles on one cylinder to the next control, but as he desired to have the credit of finishing the race he got spare parts and tools from his attendants, fixed his machine and continued. The delay of the accident had, of course, lost him all chance of first place, and the necessity of accepting outside assistance disqualified him according to the rules, but he still has the satisfaction of having finished, which made a clean score for the Indian team. Collier's disqualification gives the first three places in the race to Indians ridden by Godfrey, Franklin and Moorhouse.

1. Right, Charles Bayly Franklin's birthplace at 18 Whitworth Road, Drumcondra, Dublin; Scout 45 by courtesy of Tim Raindle. (Photo Tim Raindle)

2. Opposite, the building at 10 Wicklow Street where the Dublin Indian Depot was set up by Franklin in 1915. (HH)

3. Right, Devil's Elbow, the infamous bend in the Isle of Man TT St. Johns course, where Franklin came to grief after a tyre burst during the 1910 TT race. (HH)

4. Peter Gagan's replica of Oliver Godfrey's winning 1911 TT machine, on display at 'Legend of the Motorcycle' Concours D'Elegance in California (Photo Allan Rosenberg)

5. Charles Gustafson Snr emulated Cyclone with this overhead-camshaft eight-valve experiment in 1915. However, it remained a one-off, for the pushrod eight-valve was already doing well for Indian in US racing. (Lindsay Urquhart collection)

6. The engine of this bike was one of two 1915 small-base eight-valves sent to Rhodes Motors in Australia, and is reputedly the one used by Jack Booth to exceed 100mph in early 1916. (Lindsay Urquhart collection)

7. Top, the standard road-going Powerplus engine and timing chest, showing its single camshaft layout. (Photo TP)

8. Below, as heavyweight of the range from 1916 to 1923, tugging a side-car was the Indian factory's most highly recommended use for a Powerplus. (Photo TP)

9. Two photos of an original and unrestored example of the Indian Light Twin, showing its advanced double-loop full-cradle frame but 'un-American' engine. (Photo Tim Raindle)

10. A selection of the medals and badges won by Franklin in Irish, British and European competition up until 1914, on display in the Lyman and Merrie Wood Museum of Springfield History. (EMIMA)

11. This cartoon of Billy Wells was drawn in the mid-1920s by an artist with the magazine Motor Cycling (Photo David Wells)

12. An example of the early-model Indian Scout (TP)

13. Below, this glass-slide cinema advertisement, used in Australia in 1921, capitalises upon Shrimp Burns' 102.6mph race record to boost the Indian Powerplus. (Darryl Woodhouse Collection)

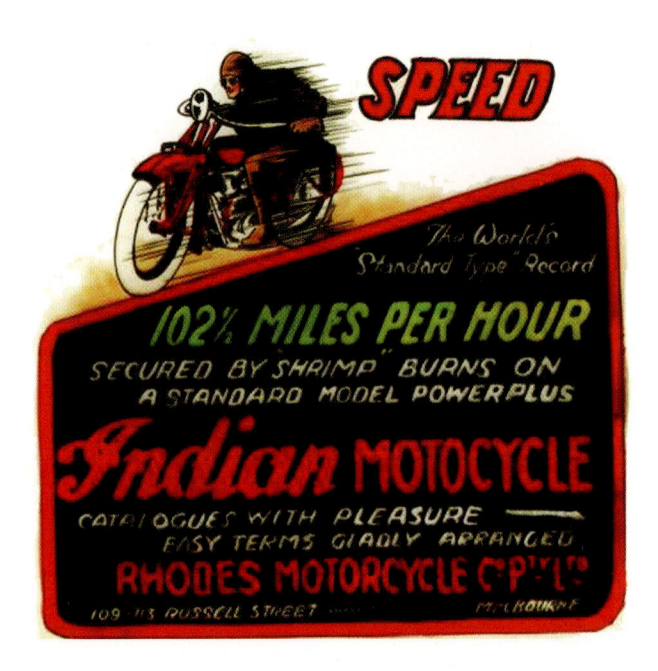

14. Above, Freddie Dixon's 1923 TT machine at 'Legend of the Motorcycle' Concours D'Elegance (Photo Fred Johanssen)

15. Right, a close up of the engine. (Photo Allan Rosenberg)

16. Left, the engine of the Indian Chief, 'embodying the highly desirable features of the Scout in increased proportions'. (TP)

17. Above, a 1927 example of the Prince, Indian's 'British bike'. (TP)

18. Left, a close up of the Indian Prince motor, showing its single-cam timing-chest layout (TP)

Godfrey, the winner, is small in size, but a bunch of muscles and nerves and a magnificent rider. He has ridden in the Tourist Trophy race before, and in many other prominent events.

Franklin, the second man, is a native of the Emerald Isle, and has figured prominently in many motor cycle events during the last few years. About two years ago, he became an Indian convert, and his Indian has carried him to many victories. He is a quiet chap, but his performance shows a fearless rider with plenty of good judgment. In the races he ran with the regularity of a well-timed express train, there being but a trifling variation between any two laps.

The performance of Moorhouse was especially fine as he is a heavy weight, carrying at least 60 pounds more than Godfrey. Moorhouse has been widely known as a prominent amateur rider in the more notable English events, and he is especially noted for his superb corner work on the difficult course. During the race he had one spill on account of another rider falling in front of him, and but for this would have pushed the leaders very closely.

At the finish of the race Godfrey's machine was in absolutely perfect condition, and could have repeated the performance without the slightest difficulty, as there was not the most trifling adjustment necessary. The same can be said of Franklin's machine and of the others the only things amiss were the results of the falls. As for mechanical troubles, none of the five machines had a second's delay on this account, and the fact that the entire Indian team finished the race is a record that has never been equalled by any other machine. The team was managed and cared for by W.H. Wells, London Manager of the Hendee

6   THE MOTOCYCLE NEWS

UP SNAEFELL

FRANKLIN

Indian

and

APPLEBEE

Scott

Franklin climbs Snaefell hotly pursued by Applebee (Scott) in the 1911 TT. This elbows-out knees-in riding position was very characteristic of Franklin. (EMIMA)

> **A HALL OF FAMER**
>
> OLIVER C. GODFREY, WINNER OF THE INTERNATIONAL TOURIST TROPHY, ISLE OF MAN, ENGLAND, IN 1911 WITH SOME OF HIS FRIENDS. WRITE-UPS OF HIS VICTORY SAID HE RODE A "PALPATING RED INDIAN".

Godfrey in triumph at the finish of the 1911 TT, with Billy Wells and Julia Hedstrom. The photographer was Oscar Hedstrom. (EMIMA)

Mfg. Co., an American by birth, although an Englishman by adoption, and the results speak highly for his foresight and care.

The results of the 1911 Senior TT race were sensational, and much was made of them in the press of the day. It established a number of 'firsts', including the first ever clean sweep by a factory team, first TT win by a foreign manufacturer, first Senior TT win, first win on the Mountain course, and first Mountain course race record (though Frank Applebee's Scott set the first Mountain course lap record). For Charles Franklin, his 2nd place was to be his best ever TT result.

The Hendee Mfg. Co. played up these race results for all they were worth in their advertising promotions, as you'd expect. The above race report can be viewed as an official Indian factory version of events (it appeared in the Hendee Mfg. house organ *Motocycle News* and was reprinted in the Indian UK sales catalogue for 1912). For a piece of factory propaganda, it is surprisingly factual with its errors being ones of omission rather than of fact. For example, the race was not an Indian-only affair and the performances of the Scott motorcycles were as much talked about as Indian's victory. It also glosses somewhat over the fact that Charlie Collier had dogged the Indian team's steps every inch of the way, and it was only sheer bad luck that prevented Matchless from sharing the podium with Indian.

Other writers have frowned upon de Rosier's poor placing and disqualification, yet his was a

The cover photo of this 'Clean Sweep Number' of Indian's in-house publication The Motocycle News shows Oliver Godfrey crossing the finish line of the 1911 Senior TT race. (EMIMA)

very plucky performance in unfamiliar surroundings. Jake proved his mettle beyond doubt the very next day when, despite his physical injuries and riding in damp and treacherous 'Isle of Man' weather and road conditions, he took on all-comers in sprints along the Douglas promenade and emerged victorious at a jaw-dropping 75.57 mph.

The 'official Indian' race report is useful to us in another respect, for it gives one of the very few available contemporary summations of Charles Franklin's personality and character. The words used are tantalizingly brief, but bear repetition:

> Franklin, the second man, is a native of the Emerald Isle, and has figured prominently in many motor cycle events during the last few years. About two years ago, he became an Indian convert, and his Indian has carried him to many victories. He is a quiet chap, but his performance shows a fearless rider with plenty of good judgment. In the races he ran with the regularity of a well-timed express train, there being but a trifling variation between any two laps.

There it is again, that word 'convert'. The overall impression conveyed is mild-mannered, taciturn, reserved, a person of gentlemanly demeanor. But there are none so zealous as the converted.

For a summation of the impact of the 1911 TT on the broader motorcycling scene, let's again defer to Ixion who was there at the time as an eyewitness to all these events.

> The Manx week of 1911 brought a thunderclap. Various British gears, mostly of the improvised type, performed with slight credit in the Junior event, won by a new 2 ½ hp Humber with a light multi-speed hub. But intense humiliation marked the Senior race. First second and third places fell to Indian machines, produced by the Hendee Manufacturing Co., of Springfield, Ohio (*sic*). The fact that they were ridden by three Englishmen - Godfrey, Franklin and Moorhouse - was no great consolation. But their victory was a blessing in disguise. They were fitted with countershaft gear boxes, and their transmission was all-chain - with only two chains at that!
>
> What America had done, Britain could surely do? Even then we learnt our lesson slowly. Before war broke out in 1914, several leading firms had produced excellent three-speed countershaft gear boxes. In 1920 some of the leading factories boldly came out with three-speed countershaft gear boxes and a properly cushioned all-chain drive. Everybody wondered why so simple a design had not appeared ten years earlier.
>
> Perhaps one strand in the answer was that earlier engines might have run red hot in private ownership, if flogged up steep hills on gear ratios as low as 12 or 15 to 1. But aircraft-engine experience during the war soon taught us how to minimize heat distortion in air-cooled engines, and a manufacturer could now trust his stupider customers with the combination of an air-cooled engine and a low gear ratio equal to climbing anything short of a vertical precipice.
>
> The battle of variable gears was now won! It had been a long battle, with plenty of sound argument on both sides.

Just as he'd been present when the very concept of the TT races was first dreamed up, Franklin was once again in the right place at the right time to help shape the future of motorcycling. Wholesale adoption of countershaft transmission with variable gears, clutches and rear-wheel drive by chain was now inevitable. This so greatly broadened the appeal of motorcycles that by 1920 the annual *Motorcycling Manual: All about the Motorcycle in Simple Language* was able to comment:

> motorcyclists nowadays do not appear to be so sporting as were the past generation, and they also demand an engine that will take them anywhere without the necessity for acrobatics ... they wish to possess machines on which it is not necessary to perform such antics as a running start.

At the conclusion of the TT races Oscar Hedstrom and wife Julia departed the Island on a Grand Tour, and soon returned to the USA. They arrived back at Springfield in time for photographs taken by Oscar of TT Indians in action at the Island to be used for a 'Clean Sweep Number' of the factory's own magazine *The Motocycle News* (Vol. IV No. 12, July 1911). However de Rosier stayed in England for another two months.

Just as Lee Evans and the others had sought to overcome their 1910 TT disappointments by racing and beating anything that moved at Brooklands over subsequent weeks, so too did Charlie Collier and de Rosier elect to move their contest to this same venue. De Rosier had already announced upon arrival in England that, as soon as this TT business was out of the way, he'd be ready to race anybody, anytime, anywhere. It was Collier 'the English Champion' who stepped forward to take him up on this, and soon it was announced that three match races would be run between the two at Brooklands for £130 in prize money.

But first, de Rosier was going to have a go at setting some world speed records at Brooklands. The occasion chosen for this was a Motor Cycling Club (MCC) race meeting on Saturday 8th July. He used his own 'seven', the 994cc Indian track racer 'No. 21' that he'd brought over from the States for any post-TT match racing that might come his way. Brooklands historian Peter Hartley provides a description of this bike.

> Only the bare functional necessities found a place on Jake's machine. It had a 994cc (82.5 x 92 mm) o.h.i.v. engine with nonadjustable tappets and auxiliary exhaust ports drilled in the cylinder walls. All touring accessories had been removed and the carburettor was completely devoid of throttle control. The only concession to comfort was the use of the latest pattern leaf-sprung Indian front fork. The exhaust pipes were only three-inches long and unsilenced. Final drive, as with all Indians at that time, was by chain, and a mechanically-driven oil pump was fitted, with an oil-tank-mounted hand pump for emergencies.

On this machine Jake set new flying-start world records in Class E (1,000cc) over the following distances: 1 km - 85.32 mph; 1 mile - 87.38 mph; 5 miles - 80.72 mph. De Rosier's one-mile record broke the long-standing mark of 87.32 mph set on 27th July 1905 by Frenchman Henri Cissac over a one-way flying kilometer along Blackpool seafront on a monster 16 hp Peugeot V-twin. It nevertheless ought to be mentioned that American Glenn Curtiss had in 1906 allegedly taken a V-8 shaft-driven motorcycle of his own design along St Ormond Beach, Florida, for a one-way run of 136 mph, a motorcycle speed record that would stand for another 30 years. In these early days of record breaking, the requirement that any record accepted be the average of two runs in opposite directions was not yet strictly adhered to.

The match races between de Rosier and Charlie Collier took place one week later, at the BMCRC-organised race meeting held at Brooklands on Saturday 15th July. The outright winner was to be determined by the best-of-three races run over two, five and ten laps of the 'Bumpy Bowl'. Because we are now running low on superlatives after describing the 1911 TT outcome, we will refer you to a race report entitled 'An American Victory' that appeared in *MotorCycling* a couple of days later.

> All motorcycling roads led to Brooklands last Saturday, where the champions of England and America were to meet in a series of three matches, over distances of two, five and ten laps. As 3 o'clock drew near, the excitement became intense, and when the two great rivals appeared a crowd at once collected round each man, who, waiting with their machines, received the good wishes for success from their friends.
>
> Jake de Rosier said that, though he was not confident of winning, he was going to do his best. He

was very pleased with the way his Indian was running. His back tyre was a new Blue Streak, with a six ply tread, the front one having only four plies. He put this new cover on as the one he had been using the previous week was slightly worn. Except for this change, de Rosier assured us that his machine was in exactly the same condition as when he broke three world records the previous Saturday. The engine is fitted with auxiliary exhaust ports drilled in the cylinder, and the exhaust pipes are only 3 inches long, and discharge straight into the open air. A present to him of a pair of knee grips was secured to the tank, and this is a wrinkle he has picked up over here. He finds them most comfortable, and they give him a greater sense of security. He has discarded his narrow handlebars in favour of a wider pair, as the narrow ones are difficult to steer with on a bumpy track like Brooklands. Jake says his back wheel is thrown so high off the ground that it spins around in mid-air, and distance is lost accordingly. He used Pratt's petrol and Wakefield oil.

Charles Collier had a beautiful spick-and-span Matchless. There were no auxiliary exhausts, but the long exhaust pipes had the shells of silencers on them. An AMAC carburettor fed Pratt's spirit to the engine, and Hutchinson tyres were shod to the wheels. The Matchless spring fork was used, and Vacuum oil lubricated the engine bearings.

But the race! It is impossible to do it justice, so magnificent a spectacle did these two giants, battling out the greatest motorcycle warfare ever seen, present. At the start, Harry Collier wheeled his brother's machine down to the far end by the bridge over the Wey, and Garret did the like with the Indian, while the two rivals walked down together, chatting to one another. The starter's car was also there, and presently it was seen that all three were coming nearer; faster and faster they went until, when the two competitors were dead in line, down went the red flag in the car, and the race was begun. They crossed the line together, with 'C.R.' perhaps a shade ahead.

The exuberant feelings of the crowd gave vent in cheer after cheer, the bookmakers shouted louder than ever, and two small dots flashed out of sight round the hill. A few seconds elapsed, and then they came out from under the bridge, and were 100 yards beyond before the sound of their exhausts reached the listening ears of those at the fork. Jake was a couple of lengths behind, but began to close the gap quickly.

They went out of sight again down the straight, and, when next viewed by the aero sheds, the Englishman was 10 yards ahead. They tore past the judge's box with Jake taking Collier's shelter, but, on leaving the big banking, the Indian got a wheel ahead for a few seconds. The Matchless, however, quickened up, and was in front at the aero sheds, and came into the straight first. Then came a most magnificent piece of riding by Jake, for he suddenly dashed away, and, before Charlie could quicken up, had got to the front.

Collier tucked his head down lower and made a final spurt, but it was too late, for, although he seemed to be catching up quickly, the Indian crossed the line first, though there was not daylight between them. It was a splendid finish, and both men came in for a lot of cheering, and, though the majority of the spectators would rather have seen the Englishman win, the splendid riding of the American called for admiration from Briton and Yankee alike.

The second race was five laps, and again a very level start was made. Collier made the pace very hot at first and led, amid the frenzied shrieks of the crowd, who were now dead set on him winning this race and drawing level. Past the judge's box for the first time they both struck two bad bumps, and Jake wobbled badly. It was very noticeable, however, that, whereas Collier rode very straight indeed, de Rosier by no means followed a perfectly straight line. Perhaps this was because the atmosphere behind Collier was changeable, owing to the draughts created by the leading rider and machine. Whatever it was, it was remarkable, for, looked at from in front, one could see the Englishman coming towards one riding perfectly straight, while every now and then the little, crouched-up figure on the

Indian would appear first at one side and then at the other, though he never for a second deserted that back wheel of the Matchless. It was great - it was magnificent! At 80 miles an hour this masterpiece of American track riding was sucking away at the power of the Matchless, letting his rival draw him along in the vortex that his wild rush through the air created.

Down the railway stretch, with the wind behind, the speed must have been 90mph. Though the crowd yelled madly and joyously every time Collier passed them ahead of his rival, the wiseacres shook their heads, for they knew who was doing the pacing work. So the tearing, roaring race went on.

Suddenly a shout, then a wild yell as a babble of voices shriek, 'Where's Jake?' He is stopping on the far side of the track. 'What has happened?' Then a British cheer as the Matchless sweeps past on its last lap. 'Has his engine seized?' 'Jake's given up.' These are the hysterical remarks bandied from mouth to mouth. A few more moments of suspense, and the English champion roared home the victor to a deafening storm of applause from the supporters of home industries. Then slowly up the track is seen the worthy Jake carefully picking his way, with foot extended, and, trailing on the ground, caught between the spokes and the right fork, is his front cover, and dangling from the hub are a few shreds of what had once been a tube. Yes, riding on the rim, with not a scrap of rubber between the metal and the track, came the tough little man from over the water, and, with never a word of anger or annoyance, explained that his tyre had suddenly burst, and the cover come off the rim. Think of it! At 80 miles an hour, Jake the redoubtable held up his racer when the tyre left the rim. 'Miraculous!' 'Incredible!' were the expressions used by the racing men when they had fully grasped the meaning of it all.

One match each and one to go. What better sport could be hoped for? The wired on Blue Streak was cut off the wheel by Jake's orders, the wheel extracted and another front wheel, shod with a Continental, substituted for it.

The final had now to be run off, and all was ready for the start when it was discovered that the Indian machine was loose as to some of its nuts, so that a spanner had to be procured, for these racers do not carry tool-bags. Then, after a false start, it was ascertained that the trailing cover had broken one of the carbon brushes in Jake's magneto, so another journey had to be made to get another one. Off at last. What a shout! What terrific excitement among the crowd is now caused by these two machines rapidly gaining speed - speed so abnormal that before everyone was aware that these two motorcycling giants had really started on their great deciding battle their engines were roaring under the bridge, and in less time than it takes to write, they were back again past the judge's box, neck and neck, though, after taking the hill and the big banking, the wily Jake tucked in behind the Matchless once more!

In this order the second lap was run, but the sight of the little brown-clad man, with his leather helmet, on his great wobbling racer keeping less than a wheel's length behind his rival, sent many a thrill through those who saw him. The next lap it was Jake who crossed the line first, but Collier came down the straight 10 lengths ahead, and the over-hopeful Britishers shouted for joy. 'C.R.' (Collier) did this half-mile in 84.8mph, but that relentless Yankee racer was on his back tyre again at the aeroplane sheds.

Taking the big banking for the fifth time, Jake lost no distance, as he had previously done, and so the great race went on. But trouble was in store for the Englishman. His machine was missing badly. Glancing down, he saw what was the matter - the high-tension wire had come off a plug, and though the engine conked on the hill, Collier never stopped, though he was barely able to keep going, and at last, in spite of shocks from the magneto, he got the errant wire in place and screwed the nut. But he had lost fully a mile, and there were but four more laps to go. It was quite pathetic to see this great champion trying to make up time lost for such a trifling cause, and try he did.

When it came to the end of the seventh lap the little man in the airman's suit was but 20 seconds ahead, and he was looking behind him for quite long stretches to see where his opponent was. Looking round over his shoulder, without going out of his course and at 80 miles an hour! What a skill! What daring! In this eighth lap the champion of the home side came up on the machine of the American, but receded on the penultimate circuit. And so, without making a mistake, Jake de Rosier won the third race, the final, and the prize money.

Only one could win, and though Englishmen sympathized with their countryman, there was plenty of cheering for Jake, for he rode magnificently. C.R. Collier certainly did the pacing work, but after all it was a race to finish first, not to lead the whole way, and Jake, with his knowledge of track riding, was out to win. He nursed his engine by taking Collier's shelter, and he cannot be blamed for doing this. To say that both are magnificent riders is puerile: they are the two most magnificent riders the world has ever seen. Collier's steering was beautiful: he kept a course as straight as an arrow. Jake rode very differently; he dodged about the whole time, and even looked as if he were quizzing his opponent sometimes when he would dash alongside him for a short distance.

The styles of racing, in this country and America, are quite different. Here Charlie Collier has never had to take anybody's dust, and he invariably gets ahead and stays there. Jake, on the other hand, rides behind his most dangerous rivals until the time comes for a final dash. Collier had his best chance in the first race, and had he gone all out round the last bend he might have done it, but he made that fatal mistake of letting the backmarker get his throttle open first when but a few seconds from the finish. Whether Jake was all out even then we cannot tell, as he says nothing. The Hutchinson tyres on the Matchless behaved splendidly, withstanding the terrific speed and appearing little worn at the finish. Jake's hand was bleeding at the finish, the skin being chafed through, and his back and leggings were covered in oil, for what oil, from the auxiliary exhaust ports, escaped his leggings went on to the back wheel and was immediately thrown up onto his back.

It is the opinion of the very best judges that there is not a difference of one mile an hour between the two machines, and this seems to be fully borne out by the results. Jake will presumably go back to America and sigh for more champions to conquer, but it is now certain that all doubt has been removed from the minds of those who were at one time disbelieving of the wonderful tales told of his prowess. He has beaten our records on our own track under our own timing, he has conquered our champion, and he has established a reputation for road racing in the few weeks that he has been here.

A month later, on Wednesday 19th July, Jake indulged in some regular Brooklands competition by taking part in two handicap races for motorcycles. Peter Hartley records the field and handicaps for the Short Handicap Race (5 ¾ miles) as including: Jake de Rosier (994 Indian) at scratch, Charlie Collier (998 Matchless-JAP) with a 2-sec start, Harry Collier (580 Matchless-JAP), Gordon Bell (580cc BAT-JAP), Sidney Tessier (580cc BAT-JAP), G. E. Stanley (499 Singer), Jack Haswell (499 Triumph), Harry Martin (345 Martin-JAP), and Frank McNab, R.N. Stewart and A. Baker White (all on Trump-JAP). Gordon Bell won, with Collier 3rd and de Rosier in 5th place. There was later on a Long Handicap over 8 ½ miles, after riders' handicaps had been re-calculated by official starter 'Ebby'. Neither Collier nor de Rosier placed in the top three, but this time de Rosier got in just ahead of Collier after slip-streaming him for most of the race.

De Rosier was due to leave England bound for America on Saturday 5th August, so went down to Brooklands the day before his departure with his Indian 'seven' for a last effort at further improving on his world records set on 8th July. He was able to lift the marks for the Class E (1,000cc) records for the flying-start kilometre and mile to 88.77 mph and 88.23 mph respectively.

It's reported that, before leaving England, Jake tried to persuade Charlie Collier to come over and race in the USA, which Collier politely declined. Jake also wanted to buy Collier's Matchless racer, but this was earmarked to go on display at that year's motorcycle trade show in London.

It was just as well that Collier did not part with his Matchless-JAP, for no sooner had Jake left England than Charlie got this motorcycle running really well. On Friday 11th August he took it down to Brooklands and toppled each and every record set by Jake just one week previously. These were the flying-start 5 miles British record (83.72 mph), the kilometre world record (89.48 mph) and the mile world record at 91.31 mph. The mile record Collier set on his belt-drive machine was the first occasion on which any motorcycle officially exceeded 90 mph in Britain.

One can well imagine the chagrin of the Collier brothers at finding this much extra 'steam' only right at the end of what was to go down in history as 'the Indian Summer'. But that's racing for you.

Charles Franklin - Indian's Man In Dublin

Meanwhile, where was Charles Franklin all this while? There are no reports of him participating in any of these post-TT Brooklands races or record attempts as a rider. Neither does his name appear again in any Irish competition events until 2nd September, almost a full month after de Rosier had sailed for New York.

Assuming Franklin was not already back in Dublin and catching up on business at his Indian agency, the best theory is that he helped to man the pits as part of the Billy Wells sponsored 'We Support Jake' *équipe*. We have no proof either way, but if America's greatest track racer of the age was in town as a member of your own race team and were taking on the main champion of your chosen marque's nemesis, Matchless, in a series of duels, where would you rather be?

Nowadays riding Indian exclusively, Charles Franklin again became active in Irish competition, with the following results. He entered a 7 hp Indian into the Dublin & District MCC Hill-climb at Ballymacroe Hill, run over 1,144 yards on 2nd September 1911, gaining 2nd in Heat Two and 1st in Heat Four. In the Dublin and District MCC Speed Trials at Portmarnock Strand on 7th October 1911, he won the Two Miles Handicap, and came 2nd in the 100 Miles Handicap for the Rudge-Whitworth Cup, all Indian-mounted. The *Irish Cyclist* had this report:

> In addition to the 100 miles, there was a two miles handicap as a kind of pipe-opener, and it gave Franklin an opportunity of adding another to the long list of races he has won at the Velvet Strand. Franklin maintains his enthusiasm for the sport in a wonderful manner. He has been competing at Portmarnock since the days Bob Stevens discovered its possibilities as a race track. All of those who competed against him at the earlier meetings have long since ceased to take part in competitive events, and many of them have even deserted the motor cycle only to return to it again. He is quite the most consistent winner Portmarnock has ever seen, a fact that is mainly due to the infinite pains he takes in the preparation of his machine. On Saturday he had his Indian tuned to perfection, and it was quite a treat to see the way he made it jump into its stride before he had gone 100 yards in the race. With a delightfully healthy roar it was going at full speed in a quarter of a mile, and rounding the bend with his usual skilfulness, Franklin was amongst his men in the last third of a mile and ran out an easy winner from J. J. Harvey (8 hp BAT) and P. Brady (3.5 hp Rudge). Franklin's time was 2m. 4 secs.

In the Dublin & District MCC Winter Trial in Co. Wicklow on 27th December 27, 1911, C.B. Franklin was the winner on a 7hp Indian and gained a Gold medal after completing the 100 miles event with no loss of marks. In 1912 C.B. Franklin retained his position as a vice-president of Dublin and District MCC. The 1912-1913 Irish Motor Directory listed him as living at 2 Vernon Terrace, Rathmines. His motorcycle registration number was IK40.

Two incidents now occurred which highlight the fact that motorcycle racing at Franklin's level was dangerous, and that it required courage as well as great skill for a rider to be successful. The speeds of the day do not seem all that high by today's standards, but this can quickly be set in perspective by the statement 'you try riding a bicycle at 80 mph'.[27]

On Saturday 20th April 1912, Indian rider Arthur Moorhouse was killed. It was the first ever motorcycling fatality to occur at the Brooklands Track, and the story of how it happened is told in *Bikes at Brooklands in the Pioneer Years* by Peter Hartley.

> Four events were included in the programme of the BMCRC's Second Monthly Race Meeting of 1912 on Saturday, April 20th. The June-like and almost windless conditions proved ideal for the setting up of high speeds in the first event: the first in the 1912 series of Record Time Trials.
>
> There then came the tragic hour race in which Arthur Moorhouse was killed. The event was for all classes, machines of various capacities running simultaneously on the track.
>
> The engine of Moorhouse's 994cc Indian was running badly before the start, and he was the last man to line up. Nevertheless he got away fairly well and was soon in the lead, reeling off laps at around the 70 mph mark. By the seventh lap the leading four were Moorhouse, G. E. Stanley (499 Singer), Harry Collier (741 Matchless-JAP) and Sidney Tessier (741 BAT-JAP). The next thing seen by spectators at the Fork was a big blaze at the start of the Railway Straight and a column of smoke. The first facts came from W. O. Oldman, who said Moorhouse was seriously injured in a crash and that the race had been stopped. Later it was learnt that he had been killed.
>
> Years afterwards Harry Bashall, who rode a 340cc Humber in the race, recounted what had in fact happened: 'In the course of the race Moorhouse's Indian had lapped my Humber several times. When it passed me on the seventh lap, I noticed that its back wheel was canted over in the frame fork ends, as if the spindle nuts had worked loose. It seemed as if the pull of the driving chain was the only thing keeping the wheel in position. Then, as Moorhouse went up the Members' Banking prior to sweeping down on to the Railway Straight, the wheel must have come loose, for he went at full speed into a telegraph pole on the inside of the track and was killed outright. His machine burst into flames.'
>
> It is part of the Brooklands' folklore that Moorhouse's machine was buried by his friends beneath the telegraph post that killed him, and which was said to bear the imprint of his goggles from the impact. If true, the machine may still be there to this day.

Charles Franklin was riding in the same race, a fact noted by *Irish Cyclist and Motor Cyclist* which reported this version of events in the race:

> About half-way through the race the silencer on Moorhouse's machine became loose, and when passing the judges' box he leant over to examine or adjust it. This was a very risky proceeding, seeing that he was travelling at a speed of 70 mph at the time. When coming down the back straight it appears that he must have leaned over too far and lost control of the steering. He crashed into a telegraph pole. The back wheel was wrenched out of the frame and flung 30 feet from the machine. Moorhouse was killed instantly due to a fractured skull.

Covering the Portmarnock Speed Trials held on Saturday 27th April 1912, *Irish Cyclist and Motor Cyclist* reported that:

> C.B. Franklin, who usually appears in the role of a competitor rather than that of a spectator, was present, but only in the latter capacity, all Indian trade riders having agreed to abstain from taking part in any events for a definite period in respect for the memory of poor Moorhouse who met so tragic an end at Brooklands'.

Next, tragedy befell Jake de Rosier in the early part of 1912. Very soon after his return to the USA in August 1911 there was a falling out between him and the two founders of Indian. One version is that they were disappointed at his low placing and disqualification in the 1911 Tourist Trophy race. But this has to be balanced against his subsequent racing and record-breaking efforts at Brooklands where he was a fabulous ambassador for Indian, plus the fact that by the end of 1911 Indian held all 121 recognised categories of American speed and distance records.

At least one US newspaper report does make it clear that, far from being a disappointment, Jake was welcomed home as a conquering hero. In American eyes, he was now world champion. This piece appeared in *The Washington Post*, 27th August 1911:

> **De Rosier's Motorcycle Honors**
> Jake De Rosier will return to America with the world's professional motorcycle track championship as a result of his victory at Brooklands, England, over C. Collier, the English champion. De Rosier broke the world's record for the mile and the kilometer with a flying start, covering a mile in 40 $^4/_5$ seconds, at a rate of 88.24 miles an hour, and the kilometer in 25 $^1/_5$ seconds at a rate of 88.77 miles an hour. American-built motorcycles took first, second, and third place over a field of 67 starters in the tourist trophy race. De Rosier will appear on many of the tracks on his return.

Another story is that Hendee and Hedstrom decided not to issue Jake with one of the first small batch of Indian eight-valve racers developed during 1911, and he had an argument with them about it. The eight-valve engines had been under development by Hedstrom and his engineering assistant Charles Gustafson Snr since late 1910, to meet the challenge posed to Indian prestige on America's board tracks by the ioe 'Big-valve' Excelsior models now being campaigned by Ignaz Schwinn's Chicago factory. Finally made ready by Charles Gustafson Jnr and Charles Spencer of Indian's race department while Hedstrom and de Rosier were both away at the TT races, two amateur Indian riders Eddie Hasha and Ray Seymour had started using them instead. Yet another version of this story is that de Rosier got off-side with his employers by accepting a ride on an Excelsior machine at a race meeting, when he was contracted to exclusively ride for Indian.

Whatever the truth, the outcome was that Jake suddenly left Indian and by September 1911 he was in the employ of the Excelsior company. Further development of the Big-valve Excelsior motor, combined with de Rosier's board-track riding talent, kept both him and them at the fore-front of US racing.

But press coverage from the last quarter of 1911 shows that de Rosier is now falling from grace in the eyes of the motor-racing public. On the very same day as the 'conquering hero' report above, other newspapers on 27th August reported from Chicago's Riverside track that, in front of 10,000 spectators, Excelsior's Joe Wolters had with apparent ease broken by 2 seconds the 3-mile and 5-mile records set by De Rosier way back in February. Jake now had a problem and his name was Joe Wolters, as the *Olean Evening Times* of 7th October makes plain:

> NEW RIVAL FOR CYCLE HONORS
> Even Jake De Rosier Forced to Take Notice of the New Star, Joe Wolters.
> One of the motorcycle sensations of this year was the riding of 'Farmer' Joe Wolters who, in a night, jumped into prominence among the world's best and fastest riders at the Chicago Motordrome. Even Jake DeRosier, the old 'war horse' fresh from his victories over Collier, the English champion, was forced to 'take notice' and settle down in Chicago to defend his laurels.

> The season finished the other day at the Chicago Motordrome with a din from DeRosier and Wolters still reverberating through the motor-cycle world. DeRosier and Wolters as a team challenged any other two riders in America to engage in an Australian pursuit race of not less than five miles or more than fifteen miles.
>
> Many records were announced from Chicago during the carnival of speed this summer, but they have not yet been announced as official by Chairman Thornley of the Federation of American Motorcyclists. It is admitted, however, that the time was very fast and in the light of this fact it is a matter of satisfaction among motorcycle enthusiasts that motorcycle racing can be conducted with little danger to the participants.
>
> The new Chicago board 'saucer' held the speeding riders safely, and under the careful supervision of the Federation of American Motorcyclists there was no case of serious injury. DeRosier and Wolters are only two among many who whirled around the saucer to the delight of thousands—and they came through the daily test as safely as though they had been participating in an FAM national tour. The track contributed to this end. Another element was the skill of the riders, and the third was the high state of perfection now reached in motorcycle construction. Only on machines absolutely dependable and under perfect and easy control would such deeds be possible in safety.
>
> Wolters' rise was phenomenal. One day he was practically an unknown rider. The next day he was heralded as having 'walked away' from several other astounded 'stars.' And he just kept it up until DeRosier arrived from England to take a hand in the proceedings.

The homily about safety is somewhat ironical, given the fate soon to befall De Rosier and several other big names of racing in those times. But the main point is that, from this time on, press reports start to refer to de Rosier as 'the former champion', 'the old war-horse', or 'formerly motorcycle speed king and holder of many of the *old* world's records' (our italics). This appeared in the *Oakland Tribune* of 7th November 1911:

> 'Farmer Boy' Wolters is now proclaimed as the motorcycle champion, having earned the honor by decisively beating the old time war horse, Jake De Rosier, on the Riverview track.

One soon starts to gain an impression of a beleaguered stag taking increasingly desperate measures to keep the pack of wolves at bay. On 12th December 1911 it is again the *Oakland Tribune* that summed up the end of the 1911 US racing season like this:

> One thing is certain, Wolters is in a class by himself when it comes to judging the merits of the various riders. Jake de Rosier, the former champion, is not to be compared with the 'Farmer Boy' rider, figure them out any way you will. In the opinion of many local motor experts Earl Armstrong and Seymour can more than hold their own in a battle of speed with the Frenchman.

In February 1912 the Excelsior team went out west to Los Angeles for a series of races on a newly-constructed board track there, the L.A. Motordrome. The 12th February 1912 edition of *Galveston Daily News* proudly picked up the story going out from the first day of competition, about a fresh young contender and native Texan who came out of nowhere to topple the big names:

> ***New Motorcycle Champion Springs Into Fame at Los Angeles - W. E. Hasha Defeats Rosier.***
> Los Angeles, Cal.,.Feb. 11.—A new motor cycle champion sprang into fame here today, at the opening of the new one third mile stadium saucer track; when W.E. Hasha of Dallas, Tex., decisively defeated Jake de Rosier of Indianapolis and established what were declared to be four new world's records made

in competition. The new marks set were given out as follows: One mile, 39 $^3/_5$; two miles, 1:19$^2/_5$; three miles, 2:01$^3/_5$; four miles, 2:40$^3/_5$. The records declared to have been shattered were the one-mile, 45$^4/_5$; two miles, 1:23 $^4/_5$; three miles, 2:05; four miles, 2:47. De Rosier and Joe Wolters of Chicago were heralded as the stars of the meet. Hasha came here as a stranger.

During the series of race programs organized at this new venue over the next couple of weeks, de Rosier began to stage a minor come-back, as described by this report:

A NEW WORLD'S RECORD.
Los Angeles, Feb. 29.—Joe Wolters last Sunday established a new world's record at the Stadium when he won the three-mile professional race in 1:59$^3/_5$. Jake De Rosier, the veteran racer, came back into his own at the meet. He won the two mile match race from Joe Wolters in 1:21$^1/_5$, and took the six-mile event in 4:08$^3/_5$.

And then - disaster! For what happened next, available published accounts all echo the version related by Stephen Wright in his book *American Racer 1900-1940*, in which de Rosier apparently did not get along very well with another Excelsior team member, Charles 'Fearless' Balke. Promoters played up this well-known rivalry by staging match races between the two and, in one of these on 10th March 1912, a mistake by Balke led to the two machines colliding at high speed.

Whatever the background to the incident, the bald facts are set out in a short report that appeared as far afield as the *Fort Wayne Journal-Gazette* of 11th March 1912:

JAKE DE ROSIER HAS LEG BROKEN
LOS ANGELES, Cal., Mar. 10: - Jake De Rosier, holder of many world's motorcycle records, was badly injured at the stadium saucer track today. In the second heat, his match race with Charles Balke, the latter's wheel slipped. De Rosier ran into it and both men slid around the track for 500 feet with locked wheels. De Rosier's left leg was broken in three places.

De Rosier's multiple breaks in his thigh bone required immediate surgery on a scale that was life-threatening in those pre-penicillin days. After several months of convalescence, there were complications. Further surgery was needed, following which he was able to be moved back east to his home in Springfield, Mass.

During this time of enforced idleness he mounted a campaign calling for improved safety for racing motorcyclists. Doubtless he looked forward to being up and about eventually, and able to again throw a leg over a motorcycle in earnest. After all, he'd been through other scrapes that had sentenced him to a lot of bed-rest, and he'd always pulled through.

In mid-1912 Oscar Hedstrom sent Billy Wells an allotment of the new Indian eight-valve (that is, four overhead valves per cylinder) race engines to play with. And so it was that on Thursday 20th June 1912 Charles Franklin went down to Brooklands with one of these eight-valve motors in a track-racing frame, to have a go at raising the 6 hours motorcycle speed record. In this he succeeded, riding the Indian track racer around the Bumpy Bowl with no stops except briefly for fresh fuel, oil and tyres, to accomplish a distance of 373 miles and 1,725 yards by the time the 6 hours was up. This exceeded the previous best of 322 miles 603 yards set by W.L. Rhys (Rudge).

Franklin's average speed over the whole 6 hours was 62.33 mph, and it represented a feat of considerable endurance to keep up that pace for six straight hours on Brooklands' bumpy surface

Franklin awaits his start in the 1912 Senior TT race. (Photo Stilltime)

astride a bicycle-framed speedster with almost no suspension and only the merest suggestion of a saddle. During the run Franklin covered 300 miles in 283 minutes, which was itself a world record. He had surpassed for the first time what was then considered an important speed barrier, by becoming the first rider in history to exceed 300 miles in 300 minutes. Franklin could now enjoy the fame of being the fastest man alive on two wheels for that time and distance.

In addition to the 6 hours record and the 300 miles in 300 minutes achievement, in the same run he also took the world's records for 2, 4, and 5 hours, and for 250, 300 and 350 miles, prompting *Irish Cyclist and Motor Cyclist* to opine:

> It is most encouraging to see an Irishman going over to Brooklands and beating the world's record. Franklin is riding in the TT race. His mount will be a 3.5hp twin-cylinder Indian. We wish him the best of luck in this classic event and are assured that he will prove an able exponent of Irish skill, pluck and dash. He was always a good man at fast corner work, and the forthcoming TT will give him every scope for his abilities in this direction.

The Tourist Trophy Senior race for 1912 was held on Monday 1st July, and was again to be on the Mountain course despite opposition from some British manufacturers that, if it continued to be run on this route, then they would no longer support the event. This was a moment of crisis for the TT races and it threatened their very future, but the ACU stood firm. The event went ahead as planned, with a resultant lower number of entries which by race day stood at only 49 riders. Rules this time stipulated that singles and twins would now be given the same engine capacity limits, and these were set at 500cc for the Senior race and 350cc for the Junior.

The race was billed as another clash of the Indian and Matchless (Collier Bros.) titans, however times were already moving on and new protagonists were entering the fray. Indian was now without de Rosier and Moorhouse, though could field a team that contained the experience of Charles Franklin and Jimmy Alexander along with two others, Alfie Alexander and Jack Sirett. Jimmy and Alfie were Edinburgh's Indian dealers. Oliver Godfrey did not get to compete in the 1912 Tourist Trophy, apparently due to engine trouble just beforehand. Nor did Oscar Hedstrom come over from the USA, since he was preoccupied with design and production matters at the Wigwam in Springfield. Billy Wells supported the British Indian riders, but did so in his capacity as manager of the London Indian Depot rather than with the full might of the Indian factory behind him.

In the event it was the Scott two-strokes of the two Franks, Applebee and Philipp, who got out in front and stayed there. The Scott machines were both fast and nimble in their handling. They led all the way until, not far from the finish, Philipp's rear tyre blew out. This let Haswell's Triumph into second place behind winner Applebee. The best Indian was Jimmy Alexander at 8th place, with Alfie 10th and Sirett 13th, while Franklin had a spill on Snaefell during the fourth lap. His front wheel was badly buckled, and officials judged that it was not safe to allow him to continue. Commenting about their champion, *Irish Cyclist and Motor Cyclist* reported that:

> Franklin was unfortunate. He was regarded generally as the pick of the Indian team and, indeed, was hot favourite for premier honours. On the first lap he had to change a plug, but he ran into fourth place. At the end of the second circuit, rounding the mountain road near the Bungalow, he skidded, ran into a bank and buckled his wheel so badly that the judges called him off – to his disgust, be it noted, for Franklin considered the wheel quite safe enough to carry him through. It was not an Indian day, and Franklin shared the minor misfortunes that dogged the team.

It just so happened that 1912 race winner Frank Applebee, though a disciple of Scott, was a partner with Oliver Godfrey in a motorcycle dealership in London that they established together in 1910. Godfrey was killed in action in 1916 while flying for the RFC during WWI, however the business that bore his name, Godfrey's Ltd, continued trading until the 1960s. In a 1920 magazine advertisement, Godfrey's Ltd laid claim to 'a thorough knowledge of the motorcycle trade ... including winning the Tourist Trophy Race in the Isle of Man in 1911 and 1912'. Their business address was 208 Great Portland Street, just yards away from Billy Wells' Indian emporium at No. 178. This must have made for some very interesting lunchtime conversations between these great motorcycling competitors.

Charles Franklin had two younger brothers, of whom it's already been mentioned that the youngest, Rupert Fairfax Franklin, competed occasionally in Irish motorcycle events on an FN in company with Charles before removing to England's midlands in 1906 to take up a position with an electrical power company. The middle brother, Lorenzo Bruce Franklin Jnr, a clerk by occupation, was Charles' junior by two years. On 23rd October 1907 he had wed Elizabeth ('Elsie', 'Frances') Graham, whose father's name was Hugh Graham of Rostrevor, County Down. While living in Dundalk, Co. Louth, they had two children, a daughter they named Honor (born in September 1908) and a son Hugh G. (born in January 1911).

In 1912 Lorenzo migrated to the United States. He sailed from Londonderry aboard the *SS California* on 21st September 1912 and passed through US Immigration in New York City on 30th

Franklin competing in the Brittas Hill-climb in Ireland on 27th March 1912. (NLI)

September. On his Immigration arrival form he stated that his destination in the US was Pontiac, Mich., and his 'friend in the U.S' was a Robert Scott of the Oakland Motor Co. Presumably he had been promised a job there. Oakland was an early car maker, soon bought up by Willy Durant's General Motors Group in 1908. In 1926 Oakland under GM, introduced a cheaper Pontiac model which soon outsold their own Oakland . The Oakland name was dropped in 1931.

Lorenzo's wife and children followed him out in 1913, arriving in New York on 6th May. They were accompanied by Elizabeth's brother, also named Hugh Graham (age 19, clerk). Their final destination was 'Husband L.B. Franklin, 337 Clay Ave., Detroit.' Descendants of Lorenzo Jnr and Elsie are still living in Detroit, Michigan, and in Richmond, Indiana.[28] The departure of his two brothers for other shores left Charles as the sole remaining member of the Franklin family still living in Ireland.

The Annual Dinner and Prize-giving of the Dublin & District MCC was held at the Dolphin Hotel in Essex Street on 14th December 1912, an event covered by *Irish Cyclist and Motor Cyclist* which reported that Charlie Franklin 'modestly disclaimed any particular credit for his many brilliant performances during the season'. The successful competitors, on coming up to receive their awards, were vigorously applauded, while the big winners of the year, such as Roche, Franklin, Green, Walker, Healy, and Dunphy Jnr, were received with great applause. Franklin and Healy were forced to make speeches in response. Their remarks can be summed up in the words of the poet 'of their own merits modest men are dumb'.

Indian continued to expand the quality and quantity of its factory output in the years leading up to WWI. The Hendee Mfg. Co. produced 19,500 machines in 1912, heading to their all-time high of 32,000 in 1913. Buoyed up by these sales, Hedstrom's quest for technical excellence also continued. He insisted on the best possible materials and production methods, even though these rendered Indians an expensive product. In 1913 a swinging-arm spring frame was introduced on all Indian models, a concept that was years ahead of its time. Other manufacturers demurred and generally stuck with the simplicity, lighter weight and lower cost of rigid frames until 1954, when there was finally an almost over-night and industry-wide transformation to swinging-arm suspension on both sides of the Atlantic.

Other Indian improvements included better brakes, updated carburettors, and revised valve timing. The most radical move, beginning from early 1913 at the instigation of president Hendee, was the devising of an electric-start mechanism. The idea was a clever one since, after getting the engine started, the starter-motor then functioned as a generator to run all-electric lighting. Hedstrom was not so keen, being reportedly dubious about the capabilities of the lead-acid batteries then available. Sure enough, electric-start proved too far-thinking for the technology of the time and the resultant Hendee Special model was one costly Indian innovation that bombed. The idea of electric start as standard equipment on a motorcycle did not re-surface again until the 1960s, when the Japanese invaded America.

Hedstrom's and Hendee's purist approach to design and production matters apparently brought them into increasing conflict with other directors of the company, particularly those who'd bought their way in recently by virtue of the share floats that financed the factory's huge expansion. Businessmen first and foremost, with no empathy for motorcycles *per se*, they argued for cost-cutting to improve the margins for profit.

History does not treat such people kindly, since motorcycle historians tend to be hobbyists hung up on the exclusivity and prestige of their favoured marque (yes, we are guilty as charged). But *successful* motorcycle factories are run as profitable businesses, rather than as the self-funding hobbies of their motorcycle-enthusiast founders.

By the same token, the motorcycle market has always been a unique one. This is a fact which many people otherwise well-versed in the running of businesses often do not quite come to understand. Motorcycle customers make purchasing decisions based as much, if not more, on 'illogical' matters of emotion and image as they do on 'logical' matters like price and engineering attributes. Once the 'transport for the masses' rationale for motorcycle sales had fallen away, it really did take an enthusiast to know what enthusiasts would want to buy. Some of the major blunders in motorcycle manufacture, such as the downfall of BSA, Triumph and Norton in the 1970s, can be ascribed to otherwise astute business managers jumping from manufacturing sectors like automobiles or aviation into an industry requiring specialist marketing knowledge which they scarcely understood, elbowing aside that industry's knowledgeable but 'unbusiness like' enthusiasts in the process.

It is this need to understand a motorcycle product's *je ne sais quoi* that makes the re-launching in modern times of famous old names like Triumph, Norton, Excelsior-Henderson, and (underline this word three times in red ink) Indian, so fraught an undertaking for those business people trying to cash in on the cachet of these famous marques.

In any case, the manner in which Hedstrom and Hendee were running Indian had not exactly been unprofitable. Customers were willing to pay a premium for the quality and excellence of an Indian motorcycle, and this resulted in the factory becoming the biggest in the world. Its position in the global motorcycle industry by 1913 was equivalent to that held by Honda of Japan from the 1970s to the present day. This was not enough to satisfy the new investors however, and Hendee Mfg. Co. board meetings became increasingly turbulent affairs during this period.

In February 1913, Jake de Rosier entered hospital in Springfield for a third operation. He seemed to pull through at first, but then his condition suddenly deteriorated and he passed away on 25th February 1913.

Not a quitter - he only left the motorcycle racing game because he died. Hundreds attended his funeral in Springfield. Work at the Indian factory ceased, and their flag was lowered to half-mast while the funeral procession passed by.

On the same day that de Rosier was buried, Oscar Hedstrom announced his retirement. His last contract to Hendee Mfg. Ltd as Mechanical Engineer, signed on 27th January 1910 with a term of 5 years and a salary of $6,000 per annum, shows that it was terminated at his request with effect from 1st March 1913.

Franklin opted to ride a single-cylinder 500cc Indian for the 1913 TT (Photo Jonathan Bewley Collection)

Although various theories have been proposed to explain Hedstrom's sudden departure from Indian, no one has ever discovered the specific reason for his retirement at the young age of 42. Though he lived to be 91 (he died in 1960) Hedstrom never spoke on the subject. One plausible theory for his departure is that he had ethical concerns about manipulations of Indian stock by the new board members. Maybe so, but timing his resignation for the day of de Rosier's funeral is spooky, to say the least.

Engineering research and development at Indian became the responsibility of Charles Gustafson Snr, who had long been Hedstrom's assistant. The Indian factory now entered a period where other big changes were in the wind.

According to the reminiscences of former Indian factory staff who worked with Charles Franklin in the 1920s[29], it was from around 1912 onwards that Franklin became preoccupied with matters of motorcycle design. He apparently would have stimulating discussions with his mentor and immediate superior Billy Wells, in which they speculated about the ultimate form of the 'perfect motorcycle'.

Franklin's thinking tended along the lines of a semi-unit construction whereby the engine and gearbox would form a discrete 'power plant'. In contrast to the overhead-inlet-valve side-exhaust layout of de Dion Bouton then current on many American brands including Indian, the elegance, simplicity and cleanliness of the Peugeot-type side-valve layout appealed more to his mind. This would be very much in keeping with both his and Wells' own positive experiences of JAP and the

Peugeot-powered Vindec in Britain. As soon as Franklin had pencilled-in these main design decisions upon the drafting board of his imagination, he had the general outline of what would one day become the famous Indian Scout.

At least one Indian project, in which it has been claimed that Franklin had a lead role, did actually make it into metal during this time when Franklin was still in Ireland. This was the short-lived two-stroke Indian Model K lightweight, released for sale in 1916. Since the chief designer at Indian was now Charles Gustafson Snr, responsibility for the design and production of the Model K must ultimately have rested with him. Even so, the machine is just so 'English' in concept and execution, and bears such a strong resemblance to contemporary Villiers-powered British lightweights like the 'Sun', that a very strong case can be made for this bike being the brainchild of either Franklin, or Wells, or both. Design credits have certainly been given to Franklin by historians, despite the fact that he was still a dealer in Dublin when the Model K went on sale. He did have Wells' ear on technical matters, however, and Wells in turn had George Hendee's ear by virtue of his place on the Indian board of directors.

The 1913 Senior TT race was run on the Isle of Man on Friday 6th June, with a strong entry overall of 97 machines in total (showing that the manufacturers' boycott crisis of 1912 had now abated) and a strong turnout by Indian riders. Old hands Godfrey, the Alexander brothers and Charlie Franklin were there, along with Ossie Braid, Noel Brown, Sydney George and Jack Sirett. This year Franklin rode a 3.5 hp single-cylinder model of Indian - a 'half-twin' with rearward sloping cylinder.

Not content with all the hoo-hah they'd caused by moving the races onto the Mountain circuit in 1911, the ACU now made another controversial rule change. This year, the Senior race would be run over 7 laps, instead of the usual 5 laps, to provide an even more severe test for the machinery entered. Further, 3 laps would be run on one day, the machines would then be locked away for two days, and then the remaining 4 laps would be run.

Expected this year to be a shoot-out between Indian and Scott, the 1913 TT entry contained wild cards in the form of new riders mounted on Rudge singles. The race was a nail-biter as the lead rotated between these three marques until finally, at the very close finish, the order was T. Wood (Scott) in first place followed 11 secs later by A.R. Abbott (Rudge) in second place and, after another 21 secs, A.H. Alexander (Indian) in third place. Abbott had been set to win but blundered by overshooting a corner. Alexander for his part might have repeated Godfrey's 1911 feat for Indian, had he not been slowed by dirt in his carburettor during the last lap. Charles Franklin finished fourth, and had been in the running throughout. The other Indians all finished far down in the field, except for Godfrey who retired.

The 1914 Senior TT race was run on the Isle of Man on Thursday 21st May 1914, and this time the Rudge team was favourite owing to their strong performance the previous year. Neither the Indians nor their old adversaries the Matchless machines of Harry and Charlie Collier and Bert Colver could be written off, however, and Scott would again prove dangerous. *Irish Cyclist and Motor Cyclist* made this report on 29th April 1914:

> Indian machines for the TT will have twin cylinders, 69.85 x 65mm giving 498.86cc The Indian riders will be: C.B. Franklin, J.R. Alexander, A.H. Alexander, O.C. Godfrey, Noel Brown, S. George, J.T. Bashall, P.J. Derkum (a rider from the States who has a big reputation).

The race was good entertainment for those who'd made the trip to the Island, as the lead got swapped around between C.G. Pullin on a Rudge, T. Wood's Scott, and Harry Collier. Snapping

Billy Wells and Franklin in conversation during practice for the 1913 TT race (NLI)

C.B. Franklin filling up at Kirk Braddan during the 1913 TT (NLI)

right at their heels throughout were Oliver Godfrey on an Indian, and a rider later famous in the 1920s named Howard R. Davies who this time was on a Sunbeam. The leading Scott retired with a dud magneto, leaving the race to be won by the Rudge of Pullin by a seven minute margin at a speed of 49.9 mph. Godfrey came second. A lot of eyebrows were raised by the Sunbeam of Davies which got past Collier's Matchless and ultimately came third, for Sunbeams had been created and promoted as luxurious gentleman's tourers and possessed no racing credentials at all until that moment. C.B. Franklin (Indian) had been holding 5th place on laps 2, 3 and 4, but got home in 8th place at a speed of 46.12 mph after a puncture during the fifth lap put paid to his chances of a higher placing.

A quote about Charles Franklin by Noel E. Drury appeared in *Irish Cyclist and Motor Cyclist* of May 27, 1914. Drury had watched the first lap of the 1914 Senior race at Windy Corner. He wrote

> Franklin, on his Indian, came 11th (*sic*) having passed fourteen other men in three-quarters of a lap. He was going fast and steadily. All the Indian machines held the road excellently and contrasted favourably in this respect with most of the other machines. Franklin sits on his machine with a peculiar crouch, his elbows out and knees in. He is recognisable a long distance away, and appears glued to his machine on a rough road.

In the same issue, Drury wrote in a column 'Some impressions of the Senior' that

> The hopes of the Irish contingent rose high when it was seen that Franklin was doing so well and riding in his usual steady manner. We had almost finished arranging a dinner in his honour at the Red Bank when we heard that he had suffered a badly gashed back tyre, and thereby lost a lot of time and was put quite out of the running for the Trophy.

(The Red Bank was a well-known and popular restaurant in Dublin at the time, much used for functions by the Motor Cycle Union of Ireland and the Dublin and District Motor Cycle Club).

Famous American racer Paul 'Daredevil' Derkum, overlooked in favour of Jake de Rosier for the 1911 TT Indian team and by this time a race promoter in Los Angeles, finally got his chance to compete in a TT and was captain of the 1914 Indian team. He placed 31st. Of the Matchless team, Colver was 4th but both Colliers failed to finish. Of the 96 riders who entered the race, 51 finished.

This was the last TT held before the outbreak of WWI. The world was to be a very different place when British racing resumed seriously in 1920. The mantle would pass to a new generation of speedsters, and very few of the big names of 1907 - 1914 racing would reappear after hostilities had ceased. To mark the end of this era of motorcycling competition and development, let's give the final say to Ixion:

> The men who organized the first TT race in the teeth of ridicule, opposition and indifference, may well feel proud when they reflect how the Manx event has transformed motorcycles, and especially their engines and gears. The same coterie of enthusiasts were largely responsible for maintaining our representation in the old International Cup Trials, and they must have felt inclined to despair when their best efforts only procured four or five entries for an eliminating trial, and a few miles of park roads for them to race over. In 1914 there were no fewer than 158 entries for the Manx races: everybody of importance in the trade crossed to the island, and thousands of amateurs arranged their holidays so as to be present. Moreover, the British-built machines can now more than hold their own with those of any other nation, and fear comparison with none in the world.

Franklin commences his start (from 'scratch', as usual) in a Portmarnock handicap event. (NLI)

Franklin's care in rounding the flags was legendary in Portmarnock racing, and he rarely fell off in these treacherous turns. (MMG)

Franklin with an Indian eight-valve in the paddock at Brooklands, with the Members Hill behind him. (MMG)

At Brooklands on Wednesday 17th June 1914, Charles Franklin set out to break Harry Collier's solo 24-hour record, but the attempt was brought to a premature end after three hours. While Franklin was circulating the track at high speed on the Indian 'big-base' eight-valve machine prepared for the occasion, a petrol pipe broke and this caused a fire that engulfed both bike and rider. With only engine-braking available to bring himself to a halt, Franklin leapt off as quick as he could and rolled in the trackside grass to put out the flames that were covering him. The smouldering remains of the bike were completely unrideable for the time being. It's not known whether the rider suffered very much damage but evidently not, for later that day another 998cc eight-valve Indian was wheeled out and with this he set a new 10-mile standing-start world record in the 1,000cc class in 7 mins 41.8 secs, equating to 77.95 mph. The previous best was 74.04 mph, set by E.F. Remington on a Matchless.

Apart from the drama of bursting into flames, this story is significant in that it illustrates how much influence Billy Wells had at the Indian factory. Scarcely a dozen 'big-base' eight-valve machines were ever built and none of them were made available to Jake de Rosier, yet Wells was issued with at least two. The surviving example from this 1914 record attempt was still going strong in 1921, when it generated even more drama in the hands of a person, still a very young man in 1914, but already competing at Brooklands - Herbert Le Vack.

On 25th November 1914 a news item appeared in *Irish Cyclist and Motor Cyclist*:

> The Hendee Manufacturing Co. have decided to open a wholesale and retail depot in Dublin. The depot will be under the management of Mr. C.B. Franklin. The location has not yet been decided. Mr. Franklin's many brilliant performances on Indian machines have helped to bring it into the prominent position it now occupies in the United Kingdom. Mr. Franklin's exclusive services will be at the disposal

of the Hendee Co. and, in addition to managing the new depot, he will travel in Ireland. The new depot will have a fully equipped repair shop. Mr. Franklin's long experience as an electrical engineer should particularly qualify him for his new position. Any agents anxious to handle the Indian in Ireland are asked to contact Mr. Franklin at 8 Vernon Terrace, Rathmines.

And then, on 9th December 1914, the same magazine reported that Mr. W.H. Wells of the Hendee Co. paid a visit to Dublin that week from London in connection with the new depot he is opening under the management of Mr C.B. Franklin.

This was big news for Irish motorcycling, and a bold move by Wells given the deteriorating situation in war-torn Europe. A 'depot' implies ownership, and therefore investment, by the Hendee Mfg. Co. in the new Dublin venture, and also implies that Franklin was now entering the Indian company as a salaried employee. This arrangement would contrast with the Indian agency Franklin had been running from his suburban house in Rathmines, for this agency would have been his own stand-alone business.

The Dublin and District MCC held its annual dinner at Jury's Hotel on Saturday 19th December 1914. Mr. C.B. Franklin was among those present, and was again a vice-president of the club. This event was commemorated in a cartoon showing caricatures of various club personalities. Franklin is featured in the garb of an Indian brave, and accorded the title 'Red Indian Franklin'.

The *Irish Cyclist and Motor Cyclist* of 10th March 1915 announced that the Hendee Manufacturing Co. is to open their new depot at No. 10 Wicklow Street. The report reads:

Franklin at Brooklands in June 1914 on an eight-valve Indian, having just set a 10-mile standing-start record at 77.95mph. To his left is 1911 TT winner Oliver Godfrey, on his right is Billy Wells. Official timekeeper A.V. 'Ebby' Ebblewhite is seated in the sidecar. (Photo MMG)

Franklin has just won a three-lap Class E scratch race at Brooklands, 28th March 1914, on his Indian 'big-base' eight-valve racer. (Photo Stilltime)

Indian eight-valve cylinder heads showing the very flat combustion chamber shape dictated by use of parallel overhead valves, rendered out of date by aero engine research during WWI when splayed-valve hemi-head arrangements were developed. Yet the venerable Indian eight-valve continued to kick butt. In 1921, Bert le Vack's 'The Camel' was the fastest bike in Britain. (Photo Mick Atkins Collection)

THE INDIAN DEPOT
The Hendee Manufacturing Co. have secured premises for the depot they propose to open in Dublin at 10 Wicklow Street, and expect to be able to open them with a full stock of 1915 pattern Indians in about a fortnight to three weeks from the present date. The situation is a very central one, and although the frontage is not extensive, there is great depth in the premises and they should provide a very suitable depot for Indians in Dublin.

The building chosen for the Indian depot still stands, and is today is in a fashionable area regarded as being the 'Carnaby Street' of Dublin. At the time of writing there is a shoe shop on the ground floor and a bridal shop upstairs on the first floor (see colour photo 2).

The *Irish Cyclist and Motor Cyclist* reported on 19th May 1915 that the new Irish depot of the Hendee Manufacturing Co. has opened at 10 Wicklow Street. The report stated that Mr. Franklin has had difficulty in accumulating much in the way of stock, but the machines in the depot included samples of most of the Indian range. The phone number was 4709 and the telegram address was 'Hendian, Dublin'.

On 9th June 1915 *The Irish Cyclist & Motor Cyclist* marked the opening of the Dublin Indian depot with a retrospective article looking back over Franklin's motorcycling career to date:

C.B. Franklin - An appreciation of Ireland's foremost racing crack.
It is not any exaggeration to say that the performances of C.B. Franklin on the road and the race track during the past twelve years have been the means of making more converts to motor cycling than the performances of any rider in the United Kingdom. Indeed, it is hardly fair to suggest that the influence of his performances has been confined to our own island, for his feats in the Isle of Man, at Brooklands, and on the Continent have won recruits for the sport far outside the four seas of Ireland. Anything in the nature of a review of a career so extended must necessarily be brief, for to deal at length with Franklin's connection with the sport would be to write a history of motor cycling in Ireland.

Franklin does not claim to be a pioneer of the motor bicycle, but he can certainly be ranked amongst its very earliest users. Originally trained as an electrical engineer, to which profession he devoted his attention until he entered the motor cycle industry, Franklin was much sought after in the early days of the pastime by his friends who possessed motor bicycles. Those were the days when electrical knowledge was of the greatest value. The ignition was the part of the machine that called for constant attention, and as most of us knew very little of the mysteries of primary and secondary circuits, condensers, coils, etc., we took our troubles to Franklin in the sure and certain hope that he would be able to find the cause of the trouble that mystified us. Nor did we go in vain. Many of Franklin's friends consulted him in this way in the early days, and he got a good deal of riding on crocks that the owners could not make go. He bought his first machine in 1903, an FN, and at once entered for a hill climb at Glenamuck, an event that was stopped by the police. If our memory does not deceive us it was in this year that the first races were held at the Velvet Strand, Portmarnock. Franklin was amongst the competitors, and bringing his machine to the post in the perfect tune that we have since come to regard as a matter of course, he made an impression that is remembered today. Since then Franklin has been a regular competitor at the races on the sands, and it is rarely, indeed, that he does not win one or more events. In fact, his persistent successes at one time looked like killing all interest in the racing at Portmarnock. If one were to be asked for the cause of his consistent success the answer would be in his painstaking attention to detail. He invariably brings his machine to the post in apple-pie order, and if he fails to finish in a race one may safely bet, without making enquiries, that the cause was due to something beyond his control.

Franklin's successes at Portmarnock are literally without number. Perhaps his biggest score at that venue was at the two-day meeting of the Irish Automobile Club in 1904, when he won each of the two races on both days. He must have ridden many thousands of miles on the Velvet Strand, and yet we cannot recall his ever having fallen at the turns that bring so many to grief. Caution is his motto, and in cornering he plays for safety rather than spectacular effect. Of his successes in reliability trials and hill climbs it is superfluous to write. A list of them would fill a volume.

Franklin's first appearance in an international race was in 1905. The trials for the British team were held in the Isle of Man in May of that year, and after leading from the second to the fifth circuit of the course, the set screw of one of the gudgeon pins came loose on the last lap and he did not finish. His consistent running, however, won him his place on the team, and he competed in the race in France. The race was won by Vondrich on an Austrian machine, and the 1906 race was run in that country. In that year Franklin was again selected as one of the British representatives for the international event. He did not secure any high honour in the actual race, as his engine broke down in the first ten miles.

Franklin has, we think, as consistent a record in the series of races for the Tourist Trophy in the Isle of Man as any rider with the possible exception of the Brothers Collier. With them he ranks as one of the veterans of the event, having ridden each year without a break from 1908 to last year, and although he has never actually won the event, he has finished 2nd, 4th, 5th, 6th and 8th. The two occasions on which he did not finish were in 1910 when he had persistent tyre troubles, and in 1912 when he fell in the mist on the mountain and was not permitted by the judges to continue, as it was considered that his machine was not safe to ride on account of a buckled wheel. In his first TT race in 1908 the event was run on petrol consumption. Franklin was overcautious with the spirit and finished sixth, averaging 126 miles to the gallon against the 100 miles asked for. In the following year, riding a Triumph, he was fifth and won the Private Owner's prize. Tyre trouble put him out of the race in the next year, but he almost won the event in 1911, finishing second on an Indian, Godfrey, on a similar machine, winning. In 1913 he was fourth, and last year, as will be remembered, he was eighth, a puncture on the fourth lap destroying his chances of the premier honour. Caution has always been a feature of Franklin's riding in the Isle of Man,

Franklin chats with S.L. Hutchinson at the Portmarnock Silver Strand. (NLI)

The Irish Cyclist & Motor Cyclist.   2   AUGUST 5, 1914.

Indian
SPEED
ON PORTMARNOCK SANDS.

C. B. FRANKLIN ON AN INDIAN WON
TEN MILES OPEN SCRATCH RACE
finishing a mile in front of the Second man.

The "*Irish Cyclist and Motor Cyclist*," says:

"The scratch race resulted in an easy win for C. B. Franklin ($3\frac{1}{2}$ Indian), as every scratch race at Portmarnock does."

AND THE INDIAN PUT UP FASTEST TIMES AT BROOKLANDS ON SATURDAY, AT THE B.M.C.R.C. MEETING.

1,000 c.c. 10 Miles Race.

S. George, INDIAN, FIRST. 77·56 m.p.h.

1,000 c.c. Flying Kilo.

S. George, INDIAN, FIRST. 88·01 m.p.h.

Catalogue with full information about the speedy Indian sent post free anywhere.

HENDEE MANUFACTURING CO.,
"INDIAN HOUSE,"
366-368 EUSTON ROAD, LONDON, N.W.

'Phone: Museum 1743.
DUBLIN: C. B. Franklin, 8 Vernon Terrace, Rathmines.
F. A. Wallen & Co., 6 Nassau St.
T. D. Rollins, 133 Stephen's Green.

Telegrams: "Hendian, Eusroad, London."
BELFAST: Stanley Motor & Cycle Co., 17 Great Victoria Street.
CORK: P. J. O'Hea, Crane Lane.
ATHENRY: W. P. Higgins.

A1   MENTION THE "IRISH CYCLIST AND MOTOR CYCLIST" WHEN WRITING.

(From the NLI Collection)

Franklin and 5 hp Indian get underway in the MCUI Easter Trial of 1915 (NLI).

and while riding with plenty of dash he has never overlooked the fact that the man who falls cannot finish, and the man who doesn't finish cannot win. He has left less of his skin in the Isle of Man than any rider who has competed there.

At Brooklands Franklin has a record of successes quite as consistent as elsewhere. He first rode there in 1910, when he finished third in a 160 miles race. In 1912 he broke a series of seven world's records, including the six hours, and last year he put up a new record for ten miles, doing 77.95 miles per hour from a standing start. He won the last three scratch races in which he competed at Brooklands, each on a 7-9 hp Indian. He has given up riding in handicaps there.

In 1911 Franklin rode in the French Grand Prix at Fontainebleau. The distance of the race was 280 miles. At 220 miles he was leading by twenty-five minutes, but a series of punctures robbed him of victory, and he only finished third.

The opening of an Irish depot by the Hendee Manufacturing Co. with C.B. Franklin in charge as manager, makes it an opportune occasion to present to the readers of the IRISH CYCLIST AND MOTORCYCLIST a brief review of the career of one who has played a very prominent part in the development and popularising of the motor bicycle in Ireland. Franklin is more than a clever rider. He is a first class mechanic, and his ability to diagnose the cause of trouble in a motor bicycle is almost uncanny. That he is eminently qualified to manage the new depot of the Hendee Manufacturing Co. goes without saying, and we feel pretty sure that his closer association with the Indian will result in that machine attaining to a still greater degree of popularity in Ireland

The comment that Franklin had given up racing in handicap events at Brooklands is a telling one, and indicates that he was being handicapped out of the running by virtue of being too successful. This was one of the ironies and drawbacks of the handicap system operated at Brooklands. Any improvement by rider or machine would enable them to secure a win or maybe two, and then the handicaps would all be re-adjusted to put them out of the running again. Top racers of motorcycles and cars alike, such as the famous driver Prince 'Bira' in the 1930s, thoroughly disliked the handicap system for this reason. Others, like Norton rider Charles Mortimer Snr, made serious study of form and continually looked for ways to out-smart the handicapper 'Ebby' Ebblewhite, not only to win the race and get their photo in the *The Motor Cycle* or *MotorCycling* weeklies but also to win hard cash from the bookies that frequented the Brooklands paddock. 'Ebby' never did much like being out-smarted, however, and would usually be on to such schemes in a flash.

In November 1915 *Irish Cyclist and Motor Cyclist* reported that C.B. Franklin had cancelled his attempt to reach a 100 mph speed on his eight-valve Indian at Brooklands, due to the poor state of the track caused by the solid-tyred heavy lorries in use by the RFC coming and going from the airfield and aeroclub in the centre of the track. This was where pioneer aviator A.V. Roe had been based and where the world's first-ever commercial-flight ticket office had been built. Now that England was at war with Germany, track owner Hugh Locke-King had given this airfield over for use by the Royal Flying Corps. It was for this reason that motoring competition at Brooklands could not resume until 1920, nearly two years after WWI ended. By that time, Franklin was in America. It then fell to a new and upcoming young rider/tuner in Wells' employ, the afore-mentioned Bert Le Vack, to take over Franklin's 1911 eight-valve racer and resume this quest to be first to officially reach 100 mph in Britain.

Contestants reaching the finish of the Dublin and District MCC Easter Trial event on 24th April 1916 were astonished to hear news that the General Post Office and other government buildings in downtown Dublin had been occupied by armed Republicans. There was now heavy fighting going on between them and the British authorities, who quickly declared martial law in Dublin. The events later known to history as the Easter Rising began on this day.

The Rathfarnham Trial for the Rudge Cup featured the first appearance of the two-stroke 2.25 hp Indian Featherweight Model K in a British or Irish trial. Ridden by C.B. Franklin, he won a silver medal and the lightweight prize (Gerald Mayne's prize for best performance by a machine under 300cc).

This was the last Dublin & District MCC event for three years, on account of the hostilities in Europe. By this time many of Franklin's peers and club-mates (such as Noel Drury and Oliver Godfrey) had already joined the military. Conscription was never imposed in Ireland (it was ultimately legislated for and about to be implemented in 1918, when the war ended), however there was no shortage of volunteers. By April 1916, 150,000 Irishmen of all political affiliations had already stepped forward to serve in the British army.

One such was Franklin's brother Lorenzo who in July 1917 mysteriously reappeared in Ireland from Detroit, where he was by now Asst. Paymaster at Cadillac. He enlisted on 4th February 1918 at Grove Park, Dublin, and spent a comfortable war based in London as a storekeeper for the RASC (Royal Army Service Corps). He was medically discharged on 1st July 1919 for epilepsy, from which he'd suffered since 1905.[30] Lorenzo subsequently returned to the US, and in later life he worked at Ford.

Charles, on the other hand, did not follow suit and enter the military. It is not known whether this was by inclination, or whether he was considered medically unfit for military service by virtue of damage to his lungs caused by pneumonia when a teenager. Most likely it was the latter, for the expectations of one's peers among the gentlemanly social network to which Franklin belonged in Ireland would have made it unthinkable that one would not join up and fight if one were able to do so.

Franklin Goes To America

More changes were occurring at Indian, beginning in August 1916 with the resignation and retirement of company president, Big Chief Hendee. Approaching the age of 50, it appears he was tiring of boardroom battles and was ready for a change of scene. Before stepping down, he took care to ensure that good people held various key posts who could 'hold the fort' regardless of who succeeded him as president of the company. Treasurer Frank Weschler proved to be the lynchpin here. He'd been fulfilling the role of a General Manager from when the Big Chief's mind had first started going into exit mode. The newly Board-elected President was a New York City financier named John Alvord who, starting a trend for absentee ownership of Indian, was content to stay in NYC and leave the day to day running of the company with Weschler. Sales and marketing were secure with people like Frank Long, Tommy Butler and William McCann but, in Hendee's mind, a question mark still hung over the matter of chief engineer responsible for design.

Charles Gustafson Snr, Hedstrom's former assistant, had become chief engineer when Oscar Hedstrom left in 1913. Gustafson was a tradesman who was very handy in a machine shop, just as Hedstrom himself had been. When it came to the esoterics of internal combustion – gas-flow, metallurgy, load characteristics, and so on – both men were self-taught, however. Their approach to these subjects was empirical. Or, in other words, they were graduates from the Engineering School of Hard Knocks. Gustafson's employment at Hendee Mfg. Ltd. dated from 1903, and prior to this he'd been a bicycle repairer. Immediately before joining Indian he'd been working at George Holden's bicycle business at 17 Dwight Street, during the time when it became the world's first dealer of Indian motocycles. He'd taken a year of time-out in 1906 to join the Reading-Standard company in Reading PA., then returned to Hendee Mfg. Co. to become a right-hand man of Hedstrom's in the engineering department.

Indians continued to be fitted with the Hedstrom inlet-over-exhaust or 'F-head' motors of de Dion pattern through the 1914-15 sales season. The grumbles of the new Indian board about the need for cost-cutting were beginning to hit home however, and Hendee wanted something done about it. Both the F-head Hedstrom engine and the Hedstrom-designed carburetor were costly to produce. Though reckoned to be generally excellent and thus worth the cost, they did have one weakness shared by all ioe engine configurations including the Harley J-model and the Big-valve Excelsior - the inlet valve pushrods and rockers were external to the motor and thus exposed to the elements. Road dust adhering to these moving parts soon formed a grinding paste that caused rapid wear. Owners needed to be continually cleaning, re-lubricating and adjusting the inlet valve trains if their engines were to remain on song.

Gustafson was by now inclining toward a different school of thought than de Dion disciple Hedstrom. The motors he'd worked with at Reading-Standard had followed the Peugeot pattern of side by side valves sitting atop the timing chest. Giving the matter some thought, Gustafson reasoned that this arrangement could be simpler, more elegant, and therefore cheaper to produce than the

George Hendee (2nd from right) with Frank Weschler (1st on left) and other Indian staff admire the new for 1916 Indian Powerplus model. (EMIA)

Hedstrom ioe arrangement. It need not be any less efficient combustion-wise, and would bring an added benefit that all valve-train parts could be enclosed inside tubular covers that shielded them from road grit. By becoming part of the inside of the engine rather than left on its outside, these valves would now be kept lubricated by oil mist wafting up from the timing chest.

The prototype lived up to its promise, and a new Indian engine was born that was both cheaper to make and more powerful than its predecessor. Dubbed the 'Powerplus' (for obvious reasons), they went into production in the autumn of 1915 for the 1916 sales season. Conservative Indian fans and die-hard Hedstrom devotees were soon won over by the increase in power and less need for valve adjustment. Apart from the new engine, the rest of the bicycle was the same frame and running gear as used for the Hedstrom big twins, which further eased the transition in the minds of customers. Similar transitional policies have been used by Harley-Davidson in modern times, for example when they introduced the new Evolution motors into the old Shovelhead frames for 1984.

Gustafson did good work with the Powerplus, which became Indian's mainstay as 'heavyweight' of the range for the next six years. Hendee was nevertheless still concerned that Indian's technical staff to date had never included any formally trained engineers. For example, one apparent shortcoming of Gustafson's was in carrying out the drafting work needed for laying out new engine designs and bringing them into production.

Meanwhile it appears that Billy Wells had been keeping Hendee informed about his own ongoing exchanges with Franklin on design matters. While running Indian's affairs in Dublin, Franklin continued to dream and scheme about his own 'perfect motorcycle'. As Indian's man in Dublin he would have been in regular contact with Wells on many matters, including this one. Wells, as a Hendee Mfg. Co. director, was entitled to make trans-Atlantic trips to attend board meetings in Springfield. Wells and Hendee would doubtless have got to talking, and in this way the suggestion must have been made to Hendee that Franklin be transferred to the Wigwam, due to his educational qualifications, his extensive practical experience with motorcycle repair, sales and service, and his outstanding record in competition both as a rider and an engine tuner. An Indian devotee since 1910, Franklin's loyalty to the product could not be questioned.

Concerning Hendee's job offer to Franklin, previously published accounts have been unclear about how hard or easy it had been for Franklin to make a decision. Some imply that it was a tough decision, because he was giving up a tenured civil service post with a guaranteed pension. But technically speaking, as manager of the Dublin Indian depot, Franklin already held a post within the Indian company. He had in fact relinquished both his life-time civil service career in electricity generation, and his own Indian agency, quite some time earlier (in 1910, and in 1914, respectively). This was not a question of moving *in* to the Indian company, but rather one of moving *up*.

One can well imagine Franklin's excitement at the prospect of working as a design engineer in what was then the biggest and best motorcycle factory in the world. How was it that the Hand of Fate had pointed his way, right across the Atlantic to Ireland, when President Hendee sought to further boost his company's engineering credentials? Franklin had certainly parleyed his TT second-place-getter fame into first a Dublin Indian dealership and then as Depot Manager, but for most successful racers or ex-racers this would have been as far as it went. To be offered an opportunity to actually design the next generation of the very products upon which Franklin had gained his competition successes must have come like a bolt from the blue, like winning a major lottery prize.

If there was any reluctance on his part, could it be reluctance to uproot his family from their familiar surroundings? On the other hand, the 1916 Easter Rising had led to a violent trashing of downtown Dublin. Barely a couple of blocks away from his Indian Depot at Wicklow Street, major buildings had been almost completely demolished by artillery shells fired by the British military at the holed-up rebels. More bloodshed and destruction lay ahead.

As it happened, the deciding factor turned out to be very simple. In late 1915 there had been a change in government policy on imports of foreign vehicles including motorcycles, as part of wartime austerity measures (the 'McKenna Duties'). Appearing too late to affect the 1915 motorcycle selling season, a new and substantial import tax now began to bite in 1916 and in Wells' view this rendered the recently-opened Dublin depot unviable. He decided to close it down, and retrench all British Indian activities to his London operation. Franklin was going to be out of a job anyway.

So if Franklin hadn't made his mind up, it would have been made up for him. He accepted Hendee's offer to travel to Springfield and join Indian's design department. These events were duly reported in *The Irish Cyclist and Motor Cyclist* which, for 18th October 1916, carried this report:

> Hendee Manufacturing Co. – Irish depot to close – Franklin goes to America.
>
> Owing to the restrictions relating to the importation of motorcycles made abroad, the Hendee Manufacturing Co. has decided to temporarily close its depot in Wicklow Street, Dublin, and at the end of the present week the business will be transferred to the British headquarters of the firm at 366 Euston Road, London NW, where all correspondence relating to the Irish business should in future be addressed.

An item of news that may be learned with considerable interest is that C.B. Franklin, who has acted as representative for the Hendee Manufacturing Co. in Ireland since the opening of the depot, and who for many years previously was identified with the Indian as a rider of it in competitions, is going to America to take up an important position at the Indian works in Springfield, Massachusetts. Franklin tells us that he will be in America for a period of six months, from which we may conclude that at the end of that time we may anticipate developments of an interesting character in the Hendee Company's business on this side of the Atlantic.

On Wednesday 25th October 1916, the Dublin & District Motor Cycle Club held a farewell dinner for Charles B. Franklin in the Dolphin Hotel, Essex Street, Dublin. Mr G.A.M. Curtis, president of the club, chaired the dinner. Mr Franklin made a brief speech in which he expressed the hope that he would meet in America as good fellows as he had found in Irish motorcycling, and that good fortune would again bring him back amongst them. After the dinner the company adjourned to the Theatre Royal.

Franklin travelled to New York on board the White Star liner *RMS Adriatic*, which sailed from Liverpool on 1st November 1916. His wife Nancye and daughter Phyllis remained behind in the family home in Rathgar. He arrived in New York on 16th November 1916.

The *Irish Cyclist and Motor Cyclist* reported on 20th December 1916 that C.B. Franklin had written to them to inform them of his safe arrival in Springfield, Massachusetts, and he asked them to convey to all his friends in the old country his cordial greetings for the festive season.

On departing Ireland's shores, it was apparently Franklin's intention to return after only about six months. In any case, he was sure it would not be too long before he saw all his old friends again. As it turned out, this was the last that Ireland ever saw of him. He was never to return to the island of his birth.

To wrap up this phase of Charles Franklin's career we'll again give the last word to Ixion who, writing in 1920, summarised the motorcycle racing scene thus:

> Road-racing has developed into a highly dangerous sport, demanding physical and mental qualities which are the property of the few, and which increasing years rapidly impair. The career of the road racer resembles that of the prize-fighter. New men flash into fame, stay a year or two at the top of the tree, and swiftly pass into the ranks of the has-beens. Some of them face the facts with a good grace. A few try to prolong their waning courage with whisky, and only hasten the inevitable downfall. After the twenty-fifth birthday only one man in a thousand can continue to race on motorcycles and display any real skill. The strain is as great as that of flying a scout aeroplane over the lines.

Franklin's racing career lasted from 1903 to 1916. When he finally hung up his distinctive collarless, double-breasted leather jacket for good, he was 36 years of age. By Ixion's reckoning, then, Charles Franklin, the Irish Champion, was literally one man in a thousand.

Manifest of Alien Passengers for the United States, New York, 16th November 1916:

Franklin, Charles Bayly, 36, Male, Married.
Occupation, Manager. Able to read and write? Yes.
Nationality, British. Race, Irish. Country. Ireland.
City, Dublin.
Wife, Mrs A.W. Franklin, 8 Vernon Terrace, Rathgar, Dublin.
Final destination, Springfield Mass.
Whether have ticket to final destination? No.
By whom was passage paid? Hendee Mfg. Co..
In possession of $50? Yes.
Whether ever before in the United States? No.
Whether going to join a relative or friend? Hendee Mfg. Co., Springfield Mass.
Height, 5'10'. Complexion, Pale. Hair, Dark brown.
Eyes, Hazel. Place of Birth, Dublin Ireland.

This cartoon depicting prominent personalities of the Dublin & District Motorcycle Club in 1915 includes a character named 'Red Indian Franklin'. (NLI)

Franklin's Competition Career Summary

The major competition successes of Charles Franklin are presented in the foregoing narrative. For the sake of completeness, we list here the other race events he participated in for which results are available. These provide a useful record through time of Franklin's changing tastes and loyalties toward particular motorcycle marques.

Motor Cycle Union of Ireland (Dublin Centre) Reliability Trial from Dublin to Maryborough, September 1903:

1. H. Huet (James) - lost 135 marks
2. R. W. Stevens (Star Griffon) - lost 135 marks
3. L. R. Oswald-Sealy (Brown) - lost 160 marks
4. A. Summers (Triumph) - lost 185 marks
5. T. W. Houghton (FN) - lost 230 marks
6. J. J. Cahill (Roebuck) - lost 250 marks
7. H. Shaw (Excelsior) - lost 260 marks
8. C.B. Franklin (FN with forecarriage) - lost 265 marks
9. E. Martin (Excelsior) - lost 275 marks

Motor Cycle Union of Ireland (Ulster Centre) Belfast to Dublin Reliability Trial for the Canning Cup, 10 October 1903.

1. R. W. Ireton (Riley) - lost no marks
2. C.B. Franklin (FN) - lost no marks
3. T. Ireland (Humber) - lost 5 marks
4. A. Summers (Triumph) - lost 5 marks
5. J. Stewart (Centaur) - lost 5 marks
6. T. E. Denby (Excelsior) - lost 5 marks

The Ulster Centre team won the Canning Cup

Dublin Centre MCUI Motorcycle speed trial, Portmarnock Strand, Saturday 14th May 1904.

Winners:
Class A - W.B. Martin (FN)
Class B (under 150 lbs.) - C.B. Franklin (FN)
Class C (unlimited weight) - C.B. Franklin (FN)

Competitors:
R.W. Stevens (cycle agent of Aston Quay), (2¾ hp Griffon); N.E. Drury, (2 hp Triumph, Minerva engine); J.B. Dunlop, Jnr, (1¼ hp FN , flat belt model); Oswald-Sealy, (2¾ hp Brown); W. Ladley, (2 hp Minerva); E.A. Wallen, (2½ hp Triumph, JAP engine); Alfred Summers, (2 hp Triumph, Minerva - Wallen and Summers were in partnership as Triumph agents in Nassau Street, Dublin); R.W. Ireton, (2 hp Royal Riley); T.C. Furlong, (2½ hp Wearwell); H.S. Huet, (3 hp James); H. McAllen, (3 hp Centaur); Charles B. Franklin, (2¾ hp FN) ; W. Ladley (again), (3 hp Hamilton); R.W. Stevens, (2¾ hp Phoenix); A. Flood, (2¾ hp Excelsior); C.W. Mercier, (2¾ hp Bat, JAP engine); C.J. Ball, (2¾ hp FN); Hampden Shaw, (3 hp Excelsior).

Franklin rode six trials that afternoon. His times were: 1min 45secs, 1min 48secs, 1min 42secs, 1min 46secs, 1min 43secs, 1min 45secs.

Portmarnock Speed Trials, 11th June 1904:

Class B (one mile, standing start, machines of 150 lbs. or under) - 1st C.B. Franklin (FN). In this class, C.B. Franklin failed to get off with his customary smartness and Frank Wallen (Triumph) got a long lead. However, Wallen's carburettor leaked and this gave Franklin the chance to get home by 10 yards. His average speed was about 37 mph

Class C (one kilometre, 1,096 yards, with flying start, unrestricted weight, horse power limited to 3.5) - 2nd - C.B. Franklin (FN). In this flying kilo event, Oswald-Sealy (Excelsior) beat Franklin by 0.4 of a second.

Kilmacanogue Hill-climb, Saturday 9th July 1904:

Pedalling class - 2nd - C.B. Franklin (FN)
Non-pedalling class - 2nd - C.B. Franklin (FN)
Franklin finished second in both classes, 'and the fact that the little pedalling he did in the first class improved his time by only 2 seconds, shows how well his FN travelled, and at the same time testifies to his consummate skill as a driver'.

MCUI Speed Trials, Portmarnock, 23rd July 1904:

Class B (150 lbs. or under, one mile, standing start) - 2nd - C.B. Franklin (FN). Class C (no weight restrictions, one kilometre, 1096 yards, flying start) - 3rd - C.B. Franklin (FN). In this class there was also an R.F. Franklin (FN), Charles Franklin's brother, who finished 6th.

MCUI Dublin-Waterford Reliability Trial, 2nd August 1904:

FN Team No. 1 - C.B. Franklin, his brother R.F. Franklin, T. Turpin, W.B. Martin
FN Team No. 2 - E. Oates, A. Hamilton, R.E. Price
Triumph Team No. 1 - F.A. Wallen, R.W. Stevens, R.M. Talbot, T.W. Murphy
Triumph Team No. 2 - A. Summers, L. Summers, J.G. Drury, G. Mayne

Result:
1. Triumph Team No. 2 - all scored 100 marks
2. FN Team No. 1 - both C.B. Franklin and R.F. Franklin scored 100 marks

MCUI Hill-climb, Saturday, 27th August 1904:

880 yards long course leading from the Waterfall Gate of the Powerscourt Demesne, Co. Wicklow:
Class B (76x76mm) - 1st C.B. Franklin (FN)
Class C (84x84mm) - 1st C.B. Franklin (FN)

Crystal Palace, London, 24th September 1904.

Five Miles Race for the Motor Car Journal Challenge Cup:
1. C. Collier (Matchless)
2. J. F. Crundall (Humber)
3. C.B. Franklin (FN)

One Mile Time Trials for the Automotor Journal Challenge Cup

1. C. Collier (Matchless)   1 min 15 secs.
2. W. W. Genn (Minerva)   1 min 16.6 secs
3. H. Martin (Excelsior)   1 min 17.6 secs
4. H. C. Tyler (Humber)   1 min 20 secs
5. S. Varney (Kerry)   1 min 20.4 secs
6. C.B. Franklin (FN)   1 min 21.4 secs

MCUI (Dublin Centre) Hill-climb at Stepaside, 23rd September 1905.

1. W. H. Meredith (Triumph) -   1 min 38.4 secs.
2. C.B. Franklin (FN) -   1 min 39.4 secs
3. J. G. Drury (Triumph) -   1 min 42 secs
4. C. G. H. Lewis (FN) -   1min 48.8 secs

MCUI Speed Trials at Portmarnock Strand, 30th September 1905:

One mile scratch (Wheatley Bowl) - 1st C.B. Franklin (6 hp JAP)
10 mile members handicap - 2nd C.B. Franklin (FN)

Motor Cycle Race Meeting at Canning Town, 4th May 1907

C.B. Franklin competed in a series of three races against C. R. Collier. The distances of the events were one, three and five miles, and in each Collier was successful. At the same meeting Collier rode a mile, with a flying start, on a machine fitted with a 76 x 76 mm engine in 64.2 secs., and won the open five miles scratch race.

Canning Cup Reliability Trial, MCUI (Dublin Centre), 25th May 1907:

Three riders completed non-stop runs
C. Murphy (Triumph), C.B. Franklin (JAP) and D. Leavy (Triumph).

MCUI Speed Trials, Portmarnock Strand, 3rd August 1907:

2 miles Members Handicap - 3rd C.B. Franklin (JAP)
20 miles Members Handicap -2nd C.B. Franklin (JAP)

MCUI (Dublin Centre) Hill-climb, Saturday 17th August 1907

On the old military road from Lower Lough Bray to Sally Gap:
4th place - C.B. Franklin (JAP). He rode the machine he had built for the TT race.

MCUI Speed Trials, Portmarnock Strand, 24th August 1907:

20 miles Members Handicap (Kavanagh Cup) - 1st C.B. Franklin (JAP)

MCUI (Dublin Centre) Hill-climb, Long Hill, Sugarloaf Mountain, 21st September 1907:
Pedalling class - 2nd C.B. Franklin (JAP)
Non-pedalling class - 3rd C.B. Franklin (JAP)

MCUI Portmarnock Speed Trials, 5th October 1907:
2 miles Members Handicap - 4th C.B. Franklin (JAP)
20 miles Members Handicap - 4th C.B. Franklin (JAP) This race was won by N.E. Drury (5 hp Vindec Special).

MCUI Speed Trials, Portmarnock Strand, May 30, 1908:
20 miles open race - 4th C.B. Franklin (JAP)

MCUI Hill-climb, Sugarloaf Mountain, 1st August 1908:
5th place - C.B. Franklin (Minerva).

MCUI Speed Trials, Portmarnock Strand, 22nd August 1908:
C.B. Franklin (JAP) won three events - the 2, 4 and 20 miles handicaps.

MCUI Hill-climb, Long Hill, Sugarloaf, 29th August 1908:
1st C.B. Franklin (JAP 3.5 hp)

MCUI (Dublin Centre) Hill-climb, Sugarloaf, 8th May 1909:
Both classes were won by C.B. Franklin on a Triumph.

Dublin and District MCC Reliability Trial for the White Cup, 31st May 1909:
From Dublin to Lisburn and back (180 miles), the winner was C.B. Franklin on a 3.5 hp Triumph, registration number IK 352. It rained all day. The start was at Drumcondra Bridge at 9 am. The roads were a quagmire. 'The competitors presented a very travel-stained appearance when they arrived back at Drumcondra. Water oozed from every part of their garments.'

MCUI (Ulster Centre) Irish End-to-End Trial, 13th July 1909:
From Mizen Head, Co. Cork, to Fair Head, Co. Antrim, a distance of 395 miles. On a Triumph, Franklin found this ride a much easier affair than when he first attempted it on his FN five years earlier. There were 16 starters assembled for the off at 1 am from Rock Island Coastguard Station, and they proceeded from there to Mizen Head, Cork, Fermoy, Cahir, Cashel, Durrow, Abbeyleix, Maryborough (Portlaoise), Naas, Dublin, Drogheda, Dundalk, Belfast (Balmoral), Antrim, Ballymena, Armoy, Ballycastle, Ballyvoy, to arrive at Fair Head. Of the 16 starters, six completed the distance without loss of marks. As a result of this 'draw', a hill-climb was held on Wednesday, July 14, at Quay Hill, Ballycastle to decide the winner. Times:

Charles E. Murphy (Triumph)	39.8 secs	J. Lavery (Triumph)	52.8 secs
C.B. Franklin (Triumph)	52 secs	T. A. Govan (Triumph)	55 secs

Final result of the End-to-End Trial (after the hill-climb):
1. C. E. Murphy (Triumph) - 51.06 pts. (Palmer Trophy)
2. J. Lavery (Triumph) - 62.99
3. T. A. Govan (Triumph) - 69.81
4. C.B. Franklin (Triumph) - 72.58
5. R. M. Talbot (Triumph)
6. J. E. Coulter (Triumph)

Dublin and District MCC Hill-climb, 4th June 1910

Held at Long Hill, Sugarloaf Mountain, Co. Wicklow, Charles B. Franklin presented a silver medal for the event. He did not take part, but was time-keeper at the top of the hill during the competition. Winner of the event was J. Browne on a Scott. After the competition was over, Franklin got out his 5 hp Indian and made an attempt to break his own 1909 record of 2 min 15.2 secs., which he'd set using a 3 ½ hp Triumph. In this he succeeded, setting a new time of 2 min 10.2 secs. - an improvement of 5 secs. M.J. Chambers acted as starter and timekeeper.

Dublin and District MCC Speed Trials, Portmarnock, 18th June 1910

One mile handicap - 3rd - C.B. Franklin (5.5 hp Indian)
20 miles (out and home) handicap, one mile course - 3rd - C.B. Franklin (5.5 hp Indian)
From *Irish Cyclist & Motor Cyclist*: 'Franklin did fastest time for the 20 miles - he covered the distance in 25 mins. 55 secs, which, of course, is by a long way the fastest time that has been accomplished at Portmarnock. His 5.5 hp Indian travelled at a surprisingly fast pace in the middle part of the course - he must have been doing well over 60 mph at times - but he took the bends very cautiously.'

Brooklands 60-Lap TT Race (Isle of Man TT Regulations), 22nd June 1910, over 163 miles and 103 yards. Fork start and finish.

Multi's (up to 670cc) — Speed (mph)
1. A.J. Moorhouse (639 Indian) — 56.72
2. H.H. Bowen (666 BAT-JAP) — 49.56
3. C.B. Franklin (639 Indian) — 49.01

Singles (up to 500cc)
1. F. A. McNab (488 Trump-JAP) — 53.71
2. J. Marshall (499 Triumph) — 52.66
3. A.R. Abbott (499 Rex) — 54 laps

Dublin and District MCC Hill-climb, 17th March 1911:

Held at Ballinaslaughter Hill on St. Patrick's Day, 4th was C.B. Franklin riding an Indian.

Portmarnock Strand Speed Trials, Saturday 29th April 1911:

4 mile scratch race (up to 520cc) - 1st C.B. Franklin (Indian)
Open 26 miles handicap (13 laps of two-mile circuit) - 3rd C.B. Franklin (Indian)
Irish Cyclist report of the 26 miles handicap event: 'C.B. Franklin's exhibition on his 3.5 hp Indian was the subject of much comment amongst the spectators. Not only did he excel from the point of view of speed, but also in the matter of cornering.'

Dublin and District MCC flying half-mile, June 1911:

Held on a deserted road in Co. Dublin in Unlimited cc:
1. F. J. Walker (8 hp JAP) — 26.9 secs
2. C.B. Franklin (7 hp Indian) — 27.2 secs
3. R. Dunphy (Triumph) — 29.8 secs

Dublin and District MCC Hill-climb, 18th March 1912, at Brittas:

Class C (over 520cc) - 2nd C.B. Franklin (Indian).

Dublin and District MCC Portmarnock Strand Speed Trials, Saturday 13th April 1912:

One mile scratch (under 520cc) - 1st C.B. Franklin (Indian)
One mile scratch (unlimitedcc) - 1st C.B. Franklin (Indian)
20 miles handicap - 5th C.B. Franklin (Indian)
Irish Cyclist and Motor Cyclist commented: In the 20 miles handicap, C.B. Franklin was riding a new 4hp Indian. He was always recognisable, even at a distance, by the trail of blue smoke he left in the wake of his machine, showing that he is a believer in the eminently sound practice of copiously oiling the engine while racing.

Dublin and District MCC Portmarnock Speed Trials, 20th July 1912:

A large crowd attended to see 15 starters contest the 100 miles race. There was water on the course, several inches deep in places, which gave chain-drive machines an advantage over the belt-driven ones. There was a close and exciting finish between C.B. Franklin and W. Curtis, also on an Indian.

1st	C.B. Franklin (3.5 hp Indian)	2 hr 9 min 13 secs	46.43 mph
2nd	W. Curtis (5 hp Indian)	2 hr 15 min 43 secs	44.21 mph
3rd	T.E. Greene (3.5 hp Rudge)	2 hr 18 min 46 secs	43.24 mph.

French Grand Prix, Forest of Fontainebleau, 25th August 1912.

Indian placed entries in this race, run over a distance of 279 miles. It was won by Oliver Godfrey, with Franklin in 3rd place.

1st.	O.C. Godfrey (England) Indian	6 hr 34 min 59 secs
2nd.	Devay (France) Triumph	6 hr 35 min 14 secs
3rd.	C.B. Franklin (Ireland) Indian	7 hr 5 min 24 secs
4th.	Bloch (France) Gillett	8 hr 9 min 42 secs

Brooklands Race Meeting, 9th November 1912:

Sidecars up to 1,000cc - 3rd C.B. Franklin (Indian)
1,000cc scratch race - this was won by H. Reed (Dot-JAP) at 74.97 mph, while C.B. Franklin (994 Indian) was second at 74.60 mph

Dublin and District MCC Hill-climb, Glencullen, 17th March 1913:

Class One - 3rd C.B. Franklin (3.5hp Indian).
According to *Irish Cyclist and Motor Cyclist* 'Franklin made an excellent climb, but his time would have been slightly better had he taken the first bend wider. The class was won by G. Roche (Rudge)'.

Brooklands, Easter Monday 24th March 1913

C.B. Franklin (Indian) took part in the 8.5 miles handicap, starting from scratch. He had some machine problems in the early stages, however he covered the last lap at 80 mph and passed several of the competitors, though too late to secure a place.

Dublin and District MCC Speed Trials, Portmarnock, 19th April 1913:

Two miles scratch race - 1st C.B. Franklin (Indian).

Dublin and District MCC Speed Trials, Portmarnock, 3rd May 1913:

One mile scratch race (500cc) - 1st C.B. Franklin (Indian).

In 1913 C.B. Franklin was again a vice-president of the Dublin and District MCC.

Dublin and District MCC Reliability Trial, Co. Wicklow, 19th July 1913:
C.B. Franklin (Indian and sidecar) was one of four riders who scored full marks.

Dublin and District MCC Speed Trials, Portmarnock, 30th August 1913:
C.B. Franklin (Indian) won both the unlimited cc two mile scratch and the 100 miles open handicap events.

Brooklands, Saturday 13th September 1913:
Senior one-lap race - 1st C.B. Franklin (Indian) - 71.94 mph
Senior one-hour team race: The Indian team finished second. The team members were: C.B. Franklin, S. George, B.A. Hill.

Dublin and District MCC Speed Trials, Portmarnock, 11th October 1913:
Six mile scratch race - 2nd C.B. Franklin (Indian).

Brooklands, Saturday 28th March 1914:
501-1,000cc handicap (solos) - 3rd C.B. Franklin (Indian).
1,000cc scratch - 1st C.B. Franklin (994 Indian) at 79.90 mph
At the Dublin and District MCC annual general meeting on 22nd October 1913, C.B. Franklin was re-elected a vice-president.

Dublin and District MCC Speed Trials, Portmarnock, 25th July 1914:
10 miles scratch race (under 500cc) - 1st C.B. Franklin (Indian) - 13min 0 secs

Portmarnock Speed Trials, 19th September 1914:
6 miles open scratch (under 500cc) - 1st C.B. Franklin (Indian).

Dublin and District MCC Easter Monday Trial, 5th April 1915:
C.B. Franklin (Indian) was one of six riders who had non-stop runs.

Dublin and District MCC Glencullen Hill-climb, 17th April 1915:
5th - C.B. Franklin (Indian). He also set the fastest time of the day in 41.8 secs

Dublin and District MCC Sidecar Trial, start at Donnybrook, 1st May 1915:
1st - C.B. Franklin (Indian) - 100 marks

Portmarnock Speed Trials, Saturday 15th May 1915:
50 miles open handicap (unlimitedcc) - 1st C.B. Franklin (Indian).

Cork 20 Hours Trial, 24th May 1915:
The start was from the Imperial Hotel, Cork, and ran over a 344.5 mile course. The winner was W.H. Freeman (7/9 hp Indian). C.B. Franklin (7/9 hp Indian and sidecar) was one of the finishers and won a gold medal.

Dublin and District MCC Speed Trials, Portmarnock, 12th June 1915:
100 miles handicap race (unlimitedcc) - 2nd C.B. Franklin (Indian).

MCUI (Ulster Centre) End-to-End Trial:
This started from Rock Island Coastguard Station, Goleen, Co. Cork, on Tuesday 13th July 1915. C.B. Franklin rode a 7 hp Indian and sidecar (registration number RI 3639) and won a gold medal.

Cork Hill-climb, 8th September 1915:
This event was held on the road from The Lough to Ballinhassig.
Under 600cc class - 1st C.B. Franklin (Indian).

Dublin and District MCC Speed Trials, Portmarnock, 11th September 1915:
10 miles scratch (under 600cc) - 1st C.B. Franklin (Indian).

Liverpool MC Hill-climb, held at Pen-y-Ball, Holywell, Wales, September 1915:
500cc - 1st - C.B. Franklin (Indian)
1000cc - 2nd C.B. Franklin (Indian)

Dublin and District MCC Winter Trial, Co. Wicklow, 27th December 1915:
C.B. Franklin (7hp Indian and sidecar) was one of the finishers.

Dublin and District MCC Easter Trial, Easter Monday 24th April 1916:
This event took place in the Dublin Mountains and was won by C.B. Franklin (Indian).

Dublin and District MCC 24 Hours Reliability Trial, 23rd June 1916:
Competing for the Rudge Cup, the start was at Rathfarnham. Winner was W. H. Freeman (Indian).

American Motorcycle Designer

Springfield In 1916

Upon arrival in New York City, Charles Franklin was met by Thomas Callaghan Butler of the Hendee Mfg. Co. They travelled by train to Springfield, Massachusetts, home of 'The Wigwam' at the intersection of State Street and Wilbraham Road where Indian 'motocycles' were being manufactured.

Springfield lies inland from the Atlantic coast, about 90 miles west of Boston, in the New England region of the north-east United States. New England was the first part of the New World to be colonised by Britain and, after Independence, the first to become industrialized. Situated on the banks of the Connecticut River in western Massachusetts, Springfield is about 70 miles upriver from the mouth at Long Island Sound and 26 miles upriver from the next decent-sized city of Hartford, Connecticut. Geographically and economically, Springfield has always been closely linked with Hartford, much more so than with its own state capital of Boston.

Springfield was chosen as the location of the National Armory during the presidency of George Washington, and this led to the town becoming an important cradle of the industrial revolution in the United States. The Springfield Armory gave rise to a cluster of artisans and metal workers (such as machinery inventor Thomas Buchanan) up and down the Connecticut Valley, and in the 19th century was a key player in the emergence of the American System of Manufactures. Centered upon interchangeable parts made by machine tools, this system laid the foundation for modern methods of mass production. The industrial revolution brought New England to a position of national strength, making it by 1860 the region most highly industrialized and urbanized, and attracting more immigrants (including many from Ireland), than any other part of the USA. By 1920, more than two thirds of the Massachusetts population were first or second generation immigrants.

Springfield today dubs itself *The City of Firsts*, for the number of inventions and pioneering achievements that originated there. These include the invention of the game of basketball, and of the first American automobile. Built by the Duryea brothers in 1893, this latter Springfield creation also became the first US automobile ever to be offered for sale to the public. Smith & Wesson chose Springfield as its base, and in time became the largest small-arms manufacturer in the US. At the close of the 19th Century Springfield was a hub of manufacturing industries that, in addition to firearms, included automobiles (the Knox company, and later, the US plant of British car maker Rolls-Royce), bicycles, clocks, sewing machines, and machine tools. It was entirely logical that George Hendee, the man who hired Charles Franklin, should have chosen Springfield as the location to build America's first big-selling motorcycle, and to build the aero engine that powered the first ever airmail flight in North America.

New England's pre-eminent role in the American industrial revolution had been founded upon its Atlantic seaboard location, which made it the then most populous region of the newly-colonised New World, and on its many streams and rivers which provided water-wheel power for the emergent factories and mills. By the second half of the 19th Century however, the Great Lakes region had emerged as a far greater nexus of the three ingredients so essential to large-scale industrialization - iron ore, coal, and water-borne bulk transport.

The fact that the Hendee Mfg. Co. Ltd, a mere motorcycle manufacturer in an America that now churned out automobiles in the hundreds of thousands, had by 1916 become Springfield's leading employer is perhaps indicative of the industrial decline by now setting in across the north-east. When Charles Franklin's brother Lorenzo landed a job in the US auto industry in 1912, he did not go to Springfield. He went to Detroit. For New England this process of decline was accelerated by the Great Depression, and the economic situation of Springfield itself was further worsened by closure of its National Armory in the 1960s. This atmosphere of having seen better days continues in contemporary Springfield, only partially off-set by an emergence of technology and electronics 'smart industries' buoyed by its location in the Connecticut Valley's 'Knowledge Corridor' of seats of higher learning.

But none of this would have been apparent to Charles Franklin in 1916. His Springfield was one of large and elegant Victorian houses, many of which are still standing and give rise to Springfield's other nickname *The City of Homes*. Most importantly to him, it was home to the Hendee Mfg. Co.'s factory on State Street and Wilbraham Road, and another smaller plant in East Springfield. Indian was by now the biggest and best-equipped motorcycle producer in the world, the acknowledged industry leader and innovator with a global position similar to that held by Honda in modern times. Only three years earlier Indian had enjoyed its best ever sales year of almost 32,000 motorcycles, and completed the expansion of its production facilities to one employing 3,000 people and capable of producing 100,000 units in a year.

One can only imagine Franklin's excitement at joining the staff at the Wigwam. He had been one-eyed in his devotion to the Indian marque since 1910, his engineering proclivities totally won over by the advanced technical specification, toughness, sheer speed and dashing good looks of Indian's products. Now he would really be able to play a key role in developing those products further.

Franklin is first recorded in the City Directory as living at the Oaks Hotel on State Street at the corner of Thompson Street, about five blocks away and thus an easy stroll from the Indian factory. Since period advertisements for the hotel reveal that this would have been costing his employers between $1.50 and $4.00 per day (depending upon meal plan), it is likely that his stay there was only a matter of a few weeks or months at the most. It is unclear where he moved to from there, however by 1919 Franklin was a lodger with Eugene and Candace Fark in their big Victorian home at 53 Thompson Street.

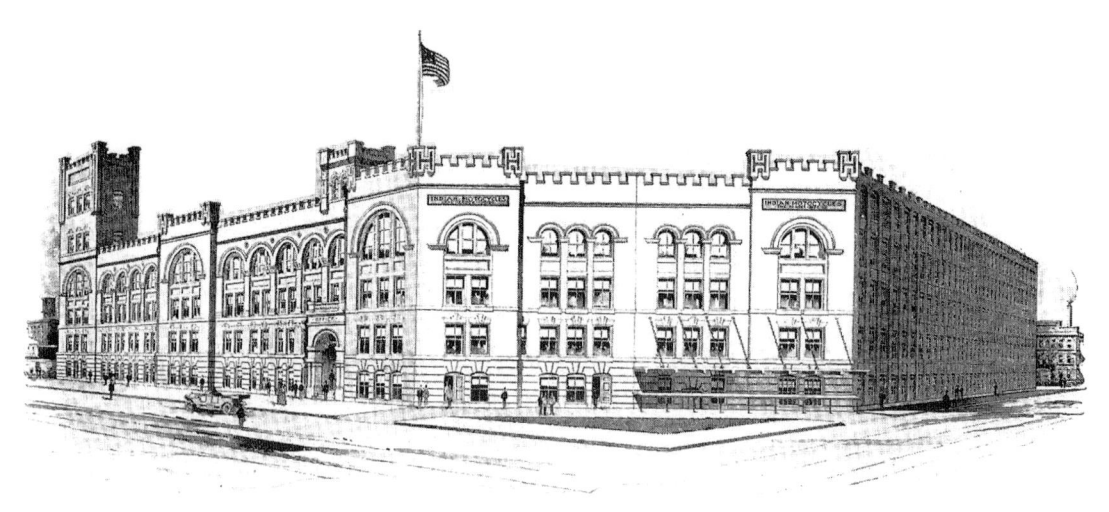

The frontage of The Wigwam in Springfield MA, as it appeared to Franklin when he reported for duty there in November 1916. (Indian Factory Archives)

Settling In At Indian

What was the Indian factory like in those days? A massive and castellated structure, the complex had been built in two main phases beginning in 1902 and in 1910. Five storeys high, its four main buildings were arranged in the shape of a letter 'V' on a triangular plot of land at the convergence of State Street and Wilbraham Road. Bisected by a convenient railway line halfway along the two sides of the 'V', the two pairs of mill blocks that made up each side were bridged over the railroad track by covered walkways between their upper storeys. Uniting the ends at the apex of the 'V' formed by these four mill blocks was an office block, leaving a triangular plot (then called Winchester Park, later the site of a firehouse) where the two main thoroughfares merged.

The factory buildings were comprised of solid brick walls, with internal wooden frames and joists to support the floors and interior walls. Mill blocks 1 and 3, and the office block, also had underground basements that effectively gave them an additional floor each. The open courtyard space between the four major blocks was built on and added to in places, for example by a boiler house, punch-press building, and storage areas.

Indian staffer Allen Carter was interviewed by *Indian Scout* author Jerry Hatfield, and had this to say about entering the Wigwam from its front street entrance on State Street at the Firehouse end of the complex. He speaks of the Wigwam during the 1930s and 40s, but it was little changed since Franklin's time except for the condition of the machinery.

> You walked through the main door and turned right. They had a receptionist there, and the rest of the room was the sales manager and all their offices, and the comptroller was there. There were a lot of old motorcycles around in this reception thing. All the offices on that first floor in that section were beautifully done, with oak paneling.
>
> When you came in, on the first floor there was a big wide pair of steps that went up to the second floor. On the second floor there was a landing. When you went into there (to the right), that's where the design engineers had an office. That's where Briggs Weaver was, and Bob Powell.
>
> On the third floor we had the blueprint room, and we had some detail draftsmen up there that detailed various things - drawing storage, factory control stuff. Off of that, in the back of it, we had the experimental room - the machine shop. And then, from then on it went over to the dynamometer room and on down the side of the building where we made the experimental frames and things of that nature.
>
> The fourth floor was just storage up there. That's where we had all the old hillclimb machines and everything else. I used to go up there and look at all these old machines laying up in there. Whatever happened to them, I don't know. Somebody junked them, I think. Rogers came in and they hauled them away and junked the things. There must've been a dozen of them up there, different old racing bikes.
>
> When you went in the front door, the stairway was there, built along the partitions. On the left side (on each floor) you went through doors and went right out in the factory.

Everything had to come up and down on elevators. And all those columns inside; you always had to work around those; it wasn't good at all. To heat the thing was unreal. You had high ceilings; the ceilings were about fourteen feet. They had two steam boilers down there - they were enough to run five locomotives - to try and heat the thing.

It was an old worn out plant when Mr du Pont took it over (in 1930). Nothing had been replaced. When I was up there during the war, we were still struggling with some of those old turret lathes and stuff that Hendee had bought. We had a whole damn big factory full of old worn out machines. We couldn't hold the tolerances; we just didn't have the machines that would do it.

Almost every machine in there made more than one part. You had to set them up and break them down, set them up and break them down. If they had a milling machine set up, that milling machine had enough tools to make maybe five parts. They would build maybe a hundred motorcycles at a shot. You would have one machine operator, and he would be in a place maybe as big as twenty feet by thirty feet, and he would have three or four machines. So the machine operator would get an order and a number for a certain piece that he was going to make. He would go down behind the machine and pick up these jigs and things and put them on the machine, and clamp them on, to make that part. That one machine might make five or six different parts, by adding and taking away different fixtures from it. And the whole plant was that way.

All this was, for the 'teens', a considerable advance on the cramped, dimly-lit Victorian sweat-shop conditions seen at British motorcycle factories like Norton and Velocette right up until the 1950s. All manufacturers in those days (Indian included) used general-purpose machinery, in which a run of parts was made by an artisan skilled in the set-up for, and machining of, that particular piece. It was the Japanese and Germans, making a fresh start during their post-WWII industrial reconstruction, and building in big volumes for a healthy domestic market for small-capacity machines, who took motorcycle manufacture into the modern age of special-purpose machinery (one machine, one part). These require a bigger capital outlay, but need less skill to operate and have no down-time for set-up between batches. For large production runs, they are more cost-effective in the long term. All this was in the future, though. For 1916, the sheer spaciousness of the buildings and the plethora of machinery at the Wigwam made Indian's factory state-of-the-art.

And how about that dynamometer! Luxury indeed. A dynamometer is an expensive piece of kit, which the majority of motorcycle factories in the world in those early times would simply have had to do without. When Arthur Lemon joined the Ace company in 1922 a dynamometer was something they lacked, it was one of the first things he insisted upon, and it cost Ace's backers a cool $7,500 to get one for him (almost $100,000 in today's money). Oscar Hedstrom's wish-list had certainly been fulfilled with no stinting when the full-size Wigwam was completed and equipped in 1913.

Franklin arrived at a Hendee Mfg. Co. that was in transition. President Hendee had now retired to his Hilltop farm, leaving faithful Treasurer Frank Weschler in charge as General Manager. The Engineering and Design Department on the 2nd and 3rd floors was now headed by Charles Gustafson Snr, a long-time Indian staffer who had worked closely with Hedstrom on development of the various Indian inlet-over-exhaust road and race models.

A believer in the advantages of enclosed side-valves instead of open-to-the-elements actuation of over-head valves, Gustafson Snr designed the new Indian Powerplus engine which, from the 1916 model year forward, was being fitted into the frames and running gear where previously had sat the Hedstrom ioe big twin motors. In taking this initiative he had been enthusiastically supported by Thomas Butler in the sales department, who had enough engineering background and common sense to recognize a better mousetrap when he saw one. The Powerplus was not only true to its name, it was also cheaper to manufacture, more rugged, and easier to maintain than the Hedstrom motors.

There was another new model also introduced for 1916 - the little two-stroke Model K. Described in factory advertising as the Indian Featherweight, it was offered for $150 as compared with $250 - $275 for a Powerplus. In contemporary UK magazine reports the Featherweight was 'puffed' by Billy Wells as the ideal city commuter or telegram boy's bike. Certainly it was too small and low-powered to be of much use on the ox-cart tracks that still made up the major portion of America's rural roads. It would only have been effective on relatively well-paved urban streets but, even so, it would have been no less useful for all that.

The Featherweight was uncannily similar to the contemporary British Villiers proprietary engines being fitted to makes like the Sun, so it is logical to conclude that it was aimed at capturing a bigger share of British and European export markets where the average journey was shorter and the roads much better. In this it was ill-timed, since Europe in 1916 was in the midst of a conflagration - the largest and bloodiest war the world had yet seen. This would have left only the Australasian market, except that road networks Down Under were as undeveloped as those in the USA so motorcycle buyers showed a marked preference for large American V-twins.

It did make sense in America for Indian to offer a lightweight model. The Indian line had been transformed in 1909 from neat little mopeds to tall, heavy, fire-breathing rip-snorters suitable for 'real men'. This was fine and dandy if you were a real man, but there were many people likely to need personal transport who were not so rugged or athletic in their physique. Sure, the Powerplus motors were also offered as a more user-friendly single-cylinder 'half-twin', but this was still housed in the same tall bicycle as the big twin.

Billy Wells was interviewed by English magazine *The Motor Cycle* at the beginning of 1916, and he was asked to comment upon the state of the US motorcycle industry. Appearing on 3rd February 1916, this article provides us with his impressions of the intended role of the Featherweight, but without going so far as to admit that he might have been one of the brains behind it.

Developments in the American Motor Cycle world
Mr WH Wells recounts Impressions gained during his Latest Visit to the USA
We recently had a chat with Mr W.H. Wells, who has lately returned from a short visit to the Hendee headquarters in Springfield, Massachussetts. Asked about the present condition of the motor cycle industry in the United States, Mr Wells stated that the demand for motor cycles and cars was as great as ever, but the difficulty was a shortage of material, which was almost as bad as it was in Great Britain, owing to the very large quantities required for munitions for the Allies.

We then asked Mr Wells if there were any indications of the American manufacturers devoting their attention to the medium-powered machine. The answer was in the negative, and he went on to say that there appeared to be a good prospect of the lightweights attaining a certain degree of popularity for use in districts where the roads were good, but that the medium-powered machine was simply non-existent.

In his particular case, the 5 hp model Indian, which has met with so great a success over here, is not sold at all in the United States. For the coming season 1,000 Indian two-strokes were laid down, but, owing to the demand being much greater than had been previously anticipated, provision had been made for the building of an additional 2,000. It is interesting to note that all Indian two-strokes, for both over here and in America, will be fitted with AMAC carburetors. Altogether the Hendee Co. hopes to turn out 30,000 motor cycles this year, provided the necessary material can be delivered.

One of the materials in which there is certainly a great shortage is aluminium, but, fortunately, the Hendee Co. has a heavy stock to fall back upon. Mr Wells then went on to make the interesting statement that he thought that the pistons of the future would be made of die-stamped aluminium. Such pistons were already used successfully in the 12-cylinder Packard car. He also stated that carbon deposit does not adhere to the tops of these pistons to the same degree as an ordinary piston.

We interrogated Mr Wells concerning the condition of the roads in the United States. He assured us that the making of good roads was progressing by leaps and bounds, and the reason for this was that the necessity for well-kept highways had been forced upon the authorities by the massive increase in the use of motor vehicles, with the result that many miles of Tarmac highways are now being laid down. The grand Lincoln highway, which is to extend right across the continent, is rapidly approaching completion, and when this is finished it will indeed be worth travelling over.

One has to wonder whether Billy Wells' bleak analysis of the prospects for a middleweight motor cycle in America was coloured to any degree by the fact that the Indian range for 1916 comprised a heavyweight and a lightweight model, but no middleweight. Later, once the Hendee Co. had commenced production of the Scout, you could be forgiven for thinking from Indian advertising that a middleweight was really the only type of motorcycle worth having!

The Featherweight appears to be an attempt to hark back to Indian's cuter, cuddlier roots when the camel-backed models were, quite literally, motor-bicycles. This impression is reinforced by the fact that sales of the Featherweight were handled not only by Indian's motorcycle dealer network but also by bicycle dealers. Indian's advertising nevertheless took care to stress that this is 'a lightweight *motorcycle*, not a motor-bicycle'.

Unfortunately the 'power' of the Featherweight was somewhat underwhelming for American tastes. Factory advertising tried to turn this into a virtue by describing it as possessing 'power and speed in modified form'. There were dealers whose relationship with their local newspaper must have been a cosy one, for they managed to pull off some news coverage to suggest that the Featherweight, despite being a featherweight, was still capable of handling the rough stuff. This is what *The Bakersfield Californian* of 8th April 1916 had to say about the Featherweight. Though presented as a genuine news report, the second sentence of this article repeats Indian advertising copy *verbatim*.

Indian Lightweight Makes Decided Hit
The Indian Featherweight model which has been on display at the Berges Motor Supply company's salesrooms has made a decided hit especially amongst the younger set of motorcycle enthusiasts who have caught the bug from their big brothers who ride regular models. The lightweight incorporates all the advantages which have made Power-plus model so popular but with power and speed in modified form and extremely simple mechanically. It makes an ideal machine for town use but if a cross country trip were required of it there is no doubt but what it would uphold the dignity and records of the other Indian models in that capacity. The Junior member was taken out to China grade this week with a good sized man astride and it behaved like a thoroughbred on the long grade.

There is even one report of competition success for the Featherweight, in *The Hutchinson News* of 9th August 1916. The incredulity shown by the 'big brothers who ride regular models' about this two-stroke tiddler bettering the likes of Ralph Hepburn is plainly apparent.

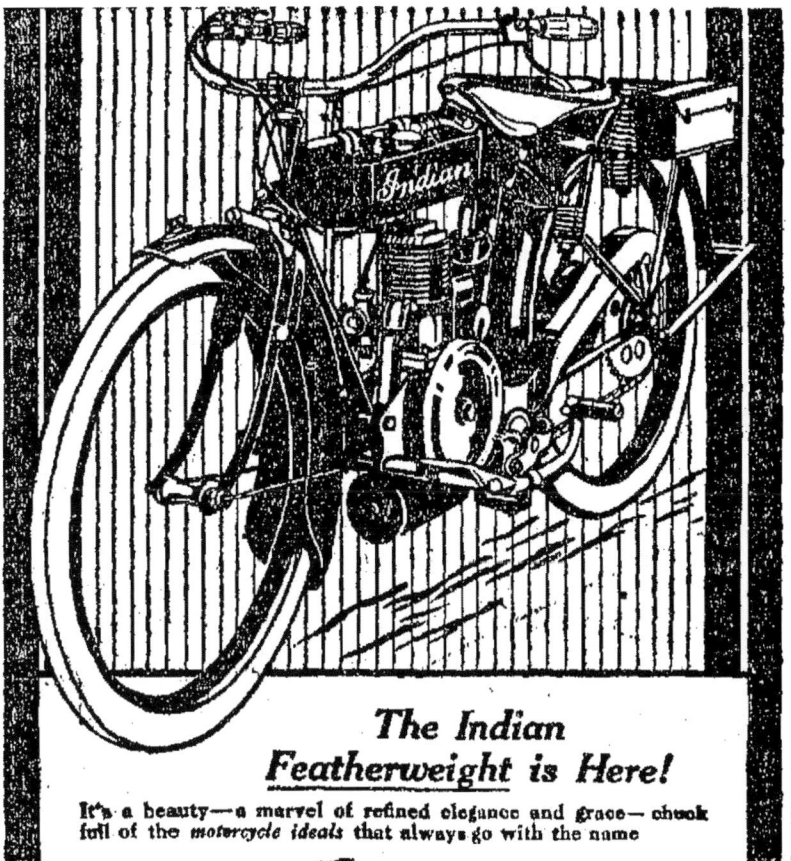

The Indian Featherweight offered 'power and speed in modified form' and 'mechanical simplicity'. But American customers prefer power that's been modified upwards, not downwards. (Indian Factory Archives)

The Indian Featherweight is Here!

It's a beauty—a marvel of refined elegance and grace—chock full of the *motorcycle ideals* that always go with the name

Indian

We don't want you to confuse the Featherweight with a *motorbicycle*, for the Featherweight is a real, true *motorcycle*—an *Indian* motorcycle—developed on *motorcycle* lines. We want to give you an actual demonstration of this perfected machine—want you to handle it—ask questions about it—*study it at close range!*

The Featherweight was made to meet the demand of you fellows who want *Indian* quality, but power and speed in modified form; who want mechanical simplicity; who want an easy-to-handle machine, comfort, convenience, lightness in weight, at a moderate price and low upkeep, linked with substantial design and building. That's the Featherweight—*Indian built* from start to finish! A world-winner whirlwind of *motorcycle* values!

GEORGE N. HOLDEN, 190-192 Massachusetts Ave.

HUB MOTORCYCLE CO., 258 Columbus Ave., Sub-Agents.   CROUT MOTOR CO., River St., Mattapan, Sub-Agents.

'RED' ALEXANDER WON THE SILVER TROPHY
Rider on a Featherweight Machine Won the Endurance Run.
'Red' Alexander won the Central Kansas Motorcycle club's endurance run trophy, a silver cup, in the two day's run which included an hour's stop in Hutchinson last Sunday. Alexander won the first prize at the finish of the run at Ellsworth. His home is in Dodge City, and he rode an Indian featherweight.

Ralph Hepburn, another Dodge City rider, on a twin cylinder Indian, took second prize. Both machines made perfect scores, but the Featherweight scored a half point higher than the Powerplus for consistent running, There were twenty-two entries and all makes of machines were entered. The course was from Ellsworth via Salina to Wichita and back to Ellsworth via Hutchinson, a distance of 300 miles. The roads were in poor condition and at the start Alexander's light car was not supposed to have a chance to win.

We have already speculated that Billy Wells and Charles Franklin must have both had considerable say in the inception of the Featherweight, although it was brought into production with Gustafson at the helm as chief design engineer. It begs the question of whether, upon arrival at the Wigwam, Franklin ever had any direct hands-on engineering role in its continued development to provide it with more sales appeal.

This question can be answered by looking at the timing of investment by Indian in advertising the Featherweight, because advertising and promotion of any model closely tracks the investment in its engineering and production. With these events having occurred almost a century ago now, engineering effort is difficult to discern but advertising effort remains very visible. We looked through period newspapers for indications of just when the Indian sales department started heavily promoting the Featherweight, and when they stopped.

We found that dealer-sponsored advertising for this two-stroke model of Indian occurred only in the Spring of 1916, starting from the media build-up to Indian Day on 22nd February. Indian Day was an annual event held every Washington's Birthday by Indian dealers to signal the start of the Spring selling season, and it was marked by open-house promotions, organized activities and souvenir give-aways. The occurrence of Featherweight advertisements peaked in April (at about the same time that Franklin himself was promoting the model in Ireland by riding it in the Rudge Cup Reliability Trial) and ended in mid-June. Over the summer of 1916 there is a handful of news reports that mention various deeds of derring-do done by people mounted on a Featherweight (see the two examples above), but these soon dwindle away, and for 1917 - nothing. This indicates that by the end of 1916, which is when Franklin arrived in Springfield, the Indian factory already regarded the Featherweight as a lost cause.

Sure enough, Indian Day newspaper announcements for 22nd February 1917 speak only of a new baby Indian, the Light Twin. Charles Franklin had far too much on his plate getting that bike ready for production, given that he'd only just arrived at the Wigwam in late November. If he'd done any tinkering with the Featherweight at all, it could only have been during the summer of 1916 and from the depths of 10 Wicklow Street in Dublin. By year's end of 1916, it's pretty clear that the Featherweight had been well and truly dropped.

The 10th January 1917 issue of *Irish Cyclist and Motor Cyclist* contained this item:

FRANKLIN'S GREETINGS
Accompanying a Christmas card to wish 'Irish Cyclist and Motor Cyclist' the compliments of the season was a letter in which 'CB' says: 'I am just beginning now to be able to find my way about the Hendee factory, but even still I come across new departments now and then. I will write more fully later on when

I get better acquainted with the factory, as no doubt some of the readers of the good old *Irish Cyclist and Motor Cyclist* would like to know how Indians are built.'

Another item in the same issue discussed arrangements to continue serving Indian customers in Dublin now that Ireland's 'Mr Indian' had emigrated:

Mr. S.J. Redmond, who was in charge of the repair department of the Irish depot of the Hendee Manufacturing Co., has now opened his own Indian repair business at the rear of No. 40 Dawson Street, Dublin. He had taken over the bulk of the spare parts of the Irish depot when it closed down.

The name 'Steve Redmond' starts appearing among racing results reported in *Irish Cyclist and Motor Cyclist* in 1916, when he himself was only 16 years old. When racing resumed in Ireland in the post-war period after a 2-year lapse, Redmond quickly established himself as Ireland's leading Indian exponent. From 1919 into the early twenties he and his 500cc Indian single, which he race-tuned himself, dominated competition at Portmarnock and at other venues like the Magilligan Strand Co. Derry where he won the 50 Miles Championship of Ireland two-years running. This moved *Irish Cyclist and Motor Cyclist* to comment that 'if Redmond continues in his present form he will be the only man to touch Franklin'.

Redmond, a Roman Catholic, saw active service in the Irish Republican Army (IRA) during the War of Independence, and in the Civil War for which he took an anti-Treaty stand. He was jailed at least once, in November and December of 1922, and while in jail he survived a 40-day hunger strike. His skills with motors, and in the very fast driving thereof, came in handy for various 'projects' the IRA was engaged in during this period. When the Leinster Motor Club was set up in May 1921, the reason for its establishment was that founder Nathan Lepler had been declined membership of the largely Protestant Dublin & District MCC on account of his being Jewish. So Lepler started a club of his own which allowed everybody. Redmond attended the first meeting of the Leinster club and was elected one of its first committee members. In later life he became concessionaire for Silvertown Oils, was very well known in the motor trade, and ultimately moved into the construction business. He died in 1973.

Steve Redmond, Dublin Indian Depot workshop foreman (here photographed circa 1940), took over the 'Ireland's Mr Indian' title after Franklin emigrated to America. (Photo courtesy the Redmond family)

In connection with his competition career on Indians, Redmond was described as 'an experienced engineer and an expert on secret tuning'. Clearly there'd been thorough mentoring by Franklin, the master of Indians in Ireland, during Redmond's year-and-a-bit stint in the workshop at the Dublin Indian Depot at Wicklow Street. Presumably the two men avoided discussing politics. Since Redmond was still a youngster at the time and Franklin was Depot Manager, it is likely the relationship was mainly one in which Franklin spoke while Redmond listened.

In the period immediately following his arrival at Indian in Springfield, Franklin's main activity almost entirely concerned the new lightweight model with which Indian had decided to replace the recently dropped Featherweight. Once that was in production, he'd next have found time for further development of the Powerplus. In this he worked closely with Gustafson Snr, whose design it was.

Franklin had much to contribute to Powerplus development in the areas of breathing and flow-metrics, being a seasoned engine builder and tuner as a result of past campaigns in Irish racing and in the crucible of Brooklands competition. A side-valve engine format held no surprises to him, since in those days it was far more common and accepted in Britain and Europe than in the USA. Gustafson was no slouch as an engine-tuner either. His earlier service at side-valve oriented Reading-Standard in 1907 had been both preceded and followed by several years as a 'sorcerer's apprentice' working at the elbow of the great Medicine Man, Hedstrom himself.

Although the design department's wings had become somewhat clipped by sourpuss accountants on the Board after Hendee's departure, there was in 1916 still some scope to indulge in the fun and glamour of racing. Treasurer and General Manager Frank Weschler believed in racing. Though not himself a motorcyclist, he was nevertheless staunch in pointing out to the Indian Board the importance of racing for advertising promotion, and as a spur for product development.

As a result of this support Gustafson was authorized to build two further batches of eight-valve race bikes, one batch in 1915 and then a second in 1916. In contrast to the first 'big-base' eight-valve engines developed by Hedstrom and Gustafson during 1910-11, these later batches both used smaller flywheels in standard production crankcases so have been dubbed 'small-base eight-valve' motors. The 1915 batch, like the 1911 eight-valves, were very limited-edition and their use was restricted either to Indian's own factory race team or to a select few favoured Indian dealers. For example, Rhodes Motors in Melbourne, Australia, was allocated two of the 1915 bikes and it was one of these (see colour photo 6) that Jack Booth used to set a record in South Australia of 102 mph in 1916. This record was never ratified internationally, but it was bragged about in Indian advertising in the US.

From the 1916 batch, some machines were offered for sale to the public at the steep, but not astronomical, price of $350 each. That there were indeed two separate batches is evidenced by a change in cylinder head design. On the 1915 small-base bikes the rear cylinder exhaust-port exits on the left-hand side, whereas on the 1916 bikes it exits on the right-hand side.[31]

In some published accounts, the re-design of Hedstrom's big-base engine into the small-base version has been attributed to Charles Franklin. There appears to be a lack of specific information to

Charles Gustafson Jnr at Springfield Stadium seated astride a small-base eight-valve Indian (EMIA)

Franklin on a Powerplus in America. (RHC)

guide Indian authors on this point one way or the other. With the first-hand witnesses all now long deceased, the best hope to settle the issue nowadays lies in making an educated guess.

Our best guess is that it was Gustafson who was responsible for the small-base eight-valve. Firstly, because Gustafson had already worked closely with Hedstrom to develop the original big-base motor, so he was no dummy when it came to deciding how best to take the concept further. And secondly, because Franklin was still in Ireland at the time. He didn't arrive in the USA until November 1916, by which time both batches of small-base machines had already appeared. There's only one way he could have played any role in design of the small-base motor, and that is by letter, postcard or telegram from Dublin.

What Franklin certainly did do, once he'd arrived in Springfield to take up his new post of Design Engineer at the Wigwam, was collaborate with Gustafson in the further tuning and development of these engines. He already had an easy familiarity with the Indian eight-valve racers, so would have slotted right in to this development programme and felt perfectly at home. He'd tuned, raced, set world records with, and even been set on fire by, the 'big-base' bikes of which at least two, out of probably no more than a dozen ever built, had been allocated to Billy Wells of the London Depot for use at Brooklands.

But the new Powerplus engine soon showed that it also had room for dramatic power improvement, if appropriate attention were given to cam timing, porting, and combustion chamber shape. Gustafson and Franklin found themselves embarked upon two parallel lines of development, exploring both the overhead-valve and side-valve engine formats for their speed possibilities. The results of this were to be surprising, and it had ramifications for the US motorcycle industry that would last for decades to come.

Much of this work had to wait, however. Within a short time of Franklin's arrival, the USA entered World War One and racing development at Indian was suspended for the duration of the war.

According to conversations held with Indian staffers later in life, Franklin soon formed a close working relationship with Tommy Butler in the sales department. Butler had an engineering background, so was able to immediately grasp the inner workings of any new development as well as judge whether or not it would translate into sales. Personality-wise, he complemented Franklin's quietly spoken, reserved and gentlemanly demeanour with a brash, up beat character and knack for promotion. Theirs was an alliance in which he took on the front-man role of doing the talking, attending the meetings, and writing the letters and memos, as required for new technical developments to gain the support of Indian's non-enthusiast corporate management. This freed up Franklin to focus upon the generation of ideas and designs, aloof and sheltered from the managerial level street-fighting.

Apart from Butler, Franklin did not form much in the way of close personal relationships with any other Indian staff. He was nevertheless generally well-liked, and highly regarded for his abilities. Of course he had one other valuable ally within the Indian organization, and that was his old friend and mentor Billy Wells. Press reports and trans-Atlantic passenger manifests show that Wells was a very frequent visitor to the Wigwam, and he was entitled to a seat at all meetings of the Board of Directors. Both Wells and Butler could be relied upon to go out and bat for Franklin at the senior management level, if the controlling business types needed to be convinced of the need for a new course of action.

The relationship between Franklin and Gustafson Snr was less straight forward. Bear in mind that Hendee brought Franklin into the design office as a response to perceived deficiencies in Gustafson's range of skills. A journeyman and self-made 'hard-knocks' graduate of no mean ability, he allegedly left some gaps that needed to be plugged in the technical design and layout aspects of the design office's role. Franklin was the first designer to work at Indian who had formal tertiary qualifications. Franklin's good manners and soft-spoken ways would have helped to avoid actual confrontation, however it's to be expected that long-time Indian staffer Gustafson may have felt a little defensive about Franklin being treated like a prodigal son of Hendee and Wells.

Franklin may not have formed close friendships with other Indian staff besides Butler, however he was certainly sociable. Doubtless he would have missed the English gentlemen's club atmosphere of the Dublin & District Motor Cycle Club. At the Indian factory there was an 'Outing Club', formed by senior management figures as a kind of corporate team building exercise. Established in May 1914, the Club charter allowed for 50 members and set up the following committees: Field Day, Fishing Day, Hunting Day, and Semi-Annual Dinner. The Initiation fee was somewhat steep at $40, however this gave the new member forty $1.00 shares in the Club House which was a lakeside cottage on the scenic Congamond Lakes south-west of Springfield. There was to be no gambling or profanity, and it was Men Only, except for Ladies or Open days, from Sunday to Wednesday.

The main activity appearing in club minutes is the Fishing Contest. Membership was divided into two teams, the Blues and the Reds. They fished from 1 pm to 11 pm and then counted up the numbers of fish. The losing team bought dinner for the winners. Charles Franklin was voted a member on 12th July 1917. Given that his wife and daughter had not yet joined him in the USA, it would presumably have been no problem at all for him to stay out fishing with the lads until well past 11 pm at night. Other club members included Frank Weschler, Gustafson Snr, and Theron Loose. George Hendee after his retirement was invited to some events. One can be certain that a great time was had by all.

Though Franklin lived at an address located an easy stroll away from his workplace at the Wigwam, it was clear he'd need personal transport to travel further afield to scenic places such as the Congamond Lakes. It is known that, not too long after arriving in Springfield, he acquired an automobile. It was *not* a Model T Ford! No, it was a Maxwell.

Produced by a company founded in 1903 which ultimately morphed into Chrysler[32], in its day the 'good Maxwell' car had a definite sporting reputation. In choosing one as his personal automobile, Franklin may well have taken into account the fact that, in 1916, a Maxwell touring car had set a new USA coast-to-coast record of 10 days and 16 hours. Another Maxwell attempted to outpace one of Pennsylvania Railroad's top locomotives over the forty miles from Washington to Baltimore, and lost this contest by only four minutes. The marque even became the subject of a popular song entitled 'Mack's Swell Car was a Maxwell'. Model prices ranged from $900 to $1400, at a time when a Model T Ford cost around $300. The Maxwell was not an automobile that one acquired for mere transport. Charles Franklin was like a kid with a new toy. Tommy Butler recalled that Franklin quickly became 'addicted' to cars, once he was in the USA and able to indulge in this new passion. In America, automobiles were so much more affordable than in Britain.

From *Irish Cyclist and Motor Cyclist*, 14th February 1917:

> C.B. Franklin now holds an important position in the Hendee Manufacturing Co. factory in Springfield. He wrote a letter to 'Irish Cyclist and Motor Cyclist'. The letter was dated 7th January 1917:
>
> 'I have not been getting the Irish Cyclist and Motor Cyclist regularly, and found they were being taken in the office here. It is one of the most popular papers that are received, and the copies circulate around the whole factory, and there is keen competition to get hold of it. You see it is quite different from all the other motor cycle papers, and its chatty articles, humorous paragraphs, etc., are greatly appreciated. The local papers have a great tendency to boost some particular machine that they happen to be interested in, and so few of the public buy them. I believe if a paper was started over here that would be quite unbiased it would have a ready sale. I know I read my Irish Cyclist and Motor Cyclist from cover to cover, and one needs to be away from home to fully appreciate all the advantages of living in 'dear, dirty Dublin'.
>
> 'I find it hard,' adds Franklin, 'to get the people here to believe I am Irish. One gentleman that Wells introduced me to told him afterwards that he could not believe I was Irish, and that Wells was just pulling his leg. When asked to explain why he thought I wasn't Irish, he said 'Why, he speaks quite good English.' I wonder what kind of savages some of them think the Irish people are?'

Here Franklin provides us with a contemporary opinion about the standards of journalism in the US specialist motorcycling press of those days. With our benefit of hindsight, it can be seen that these magazines were not particularly free, frank or fearless in their reporting. They would blatantly promote the views of the main manufacturers, and rarely spoke ill of their products. It appears that Franklin was on to this in a flash. Franklin's own employers, however, were one of the guilty parties in this state of affairs.

We also have direct evidence here that Franklin's manners and speech (what the English would term 'breeding') were somewhat different from the perceived national average in his native Ireland. We know nothing of Franklin's politics or personal views, however it's clearly apparent that he came from a privileged social background. Protestant, public-school educated, and descended from English plantation families, it's reasonable to assume that Franklin was of a class not wholly unsatisfied with the *status quo* in Ireland prior to the 1916 Easter Rising. Americans unaware of these complexities in Ireland's social and political make-up were clearly bewildered that he did not match the 'Irish navvy' stereotype apparently projected by others among his compatriots on coming to the New World in search of a better life.

Powerplus and Light Twin

With the Powerplus engine established as the core product in Indian's business of selling motorcycles, Gustafson and Franklin's main responsibilities to the company were two fold.

Firstly, any newly introduced motorcycle needs refinements to iron out any bugs, and annual improvements to make civilian customers feel that next year's model is an advance upon the previous year's. The Powerplus was destined to be Indian's mainstay as heavyweight of the model range from 1916 up until 1923.

Secondly, they were to come up with another lightweight design with more pep than the Model K Featherweight, but still user-friendly enough to attract newcomers into the world of two-wheeled transportation.

Detail improvements to the civilian Powerplus focused upon making it more stylish, yet cheaper to produce. It cannot be determined after all this time whose idea was whose, but it can be supposed that Gustafson and Franklin worked together and jointly made these changes. Among other things, in 1917 the between the rails gas tank was changed for a more rounded one that shrouded the top frame tube, updating the look of the bike. This change anticipated the later saddle-tank era of the late 1920s in execution, but not in concept since the bike's frame and overall appearance was still firmly in the 'vintage long-tank' era. Made of large-section steel stampings rather than small hand-formed and soldered pieces, this new tank didn't cost as much to make. Aluminium pistons were tried out for the first time. The following year the intricate handlebar controls system of solid rods and bell-cranks, a trademark Indian feature since twist-grips first debuted on their 1905 models, was done away with. It was replaced by the lower cost and longer wearing flexible cable system, which used a piano wire cable inner that could both push and pull. Harley-Davidson had adopted this system in 1914.

The Powerplus is a fine motorcycle and at the time it was deservedly popular with big-bike buyers. But US motorcycle manufacturers could see they had to broaden the appeal of motorcycles, and needed more options than the now traditional heavyweight V-twins, if they were to claw back anything at all from the wholesale shift to automobiles as America's preferred means of transportation. This change in thinking can be seen in period motorcycle advertisements. Rather than run ads boasting of technical or race achievements to simply help sell 'motorcycles', companies like Indian started using lifestyle type advertising themes that they hoped would be able to sell 'motorcycling'.

Although Charles Gustafson Snr was Indian's chief designer at the time, no one has ever disputed that the design and execution of Indian's next attempt at a 'Motorcycle for Everyman' was almost totally a Franklin effort. It represents Franklin's first ever ground-up design exercise. The main evidence for this is that, like the Featherweight, the new 'Model O' (or 'Light Twin', as it was called in factory advertising) is just so terribly English.

Franklin was very quick off the mark in designing the Light Twin and bringing it to production. He arrived at the Wigwam in November 1916. By Indian Day of 22nd February 1917 the Light Twin was being announced as an actuality, with examples on display at dealerships throughout the land.[33]

This is an incredibly short time for a factory to design and build a new model of motorcycle. So short, that Franklin must surely have walked down the gangplank at Port of New York with the blueprints already in his suitcase. Maybe he even hand-carried a complete set of machined castings over with him from Dublin, from which to assemble a prototype! Even then, getting a new design off the drafting table and on to the factory floor is a task that usually takes a year or more. Just how he achieved this feat is a mystery. It's little wonder Franklin did not find time to join the Indian factory's Outing Club until July 1917! Another explanation is that he'd been in close communication with Gustafson from Dublin, to kickstart the Light Twin development process from the instant his appointment at the Wigwam had been announced.

Its engine is of the Douglas type, an in-line flat twin which 'Duggie' exponents had been using to good effect in British competition. Douglas machines became top contenders in Isle of Man TT races immediately pre- and post-war, served with distinction in the war itself, later were successful in speedway, and were not considered too weird looking to sell moderately well as street-bikes in Britain and Europe. Scaled down to 15 cu in (250cc) for the Indian incarnation (see colour photo 9), the result was tame, inoffensive, and it did the job it was designed for fairly well.

As any small-engine textbook will tell you, the flat twin layout then being used by Douglas in-line, ABC across-the-frame, and very soon German newcomer BMW (also across-the-frame) has, as its main advantage, perfect primary balance of its crankshaft assembly. The main source of engine vibration, which can get severe on traditional big singles and V-twins, is limited to a mild rocking-couple caused by the two con-rod big-ends sitting side-by-side on the crank. Combined with its modest displacement, this engine was going to be smoooooth. Flat-twins also give the lowest possible centre of gravity, making parking space manoeuvres easy to manage for even the klutziest of newbies to motorcycling.

They are so rare these days that it's hard to locate one and find out what they really do run like, however a Light Twin was rallied regularly in the South Island of New Zealand for many years. According to a report published in *Indian Motorcycles Illustrated*, the machine when seen in the metal appears light and delicate, yet its engineering exudes quality and on long runs this Model O has proved tough and reliable. The full-loop double down-tube frame was particularly innovative for its time. It cruises comfortably at about 35 mph and, though it has to be dropped down a gear to make headway into the teeth of a stiff Canterbury Plains nor'easter, it would always get its rider home.

The Light Twin is thus remarkable mainly for its remorselessly logical flat-twin layout, since frame, transmission and running gear borrowed heavily from the defunct Model K. With functional attributes sufficient to have made it the Honda CB200 of its day, it could be said to have been designed by Franklin's head but not by his heart. For a design brief that called for a pussycat and not a tiger, the Light Twin fitted the bill perfectly.

There-in lay the problem. The sweetly competent little Light Twin failed to stir the blood of two-wheeled enthusiasts. It can be seen from newspaper classified advertisement columns in 1917 and 1918, when these bikes were still brand-new, that scarcely used Light Twins were being quit by their owners at heavy discounts. Four examples are shown here, in which the strict economy of words typical of classified ads cannot conceal the sellers' disappointment in their Light Twins or disguise their eagerness to be rid of them.

> THE INDIAN LIGHT TWIN
> A Motorcycle for Everybody
>
> THE INDIAN and WAVERLY BICYCLES
> Can be Bought on Easy Terms.
>
> We can furnish anything you want in Tires,
> Horns, Lamps, Etc.
>
> Bicycles **TULLOCH** Insurance
> Motorcycles   Real Estate
> 117 W. Central Ave.

What kind of customer was the Indian Light Twin aimed at? Everybody. Who bought it? Nobody. (Indian Archives)

FOR SALE Motorcycle, Indian light twin, nearly new. Fully equipped. With equipment cost $270, Sale price $175. Call Main 4543.

FOR SALE My Indian light twin opposed motor, bought last month, cost $230; best offer takes it; home Sunday from 2-6 o'clock. 81 Anderson St., West End.

$125 INDIAN light twin; cost $210 a short time ago. F M DURKEE, 20 Aberdeen St., tel. Back Bay 178.

INDIAN, light twin; perfect condition; price right. North 8801.

Nor did the Light Twin catch the eye of very many of the new type of customer Indian's management was going after, of whom it was hoped that they might pick one of these instead of using the money as a deposit for a Model T Ford on a time payment plan. The factory didn't make huge efforts to promote it, because they were by now switching over to a war production footing. Indian's traditional customers, and even their dealers, thought of it as a lady's bike and ultimately this was the kiss of death for any chances the Light Twin might have had with those prospective customers who already did like motorcycles.

Which goes to show that creating a successful motorcycle is a bit like making a rock'n'roll hit record. It's really hard to know by formulaic means what exactly it is that people will go for. To this day, both fields of marketing endeavour remain more of an art than a science. Released for 1917 the Model O, cruelly dubbed the 'Model Nothing', struggled on with very slow sales until 1919 and then disappeared from the catalogue.

The main lesson for Franklin? That the US market was not the same as the British one. What works back home may not necessarily work over here. More than technical competence is required if one is to come up with a sales 'hit'.

Meanwhile, the USA entered World War One in a combatant role in April 1917. Uncle Sam was going to need military motorcycles. Indian anticipated these events during 1916 by developing a military-spec Powerplus from the civilian version released in late 1915 as a 1916 model, and by gearing up to produce it in quantity to fill military contracts for supply to the US forces. In 1917, once the Light Twin had been introduced, further major work on civilian road models or race engines was suspended in order to concentrate on the military Powerplus.

Indian's directors, now a consortium of investors and financiers not well versed in the pastime of motorcycling, immediately saw great potential in selling motorcycles to Uncle Sam. Indian's marketing department was instructed to pursue military contracts with all possible vigour. It appealed to those calling the shots at Indian that a 'one customer' policy would greatly increase the profit margin on every machine sold. Only a single model had to be produced rather than a whole range, thus providing greater production efficiencies. Heavy advertising and promotion (for example, by running a race team) to win sales would no longer be necessary. The sheer number of motorcycles projected to be required by a US Army newly convinced of their utility, was the answer to the prayers of those who were concerned about the post-1914 flattening-out of motorcycle sales in America.

With war looming, things looked good for Indian. Or so the company's directors thought. What could possibly go wrong? All Indian had to do now was produce the requisite number of motorcycles.

This proved to be more of a problem than anticipated. The move to a war economy placed inflationary pressures on costs like raw materials. Indian's staff responsible for sales projections and materials acquisition were apparently unaccustomed to the new economic ground rules, and found it hard to forecast an accurate cost per unit as a basis for negotiations with government about selling price. These and other problems in gearing up for the first military contract for 20,000 motorcycles led to Indian's President Weschler asking founder Oscar Hedstrom to come out of retirement to sort things out. This he duly did, for an unspecified period that was first announced in *Motor Cycle Illustrated* in their 6th July 1916 edition:

> OSCAR HEDSTROM AGAIN WITH HENDEE CO.: Motor Wizard, Who Retired From Springfield Concern About Three Years Ago, Is Back Now In His Previous Capacity; Indianites Are Elated.

The precise dates of Hedstrom's return to the Wigwam for active duty are not known. An official company letter bearing his signature, and concerning delivery of a race machine to a factory-sponsored rider, is reprinted in Wright's *American Racer 1900-1940* and is dated 19th September 1916. A report in the *Springfield Union* states that Hedstrom was made a member of the Board of Directors of Hendee Mfg. Co. in October 1916. For such an appointment to be made now, given that he'd severed his official ties with the factory in 1913, is an indication that he was important to them at this time and that his role within the company was intended to be an on-going one.

Although the timing can't be proven, it raises the tantalizing prospect that Indian's three all time greatest motorcycle designers Hedstrom, Gustafson Snr and Franklin, whose Indian models collectively spanned 1901 right through to the final cessation of production in 1953, were all working at the Wigwam at the same time.

What can certainly be proved is that during 1917 all three men had accommodation only a few blocks from the Indian factory, and from each other. The 1917 City Directory places Hedstrom as renting a room in the big home of Mary E. Neylon at 8 Buckingham Street, just a hop, step and jump away from the Indian factory. Franklin is two blocks closer to town at Thompson Street, and Gustafson is about five blocks away from Hedstrom in the other direction, at Montrose Street. For the years 1914 - 1916 Hedstrom is listed as renting apartment No. 17A at 820 State Street, which overlooked Winchester Park and the Indian factory's front entrance.

Common legend has it that Hedstrom retired to the Big House in Portland CN in 1913 and stayed there, content to potter around the house, invent gadgets and build motor-boats. He must have been spending a large number of his post-retirement week days in Springfield however, if he needed to retain a small place of his own in which to spend the night. To have maintained lodgings in Springfield so close to the Wigwam and for so long a period, Hedstrom cannot have been as disinterested in what was going on at Indian as has previously been thought. Did he have occasional need in the middle of the night to borrow the use of a dynamometer, perhaps?

Given that Hedstrom probably commuted back to Portland each weekend for family time but was effectively a bachelor on week nights, and that Franklin was similarly a 'bachelor', one has to wonder if there were any occasions when all three engineers might have unwound from a long day at the office by slipping across to the Oak or Highland Hotel for a pilsener or seven before wending their way homeward. Under this scenario we have seated in conversation at the bar the inventor of the Indian eight-valve race motor, together with his design assistant in that particular exercise, and the man upon whom responsibility would soon fall to again make the Milwaukee 'Wrecking Crew' eat its dust. What would you give to be a fly on the wall during that kind of discussion?

The task that all three men were currently drawing salaries for, however, was that of getting Powerplus models out to the US military in quantity. In this they were helped by the fact that the Powerplus did not need drastic changes to make it suitable for the glutinous mud of the Western Front. It had already proved its worth in the glutinous mud of the American mid-West during the coast-to-coast record attempts by Erwin 'Cannonball' Baker. Main changes were a lowering of gear ratios and fitment of flat section trailer-type mudguards, along with the other detail changes adopted for the civilian models.

Of course the military was going to need help with training in the operation and maintenance of its motorcycles. This was an era when horse-drawn transport still predominated, and the majority of army recruits could not be assumed to have any driving or mechanical skills. It is within this context that the name of Charles Franklin next crops up in his fan-zine, *Irish Cyclist & Motor Cyclist*, in their issue of 31st October 1917:

FRANKLIN'S NEW JOB
C.B. Franklin is going to France to assist the military authorities in repairing Indian motorcycles in use on the Western Front. He has been busy organising the tools and spare parts to equip the workshops in France.

'I have often been greatly cheered up,' writes Franklin, 'by receiving the Irish Cyclist and Motor Cyclist. I know most of the places shown in the paper in each issue, and it almost seems I am back again amongst my own friends, and happy recollections keep coming into my mind as I look at them.'

This is certainly a sign of Indian's heavy commitment to the US war effort, that it be proposed for so senior a staff member be sent abroad to oversee the servicing of the many Indian machines now in military use. It didn't happen that way however, as the next cutting about Franklin from *Irish Cyclist and Motor Cyclist,* on 30th January, 1918, shows:

> AN HONOUR FOR C.B. FRANKLIN
> A couple of months ago we announced that C.B. Franklin had been appointed to a position on the staff of the American Army in France, and that his duties would be the supervision of the motor cycles in use by that force. Apparently the arrangement has been varied, as our latest mails from America advise us that Franklin has been nominated by the United States Government as one of the engineers on the Standards Board appointed to design and get out a standard army type of motor cycle. Franklin's appointment is a great tribute - not only to himself, but to this country. He is universally recognised as one of the cleverest experts in connection with the tuning of machines for racing and reliability competitions and his uniform success in Irish competitions will be remembered by those familiar with racing at Portmarnock and elsewhere. In combination with an Indian motor bicycle, he held most of the British long-distance records, and it was only just before the outbreak of war that he tuned up one of the eight-valve Indian racers to such a pitch that he felt sure it was capable of doing over 100 miles an hour for the kilometre or mile. On the closing of the Dublin depot of the Hendee Manufacturing Company fourteen months ago, Franklin went to the headquarters of the company at Springfield, Massachusetts, and since that time has been in the engineering department and has had every opportunity of studying American methods of production.

So he didn't get his trip to Europe after all. Instead this task was given to Tommy Butler, who was assigned to the US Army as a special advisor to set up and run a service organization for the upkeep of all the military's motorcycles, not just the Indian ones.

Neither did the 'standard army type' of motorcycle ever eventuate. This was to be dubbed the 'USA', powered by a 'Liberty' motor that was supposed to be an amalgam of all the best features of the Big Three's products. If Franklin ever attended any meetings of the 'Standards Board' in connection with the 'USA' then he must have suffered from very bad laryngitis at the time. This is because available photos show that the 'USA' ended up being pretty much a modified Harley-Davidson ioe engine in an Excelsior frame, with scarcely any Indian influence whatsoever. The cost-saving, better-wearing and longer-lasting side-valve set-up of the Powerplus, already the predominant model in use by the American military, was the natural choice for such a motorcycle but it was overlooked. By way of eerie coincidence, the head of the Society of Automotive Engineers Committee on Standardized Military Motorcycles was a gentleman named William S. Harley. As it turned out, WWI ended before the mooted design exercise could make much progress, and the project was shelved.

What is prophetic here is Franklin's pre-war remark that his eight-valve Indian racer was capable of reaching and holding a speed of 100 miles per hour. The very motorcycle of which they wrote certainly did go over 100 mph but not until seven years after Franklin last rode it, and not with Franklin in its saddle.

In the US domestic market once peacetime returned, Indian's main price-point equivalent competitors in the heavyweight division were the ioe Harley J-Model, and trailing in third place the big ioe twin made by Excelsior. Between them, these three accounted for 90% of US motorcycle production. Others like Reading-Standard and Cleveland were still around, but struggling to make ends meet.

In the smaller classes, just as Indian took their Model O flat-twin off the market, Harley-Davidson in 1919 released a flat-twin of their own. Quite why they followed Indian's lemon with a similar model was never recorded in the minutes of the regular H-D board meetings of those times, but perhaps H-D thought the Model O was right in concept, only wrong in execution. The Harley Sport was much bigger at 35 cu in (600cc) compared with the O's 15 cu in (250cc), so was a middleweight rather than a lightweight. It was innovative in introducing America to unit construction of crankcase and gearbox, a 'wet' clutch (running in oil) and a gear rather than chain driven primary drive. It was better timed in that it was released during the post-war economic recovery period. Unlike Indian's flat-twin, the Sport had enough power to live up to its name, and it got the backing of Harley dealers who promoted it well. Initially, it sold okay, despite its un-American looks and sound. Unfortunately for the longer term prospects of H-D's middleweight, in 1919 Charles Franklin was already at work on designing the Indian Scout.

Historians mainly agree that 1915 was the year by which the main design elements that constituted Harley's J-Model finally coalesced from its various pre-cursors, becoming from this time forth an F-head V-twin of about 61 cu in (1,000cc), with three-speed transmission, electrical lighting, and improved oiling. From then onwards, until they finally pulled the plug on the J-Model in 1929, H-D's approach was one of steady improvement, enlargement (74 cu in or 1200cc by 1923) and refinement to keep the basic design platform competitive. Even in those days, Milwaukee was into evolution, not revolution.

Ironically 1915 was the year when Indian took a completely different tack and killed off its founding F-head concept altogether. It can be fairly convincingly demonstrated that the Powerplus was better and more modern than the J-Model, as well as more economical to manufacture. Its side-valve layout protected the valve gear under covers where lubrication could be by internal oil mist, and this both kept the outside of the engine cleaner and reduced valve-gear wear from road dirt. Performance of standard versions of the two was on a par, but the Powerplus won out in reliability and longevity. In racing, Franklin would soon have great fun tuning the sv Powerplus to the stage where it ran stronger and for longer than Harley's J, or indeed either Harley's or Indian's futuristic overhead eight-valve racers. To rub in the point about the technical sophistication of the Powerplus, Indian offered it with the Hedstrom twin's swing-arm rear suspension, having already dabbled with electric start on the previous, but short-lived, Hendee Special.

Did the Milwaukee Motor Company care about the Powerplus's 'pluses', or take any notice? Nope. Because unfortunately for Indian die-hards, having a better product does not guarantee commercial success. The advent of the Powerplus in mid-WWI was also the time that Indian's new management turned its back on its US dealers and customers in order to sell this model almost entirely to the military. This story is told by the wartime sales statistics, in which the 70,000 or so motorcycles purchased by the government from 1916 to 1919 comprised almost 50,000 from Indian, about 20,000 from Harley-Davidson, and a few from Excelsior. Hendee and Hedstrom would never have stood for it, but Indian's new controlling financiers didn't care less about the company's US dealer network. For three years they had no product to sell, and consequently they starved. H-D also manufactured about 50,000 motorcycles during this period, but 30,000 of these were sold to the civilian market. Harley's US dealerships were sustained and even increased in number, right as Indian's were dropping like flies. This increase in H-D sales from 1914 to 1919 justified their investment in a factory expansion which, upon completion in 1920, became in floor-area terms the new Biggest Motorcycle Factory in the World.

The whole problem with wars, from the point of view of industrialists selling to governments, is that sooner or later they end. Indian had made good money from its war department contracts, but now what? When peace returned, late-model Harleys were conspicuously more numerous than Indians on the roads of America. H-D's dealer network was intact, loyal, and well-placed to cash in on returning dough-boys eager to spend their discharge money. Many of Indian's dealers had gone to the wall, or had switched loyalty to H-D. More H-D dealers, with a larger and more prosperous look about them, meant more fellow customers and more dealer-supported H-D riding clubs, adding up to more like-minded fellows for a new bike owner to go out with and have a weekend of fun.

This was the period when H-D, Number Two of the Big Three (Indian, Harley Davidson and Excelsior), caught up with and overtook Indian to become Number One in the US market. From now on, Indians needed to be significantly better motorcycles than Harleys if they were to have any chance of attracting customers away from the showrooms of the Harley dealerships. For H-D to win customers, on the other hand, their motorcycles did not now have to be any better than an Indian. They only had to be *as good* as an Indian, and the balance would be tipped by the additional customer support advantages stemming from Harley ownership in the US having reached critical mass. Indian would never fully recover from this situation.

Billy Wells was finding the Powerplus a steady seller in immediate post-war Britain. Exuding an air of quality and dashing good looks in its scarlet and gold livery, it was an expensive but sound option for the discerning enthusiast, either as a long-distance solo mount or tugging a sidecar as a capable but cheaper alternative to the British small car. Its indestructible clutch which, unlike British machines, had been designed to be slipped under load to offer low speed fine control additional to that of the throttle, was particularly praised by those who'd had a chance to sample it. The British industry at that time did not have any home-grown V-twins of similar quality, ruggedness or reputation as the Powerplus. The situation was summed up in John Harrison's otherwise jingoistic 1928 *The Boys Book of the Motorcycle* (Oxford University Press) when he wrote of Well's establishment in the UK as concessionaire for Indian:

> It marked the commencement of the American invasion which at its zenith so influenced the British motorcyclist that it was next to impossible to sell a big British machine to a discriminating buyer.

Expecting further expansion of sales in Britain and feeling that more spacious premises were going to be called for, by 1915 Wells had moved the London Indian depot from Great Portland Street to another location around the corner at 366-368 Euston Road.

This same building later became the used-car department of motorcycle dealers Godfreys, whose main new-motorcycle showroom was in Great Portland Street a stone's throw from the premises Wells was moving out from. His son George Hendee Wells, born and raised in one of the apartments upstairs in Portland Court, has this to say about the new Euston Road address for the London depot of the Hendee Mfg. Co. Ltd:

> Go north along Great Portland Street and you run into Euston Road at the Metropolitan Railway Station. This railway ran for some distance in the open and just under the surface. Euston Road had a variety of shops. First of all there was *Bonds*. They sold all sorts of model railway bits and pieces together with the tools and materials to make practically anything. Metal and brass in many shapes and sizes, and screws and nuts and spring wire to make your own.
>
> Another very good shop was *Buck and Ryans*. They held a very good stock of all kinds of tools. There was a post office, and the area was generally well served. One of the most important establishments in the Indian story was *Euston Ignition* owned by Fred Kirby. They not only stocked all the electrical things

for the new owners of motorcycles and cars but were able to diagnose troubles. Only once do I recall, as a boy, seeing the inside of their works. I already knew a bit about magnetos and often wondered how they got the magnetism into the big magnet and I was just in time to see them 'servicing' a magneto. There was a huge electro-magnet and the magnet was pulled across it.

It was a good area for the Indian Motorcycle Company to open up its business and there it was about halfway along with a big shop window and the name blazoned on it - THE HENDEE MANUFACTURING COMPANY.

I can remember the premises quite well. I think it was quite an impressive establishment. There was a showroom at the front and between the motorcycles was a model of the Springfield Factory which had lights inside the windows of this rather box like building. It was very intriguing to this young boy. There was a leather settee - bright red for Indian - and it was covered in little scratch tears. I was told the firm's cat had done it. I never see our cats about to sharpen their claws without recalling that disaster.

At the back of the showroom was an open plan office area reached through a low barrier of the kind I have only seen in American films. The rear of the office led through to the 'works' and this was the first place I had ever been in where they 'did mechanical things'. To me it was vast but was probably quite a small machine shop for servicing and repairs. There was a big electric motor at one end and this drove an overhead shaft which ran the length of the works and fed the various drills and lathes via belts. I suppose this was a hangover from the earlier machine shops where you had one steam engine to supply all the power. I asked my father why the belts did not come off the unflanged pulleys and he explained how they were 'domed' and the belts went to the highest point. I never quite understood why but certainly found the information very useful in later life when dealing with machines for processing photographic paper. The most exciting machine was the grindstone with its stream of white hot sparks and you could put your hand in the sparks and not get burnt!

On the upper floors were the stores and servicing areas and these were reached by a lift. Of course I wanted to know how it worked and was told that it was 'hydraulic', which meant it somehow operated on water pressure. I believe at that time the mains pressure could be used for this purpose. Certainly, to me it was magic that all you had to do was turn a tap like on the bath and up we slowly went. In later life as an industrial photographer I have always been interested in manufacturing processes, and have been suitably impressed with the way men have shifted enormous weights and moulded tons of steel, but that early experience in the Indian works was an exciting introduction.

As a boy my memory of the Indian establishment was that it was very big and important, and if you started up a motorcycle inside it was very loud.

US Motorcycle Competition Up To 1919

Upon arrival in the US, Franklin first sang for his supper by working on the Light Twin, by helping Gustafson refine the Powerplus model both as a civilian street-bike and as a military machine, and by providing logistical support for the many Powerplus machines already supplied to the US Army. At heart he was a racer and a speed freak, however; so he must have been itching to continue his involvement in motorcycle competition. What kind of a racing scene did he find in the USA from the end of 1916 onwards?

Historically-important motorcycling competition in America has been of six main types. In approximate chronological order of first appearance or dominance, these are; inter-city reliability runs, board-track racing, trans-continental record setting, dirt-track (flat-track) racing, hill-climbing, and asphalt road or closed-circuit racing.

In the beginning, motorcycle competition in America followed a parallel line of development with Britain and Europe. But very soon US competition went its own way, owing to the very different riding conditions and consequently the different type of machines that were evolved to cope with them. American motorcycles needed to be larger, heavier and more powerful. The extra power was not necessarily there to make them go any faster than European machines, but rather so they could haul bigger loads, penetrate deeper muck, and work harder for longer without breaking down.

At first, as in Europe and Britain, reliability was the goal of US competition and speed was an unexpected bonus. The first major contests were thus an equivalent of Reliability Trials, which in the US have come to be termed 'enduros'. There were large and well publicized city-to-city events during the early 'noughts', in which Indian as industry leader was the dominant force. One example was a New York - Springfield - New York event in 1903.

As the battle for reliability was won and speed became the thing, proper 'races' came to be held on country horse tracks as ready made, albeit rough, venues. The glamour speed events that gained prominence from 1908 onwards, however, were on tracks built from wooden boards. Such tracks had been around for bicycle racing for quite some time, and these featured the very earliest motorcycles as pacing machines even before motorcycles ever competed against each other. Cycle board tracks were short, were not steeply banked, and mostly built so narrow that only two motorcycles could safely compete at a time.

The opening in L.A. of the first board track designed especially for motorcycles (by impresario Jack Prince) started a fad that soon took the country by storm. Featuring very high speeds, thrill, spills, and very real danger, these came to be known as 'Murder-dromes'. This appellation followed in the wake of some high-profile catastrophes, like the notorious incident in New Jersey in 1912 when Eddie Hasha and others (including some spectators) lost their lives. Despite losing some of its lustre in

Charles Gustafson Snr and Jnr at Springfield Stadium, posing with a Hedstrom ioe single-cylinder board-track racer. (EMIMA)

this way, board track racing continued to be an important form of competition through to the 1930s, when Depression-era economics finally killed it off. The emphasis then shifted to the lower-cost, more accessible 'run-what-you-brung' Class C racing on cheaper-to-build-and-maintain dirt tracks.

As motorcycles got still tougher and the national road networks improved, distance events came into vogue. These were record setting attempts for crossing the continental US from coast-to-coast, or the Three Flags run from Canada to Mexico. The golden years for such events were from around 1915 through to the mid-twenties, when law enforcement agencies started to clamp down on high speed use of public thoroughfares.

Another major form of competition was hill-climbing. Initially these were timed events from a 'start' to a 'finish' on proper roads, as in Europe. But in the US hill-climbing soon evolved into off-road events held on hills so steep that 'topping' them, that is, reaching the finish line, was usually impossible - the winner was the person who managed to get closest to the finish before falling off. Hill-climb competition became important enough to earn worthwhile prestige for the manufacturers of winning machines from around 1920 onwards.

Following the Depression years, flat-track racing on oval dirt tracks became the main form of American racing, a situation which persists until this day. Road racing in the European sense, either on real public roads or on closed circuits of tarmac, was never a significant form of racing in the US until well after WWII. The closest such pre-war event was the Daytona 200-mile race, inaugurated in 1937 and run on a surface that was hard sand beach for half of each lap, and a tar-sealed public road for the other half. Earlier 'road' race events, such as at Marion IN. in 1919 and 1920, were held on rural dirt roads.

The first significant period of US racing on board tracks was in the main a two-horse contest between Indian and the Chicago based marque Excelsior, although up to a dozen marques would

A dirt track venue of the type typical in US racing in this period. Charles Gustafson Snr is 4th from the left. (EMIMA)

put up entries. Indian's first 'big-base' eight-valve V-twin race motors of 1911 arose from a need to maintain Indian supremacy in the face of serious challenge to the ioe Hedstrom motor racers from the 'big-valve' ioe race machines being fielded by Excelsior. Their star rider, Joe Wolters, became fairly unstoppable during this year. Insult was added in 1912 when one of these Excelsior racers, in the capable hands of Lee Humiston at Playa Del Rey board track, beat Indian to the punch by becoming the first officially timed motorcycle in the USA to cover a one mile distance at over 100 miles per hour.

In 1911 Indian 'owned' all 121 of the FAM speed record categories, but by 1912 the majority were taken over by Humiston, Wolters and de Rosier (now also riding for Excelsior). The Chicago machines were bettering Indian's best in many race events, too. Excelsior's racing fortunes reached their high point during the 1915 season, but faded thereafter.

During the very early years at H-D, Walter Davidson had taken part in mid-west motorcycle competition just for the heck of it. When it came to corporate sponsorship of a racing équipe, however, the Harley Davidson Motor Company professed to be uninterested. Their advertising instead extolled the strength and reliability of their grey-hued machines, occasionally making reference to some privateer's competition success with a slogan like 'Not bad for a company that doesn't race!'

This all changed in 1914. Beginning by giving support to tuned ioe (or 'pocket-valve') dealer entries, the founders started showing up at major meets in person to check on their progress. In a rare show of delegation of some of his engineering responsibilities, William Harley hired Bill Ottaway, then in charge of racing at Thor, and set him the task of injecting more speed and reliability into the H-D V-twin production engine. Next, an official 'works' team appeared for the first time ever at one of the final events of the year, the Savannah 300-mile race. Although they came third after Indian and Excelsior, it was clear that H-D were not kidding around. The level of staffing and resources put into this effort showed they were serious about winning, and that money was no object. Their professionalism and determination had paid off hugely by the middle of 1915 when, at the Dodge City 300 (run on an oval dirt track), H-D ioe racers came 1st, 2nd, 4th, 5th and 6th. These results caused a sensation, and placed the Motor Company (H-D) well and truly 'on the map' of US racing.

Why the sudden and dramatic reversal of H-D's 'We don't race' policy? Throughout its century-plus history, the Motor Company has consistently never done anything not calculated to have a clear benefit for their financial bottom line. This is how they got to have a century plus history in the first place. Back in 1914 when the overall leveling-off of motorcycle sales against the continued meteoric rise of the American automobile was becoming apparent, the four founders decided their long-term survival depended upon increasing their market share. To do this, they needed a share of the attention that rival marques were getting for their products by bragging about achievements in racing. Avoiding the very high speed board track events for the time being, the staying power of HD's ioe big twin, backed by a highly-organized pit crew, produced good results in dirt-track and road race events run over longer distances (50 - 300 miles). In the space of only two race seasons H-D went from wallflower to belle of the ball, showing themselves capable of winning America's most prestigious racing events. The gratifying result was some pick-up in sales of their road bikes.

In 1916 H-D further demonstrated their seriousness of intent by designing an ohv eight-valve racer of their own. Indian could sneer that they'd thought of it first, way back in 1910. Annoyingly for Indian, H-D's tardiness was perfect timing to adopt new combustion-chamber innovations emerging from military aero engine development undertaken for the Great War. Indian's eight-valvers, which had been having a tough fight on fairly equal terms with the Excelsior and H-D ioe pocket-valve racers despite their theoretical advantages, followed a pre-war ohv practice of placing all their valves vertically in the cylinder head (that is, the inlet and exhaust valves ran parallel to each other), leading to a less efficient flat-roofed combustion chamber shape and a spark plug placed off to one side.

Harley splayed the valves at 45 degrees from the vertical (that is, sloping toward each other with an included angle of 90 degrees) in a pent-roofed combustion chamber, with higher compression provided by a domed piston. This, a more modern arrangement than Indian's, reduces heat loss and makes possible higher compression and superior flow-metrics. Though in fairness to Indian, it is argued by race bike collector Daniel Statnekov that Hedstrom's choice of four valves per cylinder was mainly driven by the fact that four smaller valves have better heat dissipation properties than two big ones. The woeful metallurgy in those days meant that warping and scaling of valves in the heat of combustion under racing conditions was a major source of breakdowns. The main driver for adoption of four-valve heads in 1911, according to Statnekov, was better reliability and stamina. That they also gave better breathing, particularly at lower valve lifts while opening and closing by virtue of their greater total circumference, was a bonus.

Thus by 1916 Indian had seen their main rival Excelsior's fortunes fade, only to be replaced by a pattern whereby Indian's riders had the speed and daring to win in short events but H-D's pocket-valve machines had the stamina to take out the prestigious longer races. It was high time that Indian's race department gained an injection of fresh ideas and enthusiasm. The advent of the side-valve Powerplus and the 1915 make over of the eight-valve Indian (Gustafson initiatives both) provided promising lines of enquiry from which Indian could be poised to reclaim their top spot.

Unfortunately for Franklin, his arrival at Springfield was followed within months by USA's entry into the First World War. By mutual agreement the Big Three of Indian, Harley-Davidson and Excelsior did not provide any official 'works' support to national racing for the 1917 and 1918 seasons, as a patriotic gesture in support of the war effort. Certain key dealers continued to fly the flag for their preferred marque however, by sponsoring local riders in races and record attempts.

Indian now threw all its effort into production of motorcycles to fulfill its military contracts. As far as can be determined, there was little or no work done during this period to develop the Powerplus or eight-valve motors for racing. That had to wait until peacetime returned.

Harley-Davidson, on the other hand, supplied some motorcycles to the military but predominantly they made civilian models for domestic sales, and they continued with development of the eight-valve race motor. H-D race-shop manager and engineer William Ottaway, soon to be Charles Franklin's opposite number and nemesis in a post-war clash of the titans, used this time to design and build a two-cam version of the eight-valve. H-D built a batch of pocket-valve racers with this new timing-gear configuration as well.

Meanwhile, Franklin had to wait until the resumption of top-level competition in the 1919 season to really get out amongst it and test his mettle as a tuner of bikes for the board- and dirt-tracks of the prevailing US racing scene.

But then, from 1919 onward, the US motorcycle industry nearly died.

In 1919 this Indian advertisement claimed Jack Booth's 1916 speed record, set in Australia on a Rhodes Motors small-base eight-valve, as the fastest speed ever on a motorcycle up until this time. If so, then Booth, on an Indian, was the first British subject to officially exceed 100mph on a motorcycle, six years before this feat was accomplished in Britain by Doug Davidson on a Harley-Davidson. (EMIMA)

Indian Scout

The Marvel Of Motorcycle Engineering

That the American-made motorcycle was in trouble is evident with the benefit of 20:20 hindsight, just by looking at the sales figures of the Big Three. Production was now way down on the numbers rolling out of their doors in the golden decade up to 1914. In 1913 Indian alone had sold 32,000 motorcycles, with Harley-Davidson still a fledgling brand at 13,000. In 1922, all US makers put together produced only 25,000 motorcycles in total. Globally, 1921-1923 was a recession that led to a slump in motorcycle sales generally. Even the British industry, now confirmed as the world's leader, was affected. However their 'slump' was a fall from around 100,000 in 1920 to 60,000 units per year, and by 1924 they'd bounced back to 120,000 of which 50,000 were export sales. The US industry slumped, but never bounced back.

Also chilling was the extinction rate among American motorcycle marques, which had dwindled from almost a hundred to a couple of dozen, and now there was barely room even for only three major producers to remain in business. This represents a 97 per cent mortality rate within barely two decades.

According to most historians, this parlous state of affairs for the US motorcycle makers came about because of the mass production techniques adopted by the US auto industry. With any motorcycle sales growth after 1914 being measured in terms of 2 or 3 % per year, the carmakers at times could show 65% growth. Detroit's new methods and growing markets provided such economies of scale that automobiles became genuinely affordable to the average man in the street. This left the motorcycle factories without much of their market.

That the seriousness of the situation was very apparent to industry leaders at the time is proven by the fact that, for the first time ever, the Big Three got together into a secret huddle and agreed to cooperate in a marketing study whose aim was to increase the size of the whole motorcycle market. Previously, their concern had been only to increase their own market share. Sales representatives of the Big Three, plus Reading Standard, met clandestinely in NYC and entrusted their confidential sales figures and projections to the hands of an independent consultant named Norman Shidle. After due consideration and analysis, the consultant returned a report (ultimately published in 1921) saying the problem was that motorcycles had gotten too heavy and powerful for most people, and only attracted a small market segment of athletic young hell-raisers. Promoting motorcycle products via racing provided good entertainment, but it fostered an image of danger that discouraged actual participation in the sport of motorcycling. What was needed were small, lightweight, smooth running, easy-starting motorcycles that would appeal to the wider population, he wrote.

How motorcycling's captains of industry reacted to this, having just gambled and lost on such cuddly concepts as the Featherweight, Light Twin and Harley Sport, has not been recorded. Maybe it couldn't bear repeating in polite company!

At this juncture it's worth exploring just who in the Western world was buying motorcycles. In the beginning when motorcycling was an adventure, they were playthings of rich and athletic young dilettantes who relished a challenge. When motorcycles first became practical, and for so long as cars remained expensive, there then ensued a boom in the motorcycle industry. But the 'masses' that took to getting themselves about on two wheels were not motorcyclists. They were people who could not yet afford cars. When they could afford cars, motorcycling was abandoned.

If you want to see a booming motorcycle industry nowadays in the new millennium, you need to go look in Asia. There you will find a lot of people who cannot yet afford cars. Cities like Bangkok or Hanoi are teeming torrents of light motorcycles and scooters. Enfield India in Chennai has consistently sold 20,000 - 30,000 Enfield Bullets every year from 1958 to the present day, compared with only 10,000 'Made in England' Bullets ever sold *in total* during this model's entire fourteen-year (1949 - 1963) production run at the parent Royal Enfield factory in Redditch, UK. The difference in approach to motorcycling compared with the modern-day West is illustrated by this passage from Gordon May's book *Made in India - the Royal Enfield Bullet* (RG Publishing):

> The 350cc Bullets are far more popular in India than the 500cc models. This is because in India the bikes are mostly used as commuter transport rather than as a leisure or hobby item - the usual reason overseas buyers opt for a Bullet. The 350cc engine is more fuel-efficient than the thirstier 500 and it is difficult to get the most out of the larger engine's performance due to the country's slow road and traffic conditions.

This was equally so in Britain from the 1920s to the early 1960s. During this era the catalogues of every major British manufacturer listed a 350cc single along with a companion 500cc model - both used the same frame and running gear components and looked almost identical. Of the two, the smaller engine capacity consistently outsold the larger model by about four to one.

The rise and fall of motorcycling by the masses in Britain was a process that took fifty years. It's commonly stated that it was the advent of the new Morris Mini car in the late 1950s that sounded the death-knell for many British motorcycle firms. But people who were there at the time in fact recall that the abandonment by sensible family men of the once ubiquitous motorcycle and sidecar combination was due more to increasing post-war prosperity, combined with a big drop in the price of older second-hand cars.

A similar historical process occurred in the USA, but it was here compressed into barely twenty years. The US motorcycle industry's rise was meteoric in that very first decade, and subsequently proved to be a flash-in-the-pan. Post-WWII it took imported bikes, firstly Triumph and then Honda, to revitalise the US motorcycle market. The market malaise that Soichiro Honda sought to snap the USA out of is illustrated by global motorcycle registration statistics for 1961 - a year that falls just prior to Honda's hot inroads in the US, yet comes at the start of Britain's decline. In 1961 motorcycles in the USA (pop. 183,691,481) numbered only 565,400, or 3 per 1,000 people. In Britain (pop. 52,700,000) there were 1,360,000 registered motorcycles, or 29 per 1,000 people.

Back in 1920 nobody in their wildest dreams could ever have predicted even a future British invasion of the US motorcycle market, let alone a Japanese one. What was becoming clear is that motorcycling in the US for the foreseeable future was going to be the preserve of that small bunch of diehards whose love of motorcycling stems from reasons of sport and hell-raising, not from everyday requirements for practical transport. Indian would struggle to sell 7,000 machines per year from then on until their demise, and would require only 5% of their huge factory's capacity to do it. But making, selling and riding even so few Indians was a whole lot of fun for all those concerned. Looking back, one can be sure they wouldn't have missed it for anything. We have to be glad they stuck it out.

L.J.K. Setright sums up this remaining market well, in describing the kind of fellow who might have bought brand new the horrendously expensive Brough Superior. This was a rorty heavyweight V-twin whose engine was designed by Val Page and Bert Le Vack in 1922 as Britain's answer to the American 'V's and, according to L.J.K., was a machine

> 'catering for the requirements of a special class of motorcyclist, one that had been slow to grow, would never reach large proportions, and would slowly die away.'

Of this type of motorcyclist, Setright goes on to say:

> The motorcyclists of the real pioneer days had been largely men in the trade, augmented as time went on by a sprinkling of sons from what were by the standards of the time reasonably well-to-do families. After the war the upper and middle classes preferred to see their sons in motorcars, and since the sons themselves could not fail to see the advantages of a four-wheeler as a means of conveying the gentler sex, the preference was one to which they readily acceded. In consequence motorcycling was growing to be a proletarian activity. Nevertheless there remained a sizeable number of gentlemen, young and not so young, who regarded poodle-faking[34] and the weather protection of the motor car with scorn. Believing that 'he travels fastest who travels alone', they managed to satisfy themselves - if nobody else - of their sturdy masculinity by bestriding a good lusty motorcycle. However, their standards were high: they demanded good performance, good looks, lasting reliability and a high standard of finish. There were not many machines that could satisfy them.

On the US side of the Atlantic, the top-priced models of Indian, Harley-Davidson and Excelsior certainly had massive appeal to just such a gentleman. But not, apparently, the Indian Featherweight, Light Twin, or the Harley Sport; yet these did not get many takers among the American proletariat either.

Sportsman/hell-raiser? Or cash-strapped commuter? It was Honda in the 1960s that finally broke down the constraints imposed upon manufacturers by these two traditional motorcycle markets, and made the sky the limit in the US by creating a third, new leisure market in which motorcycling epitomised wholesome recreation and genuine middle-class family fun.

If the Big Three American motorcycle manufacturers of 1919 were collectively feeling nervous, then Indian itself was in a position of double jeopardy. Not only had the size of the overall market shrunk. It was now clear that Indian had just lost their pre-eminent road-bike sales and racing results position, which it had owned as if of right since 1901, to that provincial blue-collar gang-of-four Mr Harley and the Davidson brothers. Thanks to the medium-term folly of the 'One customer: Uncle Sam' business strategy which saw the Indian dealer network wither on the vine, and thanks to the money and resources now being poured into the H-D racing effort, Indian was having to adjust itself to the idea of being Number Two.

Franklin himself must have been feeling pretty nervous by this time. Consider his position at the Indian factory in early 1919. Since being brought in at the end of 1916 as some kind of *wunderkind* to get Indian's product line jazzed up with new and hot-selling designs, what had he actually done? He'd been closely associated with the launch of not one, but two new Indian models, both of which had bombed. If this continued, he would surely be finding himself back on a boat to Ireland before long. A case of 'third strike and you're out!' It is significant that Franklin had not yet brought across his wife Nancye and daughter Phyllis to the US as yet. It was as if he still regarded himself as 'on probation' and not yet firmly enough established at the Wigwam to make any permanent plans.

For Franklin, it was more than just a case of needing to be third-time-lucky. He would have to make absolutely certain that the next design effort to emerge from his draughting board would save the Indian factory, and save himself in the process.

Looking back at the immediate post-war period in America from an early 1970's vantage point, L.J.K. Setright wrote:

> 'Only Indian and Harley Davidson remained as substantial protagonists of a two-wheeled way of life that even they had to modify somewhat if the last adherents were not to be seduced by the tempting four-wheelers'.

This statement well sums up the challenge facing Franklin at this point in his career.

How to modify the US two-wheeled way of life, to retain its last adherents? How to create a new model that would appeal to those put off by the he-man antics required to own and operate a big, long, loud and vibratory heavyweight V-twin? But how at the same time to retain the macho element, that certain *je ne sais quoi*, which heavyweight V-twins have in spades but functional yet soporific devices like the Model O clearly lack? How to make a smaller machine of wider appeal, yet still '100 per cent American'?

The answer, when it came, in hindsight must have seemed blindingly obvious: a smaller V-twin. A model that could bask in the glow of larger siblings; a new and more manageable package. Though not so 'new' or different that it challenged potential customers with unfamiliar concepts. Cute, cobby, non-threatening. Handsome-is as handsome-does; yet still capable of a terrier-like growl when asked the question.

Indian had tried smaller V-twins before, and had sold a moderate amount of them. These were the 'Little Twin' or Model B, a scaled-down version of the Hedstrom ioe 1000cc twins. It wasn't a flop, but neither did it cause a sensation. It had just as many intricate and rapidly-wearing parts and called for just as much mechanical and riding skill as the bigger twins, but without the performance. Margins for its maker must have been slender. The Little Twin had not survived for more than a couple of seasons.

But unlike the Little Twin, Franklin was going to start with a fresh sheet of paper. No 'parts-bin special' this. No transitional hybrid of a new motor in an old frame, like the Powerplus. No design straight jacket imposed by existing-model concepts. Franklin was going to dig back into ideas he'd been nurturing since at least 1912, and rake over all those late-night conversations with Billy Wells and other British and Irish Indian colleagues and clientele for nuggets of inspiration. He had an enthusiastic ally to bounce ideas off, in the form of Thomas Callaghan Butler.

This would be a bold departure. Franklin was going to gamble his future, and that of the Indian factory, on this new motorcycle design. This much we are able to surmise, just by placing ourselves in Franklin's situation at the start of 1919. But in detailing the genesis of what was to become the Indian Scout, we do have a problem.

As far as we've been able to discover, there are no 'Franklin Papers' to explain how this next design of his came about. No design notes, no diaries, no sketch books of roughed-out design elements. No factory correspondence detailing exchanges between designer and management, giving justifications to the accountants for doing things this way and not some other way. No interviews with the motorcycling press to whet customers' appetites with sneak peeks of snazzy new engineering features. We know more about how Leonardo da Vinci invented the helicopter.

The job of a Harley historian is much easier. Over at Harley-Davidson the minutes of monthly Board meetings got meticulously archived, and to this day they are still there to be consulted. If you really want to know what was going through the four founders' minds when they opted to drop the J Model and go ahead with the VL, or decided against buying the Cleveland motorcycle company in order to acquire a four-cylinder model, then it's still possible to go on over to Juneau Avenue and ask very nicely. Any records like this at Indian got tossed out and scattered to the four winds during the reign of controlling financiers who only looked forward to making more money from Indian, and didn't give two hoots about looking back at the company's heritage. Only when E. Paul Du Pont took over Indian was care again taken to preserve its records by a man with a genuine concern for the company and its people.

Can you imagine someone like Edward Turner, designer of the early Ariel Square Four, and of the Triumph vertical twins that took America by storm in the 1950s and 60s, remaining so tight-lipped about what he'd created and why? Sure, Turner was ego-driven and loved to talk about his favourite subject - his own design achievements. But even that taciturn elder-statesman of British motorcycle design Val Page was willing to regularly go on public record about his highly-successful JAP, Ariel, BSA and Triumph single cylinder models, and his rendering almost practical of Turner's Square-Four engine concept.

Billy Wells did 'let the cat out of the bag' quite early to the press in Britain that a new model was being developed by Franklin. He doesn't give away any of its details, however this report in *Irish Cyclist and Motor Cyclist* dated 26th March 1919 does at least help us to establish by when the design work for this project had been completed:

> Mr W.H. Wells, the manager of the Hendee Manufacturing Co. in London, has just returned to England having spent eight weeks at the factory in Springfield, USA. He stated that Irishman C.B. Franklin was now head engineer of the company. Franklin had designed a new model which would be available later in the year.

So Wells is going around telling people that Franklin is head engineer at Indian, eh? One wonders if Gustafson Snr ever read this news report and, if he did, how he felt about it. March 1919 is about one or two years too early to be declaring that Franklin is already head engineer. Although such remarks were presumably based upon popular perceptions of Franklin's contribution to engineering matters at Indian during this critical and extremely productive year, as compared with those of his nominal boss Charles Snr, it must surely have fuelled resentment.

Yet again we must bemoan the absence of any 'Franklin Papers' that shed light on the reasoning that went into the design of the ground-breaking Indian Scout model. It is such a shame we do not have any personal comments from the designer himself. We only have some telephone interview reminiscences of colleagues, of which the most valuable were those of Franklin buddy and side-kick Thomas Callaghan Butler.

We are left mainly with the hard evidence of the Indian Scout itself. Just by looking at one, we can infer what its designer must have been thinking, what options he considered and rejected, and what made him plump for the design elements finally incorporated. Our analysis of Franklin's latest design to date for Indian becomes motorcycling 'paleontology'[35]. Form follows function. Study the form of a dinosaur's jaw bone, and you can figure out what it pursued, how it must have moved, how it was best adapted to suit its ecological niche. Study the bones of a Scout, and we can soon figure out that its various adaptations arose to give it competitive advantages in its own particular market niche. Everything about it had a reason for being, and the reasons are not hard to guess. We can't help but marvel at the way it turned out.

Let's start with the engine. The engine is the heart of any motorcycle. It has to look right, as well as be right. In engineering, what looks right usually is right.

To the generality of Americans, the only right look is an in-line V-twin. This was as true in 1919 as it still is today. No flat-twin funny-business, thank you very much. No popping two-strokes. To sell a motorbike to large numbers of Americans, it will have to look American and sound American. Its engine has to fill the space in that frame just right, and at tick-over it has to go 'potato-potato-potato'.

Though not too big, please. This machine shall be of dimensions easy to manhandle and to throw a leg over. Anyone giving it the 'sit' test should find themselves nicely low and balanced, with their feet well planted on the ground. There should be little chance of this bike ever catching somebody off-balance and trapping their leg with a hot exhaust pipe. The fact it's a V-twin will certainly help here. This gets a lot of displacement into a low package, by employing two short splayed cylinders compared with one tall and upright one. A twin's shorter piston stroke, and two smaller pistons rather than one big one, would surely make kick-starting a whole lot easier. Easy starting will be an essential characteristic for this bike, if people are to feel affection for it rather than dread while getting themselves kitted-up ready for a ride.

A choice of side by side for the placement of the inlet and exhaust valves should not come as any surprise. The Powerplus had already demonstrated how ideal this valve layout was for a production motorcycle in this era. Fewer machining steps meant lower manufacturing cost. Enclosed valves means less clattery racket from the motor, and much longer periods spent running between valve clearance adjustments. Much cleaner too, now that lubrication of the valve gear is all-enclosed as well. The lack of any upstairs valves like on ioe or ohv engines contributes to keeping the cylinders short, and the bike overall quite low. Adoption of a side-valve layout was a sophisticated and industry leading choice for the Scout. By this time Franklin was becoming aware of this layout's promising speed tuning potential as well.

Let's give it two cam-shafts. Again, this is a nod toward speed tuning potential. The Powerplus (see colour photos 7 and 8) runs just fine on one cam-shaft as a standard model, however this dictates that longer and weightier cam-followers be used compared with a two-cam system. That extra weight reduces the rpm limit the motor can be spun up to, beyond which valve springs can't reverse the valve train's inertia quick enough to keep everything following the cam profile. This is a phenomenon known as 'valve float' (also known as 'valve bounce'). Two cams would not have been a design decision of great import for normal street use, however it's just one more instance where, faced with a choice of doing what everybody else does or doing 'right', Franklin opted to make this motorcycle as 'right' as possible.

The valves are comparatively large, a decision which in a side-valve motor trades off compression-ratio for better breathing. A smart choice considering that, on the 'knock'-prone fuels of that era, compression ratio could not be pushed up very high anyway. Better breathing combined with after market fitment of hot cams or cam followers spells more horse-power at higher revs, should anybody be interested.

In terms of capacity, this engine was going to be 37 cubic inches. An odd displacement, literally and figuratively. That's 600cc in metric but still odd, because there were few other machines of this displacement in the world and only one other made in the USA (the Harley Sport). Probably this size was chosen because it was small enough to keep the overall dimensions of the bike nice and compact, but still big enough to make some useable power to get through the rough stuff of America's so-called 'roads'.

So far, so fairly straightforward. This choice of engine layout is evolutionary, not revolutionary. For Indian to be the first ever go into production with a side-valve layout was Gustafson's innovation. Franklin's knack here was to recognize a good idea when he saw one, and adapt it to his purpose. The Scout engine is essentially a diminutive two-cam Powerplus, whose very appearance would echo Indian's range leader and provide a reassurance borne of familiarity to prospective customers. A chip off the old block. Coming up with a suitable engine for this prospective world-beater would have been the relatively easy part.

If the motor is evolutionary, then what here is revolutionary? To answer that, we need to look at the cycle parts. Here, we've been saving the best part of the Scout story until last.

Before we get bogged down on its detail design, it has to be said right up front that the Indian Scout is a *concept*. It was conceived holistically as a ground-up package, to provide an integrated whole. It represents an out-pouring of about seven years' contemplation and reflection upon the elements required to make a perfect motorcycle. These elements were not developed in isolation, or imposed by production constraints, or taken holus-bolus as parts left over from other Indian models or even bought in from other manufacturers (as was common-place for some motorcycle brands). Nor were they worked upon separately by members of a committee. The result encapsulated the ideas and vision of one man. The design elements of the Scout complement each other (see colour photo 12), and make the whole more than just the sum of its parts. It will become apparent just how fresh and untypical this approach to motorcycle design was in 1919 if we walk you through a detailed description, and draw comparisons with other contemporary machines.

Let's now look at the frame. After determining the engine's layout, a decision about the frame must have been the very next task on Franklin's 'to do' list. This is because there are other aspects of the Scout's design that only become possible once Franklin had settled in his mind's eye the issue of frame type.

Most bikes of the era had their frames bolted together around the engine as two-dimensional (that is, flat-plane) sections. Many relied on the engine as a 'stressed member' that held the whole bike together, linked to the frame parts by steel plates. Others used a single full loop that ran from steering head down under the engine and wrapped back up around it to the base of the seat. Formed from tubes that lie along the centre-line of the machine (apart from the rear-axle stays), this type of frame clearly betrays a bicycle ancestry. A transmission (a very recent innovation) would be hung in there someplace where the bicycle-pedals used to be, and drive chains (also adopted only recently by most makers) used to receive power from the engine and transmit it to the rear wheel. Over time things could loosen up, twist around under power, and bolt holes could wear into ovality. Tightening up frame bolts was a regular and necessary maintenance task. The Powerplus had just such a frame, as did practically every other motorcycle of the era.

The Scout's frame was different. It functioned as a stand-alone three-dimensional assembly with its own intrinsic strength, independent of any other components. This was achieved by making it a double-loop full cradle type, with not one but two tubes running down from the steering head, back along either side of the engine, and from there straight on back to the rear axle. Franklin had experimented with a twin-loop full cradle on the Model O, and was clearly satisfied that the extra metal was worth it. This type of frame is not bolted up, but permanently brazed together by cast lugs at all its joints. Its geometry is very stiff and resistant to twisting or bending forces. The engine could sit in it, but did not have to be a part of it. No worries about things getting all loose and squirrely-feeling.

The 1920 Indian Scout. Ground-breaking features include its integrated design, double-loop full cradle frame, unitized 'power-plant', helical-gear primary drive, and user-friendly middleweight size with peppy performance. (Indian Factory Collection)

But let's not call it an engine. Let's use the term Indian itself applied to the Scout in their advertising, and call it a *power-plant*. Because if an engine doesn't need to be a part of the frame, then the bike's designer has the freedom to make the transmission a part of the engine. The Scout power-plant is of what's termed 'semi-unit' construction. Its transmission follows tradition in being functionally separate from the engine, in the sense that it is still in a gear*box*. That is to say, the gears sit in their own compartment and are immersed in their own lubricant. Structurally however, this gearbox is joined onto the back of the engine rather than to the frame. This makes for a single strong, simple assembly with two big advantages.

Firstly, the number of attachment points for the engine and transmission to bolt into the frame can be reduced to the geometric minimum. A stool only needs three legs to give it 360-degree stability, and that's precisely what you find on a Scout motor. Two points at the front of the motor, and one point at the rear of the transmission. Simple. Neat. You can pull out the motor in a jiffy to get it up onto a bench for servicing, without having to take the bike all to pieces.

Left side of the 1920 Indian Scout (Indian Archives)

Secondly, such a strong and rigid relationship between engine and transmission keeps all shafts in alignment, and the distance between shaft centers remains constant. It affords a designer the luxury of choosing a primary drive system other than by chain.

Everybody was by now using chain primary drive in the post-WWI era. In the British industry of 1919 it was quite new-fangled to even have a primary drive at all however, because bikes over there had only just shed their direct-to-rear-wheel belt drives. Franklin himself had been at the forefront of that particular revolution, by helping demonstrate so clearly to 1911 TT race-goers the advantages of a two-stage all-chain drive train with free-engine clutch as seen on Indian models from 1909 onwards. In addition to being light in weight and low in internal friction, two runs of chain can tolerate a host of sins when it came to misalignment of sprockets in frames that would often twist under power or get out-of-shape from being pounded by road shocks.

The down-side of chain primaries is that nobody (except Sunbeam and P&M) did them very well in those days. Mostly they ran out in the open. This meant they wore quickly from picking

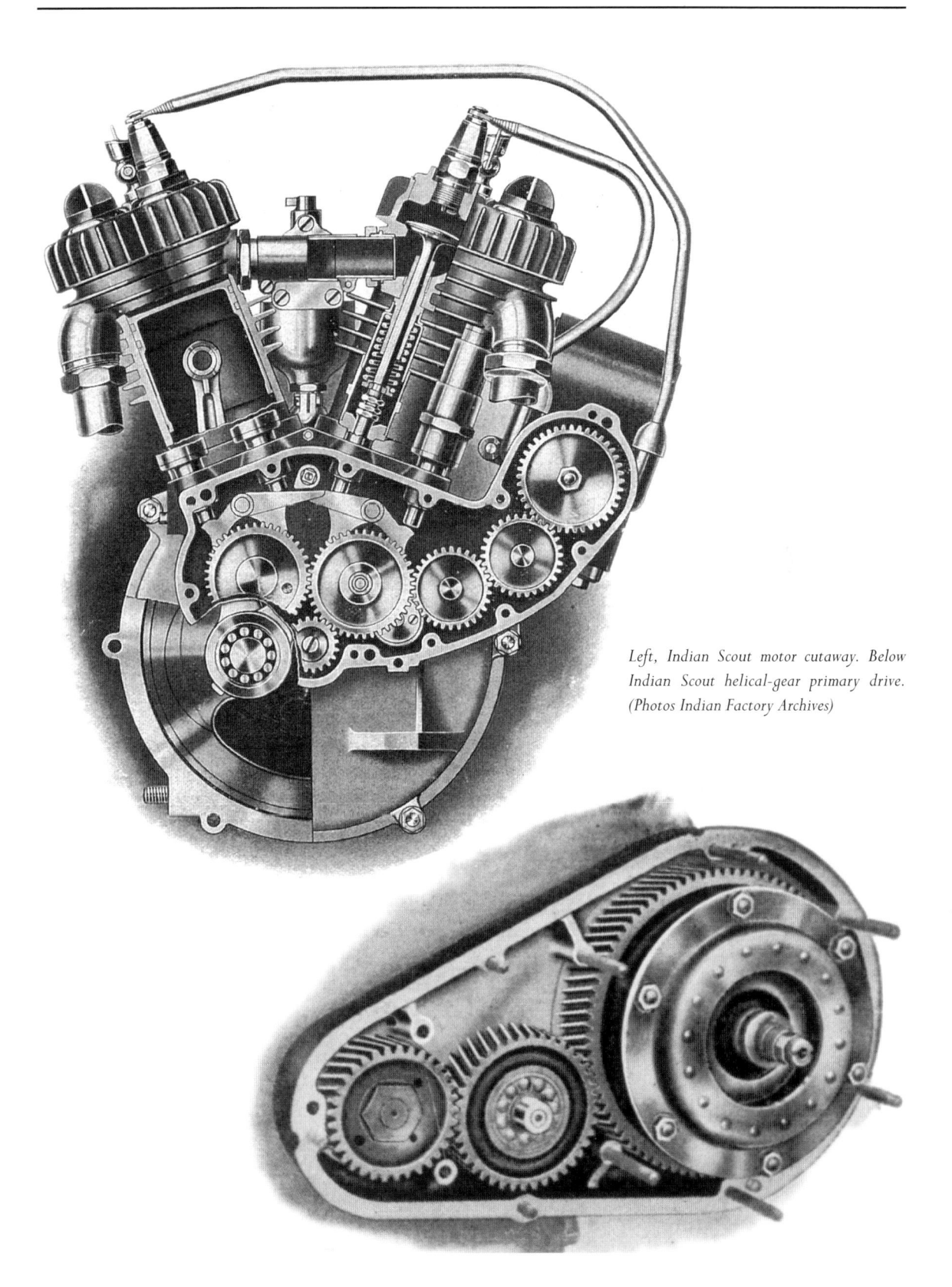

Left, Indian Scout motor cutaway. Below Indian Scout helical-gear primary drive. (Photos Indian Factory Archives)

up road dirt even if oiled regularly, and if oiled then this got thrown all over the operator's left trouser cuff. To keep this chain at its proper tension and thus stop it from flogging itself to death even more prematurely, it would be necessary to design bikes with the gearbox on a pivot. Loosening its mounting bolts and rocking the gearbox rearward would allow one to take up slack in the primary chain to compensate for wear. After tightening up the gearbox bolts again, you'd next have to go adjust the final drive chain. This is because sliding the gearbox further back will make one's rear chain go slack. The whole arrangement was not as strong or well-aligned as a gearbox rigidly and permanently bolted into place. But the latter method would leave the designer looking for some other way to keep the chain at its proper tension.

Clearly Charles Franklin had adjusted more primary chains than he cared to remember, because he made sure that, for the proud owner of an Indian Scout, such a rigmarole would be a distant memory. Having helped to make chain primary drive the industry standard, Franklin now put himself another jump ahead by eliminating the primary chain altogether! Just as H-D had done a year earlier with their flat-twin Sport, he settled upon helical-cut gears instead of chain as the means to transmit power from the engine to the clutch. The crankshaft drive gear and the clutch basket driven gear sat either side of a central idler gear, which ran backwards and so restored normal 'forward' rotation to the transmission main-shaft. This train of three gears sat in the ideal operating environment - an enclosed oil-bath alloy primary case.

This primary-drive arrangement of meshed gears was only made possible by the unique semi-unit engine construction, which keeps the distance between shaft centers constant. Semi-unit construction was in turn a consequence of the stand-alone frame design. A train of helical gears was going to be more expensive for Indian to build than a chain primary, but the bike's owner would never ever need to get his hands dirty over it. It was a maintenance free assembly capable of outlasting the rest of the bike. Again, Franklin opted to do 'right' rather than merely adopt the 'expedient'.

What about suspension? Indian had for some time now been using a leaf-spring trailing link front suspension. It worked mighty fine, having a castor action that contributed in no small measure to stable steering and sweet handling characteristics. Not as photogenic as the front suspension in use by other makers like H-D or Ace, it nevertheless had become a trademark Indian feature and an intrinsic part of the Indian 'look'. Again, Franklin recognized a good idea when he saw one, and saw the value of retaining some continuity of familiar 'Indian' features to provide a family resemblance across the model range. This same type of leaf-spring front suspension would continue to serve Indian well until the post-WWII era.

Why no rear suspension? The Hedstrom twins had been innovative in this regard, and the Powerplus had continued the trend. It's difficult to know precisely why Franklin chose to depart from what was now standard Indian practice, and instead designed the Scout as a rigid-framed bike. So we are forced to use conjecture. One relevant factor may be the persistent dissing of rear suspension by certain other manufacturers and dealers of motorcycles that did not possess this feature. Upsets high speed handling, they murmured. Causes frequent drive chain breakages, it was insisted. Unfair, but such notions can be infectious. A second factor could have been cost. Having splurged on items like a double-cradle frame and gear primary, maybe Franklin had to pare back production costs in some other area?

The third reason could be that, in the road environment and practical cruising speeds of those times, the Scout simply didn't need rear suspension. When the time is right for a design innovation, it's usual for it to be rapidly and universally adopted to become the new industry standard. This happened for drop-centre wheel rims in 1928 and for saddle-type over-the-rails gas tanks in 1929, but didn't finally happen for swing-arm rear suspension until 1954 (one year too late for Indian).

Notwithstanding Hendee's progressive thinking in 1913, the world would not be ready for electric start on a motorcycle until the arrival of the Japanese in the 1960s. Back in 1919 there were still too many hold-outs, so Indian was finding itself uncomfortably alone in continuing to root for swinging-arm rear suspension.

Those of us who ride our Indians nowadays (admittedly on much-improved roads) find that the Mesinger leather sprung saddle fitted as standard is very comfortable, so none of us really notice a lack of rear suspension. At the time, rear suspension was still considered 'weird' and viewed with suspicion by a significant number of prospective purchasers, so Franklin was kow-towing to popular opinion on this issue. The aim was for the Scout to break through into mass sales for Indian, so they could not afford for it to be too 'weird'.

Because the engine was so compact, the frame could be made quite low. This 'lowness' is accentuated by a between-the-rails gas tank typical of this 'flat-tank' era of motorcycling. Being low meant the frame could also be kept short with a wheelbase of 55 inches between axles, compared with the 60 plus inches usual for heavyweight V-twins.

It was Tommy Butler who took on the task of 'selling' the Scout design to the powers-that-be at Indian. They were reportedly reluctant to commit to the expense of bringing any new design into production at a time when the motorcycle market was shrinking. The Powerplus might have to soldier on as range leader until such time as sales improved, they reasoned. The middleweight market segment could be served by a stop gap in the form of a 'Powerplus single' of 33.50 cu in (600cc approx) single with a rearward leaning cylinder. But this was just as high, long, and off-putting to novice riders as the 'full-twin', Butler opined. If Indian's financiers wanted to accumulate, then they'd have to speculate, ran Butler's logic. You can't sit around waiting for markets to pick up. You've got to get out there and create new markets. You have to make your own luck in this world.

Fortunately for Indian's chances of survival through the global recession of 1921-22, and fortunately for those of us almost a century later who love riding our Indian motorcycles, the Indian directors were brought around to Butler's way of thinking. The strongest selling point to the Board could well have been that name. Apparently Butler had dreamed that up, too.

Scout.

What a perfect name for an Indian motorcycle.

Having got the 'green light', a prototype was built and subjected to testing. During mid-1919 several pre-production examples were out and about in Massachusetts and Connecticut, ridden hard to find out which components would be first to break. With a bottom-end, primary drive and transmission already quite substantial for an engine of this size, it was able to take everything dished out to it and passed these tests with flying colours. The go ahead was given for tooling-up to commence Scout production in the last quarter of 1919 as a 1920 model.

The Indian Scout was launched at that year's National Motorcycle Show in Chicago. It was an immediate 'hit' in the motorcycle market of 1920. Customers loved it, and dealers loved to promote it. To dealers this new addition to the Indian 'family' was one they could easily see value in having in their stores.

On the one hand, its physically small size made it nimble and manageable. Small did not mean fragile though, because this bike exuded toughness thanks to its solid frame. The engine was easy to start, and the bike felt very comfortable once you'd settled yourself on it and gotten underway. Its handling on the move was at once both agile, and stable.

On the other hand, those thinking they needed a decent amount of power from a motorcycle found that the Scout was capable of providing it. In terms of numbers its 600cc engine dimensions gave it a rating of 5 hp according to the conventions of the day, while its 'real' output as measured on the dynamometer was about 11 or 12 hp. This is less than that of any 1,000cc V-twin to be sure, and no knowledgeable speed-demon of those days would have expected otherwise. On a smooth level road these early 600cc Scouts could be wound up to a comfortable 55 mph before they started to run out of puff, and after that you'd have a while to wait before it would nudge 60. The big 'V' road models were usually good for 80 mph if the road gave them room enough.

Even so, many who tried one immediately noticed that the power and acceleration of a Scout, proportional to that of a fully-fledged heavyweight V-twin, was greater than expected. Scout power was seen as 'surprising' - the explanation, of course, lay in its good breathing. In the real world, it transpired that the power difference between a Scout and a heavyweight usually was of little account once one got out into the countryside. On only a small percentage of US public roads in 1920 could speeds higher than 50 mph be sustained by any type of vehicle for more than a mile or two. The advantage of the big twins lay not in greater speeds from point-to-point, but in better pulling-power when on steep hills or bearing heavy loads.

Here in a nutshell is an explanation for why the Scout was so well received, while the response to the Featherweight and Light Twin was so lukewarm. This was a machine 'lightweight' enough to be liked by people who might not otherwise like motorcycles, yet with power enough to forge its way through rural sand or muck on equal terms with the 'real' motorcycles. No apology need be made for owning and riding an Indian Scout.

This is not the whole explanation, however. Remember there was at this time another middleweight motorcycle in America, also of 600cc, equally capable of slithering through mid-western ruts and morass? This was the flat-twin Harley Sport. Introduced with high hopes in 1919, one selling-season ahead of the Scout, Milwaukee took it off the market in 1923 and after that said nothing more about it.

By all accounts the Sport functioned well enough as a motorcycle. It also sold reasonably well at first, especially in Europe where buyers were already familiar with the Douglas concept. Technically innovative in its use of unit construction, primary drive by gears, and side-valve configuration, the Harley Sport went well enough to even have some successes in competition.

But once the 600cc Indian Scout was released for 1920, it flat-out killed the Harley Sport in middleweight motorcycle sales. Not only did it perform slightly better, but (to American eyes) it didn't look so weird. The difference being that the Scout was progressive, without being radical.

Sure, the Scout also had ground-breaking features like semi-unit engine-gearbox construction, double-loop full cradle frame, and helical gear primary drive. Yet overall it managed to look like a slightly miniaturized version of America's familiar he-man V-twins. It had the same sound, same feel, same looks, as any UAM (Universal American Motorcycle).

It remains a fact that motorcycle customers are conservative, who choose to buy a particular model as much (if not more) for reasons of emotional attachment and image as for practical performance. We will always want something better, so long as it doesn't look too much different. Triumph's Edward Turner was another designer who found huge success by striking that skilful balance between being progressive but not radical. His own trend setting Speed Twin of 1938 managed to resemble in appearance the twin-port big singles that were by then the UBM (Universal British Motorcycle), but it ran smoother and gave more power.

As already related, the Indian Scout was a runaway success. At first, Indian couldn't make enough of them to really cash in on its success. Meanwhile in 1923 H-D quietly ceased manufacture of the Sport, with attics and yards crammed full of unsold bikes and components. Doubtless cursing their lapse into such design adventurism, they went back to evolving and refining the J-Model, building

A newspaper advertisement announcing the new Indian Scout, dated 15th November 1919. (Indian Factory Archives)

up their dealer networks, consolidating their position as USA's new Number One, and considering a fresh foray into the small-bike market with an English-style lightweight single cylinder model.

What they didn't do is directly challenge the Scout head-on. Not yet, anyway. That waited until 1928 with release of the 45 cu in Harley Model D. For the time being, H-D didn't bother with any middleweight offering at all.

What did Franklin himself have to say about the Indian Scout? Well, to be honest, we don't really know. Indian advertising did carry statements extolling the virtues of the Scout which were based upon engineering arguments, and these must have stemmed from Franklin as Chief Engineer who would probably have provided some copy for the ad boys to work with. These statements were so 'puffed' and 'massaged' by the advertising department however, that they cannot really be relied upon as reflecting any objective and hard-headed analysis attributable to Franklin. Nevertheless, it is interesting to read the official Indian factory account of why they thought the Scout was really cool,

Indian Scout advertisements, like this one from 27th March 1920, were large and lavishly illustrated. This and the previous one each took up one-quarter of a full newspaper page. (Indian Factory Archives)

INDIAN Scout—
the "handiest" of all motorcycles

THE new INDIAN SCOUT Model G-20 eclipses every past triumph in the motorcycle industry.

As a perfected middleweight, it is the motorcycle of the future. New in conception—new in design—new in construction—new in a hundred important details. Powerful, strong and sturdy—yet a hundred pounds lighter than its big brother, the INDIAN POWERPLUS. Seventy-five miles on a gallon of gasoline—an easily handled, practical, economical middleweight machine. What engineers dreamed of for years as the ultimate; what loyal dealers have hoped for; what an overcritical public demanded with ever-growing clamor, and what was called the "impossible"—here it is crystallized in this latest and most astounding motorcycle achievement.

Come in and look them over. Make your choice today—our plan of payments will put you in possession of your new INDIAN tomorrow.

MACK BROS. Inc.
Reno, Nevada

Indian Motocycle

and compare it with our own 'motorcycle paleontology' analysis. This is what 1920 Indian advertising had to say about the Scout:

Introducing the Indian Scout
Fulfilling the increasing demand for a medium-weight mount incorporating the excellence of Powerplus construction, Indian has brought out a middle-weight, the Indian Scout, rated at 5 horse power but delivering 11 on the dynamometer. This model is an *ideal solo mount* by reason of its mobility, *low saddle position* and elasticity of performance in combination with its reduced weight and handiness. It weighs 100 pounds less than the Powerplus.

For the sidecarist and the rider who desires maximum power and speed, the Powerplus Big Twin is again offered with numerous important improvements.

Expressive of the greatest number of long desired qualities in a solo motorcycle is the Indian Scout, with its graceful lines and extremely low saddle position, rugged strength and neat design. It is every inch a thoroughbred.

Fitted with a unit powerplant, its centre of gravity is low yet the clearance is ample. Scientific weight distribution ensures correct traction and comfort.

To ride the Indian Scout is to realize the marvellous fulfilment of highest expectations. A comfortable, low-hung vehicle with silent, eager power, it launches the rider into motion so easily and smoothly as to make it difficult of comparison to any previous offering of the motorcycle industry. *Perfect in balance*, it has a remarkable 'feel' and responsiveness. It glides evenly at a walking pace and *accelerates without effort* to fifty-five miles per hour on high gear. The Indian Scout is the heart's desire of solo motorcycles. It brings all the joys of riding to thousands who have hesitated at the weight, price and extreme speed of the heavier machine.

The roadability of the Scout is a revelation, even to the veteran rider.

Not bad. The only part here that makes our eyebrows arch slightly in incredulity is the bit about 'scientific weight distribution'. By and large, this advertising copy describes the Scout pretty well in comparison with our 20:20 hindsight perspective ninety years hence. It makes clear that this is a bike to attract new people into motorcycling, yet is still capable of satisfying that hard-core element who need no convincing about the fun of being on two wheels but who expect that it will indeed be fun.

During our researches we have found only one published statement containing words directly attributable to Franklin himself, on the subject of his brain child. This appeared in a letter he wrote to the editor of *Irish Cyclist and Motor Cyclist*, after it published an article on 1st October 1919 which announced the launch of the Scout and dared to do what neither US nor English motorcycle magazines of the day were accustomed to doing. It offered *objective criticism!*

An 'Indian' Medium-weight Motorcycle
574cc 'Scout' model, the product of Mr C.B. Franklin.
It will be remembered by many readers of THE IRISH CYCLIST AND MOTOR CYCLIST that Mr C.B. Franklin - the well-known Irish trials rider and racing expert - recently accepted an important position on the staff of the Hendee Mfg. Co., USA. He has already been very busy re-designing the 7-9 model, and the clean lines and British appearance of the 1920 Power-plus Indian is largely due to his supervision. His latest product - the medium-weight model illustrated below - is a most pre-possessing mount. It will be known as the 'Scout,' and is intended purely as a go-anywhere lightweight machine for solo work.

A novel type of duplex cradle frame houses the neat little 574cc power unit. The latter is a miniature edition of the well-known 'Power-plus' side-by-side valve engine. With it, as a single unit, is incorporated the Dixie magneto, 3-speed gearbox, clutch, kick starter and silencer. The K.S. itself, which is fitted on the right-hand side, is a really efficient article possessed of ample leverage and strength. Transmission is *via* a train of gears to the gearbox, and from thence by chain on the right-hand side - as on the Sunbeam and Enfield machines - to the rear wheel. As standard on 'Indian' mounts, the drive is not enclosed, efficient guards taking the place of the usual chain case. The wheels and tyres are of 26-inch diameter, and the saddle height is under 28 inches.

Although considered a lightweight from the American point of view, this model really comes into the medium-weight class. Its actual weight is 260 lbs.

On road tests it has show itself to be an extremely efficient machine, and capable of 60-65 mph all out. It has already covered 102 miles in 126 minutes, viz., the distance between Boston and Springfield. At moderate speeds it is exceptionally silent, both as regards exhaust and mechanical noise.

The only point of criticism one could possibly bring to bear against Mr Franklin's product is as regards the incorporation of 26-inch wheels. We have always found one of the greatest charms of the standard American machine to be the increased comfort provided by 28-inch wheels. Now that quite a large number of English manufacturers are fitting the larger diameter tyres on their products, it appears somewhat of an anomaly to find the originators of this highly desirable practice forsaking it in turn.

Since every detail of his creation had apparently been the subject of deepest thought, Franklin could not allow these remarks pass without further explanation. His letter of reply, which appeared on 12th November 1919, ran as follows:

Letter from C.B. Franklin
'I notice in your issue of Irish Cyclist and Motor Cyclist of October 1st, regarding the Indian Scout model, that some criticism of our adopting 26 in. wheels instead of 28 in. is made. This has been done for various reasons, principally to get greater mudguard clearance and a lower centre of gravity on the machine, and at the same time to keep the saddle position low. You do not mention the section of the tyres, but they are 3 in., and as a matter of fact, the tyres actually measure 27 in. by 3.25 in. outside. You may be interested to know that we have been using wheels of this size on some of our 7-9 hp models, and the riders like them very much indeed, and it is our intention very shortly to introduce a new-sized tyre on these machines, the nominal size being 27 in. by 3.5 in. These will fit on our regular 26 in. by 3 in. standard rims. With kindest regards to yourself and all readers of the Irish Cyclist and Motor Cyclist.'

Never mind the semi-unit powerplant. Forget about the helical gear primary drive. To heck with the double-loop full cradle frame. Frustratingly for historians, the most significant Scout issue that this correspondence could find to discuss was the tyre size!

Customers were nevertheless able to recognize qualities other than just unusual tyre size, for the Scout model soon became popular, both at home and abroad. Indian already had a significant export business and a good reputation in overseas markets, especially in Britain, Europe and Australasia. The Scout's size and power made it a handy all-rounder, for its time one of the most manageable combinations of power and agility available in any market. British markets would soon become dominated by 500cc and 350cc singles of similar physical dimensions and performance envelope as the Scout. Apart from initial ground breaking models like the Big-Port AJS (offered as a street model from 1922), these UBMs didn't emerge fully formed from the conceptual chrysalis laid down by their tall, heavy Trusty-Triumph type progenitors until about 1923-25, when a host of nimble models like the Black Ariel series and Velocette's K Model started appearing. The Scout beat such ecological equivalents into the marketplace

Parsons' Remarkable Ride

1,114½ Miles in 24 Hours

87 Miles added to previous World's Record

When E. Baker, the American Crack, covered 1027 miles in 24 hours on a 7 h.p. machine on the Mortlake Circuit (Vic.) in 1916, his ride was acclaimed a phenomenal performance, and one destined to stand many a day.

It stood four years—until the Australian Champion, H. A. Parsons, determined on tackling the stiff proposition of creating new figures—on a machine only 3/5ths of the power used by Baker.

Here's what he did

Riding a 5 h.p. INDIAN SCOUT and Ordinary Standard "Railroad"

DUNLOP TYRES

he covered 579 MILES in 12 Hours and

1,114½ Miles in 24 Hours

Riding at an average speed of well over 50 miles an hour he went right through without mechanical or tyre trouble. That's a Road Tyre test worth talking about—and again demonstrates what a great wearing cover the "RAILROAD" is. There's no tyre that approaches it for wear and economy—and MOTORISTS know it! We know it by the demand for more—and yet more "Railroads"—Your agent can supply.

* *

DUNLOP RUBBER CO.
ALL STATES   AND N.Z.

Dunlop Tyres here claim bragging rights from their sponsorship of Harold Parson's 24hr record in Australia on an Indian Scout. (Mick Atkins Collection)

by about three to five years. It was an influential model that had an impact on the offerings of other makers and can be regarded as one of the very first examples of the 'modern motorcycle'.

In far-off New Zealand, way down in the sub-Antarctic part, a brand-new 1920 Scout caught the eye of a 21 year old larrikin who thought it so handy-looking and dashing that he had to have it. It was built among the very first batch to leave Springfield and bore engine number 50R627 (the prototype Scout had engine number 50R101). He bought it for £120 and ended up owning it fifty years. His constant tinkering to make it go better raised it to a pitch where it was ultimately recognized as the world's fastest Indian ever. The man's name was Burt Munro, and his story is the stuff that movies are made of.

In nearby Australia another young chap set out that same year to do world beating things with an Indian Scout. His name was Harold Parsons, and he unfortunately didn't live long enough to be as well remembered as Burt Munro. His achievement was right up there with the best however, for he decided to have a go at beating the world 24 hours record set by 'Cannonball' Baker while riding a Powerplus. It is indeed a bold choice to take aim with a Scout at a distance record held by so proficient a long-haul cruiser as a Powerplus. One factor may have been that the triangular country-road course available to Parsons near the Victorian towns of Sale and Maffra had a decent-sized hump in it at one point where it crossed a railroad track, so that every twenty-six minutes during his 24 hr hell-ride Parsons would be launched airborne for a distance of about 50 feet. Re-entry to Planet Earth at this frequency would become fairly tiresome after a while on any motorcycle, but especially so on a big yank-tank like the Powerplus. The innovative 26 x 3 in. 'balloon' tyres fitted to the Scout as standard may have helped to soothe Parson's tender butt more than just somewhat. More important still was the fact that a 600cc machine, if it held up okay, would be able to take out records in more capacity classes than a 1,000cc machine. On 28th August 1920 young Harold duly set off and, by the time his 24 hours were up, he'd covered 1,114 miles and gone over 250 miles further than Cannonball's own most recent effort. It was a convincing demonstration of Scout stamina and toughness, and Indian made much of this achievement in their advertising.

This inaugural Indian Scout in its cobby-looking 'short-frame' guise went on sale from 1920 through to 1927 as substantially the same model. During this period its sales reached 60,000, a very respectable figure. This kept the workforce employed, the factory functioning, and allowed Indian to build up some cash reserves in its treasury. Importantly, the Scout allowed Indian to ride out the recession of 1921-22 and thus ensured that the company survived to fight another day and another decade.

From late 1919 onwards the Indian range now comprised three models. The Powerplus as range leader was available in both standard form (the Model N) or with electric lighting (the NE) at $410. Customers could choose either the standard spring frame, or a cheaper rigid frame version (not shown in catalogs but available upon request). There was a Powerplus-single commercial model, as mentioned earlier. The Scout rounded out this range as the Model G, at $310.

Having really done a decent year's hard work and doubtless by now looking to unwind, Charles Franklin got a pleasant surprise just as he and his colleagues were gearing up for the business house Christmas party season. His old race team-mate and associate, Douglas S. Alexander from Edinburgh, came to visit him at the Hendee plant. It was reported in *Motorcycle and Bicycle Illustrated* on 11th December 1919 that:

> An interesting feature of his visit was his meeting with C.B. Franklin, Chief Engineer of the Hendee Mfg. Co. The two had not seen each other since the last TT contest, over five years ago. Two of the Alexanders, Sidney George, N. Brown and the late Oliver Godfrey, with Mr. Franklin formed the Indian team that brought the coveted trophy to America.'

There it is again - 'Chief Engineer'. And in a US trade publication this time. One really has to wonder whether Charles Gustafson Snr would've had anything to say about that.

Contemporary perceptions of the Scout's most important virtues are checked off in this 1920 collection of Indian dealer advertisements, designed to be run one-by-one over consecutive days in the local newspaper. (Indian Factory Archives)

Harley vs Indian Wars 1919-22

Going back to the start of 1919, this was the year in which the US manufacturers resumed their support for national racing competition after the two year layoff for WWI. It was clear from the outset that H-D's racing effort was going to be as star-studded, as well organised and as well financed as the earlier 1914-1916 campaign that helped elevate them to their new position of US industry leadership.

Mainstream competition in this era was a mix of dirt-track oval events, a couple of 'road' races (on country lanes), and board track events. These latter contests were nowadays restricted to a relatively few venues that had bigger tracks of one mile or more per lap, which also got used for car racing. Most of the short $1/3$ mile 'murder-dromes' built for motorcycles in the 1909 - 1912 board-track hey-day had closed their doors due to declining attendances and increasing costs of repairs. H-D now went all-out to compete at all venues including board tracks, which they'd previously down played in favour of longer dirt-track and road race events.

The opening shot of the 1919 campaign was fired at Ascot Speedway in Los Angeles, a one mile banked track surfaced in asphalt, with the running of a 200-mile National Championship race on 22nd June. In front of a 10,000 strong crowd the new two-cam Harleys ran fast and well, winning the first five places (Ralph Hepburn was 1st) and only one of the H-D entries failed to finish. Ray Weishaar led for the first 30 miles, then Hepburn passed him and led for the next 50. Weishaar regained the lead until they both made pit-stops, after which Hepburn took over again and crossed the line first with an average race speed of 72.32 mph, a new track record. A hallmark of the H-D team's performance was the well-drilled precision of their pit crew, and careful attention to detail by a well staffed race organisation. The only chink in the H-D armour was the indisciplined ride of new comer Weishaar, dicing hard against his own team-mate Hepburn in an effort to make a strong impression and boost his own reputation.

The Indian and Excelsior entries were slower than the Harleys and experienced many breakdowns, not to mention silly slip-ups like Roy Artley's Excelsior getting fresh oil put in its gas tank. Pit crew lifted his bike up bodily and held it upside-down to rapidly drain it and rectify their mistake. The first Indian home (in 6th place) was ridden by a complete unknown in the USA, New Zealander Percy Coleman, who'd consequently been assigned the slowest bike out of all the Indian entries. He'd made up time on the bends by sticking to the inside rail in New Zealand grass-track style, rather than ride high up on the banking as was the convention among the American riders. This much shorter line was certainly the faster way to get around, but the need for him to slide out the rear wheel on this inner unbanked portion of Ascot's hard surface was very tough on tyres so Coleman was forced to make frequent stops for wheel changes.

The 200-mile National Road Championships held at Marion, Indiana was one of the prestigious long-distance events of the 1919 race season. This race was run out amongst farmland on a 5-mile course of narrow dirt lanes. There were 15,000 spectators in attendance to witness another H-D clean-sweep of the first three places. This time 'Red' Parkhurst was 1st, with Hepburn 2nd and Otto Walker 3rd. The race was not as dismal for Indian as the results suggest, however. Indian entrant Teddy Carroll dogged Parkhurst's footsteps for much of the race, frequently challenging for the lead.

What is surprising about this is that Carroll was riding a Powerplus-based sidevalve machine, on which Charles Franklin had recently begun devoting time and effort to its speed tuning. Several of these had been prepared for the event, with the breathed-upon Powerplus lumps installed in special racing frames of the 'key-stone' type. These had the bottom section of the frame loop cut away in order to save weight, so used the engine as a stressed member to hold the bike together. In time these came to be known as 'Marion frames', a term that is still applied by motorcycle collectors today.

The engines were essentially production Powerplus motors, but with important developments made during 1919 and 1920. Firstly, special cylinders were employed which are shorter than standard and more deeply finned. They are easily recognizable by extra cooling fins that run across the exhaust stubs (there are no fins on the stubs of standard Powerplus cylinders). The other external difference is that Powerplus race motors have naked valve springs. Since there are no valve-spring covers, consequently the pushrod guides do not have the widened, threaded tops on them for the covers to screw down onto. Internally, short aluminium pistons were used with fully floating and bronze padded wrist pins (gudgeon pins). In contrast to road-model cylinders, the combustion chamber roof has a definite step in it to blank off a portion of the piston at tdc and thus provide 'squish'. Special cams gave very long valve openings, and extended valve caps raised compression. To make room for a 'big-valve' version, special crankcases were produced in which the pushrods, guides, etc. for each cylinder were spaced wider apart.

It must have been both satisfying yet galling to witness Carroll's Indian racer, based upon a production engine race-prepped for a fraction of the time and cost that had gone into each of the new H-D two-cam eight-valvers, be put out of contention only in the second to last lap of the Marion 200 due to a broken valve spring. The Indian pit crew managed to get Carroll's bike fixed quickly enough for him to resume and secure 4th spot, however up until that point he had been on for a 2nd placing at least. Such is racing. Percy Coleman rode in this race but retired, the problem also being broken valve springs. Clearly there were some teething problems in getting the Powerplus valve-train to cope with some fierce new cam profile of Franklin's devising.

Excelsior were behind the race leaders, and not competitive with their 'big-valve' ioe racers which appeared by now to have reached the limit of their development. Bob Perry, a veteran of Excelsior's pre-war pinnacle of racing achievement, competed for Excelsior in this race. Fresh out of University, in his 'day job' he was helping designer Jock McNeil to make an Excelsior version of the Cyclone overhead-cam race motor that had caused such a sensation back in 1915. Excelsior boss Ignaz Schwinn was determined to reclaim some of his company's lost racing glories and advertising bragging rights, to remain in the Big Three and not descend to the level of the second-rank US marques of which many had by now been forced to close their doors.

Sheepshead Bay Speedway at Long Island, NY held an important series of National Championship races, run on wooden boards over 2, 10, 50 and 100 mile distances. Indian bagged the 10 mile race, and H-D took out all the rest. Of the dirt-track Nationals, Gene Walker won four out of nine races for Indian.

The year 1919 ended as a good one for Harley-Davidson. Indian had nevertheless claimed sufficient victories to have cause for celebration in its advertising, however these were mainly over shorter courses. Looking back on this season in US racing, historian and race bike collector Daniel Statnekov comments that the Indian and H-D ohv eight-valve machines were about equal in speed, with the outcome between them on any one day being determined by whoever could get their machine to hang together long enough to make it to the finish. This parity is surprising, given the much more recent genesis of the H-D eight-valver, and the continued race-shop activity over in Milwaukee during the two year lay-off in factory supported racing during WWI. Statnekov ranks the pocket-valve H-Ds as slightly faster than the Powerplus racer, but the latter was ahead in pulling power which gave it an edge in sidecar events.

Indian has to be viewed as the underdog during this period in US competition, because they simply lacked the kind of top level support and, above all, budget that H-D's enthusiast founders had committed to its post-war racing effort. H-D was going all-out to consolidate its image as the new US No. 1 manufacturer, and to heck with whatever it cost. Indian's race budget could best be described as 'meagre', and they had to make up for lost time after halting race engine development during the war-production years.

For 1920 there'd been a further full year of development by Franklin on the Powerplus however, and it was expected to be competitive. Indian now also had the services of star rider 'Shrimp' Burns, a young and diminutive but fiery rider who'd recently switched to the Indian camp from Harley-Davidson after apparently getting off-side with H-D team captain Otto Walker. Gene Walker was another Indian star who was practically unbeatable on dirt-track short races, where rider skill and tactics counted for more than possession of machinery capable of sustained blistering pace over the long haul.

Charles Franklin had by now assumed leadership of Indian's race department. In this role his closest associate was not his nominal boss Charles Gustafson Snr, but rather the son, Charles Jnr. This younger Gustafson knew how to ride, having previously competed on board tracks with Hedstrom ioe and eight-valve machinery, and he now held a post in the racing department.

Franklin took more than just a close interest in the activities of the Indian race team at each event - he was right there 'up close and personal', and would get actively involved in preparations and pit work during the running of a race. One photograph taken at the 1920 Marion races shows him holding the gasoline funnel as a Powerplus racer is being re-fueled. Continuing his pre-war tradition of meticulous machine preparation, one can be sure that under his eagle eye nothing was being left to chance. This attention to detail was picked up and commented upon as far afield as his native Ireland, where the *Irish Cyclist & Motor Cyclist* of 11th August, 1920 duly reported:

> An item culled from the American contemporary magazine, *Motorcycling and Bicycle Illustrated*, reporting the 300 miles national championship at Dodge City, Kansas, stated: 'Down the line in the Indian camp, engineer C.B. Franklin and sales manager Ed Buffam were busily grooming the Indian contenders.' Franklin appears to be following the round of American race meetings. Seven of the eight national championships to date have been won by Indians.

The year 1919 would have been a very busy one for Franklin. In addition to designing the Indian Scout and attending to all the multitudinous preparations for it to go into production, he was simultaneously reviving Indian's racing organization and trying to develop competitive machines with which to equip its team of salaried expert riders.

The hot news at the start of the 1920 race season was the unveiling of the new Excelsior overhead-cam race machines, which were by now thoroughly tested and apparently not lacking in horse-power. Ascot Park in Los Angeles was again the opening round of competition, in a week long event that included 25, 50 and 100 mile National Championships. Before the races began, Bob Perry decided to use the Ascot venue for a speed record attempt. He lost control and crashed, hitting a fence post and sustaining serious head injuries to which he unfortunately succumbed several hours later. Perry had been a favourite of Schwinn's and was being groomed for greater things within the company. It is said that Ignaz Schwinn started to lose his enthusiasm for the cut and thrust of top level, high speed competition after this. The immediate result was that Excelsior withdrew the rest of their team from the upcoming race as a mark of respect, leaving the way clear for H-D and Indian to resume their rivalry undistracted.

In the first 100-miler (a non-Championship race) 'Shrimp' Burns went straight into the lead on an Indian eight-valve machine, but before long his handlebars worked loose. Forced to halt for this to be attended to, he never regained the lead and H-D again claimed the first five places with captain Otto Walker in 1st place.

Indian did better in the shorter races at Ascot, but these got rather spectacular. Excelsior now allowed its new ohc machines to run, and in the 25-mile race it was Joe Wolters who hotly pursued early leader 'Shrimp' Burn's eight-valve. Burn's riding style during this race could best be described as 'suicidal', and he appeared continually on the verge of sliding-out. Then one of the other Indians went down after its rear tyre came off, causing burning gasoline to spill over the track. Otto Walker stepped off at speed rather than hit the stricken Indian, slid through the flames and well beyond, but got up unhurt to remount his machine and carry on. Joe Wolters also put his bike down to avoid the wreck, and similarly went a long way on his butt before coming to a stop. The outcome was that 'Shrimp' Burns crossed the line first, and set new race records for 5, 10, 15 and 20 miles in the process. Score one for Indian, in the first National Championship race of the season.

The 50-mile race was for 'standard valve' engines, that is, ones that ordinary customers could actually buy, so was a contest between pocket-valve and side-valve machines. Joe Wolters did well for the first half of the race on an out-dated 'big valve' Excelsior, however Otto Walker then took over the lead and never relinquished it, leading home Freddy Ludlow (another H-D) in 2nd and this left 3rd place for 'Shrimp' Burns on a Powerplus racer.

It was Ludlow who, in later life, explained for posterity the kind of teamwork and tactics needed in the longer races at which the H-D team so excelled. If at all possible each factory team would ride in a bunch in line astern, much as bicycle racers still do in team sprints. The leader would set the pace and push his engine to its limit, while those slip-streaming him would be sucked along in his wake with their motors having an easier time of it. As soon as the leader sensed that his engine was tightening-up or going off-song from over-heating, he'd drop to the back and the one who'd been second behind him would take over the pace-setting role. In this way all riders would work their way up the pack to assume leadership for a time, and then fall back to the rear again. If the group got broken up by forced retirements or disruptive opposition tactics, then it was every man for himself to try and get to the line in a winning position.

This type of disciplined riding was much practiced by teams between events, as was the crowd pleasing spectacle of the rapid pit-stop. None of the bikes had brakes nor any fine control over speed, since they'd been carburetted to run either flat out or not at all. Riders needed to know exactly when to hit the kill-button on making a pit-stop, so that they'd roll to a halt within easy reach of the pit crew. It would be somebody's job to stand in the way of the incoming bike, ready to brace themselves against its handlebars and prevent overshoot. In a well rehearsed scramble by as many as six crew, both of the wheels and spark plugs would be changed, gas and oil tanks replenished, the rider given a thirst quenching drink and a clean pair of goggles, then he and the bike were push started to get underway again, usually all in less than 60 seconds.

To start off each race, the bikes had to be towed by rope behind automobiles or sidecar outfits until rolling fast enough for the rider to let go the kill switch and get the engine to fire, then release his grip on the rope wound a couple of turns around the handlebar. Once everybody's engine was running, they'd circulate in a pack behind a pace car in which the official starter stood facing backward. When satisfied that a fair start was possible, he'd wave his flag and the pace car would head for the infield area, leaving the contestants free to jockey and elbow each other for a favourable position on the fastest possible line around the track*.

In 1920 the two top factories, H-D and Indian, also vied with each other in factory supported record attempts at Daytona Beach in Florida, looking for more plaudits with which to bolster their advertising copy. In February Bill Ottaway took along eight-valve and pocket-valve versions of the two-cam motor where, after waiting for bad weather to clear, Parkhurst and Ludlow ran them over a measured 5 mile distance. The eight-valves succeeded in setting records for 1, 2 and 5 mile distances. A larger than class 68 cubic inch eight-valve was timed at 114 mph. Ludlow made a one-way run of 103 mph on a pocket-valve machine.

Two months later it was Indian's turn, with their own eight-valve motors and the side-valve Powerplus. The factory took care to arrange internationally recognized officials and an electric timing system. Gene Walker used the eight-valve to good effect and exceeded by a small margin the American records just set by the Harley team. With a best one-way run of 114.17 mph with a tail wind (the return run was 93.67 mph), his two-way average was 103.56 mph.

It took them until January 1921 to make their minds up, however this speed was duly granted recognition by the FICM as an outright Land Speed Record for motorcycles. Gene Walker was officially declared the world's fastest motorcyclist, and his name went into the record books (Glenn Curtis' 1906 Daytona speed of 136 mph on a V-8 motorcycle had been the result of a one-way run, so was not FICM-recognised). In addition to their other laurels, Franklin and Gustafson (it's difficult to say if either or both were responsible) could now say that they were engine builders and tuners of the world's fastest motorcycle.

When ratified, this effort displaced from the FICM record book Britain's Bert Le Vack whose own 1911 Indian eight-valve had 'only' gone 94.79 mph, achieved at Brooklands on 23rd November 1920. No motorcyclist in Britain had yet officially exceeded 100 mph. It is most likely that the first British subject anywhere in the world to ever exceed 100 mph on a motorcycle was either New Zealander Percy Coleman or Australian Jack Booth. Before returning to the British Dominion of New Zealand at the close of his 1919 season with the Indian team, in October Coleman was timed aboard an Indian eight-valve at a track in New York at a speed of 101 mph. Meanwhile Jack Booth was reported in early-1919 Indian newspaper advertising as having covered a mile in 35 seconds, or 102.8 miles per hour, at Adelaide in Australia during 1916. This is a speed which Indian claimed was the fastest time ever made on a motorcycle up until then.

---

* *We are indeed fortunate that some 1919 film footage of board track action, shot by a Czech Indian dealer while visiting the US, came to light in recent years. Featuring Indian rider Gene Walker and illustrating many of the above points, it can be found on www.youtube.com by searching for 'Indian board track racing'.*

Gene Walker at Daytona with the Powerplus that put the 'Daytona' into 'Daytona Powerplus'. (Mick Atkins Collection)

Of the over the counter models run at Daytona, the Powerplus proved quicker than the H-D two-cam pocket-valve model over the 1 and 2 mile distances, but not over 5 miles. An indication of the extent to which side-valve motors can suffer from heat and distortion is provided by the fact that a one-way speed of 105.78mph was achieved by Walker over the first kilometre, but this dropped to 103.28 for 2 miles and 97.45 for 5 miles.

As a result of performances like this at Daytona, the race-tuned Powerplus engines came to be known among aficionados as 'Daytona' motors. We've already mentioned cylinders and pushrod guides that differ from standard production components. To this add a special Schebler 'Daytona' carburetor, forged-steel flywheels instead of cast-iron, a different transmission gear cluster, and a different clutch.

There were more race events run in the US during 1920, compared with 1919. One event to make a welcome return was the Dodge City 300-mile race, last held in 1916. Taking place in July, it shaped up to be an H-D versus Indian clash and, unusually, H-D elected to enter all pocket-valve racers. Indian bet a dollar each way with three eight-valve machines backed up by five Powerplus 'Daytona' racers. 'Shrimp' Burns and Gene Walker used their 'eights' to hold the lead on the two-mile oval track until the first pit-stops, when H-D rider Maldwyn Jones took over from the 33rd lap. Ludlow and Jim Davis slipped in behind him, giving H-D the top spots out to the 200-mile mark and establishing new race records in the process. 'Shrimp' caught Jones up at this stage and tussled for the lead for another 15 laps until he made another pit-stop to change tyres. At the 250-mile mark Jones had an approximately 2 mile lead on everybody, when his engine developed a spark plug problem. His pit-crew changed the plugs pronto but couldn't get the bike re-started, so now Jones was out of the picture.

This left Jim Davis as race leader, but Burns and Gene Walker were both hot on his heels with eight-valve Indians. Burns caned his engine hard to catch up, being timed over one lap at 94 mph. Too hard, because he next broke down and had to retire. As a result, the pocket-valve Harley of Jim Davis finished first, followed four minutes later by the eight-valve Indian of Gene Walker. A curious result, if you're a diligent student of small-engine design.

The next big event was at Marion in Indiana. Owing to the narrowness of the roadway riders could not all start together, so starting positions were allocated by drawing lots. 'Shrimp' Burns picked a number that had him starting from right at the back. Boldly he declared to all within earshot that by the end of the first lap he would be in the lead. He started out like a maniac on his Powerplus 'Daytona', riding in the rough along roadside verges and even up banks to get around anyone in his way. As promised, he took the lead from H-D's Ray Weishaar just as the second lap commenced. Burns slackened not a bit, and even set a record speed in Lap 13 plus a record time for the 100-mile distance by Lap 21. Then his final-drive chain broke, and it took him six minutes to fix it. He got back to within half a minute of Ray Weishaar, when the chain failed a second time. It caused damage to fuel lines so Burns was this time forced to retire, with 40 miles remaining. Weishaar turned the race into a Harley victory, however Leonard Buckner's side-valve Powerplus 'Daytona' snuck in to 2nd place, with Jim Davis 3rd. Despite it being a Harley-Indian contest, Excelsior 'big-valve' machines were also there and came in at 4th, 5th and 6th. So H-D grabbed the headlines, but underdog Indian provided very stiff competition.

Charles Franklin with the Indian team at the 9th September 1920 Marion road race. (EMIMA)

The Wigwam clan. Left to right, C. B. Franklyn, chief engineer, Roy Artley, Leonard Buckner, Albert "Shrimp" Burns, L. M. Fredericks, Wald Korn, Nemo Lancaster and Charles Gustafson, chief mechanic

Indian camp scenes at the big race. Upper, Captain Charles Spencer (with can) and Engineer Franklin; lower, everybody active

Preparing Indian machines at the 1920 Marion road race. Franklin holds the gasoline funnel. (EMIMA)

ome of those at Marion. Left to right, Rev. Father R. M. Botting, chief checker; R. S. McConnell, referee; C. B. Franklyn, endee Mfg. Co.; William Ottoway, Harley-Davidson Motor Co.; Lacy Crolius, Harley-Davidson Motor Co.; "Corky" Hammond, track manager, and W. H. Parsons, Chairman M. & A. T. A. (Photo by Firestone)

Charles Franklin with his opposite number William Ottoway (H-D race engineer) at the 1920 Marion races. (EMIMA)

On the 19th September 1920 the nation's top stars appeared at a dirt-track oval near Cleveland Ohio for some action-packed racing. It was a good day for Gene Walker, winning the 1-mile dash and 5-mile event, however he conceded the 25-mile race to Ludlow and Jim Davis on Harleys. The day was very notable in historical hindsight for 'Shrimp' Burns' win of the 10-mile race at a dirt-track record time of 7 minutes 53 seconds (76 mph average speed), beating H-D rider Jim Davis into second place. The reason it is notable is because 'Shrimp' was riding a side-valve Powerplus racer, while Davis was on an ohv eight-valve machine. This is another bizarre result for the technically-minded to dwell upon.

The year 1920 ended with Indian crowing about having won 14 out of 17 National Championship races. But that's only one way to look at it. Another way is to look at the track miles won. Indian gained 191 miles worth of race titles but H-D had racked up 513 miles, with 500 of those won in just two races, the prestigious and highly publicized Dodge City 300 and Marion 200 races. The four founders could feel well pleased with the publicity gained by their huge investment in racing, and doubtless looked forward to this being reflected in increased sales through bigger market share. Their other big investment of this period, a greatly expanded factory now slightly larger than the Wigwam in Springfield, was completed in this year and stood ready to cope with the expected demand.

Unfortunately for all the US motorcycle manufacturers, they were now getting killed by the US auto industry. Harley's fall-back strategy was to try and get as big a slice of the shrinking 'motorcycle' pie as possible. That meant continuation of their racing policy into 1921.

This year started well for Harley because, never mind simply going 100 mph for one lap of a race, or for one mile of a race, their star rider Otto Walker became first in the world to exceed 100 mph for an *entire* race. He pulled off this feat not just in a single race, but in four separate races all run on this one day. There was a 50-mile board track event run at Fresno CA on 22nd February, over which distance Walker averaged 101 mph. He also ran 107 mph in the 1-mile dash, 103 mph in the 10-mile race, and 104 mph in the 15-mile race. These feats gave Walker the honour of winning the most races ever at any one US racing event.

By now Charles Franklin had the Powerplus 'Daytona' machines running really well, to a pitch where they too were finishing races at sustained speeds of 100 mph. Admittedly they were a fraction slower than the pocket-valve Harleys, however they were capable of winning and there was more speed in them still to be extracted. Indian's overhead eight-valve design was now over ten years old but very much in contention. Much also depended upon the skill of individual riders like Gene Walker and 'Shrimp' Burns, whose daring and willingness to take risks to an extent compensated for Indian's more modest race shop resources, and ensured that the Harley-Indian duel remained very much a contest.

This rivalry did not seem to get at all bitter, however. Trackside photos show riders from different teams getting along very amicably, when not out riding on the track at least. Race promoters may well have billed particular contests as a 'grudge match' between riders of opposite camps but, much like modern day professional wrestlers, one can be sure they'd all head for the same bar afterwards to unwind and have a good laugh together. Such camaraderie extended to race team management who, after all, were fellow members of a very select 'club' of people able to indulge their lifelong passion for fast machinery. There is a photo taken at Marion that shows Franklin very comfortable in the company of his opposite number Bill Ottaway and another H-D figure, advertising manager Lacy Crolius. To top off all this chumminess, at around this time Franklin hosted H-D's Four Founders to a guided tour of the Indian factory. One of the early-1920s photos discovered in the apartment of Franklin's daughter in 2007 shows Franklin on a fishing trip with none other than William S Harley. This same photo appears in the Billy Wells memorabilia collection of Rick Howard, so it is very likely that Billy Wells was the photographer.

Impresario Jack Prince was still active on the US racing scene, and in fact had recently completed construction of a new 1 ¼ mile board track at Beverly Hills CA. The inaugural motorcycle meet at this venue was on 24th April 1921, and the very first race was won in dramatic style by Albert 'Shrimp' Burns on a small-base eight-valve Indian. Run over 10 laps, this was a 'Miss & Out' race in which the rider running last at the completion of each lap was flagged off the track. Burns had been trailing Otto Walker until the last lap when he moved high up on the banking for the last turn. Converting this height into added speed, he shot down the slope toward the finish line and passed Walker, winning by a bike-length. Burns' average speed over the ten laps was 104 mph. But in the 25-mile race that followed, Burns' engine seized and he got hurled down the track, picking up multiple slivers of wood from the rough-sawn lumber surface as he went. Imagine being stabbed in your arms and shoulders by a dozen sharpened pencils all at once. Just the thought of it is enough to make one's eyes water.

Lesser people would have called it a day and headed for the refreshment booth for repeated doses of some stiff 'medicine'. But Burns reappeared for the start of a 15-mile race, this time on a Powerplus 'Daytona' machine. He was heavily bandaged and iodined from where most of the larger slivers had been extracted, and he was initially content to tuck-in and hold 3rd spot behind H-D riders Ludlow and Hepburn. Then, on the final lap, Burns repeated the stunt he'd pulled in the opening race, diving down from high on the banking at the final turn to pass the two leaders and win the race just inches from the line. His average of 102.6 mph was the fastest race speed yet recorded by a side-valve machine. Leaving aside Burns' surplus of *cajones*, it is nothing short of incredible that what was essentially a production engine (though with a few tweaks by Franklin) could even come close to, let alone beat, the expensive and highly-specialised race machinery being fielded by H-D.

A movie was made of this opening event[36], and it provides invaluable historical footage of this gala occasion held under brilliant Californian sunshine. The wooden-board circuit is huge, with two straight-aways connected by steeply banked bends. The grandstand and in-field area is jam-packed with people, and a perimeter of flagpoles with flags snapping in the breeze completes the spectacle. Scenes include shots of Burns with an Indian eight-valve, and they show his duct-taped arms and hands

A smiling 'Shrimp' Burns has just won the 15-Mile race at the opening meet of the Beverly Hills board track on 24th April 1921 at 102.6mph, beating H-D eight-valve machines and setting the fastest race speed yet for a side-valve motor. The silent-movie camera pans down to show his bandaged and duct-taped arms from his 107mph spill along splintery boards in the earlier 25-mile race, and then zooms in on the Daytona Powerplus motor (revealing that the front exhaust pipe has fallen off). (Photos from film on YouTube, original source unknown)

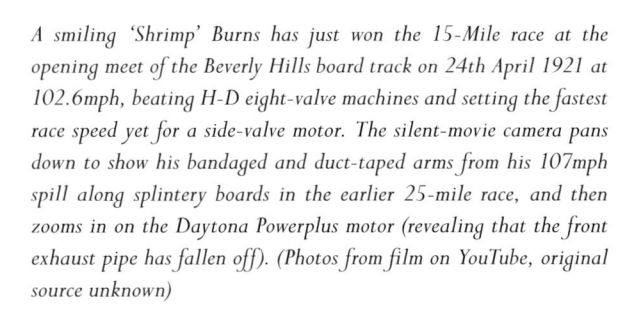

along with the Daytona Powerplus on which he performed the feats just described. A close-up of the Powerplus engine shows useful details like the tell-tale finning of the exhaust stubs, the naked valve springs, and a missing front exhaust pipe that fell off during the race.

Being a silent movie, there are on-screen inter-titles every couple of scenes which provide a written commentary. The movie-makers must have been on the company payroll, because these inter-titles read like an Indian Sales Department 'Powerplus' advertisement from start to finish. They do not fail to rub in the point about exotic, unobtainable eight-valves getting beaten by a motor that anyone could (theoretically) stroll into an Indian dealership and purchase for themselves.

Indian Powerplus triumphs at Beverly Hills Speedway. 12,000 Californians thrilled when daring riders pace fastest track in the world with terrific speed. Los Angeles California, 24th April 1921

The show begins! Lineup for the 'Miss and Out' Race

They're off! Shrimp Burns and Indian take the lead as usual!

Indian wins! Burns getting the checkered flag

Start of the fifty mile race. Burns unable to start; he spilled in the 25 mile race running 107 miles an hour BUT!-

Curley Fredericks jumps to the fore on his Powerplus Pocket Valve Indian and leads the roaring pack of eight-valves at a dizzy pace!

CRASH! Fredericks does a sensational spill in the ninth lap at 105 miles an hour!

Start of the Fifteen mile race, the sensation of the day. Burns escapes from the hospital, swathed in bandages and full of splinters.

Burns and Powerplus step out in front!

Burns rides them off their wheels - Powerplus in front, eight-valves to rear!

Burns and Powerplus win! 102.6 miles an hour.

Powerplus Indian first stock motor to do 100 mph in competition. WORLD RECORDS FALL. Powerplus breaks all records for stock machines, five, ten and fifteen miles.

Indian Powerplus is the supreme Stock Motorcycle Engine of the world!

The Dodge City race was run again, though for the last time, in 1921. It began with the startling media announcement that Indian had fired its star rider Gene Walker for refusing to ride at Dodge City. Daniel Statnekov has explained this attitude of Walker's as being possibly motivated by concern about track conditions and rider safety, or some safety concern about his own Indian machine. Walker was known to be careful about the machines he rode and the tracks he rode on, and was a strong advocate for other riders to do the same.

The magazine *Motorcycling and Bicycling* on 14th July 1921 published a different version of events. In reading this account, it must be remembered that the US motorcycling press of those days was not independent but rather were mouth-pieces of the major manufacturers. This can therefore be regarded as the Indian factory's 'spin' on events and, for this story to have been published at all, it must surely have been the version that the Wigwam wanted to have published.

Hendee Co. Release Gene Walker

Gene Walker has been dismissed from the employ of the Hendee Mfg. Co. The reason for this action is perhaps best explained in telegram sent to Walker at Hamilton, Ohio, under date of July 6, which read as follows :

'Your refusal at last moment to ride at Dodge City after agreeing through Butler to do so has seriously embarrassed this company. Consequently you deserve no consideration at our hands. Under circumstances will require your services no longer and thank you to turn machines over to Indian dealer Mr. Schaub, to whom we are writing today.'

(signed) Hendee Mfg. Co.

This is the last of a series of telegrams and letters which passed between the Hendee Company and Walker beginning 20th June. On that date Walker wired from Denver that he would not ride at Dodge City , but intended to ride at South Bend and Hamilton. *Mr. Franklin* immediately wired him to the effect that he was absolutely expected to ride the Dodge City race and to stop at Chicago Branch and see Butler on his way to South Bend.

Mr. Franklin wrote Mr. Butler to try and come to an understanding with Gene, his letter in part reading as follows:

'I need hardly tell you how embarrassing Walker's attitude is coming right on the eve of Dodge City race, but recently his actions appear to be governed more by his own self interest and he quite overlooks his obligations to the Hendee Manufacturing Company, by whom he is employed and which company pays his salary and gave him the opening and opportunity of winning a lot of prize money during the last few years.

Should Walker positively refuse to ride for us at Dodge City, and prefer to go pot hunting around the meets at that time, where no doubt he figures he can win easy money as all the competition will be at Dodge City --- and in my opinion this is what he intends to do --- then you can take this letter as your authority to inform him that as he has refused to obey instructions of his employers, that his services are no longer desired by the Hendee Manufacturing company, and that the factory machines now in his hands are to be immediately returned to the factory. Wire in result of your interview with Walker.'

Butler and Walker came to a very definite understanding, with the result that Butler wired Springfield that Gene would ride the Dodge City Race and ride to win.

Despite this understanding and promise on Walker's part to ride the Dodge City race, he again had a change of mind just a few days prior to 4th July, wiring the Hendee Company that he would not be on hand at Dodge City, but intended to ride at Hamilton, Ohio, at the Eagles' meeting in that city.

The telegram quoted in the beginning of this article was the result. Mr. Franklin, and in fact the entire Indian organization, dislike very much to lose Gene Walker. They realize that he is beyond doubt one of the finest dirt track riders in the world, but this action coming on top of two very similar cases a year ago forced drastic action by the company.

Gene Walker was an employee of the Hendee Manufacturing Company and as such was subject to their orders. Therefore, to maintain discipline the Hendee Company have been forced to sacrifice the services of a very valuable man in their racing organization.

Again bearing in mind that this is the factory's version of the story, it does reveal that Charles Franklin as a manager could rule with a firm hand if required to do so. How this whole issue was eventually resolved has not been recorded. The fact is that Gene Walker did not race at Dodge City. It's also a fact that he would be back and competing for Indian again in the not too distant future.

A team of Excelsiors had entered for the 1921 Dodge race, featuring their ohc Cyclone-inspired machines. Saying there was a team of Excelsiors is not the same as saying there was an Excelsior team. The Chicago firm had supplied the riders with bikes, but that was about it. These riders paid for fuel, spare parts, and pit-crew from their own pockets. It was a last gasp effort for the ohc 'X'. It started out in a promising fashion, however. In qualifying, Waldo Korn took almost one second off the track's lap record set by his machine's inspiration, the original Cyclone back in 1915.

The tone of the event was set by 'Shrimp' Burns on his Indian machine however, for his own qualifying lap took not one but two seconds off that record and earned him a start at pole position. Once the race was underway, Burns' eight-valve promptly broke its valve gear and left him helpless at the wayside. There was only one H-D eight-valve in the race, ridden by Ralph Hepburn. This was a change of policy for Hepburn, who for the 1919 Dodge had declined the offer of an eight-valve ride saying that he preferred the staying power of a pocket-valve, and for H-D who in 1920 had only entered pocket-valvers for this race. The policy change paid off however, for Hepburn took the lead and held it for the remainder of the race. An Indian eight-valve ridden by Johnny Seymour claimed

2nd place about 10 minutes behind the winner, and after that there was a procession of Harleys. The ohc Excelsiors simply weren't in it. It's hard to say what Indian's chances might have been if Burn's eight-valve hadn't broken, or if Gene Walker had been present. But then again, that's racing.

'Shrimp' Burns' charmed life ended six weeks later, on 14th August, at a dirt track race held at Toledo, Ohio. In one of the turns his and Ray Weishaar's machines nudged each other, with the result that Burns shot across the track and disappeared through the outer rail. Weishaar went down but got up unhurt and, looking past a yawning gap of broken timbers, saw flames and a pall of smoke rising from where Burns' machine had come to rest. He rushed over to find that 'Shrimp' had head injuries and a broken neck. Burns died before reaching hospital. The irrepressible Albert Burns was hugely popular for his hard-riding style and refusal to ever quit. Tributes flowed in the press, and some reportage even openly questioned the usefulness of high speed racing to enhance manufacturers' prestige if it only cost the lives of people like Burns.

At the close of the 1921 racing season it could be seen that Harley-Davidson had been all-conquering. They won every single one of the National Championships over all distances, including the shorter races where some Indian competitors could usually be relied upon to do well. During 1921 a Harley had been the first bike in the world to win an entire race at over 100 mph, and the first motorcycle to exceed 100 mph in Britain. H-D had been the dominant force in US racing since 1915, an accomplishment they achieved at huge expense. Their products were now bestowed with a glamorous image of speed, giving dealers another pitch to make besides just homely traits of sturdiness and reliability.

Having proved their point, the four founders now felt they could retire from racing on their laurels. By this time it was perhaps being suspected that the link between racing success and street-bike sales was not as direct as had been hoped, particularly now that a global recession had depressed motorcycle sales overall. Consequently it was announced at the end of 1921 that henceforth H-D would no longer have an official factory-supported race team. The engineering resources thus spared would be directed into further improvements of the street-able models in their catalogue.

This let Indian have everything their own way for 1922. The Wigwam continued to maintain a factory team and even gained some of the laid-off H-D stars like Ralph Hepburn and Jim Davis. Despite the lack of serious challenge to spur their efforts, the performances of Indian's side-valve 'Daytona' racers continued to climb. It was Davis who soon broke some of H-D's eight-valve race records of 1921; on one such occasion in April 1922 his side-valve Indian machine covered a mile at an incredible 110.67 mph. Harleys continued to compete in the hands of privateers but, without the backing of the well-drilled money-no-object H-D race organisation, they didn't figure much in the top placings.

This account of US racing up until 1922 has necessarily been focused mainly on the National Championship events, for reasons of space. These were the prestigious events that gained national attention for the winning marques. H-D successfully spent its way into national prominence by dominating these Championship events. But the US competition scene was much more than these relatively few major races. Across America there were a host of local events organised every weekend at small-town venues, in which the exponents of particular marques staged their own private contests. Irrespective of national dominance, and depending upon machine preparation and rider skill, sometimes Harley would win but equally likely it could be Indian, or Excelsior, or Reading Standard, or Henderson or Ace or any of the other brands still around that had any pretensions to speed. Despite H-D's expensively-bought success or Indian's valiant rear-guard actions, it was simply not possible for any one manufacturer to ever claim pre-eminence across all of US motorcycling competition.

Side-Valve Genius

A recurring theme running through this period of US racing is Franklin's great success, at a comparatively modest cost, to make the Powerplus engine competitive in top-flight national racing. That this was so is evidenced by the tally of races won and records set in the US board-track racing events we've just described, which show that Franklin's side-valve race motors often bettered theoretically superior engines, including Indian's own and Harley's ohv eight-valvers. We need only look at some of the highlights of 1920-23, re-listed here, to illustrate this point.

> On a Powerplus racer at Beverly Hills, CA in April 1920, Shrimp Burns became the first rider to win a National Championship at a speed of over 100 mph in a 15-mile race.

> On 19th September 1920, Shrimp Burns set a new 10-mile dirt-track record of 7 mins 53 secs on a side-valve racer (76 mph average speed), beating Jim Davis on an eight-valve Harley.

> On 14th April 1922 Jim Davis rode a side-valve Indian at the fastest one-mile speed ever recorded on a board track, at 110.67 mph.

These achievements are remarkable, firstly because the Powerplus had not been designed as a race motor. It was a production engine, instituted for reasons of greater reliability, easier maintenance, and cheaper cost of manufacture. All fine qualities to be sure, but secondary in importance to the one thing that matters in racing, which is out-and-out speed from an engine that only needs to hold-up as far as the finish line of that one event. And secondly, from a theoretical point of view, it is surprising that Franklin could extract so much speed from a side-valve engine layout.

This culminated in a Franklin designed, side-valve Indian turning the fastest board track lap of all time. On 21st August 1926 a two-camshaft twin-carb 'Altoona' racer ridden by 'Curley' Fredericks was timed around the Rockingham New Hampshire board track at a speed of 120.3 mph. Not simply the fastest ever lap by a side-valve machine. This was the fastest board track lap for *any* type of machine.

Such a mark should ultimately have fallen to the ohv onslaught, because the world did ultimately embrace ohv engines as the 'better mouse-trap'. The foreseeable future for side-valve engines lay not in sporting motorcycles but rather in lawn-mowers, portable generators, and water pumps.[37] The reason this record did not fall is that the whole board track racing scene fell out of favour and went into decline at the onset of the Great Depression. Frederick's achievement has remained frozen in time as a mark never beaten, and a permanent testament to the genius of Charles Franklin.

Probably no one was more surprised than Franklin himself. Nobody with any knowledge of small-engine design would have expected a side-valve layout to do well in racing against overhead-valve jobs. Sure, small-engine design was still a very new and unfolding subject, however Franklin had made it his business to be familiar with every aspect.

When motorcycle manufacture first got underway in the 'noughts, scarcely anyone really knew how to make them run well. By the mid-teens however, the laws of physics had been duly applied to the general case of gasoline internal combustion engines, and the theoretical principles that were to govern their design for the next 100 years had pretty much all been worked out. A summary of the conventional wisdom applying specifically to motorcycles in Franklin's day can be found in *Motorcycles and sidecars: construction, management, repair*, first written by Victor W Page in 1914 and then updated in 1920. This book clearly sets out the rules of practice that prevailed in motorcycle construction and operation for the US industry of that era. To understand why Franklin's success in tuning side-valve motors for speed is so surprising from a theoretical perspective, it is worth reading through Page's sections on *Combustion Chamber Design*, and *Relation of Valve Placing to Engine Efficiency*.

> The endeavour is made to use a form of combustion chamber that will provide for the least heat loss, and that will not interfere with a balanced design for a cylinder.
>
> Theoretically, any cylinders having pockets at the sides to hold the valves are not as desirable as those forms in which the valves are placed directly in the head, and where the cylinder is uniform in diameter at all points.
>
> It is contended by designers favouring valve-in-the-head location that the expansion and contraction of the cylinder will be uniform because the metal is evenly distributed whereas on most patterns, having extensions in the side, the irregular placing of the metal will mean that one portion of the cylinder becomes hotter than the other part, and as it will not cool as fast, the cylinder will not expand and contract evenly at all points. The greater the amount of metal to be heated, the more the heat loss and the less efficient the engine.

The US industry up until this time had been using three main configurations for valve placement - inlet-over-exhaust, side-valve, and overhead-valve. But only the first two of these configurations were being used in production engines intended for road use by regular customers. The overhead-valve type was built only for racing, and even there it was the exception rather than the rule. Theoretically deemed the most-desirable valve placement layout, not just for its better symmetry that avoids distortion and hotspots but also for its better 'breathing', there were practical considerations that precluded its more general use.

In Britain and Europe, the side-valve layout had become the most popular for both road use and in racing. Side-valve engines were termed 'L-head' if the inlet and exhaust valves were close together in a single pocket, or 'T-head' if these two valves were wide apart in separate pockets. The old-world industries had largely adopted the lead shown by Belgian manufacturer Minerva when, around 1903, they came up with a most-useful L-head side-valve engine which owed its usefulness to a mechanically-operated inlet valve. This was a big improvement upon automatic (atmospheric-pressure operated) inlet valves which were easier to manufacture but far trickier to operate. Correct spring pressure was absolutely critical, and impossible to set up for good running at both high and low speeds.

Over in the new world Indian, Excelsior and H-D had all established themselves as mainstream manufacturers with inlet-over-exhaust designs, also known as ioe, F-head, or 'pocket-valve' engines. It was certainly known to them and their old-world counterparts that symmetrical combustion chambers with valves-in-head are theoretically better, but designers were simply too scared to place exhaust valves in an over-head position. This is because valve metallurgy was in those days so pathetic that exhaust valves, being the hottest, could easily break. By placing the exhaust valve beside the cylinder in a side pocket, they lessened the chance of engine destruction from a snapped-off valve head falling into the cylinder. To place only the inlet valve 'upstairs', hence 'inlet-over-exhaust', was a design compromise to lessen the asymmetry of a cylinder that has the valves in a pocket, by making both valves share the one pocket.

A   **B**   **C**   **D**

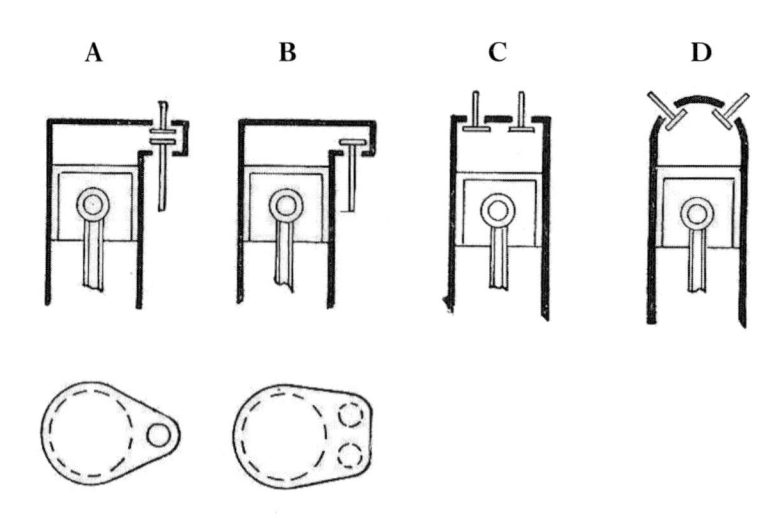

*From the dawn of motorcycling the two most popular valve dispositions for both road use and racing was inlet-over-exhaust (ioe) (**A**) or side-valve (**B**), with ioe most popular in the USA. Indian used parallel overhead-valves (**C**) in 1911 for racers only, while in 1916 H-D adopted hemi-head (hemispherical head) with splayed overhead-valves (**D**) also for racers only. Wolverhampton firm AJS prompted a wholesale shift to hemi-head overhead-valves for British road bikes after the mid-1920s. Meanwhile, Franklin's tuning successes prompted a wholesale shift to side-valve for road bikes in America. (TP)*

In these early days, engine valves were so problematic that stoppages for road-side repair or replacement were a routine facet of motorcycle ownership and operation. Valves were manufactured of ordinary carbon steels, and gave endless trouble with scaling, distortion or complete fracture of the exhaust valves in particular because these are swept by red-hot gases upon every second revolution. By the same token, it was the very softness of valve metals that made road-side repair feasible. The tool-roll provided by some makers like Ariel with every machine sold would include a hand-held device that resembled a glorified can-opener. If the machine stopped running because the exhaust valve had burned out, removing and placing it in the device and cranking its handle with mere hand pressure was sufficient to re-grind the valve edge and restore some semblance of a gas-tight seal.

In long distance track races the most common time for a valve failure was shortly after a rider had made a pit-stop. The variation in temperature caused by a piping hot engine being stopped and then re-started again one minute later was often enough to pop a valve head right off its stem. In a side-valve or ioe engine the pieces of a broken exhaust valve will just lay there in its valve-seat and guide. It won't do very much to help forward progress, but it won't wreck the engine either. Jack Marshall suffered a snapped valve head during the last lap of the 1912 TT Senior race, and it took him only 10 minutes to extract the fragments, fit a new valve, and carry on to win the race. Valves did not become components that owners could safely ignore until much later, when high-grade tungsten or nickel-chromium alloy steels had been developed.

The fact that these three main valve-placement types could co-exist in such a highly competitive industry is evidence that all three had merits as well as drawbacks. L-head side-valve disposition makes engine manufacture and operation both easier and cheaper, because fewer machining operations are needed to make the cylinder and less components are used in the valve train. For example, the close-together valves can both be actuated by a single cam, and no rockers are necessary. All parts are easily enclosed for protection and lubrication. Valve actuation is very direct, so the valve train and valve springs are simple and light. However, only this last feature is of any use for high-performance. As the great Phil Irving pointed out in his seminal *Tuning for Speed*, the valve train of a side-valve motor is 'usually much lighter than its ohv counterpart and can be screamed up to maximum revs. without danger of the valves hitting the piston or fouling each other'.

But the valve pocket area will be large if the valves are to be large for better breathing, and a large pocket means high heat loss and cylinder distortion. Flow of incoming gas is impeded by at least two or even three ninety-degree turns (for a single, or a T-manifold V-twin, respectively) from carburetor to cylinder. Raising compression in the search for more power becomes counter-productive, because reduction in combustion chamber volume only restricts cylinder breathing still further. Because of the elongated combustion chamber shape, side-valve engines of this era couldn't be run with compression ratios any higher than 5:1 or 5.5:1 without destructive 'detonation' occurring. Thirty years later, even the most highly developed side-valve engines were still limited to a compression ratio of about 6.5:1, or 7:1 at the most. Once ignited in the side pocket, the fuel mixture's flame front has to travel much further to do its work compared with a similar displacement ohv motor, so combustion is slower. Slower filling and burning means the rpm of maximum power development will be lower, at about 4,000 rpm. Long flame-travel also increases the risk of 'detonation'.

With ohv placement actuated by pushrods and rockers, large valves can be used without losing symmetry in head or cylinder. This vastly improves breathing and keeps heat loss and cylinder distortion to a minimum. Incoming mixture can fill the cylinder direct from the carburetor, with gas flow impeded only by the manifold. A bigger 'bang' and hence more power is obtained by compressing the mixture as much as possible before igniting it - this is why a higher compression ratio (calculated by dividing the volume inside the cylinder when the piston is at the top of its stroke by the volume when the piston is at the bottom of its stroke) is desirable. Overhead-valves allow for the most compact possible combustion chamber shape to be adopted, that presents the smallest possible surface area of metal to the burning mixture (reduces heat loss) and provides the greatest possible compression ratio, all with less restriction to gas flow.

The drawbacks of the overhead layout, to a manufacturer, were its extra complication and cost. In both ioe and ohv layouts, additional parts (long pushrods, pivoted rockers, etc.) are needed to transmit cam action to the valves. The greater reciprocating mass of these additional parts then demands stronger valve springs and places lower limits on revs in order to avoid valve float. For the owner, the scrubbing action imparted by rocker arms across the top of valve stems produces side loadings that accelerate valve and guide wear. The need to keep exhaust valves cool meant leaving the guides, springs and valve-train external to the engine where they are out in the slipstream. The valve-train joints and pivots then suffer from lack of lubrication and adherence of road dirt, resulting in noisy operation and more rapid wear. In the days of soft valve metals the biggest draw-back of overhead-valve placement was exhaust valve breakage, whereby the valve head dropped into the cylinder to be met by the up-coming piston. The results of that were never pretty, and always fell beyond the scope of road-side repair. It has been postulated that Oscar Hedstrom selected four valves per cylinder for Indian's 1911 eight-valve racers not so much for better breathing but for better reliability, since four small valves can shed heat better than two big ones so are less vulnerable to breakage. In addition to 'better breathing', this 'better reliability' rationale has also been put forward for Rudge's adoption of four-valve heads in the 1920s.

Inlet-over-exhaust valves were reckoned to direct incoming cool mixture straight onto the exhaust valve, reducing the valve blistering or warpage that could lead to loss of a gas-tight seal. If the exhaust valve broke then it would stay in its seat (as with a side-valve), and a removable inlet valve cage enabled access for road-side repair. On the other hand, gas flow is impeded by the fact that incoming mixture must turn sharp corners to get into and out of the cylinder. Attempts to improve gas flow by using larger valves create the same problem as side-valves in that the valve pocket must become quite large, which then increases heat loss and cylinder distortion. Inlet valves still need an external valve train, so the highly strung and temperamental nature of ohv is only halved rather than eliminated altogether as for side-valves. Inlet over exhaust is thus a compromise between the symmetry of ohv and the more livable and lovable user-friendly characteristics of side-valve.

Unfortunately, efforts to tune up and increase the performance of side-valve engines were limited by a greater propensity to detonation in this type than the other two types. By 1919 expectations about road performance had increased to the limits of what side-valve could deliver, given its elongated combustion chamber shape. Only by accepting that performance was going to be limited could their sweeter-running characteristics be retained. What was acceptable in 1909 was no longer so in 1919. With the advent of high grade alloy materials, better valve reliability was predicted to now tip the balance in favour of the improved engine breathing and less detonation prone nature of ioe and ohv combustion chambers. The side-valve engine layout was in danger of a major loss in popularity.

Such was the state of the industry in 1919, at the time when Franklin really applied himself in earnest to make Indian's racing models go seriously faster. Since the theoretical ranking of valve placement types was already well understood by 1915, it demonstrates that Indian's choice of side-valve for the 1916-on Powerplus was not for its efficiency but for its other merits of lower cost manufacture, cleanliness, and ease of maintenance in road use. That Franklin was able to tune the side-valve Powerplus to go so well in racing, which then revived the popularity of side-valve for high performance road models as well, was an unexpected bonus that changed the face of American motorcycling and further separated it from the motorcycling scene on the other side of the Atlantic.

Study of the schism that was about to develop in world motorcycling (in those days 'the world' meant British and American) necessarily begins with the 1920 Isle of Man Junior TT campaign of Wolverhampton based manufacturer AJS. The four Stevens brothers created a batch of skeletal little racers with one bold claim to sophistication - the engine was of valve-in-the-head construction with a hemispherical combustion chamber and valve actuation by pushrods and rockers.

One of these managed to win the 1920 Isle of Man Junior TT, despite the fact that all six of the AJS works entries broke down during the race. Breaking-down is what ohv engines were mainly noted for in those days, and was the main reason why none of the American manufacturers (or anyone, really) had yet seen fit to use this type of valve placement in production engines intended for normal road use.

So how did AJS manage to win the 1920 Junior? Well, when their bikes did go, they went like rockets. Of the six AJS team riders, Cyril Williams had gained such a commanding lead by the time his own engine failed that he still came first by a ten minute margin, despite having to push his stricken machine a coronary-inducing four miles to reach the finish line.

These breakdowns were caused as much by lack of AJS team discipline (needlessly dog-fighting each other when all were well to the front) as by the fragility of their new-fangled valve actuation. Blown head-cylinder joints were the main cause.

The four Stevens brothers went to work ironing the bugs out of their new creation with the result that AJS made a clean sweep of the 1921 Junior TT. One of these AJS 350cc Junior bikes was cheekily entered in the Senior race for 500cc machines, and it came first! This set a whole new trend. Across the British industry, manufacturers scrambled to develop small, efficient, reliable ohv designs of their own. Velocette then went one better than AJS by creating an overhead-cam 350cc race bike, which from 1925 they also sold as a road model for the discerning sports bike enthusiast. Rudge went down a path of four valve heads for their own efforts. The last side-valve machine to win a TT was a Sunbeam in 1922. Seeing the writing on the wall, the British factories neglected to further develop side-valve engines for greater power and efficiency, and switched their energies to engines with upstairs valves.

Not everyone was convinced that side-valve motors were dead, however. Though ohv came to dominate in racing, for street use opinion long remained divided. 'Only fit for racing, and for the mad fools who hurtle through the countryside bent on suicide' was a common view of overhead valve motorcycles, here captured in a tongue-in-cheek display of irony by a 1928 Norton catalogue. Many road-bike customers long clung to the idea that the side-valve virtues of low-speed pulling ability under heavy load and ease of maintenance and adjustment outweighed any performance advantages of the more expensive and highly-strung ohv machines. The British factories continued to find a ready market for side-valve machines well into the 1950s, including heavyweight V-twins right through the thirties. But these were utilitarian and unglamorous machines, for which the journalistic phrase 'side-valve slogger' got invented. Thanks initially to Franklin however, in the USA side-valve motorcycles retained a glamorous 'speed' image until the late 1960s.

How did Franklin work his side-valve magic? To answer this, we need to return to first-principles and brush up on some of the basics of the engine tuner's craft.

For an internal combustion engine to give of its best, the main considerations are to fill the cylinder with as much incoming charge as possible, then compress this charge as small as possible so that, when ignited, one gets the biggest possible 'bang' in a compact combustion space that loses the least amount of heat into the surrounding metal. The moment of peak energy release needs to be perfectly timed within the engine cycle for the piston and rod to impart the maximum amount of torque (twisting force) to the crankshaft.

To achieve all these considerations and thereby extract maximum performance from an engine, the three most important factors are the *shape of the combustion chamber*, the *placement of the valves*, and the *compression ratio*.

The best chamber *shape* is one in which the least amount of heat from combustion is lost into the surrounding metal, because then more of this heat is available for power development and less goes into heating up the engine itself which can lead to over-heating. Mathematically, the combustion chamber shape with the least amount of surface area of metal for heat absorption from a given chamber volume is a perfect hemisphere.

The best *placement* of the valves is therefore the one which allows the combustion chamber to most closely resemble a hemisphere. On this count, over-head valve wins because this valve placement does not require a side pocket for the valves. A side pocket increases surface area, and provides irregularities that become hot-spots which then cause power-sapping distortion from uneven heating of the metal. Side-valve and ioe are both the losers here because they both place valves in an extension of the combustion chamber into a side-pocket, which means that in cross-section the combustion chamber is shaped like a flat slab rather than a sphere.

Cylinder filling is an issue of 'volumetric efficiency', that is, the weight of gasoline-air mixture that can get into the cylinder before the valves close and compression begins. This means careful attention to 'breathing', for which the check-list includes; an inlet tract with as little surface friction and as few obstructions to gas flow as possible; the placement, size and number of valves; and the amount of lift and duration of each valve opening and closing. It is overhead-valve placement that provides the most direct passage into the cylinder and least obstruction to flow of incoming mixture and outflowing exhaust gases.

DETONATION

Detonation has come to be defined as a situation where pockets of gasoline-air mixture start combusting outside of the normal flame front as it radiates out from the spark plug. Gas pressure ideally should occur from a single explosion rising smoothly to a well-timed peak, but the effect of detonation is that multiple explosions collide. These create localized hotspots that drain energy, and shock waves that can nibble holes through pistons. Any detonations that occur ahead (time-wise) of the intended spark will meet the piston head-on while it is still moving on its way up, so will pound up crank bearings. Severe detonation can ruin a motor within seconds.

Detonation is often termed engine 'pinking' or 'knocking' owing to the characteristic tinkling sound made by the collisions between multiple flame fronts, which vibrate the entire cylinder. Strictly-speaking however, 'knocking' is not detonation but is the sound of the hammering being dealt to a big-end bearing by too-early ignition meeting a still-rising piston. Detonation is but one possible cause of 'knocking'. It can also be induced by normal ignition that is set way too advanced. In fact, a valid seat-of-the-pants method to set an engine's ignition timing is to adjust it with more and more ignition advance until road-testing reveals 'knocking', then retard the timing just a tad until the 'knocking' stops. This kind of knocking is not from detonation.

Detonation is also different from 'pre-ignition', which is an otherwise-normal flame-front caused by something else in the combustion chamber (such as a 'hot-spot', or glowing carbon build-up) igniting the mixture before the spark plug has a chance to. Detonation can however precede normal ignition if too-high compression raises the mixture to a combustible temperature before the plug can spark. This is the situation that Page describes in his 1920 treatise. He appears unaware that the phenomenon of detonation is complex and much wider in scope than merely a compression-induced form of pre-ignition. It was Sir Harry Ricardo who first realised (in about 1913) that detonation is a chemical issue intrinsic to the fuel being used, whereas pre-ignition is a physical issue related to some attribute of the cylinder.

This led to Ricardo's famous conclusion that the limit on compression is ultimately set by the type of fuel being used. For any given fuel however, careful attention to mechanical design, such as combustion chamber shape to promote turbulence of burning mixture or to keep flame travel short, and an alloy cylinder head to keep the average temperature lower, will allow an increase in the limit on compression possible with that particular fuel.

Up until the mid-1920s, standard pump fuels were desperate stuff in terms of propensity to detonate. In fact, by 1920 the burgeoning US auto industry was facing its first big fuel crisis. There were now almost ten million cars on the road. The US Geological Survey was warning that America had oil reserves sufficient to last only another 20 years at the most. Engineering advances since pioneer days had resulted in cars like the Ford Model T reaching a level of development whereby a compression ratio of 4.5 to 1 could be used, allowing production of about 20 horsepower and speeds of 40 miles per hour. Fuel scarcity during WWI led to decline in its quality however, which increased engine 'pinking' to intolerable levels. Car makers like Henry Ford were forced to reduce compression ratio to 3.8:1 to make engines run acceptably well again. This made the strategic fuel situation of the United States even worse, because lower-compression engines do less 'work' so use more fuel to cover the same road-mileage.

America was at a cross-road. Vigorous debate was going on within the fuel industry about which type of fuel:gasoline, alcohol, or benzene, or blend of these, would strategically be the better? It was during this same WWI period that Harry Ricardo first became famous, chiefly as an expert blender of fuels. He'd already shown that both alcohol and benzene had better anti-knock properties than gasoline, by virtue of their higher 'activation energy' (the amount of energy necessary to start a chemical reaction). This ranking of different fuel ingredients, or blends of ingredients, in terms of their propensity for 'detonation' led later to the octane rating system for fuels, where a higher octane fuel is one with a higher activation energy so making it less prone to detonation at a particular compression ratio.

In the US there were major supply issues for benzene and alcohol-based fuels however, which were going to take time to solve. Gasoline has a higher energy content pint-for-pint, so as an interim solution the US industry plumped for gasoline which hitherto had been a useless by-product of the kerosene industry for household lanterns. What type of engines should be developed for this fuel source? Inefficient low-compression motors that could handle the prevailing fuel quality without 'pinking', but would use up available oil reserves much faster? Or high-compression engines that would get more road miles out of these reserves, thus buying more time for petroleum exploration or to improve supplies of viable alternatives like alcohol-based fuels? If a high-compression solution were to be adopted, then something would need to be done about the terrible 'detonation' of gasoline compared to the other fuels.

The same weight of mixture can be made to do more work if it is more highly compressed before it is ignited. The reverse is also true - an engine will use more fuel to do less work if it has a low *compression ratio*. This is one reason why a disadvantage of the side-valve engine in road use is its higher fuel consumption. Another disadvantage is that, for a side-valve engine, power is a trade-off between 'compression' and 'breathing'. In a side-valve layout a reduction in compression ratio can actually result in an increase in power, if it leads to better cylinder filling. This is counter-intuitive compared with ohv motors, where breathing is largely unaffected by compression *per se*.

A bigger bang is a hotter bang, so an upper limit on compression is placed by the ability of the cylinder head material to shed the heat it absorbs and so keep the temperature of engine components within safe limits. With gases, pressure and temperature are closely linked - increase one in a closed volume, and you will also increase the other - therefore the temperature increase due to compression gets added to the temperature increase from combustion. Higher compression can be run when aluminium cylinder heads are used instead of cast-iron, because aluminium sheds heat more readily. The reason why cooler temperature safely allows higher compression is because of 'detonation', a phenomenon that plagued all the early engine designers. Management of 'detonation' in side-valve engines was the magic ingredient that set Charles Franklin apart as a motorcycle engine designer and tuner.

All else being optimal, 'detonation' is the factor that sets the uppermost limit on the amount of power that can be extracted from an engine. But in those days no one knew what caused 'detonation'. They only knew that it became worse as compression got higher.

Victor Page's 1920 book doesn't even use the term 'detonation'. His discussion of the role of compression notes only that 'more power is obtained with high compression than where the gas is not compacted to such a degree', but that 'more heat is developed with a high compression prior to ignition and it is possible to compress the gas to a point where the engine will overheat rapidly ... and the cylinder head will soon become hot enough to fire the gas without the aid of the electric spark.' This violates the fourth consideration above, that the moment of peak energy release should be perfectly timed within the engine cycle.

Page does not offer any solution to this dilemma, other than instruct readers to ensure that 'gas in the cylinder and combustion chamber is compressed to about one-fourth the volume it occupies before it is compacted'. In other words, keep compression ratio limited to a conservative but inefficient 4:1. The brevity of this discussion and the lack of options put forward is an indication that there was as yet little understanding of the whole phenomenon.

Detonation was very bad in side-valve engines up until the early 1920s because of the long path for flame travel in their elongated combustion chambers, which gave more space and more time to develop competing explosions on the shocking fuel quality then available. But then it was discovered that some measure of control over detonation could be achieved through careful side-valve mechanical design, and that this could place side-valve and overhead-valve motors together on the same rung of the performance ladder thereby confounding the combustion theorists. The leading discoverer in the automobile world was Harry Ricardo, but in the world of motorcycles it was Charles Franklin.

The sad fact for theorists was simply that ohv motors suffered their own practical disadvantages, attributable both to the fuels and the valve metals of those times. To manage detonation and thus avoid an engine being wrecked prematurely, several strategies are open to the engine's designer.

Firstly, decrease the compression ratio to reduce combustion temperature. This is like saying 'Doctor! It hurts when I do this!' and your doctor merely answers 'So don't do that'. But Ford and other US car makers had already 'not done it' in 1916 when faced with no alternative, and they weren't happy because the nation was burning more fuel as a result. For racing, low compression is hardly a solution. Tuners always pushed compression as high as they dared. Unfortunately the compression ratio of an ohv engine could scarcely be made any higher than a side-valve when run on the pump fuel then available.

Secondly, use a fuel with the highest possible activation energy ('octane rating'). In racing, fuel-blending of gasoline with either or both of benzene or alcohol, and a few other minor constituents, was very popular and was something of a 'black art' bordering upon sorcery among race-engine tuners. This was the so-called 'high-percentage' option then being considered by US auto-makers, so named because gasoline needed to be diluted as much as 30% or 40% by these other ingredients before they had much impact on 'detonation'. That was okay for racing where the fuel volumes required were small and cost counts for nothing. Alcohol had an added benefit in that it burned cooler than gasoline, so higher compression ratios were possible without 'pinking'.

As an industry-wide solution the US auto-makers hesitated to apply the 'high-percentage' option, due to the supply and logistical issues involved with these other ingredients (not so critical in Britain because they had far fewer cars and a lot of coal from which to extract benzene), and because they diluted the energy content of the gasoline. Research into oil-refining techniques to promote the presence of branched-chain hydrocarbons in gasoline was one promising line of research that did provide real gains in anti-knock properties. The industry also sought a 'low-percentage' option, of some wonder-ingredient that could be added to the gasoline in small amounts to control 'knocking' without diluting energy content or resorting to complex oil-refining processes. Over at General Motors a research group of chemists were steadily working their way down the 'carbon' column of the Periodical Table of Elements, searching for something able to bond with a short-chain organic (and hence soluble) compound that might change gasoline's activation energy for the better.

Thirdly, employ careful mechanical design to reduce detonation. In particular, develop a combustion chamber shape to promote the smoothest possible burning of fuel. Not enough was known about the chemistry of combustion or the physics of fluid dynamics for this to be calculated mathematically, however empirical knowledge generated by many painstaking experiments with different combustion chamber shapes was showing some emerging trends. It was in the areas of side-valve combustion chamber shape and cylinder breathing that Charles Franklin was particularly successful.

At the time that Franklin started out on his side-valve line of enquiry, the limits to compression on ohv engines were about 6.5:1. For example, the victorious 1921 AJS overhead-valve TT bikes used only 5.5:1, the same as for any contemporary side-valver, and only turned 4,750 rpm. This meant that their one significant edge over the side-valve competition lay in better breathing.

Meanwhile the side-valve lay-out, still equal with ohv on the issue of compression owing to the bad fuels available though always lagging behind in terms of breathing, did have a valve-train advantage that allowed it to reliably run at higher rpm for speed work. The general absence of any bending or scrubbing motions in its valve train components (in contrast to the bending of ohv rocker arms and their wiping action across the top of the valve stem) meant these parts didn't need to be as big and strong. They could be made considerably lighter without fear of breakage, and so enable higher rpm without valve 'float'. A lighter valve train allows use of a more radical cam form - a so-called 'shoe-box' cam that slams the valves open, holds them open for the longest possible time, then slams them shut again.

But side-valve and pocket-valve engines at that time had worse issues than ohv with detonation. Their elongated combustion chambers make them even more vulnerable to it - another reason why

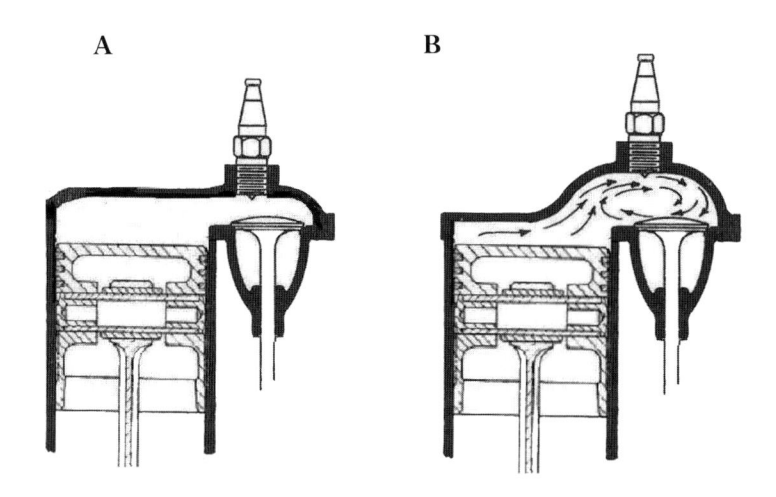

*A key to Franklin's side-valve success was an understanding of 'squish'. The standard side-valve combustion chamber (**A**) universally used up until the early 1920s was 'squish-less', in contrast with the Ricardo-type (**B**) that emerged at this time and soon became very popular. 'Squish' also benefits ioe motors, a fact Franklin had already discovered by around 1911. (TP)*

their compression ratios need to be kept lower than what one can get away with on an ohv motor. Any hot-spots due to their irregular shape could trigger pre-ignition, too.

From 1913 and culminating in the early 1920's, Harry Ricardo made a serious and rigorous study of side-valve combustion chamber shapes. He patented a design which utilized 'squish' to suppress detonation. This is widely credited with giving cheaper-to-build side-valve engines a renewed lease of life in the British auto industry of the 1920s, in the face of advancing ohv designs.

In the motorcycle world, race-engine tuners like Franklin were already onto it. Not from theory, for there were no theories of combustion back then. Everyone thought that internal combustion was a series of instantaneous explosions. Only later was it appreciated how comparatively slowly the flame front actually progresses through the densely-packed charge in a combustion chamber. This led to the understanding that it's not good to allow enough time or space for combustion to develop multiple ignition points. Even today, fluid dynamics are very difficult to express mathematically and many results seem counter-intuitive. But Oliver Godfrey has testified how, as early as 1911, painstaking trial and error by brazing metal into Indian ioe combustion chambers and smoothly contouring it had resulted in Franklin stumbling upon 'squish' principles at least a couple of years in advance of Ricardo.

Ricardo's doctrine for 'squish' in a side-valve engine is to make the combustion chamber as compact as possible, and to concentrate it over the valves and spark-plug. Rather than allow a lot of open 'attic' above the piston as was the common practice, the combustion chamber ceiling is lowered on the side opposite the valves until scarcely the thickness of a gasket (if it has one) separates the piston at top-dead-centre from the combustion chamber roof. As the piston ascends on the compression stroke, vapourised charge directly above it that might otherwise detonate outside of the advancing flame front will instead be squirted straight back into it. The resulting turbulence swirls and stirs the gases to make them burn more rapidly, more completely and more precisely (in terms of timing of maximum gas pressure). Because the combustion chamber opposite the valves will be masked off by the piston during much of the actual moments of combustion, it stays cooler and thus further reduces the tendency for detonation on that side of the chamber. The reduction of detonation and the shorter, more-precise flame-travel provided by 'squish' turbulence allows an increase in compression ratio to safely be made, and a more optimum spark timing to be employed. The result - more power.

This approach is particularly useful if the engine dimensions are 'long-stroke', that is, the piston diameter is kept small and the distance it travels in the cylinder is long. Small diameter reduces the

A   B   C

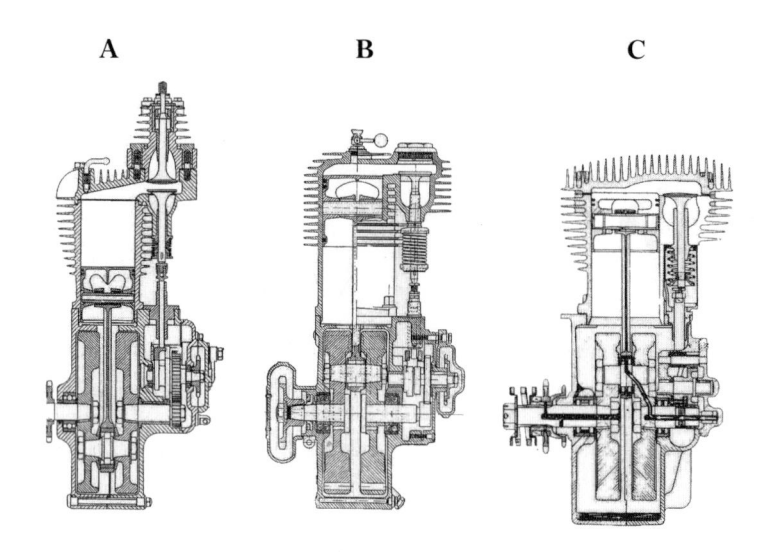

Real-live examples of motorcycle engines with (A) ioe valve disposition, (B) 'squish-less' side-valve, and (C) 'squish' side-valve. All three show just how much extra metal is used for valve pockets on the side of the cylinder, which greatly reduces thermal efficiency and increases cylinder distortion, when compared with an over-head valve disposition. But at least if a valve breaks, it will not wreck the whole engine. (TP)

distance that the flame has to travel in the combustion chamber so reduces 'pinking', and reduces the combustion chamber volume so permits a higher compression ratio without loss of breathing. The long stroke allows more time for cylinder filling and gives more efficient breathing at low revs. The downside is that a longer stroke means higher piston speed, so reduces the 'safe' rev limit of the engine.

'Squish' needs to be viewed as a general principle, because of course there are many subtle variations and interactions possible in combustion chamber size and shape, valve timings, valve-seat locations, spark-plug location, bore vs. stroke dimensions, etc., to keep an engine tuner amused while finding the best formula for an engine in a particular application. It was in this that Franklin excelled.

There are even cases in which 'squish' was known to occur by accident. One of the best-known British bike side-valve tuners of the day, Dan 'Wizard' O'Donovan, worked for Norton. The factory was at Bracebridge Street in Birmingham, but lucky Dan and underling Rex Judd were allowed to spend all their working time based over at biker-heaven, Brooklands. Batches of Norton 500cc side-valve engines were sent to them by rail freight at the rate of twenty-eight units per month. One after another they'd bolt each of these motors into the rolling chassis of O'Donovan's record-attempt bike 'Old Miracle', do 20 laps of running-in, then strip it down to check for and remedy things like high spots on the pistons, straightness of con-rod, alignment of bearings, accuracy of points and timing, etc. After re-assembly back into the bicycle, Judd then circulated the track in earnest while O'Donovan timed him. Any engine that exceeded 70 mph over a single full lap was certified as B.S. ('Brooklands Special') which, after being shipped back to Bracebridge Street for fitment into a production rolling-chassis, was sold for £68. Those that couldn't reach 70 but could exceed 65 mph were certified as B.R.S. ('Brooklands Road Special') and machines fitted with these engines were sold for £63. In their advertising copy Nortons requested customers, who might otherwise demand to know exactly which parts they needed to purchase to upgrade their B.R.S. into a B.S., to kindly not ask what was the difference in the state of tune between the two types of motors. Nortons would only say mysteriously that the difference 'is our secret, the difference is the reason for the speed, and we must ask our friends to accept the speed as the difference.'

In reality, Norton had no idea what caused the difference. It was not a result of any special parts or tuning at all, but rather because so much variation existed in the form and fit of components manufactured by the hit and miss techniques of those times. Identical looking engines could be 'good' or 'not so good' - the only way to find out was to take them outdoors and time them around a course. In his book *Flat Tank Norton*, Dr George Cohen opines that much of the difference between these engines arose from casting flaws in the one-piece cylinder/head units. If these left the combustion chamber either 'sunk' or smaller than normal, then the result could either be inadvertent 'squish', or higher compression, respectively. Harley-Davidson had similar casting issues, for at this time they were fitting different sized compression plates under the bases of J-Model cylinders. This was an effort to equilibrate accidental differences in compression ratio between front and rear cylinders, and thus get smoother running.

For his own personal race and record-attempt bikes, we don't know whether O'Donovan deliberately played around with combustion chamber shapes, or simply left them as cast by the factory and concentrated instead upon porting and cam forms followed by careful overall fit and assembly (what Americans would call 'blue-printing'). Most likely it was the latter.

Another famous British side-valve tuner was Laurence Hartley, a London Ariel dealer. His main reputation came from making Ariel ohv singles go really well in grass-track competition, however he had a soft spot for the by now 'humble' side-valve engine. His interest in side-valve tuning dated from 1932, which is later than Franklin's period, and it was something in the nature of an academic exercise. Hartley apparently felt that side-valve development in Britain had been too soon neglected by their universal switch to ohv for performance bikes in the early 1920s, leaving the side-valve format with more potential yet to be extracted. The 1926 Ariel Model A that was the particular focus of his attentions became well-known in Britain as 'The Zoomer', and its exploits are described in the 11th April 1934 issue of *MotorCycling*.

We nowadays know pretty much exactly what Laurence did to The Zoomer to make it go better, because he maintained tuning logbooks with all the details faithfully recorded. His son Peter drew upon this material when writing his book *The Ariel Story*. If only Franklin had such a son as this! Hartley Snr got The Zoomer to go 95.5 mph over a flying kilometer at Brooklands, after careful attention to porting, 'streamlined' valve guides and hotter cam profiles, and using an alcohol-based fuel of his own concoction. Apart from following the Ricardo recommendation to place the spark plug closer to the exhaust valve, he did not make any changes to the combustion chamber at all. This was a self-imposed limitation to, as much as possible, use standard parts available to customers through his Ariel dealership.

Charles Franklin certainly did explore changes to combustion chambers. In fact, chamber shape and porting had been a major focus of his tuning energies since at least 1910. Keen racing man that he was, he didn't rush to publish or patent this information but rather he kept it to himself. We don't know what became of his tuning notes, which must have been easily as copious as those of Laurence Hartley. The only available evidence of his discoveries lies in the combustion chamber shapes he evolved. These can be seen by examining the examples of Indian race engines that still survive in the hands of those people lucky enough to own them, and willing enough to open up the engine so that you can take a look. To our knowledge, there's not yet been any rigorous analysis of enough surviving examples of Indian race-bikes to piece together the full details of the evolutionary path that Franklin's side-valve combustion chambers took. This topic is deserving of an engineering monograph, but no one has yet seen fit to write it. We can see the path in general terms however, and we can apply the terminology of later tuners from the flat-head automobile world to illustrate Franklin's thinking.

Take, for example, the Austin Seven. This was one of the British light cars that benefited from Ricardo's long-stroke, small-bore philosophy and tightly concentrated 'squish' combustion chamber. It was a popular model so owners' clubs organized competition events for it, spawning an aftermarket industry of go-faster goodies. These included a host of cylinder heads, espousing different combustion-chamber philosophies. A similar thing occurred in the USA with the flat-head Ford V-eights in the rise of hot-rodding, back in the days before the 'look' of a street car stripped and modded for drag-racing degenerated into a mere fashion statement (in the way that many chopper motorcycles also did). You can still buy brand-new from any good bookstore a range of 'how-to' books written to explain the various ways of getting a lot more poke out of a flat-head Ford. Out of this side-valve tuning lore, three main principles evolved.

> First, side-valve motors have less tendency toward detonation if the spark plug is located as centrally as possible, to reduce the length of flame travel over to the far side of the piston, yet also be somewhat closer to the exhaust valve than to the inlet valve, to better scour it of combustion residues and so ensure more uniformity in the timing of the next combustion.

> Second, the cylinder head shape is critical for good *breathing* because (in contrast to ohv engines) the combustion chamber forms part of the gas route from carburetor to cylinder.

> Third, *compression* ratio needs to be as high as possible.

Since the second and third principles are trade-offs of each other, a question then arises: which of the two is more important? In the world of Austin Seven cylinder heads, two combustion chamber schools of thought are evident.

The 'compression' school follows Ricardo practice by avoiding any excess volume in the combustion chamber. There will be hardly any space above or around the back of the valves, and the roof slopes from the edge of the valves straight down to the centre of the cylinder bore. Most gas flow occurs from that half of the inlet valve circumference closest to the cylinder bore.

The 'breathing' school sacrifices compression for better gas flow. Space is provided around the full valve circumference for gas to flow up into the valve pocket area, and clearance is given for it to then flow over the top of the open valve to reach the cylinder bore. Gas taking the more direct valve-to-bore route emphasized in 'compression' engines can be further hastened by 'relieving'. This is where a shallow trench is cut in the cylinder top deck from valve-seat to a radiused cylinder edge, to further reduce restrictions to gas flow though at the expense of further lowering compression. The combustion chamber roof provides for squish, but doesn't have the same severity of angle as the Ricardo approach except near the valves, and there is greater unmasked piston area when it is at top-dead-centre.

Of the two, the Ricardo 'compression' philosophy is better suited to slower-turning production engines where mid-range power is more important. The Ariel Model A that formed the basis for Hartley's Zoomer is a case in point, concerning which *The Ariel Story* contributes this vital information:

> 'The combustion chamber followed the general principles expounded some years before by Harry Ricardo, with the combustion bowl localized over the valves and offside of the engine bore.'

In normal street-use applications, good breathing at high revs is a lesser consideration.

Franklin however was in pursuit of maximum power in engines that were going to be run at 'full chat'. He didn't care less what happened in the middle of the rev range. The pathway to maximum power for racing lay instead in a shorter stroke that, in concert with the lighter and direct-acting valve gear characteristic of a side-valve layout, would permit highest possible revs. A high-revving motor will always make more power from the same amount of crankshaft torque than a slower-revving one, but only if it can still breathe. Compression is therefore of lesser importance. The head shapes Franklin evolved were not as extreme as the Ricardo method which masked most of the piston and concentrated combustion chamber space over the valves. In Franklin's heads the chamber roof sloped gently across the whole piston, then took on a steeper slope into the valve pocket. This makes provision for some 'squish', but provides more room for better cylinder filling at high rpm. Franklin's combustion chamber designs for Indian place him firmly in the 'breathing' school of thought.

In all probability, Franklin was the very originator of the 'breathing' school of side-valve engine tuning. It can be further claimed that he was the first motorcycle designer to take side-valve engine tuning from a state of ignorance to a state of science. His only significant contemporary was Ricardo, whose own side-valve focus was on regular production automobile engines, not motorcycle race motors. From 1919 to the late-20s Franklin was the world's foremost tuner of side-valve motorcycle engines for road and track. This is shown in the chronology of his race successes and the sheer speeds his bikes were attaining. It is Franklin's side-valve race tuning methods that laid the foundation for all subsequent efforts to make side-valve motors go really quickly, from British Austin 7's to flathead Ford V-8s, and ultimately to the post-WWII KR Harleys tuned by Tom Sifton to whom it was all about *breathing*.

In the period 1919-22 when side-valve motors were still trendy and sporty in Britain, no equivalent British engines could touch the speeds that Franklin-tuned side-valve machines were producing either in America or on British home soil at Brooklands. JAP and AJS were making 1,000cc side-valve V-twins, and Martinsyde were making 1,000cc eoi (exhaust-over-inlet) V-twins, yet it was Indians and Harleys that totally dominated British Class E competition. The difference lay in combustion chamber design for enhanced breathing and swifter, crisper combustion to run higher compression without 'knock'. The Brits instead went the ohv route to knock the American big twins off their lofty perch. In moving so fast to evolve ohv motors for racing and sport, the British left the side-valve engine behind in the primordial ooze, crude and undeveloped.

Certainly there were other famous side-valve tuners around at this time. After all, side-valve machines were still winning TTs in 1922. In non-TT and second tier competition there were privateer tuners of side-valve machines whose machines continued to do well for a good many years yet. Among the factories, the delay of Norton Motors in climbing aboard the ohv band-wagon (they waited until 1922) can be explained in part by the success of 'Wizard' O'Donovan in making the Norton Model 16H go so well in racing.

But after the 1920 and 1921 performances of the AJS overhead-valve 350s in the Isle of Man Junior and Senior TT races, the mainstream British factory development engineers turned their attention to overhead valves. At the start of the 1920s decade most British side-valve motors were still direct lineal descendants of the pioneers like Triumph and Ariel, and still had crude flat-roofed combustion chambers or ran T-head configurations (the least efficient in Page's list). By the mid-1920s the makeovers of British model ranges to introduce nippy ohv sport models included significant updates to the side-valve models as well. For example new designer at Ariel, Val Page, in 1925 dumped the White and Poppe T-head powered Ariel side-valve engine and replaced it with an L-head as a side-valve variant of the new 'The Modern Motorcycle' Ariel ohv range. But neither he, nor any of the other mainstream design departments, spent long hours developing and testing side-valve combustion chambers. Instead they just adopted unquestioningly the Ricardo patented 'compression' head form as a ready-made solution, and quietly paid royalties to do so. This was not admitted publicly, rather customers were permitted to assume that these new and better side-valve engines were the result of in-house innovations. For the average Joe Blow who only wanted to ride to work each day, this was an ideal and low-cost way to provide a machine with low-down plonkability. What these bikes didn't do was go fast. Except when fettled by a very few men working privately in 6 by 8 foot garden sheds, like Laurence Hartley, who saw it as an intellectual challenge.

The difference from these other tuners is that Franklin's particular style of side-valve magic resulted in race motorcycles that went very fast indeed, and road models that were hugely influential.

This was firstly because he was not working out of a 6 by 8 foot shed. He had an entire motorcycle factory to play with, which had a dynamometer and by now was selling an entirely side-valve model range from Scout to 'half-twin' to the mighty 'full-twin' Powerplus, soon to be increased in size from 61 to 74 cubic inches. Prospective big-twin buyers could read about the race results, see that these racers' engines were essentially the same as what you could buy fitted to a road model, observe how much cleaner and quieter it was in real world riding anyhow, and wind up riding out of the nearest Indian dealer aboard either a Powerplus or (if a tad short in the in-seam) a Scout. At the close of this period 1919-1922, Franklin's side-valve machines were a major force in the battle on the race tracks of America and in British Class E track-racing, and in the motorcycle dealerships for both heavyweight and middleweight street machines. The difference lay in Franklin's discoveries and combustion chamber ideas made during this period at Indian from 1916 through to the mid-twenties.

Meanwhile, H-D's and Excelsior's own tuning efforts ignored side-valve possibilities, mainly because neither factory were manufacturing a side-valve model for road use (apart from H-D's short-lived middleweight, the Sport) and besides, for racing, ohv was the way to go, right? The Big Three were all receiving subscription copies of the British weekly magazines *The Motor Cycle* and *MotorCycling*, so knew that upstairs valves were all the rage. So for the time being they continued to refine their existing ioe production models as racers and, like the British industry, launched head-long into ohv engine development for their ultimate speedsters.

Harley already had its eight-valve motor. Excelsior developed a copy of the famous overhead-cam Cyclone engine with which to mount their fresh attack on the board-track motor-dromes in 1920. In 1915 or 1916 Gustafson converted a small-base Indian eight-valve engine into a one-off cammy experiment (see colour photo 5), in which one bevel geared drive-shaft rose from the timing side of the motor to drive the camshaft of the front cylinder head and from here a second horizontal drive-shaft ran back from the drive-side end of this cam-shaft to the rear cylinder head's camshaft. Gustafson did not persevere with this experiment however, because pushrod eight-valve and side-valve tuning was already producing such good results for Indian. Then Gustafson departed from Indian with the result that, throughout most of the 1920s in America, Franklin was going to have the side-valve speed-tuning field pretty much to himself.

Along with improved valve metallurgy, it was the advent of tetra-ethyl lead from about 1925 onwards that finally un-levelled the playing field and allowed the theoretical advantages of ohv to become actual advantages in real world riding. In December 1921 an organic form of lead soluble in gasoline was found to quell 'knock' at very low percentages of addition. Only 3 g per gallon provides an effect equivalent to 40% addition of benzene.

Reports of deaths and disabilities due to lead poisoning among ethyl-fuel, pilot production workers hit the papers during 1923-24 and resulted in a ban in most eastern-seaboard states pending a hazard assessment. The US Surgeon General's report released in 1926 concluded that the hazards of tetra-ethyl leaded fuel lay in the manufacture, with no evidence at that time of any danger from actual use in automobiles (though 'more research is needed'). With a switch-over from the dangerous open-vat to closed-vat production methods, the way was clear for Ethyl gasoline to become generally available in the US.

A satisfactory solution (from an operational point of view) to the problem of detonation in gasoline engines thus did not become routinely available in the US until 1926 at the earliest. Tetra-ethyl lead took even longer to become widely available in other places such as in Britain, even into the 1930s, due in part to the hazardous nature of handling it in bulk. Here there was much greater reliance on 'high percentage' solutions to detonation, using either benzole or alcohol as additives. Two such brands popular in Britain were 'National Benzole', and 'Cleveland Discol', respectively. Use of 'Pratts Ethyl Esso' didn't gain ground until the 1930s, nor become widespread until after WWII.

In the meantime, Charles Franklin was able to successfully tune side-valve motors for competition and have them beat theoretically superior ohv motorcycles in ways that continue to astound and amaze.

It wasn't simply that ohv development was being held back by 'detonation' and weak valves. It was also that Franklin had been taking side-valve development forward to find his own solutions to detonation. Others could have done the same but neglected to do so until, impressed by the skilful balance of power, reliability and production cost offered by Franklin's side-valve designs, there was a US industry wide switch-over from ioe to side-valve engine construction. The institutional inertia of this change over had lasting effects of which traces were still visible in the US industry in the 1960s and '70s.

The historical record shows that the two big achievements in side-valve motorcycle design in the 1920s, firstly of racing success, and secondly of high market acceptance for side-valve street bikes in the face of ohv competition, were due to the design and tuning work of Charles Bayly Franklin.

Chief Engineer

From 1920 the Indian Scout was selling as fast as the factory could make them. Which wasn't as fast as they surely would have hoped, because those in charge of forecasting demand and buying in material were again misjudging the situation in terms of both quantity and pricing. This was also a time of industrial unrest at Indian, with frequent newspaper reports during this period about workers striking for higher wages and production days being lost. Indian could've made more money than they did from the Scout during this period, nevertheless it was clear they had a sales 'hit' on their hands and this helped to tide them over through the otherwise sluggish sales period of 1922-23.

By 1920 it was obvious, and was a fact widely acknowledged by contemporaries within the industry, that Charles Franklin had succeeded in boosting Indian's fortunes by coming up with a successful street-bike. Nor was this his sole big achievement to date. He'd also re-vitalised Indian's dormant race programme, pitting it against daunting H-D opposition and so far they'd been acquitting themselves well despite being in an underdog situation.

At this time Charles Gustafson Snr resigned from the company, leaving Franklin confirmed as Hendee Mfg. Co.'s Chief Engineer.

The exact nature of Gustafson's departure from Indian is not clear. Any historical works about Indian that do touch in passing upon this event usually imply that Franklin succeeded Gustafson into the top spot by a natural progression, just as Gustafson had succeeded Hedstrom when Indian's founding engineer left in 1913.

But a closer examination of available facts makes it difficult to accept so straightforward an interpretation as this. It hinges upon the timing of his departure versus the timing of media announcements that Franklin was 'Head Engineer' at Indian.

We can't pin down the precise month or even year of Gustafson's departure, however we can say that it didn't happen any sooner than 1920. In 1918 he moved out of his Montrose Street home and went across the Connecticut River to live in Feeding Hills, beyond West Springfield. This area falls outside of the Springfield City Directory coverage so, from 1919 onwards, no further annual record of his employment details are available from this source. In 1920 however, the US Federal Census lists him still working as 'mechanical engineer' employed by Hendee Mfg. Co.

Against this, next consider that news reports from as early as March 1919 variously describe Franklin as either 'Head Engineer' or 'Chief Engineer' at Indian. Had management by now promoted him over the head of Gustafson? Tommy Butler's version, related in the 1970s, is that Gustafson had been feeling increasingly undermined now that Franklin was getting into his stride at Indian. Further, they'd had disagreements over design elements of the Scout. For example, Gustafson had not supported the idea of using spiral-cut gears for a motorcycle primary drive, but he was over ruled.

We'll never learn the full story now, yet it seems that in 1920 (or soon thereafter) Gustafson Snr finally declared 'This 'ere Wigwam ain't big enough fer the two of us' and quit. If there was any animosity then it didn't get handed down from father to son, because Charles Jnr continued working in the Indian racing department throughout the 1920s and was often seen managing the Indian entry at various race meets up and down the country.

A shake-up of managerial posts took place at this time, instituted by general manager Frank Weschler. This was done to get some tighter control of both sales and production, in order to avoid the kinds of fumbles that were making Scout production an inefficient exercise from a business point of view. Black marks appeared beside the names of sales execs Buffam and MacNaughton, while Plant Superintendent Theron L. Loose was elevated to be in overall charge of Production at Indian.

Confirmed as Chief Engineer, with both a successful road-going Indian model and a formidable race programme to his credit, Charles Franklin could at last begin to feel that he had 'made it' in America. For the first time he could regard his tenure at the Wigwam as taking on some measure of permanency. This would explain why the next significant event in his life was the arrival in Springfield of his wife Nancye and daughter Phyllis.

Manifest of Alien Passengers for the United States, New York, 15th May 1920:

Franklin, Nancye Wilson, Age 36
Female, Married. Occupation, Nil.
Read? Yes, English. Write? Yes.
Nationality, Britain. Race, Irish.
Country, Ireland. City, Dublin.
Nearest relative or friend? Father - George Kerr,
    Ashgrove Villa, Palmerston Park, Dublin.
Final destination, Springfield, Mass.
Whether have ticket to final destination? No.
By whom was passage paid? Husband.
Whether ever before in the United States? No.
Whether going to join a relative or friend? Husband -
    Charles Franklin, 53 Thomson Street, Springfield, Mass.
Length of time intended in US? Permanent.
Health, Good. Height, 5'. Complexion, Fair.
    Hair, Fair. Eyes, Blue Grey.
Place of birth, Dublin Ireland.

Franklin, Phyllis Enid, Age 11
Female, Single.
Occupation, School.
Read? Yes, English. Write? Yes.
Nationality, Britian. Race, Irish.
Country, Ireland. City, Dublin.
By whom was passage paid? Father.
Health, good. Height, 4'3'. Complexion, Fair.
    Hair, Dark. Eyes, Blue Grey.
Place of birth, Dublin, Ireland.

In coming to America at this juncture, they left behind an Ireland in turmoil. We hasten to point out that it's not our aim for this book to be a history of Home Rule in Ireland. To fully anchor Franklin's life story, from his birth in 1880 to re-unification with his family in 1920, within the watershed political events of that tumultuous period would, however, very quickly make it into one. Suffice to say that, since the 1916 Easter Rising, developments in Ireland had moved to a War of Independence which then became a Civil War between Republicans and Free-Staters. Doubtless the Franklin ladies felt that this was as good a time as any to be leaving Dublin. They boarded the trans-Atlantic liner *SS Columbia* which sailed from Glasgow on 5th May 1920, arriving at the Port of New York on 15th May.

It had suited Franklin well to have boarded with the Farks at Thompson Street, just a short stroll from the Indian factory. But now that Mrs Franklin and daughter had arrived, it was time to go and check out what else Springfield had to offer. In this matter Nancye displayed impeccable taste, for the City Directory of 1921 lists Charles Franklin now residing with his family in the Forest Park neighborhood at 111 Fort Pleasant Avenue. In 1922 he moved nearer downtown to 375 Union Street, then in 1923 moved one block nearer still to School Street where the family remained for the next 10 years. They lived at 86 School Street during 1923-24 in an eight-unit apartment building completed circa 1917, then moved next door to 92 School Street for 1925-26.

In 1927 they moved for the last time to the newly built apartment block across the street at 71 School Street - another eight-unit construction - which in 1930 was costing Franklin $65 per month in rent. This at a time when his salary at Indian was $650 per month or $7,800 per annum which is equivalent to $100,000 per annum in today's money. For comparison, the average American wage in 1930 was $1,368 per annum, equivalent to $17,500 today. No. 71 School Street is gone now, but No. 86 and No. 92 still stand. It appears that Franklin never owned property in the US - all these residences were rented. They are all located in what, during the 1920s and 30s, were considered well-to-do neighbourhoods.

Out On A High Note

Indian In British Competition 1920 - 1923

The history of motorcycle racing at Brooklands in Surrey, England, can be divided into phases according to the particular riders and marques that were ascendant at the time. The immediate post-WWI period of activity at Brooklands in the early 1920s has been labeled 'The Age of American Big Twins', because Indian and Harley-Davidson were the bikes to beat and they provided the main interest in Class E (1,000cc) races and records. Single-cylinder 500cc derivatives of the Indian twins did well in Class C at Brooklands too, and in the Isle of Man Tourist Trophy races.

The 1920s is a decade remembered very fondly by that handful of Brooklands habitués who, when those times were still within living memory, set pen to paper to record what they'd seen and done there during the track's heydays. Writers with first-hand experience like Charles Mortimer and Dr Joe Bayley recall this decade as a golden age of diversity and innovation in two-wheeled machinery, and of excellence among the riders and tuners who provided the weekly spectacle of racing and record-breaking at Britain's premier speed venue.

To this close-knit group of Brooklands insiders, there was no better place on earth. They could enjoy doing what they loved best and get paid for it, because the British motor industry now started taking Brooklands speed achievements seriously and made them an integral part of product marketing and promotion during this decade up until the Great Depression. There was no other proving ground in the British Isles where a motorcycle or automobile could be run continuously flat-out for hour after hour.

A race-winning and record-breaking industry sprang up, supported by the bonuses that manufacturers of Engine-Oil brand 'X' or Tyre brand 'Y' were willing to pay a rider/tuner to have their product associated with the establishment of some new best speed for a certain distance or new furthest distance in a certain time. There were some essential but unwritten ground rules that riders adhered to, on pain of ostracism.

> Rule One: To make the most of advertising bragging-rights, the motor-industry moguls who pledged the bonuses required that a record must stand for at least one month before there were any payouts to riders. Therefore no rider should try to beat another's record until this one-month interval had passed.

Rule Two: It was frowned-upon to break anyone else's record by more than one or two mph, because bigger margins made it too hard for the dethroned incumbent to reclaim the same record under fresh sponsorship in another month or so's time.

Rule Three: Any person who broke Rule Two, by setting the bar too uncomfortably high for others in the game, shall quietly but firmly be given to understand by these others that they no longer felt themselves bound by Rule One in connection with that person's record just set. The danger this posed of non-payment by sponsors was sufficient to make any new boy-wonder keep his enthusiasm in check.

This may make it all sound like a set-up, yet to break any record was never easy. For attempts with a duration of longer than about three hours, utmost skill and extreme care in machine preparation was a prerequisite if any machine was to last the distance and survive the pounding it would surely get from sustained high speed on that uneven concrete surface. Charles Franklin was better at machine preparation than most, yet it was right at the 3 hour mark that a fuel line broke and his 24 hour record attempt of 1914 literally went up in flames.

Long distance track races and record attempts really took their toll on riders, as well as machines. It did so in ways different from the experiences of road racers. *The Motor Cycle* journalist and early-20s TT competitor Geoffrey S. Davison wrote the following impression of competing in long-distance (200-mile or 500-mile) races at Brooklands in his book *Racing through the Century*.

> The 500-mile race must have been a shattering affair. I badly wanted to have a go at it, but I think I was lucky in not being able to touch Levis for a mount. I competed in a 200-mile race there a couple of years later and it was the most tiring event I have ever ridden in. The trouble with Brooklands - which the track fans knew well, of course, but which we road-racing 'experts' had not appreciated - was that so long as you were on the move you never changed your position. With the comfortable riding and perfect suspension of present-day machines this does not matter so much, but with high-pressure tyres, no springing and the extremely uncomfortable riding positions of 1921 models, it was agony. If all went well you travelled for two hours or so between replenishments - two solid hours with never a change of gear or easing of throttle, never a touch of brakes, never a movement of arms, legs or head. The 200-mile race was quite enough for *me* - the 500 must have been sheer murder!

The spirit of amateurism still had plenty of scope for expression at Brooklands, thanks to a racing handicap system that soon cancelled out the speed gains made possible by a professional approach and so gave everyone a near equal chance of winning. The hard core of 'track residents' could nevertheless make a living as professionals by renting small sheds and workshops within the track where they tuned their own mounts for prize money, tuned other people's bikes for payment, sought sponsors for record attempts, and used their insider's knowledge of form to try and get the better of the bookmakers who plied their trade in the Paddock on race days. Between the two world wars people like Eric Fernihough, Francis Beart, Noel Pope, 'Wizard' O'Donovan, Victor Horsman, Ted Baragwanath, 'Woolly' Worters, Bill Lacey and Bert Le Vack were members of this track community whose names became ones to conjure with.

World War One ended in November 1918, and America was straightaway able to enjoy a full season of motorcycle racing in 1919. Britain had been fighting for longer, with a much greater toll exacted upon their economy and human resources. In a nation exhausted by war, no one felt able to indulge in the frivolity of motor racing again until the 1920 season. A further calamity was the

1919 influenza epidemic which claimed millions of lives across Britain and Europe, civilian ones this time.

But once the first inter-war race season opened, a new batch of talent appeared to carve out reputations for themselves. Very few had actively raced before competition ceased in 1914 and, of those who had done, they'd been mere youngsters at the time. One such was Herbert Le Vack, then a youth in his early 20s when he competed on Triumph singles from 1909 and appeared at Brooklands on Motosacoche V-twins from 1912. Another was Freddie Dixon, who as a teenager got his own start on a 'Cleveland' motorcycle (made in Middlesborough, England) in the TT of 1912. Both would now burst onto the inter-war racing scene and go on to establish huge reputations in a range of racing formats. It was as riders and tuners of big American V-twins that both men first earned their international fame.

Le Vack had spent his war years working on aero engines. So had P.J. 'John' Wallace[38], the same P.J. who shared his reminiscences with us earlier in this book about competing in the Hundred-Mile Scratch Race at Brooklands in March 1912 when only a 16-year-old (see page 65). In 1919 Wallace applied his aero engine know-how to design an overhead-valve sports single, to be marketed as the Duzmo. He convinced the owners of a newly-idle aero engine factory to back its development, with a view to production. He hired Le Vack as 'racing engineer'. That is, Le Vack helped with detail design to improve the Duzmo's engine, and he rode it in competition events. When the 1920 TT was held, Le Vack duly entered on a Duzmo.

Interest in competing in the 1920 TT was not great, and entries were way down on the pre-war numbers. There were 32 lined up for the Junior race. The story about how AJS astounded the pundits with their nifty 350 overhead-valve machines in this race was told earlier, during the discussion of detonation (page 196).

Only 29 machines lined up for the start of the Senior race, and there were only four factory supported teams - AJS, Norton, Sunbeam, and Indian! Yes, Billy Wells had not given up on the idea of winning another TT and again sponsored his pick of riders to represent Hendee Mfg. Co. in the world's premier road race. His team contained experience in the form of Douglas Alexander (who'd visited Franklin in Springfield the previous Christmas), and Freddie Dixon from Yorkshire, both of whom had raced in pre-war TT events, plus promising newcomers Reuben Harveyson and B Houlding.

The race favourites were Sunbeam and Norton, which at the time would have seemed unusual because Sunbeam's corporate image was one of gentleman's tourer rather than racer, notwithstanding their 2nd place in 1914. Similarly Norton had won the twin-cylinder class of the inaugural 1907 event, but nothing since that. Now they both led a growing trend toward dominance by single cylinder racers - in 1920 only eight of the Senior entries were twins.

These two marques ran true to form and it was Sunbeam who picked up 1st and 3rd places, while Norton came in 2nd. Both Freddie Dixon and Reuben Harveyson were right up there amongst the leaders, but unable to secure a place. The best Indian result was the 5th place that went to Harveyson, followed in by Alexander in 6th place, while Dixon came 12th. Houlding failed to finish, and this was his one and only ever TT effort. The first three top place-getters in this race were all on side-valve 500cc singles, which still gave the best blend of speed and reliability on the valve metallurgy of those days. The Indians entered were as good a machine as any present that day. It is the nature of the TT that possessing all of speed, skill, courage and perfectionist preparation will improve your chances of winning, but will not assure it.

Bert Le Vack, on the innovative overhead-valve 3-speed all-chain-drive Duzmo, had battled to prepare the bike almost single-handedly and then battled to race it, falling once but able to continue on until the 5th lap when he was hit squarely by another bike which put him out of the race for good.

Wallace was too lightly financed to be able to afford the talents of Le Vack for very much longer, now that word had started to get around about the near-miracles he'd achieved with the virtually home-made Duzmo. In August of 1920 Le Vack was recruited by Billy Wells for Indian and added to a new post-war array of talent, which also included Freddie Dixon and Reuben Harveyson. With the resources of the UK Indian organization behind them, these men, and their London Harley-Davidson counterparts, proceeded on behalf of the USA (and by now unopposed by the Collier brothers who no longer raced) to establish a hegemony over Class E 1,000cc track races and records which the British manufacturers had little answer to. This was H-D's first factory-backed foray into competition on the other side of The Pond. The year 1914, when H-D first started to take any kind of racing at all seriously, was the same year competition had been suspended in Britain due to the outbreak of hostilities in Europe.

Indian supplied its British riders with the very latest in Franklin designed side-valve technology, in the form of single camshaft Powerplus-based 1,000cc V-twins for Class E events, and similarly Powerplus-based 500cc side-valve singles with distinctive rearward sloping cylinder for Class C track and road (meaning TT) racing. The singles in Well's stable also included at least one Hedstrom era four-valve from pre-war days - in effect a 'half-eight-valve' though it was purpose-built as a single, and was not merely made from V-twin crankcases with one cylinder aperture blanked-off.

The London Depot also still had at least one, and probably two, of the original 1911 batch of Indian big-base eight-valve ohv track racers designed by Hedstrom and Gustafson. We say 'probably two' because one of them with Reuben Harveyson on board very nearly entered Valhalla in an October 1920 incident, yet Le Vack still had one available to him in 1921 when vying with H-D for the honour of being first to go 100 mph at Brooklands.

New on the scene in 1920, Harveyson steadily made his mark as a consistent entrant on Indians right from the very first post-WWI meeting at Brooklands held on 10th April. As had been customary before the war, races under TT rules were run at Brooklands so that riders could test their mettle and their metal in the lead up to the Isle of Man TT. In the Senior One-Hour race run during the second motorcycle meeting that season, Harveyson on a single cylinder Indian placed 3rd behind Emerson and Pope. Such races were used as a barometer for the likely outcome of the 'real' TT when it took place on The Island.

Earlier that same day there had been a 2-Lap 1,000cc Solo Scratch Race for Novices in which Harveyson was an entrant, so by the race's very definition it is apparent that he had not yet been a motorcycle competitor for very long. Oliver Baldwin nabbed 1st place on a Matchless-JAP while Harveyson came in second on an eight-valve Indian, beating a Harley Sport Twin (600cc) ridden by Doug Davidson into 3rd place. Mind you, it would have been a bit embarrassing if he hadn't.

On 26th June during the third BMCRC race meeting of the season, 100-mile TT Senior and Junior races were held in which Harveyson came 3rd in the 500cc event. He was beaten by Jack Woodhouse on a MAG-engined Matchless and Jack Emerson on a flat-twin ABC, both being seasoned riders.

The Motorcycle Club (MCC) organized a meeting on 10th July in which Sydney Garrett competed on a 994cc eight-valve Indian to win the 1,000cc Solo scratch race over three laps for the O.C. Godfrey Cup. He beat Claude Temple (989cc pocket-valve H-D) into 2nd place.

The fourth BMCRC meeting of 1920 saw Harveyson get 3rd in the 500cc 10-mile Solo Scratch Race on a single-cylinder four-valve Indian, beaten by a Matchless-MAG V-twin ridden by Harry Martin and an ABC flat-twin with Jack Emerson (again).

At the race meeting held on 14th August, Bert Le Vack appeared in his first Brooklands event under the sponsorship of Billy Wells. He first rode in the 500cc Junior Open Motorcycle Handicap

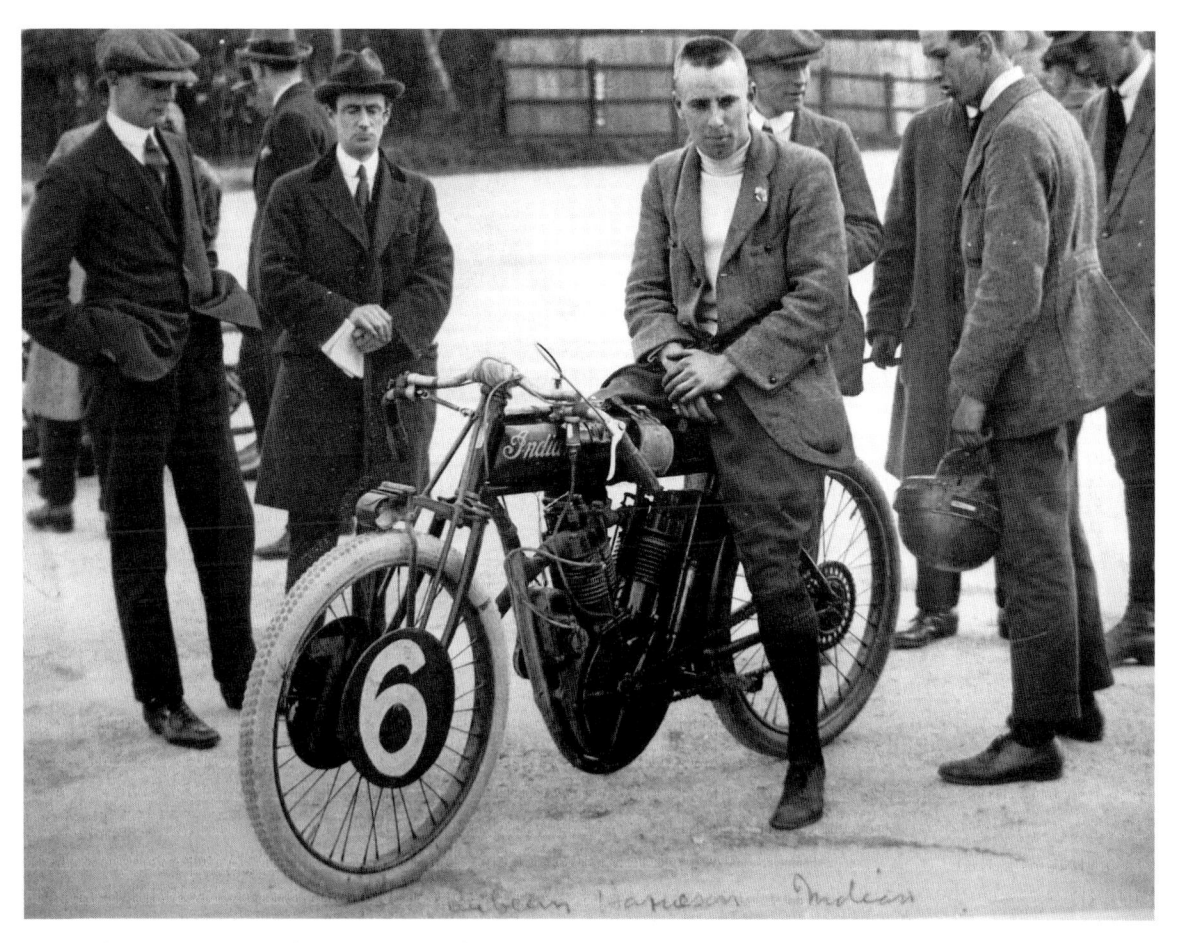

Reuben Harveyson and Indian 8-valve at Brooklands. This is the bike that shot him into orbit on 2nd October 1920. (RHC)

on the Hedstrom era Indian four-valve single used by Oliver Godfrey before the War. He did not get into the top three, beaten by a trio of Douglas flat-twins.

Le Vack then reappeared at the start line for the Senior event on a 994cc eight-valve Indian, which historian Peter Hartley states was apparently the same beast for which Charles Franklin had formerly been responsible for the care and feeding. Given a 15-second start by the handicappers over his colleague and scratchman Reuben Harveyson (998cc Indian Powerplus), Le Vack rode through the field to an easy win over Oliver Baldwin (Matchless-JAP) and Victor Gayford (744cc Zenith-JAP).

But, as he crossed the finish line, the eight-valve rewarded him in the same way as it had Franklin, by catching fire! There was an extinguisher handy so it was soon put out, however Le Vack's legs were burned. There is a photo in Morton's Motorcycle Archives of him at the Track during the race meeting immediately following his debut event, cautiously seated aboard the eight-valve (by now dubbed 'The Camel') supported by a walking stick and with both legs heavily bandaged. He was still game to get on it and ride it hard, though!

As if this were not dramatic enough, at the very next meeting on 2nd October it was Reuben Harveyson's turn to suffer the wrath of an eight-valve gone wrong. His near-death experience is vividly described by Peter Hartley in *Brooklands Bikes in the Twenties*.

Harveyson goes 'over the top'

In the 8½-mile Senior Open Handicap for machines over 500cc, a most spectacular finish highlighted the dangers of using the Long Finishing Line.

Oliver Baldwin (986 Matchless-JAP), who averaged 75.75mph from a Fork start, scraped home first just ahead of scratch man Reuben Harveyson (997 eight-valve Indian). Harveyson failed to slow down and shot up the Members' Banking into the woods beyond the track. According to the late Laurence Hartley, who witnessed the incident, Harveyson's Indian had no throttle and depended on an ignition cut-out to shut off the engine. This failed to operate, leaving him on 'full chat' at the Long Finishing Line and a sharp left-hand bend ahead where the Finishing Straight joined the Outer Circuit. Harveyson tried to lay the Indian over to negotiate the bend but, as his speed was too great, he went 'over the top'.

George Tottey, another witness to the incident, saw it all from the Paddock by the BARC clubhouse. He says that the Indian shot into the air and was practically cut in two when it hit a tree beyond the track rim. Harveyson was much luckier, for when the ambulance was called out, much to everyone's amazement he suddenly appeared out of the woods beyond the track and 'right as rain' slid down the concrete of the banking on the seat of his trousers. On arrival at the Paddock his only injuries proved to be a dislocated shoulder and torn leg muscles.

The section of track where Harveyson went 'over the top' is still intact today, thanks to the decades-long struggle by the Brooklands Society to avoid having the remaining portions of the world's first ever track purpose built especially for motor racing become completely obliterated by rapacious property developers. A visit to the Brooklands Museum site will quickly show that the Members Banking is very steep at its outer edge. After travelling up this take-off ramp under full power at a speed in excess of 80 mph, Harveyson would have gone a long way airborne before coming back down in the woods. He was lucky to live.

But what does this say about the number of big-base eight-valves that ever existed, and the quota allocated to the London Depot? Wells must have been given at least two, and possibly three, of these ultra-rare bikes. It all depends upon whether the one Franklin was riding in 1914 for his 24-hr record attempt, which caught fire, was written off or not. A second eight-valve was wheeled out that same day for him to have a go at the standing-start 10-mile record instead. So there were at least two of these bikes in Britain. If the burnt one, and the one that Harveyson bounced off a tree, both had engines able to be saved to go into another frame, then there were only ever two. If, on the other hand, both those engines had to be scrapped, then the machine Le Vack used in 1921 was the last survivor of three originally sent to England.

Harveyson had to sit out the 9th October meeting owing to the injuries he sustained from his moon-shot attempt and subsequent 'splash-down' in the woods, so it was left to Le Vack to pilot The Camel in the 1,000cc Solo Championship of 5 laps. He ran splendidly, challenged for the lead only by Eric Remington riding a NUT-JAP who was then forced to drop out with plug trouble. By the time Le Vack finished, he had set new Class E records for standing start 10-miles at 81.67 mph and flying-start 5-miles at 84.82 mph

As had been traditional since before World War One, the end of the racing season at Brooklands was again a time for record-breaking attempts as the various marques jostled for advertising and promotional copy to use at the annual Motorcycle Show at Olympia in London. Bert Le Vack duly appeared on 4th November 1920 with a Powerplus-based race machine and circulated the track, hunkered down against a large tank-top cushion, trying to remain motionless on the machine apart from subtle directional inputs, but in reality frequently flung up off the saddle by Brooklands' evil bumps, to try for a range of longer-distance records up to 3 hours and 200 miles. His preparation and determination paid off in that he recorded a new Class E highest average speed for the One Hour record of 73.69 mph, and by continuing in like fashion he was able to set new records for the other times and distances of Two and Three-Hour and 50 to 200 miles as well.

A few days later Le Vack attached a sidecar to the same machine and set new flying-start mile and kilometer records at 74 and 77 mph, then carried on to produce from the same run new speed records for the flying-start 5-mile and standing-start 10-mile distances. With the Powerplus racer still running strongly, he hung on and persevered until, by the time he'd finally had enough of being bounced around so much, he'd become the first person ever to cover more than 100 miles in 100 minutes with a side-car outfit.

Then on 23rd November Le Vack wheeled out 'The Camel' in conditions that were by now decidedly wintery, to have a go at the ultimate of high-speed marks, the Class E (1,000cc) flying-start mile and kilometer records. His best one-way runs of 95.24 mph and 94.79 mph were new British records that dislodged the pre-war effort of 91.37 mph set by Charlie Collier of the Matchless concern. To ensure the records could be internationally recognized he did two-way runs which, when averaged, left him holding the FICM flying-start mile record at a speed of 90.00 mph.

The following day Le Vack reappeared with the Powerplus sidecar outfit and repeated his efforts on the Class I records he'd just set. The Powerplus had acquired even more steam, for he maintained speeds around 70 mph while in three-wheeler guise and by the time he'd finished there were more new records for flying-start 5-miles, standing-start 10-miles, and for all the times and distances from One-Hour to Six-Hour and from 100 to 350 miles.

The result of these four months spent riding Franklin's Indians, from August to November 1920, was that Herbert Le Vack sprang from relative obscurity to establish sound credentials in the minds of the British motorcycling public as one of the fastest men on the planet.

During 1921 at the Brooklands track there occurred two of the lesser-known episodes in the famous half-century long sporting rivalry between the Harley-Davidson and Indian marques - the so-called 'Harley vs. Indian Wars'. They are lesser-known to Indianophiles because they took place on British soil rather than American, but they were no less dramatic for all that.

The link between these two stories and the hero of this book Charles Franklin, by this time absent from the track and in his 5th year of employ in the design department of the Indian factory, is of course that these feats were done on 'his' bikes - firstly the very same Indian eight-valve with which Franklin had been so intimately acquainted back in 1912-14, and secondly a track racer based on the Powerplus model which Franklin had personally developed for racing.

The first episode was the battle to be the first motorcycle and rider to officially go faster than 100 mph in Britain. Godfrey's, the motorcycle retailer in Great Portland Street established by Oliver Godfrey and Frank Applebee, had put up trophies for the first rider and machine in each of the capacity classes 250cc, 350cc, 500cc, 750cc and 1,000cc, to exceed a speed target set for each class. The target to win the Godfrey Cup in the 1,000cc class was the magical figure of 100 mph

Harley-Davidson was at this time in its corporate history very interested to stamp its brand all over two-wheeled motorsport so, in addition to the high profile race events they were contemporaneously dominating in the US, they decided to set their sights upon the Godfrey Cup in Britain. Especially for this purpose, the H-D Motor Company shipped across two of their very latest two-cam pocket-valve race machines to their London-based UK distributor Duncan Watson. These bikes and their capabilities are described in Peter Hartley's book *Brooklands Bikes in the Twenties*.

Numbered CA13 and CA14, these machines were of the short-wheelbase type popular on American board tracks. They had the usual Harley frame loop omitted, it being replaced by engine plates continuing under the engine to the rear frame tube. Their 989cc ioe V-twin engines had single Schebler racing carburetters, aluminium-alloy pistons each with two rings, and transmission by chain via a countershaft. Sydney Garrett who was to have ridden one of these machines had injured his back, so Douglas H. Davidson and Claude F. Temple were nominated to ride in the record attempts. Temple, winning a toss of a coin, decided to use machine CA14. To overcome the handling problems encountered with these machines, their engines were remounted in longer wheelbase frames more suitable for Brooklands. In that form, both achieved 104mph over the fs (flying start) kilometre in practice during the last week of April.

They were set to run under official timekeeping on Wednesday 27th April, the idea being to use the downhill approach off the Members Banking onto the Railway Straight to establish the required 100 mph speed timed over a flying-start kilometer.

They had competition, however. Bert Le Vack heard about what was going on, and became very determined that it should be he, mounted on an Indian, who would get to make history by smashing the psychologically important 100 mph barrier in Britain. He worked all of Tuesday night and most of Wednesday to ready his 1911 eight-valve, and showed up at the Track around 6.00 pm just as the wind was dropping and the Harley people were getting ready to run. Le Vack unloaded The Camel from his van and promptly turned a warm-up lap in which he unofficially went 103 mph over the requisite kilometer. Looking good. Now let's do it for real.

Only one accredited timekeeper had yet arrived. Record attempts must be timed by at least two. When both were in place and official business could begin, it was Claude Temple who was to go first. But his primary chain broke, so then Doug Davidson had a go. The run went well and his speed of 97.26mph was a new kilometer record in Britain, however it was not quite the result his sponsors were looking for.

Next it was Le Vack's turn, on the ten years older, eight-valve Indian. He bettered Davidson's effort by going 98mph, which further raised the record but still not yet enough to make history. At the end of this run his engine blew, due to a seizure in its valve gear that broke the crankcase around the timing chest. It was beyond the scope of trackside repair, so he was forced to be a spectator for whatever followed.

As it turned out, he was granted a reprieve. Davidson made further attempts, but when failing light finally halted the day's proceedings it was still Le Vack who'd been fastest and who now held the British flying kilometer record. He remained a tantalizing 2 mph short of winning the coveted trophy, however.

Le Vack had already been up the whole previous night and most of that day getting the Indian ready to run at short notice, so now he really needed to sleep. When he arose the next day, his first task was to put his Thinking Cap on and figure out why the cam-follower lever had broken like that. Racking his brains, it suddenly came to him in a flash that it must be valve metallurgy. A recent change had been made to austenitic exhaust valves. This material has a greater expansion rate in response to heat, so the clearance between valves and guides needs to be increased. This had not yet been done, so of course as soon as the motor was hard-pressed the valve train would bind up and things would start breaking. Le Vack immediately set about making the necessary changes to valve and guide clearances, and repaired the crankcase damage inflicted by his earlier miscalculation.

But Temple and Davidson were not going to sit around waiting for him. They were back out on the track that afternoon. The best of several attempts by Temple grabbed the record back from Le Vack and left him sitting on 99.86 mph Davidson was next and, before anyone knew it, he'd done 100.76 mph, sufficient to lift the Godfrey Cup and secure his place in history. He carried on circulating the track enough times to set new records over 1, 5 and 10-mile distances as well.

Bert Le Vack heard this news, and it really got him down in the dumps. The disappointment of being 'pipped' by H-D, when he'd felt himself so close, was more than he could bear. He decided there and then to give up motorcycle competition and henceforth focus upon engine development work. It was Billy Wells who took the initiative to book the timekeepers again for Friday, and who convinced Le Vack to take the repaired eight-valve back down to Brooklands and give it a really good go.

This he did, with the result that The Camel delivered a flying kilo speed of 106.5 mph. This represented an almost 6 mph margin over the best Harley effort! And it was done on an antiquated 1911 model, doing battle with the 10 years younger and very latest Harley race shop jobs! Le Vack continued riding until he'd also swiped back the 1, 5 and 10-mile records from Davidson, leaving these at 99.45, 89.50 and 86.14 mph respectively.

Indian die-hards like ourselves would say that H-D had been firmly put in their place by this stellar effort from Le Vack. Unfortunately for his and Indian's place in history, 106.5 mph is not a psychologically important speed barrier. The magical figure that everybody pays attention to is 100 mph. And it is Doug Davidson on an H-D pocket-valve track racer who gets mentioned in all the history books as setting the significant British speed achievement of that era.

It is fortunate that Bert Le Vack did not give up motorcycling altogether after this disappointment, because in 1922 he switched from Indian to designing, tuning and riding Zenith-JAP 1,000cc V-twins after landing a job in the JAP experimental department. The overhead-valve and side-valve V-twin engines he and Val Page designed for JAP became the Best of British in Class E, and were the proprietary engines of choice for Brough Superior, McEvoy, Coventry-Eagle, Zenith, and any other brands with serious road-burner pretensions. In competition, over the next four years he became acclaimed as 'the Wizard of Brooklands' and established a lasting reputation as the greatest individual rider-tuner of his generation. For his versatility across so many different capacity classes, and his virtual ownership of

Bert Le Vack and The Camel at Brooklands (Photo MMG)

the British and FIM World Speed Record books throughout the 1920s, this could even be extended to 'greatest of all time'.

Not long after this, and before the second episode in the 1921 British Harley vs. Indian Wars occurred, the 1921 Isle of Man TT race was run. We mentioned this race earlier within the context of overhead-valve engine development, particularly that of AJS who cheekily entered a 350cc Junior TT machine in the Senior TT, and won! The story bears reporting in detail, because we've saved the best news until last - Indian made a particularly strong showing in this race and came closest of any TT effort to repeating the glory of their 1911 Clean Sweep.

TT entries for 1921 had doubled since the disappointing turnout of 1920, and were back to pre-war levels at 68 machines and with twelve factory supported teams. Indian entered four riders - Bert Le Vack, Freddie Dixon, Reuben Harveyson, and N.H. Brown (who'd been in the Indian TT teams for 1913 and 1914). They again rode Powerplus-derived singles with rearward sloping cylinders, which was the only really distinguishing feature of what was otherwise, by British standards, a quite conventional and up to the minute half-litre side-valve racing machine. Except that its combustion chamber and cam profile had been developed by Charles Franklin.

Freddie Dixon took off in typical Freddie style and, again typically Freddie, was leading the race at the end of the first lap. Howard Davies on the little 350cc AJS was in second place, with Freddy Edmond on a Triumph and George Dance on a Sunbeam right behind them. By the end of the second lap Edmond had got in front and Dixon had dropped back to fourth, while Howard Davies was in second place. During the third lap George Dance fought his way into the lead and as they came past for the completion of that lap the AJS of Howard Davies was ... in second place. During the fourth lap Alec Bennett on a factory Sunbeam came up from within the ranks to lead but, lying very close behind him ... Howard Davies was in second place. In the fifth lap - incredible! Bennett was in second place, just a whisker behind ... Howard Davies, whose AJS was now in the lead! Bennett fell back even further, as did Edmond on his Triumph. A last-minute surge saw Dixon and Le Vack get in behind Davies and try to close the gap, but that was the way the race ended. The diminutive 350cc AJS of Howard Davies came home in 1st place, followed 2¼ minutes later by the two Indians of Freddie Dixon and Bert Le Vack. Brown was 15th, while Harveyson 'Did Not Finish'.

Davies freely admitted that everything went right for him in this race. The Gods simply smiled upon him as he caned his engine harder and harder. He also freely admitted that he should really have been disqualified, because his tyres, though Junior-compliant, were in fact a tad smaller than the regulation sizes allowable for the Senior race. But who would have lodged such a mean spirited protest after an achievement such as his?

It turned out that Freddie Dixon's engine had broken a valve spring after the first lap - something he was aware of during the race, but he had no choice except to ride on regardless. Although the engine held together, the mishap with the spring took about 5 mph off his top speed. There went what could have been Dixon's winning margin.

Thus the Gods smiled upon AJS and frowned upon a repeat win for Indian in the Senior TT. It was a strong showing by Indian to fill out 2nd and 3rd, and it gained them the Team Prize. Despite this, the only thing all the motorcycle history books ever written from that day forward will mention is that 1921 was the year when a 350 beat the 500s in the Senior TT. It was another bitter pill for Billy Wells to swallow, and one more thing for him to brood darkly about during his final years. But then again, that's racing for you.

The second noteworthy H-D vs. Indian episode of 1921 at Brooklands was when a motorcycle won a race over a distance of 500 miles, running flat-out to maintain 85 mph for seven hours solid.

This was a colossal achievement by both man and machine, since one has to bear in mind that, in 1921, effective motor cycle designs had only been in existence for scarcely 15 years. The man was Bert Le Vack, and the machine was a Franklin-tuned Indian Powerplus-based racer.

A 500-mile race was only ever run at the track on this one occasion, and it went down in Brooklands history as The Great 500-Mile Race. The average speeds maintained, and the percentage of entrants who actually made it to the finish line, far exceeded pre-race predictions. It was convincing proof of just how far motorcycle design had progressed, and it heralded a decade that is still referred to as the Golden Age of Motorcycling.

The idea for a race of this distance came from within the Brooklands Motor Cycle Racing Club (BMCRC) and, once mooted, everything came together quite quickly. The 1921 Isle of Man TT races had been held only three weeks earlier, so it might have been expected that everybody was still licking their wounds from this other stern test of man and machine. But there was a flood of entries across all the race's engine-size classes from 250cc to 1,000cc, so places had to be limited to 64 runners with any excess listed as reserves. All of the top British makes were represented, except AJS and Scott. Britain nevertheless lacked any Class E contenders capable of seriously challenging the dominance of the two American marques - Indian, and Harley-Davidson.

The entrants included a veritable roll-call of famous names, or soon to be famous names, spanning both the motorcycle and automobile worlds. Apart from Le Vack on an Indian there was his TT team-mate but, Brooklands rookie, Freddie Dixon, who was this time to be riding a Harley-Davidson. Kaye Don, who'd later be a leading car competitor and record breaker, had organized a ride on a Zenith Anzani V-twin. Victor Horsman, soon to gain fame as the Triumph concern's only real source of competition 'street-cred' throughout the 'twenties, was at that time still nursing hopes of a career riding for Norton. Other top Brooklands habitués included Claude Temple, Jack Woodhouse, Reuben Harveyson, Oliver Baldwin, Jack Emerson, 'Wizard' O'Donovan, the two Bashall brothers, and Frank Longman.

The massive entry of bikes would have made a fine sight despite, or even because of, the un-Godly start time of 7.00 am on 6th July when The Fork starting line was still shrouded by early-morning mist. The noise upon start-up would have made the very earth tremble. It was the biggest motorcycling spectacle to yet take place at Brooklands. Anyone still slumbering in the nearby south London suburbs, by now advancing upon once-rural Brooklands, would have found further slumber impossible.

The big Harleys and Indians were soon well out in front, as you'd expect, and tussling with each other for the lead. After the first 100 miles it was Bert Le Vack on his Daytona Powerplus who was leading the race both overall and in the 1,000cc class, lapping on average at around 81 mph. Victor Horsman's Norton headed the 500cc class at 65 mph. All bikes were being run at full throttle, so the average speeds being achieved were much higher than informed spectators had predicted. It had been assumed that riders would need to nurse their engines along carefully at speeds about 25 per cent less than maximum, and ride a clever race, in order to cover the full distance of 500 miles.

On the contrary, they just went for it. And it was not long before attrition started setting in. The Douglas of Jack Emerson came to a stop with valve-gear trouble. Kaye Don's Zenith and W. Woodhouse's Matchless were put out by plug trouble that took too long to remedy. The most dramatic incident of the earlier stages of the race was the overhead-valve JAP of Harry Reed, which lost its rear tyre at 80 mph while coming past the Vickers shed and it caused him to be thrown down the road. He got up, was attended to by the First Aid people and then continued, until the petrol tank started leaking as a result of the fall and then he had to retire.

Then a similar thing happened to Le Vack while hurtling down the Railway Straight, but in his case the tyre must have stayed on the rim for he managed to fish-tail and wobble his way to a halt without dropping the bike. He pushed his Powerplus the one and a half miles back around to his pit to get a new rear wheel fitted, by which time he'd handed Harley-riding Doug Davidson a six-lap lead. Davidson stayed in front for a good long while, however Freddie Dixon slowly but surely reeled him in until, by the 200 mile mark, it was Freddie who now had the lead. Victor Horsman was firmly in control of the 500cc class, maintaining about 63 mph when averaged to include stops made for replenishments, and steadily increasing his own lead within this class.

The Bashall brothers and Harold Bowen had entered the race as representatives of a new marque of eoi V-twins manufactured by aviation company Martinsyde, and they too had their share of dramas. Harry Bashall got hit on the shinbone by a piece of cement thrown up by another bike, and now his leg hurt like hell. He pulled over for medical attention and was urged to retire. But after a half-hour rest he got going again, hoping that Martinsyde might still be eligible for the Team Prize if he could at least finish.

This was Freddie Dixon's first-ever race at Brooklands, and he'd been troubled during practice by a tendency to slide off the back of his Harley's seat as they bounded along over the bumps together. He'd cured this tendency by gluing a sheet of emery paper onto the smooth leather of the seat. As the race progressed however, he suddenly found himself experiencing 'ass-burn'. The emery had eroded first his trousers, then his underwear, and was now about to render Fred himself even stockier than he already was! A quick pit-stop was called for, in order to urgently work out an alternative seating arrangement. It is perhaps fortunate for Fred that super-glue had not yet been invented.

There were more bikes dropping out of the running now. This race marked the appearance of the Harry Ricardo designed four-valve Triumph singles, but the example being ridden by C. Sgonina seized its engine, as did the DOT-JAP of Alan Prestwich, son of the firm's founder. Claude Temple was lying in third place when his big Harley was put out of the running by engine trouble.

The race leaders passed the halfway mark of 250 miles by 10.30 am, leaving the rest of the field right down to 250cc tiddlers strung out way behind them. When the 300-miles was reached, first was Harley's Doug Davidson who had managed to catch up with and pass team-mate Freddie Dixon. Soon after, Freddie had the front tyre of his Harley let go just as he was coming off the Members Banking - the fastest part of the entire track. He fought to keep the bike upright but then was spat off and he and the bike needed most of the length of the Railway Straight to, literally, 'scrub off speed'. Dixon tumbled in somersaults across the unyielding cement before springing to his feet again. After a brief pause to loudly tell God all about it, he cut the tangled tyre away, got the bike started again and motored it around to the pits on the bare rim to get a new front wheel fitted.

In the meantime Le Vack's Indian had closed up de Rosier-like upon race leader Doug Davidson, to snap at his heels and mount psychological pressure in an effort to have the Milwaukee machine crack-up under the strain of trying to stay in front. It must have worked, for a valve broke and this left Davidson completely and utterly side-lined. Le Vack could afford to ease off now, and nurse his engine for a bit. He fell into step with the other Ricardo Triumph being piloted by George Shemans, and they circulated together for a good few laps. Commentators later wrote about being impressed with the way that the British Triumph kept pace with the American Powerplus despite its 50% capacity deficit, however they were misled by the fact that Le Vack was ambling along at this point in the race.

Dixon, however, was riding like a demon to catch up the time he'd lost by turning somersaults. He had much ground to gain, and for the moment Le Vack looked to be an easy winner. But after passing his pit as regular as clockwork until his 182nd lap, Le Vack then failed to reappear. Where was

Bert Le Vack at the finish of the Great 500 Mile Race at Brooklands, flanked by Billy Wells and Ernie Bridgeman. (Photo MMG)

he? What had happened? Fellow Indian rider Reuben Harveyson came past, gesticulating behind him. The Indian pit-crew set off along the aerodrome road toward the Byfleet Banking in a sidecar outfit loaded with all manner of spares, wheels, tools etc to go and look for Le Vack. Meanwhile, the H-D people were getting excited because Freddie Dixon was still riding strongly.

It turned out that Le Vack had oiled up his spark plugs. He'd stopped behind the aero sheds to change them, took some time out for a quick puff of a cigarette, then push-started the bike to get going again. Soon the waiting crews at The Fork pit area caught sight of Le Vack's Powerplus, once again with a full head of steam, coming around the Byfleet banking toward them. There were only a couple of laps to go to complete the full set of 186 which he duly did and, in so doing, took the chequered flag.

Le Vack's time for the race was 7 hrs 5 mins 59.6 secs, 9½ minutes ahead of Dixon's Harley-Davidson, with the Indian of Reuben Harveyson third, giving a 1-2-3 clean-sweep to the USA in Class E and with Indian taking line honours for the race overall. Victor Horsman was fourth; his Norton was the first British machine to finish. Le Vack established new Class E records from 50 miles (at 80.93 mph) to 500 miles (at 70.42 mph) and the Class E Hour record at 80.39 mph. Freddie Dixon did not come up empty-handed. In addition to 2nd, he broke the Class E 200-mile record with an average speed for this distance of 74.31 mph. Victor Horsman enhanced his own reputation and that of Norton Motors with Class C records in a range of distances and times, at speeds in the neighbourhood of 62 mph. Winners of the smaller capacity-classes of 350cc and 250cc did exceedingly well and performed beyond expectations in terms of both speed and reliability.

Given Geoffrey Davison's earlier remarks about the excruciating agony inflicted on Brooklands riders by a race of just 200 miles, these finishers must have been Men of Steel to have even walked away from their machines without assistance. Le Vack hid his discomfort well, and was all smiles in the winner's circle. Freddie Dixon, renowned for his toughness and physical strength, was none too steady on his feet at this particular time. Mind you, he had a very good excuse because he'd hit the concrete rather hard after his front tyre came adrift at around 95 mph at the start of the Railway Straight. Reuben Harveyson had been through less drama than these other two and had simply ridden steadily throughout but, comparatively-speaking, he was a physical wreck.

The noise of this race was its downfall. The stragglers were finally brought to a halt by 6.00 pm, which was when neighbouring residents could at last hear themselves think. Their collective outrage at eleven hours of the sound and the smell of so much Castrol-R being consumed brought two major consequences. Firstly, motorcycles would henceforth be required to wear a giant silencer of a type soon dubbed the 'Brooklands Can' (as in 'tin can', not 'toilet'). Secondly, no 500-mile race would ever be run again for either motorcycle or automobile, except in two 250-mile stages run on consecutive days.

It was during the Great 500 Mile Race that Le Vack had an epiphany. It can be supposed that spending seven whole hours holding oneself motionless and steady aboard a slender two-wheeler, hurtling down what seems to be a tunnel of rapidly-unfolding but monotonous grey cement, certainly gives one a lot of time in which to think. What Le Vack thought, despite the fact that he was mounted upon an Indian propelling him toward glorious victory, was that the JAP V-twin machines entered in the same race had a lot of potential. Best of all, in the eyes of a true patriot - they were British. What they really needed to go decently well was the attentions of a talented engine man. Somebody such as himself, for example.

Sometime after the race Le Vack wrote to John Prestwich, to tactfully suggest that the best possible move JAP could ever make at this point in their history was to give the under-signed Herbert Le Vack a job as development engineer. Prestwich considered this advice dispassionately, and swiftly reached the same conclusion. An offer was made, and accepted. As would become clear from 1922 onwards, both men were to be proved absolutely correct.

But first, Le Vack completed the 1921 season riding for Indian, during which his main opposition was people like Claude Temple and Doug Davidson on Harley-Davidsons. His crowning achievement for Indian came during the end of season record-breaking period at Brooklands when he got The Camel tuned to a pitch that, on 17th November, he increased his own flying-start one-way mile and kilometer records to 102.27 mph and 107.55 mph. After a return run this raised the two-way mile average to a new record at 98.90 mph.

Billy Wells could derive much satisfaction from the performances of his riders and of Franklin's Indians during this 1921 race season in Britain. Sure, Indian had been overshadowed in the headlines by AJS at the Isle of Man and by Harley-Davidson in the matter of the Godfrey Cup. But let's look at the two keynote events of the 1921 British racing calendar. In the Great 500-Mile Race, Indian were 1st and 3rd. In the Isle of Man Senior TT, Indian was 2nd and 3rd. In record-breaking, Le Vack's aging 1911 eight-valve, The Camel, finished the year as the fastest bike in Britain, out-pacing the very latest two-cam Harleys and nothing Made in England had even come close. During 1921 Indian were certainly a dominant force in British motorcycle racing, on both road and track.

All this was to change for 1922. So much so, that the chapter covering 1922 in Peter Hartley's *Brooklands Bikes in the Twenties* is entitled 'The resurgence of the British big twin'. The man responsible? Bert Le Vack.

From now on exclusively riding JAP-powered brands, for the 1922 Isle of Man TT Le Vack rode a cammy New Imperial in the Junior race (he broke down on the 4th lap while in the lead). In the 1922 Senior race Indian had a strong entry, although the dominant marques numerically were Norton, Sunbeam and Rudge. The four Indian entrants were Freddie Dixon, Doug Alexander, C.S. Stead, and Doug Davidson - the same rider who'd been Le Vack's nemesis in the battle for the Godfrey

Cup. Obviously there were no hard feelings or irreconcilable brand loyalties between the Harley and Indian camps in Britain. Dixon also raced both Harleys and Indians during this period. Other top heavyweight class jockeys like Frank Longman and Reuben Harveyson could easily and comfortably switch between the two marques, according to circumstance.

Once the Senior race was underway, the Sunbeam of Irish-Canadian rider Alec Bennett was leading after the first lap, and he built this up to a 2½ minute lead after the second. Two-stroke Scotts took up the next two places, until the fourth lap when Freddie Dixon suddenly surged up with a lap time two minutes less than that of the race leader, to assume second place less than a minute behind Bennett. But Freddie slowed after that and was forced to retire during the final lap. Alec fulfilled the bookies' predictions by coming 1st in convincing style. His 500cc Sunbeam was destined to be the last side-valve machine to ever win a Senior TT race, although in contemporary eyes a side-valve single was still viewed as the engine layout 'most likely to win' in a long road race such as the TT.

Of the Indian entries, only Doug Davidson finished (he was 11th), and the other three were all DNF (did not finish). Nevertheless it was another solid effort by Indian, in which the results did not reflect the strength of their challenge. The main point for our tale is that, at this time in Indian's corporate history, the record shows their bikes were still right up there as contenders of the very first rank amongst the Best of British.

Le Vack had switched to riding 350cc 'tiddlers' in the Junior events at the Isle of Man from 1922 onwards, thereby adding to his own stature through sheer versatility across all engine classes. A particular fancy of his was a high-tech ohc 350 engine, from the board of JAP's main designer Val Page and installed in a bicycle made by New Imperial, which became the focus of his TT race efforts. In truth, Le Vack was always more of a track racer than a road racer. It was in track racing at Brooklands that he immediately began to cause problems for continued US hegemony in British Class E events.

This became readily apparent at the very first BMCRC meeting of 1922 at Brooklands on 8th April. In the 3-lap Solo Handicap race and the 3-lap Solo Scratch race run for 1,000cc machines that day, Claude Temple won both of these events on a Harley-Davidson, while Kaye Don similarly came 3rd in both events on a Powerplus-based Indian. But splitting up their placings, in what would otherwise have been the usual 1-2 Milwaukee-Springfield Benefit, was Herbert Le Vack who came 2nd in both races on a side-valve Zenith-JAP This was the first appearance of the new KTC engine designed by Val Page, with distinctive 'fir cone' valve caps.

In the 200-Mile sidecar race on 17th June, a similar thing happened. This race was won by Indian-mounted Doug Davidson, while Tommy Allchin claimed 3rd spot on a Harley, but again Le Vack was in 2nd place with his side-valve Zenith-JAP. His Zenith clearly had the legs on the two American machines during this race, but twice he lost ground due to tyre trouble.

It's not necessary to mention everything that Le Vack did for JAP in 1922, for much of his track time was now being devoted to cleaning up in the 350cc Class B. An important highlight is that, in 1922, Le Vack on a 1,000cc side-valve Zenith-JAP became the first rider in Britain to officially exceed 100 mph on a *British* machine. He also made history by turning the first ever of what would soon become defined as a 'Gold Star' lap at Brooklands, in which a rider must average more than 100 mph for an entire lap of the Track. This feat was achieved by Le Vack on 27th October 1922, during his attempt on the flying-start 5-mile record in Class E.

Astute readers will recall that JAP racing engines were the ones to have back in the 'noughts, when Britain still played David to the French V-twin Goliaths in the International Cup and other continental races. Charles Franklin and Noel Drury had found the JAP overhead-valve 6 hp model particularly mesmerizing. But it has to be said that during the 'teens John A. Prestwich had rested upon his laurels more than just somewhat. During these years up until 1922 the company's advertising tended to emphasise the ruggedness and unfailing reliability of their big 'V' engines, backed up by testimonials from owners in places with unspeakably hellish riding conditions like South Africa or Western Australia.

JAP advertising began to take on a new look during 1922. Competition successes, like those in the London - Exeter - London Trial, in hill-climbs, and at Brooklands, began to crop up with a new frequency that warranted mention to customers interested in a competition single or a large and fast V-twin. And then - a bold new advertisement to tell the world about 'Britain's Reply - The Super Big Twin' - an all-new ohv 986cc V-twin clearly and unashamedly conceived for anti-social purposes. This was quickly adopted by Brough Superior, Zenith, Coventry-Eagle and other bespoke chassis builders to propel top of the line sports-tourer models. And it was employed by Le Vack, Baragwanath, Brough, Temple, Wright and others to steadily erode the grip that the American Big Two held on British speed records.

The 1922 competition results in Britain clearly show that, both as a rider and as an engineer, Le Vack immediately gave JAP's speed credentials an enormous boost. He was no slouch as an engineer in his own right, as his work for Duzmo attests. In going across to JAP however, it cannot be denied that Le Vack took along with him an easy familiarity with the engine tuning secrets of the most successful side-valve motorcycle engineer on the planet - one Charles B. Franklin of Springfield, MA.

No-one to our knowledge has ever joined these particular dots before, but the question has to be asked. How much of the initial impact Le Vack made at JAP was due to the thorough grounding he'd received in V-twin side-valve and ohv tuning lore during his 14-month stint within the Franklin School of Speed? Le Vack was only just becoming known as a rider/tuner when he entered the Indian organization. By the time he left it, he was an international star and a speed sensation. Ironical to think that JAP's mighty effort to eliminate from Britain the big American V-twins, their main competitors since 1909 and literally the very reason why the street fronting the JAP factory in Tottenham was named Tariff Road[39], very probably received an unseen helping hand from Franklin, via Le Vack.

Meanwhile, Indian's own star began to wane during 1922 at Brooklands track. The resurging British twins did not have everything their own way, because the USA continued to provide stiff opposition. This was now coming mainly from H-D, however. It's not that Indians were no longer any good - in the USA they were doing extremely well - it was simply that the number of Indian entries in track competition, and the number of top riders seen aboard them, started to dwindle. The most likely explanation for this is the changing business environment in which Billy Wells was now finding things tough. Indians were quality machines and were expensively priced. In any general economic down-turn, such as the one of 1921-22, it is the high-end market segment that dries up first.

Wells' plight is illustrated by import statistics for foreign manufactured motorcycles (of which the bulk were American) entering Britain during this period. From total imports in 1920 of 4,305 machines, this fell in 1921 to 2,171 machines, and in 1922 to 976 machines. Billy Wells' business was hurting. His London dealership had been bearing the costs of maintaining a racing *équipe* on a scale similar to that of a full fledged factory. With far less fat in the operation now, Wells needed to let his business head rule his racing heart.

There was going to be one final grand roll of the dice for Indian in Britain, however. The 1923 Indian TT campaign was to be as competitive and well-resourced as anything ever mounted by Wells to date. Not only that but the hero of this book, so far absent from the action in Britain this past while, now re-enters the story directly. Charles Franklin declared his intention to come over from Springfield and oversee the 1923 Indian TT entry in person.

He must have let slip this information initially to his former racing buddies in Dublin, because the Franklin fan-zine *Irish Cyclist and Motor Cyclist* was first to pick up the story. They had this to say on 25th April 1923:

C.B. FRANKLIN COMING TO ENGLAND - MAY RIDE IN TT
Irish motor cyclists of the 'old school' will be interested to hear that C.B. Franklin, who left Ireland in 1916 to take up the position of head engineer of the Hendee Manufacturing Co. in the States, will arrive in England about May 21st to look after the Indian team in the TT race in the Isle of Man. He has himself entered as a reserve rider, and it is quite possible that he may compete in the Senior race. Those who know C.B. will mentally decrease the odds against an Indian win. We do not know yet whether he will visit Dublin before his return to the USA, but it is most probable. According to our information, Franklin has not changed in appearance since he left Ireland, and is still as young and lively as ever.'

Okay, Franklin may still have been as young as ever, but he'd got to be kidding about entering the TT as a rider. By this time he was 43 years old. There is no record of him competing at all in the USA these past seven years, or doing anything to keep himself in the peak of 'match fitness' necessary to absorb the physical hammering dealt out to any that dared cheat the TT course of time. His personal lust for speed was these days being sated by a series of large and powerful American automobiles. Franklin's entry for the TT could best be interpreted as a nostalgia trip on his part.

Irish Cyclist and Motor Cyclist, May 9, 1923:
The TT Indian, designed by C.B. Franklin for the TT Races, is 497cc - 79.29 mm x 100.81 mm.

With this particular machine (see colour photo 14), Franklin had pulled out all the stops. It was a purpose designed and built TT machine, with a new and completely different motor from the one-camshaft Powerplus-derived singles that preceded it. The obvious superficial difference is that its Powerplus Daytona side-valve cylinder was now mounted conventionally as an upright vertical cylinder, like almost every other British 500cc single. This is a visual contrast with the rearward sloping 'half-Powerplus' configuration of the 1920-22 Indian TT entries, or the small batch of 1913 Hedstrom era four-valve race engines that continued to be used with good effect in US dirt-track racing up to at least 1924 by the likes of Gene Walker.

But look closer. The difference is not merely superficial. It is total. This engine has two camshafts, compared to the single camshaft Powerplus arrangement. The cams and followers are enclosed in a rectangular box-like timing chest with a timing cover cast in bronze. There is no train of gears taking drive forward to the magneto, as was done on the Powerplus family of engines. Instead there is chain drive from a sprocket mounted on the end of the front camshaft, enclosed in a neat little chaincase. The new motor is more tunable and rev-able with its two-cam layout, and has less internal friction and more resilience to distortion due to use of self-aligning ball bearings for crankshaft and cams and use of chain drive to the magneto. Quite why bronze was chosen as the material for the timing cover is unknown, for bronze is heavier than aluminium and conducts heat less readily. Perhaps it was to make the engine look 'special', and thereby psyche out the opposition!

The whole bottom-end, particularly the timing chest layout, looks uncannily like the famous 'long-stroke' Sunbeam engine, winner of the 1920 and 1922 Senior TT races, except that the magneto sits in front of, rather than behind, the cylinder. It would not be the first time in his career, nor the last, that Franklin showed an ability to very quickly recognise a winning formula and then knock off his own version of it. Where this particular engine fits within Indian's race-bike evolutionary tree will be explained in the next section of this book.

The benefit of hindsight enabled future armchair experts to rule that side-valve race motors were by now antiquated and obsolete, and that AJS had served notice of this by winning the 1921 Senior with an ohv 350. At the time however, Davies' dream result was widely considered to be as much due to luck as to engine format. Certainly that was his own opinion. To the contemporary race observer, 1923 would have seemed an excellent year in which to copy a Sunbeam. At the time, there was no way of telling that Sunbeam's 1922 TT victory was going to be the last ever by a side-valve machine. Franklin's choice of design was still the best balance of speed and reliability for the most gruelling road race in the world. For him to select this design from amongst the confusing plethora of new concepts now bursting onto the motorcycle racing scene in the early 'twenties, and without any benefit of hindsight, does not necessarily demonstrate original thinking on his part but it does demonstrate astute thinking.

Before going across to the Island, Franklin first went down to Brooklands to see his bikes in action in the customary warm-up events run under TT regulations each year as preparation for the main event on the Isle of Man. He was photographed for *The MotorCycle* of 30th May 1923, with the caption 'Old habitues at Brooklands were glad to welcome C.B. Franklin, the Indian works manager, who is over here on a holiday, and to watch the performances of the TT Indians'. Then from the *Irish Cyclist and Motor Cyclist*, 6th June 1923 we hear of his arrival in the Isle of Man:

Franklin with Freddie Dixon and Ernie Bridgeman in England for the TT races in 1923, with a completely new design of Indian single-cylinder race bike. (EMIMA)

Freddie Dixon poses with the Indian race bike for which Franklin designed a completely new engine, and brought over for the 1923 TT race. (Photo Stilltime)

CHARLIE FRANKLIN IN THE ISLE OF MAN
Irish motorcyclists will be interested to learn that C.B. Franklin arrived in Great Britain according to plan, and reached the Isle of Man on Monday of last week. He is in charge of the Indian team in the Tourist Trophy race, and is entered as a reserve rider.

On the second day of practice (Tuesday) C.B. Franklin, who had arrived on the Island the previous day, was out on one of the new Indians which he had brought over from America - he did a lap in 50 mins. 39 secs.

So far the Isle of Man had done an excellent job year after year of laying on 'TT weather' of sunny and generally dry conditions. Not this year. On race day it rained steadily, and the Mountain section of the course was shrouded in cloud and mist. Douglas flat-twins were entered, along with the usual phalanx of British singles by Norton, Sunbeam and Triumph, plus AJS 350s trying for yet another year to make lightning strike in the same place twice. Indian had three riders entered, these being the indomitable Freddie Dixon, plus Frank Longman - an experienced Brooklands track rider though this is not necessarily a recommendation for the TT - and an unknown named R.G. Gelling. Apparently Freddie resented being made to fulfil his obligation to Billy Wells to ride an Indian in the 1923 TT, because he fancied that his chances would be better on a Douglas.

Franklin's new-for-1923 30.50 racer bottom-end layout bears an uncanny resemblance to the Sunbeam long-stroke engine, winner of the 1922 and 1920 Senior TT races. This example is a TT Replica model. (Photo by Tim Raindle)

The Douglases were reckoned to be fast but fragile, and true to reputation there were four of them in the lead at the end of the first lap. Jim Whalley's Douglas set the fastest lap speed of the day at 59.74 mph, which at almost a mile a minute over the 37 ½ mile course provides a lap time of about 38 minutes. This makes Franklin's effort of 50 minutes in practice look a bit sad, especially if it is remembered that for him the sun was out and shining, unlike on race day when competitors' chances of hitting a stray sheep along the unfenced gravel road course through Snaefell's mountain mist and rain were terrifyingly real.

But by the final lap all of these Douglases had fallen back except one, ridden by a local Manxman Tom Sheard. It was Sheard who won, while the best Indian was that of Dixon who finished in 3rd place in a time of 4hrs 7mins 2secs and average speed of 55.01 mph, giving an average lap time of 41 minutes. Indian thereby made it onto the winners' podium, which was no mean feat and a result that would make any manufacturer proud. Meanwhile, Longman and Gelling were DNF.

This was the last occasion on which Indian contested the Isle of Man Senior TT. By securing a spot in the Top Three however, the marque certainly went out with a bang rather than a whimper. In British competition from 1909 to 1923, it is worth repeating that Indian was consistently among the very first rank of manufacturers who fielded teams in the Isle of Man TT.

In track racing Indian continued to be competitive for a while longer, obtaining both wins and placings in 1923 and 1924 Brooklands events. It could not be said that they dominated, since the glory of winning was in these years shared fairly equitably with H-D and the upcoming JAP-propelled devices like Zenith and Brough. A new rider W.H.A. Turner was now the most consistent place-getter for Indian in the Class E solo events, and was most often seen piloting a Powerplus 'Daytona' racer. Indian Depot workshop foreman Ernie Bridgman's name also appears frequently as a winner or place-getter in 1,000cc sidecar events, he too powered by a 'Daytona' engine. Beyond 1923 the competition successes of Indians at Brooklands sputtered on for a while, and then fizzled out.

Irish Cyclist and Motor Cyclist, 27th June 1923:
FRANKLIN MAY VISIT IRELAND
During TT week we had a short conversation with C.B. Franklin . . . we are very pleased to hear from him that there is a possibility of his being able to pay a visit to Ireland prior to his return to America in July.

Irish Cyclist and Motor Cyclist, 4th July 1923:
C.B. Franklin returns to the United States on Saturday next, the 7th inst., and will not, we regret to say, be able to pay a visit to Ireland prior to his departure.

Franklin had no immediate family left in Ireland now. He'd been the last of Lorenzo Snr's three sons to depart for greener pastures. One could be certain he'd have simply loved to join his gentlemen chums from the Dublin & District MCC for an evening of dinner and theatre, just like in old times. But his plans did not work out that way. After migrating to America in 1916, there is no record of Franklin ever returning to the island of his birth.

And what about wife Nancye and daughter Phyllis, now aged 15? Were they homesick for dear old Dublin? Was this a good opportunity for them to drop by the old neighbourhood while Dad was at the races, to visit family and look up old friends? Apparently not, for there was an item appeared in the social column of the *Springfield Republican* dated 11 July 1923 in which it was reported that Mrs C.B. Franklin and her attractive daughter Phyllis had gone for a vacation in New York City, where they planned to stay at the Ritz-Carlton 'for some time'. It's an indication of how far Franklin had come in America by 1923 that his two ladies thought nothing of a vacation in NYC, and apparently thought nothing of staying at the Ritz. Though they must have thought at least a little something about it, if they'd contrived to let slip the fact to the society columnist of the *Republican*. One can well imagine the after work dinner-time conversation initiated by Charles: 'Great news! You can both come with me to the Isle of Man!' Response: 'You run along and play with your motorcycles, dear. It's the Ritz for us!'

Upon his return to the US, the Passenger Arrival records for Port of New York now listed Franklin among the US citizens rather than the aliens:

List of United States Citizens
SS Baltic, sailing from Liverpool July 7th 1923, arriving at the Port of New York on July 15th 1923.
Franklin, Charles B., age 42, Male, Married. Naturalized, Hampton Co. Court Springfield September 1922. Address in United States, 86 School Street Springfield Mass.

The fact that in 1922 he and his family had become naturalized as US citizens is further evidence that Franklin regarded himself as a success, and that his future was now with Indian in America.

Indian Chief

A Heavy Duty Plugger

Rapid acceptance of the Indian Scout by motorcycle customers in 1920 soon had Indian aficionados wondering 'What could be better than an Indian Scout?'

For modern day Indian motorcycle collectors the swift answer to this question is '*Two* Indian Scouts'. To our minds, it's simply not possible to ever have too many Indian motorcycles laying about the house. Back in those days however, the most glaringly obvious answer to this question was 'A *bigger* Indian Scout'. Because in America, bigger is better.

To provide the answer for which Indian dealers were now clamouring, Franklin repaired to his drawing board in 1921, and came up with a motorcycle that the press described as 'basically a big Scout'. This description is very apt when the new Indian 'Chief' is compared with a Scout, or contrasted with a Powerplus.

There were some internal factory politics about the advisability of Indian introducing another new model. The Scout itself had been regarded as a gamble, which fortunately had paid off. Tooling up for a 'bigger Scout' within two years of the Scout itself was seen as even more risky, given that an economic recession was now in full swing and US motorcycle sales were falling. Since Indian already had the Powerplus to fulfill the heavyweight workhorse role, it was thought that a new model could only hurt sales of the Scout - for which Indian's management had very high hopes. It appears that Franklin's ally Tommy Butler was one of those opposed to Indian creating a new model at this time. Where Franklin stood on the issue is not clear, however if dealers had successfully gotten to the company's management and it had consequently been decreed that there shall be a 'bigger Scout', then Franklin would probably have just shrugged and then got on with the job of giving it to them. It would not have taken him very long. Design-wise the hard decisions had already been made, back in 1919.

With hindsight, it was a good move. Indian's range leader, the Powerplus, was a worthy motorcycle, but now starting to look very much like a hold-over from an earlier generation of motorcycle technology. The sleek, cobby appearance of the Scout in dealers' line-ups served to accentuate the top-heavy, itsy-bitsy construction of the Powerplus, whose frame concept (notwithstanding its swing-arm rear suspension) and power-train layout harked back to the 'look' of circa 1910 when motorcycles had only just lost their bicycle foot-pedals.

The new Chief, on the other hand, was part of the same quantum leap forward in motorcycling as the Scout. Both were third-generation motorcycles, a new wave of holistic designs taking motorcycling beyond the motor-bicycles of the pioneer days and the second generation 'parts-bin special' motorcycles that followed them. A new era was dawning in which engineers could soon be satisfied that almost all the major assemblies of their products operated reasonably well. Even electric lighting sets were

Franklin seated upon a very early Chief, possibly even the prototype, up on the roof of the Wigwam in a photograph with the background partly whited-out by the Indian advertising department. (EMIMA)

almost cheap enough and reliable enough to justify fitment as standard items! The inroads being made toward raised standards of two-wheeler technology in the early '20s meant designers would shortly be able to turn their attention to aesthetic issues, and spend time to make their creations stylish as well as functional.

The wonderfully-named Chief boasted the same innovative features as the Scout (see colour photo 16). One Indian sales brochure described it as 'embodying the highly desirable features of the Scout in increased proportions'. There was the double-loop, full-cradle rigid rear frame with its own intrinsic structural integrity, which immediately set it apart from the 1910-style bolt-up construction of its price-point competitors over at H-D and Excelsior. It had the same semi-unit engine construction with gearbox solidly mounted to the rear of the crankcase, and the same no fuss, last you a lifetime, helical-gear primary drive. The engine had the two-cam layout of the Scout, and adopted a similar cylinder cooling fin pattern to visually give the two engines a common identity. The large capacity engine was tall however, which overall made for a long and imposing motorcycle in the finest American tradition.

Strangely, the engine capacity of the new Chief was 1,000cc (61 cu in). We say 'strangely' because the industry trend in the USA at this time was for the 61 cu in range leaders of all manufacturers to be stretched to 74 cu in. Harley ioe twins became Seventy-fours in 1921, Excelsior followed suit, and Indian had already added a 74 cu in version of its Powerplus.

It appears that Indian were initially trying to be 'British' with their approach to the new and advanced Chief, adopting a very English philosophy whereby engines that are smaller but more efficient, and can perform as well as bigger ones, are much admired. The initial market appeal of the Chief was supposed to be a victory of technical innovation over brute cubes.

This again highlights the schism between the American and British motorcycling worlds, in which market requirements and riding philosophies were quite different. British motorcyclists were 'class-conscious' about engine sizes and generally felt that the owner of, say, a 500cc machine, ought to be embarrassed if it only performed the same as a 350. To increase the engine size of a less efficient model to make it out-power a more high-tech model was seen as 'cheating'. This is how John Harrison's 1928 *The Boys Book of the Motorcycle* reacted to the debut of Harley's 74 cu in models:

Above, 'The Chief embodies the highly desirable features of the Scout in increased proportions'
Below, the Scout and the Chief were race-bred motors. Here are Scout and Chief cylinder heads, showing squish. (TP)

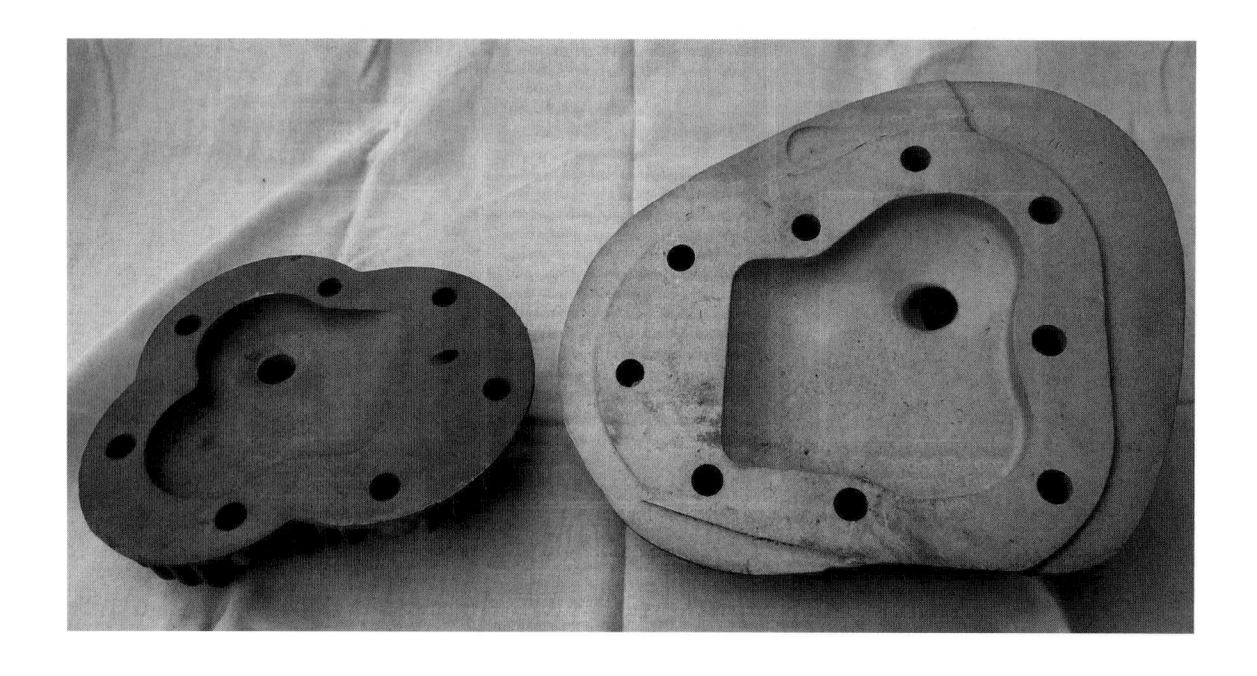

At the 1922 Olympia show the Americans committed the grave mistake of abandoning the 1,000cc limit in favour of a 1,270cc one. Rightly or wrongly the world accepted it as a gesture of defeat, for the superior speed and power of the British 1,000cc V-twin engine now seemed admitted.

To Americans there was nothing at all defeatist or shameful about this approach. Any Americans who dwelt upon the issue for more than an instant would swiftly conclude that the British capacity classes were completely arbitrary - a creation of seemingly, to American eyes, bizarre road-tax laws and tantamount to an attack on personal liberty. Since when in America - the Land of the Free - was 1,000cc ever a 'limit'?

So while it was considered 'frightfully English' to regard the engine's capacity as pre-determined and expect the designer to extract as much power from that capacity as possible, the American Way was to first decide how much power an engine needed to deliver and then select a capacity large enough to deliver it. If the result is a big lazy motor that delivers the necessary power in a relaxed, easy-going and stress-free manner, instead of a hyped-up highly-strung 'efficient' smaller engine, then so much the better. As in aviation, the engine's capacity was simply one more variable for an engine designer to play around with. If your 'Sixty-one' doesn't do it for you, get a 'Seventy-four'! It's no big deal.

Indian gave it a year to find out whether sophisticated smallness would work for them or not. Then they pinched themselves and woke up again to the fact that they are an *American* motorcycle maker. In 1923 the 1,000cc Chief was joined by a 1,200cc Big Chief model, indistinguishable except for an extra fin on the cylinder barrel.

Once the Big Chief was available it immediately became the range leader and took over the workhorse role of the Standard (ie Powerplus), which in 1924 vanished from the Indian model line-up. A report of the New York Motorcycle Show in the *Syracuse Herald* of 19th February 1923 provides us with a useful summary of contemporary perceptions about the market niche of the Indian Big Chief model.

> ***Latest Indian Model Designed for Heavy Duty.***
> A feature of the New York display was the new super-powered model, the Indian Big Chief, made by the Hendee Manufacturing Company. This is a development of the original Indian Chief, which had a cylinder displacement of 61 cubic inches. The Big Chief has an engine of 74 cubic inches displacement.
>
> It is explained that the new model was produced to fill an ever increasing demand for a machine for sidecar use. The Indian Chief formerly was used in this way, but there seemed to be need for greater power and speed. The new model embodies the same engineering principles as the original Chief, but it is designed as a heavy duty plugger, for the reason indicated.

So there you have it. The Chief is a 'heavy duty plugger'. That 0.003 per cent of the American populace who were keen observers of matters motorcycling had probably been puzzled as to why the Chief was not a 'Seventy-four' in the first place.

The phrase 'heavy duty plugger' was not the inspiration of this particular journalist, for it appears among the fine print of Indian advertisements and catalogues. For example, the British edition of the 1923 catalogue contains this quote: 'The 'Heavy Duty Plugger' is the phrase justly applied to the INDIAN CHIEF'.

The Chief became Indian's biggest seller. A general lack of model by model sales data makes this difficult to prove absolutely for the 1920s Chiefs, apart from a single factory statement that upon introduction of the 74 cu in (1,200cc) Big Chief it immediately became the top selling model in the line-up. This point is also strongly implied in the text of the same British Indian catalogue just mentioned above, which goes on to say in connection with the Chief that:

> 'In view of the fact that no alterations in design are deemed necessary for 1923 and also *on account of the large production of this model*, (our emphasis) we are able to offer it at a substantially reduced price'.

The prices were £132 for the Chief and £137 for the Big Chief, compared with £123 for the Standard (formerly Powerplus), £113 for the Scout, all electrically equipped. For the 1930s, when the series of factory leaflets entitled *Service Shots* were introduced to advise dealers about Indian technical updates, it can be directly calculated from the engine number sequences relating to announced oil-pump changes that Chiefs were out-selling Scouts by two to one.[40] It is safe to say that, from 1922 until the very end in 1953, Indian consistently sold more Chiefs than any other model.

You would never have guessed this from Indian's 1920s advertising, however. The publicity relationship between the Scout and the Chief was a strange one. The Sales Department continually 'puffed' the Scout, to the extent that one could be forgiven for thinking there were no other Indian models at all. The language chosen in advertising and in newsletters like *Indian News* either ignored the Chief completely, or inadvertently dissed it by over-praising the Scout. Here's a typical example from an Indian sales brochure of 1926:

> Those familiar with motorcycles recognize the terms 'solo' and 'side car'. It is POSSIBLE to embody in the design of one machine the necessary features to serve both purposes, but it is IMPOSSIBLE to have the one machine deliver the BEST in performance and efficiency for both solo and side car use. The added weight, strength and power, absolutely necessary for side car service is oftentimes a detriment and handicap for solo riding. While some experienced riders prefer and select the heavy machine for solo riding, the majority of motorcycle riders who are fair minded and unbiased will tell you that the INDIAN SCOUT fills every need for the most particular, exacting solo rider.
>
> That's the reason we offer the INDIAN SCOUT as the real solo machine. That's the reason we always recommend and try to persuade motorcycle riders to select the SCOUT for solo service.
>
> We can offer no better proof of the INDIAN SCOUT's efficiency as a solo vehicle than its constantly increasing popularity for police service. Police officers who have had experience with motorcycles for years have had a natural feeling that the heavy, powerful machine was necessary for the character of the work they were called upon to perform. Their experience with the SCOUT, however, has proven that its strictly solo design, its light weight and ease of handling, enable them to perform their work more efficiently and with less mental effort and strain on themselves. The INDIAN SCOUT is designed from hub to hub and top to bottom to deliver the maximum in comfort, performance and ease of control for solo work.
>
> It is also a very popular machine for side car work, but when used for this purpose its speed is limited. For those desiring the maximum in speed for side car service we endorse and recommend our BIG CHIEF model.

Yeah, right. This verbiage flowed from the pens of the Sales Dept. at a time when Indian was selling more solo Chiefs than Scouts! They'd have known very well their remarks didn't reflect reality. Scouts are good, but Chiefs are better. That's a statement which can still provoke controversy at Indian club post-run beer sessions or on Yahoo-Groups Indian message boards, but it's now 90 years since this issue ever really mattered so the debate tends to stay fairly good-natured. The bottom line here is that, on modern day club runs, Scout owners spend a lot of time down-shifting for gradients that Chief owners can romp up in top gear as if they were still on the flat. This provides a kinesthetic thrill that everybody should experience at least once before they die. If you want to call that Scout owner's bluff then half-seriously offer him your same year Chief in a straight swap for his Scout, and then see him quiver as he wrestles with his convictions.

A quantitative barometer of the favoured status accorded to the Scout, as opposed to the new Chief and subsequent models released in the 1920s, is the amount of column inches purchased for newspaper advertising. In the ad campaigns run by either the factory or its dealers in daily newspapers both major and minor, advertisements for the Scout were attractively illustrated and were quite large, at approximately 6 x 8 in. or fully one-quarter of the total area of one newspaper page. Often a smaller-sized Scout ad was run daily as a series for as many as ten consecutive days, with text changes in each subsequent ad. For other models in the 1920s range, by way of contrast, even the first advertisements which announced their debut tended to take up no more than a column inch or so, and they economized on graphics.

A further example of the Indian Chief's Cinderella status comes in the headline tag or advertising slogan bestowed upon the various Indian models offered during the 1920s. The Scouts from the start were consistently billed as *Indian Scout - the marvel of motorcycle engineering*. The Prince 350cc single introduced in late 1924 was *Indian Prince - The Personal Motor*, and then *The Solo Single*. The four-cylinder model of 1927 onwards was *The Collegiate Four*.

And the Indian Chief? What slogan did they give it? What was it billed as?

Nothing. Zip. Nada.

Just 'Indian Chief'.

Not even deserving of a slogan. As if to say, 'people already know what the Chief is for, and it isn't very glamorous'.

Business-wise it appears to make no sense for a manufacturer to promote a middleweight motorcycle in a way that denigrates its own heavyweight offering. The 'price-point' system, introduced by General Motors for automobile marketing, now extended across into motorcycling as well. Customers had become acclimated to a mind set whereby they would happily pay 25% more for a 1,000cc motorcycle than they were prepared to pay for a 750cc motorcycle, because it was 25% larger and more powerful. The fact that both machines had exactly the same number of parts and machining steps, so differed in production cost by only a very few dollars worth of extra metal, did not really enter into the selling-price equation.

It meant that, at the production volumes typical of the American Big Three between the two World Wars, the biggest profit margins were to be gained in the large classes of 1,000cc and up. Only the Japanese and the French post-WWII ever achieved production volumes of small machines in the millions required for them to stand on their own two feet and not be subsidized by sales of larger-capacity machines (for example 50 - 100cc Honda, Peugeot, Terrot, etc.). When Harley-Davidson declined to counter the 1920s success of the Indian Scout with a middleweight model of their own and instead stuck to turning out the 74 cu in J-models, it appears they had sound business reasons for being so boring and unadventurous.

It is now not really appropriate, and 90 years too late, to try and second-guess the thinking of Indian's Sales Department, or claim that they got it all wrong. We must give them some credit for knowing what they were doing. The Chief was selling quite well to that small percentage of Americans who already liked motorcycles, so perhaps it didn't really need any promotion? The type of customer who wanted a Chief was unlikely to be swayed by ads that claimed the Scout made a better solo. One test ride would show them the difference.

This argument may seem contradictory on the face it, but it is not. In boosting the Scout the sales people were aiming at customers who were not yet motorcyclists, whereas the Chief had strong appeal to those who were already motorcyclists. It was a case of two separate strategies for two separate markets.

In promoting a less profitable middleweight apparently at the expense of their steady selling heavyweight, Indian was being strategic rather than tactical. Their strategy here was to try and increase the overall size of the motorcycle market pie, dangling the Scout as user-friendly 'bait' to draw newcomers into the pastime of motorcycling. Those that came in and stayed in would surely want to trade up to a Chief before very long. In this way, the factory would get to sell two motorcycles to the same customer.

Who was right? Harley-Davidson, or Indian? The H-D company is still with us, whereas Indian is not. That outcome wasn't determined by this one issue alone, however. It needs to be acknowledged that Indian was inventive, and adopted strategies intended to make the world a better place for all motorcycles and not just their own. It is interesting to note that H-D nowadays heavily promotes its Sportster model, unfairly derided by hard-core H-D cognoscenti as a 'ladies bike', as their entry-level machine to tempt unbelievers into the Harley fold by offering the V-twin experience at a greatly discounted price. This is done in the expectation that each H-D rookie's hankering for an expensive and high profit margin Big Twin will sooner or later become overwhelming.

Meanwhile back in 1923, both Harley-Davidson and Indian were struggling. H-D's founders were disappointed that their massive investment in racing, to bestow their hitherto worthy but staid products with a new 'speed' image, hadn't resulted in the upswing in sales needed to justify their matching investment in a hugely expanded factory. After Indian's all-time high of 32,000 units in 1913, they'd maintained sales around 15,000 - 20,000 per year up to 1920 but these had now dwindled to around 7,000 in 1923. The bright spot for Indian was that Weschler's recent efficiency drive had ensured that even this level of production was nevertheless profitable.

Another bright spot was that Indian was well established in export markets. We've already discussed Britain, where Billy Wells had prospered as a result of the strength, ruggedness and sporting connotations of the sought after Indian range. We have to say 'sought after' rather than 'popular' because, to be popular, a motorcycle has to be affordable as well as top-quality.

Other steady export markets were those parts of the globe where rural road conditions were as atrocious as America's own. Places where distances were vast, good roads were few, the landscape variable, and a decent bit of power as well as stamina was needed to haul bike and rider hundreds of miles through the rough stuff. Indian motorcycles fitted the bill and were highly appreciated in Scandinavia, South America, Australia, New Zealand and South Africa. Of the major American manufacturers (all three of them), Indian was the most export oriented. In the early twenties, about half of Indian's production was earmarked for overseas markets.

USA hill-climb events began to gain a higher profile from 1922. This really suited third-string manufacturer Excelsior, who could not afford to maintain a racing effort in high-speed board track events capable of leap-frogging the engineering advances of the other two among the US Big Three. Hiring Maldwyn Jones as a hill-climb exponent, and developing some torquey and fire-breathing 80 cu in and 61 cu in contenders from their standard road-model range, Excelsior was able to claim some significant advertising bragging rights at a relatively reasonable cost.

Hill-climb events became attractive because they were held off-road on low cost 'natural' surfaces (that is, grass or dirt) that only required a set of flags or marker ropes to be staked out. Speeds were relatively slow and therefore safe, with fatalities almost unheard of. Yet the action was spectacular and crowd pleasing, with the selected gradients usually 'un-toppable' so that almost every run climaxed in a spectacular, yet low-speed, 'get-off' by the rider, with associated acrobatics by both him and his machine as they struggled for sufficient balance and traction to conquer gravity for as long as possible. The rural environments selected, and the large amount of space available in pleasantly scenic surroundings, drew crowds of up to 30,000 for a wholesome family day of sunshine and frolics in a picnicking atmosphere.

Indian was also able to gain advertising mileage from hill-climbing, coming up with side-valve Daytona powered variants for this highly specialized sport. On one of these bikes a young Floyd Clymer, at that time just beginning to make his way in the world, won the prestigious Capistrano hill-climb event of 1922 in California. Orie Steele is a name that became perennial throughout this decade as a consistent hill-climb winner who rode Indians in 37, 61 and 80 cu in classes, starting from about 1920 onwards.

In November 1923 the entire Hendee-founded company was reorganized and, to attract additional capital for product development and expansion, it went public with a share float on Wall Street. The very name was changed, from Hendee Mfg. Co. to Indian Motocycle Co. General Manager and Treasurer, Frank Weschler, was elevated to company President and awarded a bonus in the form of a shareholding worth $100,000 which, though way insufficient to give him any control of the company, nevertheless gave him voting rights on the Board of Directors.

In the same re-shuffle, Billy Wells was somehow overlooked for continued inclusion in the company's Board of Directors. He'd been a Board member since 1911 at the instigation of the man he regarded as his very best friend, George Hendee. But Hendee was no longer around. The company's very re-naming symbolized that fact, and set the seal upon it.

Re-united: Charles Franklin with wife Nancye and daughter Phyllis on an outing in Forrest Park, Springfield, January 1922. (Photo courtesy of Carol Northern)

Notwithstanding the long-running and much-ballyhooed Indian-HD rivalry, the relationship between factory executives was a chummy one. Here is Franklin on a fishing trip with his opposite number, H-D Chief Engineer and co-founder William S Harley (2nd from right). The photo was very probably taken by Billy Wells. (Photo courtesy of Carol Northern)

Overhead Valve Racer Experimentation

In American National racing from 1922, Indian dominated. But this was due to Harley-Davidson's withdrawal from direct involvement in competition. They had proved their point comprehensively yet expensively from 1919 up to the end of the 1921 season. It is therefore unsurprising and relatively unexciting that the record shows this to be a new period of Indian dominance in racing at this level. This period is nonetheless interesting in that, despite the lack of serious competition as an impetus to excel, Indian-mounted racers continued to post higher and higher speeds using Franklin-developed and tuned machinery. The side-valve Powerplus-derived Daytona race engines stood out in particular, with Jim Davis (freshly laid off by H-D and quickly recruited by Indian) achieving the fastest board-track mile to date of 110.67 mph on 14th April 1922 at Beverly Hills using just such a machine.

A new development in US racing in 1922 was the granting of National status to some 30.50 cu in ('Thirty-fifty' or 500cc) events, the idea being to reduce the danger of racing by a shift in emphasis toward smaller engine classes running at slower speeds. The Indian machines used in the unsanctioned 30.50 events held prior to this had typically been either Hedstrom era four-valve singles with rearward sloping cylinder, or similarly rearward sloping Powerplus singles similar to the type employed by the Indian teams during 1920-22 for the Isle of Man Senior TT races. Initially, this trend continued in the new sanctioned events. In 1924 there were no sanctioned 61 cu in events at all, with the National series being entirely 30.50 class races.

Given that the main impetus for the newly elevated status of 30.50 racing had been safety concerns, it is ironical that high profile fatalities continued. Ray Weishaar, an outstanding and popular rider of Harley-Davidsons, and Gene Walker, who'd returned from his earlier disgrace in 1921 to again be Indian's best dirt-track exponent, both met untimely ends during the 1924 season. Weishaar hit a bump coming out of a turn in the midst of a bunch of riders at a short-track event in Los Angeles on 13th April 1924. He struggled to regain control but he and his bike punched a hole through the boards of the outer fence and flew down a bank beyond. He sustained broken limbs and internal injuries, and succumbed to the latter several hours later. Then, on 7th June, Gene Walker died in a practice session while riding alone on a dirt-track in Pennsylvania. Apparently someone tried to cross the track and he was forced to swerve in order to avoid them, hitting a tree stump as a result. Neither of these incidents could have been prevented by the new small-engine racing format, however. There are days when it's better to simply not get out of bed in the morning. But one can miss out on an awful lot by taking that approach to life.

In 1924 H-D returned to sponsor selected riders aboard factory developed machines in the 30.50 class, and also in 1925's reinstated 61 cu in class, but at much reduced levels of expense compared to the glory days of their unstoppable 'Wrecking Crew'. They were nevertheless successful in picking up most, but not all, of the National events run in these seasons, making a clean-sweep of the 1925 61 cu in events.

Indian, on the other hand, gained 4 out of 5 of the 30.50 events.

In obtaining these results Indian's factory supported riders were greatly helped by a completely new breed of 30.50 overhead-valve engine (see colour photo 19). Technologically more advanced than the older single-cam Powerplus single or the older still Hedstrom era four-valve single, the most immediately obvious features setting this new generation Indian race motor, apart from the two earlier types, are its vertical cylinder, and overhead-valve detachable cylinder-head.

Several different valve and porting configurations are known to exist. They provide evidence that their designer was at this time trying out almost every trick in the book for overhead-valve two and four-valve formats. These *à la mode* top-end variations shared a common bottom-end assembly - the same two-camshaft bronze timing cover arrangement as that used with a side-valve Daytona cylinder on the bikes of Dixon, Longman and Gelling at the 1923 Isle of Man TT Senior race.

It appears, then, that Franklin's new race motor first came out in the summer of 1923 as a side-valve variant, of which probably only three or so were ever made. As reported earlier, the example ridden by Freddie Dixon achieved the creditable result of 3rd place in the 1923 Isle of Man senior TT race, and 1st place in the Belgian Grand Prix of the same year. The upright cylinder of the 1923 Dixon bike, which still exists in California, is in marked contrast with the rearward sloping Powerplus-single machines campaigned in the TT races of 1920-22. The Indian TT machine of 1923 can therefore be regarded as a composite of a completely new bronze-cover two-cam bottom-end and the 'old' Daytona Powerplus top-end used on the previous sloper single race motors.

With this new Sunbeam-like crankcase assembly as a foundation, Charles Franklin next began developing overhead-valve designs for it with a vengeance. At Indian during 1923 and 1924 there was a sudden flowering of experimentation and technical innovation the equal of anything happening anywhere else in the global industry. Franklin scrapped the rearward leaning Hedstrom and Gustafson descended single-cylinder designs that Indian had used so far in its racing history, in which he had personally invested so much time in their development. He now started afresh.

In terms of its significant design details, the new Indian 30.50 racing bottom-end is characterized by a two-cam timing chest layout, bronze timing cover, chain drive instead of gears to the forward mounted magneto, and use of self-aligning ball bearings for the crankshaft mains and for the two camshafts. This two-camshaft bottom-end design platform, in both single and twin cylinder guises, was destined to see out the 'twenties as the basis for all of Franklin's significant Indian racers from this point on.

It is commonly reported in Indian marque literature that the advent of self-aligning ball bearings was in 1926 on the famous 'Altoona' side-valve racer. In fact they are already in evidence on these 1924 singles, and so is the Altoona's trade-mark timing cover cast in bronze. Early, low engine number motors exist in which the boss for each camshaft bearing housing in the crankcase and timing cover was cast and machined to a much wider diameter than that required for a plain-bush arrangement, so these are not merely plain bush motors retrofitted with ball bearings later in life.

Why use a self-aligning ball bearing set-up? When compared with a roller bearing or a plain bush for main or camshaft bearings, a ball bearing reduces rotational friction by having a smaller contact area. While this gain comes at the expense of load capacity and longevity, the trade-off is worth making in a race motor because they get routinely rebuilt after every race anyhow. Self-aligning ball bearings are claimed by their inventor SKF to be 'particularly suitable for applications where considerable shaft deflections or misalignment are to be expected. Additionally, the self-aligning ball bearing has the lowest friction of all rolling bearings, which enables it to run cooler even at high speeds'.[41] These two properties are most definitely worth having in a race motor.

Franklin's new 1924 four-valve detachable heads are a quantum leap forward compared with the combustion chamber configuration of the Hedstrom era eight-valve motors, because the inlet valves are splayed apart from the exhaust valves rather than being in parallel, though they do sit at a narrower angle to each other than the later two-valve heads of 1926 on. The combustion chamber is of the 'pent-roof' type where the two inlet valves are parallel to each other, as are the two exhaust valves. Because in those days gasket materials that actually worked were limited to annealed solid copper sheet, but this could still blow, a pattern of concentric grooves was machined into the gasket face of the cylinder to provide additional grip.

The valve stems and valve springs are external to the cylinder head so are exposed to the elements, in accordance with standard practice to keep them cooler and reduce the incidence of valve or spring breakage. They were also fitted with a serrated heat washer under each valve spring to reduce the amount of heat transfer radiated up from the cylinder head. The valve rockers are supported by four steel pillars or studs screwed into the top of the cylinder head. It appears that no two motors were built the same, each being a one-off intended for a specific application or format of racing. Franklin was using these bikes as rolling laboratories of modern combustion chamber and porting design.

Some of these four-valve single cylinder 30.50 versions even had twin carburetors (see colour photo 19). This is an idea that re-surfaced again in the mid-1980s on the Yamaha SRX 600cc four-valve road single that replaced their popular SR 500 two-valve single. The outcome of innovations like this for the new Franklin-era four-valve racing singles is that they were certainly rapid. Despite the rationale that a 30.50 class would be safer for riders because they went slower, one of these four-valve Indian 30.50 singles ridden by Johnny Seymour at Daytona Beach in January 1926 showed itself capable of 112 mph. This is indeed an impressive speed, which the 60 years younger Yamaha SRX will only match if tossed off the top of a very high cliff.

H-D's own 30.50 racers at this time were relatively crude by comparison, being literally 'half-twins' whereby a 61 cu in twin had the front cylinder removed and the hole this left in the crankcase blanked off with a bolted-on flat steel plate. Though crude, they were none the less effective and they still gave Indian's special 30.50 racers a run for their money.

The overhead-valve cylinder head for the new Franklin-era Indian four-valve single-cylinder engine was cast in a manner that gave it bilateral symmetry. Cut-aways to provide clearance for push rods are present on both sides of the head, rather than just on the timing-side as is usual. The inlet port (for the single inlet port version) is centrally located. This makes them reversible. One head can be turned around to make a perfect mirror-image of another, and thus instantly provide 'front' and 'rear' cylinder heads for a 61 cu in V-twin.

Just such a 61 cu in twin appeared in Australia in early 1925, under the *aegis* of Indian agents Rhodes Motors in Melbourne, in conjunction with the Indian factory. Rhodes were fairly 'in' with the Indian factory because during the period from the early 'teens through to the late 'twenties they sold quite a lot of motorcycles for Indian in Australia. Their degree of 'pull' was such that anything Rhodes asked for from the factory, they stood a very good chance of getting. Testament to this is the fact that they were allocated two of the 1915 batch of small-base eight-valve racers (Nos. 73H and 76H). Australia was important to Indian in the 'teens and 'twenties, both as a significant export market and as a hot-bed of Indian racing and record breaking activity. This aspect of the Indian story has been under-reported in the marque histories published to date.

Paul Anderson seated upon the eight-valve Indian A61-5, with Rhodes Motors staff at Sellicks Beach in South Australia. The 30.50 four-valve single also run on this occasion can be seen on the right. (Photo Mick Atkins Collection)

    The Rhodes 61 cu in motor used two four-valve single inlet tract heads, however the rockers were supplemented by flat steel side-plates of unique shape in addition to the four upright pillars seen on other Franklin era four-valvers. The bottom end employed by Indian for this Rhodes Motors' bike, typified by the example shown in colour photo 27, used the two-camshaft timing chest arrangement (but with four cam lobes, two per shaft), the bronze timing cover, and the self-aligning ball bearings of the single-cylinder racers. This format was later made famous by the twin-carb Altoona engines of 1926, but the Rhodes bike pre-dated the Altoona by over a year. The magneto drive adopted for this new V-twin incarnation of Franklin race motor was different from the singles, however. Instead of chain drive in a separate chain-case mounted outboard of the cam gears, the two cylinder versions of Franklin's bronze-cover engine retained the earlier system of taking drive forward to the magneto via a train of gears driven off the front cylinder's cam wheel.

    In late 1924 the unveiling of banked concrete motor-dromes in Melbourne and near Sydney, in addition to the existing dirt tracks, led to four top American riders of Indians being invited out to Australia by Rhodes Motors. Paul Anderson, Johnny Seymour, Ralph Hepburn and Jim Davis remained for three months as star attractions in Australian speedway competition. Rhodes took Paul Anderson, the 61 cu in eight-valve ohv twin and a 30.50 four-valve single over to Sellick's Beach in South Australia for a crack at the world's motorcycle speed record. Stephen Wright's *American*

Top, the A61-5, the Sellicks Beach Anderson record-breaker.
Below, the A61-5 record-breaking engine up close, showing details of the frame scratch-built for it by Rhodes mechanic, Frank Barnes.
(Photos Lindsay Urquhart collection)

Racer reports a one-way run of 128mph, and two-way average of 125 mph, for the twin. A side-car was fitted, and the same bike ran 118 mph. The 30.50 single managed 105 mph. All were Australian records, and the solo 61 cu in effort a world record, if ratifiable.

Rhodes Motors put out a press release picked up by *The Sydney Morning Herald* on 31st March 1925 in which the point was firmly made that these speeds, measured over a half-mile distance, bettered those of the current world's record holder, JAP-propelled Bert Le Vack.

WORLD'S RECORD SPEEDS
The Rhodes Motor Cycle Company, Melbourne, writes:-'On March 28, at Sellick's Beach, Adelaide, Paul Anderson on his Indian made a new world's speed record of 125 mph, thus beating the world's record made by the famous English rider, Le Vack, at 123 mph During the same afternoon Anderson broke the world's lightweight speed record on a 500cc Indian at 105 mph The previous speed record for this class of machine was 101 mph, made on an English machine. The weather was dull and cloudy, and conditions on Sellick's Beach were bad for racing.'

Another example of this same type of pent-roof eight-valve engine was next run by Paul Anderson in a record attempt at Arpajon in France, where it set a suspiciously high one-way speed subsequently found to be the product of somebody's foot on the timing tape. The story of Anderson's Australian and European exploits with the new 61 cu in eight-valve motor and a 30.50 cu four-valve was told in an article run by *The Brisbane Courier* on 20th January 1926:

MOVING AT 159.08 MPH - MOTOR CYCLE EMULATES AEROPLANE'S SPEED.
The 'American Motor Cyclist and Bicyclist' waxes enthusiastic over the latest wonderful achievement of the most outstanding motorcyclist in the world, Paul Anderson, in making a world's record of 159.08 mph on Arpajon Speedway, France, late last year. The following article, reprinted from the periodical named, is written in typically American style, but if the reader will make allowance for the pardonable exuberance of an extravagant nation over a truly noteworthy performance, he will find the reading full of interest.

Back in 1920 the late Gene Walker astonished the world with his record breaking time of 115.79 miles per hour at Daytona Beach, Fla. That it was a truly great speed was proven in that it remained a world's record until Paul D Anderson, on the Annual Day of Records Speed Trials, October 11th, at the Arpajon Speedway, near Paris, entered the kilometer and mile record trials on his 60.90 cubic inch 997.64cc Indian.

The Trials were held under the auspices of the Motorcycle Club of France and sanctioned by the Federation International des Clubs Motorcyclists. Courses were accurately measured and electrical timing was used.

Zipping over the kilometer he crossed the line, clocked at 194.594 kilometers per hour or 120 miles per hour for a mean average of two ways.

This was only a teaser for Paul - he was out for real 'meat' that day. Anderson whisked over that mile stretch like a flash of lightning and as he roared over the finish line the clock spoke the world's fastest time ever made on wheels - 159.08 miles per hour. After making it the other way a mean average was produced at 135.71 miles per hour.

Some idea of the keen competition at these trials and their renown may be gained from the fact that twenty eight new records were established on this occasion and Anderson's performance on the Indian motor cycle was the best, as he scored the fastest time of the day which incidentally is the fastest time ever officially recorded regardless of type of vehicle or size.

ANDERSON'S CAREER.
Paul Anderson is a native of Rochester, Indiana, a little town of 30,000 located in the vicinity of Lake Manitou, favourite summer and fishing resort. As a boy he had always liked speed, but it wasn't till around 1920 that he actually developed the 'racing bug'.

When the big Marion race meet was held he experienced his first big thrill in 'the game'. Though he only made fifth place it served to spur him on. He entered many meets that year and while nothing astonishing was performed his ability gradually improved and victories increased.

Up to this time Anderson had had a few minor spills, but nothing of a serious nature. However, he was not to go unscratched for, early in 1921 at South Head, just two days before Hammond Springs met with the accident which sent him to the 'great beyond,' Paul Anderson struck a hole in the track and was thrown. Had he remained in the sideline where he had rolled he perhaps would not have been injured for at that time he was merely stunned. Like all clean racers, there dwelled that one thought in his mind to clear the track especially while the dust completely engulfed the wrecked machine. Knowing that a rider was directly behind him he was just about to drag the machine away when the late Gene Walker who was in the race ploughed right into him and machine. Both the riders were seriously injured and confined to the hospital for some time.

The following years, up to July of last year, Anderson led an eventful racing career. Numerous victories fell to his daring and ability, together with several records which included the three, five and ten mile, in the 30.50 class.

ANDERSON VISITS AUSTRALIA
In July of 1924 Paul, together with Ralph Hepburn, Jim Davis, and Johnny Seymour, made arrangements for a season of racing in Australia.

"No" answered Paul, to a question put him, "I did not find it difficult to ride the grass track". As a matter of fact he liked it. Among his first victories of note in Kangaroo Land were those at Ascot Vale, Foundation Day, January 24, 1925, where he made the best time - 4min $38^{3}/_{5}$ sec. in the under 600cc Australian solo championship, five laps. He also entered a solo handicap in the same class, also five laps, and crossed first with the time of 4min $41^{2}/_{5}$ sec.

His final achievement before he left the great continent which treated him so well was at Sellicks Beach South Australia, on March 20, when he made a sweep at the Australian half-mile records, and annihilated three of them, establishing new records for Australia. In the under 1,000cc solo, he averaged 15.9sec two ways. In the under 500cc solo his average for two ways was 18.5sec , and in the under 1,000cc sidecar the average was 18sec flat. These trials were under the auspices of the South Australian Motor Cycle Club over a surveyed course. They were recognised as the first Australasian record for over two miles per minute, the first lightweight to go over 100 miles per hour, and the first sidecar reaching over 100 miles per hour.

SUCCESSFUL EUROPEAN TOUR.
On returning to the United States, Anderson made plans for a scheduled racing season in Europe. He made his first headquarters in Copenhagen, Denmark, where he entered a meet on June 10, winning both the 1,000 and 500cc in the annual Danish championships.

Anderson next journeyed on to France where he spent a pleasant three weeks The races he was scheduled for here were held at Montlhery, a long winding 90 kilometre course about 150 miles from Paris. This course had numerous sharp curves which necessitated 'shutting off' almost constantly. Tyre trouble developed, and little was accomplished.

Belgium's 15-kilometre course near Spa, up in a hilly, wooded section, picturesque enough for the 'artist', more than pleased our little racer. He remained there three weeks and copped a number of races, none of them, however, of any importance.

After a few day's rest he packed his machines and shipped them on to Holland. There he came face to face with the familiar grass track which he had come to know so well in 1924 when racing in Australia. This was peculiar in that it could be made into either a 1 kilometer or an 800 metre track. A fence on the outside of the kilometer track was moved to an inside circle, making the smaller track. After showing what he could do, making several winnings, Anderson next packed for Italy. Nothing very exciting happened there except that Paul for once during his tour actually took a couple of days from his strenuous schedule for a bit of sightseeing. So, together with his wife, who had been with him since leaving America, he journeyed to Venice.

However with all the enjoyment he derived from Venice he left rather hurt in body. The natives treated both himself and wife as royal guests, but the mosquitoes seemed to have a grudge of long standing against Americans, for they were sure out and attacking with 'blood in their eyes'.

Paul arrived in Switzerland the later part of August just in time for the Swiss kilometer record trials. Entering in the 1,000cc class he established a new Swiss two way kilo record averaging 173 kilo or 107.133 miles per hour. This track, located near Geneva, was queer in that both start and finish were set at the bottom of a rather abrupt incline.

Last on his schedule was a return to France where the Annual Day of Records Speed Trials were to be held on October 11 at the Arpajon Speedway, near Paris. As has already been told it was there that Anderson made the record that is now being broadcasted throughout the world. With a few weeks on his hands, Anderson and his wife made a visit to Paris and spent some time in seeing the sights of the famous city.

Anderson returned to the US without gaining FICM ratification for any of his 1925 speed efforts in France or in Australia, yet the two-way average speeds he consistently achieved in both countries were around 125mph. This is indeed impressive when compared with the prevailing 'official' world's record holder Bert Le Vack's two-way average of 119 mph (and best one-way of 122.44) set at Arpajon in 1924, not 'officially' toppled until 1926 at the same venue by Claude Temple with a 121 mph two-way average.

The whole saga raises almost as many questions as it provides answers. Who sponsored Anderson to go on this Grand Tour of Europe? It cannot have been cheap to take such an extended and leisurely itinerary, lingering to see the sights in-between various European race and speed meets. Was the Indian factory backing him? Or was he funding it himself, and hoping to recoup his investment with prize money? Were European Indian dealers lending him a hand, and ensuring he got treated like royalty, just as Rhodes had done for him and the other three musketeers while in Australia?

Questions also surround Anderson's bikes. However, we can piece together most of the important details from direct evidence gleaned from these engines' detail design, and from reminiscences of former Rhodes mechanics like Eric Price and Jack Morris collated by Lindsay Urquhart and other enthusiasts in Australia. This is the picture that emerges.

The eight-valve engine used to set the records at Sellicks Beach in Australia was most likely built at the Indian factory and brought out to Australia by Anderson and his colleagues in late 1924. The alternative explanation is that it was built up in Melbourne by Rhodes out of spares from the Indian single-cylinder four-valve speedway bikes, using a special one-off set of V-twin crankcases. It's more likely, however, that this engine is one-hundred percent an Indian racing department effort. This is firstly because, although the crankcase is completely new, special and never before seen, over two dozen more of them were to emanate from the Indian factory in the months and years to come. Secondly, it's because the cylinder heads used on it were not simply speedway single heads with one of them reversed.

A61-5 was later used to power a racing sidecar outfit, here seen at the Melbourne Motor-drome piloted by Sid Gower with Gordon Urquhart as passenger. (Lindsay Urquhart collection)

They are 'handed' for a V-twin. For example, there are no push rod cutaways on the left hand side of the rear cylinder head (see colour photos 20, 21) as there would be if this were really a reversed single-cylinder 30.50 head. It adds weight to the theory that this engine is a Wigwam Race Shop job.

The Rhodes motor, which bears engine number A61-5, was built into a suitable frame by Rhodes mechanic Frank Barnes who simply laid the motor down on the floor and drew around it with chalk. A side-car was made ready for attachment, to tackle three-wheeler speed records as well. After Anderson was finished with it, engine A61-5 remained with Rhodes in Australia. They installed it in another frame that is rather rough looking (a bit of Powerplus, a bit of this, a bit of that) but effective none the less. In this guise (see colour photo 22) it was raced by Sid Gower in side-car events at the Melbourne Motordrome and other venues with Lindsay Urquhart's father Gordon as passenger. When Rhodes quit their Indian franchise altogether in the late 'twenties and had a big sell-off of race bikes, A61-5 went firstly to Parkers, Indian dealers in Colac, Victoria, and then north to Queensland which is where the bike remains to this day.

According to Stephen Wright's *American Racer*, the Arpajon bike had engine number A61-3. Presumably Anderson picked this one up from Springfield after he'd returned from Australia and while on his way to Europe. That there was more than one of these engines in existence by mid-1925 adds further weight to them being built at the Indian factory's race department. Which then begs the question - where are engines A61-1, -2, and -4? There's no guarantee, however, that A61-1 through -5 were quintuplets, all fitted with ohv four-valve top-ends. In view of the diversity of applications and specifications exhibited by this same basic V-twin bottom-end from this time forward until the end of the decade, it's equally likely the other three were fitted with Daytona side-valve top-ends and got used for US hill-climbs (see, for example, colour photo 30). Lindsay Urquhart's compilation of Rhodes mechanic reminiscences, and intra-Club knowledge about the whereabouts of extant examples, point to several such motors coming out to Australia in the mid 1920s. Apart from A61-5 there was a 61 cu in side-valve, and an 80 cu in side-valve (A80-5) that used the same new bottom-end. A45-7 and A45-23 are also in Australia. A80-5 was an ex-Orie Steele motor but got blown-up shortly after arrival in Australia and was re-built by Rhodes using Rudge four-valve heads. Another eight-valve 61 apparently was released in the US to some lucky person in late 1924, however its race history and ultimate fate are not known.

The final question, and it's a significant one for patriotic Englishmen: if Anderson thought he was such a hot-shot, then why did he not go to Le Vack's stamping-ground of Brooklands in England and mount a direct challenge to him there?

We think the answer lies in the fact that Brooklands had originally been designed for speeds less than 120 mph and was now being out-grown by the record-breakers of 1925. In fact, the all-time two-wheeled lap record at Brooklands was set in 1939 by Noel Pope at 124.5 mph using a super-charged Brough Superior. It was an extremely hazardous undertaking for Pope to get the Big Bad Brough around the Bumpy Bowl at this velocity, yet Anderson on Franklin's eight-valve was already capable of similar speeds in 1925 (in a straight line, at least). Le Vack himself quit Brooklands and went instead

An unknown Australian rider on an Indian ohv 4-valve dirt-track bike in the mid-1920s (Photo Lindsay Urquhart collection)

Johnny Seymour at Daytona with the 30.50 four-valve machine he used to set records in early 1926. (Photo Mick Atkins collection)

to Arpajon for the record attempt of 1924 that yielded him official FICM recognition at 119 mph. By appearing at Arpajon for the Speed Trial of October 1925, Anderson was indeed directly challenging world's record holder Le Vack on his own turf.

So was Anderson's European odyssey really just a free-lance racer's summer holiday and promotional trip, bankrolled by prize money and some friendly Indian dealerships? Or was the entire episode a Wigwam organised and financed full-on assault to seize for Indian the out-right Land Speed Record on two wheels? It can be strongly hypothesized that, after the very encouraging but unratifiable results gained at Sellicks Beach, Indian management became very determined to repeat this effort at an international speed arena run under organisation capable of securing FICM recognition without any 'ifs', 'ands' or 'buts'. Anderson was not in France for the fun of it. He was a man on a mission. Such a pity the time-keeping got so messed up. Once again, one of Franklin's Indians was denied its place in history through sheer bad luck.

Once back in America and fully recovered from the leg injury he sustained while trying to out-grass track the Aussie grass trackers, Johnny Seymour had good 1925 and 1926 race seasons on the new Franklin four-valve 30.50 vertical-single in the US Nationals. His results are detailed on p179 of Stephen Wright's *American Racer 1900-1940*. In January 1926 he went to Daytona with a 61 cu in eight-valve and a 30.50 four-valve, tended by Charles Gustafson Jnr. The eight-valve was the Arpajon motor A61-3, further proof that this racer was doing a lot of international travel at this time. Though the runs were one-way so were not FICM ratifiable, he reached speeds of 132 mph with the twin and 112.6 mph on the single.

While the full story is not known about these forays into overhead-valve exotica by Indian and questions do still remain, what clearly emerges from these events is that Franklin was now coming into top form as a designer of truly fast motorcycles. The overhead-valve racers he produced at this time, such as the examples that featured in the 1925 campaigns of Anderson and Seymour, were good enough to pose serious challenge to the very best in the world.

This new overhead-valve line of exploration starting in 1924, which occurred in parallel with continued side-valve vee development that used the same bottom-end, became the main focus of Indian race engine development in both singles and V-twins from this time onward to the end of the decade. As an engine development program it succeeded the previous two parallel programs run jointly by Franklin and Gustafson Snr, based around exhaustive and incremental improvements to the Hedstrom era eight-valve race motor and the Powerplus side-valve production motor.

It is tempting to hypothesize that this new burst of overhead-valve engine development at Indian was made possible by the advent of tetra-ethyl lead fuels, which became available for sale to the public in 1924. This innovation probably had highest impact among high performance road models, however. For racing, the limited supply and higher cost of the contemporary 'high-percentage' solutions to engine detonation at high compression ratio, that is, blends of gasoline with alcohol and/or benzene and other additives like aniline, were no impediment due to the smaller quantities demanded and the deeper pockets provided by factory race teams. Specially blended race fuels that did not depend upon tetra-ethyl lead were as available to American racers as they were to their Brooklands counterparts. It was in race events where the rules called for standard pump fuel to be used, such as in the Isle of Man TT races from 1926 onwards, that newly available tetra-ethyl leaded fuels gave the most significant advantage.

It makes more sense to attribute the timing of this new overhead-valve line of exploration to new inspiration resulting from Franklin's 1923 visit to the UK for the Isle of Man TT. Such a visit must certainly have been a real eye-opener for him regarding the current state of top-flight British motorcycle race engine technology. It is one thing to read about such machinery in the Indian factory's weekly subscription copies of *The Motor Cycle* and *MotorCycling*. It is quite another to see these bikes in the metal, hear them being revved up in the pit area, witness their comparative performances in real-live racing situations, and discuss their finer points of design over a pint of ale with like-minded people from the other race teams and sponsoring manufacturers. He'd arrived in the UK with a side-valve racer, but then gained up-close and personal experiences with a host of exotic overhead-valve machinery. He would have returned to Springfield with his mind buzzing full of ideas about things to experiment with and immediately put into practice. The sheer diversity of features and detail design variations between his superficially similar race engines from this 1924-25 period shows that Franklin was testing and evaluating each of the latest innovations in overhead-valve technology during this phase of his career.

Indian Prince

The Personal Motor

While he was there at Brooklands, the Isle of Man, and in London's West End motorcycle showrooms along Great Portland Street and Euston Road, Franklin would also have checked out all the latest road-going motorcycle designs then appearing in Britain. By this time, ohv singles by AJS, Norton and Velocette represented the new frontier of sporting road bikes. This 1923 'sabbatical' by Franklin was a valuable opportunity to study all the latest British models at first-hand.

The most conspicuous feature of the contemporary UK market was the increasing popularity of relatively high performance 350cc models for both commuter and sporting road use, superseding the vintage 'Long Tanks' - heavyweight 3 ½ hp (500 - 550cc) singles epitomized by the Trusty Triumph - which had held sway since 1907. From the mid-twenties the 500cc class lost its former popularity as *the* general utility machine. Viewed dispassionately by penny-wise purchasers, this class now had few advantages over lighter, handier and more economical 350cc machines to offset the greater cost of purchase and operation, except for rapid long-haul work or if expected to routinely shoulder the load of either a pillion or side-car passenger.

Historian James Sheldon in *Veteran and Vintage Motorcycles* describes 1923 as 'the 2¾ year' (2¾ being the nominal British hp rating for a 350cc motorcycle engine) during which, in addition to those manufacturers already offering a 350cc machine, new models in this class were announced by BSA, Matchless, New Hudson, New Imperial, Sunbeam and Zenith, followed in 1924 by Rudge and Triumph. By the mid-twenties it had become obvious that 350cc singles were the most popular and top-selling 'all-rounder' models in British, continental European and colonial motorcycle markets.

For the next three to four decades, anytime that new bike buyers were lured into showrooms by the latest hot 500cc sporting singles, there were never more than a quarter of such customers who actually rode out of the dealership on one. The other three-quarters prudently opted for the sweeter and more frugal running of the 500's companion 350cc model, inevitably displayed slightly to one side and just out of the spotlight, but wearing a decidedly more affordable price tag and petrol consumption specification. This state of affairs in world markets for British bikes persisted until the late 1950s, by which time the higher revving and smoother running properties of Edward Turner's Triumph Speed Twin, its various progeny, and its imitators, were becoming widely appreciated.

Nowadays the bread and butter 350cc pushrod single is a genre somewhat under appreciated in the British classic bike scene, simply because antique motorcycle enthusiasts are *not* people who view motorcycles dispassionately. For this reason the 350s get over-shadowed by the snob appeal of their sexier 500cc brethren. This keeps their prices lower, yet they are capable of giving much satisfaction to anyone seeking the classic bike experience. While the average 350cc ride to work single cylinder model cannot ever really be viewed as 'exciting', it is difficult to imagine any other type of machine that is as faithful in its service or as satisfying to ride. They will steam along at a relaxing and stress-free 55 mph while imparting a sense to their riders that they'd willingly carry on at that pace forever, provided that 55 mph is the speed at which you want to ride. The completion of every journey brings a sense of achievement, and we mean that in a good way. Not for nothing was the British 350cc single as popular as it was, for as long as it was.

Observation of this emerging new trend in the early to mid-1920s by those in charge of design at Indian and Harley-Davidson led these two marques to make fresh attempts at a popular lightweight model. Their aim was this time to achieve company expansion through export sales, since the domestic market was now so flat and static. Both companies soon released 350cc single cylinder models, designed not for America but for Britain and her Dominions.

Which company was first? Did one factory take the initiative, with the other forced to respond with a copy-cat model just to keep pace in the evolving marketplace? If so, then who copied whom?

Some published accounts imply that H-D was proactive, and Indian reactive, in starting a mid-'twenties trend for a Made in USA 'Twenty-one' single cylinder model for road and race track. H-D Motor Company archives document a world tour by their Four Founders during the northern summer of 1924, in which they split up to personally visit foreign motorcycle market countries and ascertain any potential export opportunities. For example, William Harley and Walter Davidson visited Britain and Europe, while Arthur Davidson went to Australia and New Zealand. After returning to Milwaukee and getting into a huddle to swap notes, they reached the conclusion that what the world wanted was a 350cc single cylinder model, and that Harley-Davidson should definitely do its bit to give it to them.

That much is certainly true, but it should not be assumed that Indian was sitting quietly at home all this while, until they suddenly heard about H-D's new initiative and rushed to counter it with a similar model of their own. We have already shown you evidence that Franklin also went on a foreign market study tour. Except that his trip took place in the summer of 1923, a full year earlier than that of the H-D Founders.

The matter is settled conclusively by the timing of newspaper advertising to promote the new Indian 21 cu in single which, as for the Featherweight, is very closely linked to the time when the model in question actually went into production. Announcements of Indian's Prince model started appearing in newspapers across America from September 1924 onwards, and use wording which makes it clear that the bikes definitely existed 'in the metal' by this time. The earliest date that can be found in newspaper archives for similar advertising by Harley-Davidson for their own 'twenty-one' single cylinder models is September 1925.

The apparent confusion leading to assumptions that H-D led, while Indian lagged, with a 'Twenty-one' street-bike may stem instead from the timeline related to overhead-valve variants derived from each company's side-valve 350 model. Indian did indeed appear to wait for H-D to add upstairs valves to the khaki-coloured 'Twenty-one', before deciding to match it with a similar-spec version of their own rendition in scarlet.

So Indian definitely had a 350cc 'Twenty-one' single in production as a 1925 model by the Fall of 1924, *one full year* before H-D had their own 'Twenty-one' ready to go as a 1926 model in the Fall of 1925.[42] The great influence that we already know Charles Franklin had on the US motorcycle industry can now be extended further than previously thought. In addition to his other recognised achievements in motorcycling, we can also give him credit for introducing to America the 'Twenty-one' single cylinder concept which, though not intended for the US domestic market, did enjoy some popularity in 1920s US road riding amongst the nerdier element of new-bike clientele, and it did lead to creation of a new capacity class in dirt-track racing.

Indian's bid to enter a global general utility market with an export oriented 350cc single, which they blessed with the model name 'Prince', did not follow the same holistic and progressive concept that unified the Scout and Chief models in the Indian range. The Prince is quite conventional, in that it adheres to standard English practice for this size class (see colour photos 17 and 18). The frame is not full-loop, but rather is open in the middle. The gap between front down-tube and seat tube is filled by the engine, held in place by flat steel engine plates. In American parlance this frame is known as the 'keystone' type. English style girder forks are employed, rather than a scaled down version of Indian's range-unifying leaf spring front suspension.

The engine similarly follows English convention in being side-valve, then still the norm for the average British street bike, and in having a separate engine and transmission with chain primary drive. There was no attempt at semi-unit construction as with the Scout and Chief. For an engine of this size the opportunity could even have been taken to adopt completely unitary construction, as was used at about this time for the popular Motobécane B-bloc range in France. US customers would not have cared less either way, because they did not have any strong domestic tradition or expectation of what a 350cc single ought to look like. British markets did have such an expectation however, and it is epitomised in the pattern adopted by AJS, Norton, Velocette, the Black Ariel range, and others. If Indian had its sights firmly set on export markets for this machine, then it may have felt it needed to conform with the design conventions already fashionable there. Cost would also have been a factor - this was to be an economy machine.

The economy theme continued in the timing chest layout, which was single camshaft. Drive was taken to the forward mounted magneto by a train of gears. Oiling was total-loss from a slow turning drip-feed pump, as used on Indians since Hedstrom days.

In a further break from the modern new 'look' of the Indian range exemplified by the Scout and Chief, the Prince of 1925 debuted with a straight sided, 'wedge' shaped fuel tank instead of the pleasing semi-teardrop profile of the two larger models. There must have been buyer and dealer resistance to this styling, for it was quickly dropped. From 1926 on the Prince gas tank and frame top-tube was re-configured to echo the profile of its two bigger brothers, and again in 1928 to conform with the shorter-tanked and sleeker 101 Scout.

A Prince innovation was the first-time use of a detachable cylinder head on a production Indian model, in which the head is a separate casting from the cylinder barrel and is bolted down onto it. This makes side-valve motors so much easier to work on for de-coke, re-bore, or any attention to valves and seats. It makes them easier to manufacture too, especially to ensure accurate casting of the combustion chamber roof, the shape of which is so critical to side-valve engine performance. It allows the possibility of casting the cylinder head in aluminium, whose superior heat-shedding properties then makes possible a slight increase in compression ratio. Parked alongside contemporary British side-valve 350s, which continued for a while to use one-piece cylinder-and-head construction, the Prince with its detachable head construction gives it a refreshingly modern look for its time.

The problems of maintaining an effective seal between head and cylinder had, to date, given the edge to one-piece cylinders. These had been the industry standard since the dawn of motorcycling. It was metal deformation, or gasket sealing problems, which required that H-D's eight-valve racer use a one-piece cylinder, for example, or that AJS's 1920 TT win would be a 'pushover'. Now that a detachable head was successfully being used on the Prince, it was not long before the Scout and Chief wore them as well.

Harley-Davidson's Model A, B, AA and BA 21 cu in series of single cylinder lightweights were laid out on very similar lines to the Prince, except that they more faithfully bask in the glow of the H-D Big Twins via the choices made for gas-tank shape, for springer front suspension, and for a wheelbase 2 in longer than the Prince. For the engines H-D used a 'modular' approach, also adopted in the mid-twenties by some British and French manufacturers like Ariel or Motobécane, whereby either sports-bike (AA, BA) or commuter-bike (A, B) editions were derived from the same design platform. Essentially similar engine cases and crankshaft assemblies supported top-ends that could be either ohv, or side-valve, respectively. For street use, a greater number of the H-D side-valve models were ultimately sold than 'sport' models. The ohv versions formed the basis for race machines, which first appeared in a local Milwaukee competition event in August 1925. These competition variants of the H-D 'Twenty-one' famously became dubbed the 'Peashooters'.

Indian also produced overhead-valve versions of the Prince, though not in the kind of numbers that H-D did for their own 'sports' variants. One theory is that Indian overhead-valve Prince 'sports-bike' production was mainly a homologation exercise for racers of their own to counter Harley's 'Peashooters' in 21 cu in racing. This 'Twenty-one' class of competition was a new development which represented a further shrinking of engine sizes, in an effort to reduce the danger to riders and thereby improve the public image of motorcycle racing.

This theory that Princes gained overhead valves in order to go racing is unlikely, however. Indian's factory supported racers never competed on Princes. At the same time as the ohv Prince was being built and released in small numbers as a sports bike for road use, Charles Franklin and his colleagues in the Indian race-shop were already at work on another similar (though not identical) two-valve ohv top-end for racing. When this was made ready it was not installed onto the single-cam Prince, however. It was instead bolted onto the bronze-cover two-cam single cylinder racer bottom-end already developed for the Franklin era four-valve racers back in 1923-24. This new two-valve top-end utilises a hemi-head layout with wide-angle splayed valves in accordance with AJS practice, itself adopted from the pioneering Peugeot race-car engines created by Ernest Henri and others in pre-WWI days.

Released in 30.50 and 21 cu in sizes as Indian's antidote to the Peashooter, these bronze-cover two-cam racers with chain driven magnetos are at times described in Indian marque literature as 'Prince derivatives'. Yet there's only one thing this next generation of two-valve two-camshaft Indian racing-single motors have in common with the Prince, and that is their valve rockers. Apart from that, they are completely different motors. The racer's cylinder head can be distinguished from the overhead-valve Prince by the fact that the Prince's head has a single vertical fin on its timing side between the pushrods, whereas the racer's head has three vertical fins. The Prince's rocker side plates are solid, while the racer's have two triangular holes cut in each plate.

If Indian already had a production 'Twenty-one' on the market in 1924, one whole year before H-D, then it's reasonable to ask - how did H-D manage to be first cab off the rank with a competition variant by August 1925? The answer for this is probably related to the fact that a 21 cu in class for sanctioned National race events did not actually exist until the following year, in 1926, so Franklin was not yet very much bothered about getting a bike ready for it. When the first 21 cu in National Championship event was finally held, on 10th July 1926 at Altoona, it was duly won for Indian by Jim Davis at a speed of 88.9 mph on an overhead-valve bronze-cover two-cam racer. Poetic, really. But although Indian's specially-built 'Twenty-one' became a winner on the track, ultimately it was the H-D rendition of a 21 cu in single that ended up winning the all-important race for sales of the street versions.

The road-model Prince is a small and dainty yet attractive motorcycle, that wears its red and gold livery well in comparison with the olive-drab of the equivalent Harleys. There are reports however that, initially at least, Princes appeared in white paintwork. All-white ohv Princes are pictured both in *The Iron Redskin* and in Hatfield's *Indian Motorcycle Photographic History*, the latter being a show model at the 1926 New York Motorcycle Show. This colour scheme did not go down well in some quarters. Ivor Dennis, an Indian dealer from Bairnsdale in rural Victoria, Australia, once recalled attending an agents' dinner in Melbourne to launch the new Prince. During the meal, the bike sat up on stage covered in a sheet. After speeches and general promotional talk, it was unveiled with some fanfare. There was a stunned silence in the room. The Prince was painted white! 'It looked bloody awful,' recounted Dennis, 'Indian's aren't meant to be white!' He was nevertheless strongly expected by Rhodes Motors to take one of these Princes which then sat in his showroom gathering dust, until he took it all apart to re-paint it red and it sold soon after. Apparently other dealers had the same experience. Painted crankcases also provoked sales resistance, with other Princes Ivor Dennis handled being torn down so the cases could be blasted back to bare alloy and then the motor reassembled. As they say in Yorkshire, 'there's nowt as queer as folk'.

The Prince is 'sized' as a 350, in contrast with many British equivalents whose 350 motors are housed in chassis intended to do double-duty for their 500s as well, thus rendering them less of a lightweight and more like under-powered 'heavyweights' (by British standards of the term 'heavyweight'). The ohv Prince really looks the business, with its taller and more prominent engine. On the side-valve model however, the engine's cylinder looks almost dwarfed by the front mounted generator and the upright pressed-steel cover for the generator drive from the magneto beneath. An ohv 350 of the Prince's petite overall dimensions can be expected to be entertainingly lively, however any contest between the side-valve 350 and the skin of an average viscosity rice pudding would be a close-run affair.

There were prettier bikes than the Prince available in this class, but not very many. Popular British class-equivalents like the Black Ariel or the BSA Round-Tank models would not have won too many beauty contests either. This was a time in motorcycling history when machines were still raw and elemental. Their engineering hearts were worn out on their sleeves, as yet unadorned by styling or artifice. The way they looked reflected the way they were engineered and the way they functioned. Because engines were not yet very powerful for their size, cycle parts remained pared to the bone to save weight. Motorcycles of the vintage era were afforded little in the way of excess baggage or tinware, which in future times would become the palette for a new type of professional in the engineering team, known as the 'stylist'.

The Prince sold acceptably well in the US, but certainly did not take the country by storm. Then again, it hadn't been intended for the US market. As it was, it provided an ideal bike for a teenager's paper round, as a utility machine for inner-city delivery boys, for college students to get around campus, or for a Reverend to visit his parishioners without upsetting the gentry or livestock. This reality contrasted somewhat with shotgun-toting hunters penetrating far out into the woods on their nimble go-anywhere Princes, as depicted in some Indian factory imagery. Period newspaper advertising emphasized the Prince's economy ('90 miles per gallon! One cent per mile for operation and maintenance!'), rather than it's speed of 55 mph downhill with a following wind and the sun's rays behind you. The other big selling point was the fact that 'you can learn to ride it in 5 minutes!'

The Prince was often selected by women riders intrepid enough to take up the sport. And intrepid they were, too. Miss Evelyn 'Bobby' Roberts of Richmond in Victoria, Australia, used her Prince to accompany about forty other Indians on a 1,500-mile 'Gypsy Tour' from Melbourne to Sydney and

In US advertising the Indian Prince selling points were '90 miles per gallon', 'cent-a-mile' running cost, and 'you can learn to ride it in 5 minutes'. Indian Factory Archives)

We're giving away this Indian Prince

To Prove You Can Learn to Ride It in 5 Minutes

TO acquaint more people with the pleasures and convenience of owning an Indian Prince — to prove that the Indian Prince is the finest solo single made — to display its simple and sturdy construction — and to prove its cent-a-mile economy — we have not only arranged for a free personal demonstration — but the Indian Motocycle Company will actually give away one of the brand new 1927 models to some person who takes his first ride on an Indian Prince during the month of October.

1927 Model Given Away FREE

You don't have to buy the Prince in order to qualify to win the solo single. We want you to hop on one of these machines and simply prove to yourself that you can learn to ride it in 5 minutes. No "ifs" or "maybes." Come in and let us show you exactly why this new type motorcycle is easier to handle than a bike and how amazingly economical it is to operate. Call at our store, ring us on the phone, or hail our demonstrators on the street.

90 Miles per Gallon

back in 1928. Hers was the only Prince among a herd of big twins, Scouts and one four-cylinder Indian Ace but she held nobody up, and managed to get through the same rough and muddy stretches as the bigger machines.[43]

With hindsight it is unfortunate that Indian and H-D both had the same good idea at around the same time, for in the US domestic market there was probably room for one or the other company to profitably sell a lightweight 'Twenty-one', but not both. Princes are in modern times an extremely rare sight at US antique motorcycle meets. This is a reflection that Indian didn't sell all that many in the first place and, being a utility machine, no one saw fit to treasure and preserve them during their unloved years when they hit the bottom of their depreciation curves.

There was a further outburst of overhead-valve experimentation by Franklin in 1925, this time relating to an overhead-camshaft layout. At least one prototype, maybe four (some reports say as many as twelve), of an overhead-cam 350 single was constructed (see colour photo 23). This was inspired by the Velocette overhead-cam 350cc Model K, which Franklin thought a really neat little motorcycle - it was also a very pretty one, incidentally.

This ohc design was far too well, and too expensively, engineered to ever go into production as a road bike. Meanwhile for US racing, the pushrod overhead-valve two-cam single was already proving more than adequate to counter the H-D 'Peashooters'.

So why was an overhead-cam 350cc single ever made? It appears that Franklin harboured ambitions for Indian to again win 1st place in the Isle of Man Tourist Trophy race. Overhead cam. construction was the level of technology by this time required to win against the top British manufacturers in this, the world's premier road race event. Construction of the ohc prototype was the opening shot of a 1926 TT Junior-race campaign by Indian that never took place.

Such a win would have been expensive to achieve. As a foreign race event, it would also have been largely irrelevant for Indian sales in the, by that time, splendidly isolated US domestic market. For Indian however, the reflected glow of a Junior TT win by this exotic ohc design is exactly what they needed to boost sales of the British-style 350cc street-single they'd just launched, for which British market success had been the main goal all along. It shows that Indian saw their future survival and growth very much as offshore-based, and the company was willing to make the necessary investment to achieve it.

It is said that Franklin arranged for the purchase of one of the first Velocette Model Ks to come onto the market in 1925, and had it shipped to Springfield for careful study. As with the Velocette, the ohc Indian single (see colour photo 24) uses a bevel-driven tower shaft to turn the upstairs camshaft from the end of the crankshaft. This is a form of construction still regarded as the ultimate in engineering quality almost a century hence. The famous bevel drive Ducati singles and V-twins use the same system of valve actuation, in their case either conventionally sprung or desmodromically (that is, valve closed as well as opened by cam action). The bevel drive system was adopted by Norton for their famous CS1, International and Manx models, and for the New Imperial JAP 350 with which Bert Le Vack so nearly won the 1922 Junior TT. Blackburne and Matchless also investigated the concept. The Indian ohc single was thus right up there with the best of major-factory entrants known to be capable of winning a TT race, for by 1925 the days of amateur entrants riding genuinely 'Tourist' models were long gone.

The fact that Franklin designed an ohc engine at all is evidence of his confidence as an engineer, and of his willingness to keep Indian at the very leading edge of motorcycle design. The 'twenties was an exciting decade in which to be a motorcyclist, or to work within the motorcycle industry. Notwithstanding that two-wheelers were now relegated to the second rank of consumer choices amongst motorized transport, within the industry there unfolded a host of technical advances and engineering experiments. At the time it was difficult to know which engineering pathways would prove most promising and ultimately take hold as the new industry standards. Apart from racing, another good reason to build an ohc engine was simply that any major factory needed to keep all these bases covered, and be prepared to either set the next new trend or be hard upon the heels of it.

In trend-setting Britain, sensible ride-to-work customers were still buying side-valve singles in droves, leaving overhead-valve 500s to that minority of hell-bent young tearaways with more money than sense. Yet as an engineer Franklin knew ohv had advantages that would see it ultimately prevail, if only from the standpoint of fuel efficiency. To be prepared for whatever which way market demand was going to pan out, Indian had to be ready with road-going models using ohv technology at their finger-tips. Marketing was not his responsibility, and international market opportunities were beyond his control. His responsibility was to ensure that, whatever opportunities emerged, Indian could respond with a suitable product.

When Franklin joined Indian in 1916, its global position was that of industry leader. A decade hence, the leadership in terms of both quality and quantity was indisputably coming from Britain. But technologically, whatever the British could do, Indian could also do. This, Franklin was now demonstrating. In later years the general British perception of American motorcycles was one of 'slow, over-weight and obsolescent'. In the mid-twenties it was true that the Indian factory's output in numbers was already pitiful, yet design-wise Indian was by no means out of it. Franklin's design efforts at this time were positioning the factory in such a way that, given half a marketing chance, Indian could rebound and again be a global force to be reckoned with.

The Prince gave Billy Wells a worthy weapon to compete with in British markets. After all, it was a 'British' bike. Princes are known to have sold quite well in the Australian states of Victoria and New South Wales, for example, where they do still turn up and, while nowadays not common, they are certainly available. In the Britain of 1925, motorcycle sales were on the rebound after the 1921-22 slump. The Indian name still counted for much in terms of a 'speed' and 'reliability' image in the minds of the motorcycling public, thanks to Brooklands and TT competition successes that were still fresh in peoples' memories. Wells managed to shift several hundred Princes in the first part of 1925.

Indian in Britain was then dealt a final and fatal blow, in this year becoming a casualty in an on-going international trade war instigated by the United States. In short, and amongst a suite of other retaliatory steps, the British government imposed a 33% import duty against all foreign motorcycles.

The background to this lay in international reaction to the Fordney-McCumber Tariff, passed by the US Congress in 1922 as a series of measures to ostensibly protect the US economy during the 1921-22 economic down-turn. A period of lobbying ensued in which international trading partners tried to convince the US to change its stance. When this lobbying failed, European and Latin American countries decided to retaliate and raise their own duties. Between 1925 and 1929 this action was taken by most of the European nations, by Latin America, and by Australia, Canada, and New Zealand. American automobiles were specifically targeted, because they were such a conspicuous component of US exports to these other nations. US motorcycles, on the other hand, were but a drop in the bucket compared to the outputs of the contemporary British and French motorcycle industries, but became entangled in the same trade politics.

The result was a return of protectionism from 1925 onwards. It was in 1925 that Conservative Party politician Winston Churchill became Chancellor of the Exchequer in Britain. A libertarian and a free-trader at heart, in this year he made two economic policy decisions which went against his grain, and he should have trusted his instincts because both ultimately proved bad for business. The first was to return Britain's currency to the Gold Standard, a popular move at the time but with hindsight it created conditions that contributed to the Great Depression following the New York stock market crash of 1929. The second was to impose a series of retaliatory tariffs against US imports which, merely for the sake of form, included motorcycles.

It was this second decision by Churchill that proved very bad for Billy Wells' business. Already expensive by British standards, the increase in sticker price of new Indians forced by this import duty resulted in sales dropping to virtually nil. The Indian London Depot had to close its doors. Franklin's overhead-cam TT racer design exercise to promote the Prince became suddenly pointless, so was abandoned. The savagery with which the axe fell upon motorcycles imported into Britain (the majority of which were American) can be seen in the following statistics.

Year	UK imports
1920	4305
1921	2171
1922	976
1923	1045
1924	543
1925	896
1926	97

Billy Wells' business was well and truly cut off at the knees, and by none other than Winston Churchill who was a man Wells otherwise greatly admired.

During this same period, total production of British motorcycles doubled from 65,000 in 1920 to 120,000 in 1926, with 50,000 of the latter being exported. The corresponding production by Indian and Harley Davidson in total struggled to reach 20,000 units per year. Eighty percent of all the world's records in every engine capacity class were now held by riders of machines that bore the label 'Made in England'. Britain's pre-eminent role and domination of the global motorcycle scene was now complete.

The loss of the London Indian Depot threw Billy Wells into a deep depression. For the better part of a year he did little but mope about it, having apparently lost the will to work. Finally his wife Clara read him the Riot Act, telling him to get out of the house and go do something useful. Billy's son George Hendee Wells has these recollections about the impact upon his father's business and subsequent events in the Wells household:

> Alas, those happy exciting days were to end when the great recession arrived and foreign imports received a further severe blow in the shape of Import Duties. My father tried to persuade the Indian Company to open up a manufacturing division in this country but as we all know only too well, recession times make everyone reluctant to take risks. And so we saw the end of an era when American motorcycles were just everywhere in Britain.
>
> But it was not quite the end for my father in the motorcycling world. He was out of work and he started a motor accessory business which had some small success. He still had something of a reputation in the realms of organising motor sport and so it was that Mr. Claude Langdon who was an entrepreneur in several activities was put in touch with him. Mr Langdon had heard of the new sport of *Dirt Track Racing* in Australia and wanted to introduce it to this country. My father was appointed to investigate the possibilities and to help guide the venture through the authorities and the body governing motor sport - The Auto Cycle Union, the ACU.
>
> There was nothing like this racing in this country and the nearest thing was Grass Track Racing. So we all trooped off one day to see a meeting at High Beech. It had not taken a lot of organising as it just required a field and a few posts to make out the course. It was fairly tame as the speeds were quite low and any excess speed and the riders slid off. The Australians had developed a new technique called 'broadsiding' but this required a dirt track. Anyway, Mr. Langdon looked for such a track and decided on Stamford Bridge - home of Chelsea Football Club - where there was an athletic cinder track just a quarter of a mile per lap. Safety fences were put up and lighting installed and in a blaze of publicity the first meetings were held. My father organised these very much as the Brooklands meetings had been held. The programmes were printed with the driver's names and the make of the machine. And there were all kinds as drivers tried to find the best combination of gearing to give them the necessary acceleration and control in the broadsiding which the Australian riders were demonstrating. In those early programmes there were very many makes of machines, but there was also an Indian. The rider was Art Pecher who had had some experience of the sport in the USA and as I remember he did quite well.
>
> Eventually all machines were replaced by the specially designed motor cycle and the sport became a contest of riders rather than the traditional contest between marques. The name of the sport was changed from Dirt Track to the more refined *Speedway*. One small facet of the racing of the past did remain and my mother always insisted it was her nagging that did it. It was very difficult to identify the riders, particularly as they all wanted to wear black leather protection. So she proposed coloured helmet cover and tunics just like the first Brooklands races when they were following the horse race tradition.
>
> When my father retired before the war he still felt the need to do something active and he became

associated with the Triumph Cycle Company and was involved in the servicing side. Of course the war halted so many things but he was still doing some cycle servicing when on the 17th April 1941 a bomb destroyed his house and workshop, at 207 Kingshill Drive, in Kenton, Harrow. Fortunately he was not hurt but a lot of the Indian memorabilia was lost. When the house was rebuilt in 1946 the first thing he did was re-establish his workshop.

> I still use his old workshop and I can still hear him over my shoulder saying 'Now do the job properly if you want it to last'. I believe the Indian success in this country probably had a lot to do with that philosophy.

George Wells' testimony about his father's contribution to the establishment of Speedway racing in Britain is corroborated by a series of articles about the racing career of Gus Kuhn entitled 'The Gus Kuhn Story' written by Cyril May. These appeared in a short-lived publication in the seventies entitled *Speedway Express*, and stated that Billy Wells held the posts of Secretary of the Meetings and Clerk of the Course at Stamford Bridge Speedway Track for several years, starting from 1928.

As George recounts above, the initial British attempts at this type of racing in early 1928 were rather feeble. Riders in Britain had heard about the necessary art of 'broad-siding' but scarcely any of them could do it. Let's face it, the technique is not easy. To attempt it for the first time takes a lot of guts, in addition to a talent for fine-balance and perfect throttle control. Dirt-track riders in Australia and New Zealand, on the other hand, were by this time quite proficient. It needed a combination of the correct loose cinder surface, and an imported crew of Australians - Dean, Meredith, MacKay and Galloway - a New Zealander 'Stewie' St George, and an American named 'Sprouts' Elder, to really get things going, initially in rural countryside settings like High Beech. The final ingredient needed to bust this new sport right out into the big-time was to provide track venues at the heart of population centers in built-up urban neighbourhoods, and run the events on weeknights under electric floodlights.

It is with this last ingredient that Billy Wells had his greatest impact on the budding new sport of Speedway. For it was at Stamford Bridge that the first such floodlit event in Britain was run, as an experiment, on 5th May 1928. As Secretary of Meetings and Clerk of the Course at Stamford, the person who dreamt-up and organized this new race-meet formula was none other than Billy Wells. Ixion of *The Motor Cycle* was there that night, and this is what he saw.

> The crowd's first impressions were the reverse of enthusiastic, for inspired showmanship held back the stars, and the early heats were contested by English novices, who could achieve no more than a few skids on the bends. Then, as dusk drew on, the loudspeakers announced that Stewart St George would give an exhibition solo ride. He rode four magnificent laps in a hushed, incredulous silence, broken only by the crazy screaming of his Douglas. When he crossed the final line, the 30,000 fans released their pent-up breath with a roar which rocked Chelsea, as they cast assorted articles from hats to newspapers into the air in such a paroxysm of admiration and wonder as is rare in British sport. When they had calmed down a little, Sprouts Elder brought out his Douglas and produced an even finer display of pluperfect technique. Both men had sprayed great black fans of cinders into the crowd on all the bends. From this moment there was no doubt that speedway racing had come to stay. Financiers connected with the entertainment business opened their purses. Star riders were besieged with offers of fantastic contracts. The crowds flocked.

The rise of speedway in Britain coincided with the demise of the record breaking bonus system at Brooklands, so there were several prominent track racers falling upon hard times who turned their hand to speedway at this time. Frank Longman was one such rider and record breaker who found that, in the late 1920s and 1930s period, British speedway racing now offered the best chance for a professional motorcycle competitor to actually make a living out of his chosen obsession. Freddie

An unknown rider flings a Franklin four-valve 30.50 sideways around the bend of an Australian dirt-track, circa 1925. It was a crew of Australians, plus one New Zealander and an American, who introduced this style of riding to Britain in 1928, facilitated by an out-of-business Billy Wells, and thus Speedway was born! (Photo Mick Atkins collection)

Dixon became manager and tuner of the Douglas works speedway team. Bert Le Vack's nephew Wal Phillips, who'd worked with his uncle at JAP and worshipped him, became well-known for designing special speedway motorcycle frames that incorporated the requisite amount of 'whip' during cornering. JAP itself scored a massive coup by designing and selling a hot 500cc alcohol-burning single that totally dominated speedway competition for many years.

If they'd each paid Billy Wells a penny for every pound they made from the speedway business, it might almost have been enough to recompense him for his disappointment at only coming second in the inaugural Isle of Man TT race of 1907.

Indian continued to sell well in Australia and New Zealand, because tariff barriers were not yet as harsh as those imposed in Britain. It was not until an even more protectionist bill, the Smoot-Hawley Tariff, was signed into law by President Hoover in 1930 that Australia and New Zealand reacted as strongly as their Mother Country. The retaliatory tariffs they erected at that time did then result in Indian and H-D motorcycle imports and sales coming to an almost complete halt in those markets.

These vicissitudes of international trade politics in large part explain the model distributions of the antique Indians nowadays extant in each of these countries. In Britain, pre-1925 Indians could not be said to be common these days but they certainly are around, whereas Indian models made after 1925 are definitely rare birds apart from any brought over from the US in relatively recent times. Similarly in Australasia, pre-1930 Indians are reasonably well represented. But then there's a yawning gap in the model line-ups seen at Indian club runs of models from 1930 onwards (apart from recent imports) until we reach 1941-44 in the Indian production timeline, which is when the military Scout Model 741 and (for lucky Australians, but not the Kiwis) military Chief Model 344, supplied to Allied armies during wartime, suddenly become relatively plentiful.

With Indian trapped in a small domestic market and with the succor of export earnings now denied them, it was the Prince's destiny to be the last ground-up, new street-bike design of Franklin's to reach production. Sure, there were to be other significant new Indian models created before his active career ended, but they were either make-overs of the existing Scout/Chief platform (Forty-five Scout, 101 Scout, Despatch Tow) or it was bought-in from elsewhere (Indian Four).

Both Indian and H-D tried very hard in the 'teens and 'twenties to break out of the unwieldy heavyweight Yank-tank image of 'they don't go, don't stop, and don't handle' into which American motorcycles would later be type-cast by future generations of British-market sports motorcyclists - perceptions which have lasted until the present day. They had the ideas, they seized the initiative, they had the right designs for the task. They were certainly not slumbering while the motorcycling world passed them by. It was international trade politics that set the seal upon US isolation from the world mainstream. Had Franklin lived longer than he did, he would possibly have found solace in another choice quote from the writings of Ixion - 'History must dwell on these economic and political menaces before justice can be rendered to the solid and brilliant achievements of our industry'.

Or, equally possibly, he would not have.

Tommy Butler resigned from Indian during 1925, after management rejected his proposal to emulate Briggs & Stratton and get into the stationary engine business. He'd been adamant that the large amount of unused factory capacity at the Wigwam during these lean years could be easily turned to manufacture of other types of engines. After all, if there's one thing Indian was good at, it's making engines.

The company didn't go for it and, frustrated that his initiatives were no longer being acted upon, Butler resigned. He was apparently a wealthy man in his own right who was working at Indian mainly for fun anyway. For Franklin's close friend who had long 'run interference' for him, being at Indian was no longer fun. Other opportunities beckoned, however the two men regularly kept in touch. When Franklin passed away, Butler made a trans-continental trip from the West Coast to attend his funeral.

Was there merit in Butler's proposal to enter the industrial stationary engine business?

H-D also came up with this idea, quite independently from Indian. Unlike Indian however, H-D actually went ahead with it. This was an uncharacteristic plunge by a cautious factory that normally let Indian take plunges first, holding itself back and only following Indian later if the new idea looked like it might be working. Examples of other concepts that were Indian innovations later adopted by H-D include ohv racer (1911 vs. 1916), side-valve vee-twin roadster (1916 vs. 1928), middleweight V-twin (1920 vs. 1928), 'Twenty-one' single (1924 vs. 1925), swinging-arm suspension (1913 vs. 1958), electric-starter (1914 vs. 1965), commercial trike (1931 vs. 1932), and enclosed body-work with automobile styling (1940 vs. 1970 Superglide).

By dabbling in stationary engines, Harley-Davidson got their fingers burnt. It's very likely that Indian would have, too. Being good at *making* engines is not necessarily the same as being good at *marketing* engines. Stationary engines, like motorcycle engines, and boat outboard-engines, are all specialized applications requiring specialized marketing knowledge to come up with the right engine at the right price. Indian and Harley-Davidson were motorcycle enthusiasts. Briggs & Stratton were America's stationary engine enthusiasts. It is unlikely that either Indian or Harley-Davidson could have made much of a dent in a market where B&S were by now pretty much unassailable, and where the cachet of Indian or H-D branding meant nothing. Mind you, in H-D's defense, there was a Depression going on at the time. They made their play in 1931, and quit ignominiously in 1932.

Meanwhile, what of Franklin's family life? His daughter Phyllis was by now 16 and attending high school. She went to the MacDuffie School for Girls, a private day and boarding school for young ladies located in Springfield, from which she graduated in 1926. The local public high school in Springfield at the time was eminently well-regarded and would have been a respectable choice for a parent who valued a sound education as much as Charles Franklin did. Both schools were well within walking distance of the Franklin home on School St. But Charles had the money, and Nancye had social pretensions, if her occasional appearances in the *Springfield Republican* society column are anything to go by, so they opted for a private education for their only child.

The MacDuffie School was (and still is) a college prep school that educated the daughters of wealthy local Springfield families. It was small and exclusive - there were 15 girls in the graduating class of 1926. Most had wealthy white Anglo-Saxon Protestant connections, and the roll bore a sprinkling of names from Springfield's 17th century founding families (Stebbins, Pynchon, Chapman, and so on). Helen Hedstrom had also attended MacDuffie, graduating in 1921. Since Franklin knew her father, Oscar, personally (the two men went back as far as 1911 and the TT races), this may well have influenced his decision regarding Phyllis' schooling. MacDuffie had close links with good colleges like Smith, Vassar and Radcliffe, plus it offered a parallel educational path that culminated in the award of a Certificate in Housewifery. This latter curriculum addressed all aspects of running a large household with servants, to prepare the school's New England blue-blood charges for the serious business of marrying well.

There are some scrapbooks of information about the Class of '26 held by the Alumni Office at MacDuffie, but no yearbooks are available for those years. Departing graduates were lampooned in a Class Prophecy, in which a crystal ball was ostensibly used to forecast where they all would be in

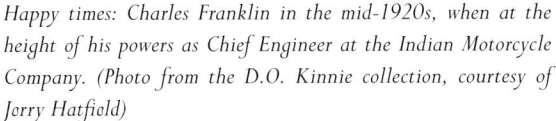

Happy times: Charles Franklin in the mid-1920s, when at the height of his powers as Chief Engineer at the Indian Motorcycle Company. (Photo from the D.O. Kinnie collection, courtesy of Jerry Hatfield)

From around 1925 onwards, Charles' daughter Phyllis (later Valerie) Franklin began grooming herself for stardom as a classical dancer. (Photo Carol Northern)

ten year's time. For Phyllis the following was composed by the budding comedienne who'd come up with this particular stunt:

> ... I am eager to know that (future) of Phyllis Franklin. Evidently the ball was active again, for the same cloud appeared and disappeared. The scene was in a gymnasium, and the instructor was Phyllis. I was astounded at this revelation for I had thought that surely she must be a scholar or an author. However, it was she, without a doubt. The picture faded, and I thought of another one of the girls ...

Given the satirical nature of such buffoonery, we can perhaps take it that Phyllis was not so bookish by nature, but had some modicum of athleticism to accompany her striking good looks. Alumni records show she passed her exams and was accepted to attend college at Radcliffe. This is confirmed by a *Springfield Republican* report about various McDuffie girls' doings at this time, but the report goes on to say that Phyllis intended going to Springfield junior high for a year and then enter Vassar as a sophomore. But she disappears from the public record at this point and we don't know what she did for the next two years, except that a letter of reference written for her in October 1932 by her Springfield dance tutor, Anatole Bourman, states that 'Miss Franklin attended school abroad and is also a graduate of the well-known Mac Duffie school in Springfield, which has the very highest of social and academic references'.

It is as a dancer that Phyllis reappears, in 1929, through brief mentions in Springfield newspaper coverage of cultural events in the city. Her performances included appearances in dance programmes sponsored by Springfield's Myron Ryder School of Dance during 1928-29, in items with titles like 'Disciples of the Scarf' (not without risk, for it entailed a dozen co-performers and a very long piece of fabric). In this devotion to dance Phyllis apparently had the full support of her mother, for Nancye also appears in print as a committee member for the organization of dance and cultural events in Springfield in 1931.

According to official public records Phyllis was not working (in terms of paid employment) since she does not appear in any of the Springfield City Directories for subsequent years from 1926. The 1930 US Census has her still living at home in School Street with mum and dad, not married, not enrolled in any educational institution, and her occupation is given as 'none'.

Scout Forty-Five and the Overhead Valve Hill-Climb Motors

In 1925 Excelsior threw a cat amongst the pigeons of the Other Two in America's Big Three. They released a novel middleweight design of Scout-like overall proportions that out-gunned the 37 cu in Scout with an engine capacity of 45 cu in (750cc). Endowed with enough pep to snap at the heels of Sixty-ones and Seventy-fours, but at a handier size, more handsome appearance and cheaper price ($285 FOB ex-factory) it was an instant sales success.

We've not said much lately about Chicago based Excelsior, the motorcycle side of Ignaz Schwinn's bicycle operation. Since 1911 the Excelsior Motor Mfg. & Supply Co. had included a big V-twin in their range, to stand toe to toe with the Other Two and slug it out in the heavyweight work-horse division. But sales-wise its nose was being consistently bloodied by a smaller production output which meant the unit price had to be higher. Excelsior also had a four-cylinder model, acquired by buying the Henderson company in November 1917. This had blossomed into America's most successful Four of the day. Under Schwinn's patronage it became deservedly popular with law enforcement officers or hard-core touring riders intolerant of the tingles and fatigue meted out by long days in the saddle of a big vee.

From the early 'twenties onward Excelsior began de-emphasizing their Big Twins in favour of the Four, which occupied a niche the Other Two couldn't fill. If Excelsior was unable to sell the same kind of machine for the same kind of price, then the only way to survive was to dare to be different. Spying another gap lying between the 37 cu in Scout and the industry staple Sixty-ones and Seventy-fours, Excelsior went for it. In 1925 the hot, feisty new 'Super-X' 45 cu in (750cc) was launched. In that same year they dropped their own Big X heavyweight V-twin altogether. To most effectively hold their own against the Other Two, Excelsior's strategy was to 'hit 'em where they ain't'.

The Super X is one of those skilful but rare offerings in the history of motorcycle design whereby features that were 'new' did not overwhelm the 'familiar'. The whole design concept is so obviously a jab directly aimed at the pre-eminence of the Indian Scout. The Scout is 'semi-unit' construction, but the Super X goes further. It is fully unit construction, with gearbox and

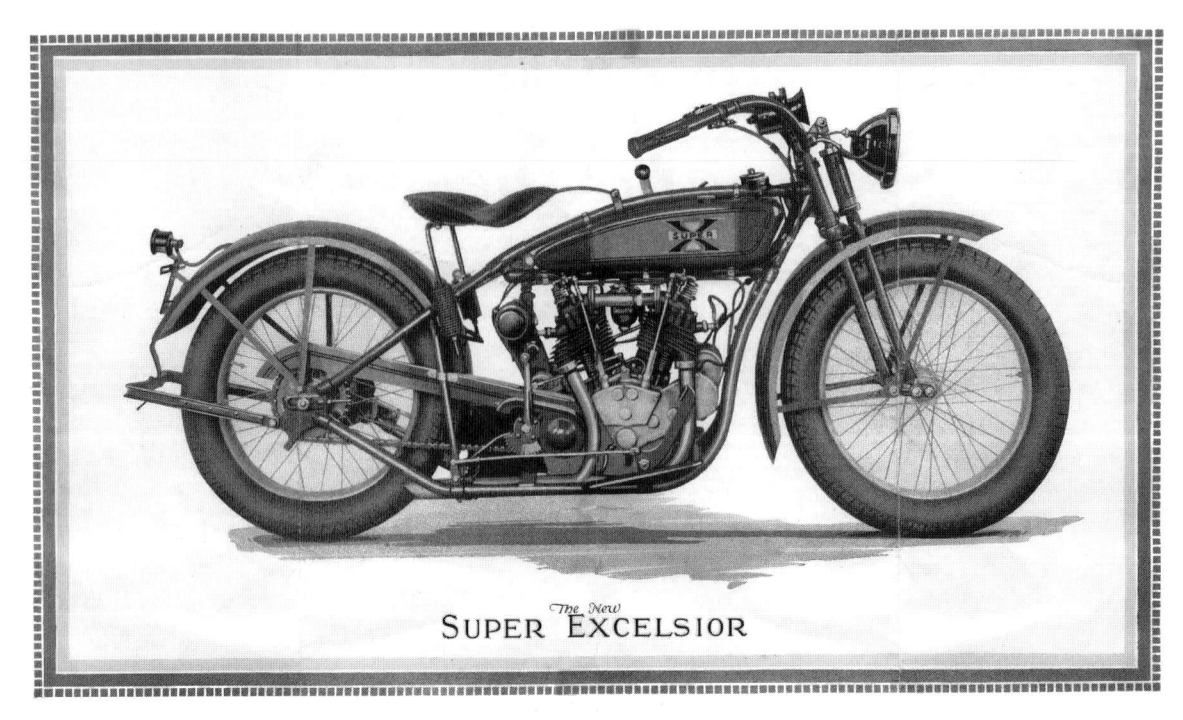

The speedy and influential 1925 Super-X with 45 cu in unit-construction engine prompted creation of a new class of racing in the US. (Excelsior factory archives)

flywheels all housed in the same set of castings. This was a US industry first for a V-twin. With crankshaft and transmission main-shaft thus on fixed centres, Excelsior could borrow the Scout idea of helical gear primary drive.

With this innovative bottom-end format married to the tried-and-true Excelsior ioe top-end, race-bred since 1912 and now unusually fierce in terms of compression, the result was a motor that worked 'modern' but looked 'traditional'. Carried in a compact twin-cradle frame, with leading-link springer forks that are an aesthetic improvement on Indian's leaf spring arrangement, the Super X scores highly in the 'looks' department. Overall the bike has such rightness about it, as if to reassure a prospective purchaser that 'what looks right must BE right!' Short, light and low, its power to weight ratio made it quick off the mark and able to set a cracking pace. It could turn 95 mph board-track laps from right out of its box. If the motor was breathed upon and put in the capable hands of riders like Joe Petrali, then this went up to almost 108 mph.

There was then no such thing as a 45 cu in class in US racing, for the simple reason that there'd never been any race-able 45 cu in machines produced in the US. So initially the Super X was instead entered in 61 cu in board-track, dirt-track and hill-climb events, and immediately began picking up wins. Then in 1926 Excelsior duly raised their hand at a convenient meeting of that industry triumvirate known as the AMA, and proposed that a 45 cu in class of racing be created. With studied indifference the H-D and Indian representatives stretched, yawned, and responded as nonchalantly as they could - 'Yeah, whatever, what the heck ...'

Behind the nonchalance, their minds were whirring. Both factories had to do something. By year's end the Super X was racking up significant sales that needed to be countered. At least by agreeing to creation of a 45 cu in class of racing, the Other Two could for now put a lid on the embarrassment of seeing their 61 cu in hill-climb and dirt-track machines getting whupped by a mere 'Forty-five'. For the battle in the streets however, H-D and Indian both needed Forty-five road models of their own.

The successful marketing of a hot middleweight by Excelsior was thus seen by both H-D and Indian as a provocative act. Far from remaining content to allow Excelsior to flourish 'where they ain't', Indian and H-D started making plans to hit Excelsior 'where they *is*'. They both set to work on adding Forty-five models to their respective ranges. Not long after, they both launched investigations into adding a four-cylinder model as well. H-D considered buying out the owners of Cleveland, a company that was already making a Four. Indian's President Weschler entered into negotiations with the receivers of the now insolvent Ace company, set up in 1919 by William Henderson after he'd split from Excelsior (themselves the purchasers of his Henderson company) due to 'artistic differences' with Schwinn. H-D decided against acquiring Cleveland, while the Indian-Ace negotiations dragged on through 1926 to a successful conclusion in 1927.

H-D had no middleweight 'V' design platform whatsoever, so in 1926 they set about designing one from scratch. Even before the appearance of the Super X, it appears the Motor Company had already been toying with the idea of a competitor to the Scout. Credence to this view is lent by the fact that their original design concept was apparently for a side-valve engine of 37 cu in. Apart from the short-lived Harley Sport, H-D had to date been fully committed to ioe valve disposition right from the very beginning of the company's existence. That they were now considering a switch to side-valve at a time when the rest of the Known World was already adopting overhead-valve, and that their initial goal was a capacity of 37 cu in, is testament to the innovation and influence of the Indian Scout and is a massive compliment to its designer Charles Franklin.

Ultimately appearing in mid-1928 as the 45 cu in Model D after three years of development, its 37 cu in origins were betrayed by the fact that it was somewhat lightly built. As a result, it suffered embarrassing teething problems and breakages. These delayed its release date, and required post-release running changes to fix various issues with power-shaft taper keys, cylinder breathing and the oiling system, as and when these matters arose on bikes already in the hands of customers. Not good. But H-D stuck at it, and in time they got the formula right. The direct lineal descendant of the Model D is still in production, nowadays going by the name of 'Sportster'.

Indian had a far easier time of it in getting out a 45 cu in middleweight. They already had a 37 cu in middleweight, it was already popular, it had been thoroughly de-bugged after six years in production, and it had been over-engineered from the outset. Indian was in a position to come up with a Forty-five at little cost and with little risk of anything going wrong, by the simple expedient of boring it and stroking it. The 37 cu in cylinder's dimensions of $2\frac{3}{4}$ in diameter by $3\frac{1}{16}$ in swept distance were increased to $2\frac{7}{8}$ by $3\frac{1}{2}$ in.

This is a dodge that led the British into trouble from the 1950s into the 1970s when their 500cc parallel twins were called upon to counter stiff Japanese competition. They responded not via a matching investment in technical innovation, but rather by 'adding cubes' American-style, firstly to 650cc, then to 750cc, and ultimately (in the case of the Norton Commando) 850cc. There's only so far a motor can be 'stretched', before certain inadequacies manifest themselves which were not apparent when the lumps of metal being flung back and forth were still only 500cc-sized.

With the Scout, this dodge worked uncommonly well. So well that one wonders why the Scout had not been made a Forty-five right from the start in 1920. Two reasons, perhaps. One being that it needed to prove itself as per the original concept before its boundaries could be safely pushed. The other being that Sales Departments do like to hold a few things in reserve, and drip-feed any

Newspaper advertisement for the new Scout 45 from 17th December 1926. (Indian factory archives)

> **Yes – It's Here With a Punch!**
> **INDIAN SCOUT 45**
> **THE POLICE SPECIAL**
>
> Not a replacement of the famous Indian Scout 37. No. Sir! A brand new model—an addition to the Indian line, offered in accordance with INDIAN policies to meet every definitely prescribed demand in the motorcycle market. This new model is a combination of Indian Scout Stamina, ease of handling, and compactness, with a brand new 45 cubic inch motor, a large brake—same design as used on the Big Chief 74, and a smoothness never before achieved in a Vee twin motorcycle—The smoothest Indian yet!
>
> **W. H. LINEAWEAVER**
> REAR 153 NORTH EIGHTH ST.

improvements onto the market so as to regularly give customers something 'new' and 'hot' that they'd then want to trade-in present models for.

First presented to the discerning public at the New York motorcycle show in January 1927, it quickly became apparent the Scout Forty-five was more than just the sum of the relatively minor changes made to the Scout 37. Suddenly it was effortlessly capable of 80 mph in road-going trim, on a par with some Sixty-ones and too good for most of the available road conditions back in those days. There was a host of other detail changes, like a lower and more comfy saddle. When the Scout became a Forty-five, a good motorcycle just got so much better.

The new Forty-five (see colour photo 33) was marketed as a 'Police Special' in advertisements and, to distinguish it from the 37 cu in model, which continued alongside it in production, it bore the legend 'Scout 45' as a tank-side transfer in gold block letters, right under the Indian script. Because police motorcycles were supposed to be fast enough to pursue and over-haul offending speedsters, and were often specified to be built with looser tolerances as on race motors, 'Police Special' was an appellation that evoked 'high performance'.

Many police departments did indeed find Scout 45 performance sufficiently up to par that it could be adopted to perform many of the duties formerly the preserve of big Seventy-fours, while being both cheaper and more nimble. Perversely this ate into sales of the Indian Chief, a situation which would have cost Indian money given that a Chief sale had a bigger profit margin. Brand loyalties were such that if Indian thought those police departments with Harleys would stop buying Harleys in order to get Scout 45s, then for the most part they were mistaken. In Police sales the Scout's main competitor was, unfortunately, the Chief.

We'd be the first to tell you that Charles Franklin is a genius, yet we're forced to concede that dumb luck also played a role in the success of the Forty-five Scout. Why was $2^7/_8$ x $3^1/_2$ in. chosen as

Erle 'Pop' Armstrong and son Bob, with a Scout 45 and a small selection of Bob's hill-climb trophies. (Photo EMIMA)

the 'magic formula' to achieve the 45 cu in capacity needed to match the Super X? Because $2^7/_8$ in. is as far out as it's possible to go before there's only a sliver of metal left in the cylinder top deck between valve seat and cylinder bore. So how far does incoming charge then have to travel, in order to get out of the inlet tract and into the cylinder? Past only a sliver of metal. The result? Even better breathing from an engine that, for a side-valve, already breathed well.

Did the larger and weightier pistons cause any problems compared with the sweet-running 37 cu in Scout? Not at all. This engine had been over-engineered from the beginning. Although no further increase in cylinder bore is possible without redesigning the crankcases, re-locating the engine's valve-gear, and essentially creating a whole new engine (Hey, good idea! Let's call it a 'Chief'!) it did later become trendy to stroke Scout motors using turned-down Chief flywheels, to provide crafty owners with a 'street sleeper' of 57 cu in (almost 900cc). That really is stretching things to the limit. The 750cc Forty-five Scout, on the other hand, was a natural from the start.

Thus Franklin lucked into a 'happy combination'[44] of motor dimensions and flow characteristics. It has been described as Indian's best motor ever. In lay-person's terms, the new Forty-five Scout went like a cut cat. And it did so with utter reliability, with none of the teething problems that would otherwise have been associated with creation of a totally new model. Over at Harley-Davidson, they must have been having fits.

The Super X was only made for six years. In 1931, when America was in the depths of the Great Depression, Ignaz Schwinn's overly pessimistic assessment of the prospects for economic recovery led to his famous staff meeting where he abruptly announced 'Gentlemen, today we stop'. The Super X was nevertheless a very influential model that changed the course of American motorcycling history. It established a market niche for 45 cu in road models where previously none had existed, which very quickly led to the creation of a 45 cu in class in board-track, dirt-track and hill-climb competition. The 45 cu in dirt-track class became a hugely popular class of racing, once H-D and Indian picked up the gauntlet thrown down by Excelsior and produced 45 cu in race bikes of their own. For decades this class of racing practically *was* US motorcycle racing, and pretty much still is.

The models created to go head to head with the Super X also had a lasting influence still being felt today, eighty years later. Indian's Forty-five Scout was reconfigured into the Sport Scout, which won the inaugural Daytona 200 and remained competitive in dirt-track racing well into the 1950s. H-D's Model DL led to the legendary R, WR, KR, and XR racers of which descendants are still racing competitively today. De-tuned military WLA and WLC versions helped to liberate Europe and the Pacific, and then kept up the daily fight across America to issue parking tickets by powering a three-wheeler called the Servicar. The Servicar remained in production until 1973, and in use until the 1990s.

At the same time as Indian's best ever road-model engine, the Scout 45, was under development during 1926, work was also underway to build Indian's best-ever race engine - the 45 cu in two-valve overhead-valve hill-climb motor. Nobody seems to know any of the details now, but some of these engines are still out there, large as life and twice as handsome, in the hands of a fortunate few collectors. Like the discovery of a new fossil, these motors have a form that follows their function. Through careful examination of their form, and of the context within which they appeared in Indian's evolutionary timeline, a good idea of their function and *raison d'etre* can be gained.

The task of designing and building these engines was undertaken because, thanks to Excelsior, a 45 cu in class of National racing had been newly established, so Indian needed a purpose built 45 cu in contender. Strange to relate, however, that the inaugural 45 cu in National event, a 20-mile race run at the Rockingham board-track, was not won by a Super X. Indian, which then lacked a 45 cu in racer, instead entered a 30.50 cu in overhead-valve single. Despite its 50% capacity deficit this machine, piloted by everybody's favourite rider Jim Davis, won first place.

When the new Indian 45 cu in race motor did reach the race venues of board-track, dirt-track and hill-climb competition in 1927, these overhead-valve machines were billed as 'Scouts'. This strongly suggests the main aim of the whole exercise was to promote the road-model Scout 45, by creating for it a 'speed image' based upon actual competition success. In reality these race-shop engines share nothing with the production Scout motors, apart from having two cylinders in the shape of a vee. They use the same two-camshaft bronze-cover bottom end apparently pioneered by the Rhodes/Arpajon 61 cu in motors A61-5 and A61-3 of 1924-25 (see colour photo 27), combined with an adaptation of the new AJS-type two-valve hemi-head designed in 1926 for the single cylinder racers (see colour photos 25 and 26).

Alongside this new burst of overhead-valve race engine development, Charles Franklin continued to develop side-valve cylinders for use on these same two-camshaft bronze-cover crankcase assemblies. He continued to surprise both himself and everybody else in US racing with the speed yet able to

Jim Davis and an Altoona, the side-valve 61 cu in version of the two-camshaft vee-twin race motor, here seen with twin carburettors.
(Photo Mick Atkins collection)

be extracted from the supposedly obsolescent side-valve layout. The parallel lines of side-valve and overhead-valve race engine development initiated by Franklin in 1919 were both, almost a decade later, continuing to yield such good results that neither evolutionary strand could yet be discounted. That the side-valve engine was thus able to maintain a 'speed image' among US motorcycle buyers, which directly influenced H-D to adopt side-valves firstly for their own 'hot-rod' 45 cu in Model D and next for their J-Model replacement, the VL, in 1930, was entirely due to Franklin's success in tuning firstly the single-camshaft Powerplus derivatives and secondly this new generation two-camshaft side-valve motor to go extremely quick.

So let's talk first about the latest Franklin side-valve race motor. Its predecessor had been dubbed the 'Daytona' engine, after the successful world speed record attempt by Gene Walker in 1920. By 1926 the 'Daytona' engine was history, for it was now replaced by the 'Altoona' motor. This new name was given in honour of its first public appearance, which was at the 1¼ mile Altoona board-track in Pennsylvania in July 1926. The occasion was an auspicious one for, in the capable hands of 'Curley' Fredericks, the 61 cu in 'Altoona'-equipped Indian machine unleashed that day ran a best lap speed of 114 mph. The previous 'best' speeds had been figures of around 110 mph.

These additional few mph of the Altoona over and above the Daytona - where did they come from? Firstly, from the choice of bearings. The crankshaft and the two camshafts were supported by self-aligning ball bearings, conferring the advantages described already for the bronze-cover two-cam singles. The entire bottom end was, of course, pretty much the same as that first appearing in 1925 on the Rhodes/Arpajon 61 cu in eight-valve.

Secondly, the cylinder heads were detachable. This conferred the same advantages as listed above for the Prince, first Indian model to have this feature. The combustion chambers incorporated the very latest in a long line of incremental improvements in Franklin's own rendition of 'squish' principles, with the emphasis upon best possible breathing at high rpm

Thirdly, to make the best possible breathing even better, some of the 'Altoona' motors were fitted with twin carburetors! One such was the updraft-Zenith equipped 61 cu in example in board-track guise now being campaigned by Mr Fredericks. As mentioned earlier in this book, a month after its debut at Altoona the same machine and rider appeared at the Rockingham board track at Salem, New Hampshire, where they were timed at 120.3 mph - the all-time fastest speed ever recorded on a US board-track by any type of motorcycle.

The twin-carb detachable-head 'Altoona' engines were all of 61 cu in capacity, however other side-valve racers using that same bottom-end appeared in a variety of versions and capacities up to 80 cu in and were employed for hill-climbing, dirt-track and board-track racing, presented in a variety of chassis to suit. For example, there are 80 cu in hill-climb versions of this motor which continued to use the one piece 'Powerplus Daytona' type of cylinder castings (see colour photo 30). Despite this diversity, one feature these motors all had in common was a bottom-end with two-camshaft timing chest and a timing cover cast in bronze.

The new for 1926 45 cu in ohv race motors also used this bottom-end. They were produced in a limited-edition batch of about two dozen examples, either all at once during 1926 or in small batches spread out to as late as 1931. An engine numbered A45-31 is known to exist, so more may well have been produced than the oft-quoted figure of 'twenty-six engines in 1926' attributable to Sam Pierce. Because the bulk of them, except two or three, were fitted into hill-climb bikes and because, unlike the Altoona, these engines never received a formal name or even a nickname, they've come to be called 'the Indian 45 overhead-valve hill-climb motors'. Because the two camshafts bear a total of four cam lobes, another moniker used to distinguish these engines from earlier Powerplus derivatives is 'the four-cam race motors'

The cylinder heads are made of cast-iron, and are of the same overall design and layout as the two-valve AJS-style components just recently developed by Franklin for the Indian single-cylinder racers of 1926. The skull-like and sparsely finned heads contain a hemi-spherical combustion chamber which breathes through widely-splayed inlet and exhaust valves, of which there are two valves per cylinder. As was then the convention for all ohv layouts, the valves, rockers and pushrods sit outside in cooling breezes, forming a superstructure supported by flat steel plates which sandwich the rocker spindles and bolt to the sides of the cylinder head casting. Naturally these reciprocating components are completely exposed to the elements and to the abrasive properties of dust and dirt, but that only mattered if you were a private owner who needed dependable daily transport - these race engines were as far removed from that as it was possible to be in 1927.

Castings for the engines were not made in the Indian factory but were specially commissioned from Browne & Sharpe, whose initials can be seen stamped in the major components. Items like magnetos and carburetors were similarly bespoke - each engine was carefully matched to a particular magneto, which was then stamped with the engine-number. In terms of tuning variables like valve lift, valve duration and overlap, compression, and so on, a range of specifications and states of tune can be expected. This is because these engines were each hand-built as one-offs for a particular application - hill-climbing, dirt-track, board-track, and at least two were destined for road-racing in Europe. One of the two is A45-21, shown in colour photo 29, which went to Czech dealer Frantisek Marik of Prague in 1927 or 1928, and is now in Germany.

The hill-climb motors of this series have solid flywheels that are quite heavy. This type of crank assembly is designed to be spun-up on the line so that its sheer momentum will take the bike straight up to the top from a savage take-off. Hill-climb cylinder heads ran higher compression because these motors did not need to be civilized or tractable, and the compression increase was achieved via shallower combustion chambers rather than by higher piston-crowns. The intake manifolds were of larger diameter to better gulp air at a wide throttle opening that wouldn't need to be closed again until about seven seconds later when the rider fell off.

Road and track racers, on the other hand, had lighter webbed flywheels for faster pick-up in repeated accelerations and decelerations over the long haul, in contrast to the single burst of outright speed needed by hill-climbers. The need to perform well over a wider range of revs calls for an engine that is more tractable. Compression was lower by virtue of a deeper, wider combustion chamber, and the intake diameter was narrower. Or, should we say, compression was 'high' vs. 'higher', for both types of motor were set up to run on alcohol fuel.

A45 ohv flywheels are solid and heavy for hill-climbers, but are webbed and lighter in weight for the road-race versions. (TP)

The hill-climbers didn't really need an oiling system, in fact they tended to run better without the internal friction created by oil drag. A couple of squirts from the hand-pump just prior to start-up, and then they were on their way. Bikes built for dirt-track racing still got by with total-loss oiling up until this time, since oil pumps could be set up to cope with the one speed required (full speed). Their oil was pressure fed into the end of the crank mainshaft to the big end from an oil reservoir by a slow acting oil pump, and it was calculated for this oil to be burned off at a rate that neither seized the motor nor oiled the plugs. The road racers needed more help than this, however. For reliability over the longer distances and more variable speeds of road races, a higher volume feed to the big-end was essential and this oil then needed to be scavenged and returned to a reservoir. This mid-twenties period marks the first appearances of recirculating dry-sump oiling on an Indian motorcycle.

The road-race twins can thus be recognized by two oil pumps, a feed pump and a return pump. These could be either two separate pumps of the standard Indian type, mounted on the bronze timing cover with one driven off the front camshaft and the other off the magneto idler gear. Or, like on some road-race singles, they could be a box-like double-plunger oil pump driven off the rear camshaft. How these were set up depends on whether they were intended for track races over short distances, or for road races. A 1928 road-race Twenty-one single exists (see colour photos 31 and 32) that has nine (9!) different oil lines connecting to the engine. One line goes from the oil pump to the timing cover to feed the crank end to the big-end bearing via drillings in the shafts and flywheels. Two go to the base of the cylinder, one at the front and one at the back. One goes to the crankcase on the drive side. There are two returns from either side of a sump chamber added to the bottom of the crankcases (should this then be called a 'big-base' single?). Finally a hand-pump mounted on the drive side of the under-seat oil tank has a line running to the top of the drive-side crankcase, to enable the sump to be filled to the right level (a sight-glass is provided on the lower timing-side crankcase) before the bike is brought to the line for start-up.

The small handful of road-race versions of the four-cam Forty-five twin and the single cylinder 30.50 and 21 engines represent the pinnacle of Franklin's achievements as a race engine designer, measured in terms of technical sophistication in design. This sophistication comes mainly from their oiling systems and from the skilful balance of engineering compromises in their other design parameters, necessary to make these bikes fast enough, tough enough, yet tractable enough for road racing conditions which are the most demanding of any form of racing. The dirt-track and hill-climb engines are no less worthy of praise, however the demands placed upon them are simpler and they can be made to run competitively well with less recourse to sophistication.

Some of the four-cam Forty-fives are nowadays photographed with alloy heads, which appear to have been factory-fitted to later motors in the series. Lindsay Urquhart tells of a further development of these alloy two-valve heads, whereby an alloy four-valve head was created with similar appearance but with cooling fins increased in size. At least one of these motors went to Europe for road racing, and is now in Switzerland. Lindsay was able to borrow these heads to make a pattern, and has built two replica four-cam motors with these four-valve aluminium heads (see colour photo 28). One of these replica engines was used in a machine that ran 158.8 mph at Lake Gairdner in Australia in recent years.

As for any race engine, once in use the four-cam 45 motors' only constant would have been change. Such changes were implemented virtually after each meeting, in the continual quest for speed and to be one step ahead of the competition. Chassis showed similar variations, depending upon intended application. There was never any such thing as an 'Indian race-frame'. They were cobbled-up as one-offs, for example by using a Powerplus seat down-tube and bracket to mount the gearbox, a Hedstrom era rear sub-frame to keep the wheelbase short, Scout top-tubes to suit a Scout or 101

19. Franklin pushrod-single race motor. Clockwise from top left:

This two-camshaft, bronze cover, bottom end replaced the earlier Hedstrom and Powerplus sloper singles, and became the foundation for almost every new single-cylinder 30.50 or 21 cu in Indian racer built from 1923 until Franklin's death in 1932.

A four-valve 30.50 cu in version of the 1923-on two-camshaft single-cylinder Indian race motor.

Franklin was trying every overhead-valve trick in the book during 1924-25. This 30.50 four-valve single has twin carburettors!

An example of the 1924-25 Indian four-valve cylinder heads developed by Franklin.

Pent-roof combustion chamber of the four-valve cylinder head, as used on 30.50 singles and on the Sellicks Beach and Arpajon eight-valve V-twins. (Photos TP)

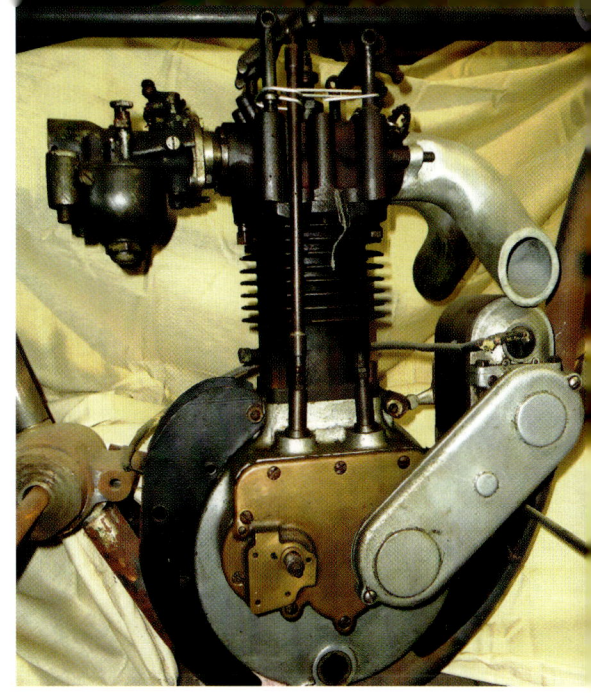

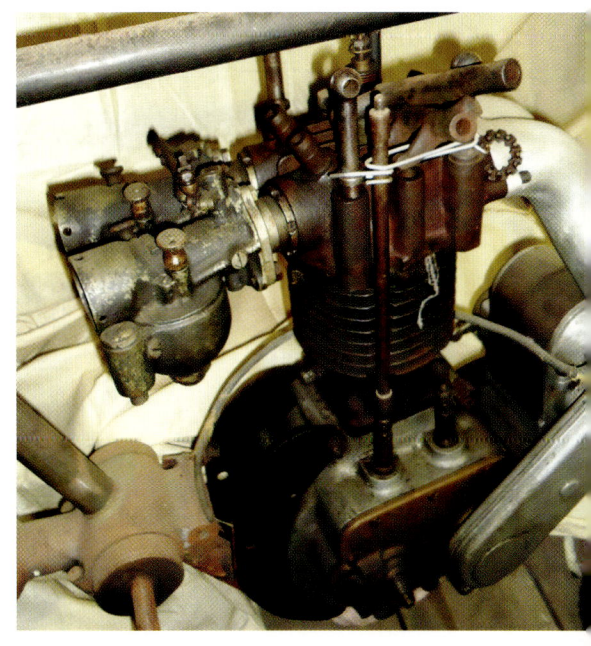

20 and 21. Above and left, the Paul Anderson Sellicks Beach record-attempt engine A61-5. Note 'handedness' of cylinder heads, for example, there are no pushrod cutaways on the left side of the rear head. (Photo Lindsay Urquhart collection)

22. The A61-5 engine in the frame subsequently built for it by Rhodes Motors to race in side-car events at the Melbourne Motor-drome (Mick Atkins collection)

23. Above, an impression of what the Franklin-designed overhead cam Indian 350cc Isle of Man TT racer might have looked like, had it ever run there in 1926. (Photo Fred Johanssen)

24. Below, the overhead cam racer engine (Photo Allan Rosenberg)

25. Above left, Indian's best-ever race motor, the 'four-cam' forty-five hill-climb engine, of which roughly thirty or so were built from 1926 onward. (TP)

26. Above right, details of the AJS-inspired two-valve hemi-head top-end used for the 'four-cam' forty-five race motors. (TP)

27. Left 'Four-cam' forty-five crank-cases. The same type of cases were used for all of Franklin's vee-twin race motors from 1924 onwards, be they pent-roof eight-valve 61s, hemi-head four-valve 45s, detachable-head side-valve 61s (the 'Altoona'), or one-piece cylinder/head ('Daytona') 61s or 80s.(TP)

28. Above. Road racer A45-21 is one of the most highly developed and sophisticated of the Franklin vee-twin race machines still extant. This bike was originally delivered to Czechoslovakia in 1927 or 28, and is now in Germany. (Photo Paul d'Orleans)

29. Above, a replica of the alloy four-valve cylinder head Franklin created for fitment to one or two of the A45 engines earmarked for European road racing, which represent the ultimate in Franklin race motors. (Lindsay Urquhart Collection)

30. This side-valve hill-climb motor of 80 cu in capacity uses Daytona-Powerplus style one-piece cylinders/heads on the same type of bottom-end as the 61 cu in eight-valve, 61 cu in side-valve, and 45 cu in four-valve hill-climb motors. (TP)

31. Above, re-creation of this B21 two-valve road racer is still a work in progress, but enough of it is now there for it to exemplify the most highly developed of the single-cylinder Franklin-designed race machines, and to thereby represent a pinnacle of his achievements. (TP)

32. Right, the B21 bottom end is of the same type as the side-valve 1923 TT bikes and the four-valve 30.50 bikes campaigned by Anderson and Seymour in 1925-26, but this is a 'big-base' version that's been cast with scavenge sump for a re-circulating oiling system. The double-plunger oil pump, also seen on A45-21, is of aviation origin. (TP)

33. Left, the Scout 45 'Police Special'. (Photo Annie Barker)

34. With the Scout Series 101, Franklin put Indian's best-ever engine into its best frame and running gear. (TP)

35 Franklin's Indian Despatch Tow was sufficiently popular as a utility machine that Harley-Davidson immediately copied it. (TP)

36. This 1938 Chief is representative of Indian's take on the modern new 'streamline' look, as applied to their entire range from 1932 onwards. 'The power of a Chief with the looks and handling of a Scout.' (Photo Malcolm Brown)

37. *The first and the last of the Indian Chiefs. (TP)*

38. *The headstone of Franklin's grave in Oak Grove Cemetery, Springfield, is extremely simple. (Photo Margaret Humberston)*

tank, a special casting with flattened section inserted into the lower top-tube to clear the overhead valve gear, front forks from a Scout or Prince or Merkel, and so on. Even within a genre, such as hill-climbing, there was constant experimentation with frames, forks, and wheels in search of that elusive winning formula. The historical waters have been further muddied over the years when a race motor is found at a swap-meet or tucked under somebody's bench, then a frame is built-up for it from a mix of period roadster or modern day Home Depot pieces, but this vital information does not always get imparted to subsequent owners of the bike.

Once the new Forty-five ohv racers appeared in 1927, they immediately enjoyed great success in both racing and in record breaking. In some California dry-lake speed events they were timed at around 126 mph averages on a circular course five miles in diameter (reaching up to 140 mph on the arc of the circle that had a following wind!) thus ranking among the very fastest motorcycles in the world at that time. In board-track racing they were winning as Forty-fives in both 45 cu in and 61 cu in events, and in the latter class they were beating out both H-D and Indian 61 cu in entrants. As just one example of successes in the hill-climb genre, Indian ohv Forty-fives ridden by Orie Steele and Howard Mitzel punched well above their weight to win both first and second places in the 61 cu in class of a major East-coast event. On the boards, Jim Davis and 'Curley' Fredericks continued to push back the boundaries of speed.

> *The Bismarck Tribune, 31st August 1929*
> 3 NEW RECORDS MADE BY MOTORCYCLE RACER
> Syracuse NY. August 31 - Jim Davis, of the Indian motorcycle factory team, shattered two world's records in the five and 15 mile open national championships here today at the New York state fair grounds. He was forced out of the 20-mile event, which was won by Curly Fredericks of the same team in 15:21:02. Davis added a third world's record to his list when he won the 25-mile event in 19:8:16. The time of his five mile run was 3:47:42 while his time for the 15-mile run was 11:29:35.

In 1928 and 1929 Indian won all National Championship races for two years running. This is an unsurpassed achievement in the history of US motorcycle racing. That Indian was able to pull it off was largely due to the ability of the ohv Forty-fives to win not only in one but in two classes of racing, though also due to the fact that H-D was not really playing the racing game over this period.

At last Franklin had an outright winner - the 61 cu in machines that were vanquished fair and square by this new upstart Forty-five included those fitted with side-valve Altoona motors. The issue of which valve layout was more rewarding for race engine development - overhead-valve or side-valve - had, for Franklin, finally been settled. In April 1929 Indian announced that henceforth it would only support the 45 cu in class in hill-climbing.

In a 61 cu in guise, Indian's best ever race motor could have staked serious claim to being the fastest motorcycle in the world at that time. In such an engine, Indian would have had just the device to match JAP which by now had stamped its initials all over the official world's record books. This fame could have then have been parleyed into a range of exclusive and high-priced sports tourers or road-going hotrods similar to the JAP-powered Zeniths or Brough Superiors. But the isolation of the US industry from world motorcycle sport administration, and from the export markets in which they could have capitalized upon world-ranking speed success, meant that this opportunity could not be grabbed. This is the main reason why Franklin is nowadays such an unsung hero of motorcycle history. At the very time he was right on top of his game and level-pegging with the world's best, everything in international sport and trade politics was going against him and his beloved Indian factory. Winning a few more domestic-market sales for the Forty-five Scout had to instead be the full scope of Indian's ambitions for the ohv Forty-five race-engine programme.

What if less hyper, more tractable, road versions of this ohv model had augmented or replaced both Scout and Chief at this time, to become a sport bike and sports-tourer respectively? What if they'd added 'streamline' saddle-tank styling by 1930, then by 1932 a re-circulating dry-sump oiling system, and a positive-stop foot-change four-speed transmission? What if the exposed valve gear had become enclosed inside cast rocker-boxes, similar to the neat arrangements adopted by British manufacturers like Matchless or Ariel by 1938? It was left to other manufacturers to turn this concept into a winner. The stand-out example is H-D's EL Knucklehead of 1936. Meanwhile, Indian's late-20s engineering effort became dissipated on ill-fated projects like a light-car, a refrigerator, out-board motors, and the Indian Four. There would also soon be a thing going on called a Great Depression.

The potential for Indian to have beaten H-D by ten years in release of an overhead-valve Sixty-one road model, just as they'd pre-dated H-D in practically every other significant industry innovation, is tantalizing. This is the one thing Indian didn't do that H-D did do, and it was this one thing that ensured H-D's survival through to the New Millennium. The failure to build an overhead-valve Sixty-one road model is another of those 'what ifs?' that make Indian history so painfully fascinating.

Weird Scenes At The Wigwam

Prudent management by President Weschler enabled Indian to remain profitable throughout the period after the 1921-22 economic slump so that, by 1927, a surplus of cash had built up in the company's accounts.

This is money that should have been used to update the existing Indian model range, or even introduce a completely new model like the large overhead-valve V-twin for the street as just described. A re-vamp of the Scout and Chief models in 1927-28 would have been very timely. This was a period when a host of innovations were becoming new industry standards. Indian had put a lot of effort lately into developing exotic racers, but was resting on its laurels with its main street models the Scout (apart from making it into a Forty-five) and particularly the Chief which was still substantively unaltered since its inception in 1922 and would remain so until 1931.

The engineering changes that swept through global motorcycling from 1927 through to 1934 were major, and included a dramatic change in the overall look of the motorcycles themselves. Positive-stop foot-change gearboxes came into vogue, beginning with Velocette in 1928. Clincher (or 'beaded-edge') tyres were shed in favour of well-rims with wired-edge tyres, in which holding the tyre in place upon the rim was no longer dependant solely upon high inner-tube air pressure. Better roads meant higher speeds and longer periods of flat-out running, which in turn revealed the inadequacies of splash lubrication and the advantages of dry-sump re-circulation under positive pressure. By the mid-thirties, everybody except Harley-Davidson had adopted re-circulating oiling.

In Britain the adoption of overhead valves on upright single cylinder engines had made them much taller, which encouraged the abandonment of between-the-rails 'flat-tank' fuel reservoirs. Starting with Howard Davies' little company HRD in 1925, petrol tanks were split down their underside to hang over the frame top-tube - the advent of the so-called 'saddle-tank'. This changed the whole appearance of motorcycles from 'fast-moving farm gate' to a geometrical harmony of eye-pleasing triangular themes. Their outlines now tapered back from the steering head to the rear axle, seated the rider lower to the ground so that he or she was now 'in' the motorcycle rather than 'on' it, and placed a teardrop-profiled gas tank as the crowning glory of the whole machine.

In this way, and in addition to becoming even more functional, motorcycles now started looking 'cool'. Any manufacturer that was slow to adopt saddle-tanks, opting to remain a while longer with the functionally satisfactory between-the-rails flat-tank layout, thereby condemned their products to looking decidedly old-fashioned and 'un-cool'. Manufacturers like Triumph, like Sunbeam ... and Indian.

If Indian had spent this surplus wisely in 1927, they could have avoided at least some of the fate that ultimately befell them. But no, the financiers who made up the Board of Directors thought it far more opportune to take this reserve of money out of the company and use it to play the stock market.

President Weschler fought this tooth and nail. He could see the need to re-invest some of this money both in the Indian range, and in the Indian plant itself which was now starting to get long in the tooth. He'd worked very hard for several years to ensure that the company would not only survive but would have a future, building on a product line that he believed in. To see the nest egg that he'd hoarded for product and plant development get diverted in this way was just too much. His arguments fell on deaf ears, so as a matter of principle he resigned from the company. He joined the Baldwin Chain Company, where he remained for the remainder of his career. Weschler was sorely missed at Indian, where his had been the steady hand at the helm through some very rough seas. If we had to name only five people as being responsible for Indian's greatness as a motorcycle manufacturer, they would be Hendee, Hedstrom, Gustafson Snr, Franklin, and Weschler.

When Weschler departed, so did the kind of restraint which had resulted in a firm 'no' to Tommy Butler's industrial engine idea. The men controlling Indian were financiers who saw the Wigwam's value as being that of a general manufacturing facility, rather than a specialist motorcycle maker. With the industry as a whole selling no more than 25,000 motorcycles a year, to them it made sense that a factory capable of making 100,000 per year could turn its hand to other products.

But which products? Well, practically anything, it seems.

At least the first major diversion of precious engineering money and resources was splurged on another motorcycle. Though in hindsight, it was still a diversion. Ironically it was a policy implemented when Weschler was still company President, at the start of 1927. In fairness to Weschler, it would have seemed a very good idea at the time.

The motorcycle in question was the Indian Four. Negotiations to buy the assets of the Ace company from its then current owners, Michigan Motors Corporation, were concluded in early 1927, just in time for a green-painted Ace to go onto the Indian stand of the New York Motorcycle Show. This caused a sensation, and added greatly to the impact of the Indian display at which another important model also debuted - the new Scout 45.

According to the later writings of Theodore Hodgdon, who was in Indian's advertising department at the time, production of the Indian Ace commenced in April 1927. Their advertising for this year was able to claim that Indian had the entire market covered - they offered a lightweight single, middleweight twins in 37 and 45 sizes, a heavyweight twin, and a heavyweight Four.

As purchased from Michigan Motors, the Ace design was 1922 technology, but now it was already 1927. Various detail improvements were immediately needed to bring it right up to date. From April to August the Ace was manufactured at Indian pretty much as-received. The only immediate change was from 27 in wheel rims to 25 in ones with balloon tyres, lowering the bike to give it a more modern and sure-footed stance. By now Weschler was gone, and it was newly elected company President Louis Bauer who had the honour of posing for a photo opportunity with the first Indian Ace to roll out of the factory doors on 25th April 1927.

Throughout that summer the engineering department was busy, and a factory pamphlet lists about 18 changes made at this time to things like the oiling system, saddle position, pistons and camshaft, to update various manufacturing processes, and to improve the materials used for engine components like cylinders and valves. All of this amounted to a lot of tinkering. These changes were announced to be incorporated into 1928 Indian Aces, whose build began from August 1927. This updated and improved, yet still substantively Ace-looking, Indian Ace continued to be manufactured until the fall of 1928.

For the remainder of 1927 and into 1928 the Indian design and engineering department continued to be busy, to implement a policy to fully 'Indian-ize' the Ace Four into the Indian 401. This essentially meant to make it stop looking like an Ace and start looking like an Indian, to fully integrate it within the Indian range.

On the face of it, investment in integration of the Four makes sense, since a modular range that uses common components like frames, forks, wheels, gas tanks, and so on, can save money and allow for better profit margins through simplification of production processes and economies of scale. Ariel, 'The Modern Motorcycle' and Motobécane unit-singles were applying this very approach with great success at this time.

Unfortunately for Indian's admirable aim of integration, this went awry with the Four. The new Four frame for the 1929 Indian 401 (in production from the end of July 1928) shared nothing but a general aesthetic resemblance to any other frame in the Indian range. Not only did they invest in this new frame in a way which achieved nothing in terms of production efficiencies, they also introduced a new vibratory patch in the rev range that hadn't been there before. This forced a further new frame, this time with double down-tubes, to be designed. Then later, in 1931 when genuine cost-cutting became of major importance owing to the nation being in the grip of the Great Depression, Indian again re-engineered the Four to achieve the very type of integration that could have been achieved in 1928. Indian's Four was starting a trend that would continue through to the late thirties, of sucking up an amount of engineering time and resources out of all proportion to its contribution to Indian sales and profits. Updates for other models like the Chief were moved onto the back-burner as a result.

How much say-so, and direct input, did Charles Franklin have into the re-engineering of the Indian Ace into the 401 and its successor the 402?

Nominally he was Chief Engineer in charge of design and product development, so would have at the very least overseen and approved of the changes in specifications and production methods brought to bear upon Indian's new Four. How much influence he had on company policy regarding the Four is now impossible to determine, and we can only speculate. The policy of Indian even having a Four in the first place was out of his hands - this had been President Weschler's idea and it was endorsed by the Board of Directors. Franklin had presumably been consulted, however once the decision was made then naturally he'd have fallen into line and got on with the job of making the Four work as well as possible within the time, budget and resources available.

As for the amount of direct input by Franklin into the Four's re-engineering in a hands-on way, this is also not easy to determine but our conclusion is 'probably not very much'. The reason for this is that when Indian got the Ace Four from Michigan Motors, they also got Arthur Lemon.

Art Lemon and Ignaz Scwhinn are allegedly the two people that in 1919 caused Bill Henderson to depart his exalted position within Excelsior, the new owners of his Henderson company, in a fit of pique. His original vision for his Four was that of low, light and fast hot-rod. Lemon had been associated with the Henderson when it was still a Henderson and, when it became an Excelsior-Henderson, he went along with Schwinn's new vision for a stately King of the Road heavyweight built for comfort rather than for speed. This was a successful concept, and it starting making a tidy sum of money for Excelsior from around 1920 onwards.

Bill started a new company to make the Ace, as a rival product which returned to the sizzling high performance ideals he'd had in mind for his four-cylinder machine all along. But then he was tragically killed in 1922 while out test-riding his new creation. Ace's main investor Max Sladkin head hunted Lemon from Excelsior to continue Ace development in a way that remained faithful to Henderson's vision. Lemon's design brief was to develop an Ace that was the fastest motorcycle in the world. In due course the Ace XP4 ridden by 'Red' Wolverton ran 129 mph in 1923, and there were no takers for a $10,000 wager offered by the Ace company for an out-and-out straight-line burn-off against any other motorcycle manufactured anywhere in the world. But the money side of things was less successful than Lemon's engineering or Wolverton's riding, and this led to the chain of dealings that brought both the Ace and Arthur Lemon to Indian in January 1927.

Lemon stayed at Indian as an engineer in the design department until mid-1930, during this time steadily developing the Indian Four to keep pace with the higher cruising-speed requirements now demanded by customers due to America's steadily improving roads. During his tenure, the Indian Four remained faithful to the lean, lithe and peppy vision Henderson had for his original Four and for the Ace. It was other, car oriented designers under E. Paul du Pont's presidency in the 1930s who later re-worked and doubly re-worked the Indian Four into another plush King of the Road heavyweight.

When Lemon joined Indian two top priorities were required to make the Ace engine hold up better under the higher demands of continuous flat out running now being expected of motorcycles in general. One was to replace the splash oiling with a pressure oiling system. The other was to change the three bearing crankshaft to a five bearing one. Both these changes would have been high on Lemon's 'to do' list ever since he first took over from Bill Henderson at Ace in 1922. The first item was achieved at Indian in 1927, and the second item in mid-1929 with the emergence of the Indian 402.

Franklin had just completed a busy year in 1926 with designing and developing the Forty-five Scout, the overhead-valve Forty-five hill-climber engines, and new two-valve versions of the earlier bronze-cover racing singles that first appeared in the 1923 IoM TT race. Then, in the first half of 1928, he was again flat out with transferring ideas from the Indian 401 project to his Scout (especially the rear frame section) to come up with the 101 Scout which was ready for production in May 1928, within one month of the new 401 itself in June.

By contrast, 1927 would have seemed a somewhat slow year for him. He was able to spend one whole month of it in the UK, and it is reported in the *Irish Cyclist and Motor Cyclist* of 2nd November 1927, that he attended the London motorcycle show at Olympia in November where the Indian company had a display.

Apart from that, what else did he do in 1927? There are really only two major projects in his diary that we can point to. One was to develop and fine-tune the new overhead Forty-five hill-climb motors during this first season of them being raced, and continue his parallel path of side-valve Altoona tuning which used the same bottom half as the hill-climb motors. This new and exciting race engine development would have chewed up several hundreds of hours of dynamometer time during 1927. Both overhead- and side-valve lines of enquiry were leading inexorably to a final showdown in 1928 whereby, at long last, his latest two-valve overhead-valve configuration would be declared a clear winner over his side-valve engines in US racing.

Apart from that, there was really only one other big thing for Franklin to do during 1927. This was to help Lemon update the 1922 Ace into a 1928 Ace, and advise on how best the Ace could be built differently to suit the available Wigwam manufacturing processes and materials on hand.

Lemon would have needed little or no detailed oversight from Franklin. He was already the proven master of the Ace design. So apart from looking over Lemon's shoulder, or even breathing down his neck to keep the costs under control, it can be presumed that Franklin was able to leave Lemon well enough alone to do what Lemon did best, while Franklin got on with his own forté which was developing his Indian V-twins.

The Indian Four added prestige to the Indian line-up. True to Bill Henderson's hopes for it, the Indian engineering department developed the Four and the advertising department promoted it in a way that emphasized its rapid performance and snappy pick-up and not just its smooth all-day drive-ability. The glamorous Four, not the workaday Chief, was touted in advertising as the top performer of the Indian range.

Looking at Indian's situation from 1927 through to the end of 1928, one can be sure that those in charge felt the company was riding toward an all-time high. In 1927 they'd unveiled the Forty-five Scout, the extremely rapid Forty-five overhead hill-climber race motors, and the Four as new-model additions to the existing Prince, 37 Scout and Chief, making Indian the 'World's Most Complete Cycle Line'. They had all bases covered, while H-D really only had the Seventy-four V-twin J-Model. Excelsior had a tubbier Four, and a hot Forty-five.

The problem for Indian is that they were never ever going to sell very many Fours. It was an expensive bike to build and, because motorcycles do not lend themselves to mass production in the way that four-wheelers do, its hand-crafted quality resulted in it wearing a sticker price that was more than the American public was accustomed to paying for a brand-new automobile ($420 ex-factory, compared with $380 for a Ford Model T). A customer firstly had to really want to own a motorcycle and, secondly, really want to own a *four-cylinder* motorcycle, in order to purchase either an Indian Four or a Henderson Four. Such customers really only amounted to those very few riders who needed to spend all-day, every-day in the saddle. This meant either law enforcement officers, or a tiny band of 'touring riders' whose emergence only became possible by the very recent coalescence in America of a road network even worth touring over.

This is why we describe the Indian Four as a diversion. It added prestige, but in a loss leading kind of way. There are a fortunate few among us in the New Millennium who love their Indian Fours, and the rest of us can only envy them. It is not our intention at all to rob them of the joy of Four ownership by begrudging the fact that this 'Duesenberg of Motorcycles' was ever built in the first place. Even so, it's instructive to observe which American motorcycle maker is still with us as a viable business today, and what they were doing back in 1927 that might have contributed to this longevity. Exclusively building a V-twin Seventy-four, the bread and butter model of American motorcycling, is what they were doing. By being staid and boring, once again the folks at H-D managed to do the right thing.

Meanwhile, 'from diversity comes resilience' is surely what they must have been thinking to themselves over at Indian. Of any motorcycle company in America, Indian was now positioned as the most ready to seize any opportunities the future motorcycle market may hold. The mid-twenties was intended to be their re-building phase on a climb back up into the US market top spot.

Two factors then chimed in to seriously undermine Indian's efforts on this come-back trail. One was the 1929 Wall Street Crash, which few predicted and which caught out many businesses besides Indian. The other was an increased tendency to stray into matters not part of Indian's core business. This had disastrous results, Depression or no Depression. Diversification accordingly became further diversion, at the expense of Indian's own mainstay model the Indian Chief.

After Weschler's departure the newly elected Indian company President was Louis Bauer, who soon installed his son Jack in the engineering department. Young Jack was a recent engineering graduate who wanted to build automobiles, and Daddy was inclined to indulge him in this wish.

This was not the first foray by the Indian company into automobile manufacture. Back in 1909 George Hendee had hired another expatriate Irishman, James H. Jones, under a three-year contract and paid him $5,000 per year to design and build some prototype air-cooled V-8 aero engines, and an Indian car.[45] The aero engine was used to power the first ever commercial air-mail flight in the USA. Left-over examples of this V-8 engine must have somehow found their way out of the factory at about the same time that Oscar Hedstrom did, for they contributed toward his home-built speed-boats becoming a force to be reckoned with in racing on the Connecticut River after he retired.

INDIAN MOTOCYCLE COMPANY PLANT EXECUTIVES
Upper Row (Left to right): Douglas MacGregor, Charles Gustafson, Charles B. Franklin, F. W. Fischer and Arthur Lemon.
Lower Row (Left to Right): T. L. Loose, George Anderson, W. W. Smith, C. F. Evans and C. A. Bauer.

Indian executives in 1927, including 'Four Whizz' Arthur Lemon, and wannabe auto engineer Jack Bauer. (Photo EMIMA)

The Indian car was built by Jones as requested, and was a two-seater along lines far more suggestive of Stutz Bearcat than Ford Model T. An existing photo of this car, with Jones' head bent over its open bonnet, indicates a straight-six with overhead valves. This puts it on the cutting-edge of high-performance for its time. It was clearly intended to be the type of automobile that Oscar Hedstrom might himself have wished to buy, had he been forced to purchase some other company's product rather than simply have one built for him within his own. With burgeoning motorcycle sales on their hands, Indian did not feel they much needed to diversify into automobiles at that time. As a result the 1909 - 1910 Indian car project did not progress any further.

By contrast Jack Bauer's 1928 effort was aimed at the economy end of the auto market, with a light car or 'baby' car concept similar to that of the English Austin 7. His first effort used a Chief V-twin engine with chain drive to the rear axle, but it proved far too prone to vibration in this application. Dropping that idea, Bauer the Younger moved on to a small four-cylinder concept that used a Continental engine. This too was dropped after a few were built, when it became obvious that it could not be sold any cheaper than the existing larger-sized and volume-produced American offerings of Ford and General Motors. In any case, Americans both then and thereafter were never much inclined to economize in either the physical dimensions or the horse-power output of their automobiles.

The cost of this dalliance with automobiles was apparently measurable not only in direct investment of time and money, but also indirectly in terms of Scouts and Chiefs which could have been sold that were not sold. This is because the diversion of available staff and materials meant there were orders for these motorcycles that could not be filled.

A full account of the various diversions of capital and talent in which the Indian company engaged through 1928 and into 1929 is set out in detail in *The Iron Redskin*. As a quick summary, much of 1929's resources of money and manpower were squandered on a massive automobile shock-absorber manufacturing and marketing campaign, followed by an investigation into refrigerators. Then there was a four-stroke outboard speedboat motor of a design purchased externally and brought into production by Indian, which proved firstly to be under powered for its size-class, secondly was only available in a single size-class rather than as part of a comprehensive range to suit all sizes of boats, and thirdly was offered through an existing Indian motorcycle dealership network whose locations were unrelated to proximity with boating waterways. Charles Franklin was called upon to have a gaze at this outboard motor, and see if he could get it to run any better. Meanwhile, changes of direction came fast and furious during a period of 'revolving door' top management at Indian, with no perennial anchor man like Weschler to provide stability or continuity in day to day policy and operations.

> *The Daily Northwestern, 22nd June 1929*
> J. Russell Waite has been elected president of the Indian Motorcycle company, of Springfield, Mass, succeeding Louis E. Bauer, who had resigned.

Other projects that were in the pipeline, which absorbed much energy from higher management but never made it to the factory floor, included a grandiose aviation project using a design that unfortunately was not ever going to gain federal aviation approval.

> *The Lowell Sun, 9 May 1929*
> The New York World said today that reports were current that Charles A. Levine, first transatlantic air passenger, had purchased the Indian motorcycle company of Springfield. Mass., and would convert it into an aircraft and aircraft motor factory.

> *The North Adams Weekly Transcript, 29 June 1929*
> LEVINE CONSIDERS AIRPLANE MOTORS
> North Adams Native to issue Statement about Springfield Plan
> Charles A. Levine, a native of this city who gained prominence as the first trans-Atlantic air passenger and who is now president of the Columbia Air Lines, Inc., during a visit to Springfield yesterday announced that he would make a definite statement next week in regard to his plans for the building of airplane motors at the Indian Motorcycle plant in that city. He spent several hours conferring with Louis E. Bauer, president and general manager of the Springfield concern. He was unable to take off from Dunn field for a trip back to New York because the engine of the plane failed to turn the propeller fast enough.

Maybe that airplane knew something that investors didn't, for Levine's plan to turn Indian into an aircraft factory also did not take off.

> *The Charleston Daily Mail, 12 November 1929*
> Charles A. Levine, (much before the public in connection with junk (bonds) and trans-Atlantic flights), and his associates, have sold control of the Indian Motorcycle company which they had obtained last summer.

What became apparent was that sales and service in Indian's core business, the motorcycles, suffered during this time. Experienced section heads were co-opted into non-motorcycle projects and this left institutional speed-wobbles when they were back stopped by others less able to perform their tasks. Fewer motorcycles were produced than could be sold, and dealer back-up by the factory with spare parts and major repairs became chaotic. The factory started demanding cash up-front for motorcycles delivered to dealers, who then found that some were wrongly assembled or even had parts missing. Relations with Indian dealers became strained as a result, and some gave up their franchises.

When run by Frank Weschler during tough times in the early 'twenties, the Indian company remained profitable for the most part. But Indian, under the successive new regimes after Weschler departed, started to consistently lose money. This report was picked up off the wire services by a good many newspapers across America, including this one:

> *The Daily Northwestern of 28th November 1930*
> Indian Motorcycle company and subsidiaries reported for the nine months ended Sept. 30 loss from operations of $479,434 and total loss, including loss on sale of securities, of $492,599. For the nine months ended Sept. 30 last year, the company reported an operating loss of $405,957 and net loss of $193,960 after $211,007 profit from the sale on securities.

Some of the diversification ventures were not really intended to succeed. Rather, they were instituted to lend credence to manipulations of Indian shares on the New York stock exchange. Indian became frequently reported in the newspapers, not for their famous products but for the various ways in which their shares were being traded. 'Pool operations' were (and still are) a common tactic for stock market speculators to engage in, and were perfectly legal during the 1920s though measures to combat such stock manipulations were one of the first things to be implemented in post-Crash efforts to establish the Securities & Exchange Commission or SEC.

A pool operation is a 'club' of investors, usually made up of some insiders of a company and their friends and associates, who drum up publicity about that company using plausible facts drawn from their inside knowledge. They next manipulate the share price via furious but coordinated buying and selling of the company's stock between themselves to generate volume and give the impression of a rising stock. Others swoop, the artificially increased demand leads to a share price rise, until by pre-arranged signal those 'in the know' all sell. That makes the price slip, then tumble, and within a few days it has settled back to its pre-operation level, leaving those inside the pool a few millions richer and those outside the pool 'holding the baby'.

According to *A financial history of the United States* by Jerry W Markham, paid publicists were an important component of pool operations. They planted stories with journalists, and spread rumours about a company's prospects. Financial journalists and radio broadcasters were directly paid 'by the story' to disseminate particular investment tips to the public at the behest of the pool operators, or were themselves members of the pool for which they were running the story. Markham names the Indian Company as prominent among the stocks manipulated in this way by a well-known Wall Street publicist named A. Newton Plummer. This particular gentleman was paid a total of about $300,000 to have stories about Indian and other companies placed in *The New York Times* and *Wall Street Journal*, from where they would get picked up by as many as 700 other newspapers. Plummer later wrote a book in which he revealed the 'systematic bribery of financial reporters by Wall Street interests'. We scanned through some newspaper archives of the era and, sure enough, it did not take us long to find news items like these three below, which provide direct evidence of the kinds of manipulations that were going on in connection with Indian stock.

> The San Antonio Light, 29th January 1930
> A trading play in a low priced stock for the really small trader is recommended here today for the first time in many weeks. Indian Motorcycle, which has seen a long period of dark days marketwise, is about to move upward under the sponsorship of a strong group. The company has unfilled orders that are 65 per cent greater than those of a year ago, according to President Norman T. Bolles. Sales of the Indian 'Scout' cycle and the new 'Silver Arrow' outboard motor will exceed those of 1929. Book value of the common stock is placed at $14 a share. Earnings for 10 years have averaged $2.26 annually, while the stock's price has been around $23. At yesterday's close it was selling under $7 a share.
>
> 31st January 1930
> Spectator is rather proud of his tip on Indian Motorcycle, a stock which had not moved in many months. Yesterday, after it was recommended here as a good bet for a trading play, it advanced from $7^1/_8$ to 9, a rise of $1^7/_8$ points and closed at $8^1/_2$ for a net gain of $1^3/_8$ points. It was the best recommendation thus far this year for the small speculator.

And doubtless the best little earner thus far for the article's author, and for those in the company who fed him the 'news-worthy information' along with advice to buy now while still at $7 but not hold on to it for too long.

> Appleton Post-Crescent, 5th March 1930
> POOL OPERATION ON INDIAN MOTORCYCLE FAILS AS STOCK BREAKS
> By Stanley W. Prenosil, Associated Press Financial Editor, .New York - The recovery in stock prices assumed rather impressive proportions in today's stock market despite the collapse in a recent pool specialty. Indian Motorcycle Common broke 63 points to 9 and the preferred 23 points to 52, on what appeared to be the collapse of a pool operation in that issue.

There are those who, consistent with a few selectively-chosen tenets of Nietzschian philosophy, can easily rationalize pool operations and other stock manipulation practices by the Latin phrase *caveat emptor*. What could not, and still cannot, be ignored by stock market regulators is that the money to be made from these practices is the direct result of deliberately and calculatingly setting out to fool people.

By 1929 Bauer had resigned as President, however stock manipulations continued under succeeding Presidents J. Russell Waite and Norman Bolles and their respective controlling-interest shareholder groups. Things were at low ebb. Indian stock had been brought into disrepute. The price of Indian shares on the New York Stock Exchange crashed during 1928, recovered on the back of renewed publicity about various diversification projects, but crashed again in mid-1929 and was already worth almost nothing by the time Black October came around. The failed projects had wasted well over a million dollars of the company's money. There was no longer any financial surplus in the Treasury, and the company began struggling to meet its payroll. Leading west coast dealer Hap Alzina personally made transcontinental trips bearing cash raised in short-term loans from San Francisco banks, because no Springfield banks would lend to the Indian company.

This was the new situation facing Indian even before the Crash of October 1929. It's no wonder they didn't quite get around to updating the Indian Chief just yet, what with all this dilly-dallying with shock absorbers, refrigerators, outboard motors, and automobiles.

Charles Franklin's own personal love affair with fast American automobiles continued unabated in the late 'twenties. In about 1927 he acquired a Roamer, the car he still owned at the time of his death.

It is said that you can tell a lot about a person from the car they drive. What can we tell about Franklin from a Roamer?

They were exclusive. They were powerful. They were custom-built using the best of components. Made by the Barley Motor Car Co. in Kalamazoo MI, the Roamer was named after a famous race horse and was 'designed for racy sportiness'. Advanced features for the 1920s included synchro-mesh transmission, and hydraulic brakes. In styling its hood and radiator grill profile was reminiscent of a Rolls Royce Silver Ghost. Film stars owned them, including Buster Keaton and Mary Pickford. Advertised with the slogan 'America's smartest car', they were priced between $4,000 and $6,000 (depending upon model and specification) at a time when a Ford Model T was $380.

Several engine options were offered from the best then available, including straight-sixes like the Rutenber motor for touring. Franklin had selected the hottest set-up, naturally. His came fitted with the more powerful and more expensive option of four-cylinder Rochester-Duesenberg engine. Nancye sold this car soon after Charles' death and it was taken out West where it ended up in law enforcement, used to pursue and apprehend offenders breaking the speed limit.[46]

What does a Roamer tell us about Franklin? That he had taste, and liked to go extremely fast.

It helps to confirm what we pretty much already know.

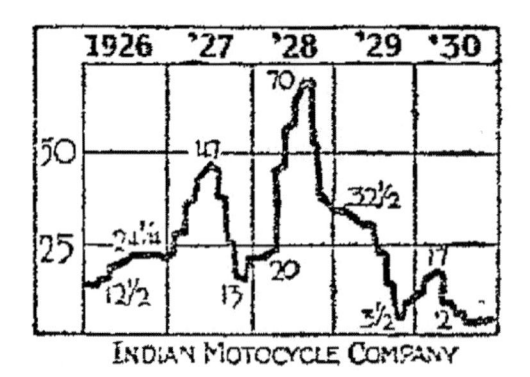

The 'Stock-a-Day' column of the Appleton Post-Crescent of 13th January 1931 published this chart of Indian stock prices over the previous five years. Due to various stock manipulation scams by company directors, Indian stock had already hit rock-bottom even before the Wall Street Crash of October 1929. (Indian factory archives)

The Immortal 101 Scout

The Indian Scout Series 101 is Franklin's masterpiece.

This was widely acknowledged to be so during his lifetime, and it has been re-affirmed over the years amongst those with a wide general knowledge of motorcycles. Anytime that a list is compiled of the world's best ever motorcycle models, be it for a magazine article, or a book, or in a late night conversation around a rally campfire, the Indian Scout Series 101 will almost certainly make it into the Top Twenty, and at times even into the Top Ten. It is consistently placed alongside the likes of the Honda CB750, Triumph Bonneville, BSA Gold Star, Vincent Black Shadow, Brough Superior SS100, 'Trusty' 3½ hp Triumph, Ariel Square Four, 1938-40 Indian Four, Honda 50 Step-thru, and H-D EL Knucklehead, when motorcycles are called to mind as being the most influential, most fondly remembered, or most 'classic' (an elusive and much-abused term).

Not bad for a motorcycle that was only made for three and a half years, from mid-1928 to 1931. Not bad given that it was not even a fresh design, but rather a make over of the Scout that had already been in production since late 1919. Call it inspiration or luck or a combination of both, but in 1928 Charles Franklin took Indian's 'best ever' production engine and dropped it into their best ever frame and running gear. The result is one of the best balances of speed, handling, power, weight, stability and agility ever to have been wrapped up into a single motorcycling package. This is both when judged by the standards of the era, and for decades hence.

Even today, the Scout 101 has a loyal following and holds a special place among Indian enthusiasts. It is prized by people who value an antique bike not just for collectability but for its all-round usability and for whom its lithe and graceful lines are just the icing on the cake. Apart from the Scout 101 there is no other model of Indian, and few other models of any marque, for which a thriving international club exists exclusively for that one model.[47] Prices of mechanically sorted and sensitively restored 101's are nowadays on a par with those of Indian Chiefs, bucking the price-point system habitually operated for the different capacity classes by motorcycle dealers when these bikes were brand new.

If, like at least one of us among this book's authorship, you're over 6-foot and fifteen stone (we won't say by how much) then you'll still prefer a Chief for real road riding. Yet the 'twenties Chief looks so comparatively utilitarian and, well … ordinary, when stood next to the lean, lithe lines of a Scout 101. Even when standing still, they are so graceful and appear poised as if for flight. You will glance across at the contemporary Chief and find yourself wishing it were not quite so high or so straight in its backbone. You'll wonder why it was not contrived to have more of a triangle and less of a parallelogram in its silhouette. It's not until 1932 onwards that the Chiefs can really be said to have become handsome, when they picked up on the triangular themes first initiated by Indian on the Scout 101.

So how did all of this come about? What was going through Franklin's mind when he decided, right in the middle of a model year, to take the Scout and completely re-vamp it into the 101? We will never know for sure, because it has not been recorded. All we can do is look at the bike itself, in terms of its dimensions and its characteristics. And we can look at what other projects Franklin had going on at the same time as the 101. And then we can make an educated guess.

1927 was a relatively light year for Charles Franklin. He'd worked hard in 1926 to develop not one but two new 45 cu in engines, one being the Forty-five Scout and the other the overhead-valve hill-climb race motor, plus the two-cam two-valve 30.50 and 21 cu in racing singles. In 1927 there was a flurry of activity surrounding the updating and the ongoing Indian-ization of the Ace Four. Arthur Lemon was there to take the lead on that, however Franklin would have been on hand to contribute his knowledge of the Indian plant, its production processes, and the available raw materials. He certainly would not have been uninterested in the Four, since he ate, breathed and drank all powerful two-wheeled mechanical devices.

There was some work done on detail improvements to the Scout and Chief during 1927, however. The year 1928 thus began normally enough with these changes appearing on the new models. Most significant of these was the first-time appearance of a front wheel brake on the Indian road bikes. It's not that the Americans did not know about such things before this, it's just that front brakes were honestly not really needed so far. Their appearance suggests that by 1928 America's road networks were improving and the number of cars upon them were increasing, to the point where American motorcycles now did need a larger quantity of 'stop' to accompany their 'go'. Another significant one for 1928 was a change to the front engine mounts, to dispense with detachable engine brackets and instead add a 'nose' to the front of the crankcase castings to act as the frame pick-up point for the front engine mount. This change necessitated some minor alterations to the frame as well. Other detail changes also took place for the start of this model year, but will not be further described here because they are already covered in other books like *The Iron Redskin* or Hatfield's *Indian Scout*.

Then, into the first half of 1928, work continued apace on the transmogrification of the already once-revised Indian Ace into a fully-fledged Indian Four. A completely new frame was

Indian Four Series 401 frame geometry was adopted for the Scout Series 101. A great move. (Indian factory archives)

In this side-by-side comparison it can be seen that the 1928 Series 101 Scout (above) is longer, lower and altogether more svelte than the stubby Scout 45 of 1927 (below). (Indian factory archives)

being worked-on which, allied to the Indian trademark leaf spring front fork, was supposed to complete the induction of the Ace into the Indian line-up.

At some point during the first quarter of 1928 Charles Franklin must have wandered across to the 401 prototype, then over to the Scout production line, and finally back to the 401, and then stood there for a while with pursed lips and a furrowed brow, and gone 'Hmmm …'. Because the essence of the Scout 101 rolling chassis is a rear sub-frame, wheelbase, and steering-head geometry all of dimensions the same as that of the 401.

It has even been said by some that the Indian Four and the Scout 101 use the same frame, but in fact they are not. Everything about the Four's frame is thicker, heavier and stronger than a 101 frame. Not only that, but the 401 frame was at this time still a single front down-tube affair.

The main effect of this cross-pollination from 401 to 101 was to lengthen its wheelbase to 57 inches, lower the seat height to 26 inches, slope the frame top-tube down from the steering head far more gracefully to the seat post and rear sub-frame, and move the engine slightly further forward in the frame. The lengthened frame then led to consequential amendments in various ancillary items like the shape of the gas tank, which became smaller and teardrop-shaped, and to the toolbox and mounting position of the battery. Although the world was now clearly switching over to saddle-tanks, the 101 retained the between-the-rails 'flat-tank' configuration, although its tank was no longer flat. This was a victory of engineering common sense over fickle fashion, for no one at Indian was yet convinced that saddle-tanks were any kind of an advance over the gas tanks their motorcycles had already.

The net result of all these changes was a motorcycle that looked even better than before when parked, and felt even better still once on the move (see colour photo 34). 'Stable, yet agile' are words often used to describe the Scout 101 in a nutshell. While maneuverable, the castor action of its front-end geometry ensures that steering the 101 can be a hands-off deal.

The Scout Series 101 became renowned as one of the most versatile motorcycles of its time. It was handy enough to be a city commuter. Roomy enough (just) and with sufficient power and stamina for the rider to really get out and tour the nation. Its power to weight ratio compared favourably with Seventy-fours and, being a lot more maneuverable, it could even out run them in tight and twisty situations. In competition it was not quite good enough to win top-class professional events owing to the weight penalty of that strong frame and ever lasting primary drive, but second-tier racers across America made it a force to be reckoned with in dirt-track, in speedway, in hill-climbing, and in road racing. As a 'California bobber' stripped to the essential items of just frame, wheels and an engine stroked with turned-down Chief flywheels, the Scout 101 could be a 'Q-ship' armed and dangerous. Out west, people like Al Crocker designed and sold overhead-valve top-end conversion kits for the Scout 101.

Why 101? Why 401? Well, these appellations came about because the Indian company in 1928 decided, as a matter of policy, to dispense with model-year designations. 'We won't make customers wait a whole year for improvements', ran the advertising, 'We'll bring 'em to you the instant they are ready!' But to let people know that the version now on offer is superior to the preceding one, a three-digit 'series' numbering system was devised in which the third digit would increase by an integer step with every set of substantive revisions to the model specification.

Thus the 1928 mid-season revision to the Ace Four went into production as soon as it was ready, which was in June, and the new machine was designated the Indian Series 401. Which is logical, because the Indian Four is, after all, a four, and the 401 is the first Indian Four.

But after that, logic sort of went out the window. Because logic would dictate that the Prince, being a single-cylinder machine, should have become the Series 101 when it in turn was substantively revised for 1928. Since the Scout is a twin, then it should have been dubbed the 201. Instead, these codes were allocated the other way around. Indian did not at this time, nor at any time before or since, have a triple in its model line-up. So what to do with the number '3'? Hey, let's give it to the Chief model. It is yet another indicator of the after-thought status accorded to the Chief throughout the 'twenties that the first digit of its series code (still being applied in the 1940s as the Model 340, 344, etc.) should be the one number left over after all the other good numbers had been taken.

Short-frame Scouts continued in production, as did 37 cu in motors. Australasia was still a viable market for Indian to export into, and a high proportion of the Scout 101 models sold there were 37 cu in versions. It is as if these were regarded as the best priced package for an Indian model with which to directly compete against the 500cc singles that formed the middleweight benchmark in these British dominated markets.

The Prince was re-vamped for a second time in 1928, by being given another new frame and gas tank of a profile that this time echoed the sleek and tapered triangular theme newly adopted by its bigger brother the Scout 101. This certainly turned the Prince into a more handsome and appealing motorcycle. Sales were still insufficient to justify its continuance in an Indian line where the short-frame 37 cu in Scout, manufactured alongside the Scout 101, had assumed the primary function of being the entry level Indian model. The year of 1928 was to be the final year for the Indian Prince.

By extending the frame and re-styling the gas tank to create the Series 101 Scout, Franklin matched a happy motor with happy running gear. The Scout shed its somewhat stumpy, sawn-off look to become long, lean, low and elegant. At the same time it gained the unique handling characteristics of being solid, yet agile. These characteristics endeared it to owners and have made the Model 101 Scout a legend to this day.

The timing was perfect because 1928 was the year that Ignaz Schwinn head-hunted Arthur Constantine of H-D's engineering department to come to Chicago and transform the Super-X and Excelsior-Henderson Four into the 'Streamline' range, which duly appeared as 1929 models. This was a far-sighted and influential move by Excelsior which once again caught the Other Two napping. It represented a final burst of major investment by Schwinn in his motorcycle range. Firstly, Constantine both updated the Four engine and at the same time returned it from side-valve to the original ioe valve layout, to become the KJ model. Secondly, he re-styled both Four and X in a way that abandoned forever the flat-topped 'flat-tank' appearance and whole-heartedly embraced the saddle-tank trend that was now all the rage in the British industry.

The triangular themed look of American so-called 'cruiser' motorcycles, that has persisted to this day in the products of not only H-D but imitators like the Honda Shadow, Yamaha Road Star, Kawasaki Vulcan, Suzuki Intruder and the like, was thus pretty much invented by Constantine in 1928. This 'look' is centered upon a frame top profile that slopes in a single straight line from the steering head back down to the rear axle, to give the machine a triangular side-on profile matched by bulbous yet shapely teardrop saddle-tanks. This Excelsior 'streamline' look was so influential in the US that H-D and Indian had both adopted it by the early thirties.

Arguably H-D had already moved in this direction in 1925, when the J-Model was given a new frame that lowered the seat height by 3-in. and allowed 'semi-streamline' gas tanks to be used. But it represents only a partial severing of this model's link to the ironing-board-flat top profile of the vintage long-tank era, which is what had prevailed on the J's until 1924. H-D retained a horizontal section in the frame top tube where it extends back from the steering head, before curving it downward to facilitate the lowered seat height and provide a sleeker overall look. It's as though they lacked the courage of their convictions about adopting this new 'look', doing so half-heartedly while keeping the J-Model firmly rooted in the past. It was with the V and VL models released in August 1929 that H-D truly got with the programme on this whole 'streamline' issue. Because Excelsior had the guts to jump in 'boots and all' with this new 'look', in a way that still looks very modern, we give them credit for being the US trend-setter in this regard.

At the time, Indian was lucky. By virtue of his various frame changes Franklin had unwittingly given the Scout 101 an approximation of the Excelsior 'streamline' look, even though he had conservatively retained the traditional and now out-dated flat-tank feature. The Scout 101 appealed mightily to the riding public and its new look made this model of Indian even more popular with both customers and dealers.

Above, Scout Series 101 engine showing its two-camshaft timing gear layout (TP)

Right, Scout Series 101 engine showing the helical gear primary drive and revised crankcases with cast-in 'nose' for the front engine mount. (Indian factory archives)

Scout 101 valves and cylinder, showing the race-bred 'squish' combustion chamber and the happily-close proximity of inlet tract to cylinder (TP)

Over at Milwaukee, these trends among the Other Two of the Big Three were doubtless being viewed with trepidation. For despite being three years in development, the new Model D had a number of teething problems that forced recalls and redesign of some components. The adverse publicity from this meant that sales were slow to pick up. Once sorted, the bike did perform well and it was not much different from a Scout 101 in terms of its quantifiable 'zing', 'zip', and 'pizzazz'. But, in terms of less tangible qualities, the new H-D Forty-five had a chronic case of the uglies when compared to the Scout now that the latter had morphed into its graceful Series 101 guise, or when compared to the equally newly-dashing streamline Super-X.

The Motor Company was never one to give up easily. It soon sorted out the problems, successfully developed the Model D for racing, and evolved it into a model that you can still go out and buy brand new today, here and now. The same cannot be said for either the Super-X or the Scout.

To be successful in business, you need more than just a superior product.

NEW *Indian* SCOUT

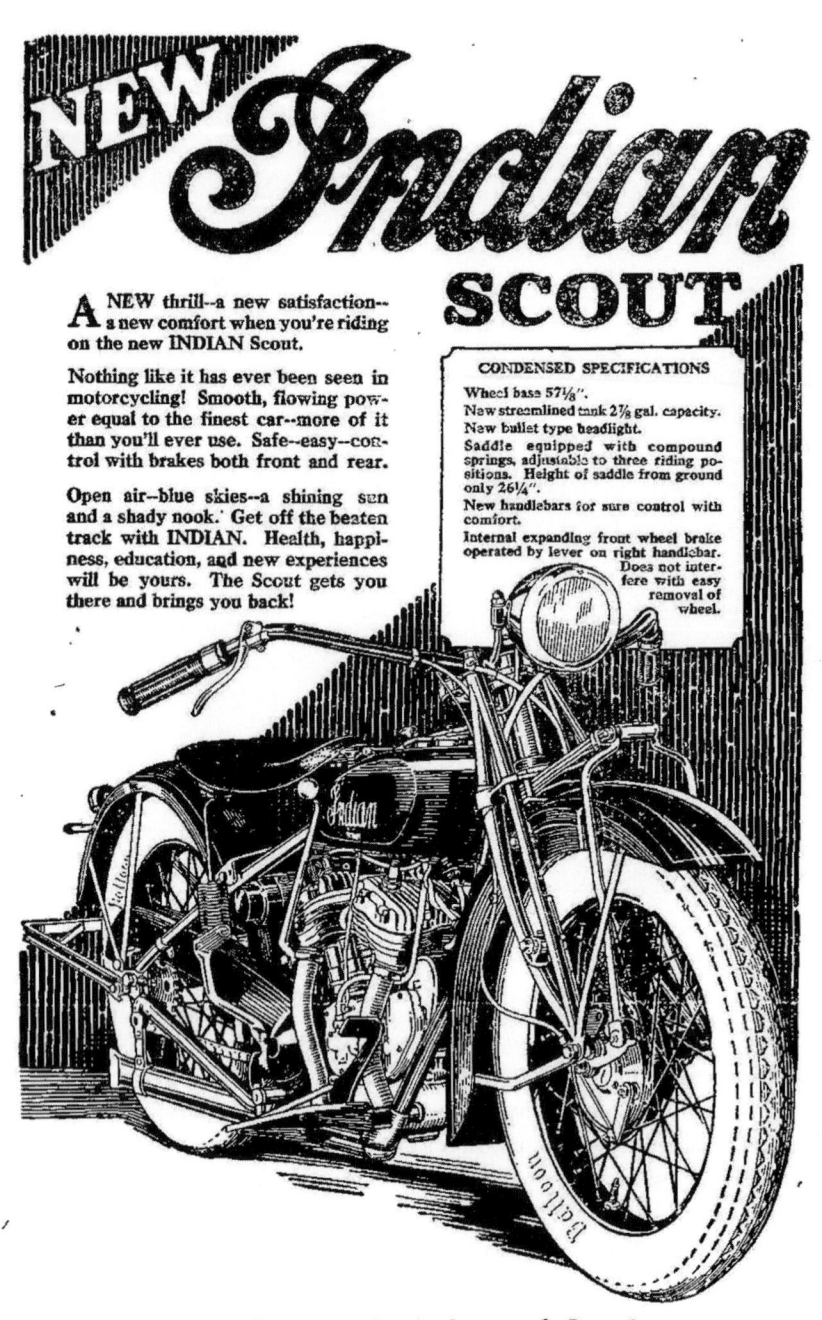

A NEW thrill--a new satisfaction--a new comfort when you're riding on the new INDIAN Scout.

Nothing like it has ever been seen in motorcycling! Smooth, flowing power equal to the finest car--more of it than you'll ever use. Safe--easy--control with brakes both front and rear.

Open air--blue skies--a shining sun and a shady nook. Get off the beaten track with INDIAN. Health, happiness, education, and new experiences will be yours. The Scout gets you there and brings you back!

CONDENSED SPECIFICATIONS

Wheel base 57 1/8".
New streamlined tank 2 7/8 gal. capacity.
New bullet type headlight.
Saddle equipped with compound springs, adjustable to three riding positions. Height of saddle from ground only 26 1/4".
New handlebars for sure control with comfort.
Internal expanding front wheel brake operated by lever on right handlebar. Does not interfere with easy removal of wheel.

Indian Motorcycle Sales and Service
North Warren, Pa., E. M. Anne, Prop.

When the Scout Series 101 first went on sale, advertisements like this one from 25th June 1928 did not use the term Series 101 at all. They simply referred to it as the 'new Indian Scout'. (Indian factory archives)

Modernisation For The 'Thirties

With the Scout 101 and mainstay Chief now the popular Indian models and selling as well as could be expected under the prevailing Depression-era circumstances, Indian next entered the du Pont era. Those holding the controlling interest in the Indian company were apparently made an offer they could not refuse. By quitting their holdings somewhat inexpensively to the du Pont brothers, E. Paul and Francis I., to seek fresh challenges elsewhere, they managed to stay one step ahead of possible legal proceedings.

Indian's newest president E. Paul du Pont was a New England blue-blood, but an untypical one in that he actually liked motorcycles. As a teenager, he'd built one of his own from scratch. But it was common sense and not sentiment that lay behind his first big policy decision, which was to renew the focus upon Indian's core business. From now on, Indian was going to do what Indian did best - design, build and sell motorcycles.

On taking over the company in April of 1930, the pressing issues facing president du Pont were both tactical and strategic. The deferred detail engineering development of key Indian models, needed to keep their levels of performance and refinement on a par with other brands, was the main tactical issue. Strategically what had to be faced was the fact that a whole new 'look' of motorcycle had evolved in which certain key functions were now taken for granted and where sheer style was all-important. Until the 'twenties it was Indian that had set the global trends. Now they were compelled to stay abreast of fashions that originated in Britain. Indian needed to invest in these new trends if it were to stay current, by either creating entirely new models or by effecting drastic make overs of existing ones. All this against a backdrop of declining motorcycle sales to levels at which continued production was barely viable. Indian's survival now depended upon the difficult task of simultaneously achieving two conflicting goals. It had to make its motorcycles more appealing, yet cheaper to build.

The first thing E. Paul had to tackle head-on was the profit margin on every Indian sold, which for some models like the Scout 101 was disturbingly slender. Now that the economic conditions of the Great Depression were really starting to bite, reduction of costs became of paramount importance. The production manager of E. Paul's luxury car enterprise, Loring Hosley, was transferred to Indian to take charge of the day-to-day running of the Wigwam and to gain efficiencies in the way Indian did things (such as in stock and materials inventories). Staffing at Indian was reduced, including some long-time staffers like Charles Gustafson Jnr who the factory let go at this time. Arthur Lemon's own prospects were inseparable from those of the Indian Four, sales of which were now dwindling. Lemon opted to jump before he got pushed. He returned to Michigan, where he entered the bicycle trade. Indian company working hours were cut to a four-day working week, and on occasion the factory was simply closed altogether for days on end, in order to help make ends meet.

NOTE: The ancient motorcycle, part of which is shown in the picture at left, is a 1902 INDIAN which now rests in the Smithsonian Institute at Washington

Loring F. Hosley
Vice-President and General Manager

E. Paul duPont
President

James A. Wright
Director of Sales and Advertising

Thomas M. Darrah
Secretary and Treasurer

Frederick W. Fisher
Factory Superintendent

Charles B. Franklin
Chief Engineer

Theodore A. Hodgdon
Assistant Advertising Manager

W. Stanley Bouton
Assistant Sales Manager

INDIAN EXECUTIVES OF TODAY

GREAT men conceive ideas—spend years shaping them into successful industries—then pass the torch to other hands.

So it has been at Indian. The men who helped to found the Indian so many years ago have retired, and their tasks have been taken over by some of the men shown on this page.

These men—and every other man in the Indian Organization—even to the faraway corners of the globe—appreciate the mighty work done by the pioneers of earlier days. They have a keen realization of the responsibility which lies with every man at an Indian post today, and they are determined that as the years roll by—more Indians and finer Indians shall go forth from the Wigwam.

Theirs is the task of carrying on the great work begun by the founder of Indian—Thirty years ago.

Indian executive staff in 1931

Indian executives in the new E. Paul du Pont team of 1931. (EMIMA)

After that, what clearly needed to be addressed was Indian's overall product quality, which nowadays was starting to suffer when compared to equivalent products from over at Milwaukee. This was a direct result of engineering effort being squandered upon diversionary projects, when it should have been going on motorcycle range improvements and updates. Now Indian would have to play catch-up football, to even up the score with H-D by fixing emerging problems with generators, vibratory crankshaft assemblies, and with oiling and breather systems. Owners and collectors of pre-war American motorcycles who have catholic tastes, and manage to stay truly unaffected by marque loyalties, do nowadays opine that H-D bikes from the 'thirties (say, the U-Model, for example) tend to be smoother, more ride-able and more rider-friendly than equivalent Wigwam ones (like the Chief) and in character a little less rough around the edges. This is a reflection of differences in the amount of detail engineering going into these models from year to year during this period.

Indian did manage to score some significant technical points over H-D however, for example by switching its entire range to re-circulating dry-sump oiling by 1933 to better cater for the increased opportunities for sustained flat out running on America's improving roads. H-D did not make this change until 1936, when it was introduced on the ohv Knucklehead. Apart from that, Indian 'progress' through the 'thirties and into the 'forties was mainly in styling. Through adoption of art deco graphics, unlimited du Pont DuLuxe paint colour options, and swoopy fenders designed by E. Paul's car people, Indian's lagging technical prowess in the 1930s was somewhat masked from the buying public by a massive injection of style.

An important factor driving this 'engineering by styling' strategy was that cuckoo in the nest, the Indian Four. In addition to the three substantive re-designs already completed in 1927 (from Ace into Indian Ace), 1928 (from Indian Ace into Indian Four Series 401) and 1929 (into Indian Four Series 402), during the 'thirties the Four soaked up engineering resources in a further three major revisions. The next one was in 1932, to 'streamline' the Four and carry out the model integration and rationalisation with the Chief that could have been done in 1928 if only the Chief had been ready for it. After that the next was in 1936, when the Four became the 'upside down' Four. And then again in 1938, when they made the Four 'upside right' again. Six major re-designs of the Four in the space of ten years! With 20:20 hindsight it can be seen that this kind of engineering investment would have been much better used to re-design Indian's top selling model, the Chief. But apart from gaining a front brake in 1928 and 'stream-line' cast-alloy gas tanks in 1930, the Chief suffered from neglect and remained unaltered while everybody ran around in ever decreasing circles working on shock absorbers, airplanes, outboard motors, and the Indian Four.

When E. Paul got down to considering which Indian models were doing well and which were not, all eyes fell upon the Scout 101. The Chief was safe, because it was Indian's biggest seller. The Four had a guaranteed, albeit limited, luxury-liner and law enforcement market, with margins apparently big enough to justify not only continuance but massive engineering development. What couldn't be kept hidden from the accountants was the fact that the Scout 101, because of its excellence, cost as much to produce as an Indian Chief. This had so far been tolerated on the premise that Scout sales drew customers in, which soon led to Chief or Four sales once the motorcycling bug had seriously bit. Now it was decided that it simply did not compute to have a motorcycle in the range that was selling at a Forty-five price while being built at a Seventy-four cost. Cheaper to produce entry level designs would need to be found. Reluctantly, for everyone knew it was such a fine and popular machine, 1931 was allowed to be the final year of Scout 101 production.

There is a paper trail for some of what went on after the du Pont takeover which, for the first time in Indian's history, affords us direct insights about how much of what went on involved Charles

Franklin. The paper trail exists because du Pont, having other business interests besides Indian, was not necessarily present at the Wigwam on a daily basis yet he cared enough to want to know what was going on. A stream of letters and memos back and forth between him and the production and engineering staff was his way of keeping a finger on the pulse. Franklin was being issued priority lists of engineering matters that either du Pont himself, or particular key-informant Indian dealers corresponding directly with du Pont, felt needed fixing fast if Indian was to have any chance at all of staying in the game during those tough economic times. These items included matters like the Chief crankshaft assembly construction, balance factor, and weight of pistons, as just one example of the up-close-and-personal level of engineering details that du Pont immersed himself in. Such a refreshing change in leadership style from that supplied by the previous string of absentee NYC bankers and financiers!

After almost one year of du Pont calling the shots, the 'Stock-a-Day' column of the *Appleton Post-Crescent* of 13th January 1931 reviewed the Indian Motorcycle Company's recent track record. Assuming this to be written by a financial columnist not in the employ of pool operators, then Indian's financial position at this time was as follows.

INDIAN MOTORCYCLE COMPANY THREE YEAR RECORD
The Indian Motorcycle Company specializes in the manufacture of motorcycles, outboard motors, bicycles, and aircooled gasoline motors for Industrial purposes. The plant of the company is located at Springfield, Mass, where are employed about 800 persons. The concern has executive and sales offices in New York City. It also has branch offices in London and owns the entire stock of a sales subsidiary and of an acceptance corporation to finance its part payment sales. Among its other assets, the company has exclusive patent rights in the United States for aircraft, motorcycles and outboard Diesel engines, for which patents are owned or controlled by the Sunbeam Motor Car Company of England.

In April 1930 the War Department let a contract to the Company to supply all motorcycles and accessories for the Army.

A new management went into operation in April 1930. The Company acquired a controlling interest in du Pont Motors, Inc. which makes automobiles on individual order. As a result of this move the previous management of the Indian Motorcycle Company retired and E. Paul du Pont became president, Francis I. du Pont vice president and Loring F. Hosley vice president and general manager. The building of du Pont cars was transferred to the Springfield plant. It is reported that as a result of this new management the company is preparing to build motor tricycles carrying two persons and provided with collapsible top, windshield and other comforts.

Operations in late years have shown losses. In 1929 these totalled $674,973 and compared with the loss of $456,390 in 1928.

There is no funded debt. Capital stock outstanding includes $735,000 in cumulative preferred stock of $100 par value and 290,000 shares of no par common. Common and preferred have equal voting power. The last dividend paid on the preferred was July 1, 1929 and the last paid on the common was July 2, 1928.

As of June 30, 1930 total current assets were $1,471,066. Current liabilities amounted to $311,574 and net working capital was $1,159,191. Book value applicable to the common stock amounted to $6-10.

It would have been far more useful if the exclusive US patent rights for Sunbeam diesel engines, purchased by Indian in March 1930 from a float of 100,000 shares, had also included cars and trucks rather than be only for motorcycles, outboards and aircraft. America has a long and proud record of employing diesel engines to power cars and trucks, but never for motorcycles, outboards or aircraft. Either Bolles and his team had blundered, or they calculatingly made this move as the basis of yet another pool operation. Certainly Indian never exercised their option to make such engines in the US. The other point to emerge here is that Indian now employed 800 people, compared with a reported 3,000 during the company's heyday in the 'teens.

Some of Franklin's design engineering work during this period included laying the groundwork for an updated Scout, which emerged later in the new decade (in 1934) as the Sport Scout. According to surviving factory correspondence from this period, Franklin was responsible for a new English-style girder fork, modern new 'saddle' gas tanks for the whole Indian range (initially these were cast in aluminum) and experiments in dry-sump recirculating oiling, which he'd already been fitting to his road racers since at least 1927. He worked on a new frame for the Chief which not only adopted the new 'look' of current motorcycling but, as a cost-cutting model-integration exercise, was intended to also house the Four and the Scout 45 motors. In other words it was Franklin, the very architect of the late lamented Scout 101, who laid the groundwork for its immediate replacement model, the unloved but under rated Standard Scout.

The saddle tanks laid down by Franklin were long overdue, since by their absence the Indian range was showing its age and lack of fashion sense. It's one example of the Sales Department driving the bikes' engineering, for the engineers were themselves quite happy with the between-the-rails flat-tank configuration. These formed a solid and leak-proof unit and besides, Indian motorcycles had no engine height issues to solve since they still used flat-head motors. But the trend setting English had established a whole new 'look' and in the US the Excelsior company had already picked up that idea and run with it. It is plain from 1930 Indian company correspondence that the Sales Department was adamant that Indians must now acquire saddle-tanks. Of course they were right but then again, so were the engineers. Indians were duly bestowed with saddle-tanks which are quite wide and of soldered construction so that, disappointingly after only eighty years or so of use, they will certainly start to leak. Anyone nowadays contemplating serious road mileage on a 1932-onward Indian will probably want to fit a set of modern all-welded reproductions, and save their original soldered tanks for 'Sunday Best'.

1930 was a US Census year, and the following was inscribed by the census enumerators for Franklin *et famille* of 71 School Street.

Fifteenth Census of the United States
21st April 1930

71 School Street, Springfield – City, Massachusetts

Franklin, Charles B, Head. Home rented, $65 per month. Radio set, Yes. Male. Race, White. Age, 49. Married, at age 26. Attended school or college since 1 Sept. 1929? No. Able to read and write? Yes. Place of Birth, Northern Ireland. Year of immigration to the United States? 1914. Naturalized. Occupation, Engineer. Industry, Motorcycle. Employment? Yes. Veteran? No.

Franklin, Nancy W, Wife. Female. Race, White. Age, 43. Married, at age 20. Attended school or college since 1 Sept. 1929? No. Able to read and write? Yes. Place of Birth, Northern Ireland. Year of immigration to the United States? 1920. Naturalized. Occupation, None.

Franklin, Phyllis E, Daughter. Female. Race, White. Age, 19. Single. Attended school or college since 1 Sept. 1929? No. Able to read and write? Yes. Place of Birth, Northern Ireland. Year of immigration to the United States? 1920. Naturalized. Occupation, None.

This is curious, for a couple of reasons. Firstly, Franklin's year of arrival in the US is stated as 1914 and not 1916. Secondly, their places of birth are given as Northern Ireland, when in fact all three were born in Dublin (located in what by 1930 was called the Irish Free State). Thirdly, daughter Phyllis told the enumerators she was 19 years of age in April 1930. We have sighted her birth certificate and it is dated 17th September 1908 so we know, as indeed she herself knew, that she was by now 21 years of age. She was still single and living at home, not attending school or college, nor was she working. She was keen on dancing, of the highbrow classical nature. She was good enough to have been the subject of several newspaper reports, appearing from 1929 onwards, about her 'interpretative dance' performances at cultural events in and around Springfield.

The errors made in this census entry had to have been deliberate. Everybody in the western world knows their own birth-year and birth-place. We can only guess at the reasons behind the responses given. Maybe the census enumerators arrived in the middle of supper, and the Franklins just wanted to get rid of them fast?

During 1931 the Design Department was again a busy place. The main project going on was the major cost-cutting range integration exercise ordered by du Pont. The same new frame, running-gear and ancillary cycle parts would now be used in common across a complete new three-model Indian range comprising the Four, the Chief and the Scout. This particular Scout is the one nowadays referred to as the Standard Scout although that phrase was not coined until later, after the advent of the Sport Scout made it necessary to distinguish the two. For now, it was simply 'the Scout'.

This major re-engineering of the whole Indian range was doubly justifiable, not only for the cost savings it would bring, but because it afforded the opportunity to increase sales appeal by adopting the modern new 'look' now prevailing in global motorcycling.

Alert readers will probably be now raising their hands to ask, 'but doesn't the Standard Scout still cost as much as a Seventy-four to produce but only fetches the price of a Forty-five?' Well, yes. But it no longer ties up factory space, personnel and resources in a separate production line for manufacture of a unique frame and cycle parts. By adopting the same components as used on the Chief and Four, economies of scale kicked in which lowered the unit price of these items across all three models.

Meanwhile, what were the Other Two up to in 1931? Well, they'd already completed modernization programs to bring their products in line with the trendy 'streamline' look. Excelsior had begun work on its 'streamline' range in 1928, and H-D in 1929. The H-D range from 1930 comprised a whole new generation of bikes and engines. Thanks to the Weschler-duPont inter-regnum, Indian at this time could only offer models of the flat-tank era with engines that dated from 1920. In 1927 the Indian range had been the most comprehensive and best prepared of the US Big Three to face the challenges of the future. Now, by 1930, Indian was the worst-prepared. Technically and stylistically, they'd gone from first to last in the space of three critical years.

But not all was completely rosy over at Milwaukee or Chicago. H-D had teething problems with the new side-valve V and VL models which resulted in a four-month suspension of production while they sorted it all out. This was a major snafu, for every bike sold up until that point had to be recalled by H-D dealers and fitted with heavier flywheels, which were wider so necessitated new crankcases, and therefore a new frame had to be fitted as well. This gave the VL a bad reputation at first, but it recovered once customers found it to be a motorcycle that really would hold up under 80mph-plus continuous running, unlike the J-Models that resented such treatment. At Excelsior, on the other hand, this was the time when Ignaz Schwinn gave his famous order to his management team 'Gentlemen, today we stop!'

President du Pont seriously considered following Excelsior's example by winding-up the Indian company altogether, in light of Depression-era sales of only around 4,000 units annually and sinking to an all-time low of 1,600 in 1933. This was Indian's darkest hour. Instead, du Pont took a gamble that this re-engineering exercise would keep the company's head above water and take it through to better days. Annual sales figures for any era of Indian production are difficult to obtain. However, those prevailing in the early 1930s compared with the late 1920s were revealed by Indian at a hearing of the National Recovery Administration (NRA) reported in the *La Crosse Tribune* of 17th December 1933.

> The entire motorcycle manufacturing industry of the United States is divided between Milwaukee and 'Springfield, Mass., and representatives of both manufacturers appeared at the Tuesday hearing on the proposed code of fair competition for the industry. Walter Davidson, president and general manager of the Harley-Davidson Motor Company of Milwaukee, formally filed the code and made a brief statement that the proposals represented a sincere effort on the part of the industry to cooperate with the NRA. He said that further grants to labor would be impossible until a general increase in prosperity brought augmented sales.
>
> The Indian Motorcycle Company of Springfield supported Davidson through its representative, declaring that annual sales have dropped from 25,000 in 1928 to less than 3,900 in 1932.
>
> The NRA Labor Advisory Board opposes the proposal to 'average' the weekly hours of labor and demanded a flat maximum work week of 40 hours with time and one-half for all overtime. The board also asks for a minimum wage of 45 cents an hour instead of the 40 cents proposed.

As a short note on Indian racing achievements during these years of re-organisation, in 1931 Burton Albrecht turned a 36 second mile on a racing 'Scout' at Oakland's Elmhurst speedway, while Miny Waln established a 21 cubic inch record for the mile using a two-cam two-valve bronze-cover 350. Franklin's overhead Forty-fives continued to do well in hill-climb completion and thus continued their role of promoting the Scout model. Excelsior's star slant artist Gene Rhyne, newly laid off from the closed-down Chicago concern, was quickly recruited by Indian. During 1931 he won all of the first places in the 45 cu in class of National hill-climb competition.

In 1931 Franklin produced one of his last original designs for Indian that made it through into production. This was a Scout 45-powered three-wheeler, termed the 'Dispatch-Tow' (see colour photo 35). The name reflects this machine's original purpose, which was for automobile service stations to literally dispatch a driver to go collect a customer's vehicle and bring it in for tune-up and lube. Servicing of the automobiles of those times was frequent, and much productivity was being lost because two employees and a company car were required to drive out to the customer's address so that one of the two could bring the customer's car back in to the garage for its tune-up and lube. The Dispatch-Tow was designed with a foldaway draw-bar at the front so that only one employee had to be dispatched on this cheaper-to-run motorcycle-powered outfit, which was then hooked up to the rear bumper-bar of the customer's auto and towed driver-less back in to the shop.

The three-wheeler layout was of the trike type with two drive wheels at the rear, and not the Morgan-type which has two steered wheels at the front and a single drive wheel at the rear. The latter type provides a much better geometry for high speed cornering, however the trike layout is fine for the modest speeds of built-up urban areas and it will cope better with a load. The Dispatch-Tow looked like a motorcycle front-half from the seat-post forward, with a two-wheeled back end built onto it in place of the usual rear sub-frame. Power is delivered by chain drive back to a differential that feeds drive out to either end of the rear axle.

Box-like bodywork could be positioned between the two rear wheels just aft of the driver's seat, making a handy storage space for packages, tools or equipment. This feature broadened the appeal of the Dispatch-Tow far beyond its original and quite specialized purpose. Its car-like stability but motorcycle-like running costs made it an economical choice in those straightened times for tradesmen, delivery men or small businesses to operate as a means to ply their trade.

The Indian Dispatch-Tow was sufficiently successful that Harley-Davidson immediately copied it, dubbing their own version the 'Servi-car' which remained in production until 1971, becoming a familiar sight across America in the hands of big-city parking meter-maids. This type of trike lends itself to recreational pursuits as well, with the possibility to mount a decent sized keg of beer as payload being a feature much appreciated among certain motorcycling cognoscenti.

Also being worked-upon by Franklin in 1931, and introduced onto the production line just as soon as it was ready, was a complete new crankshaft assembly and pistons for the Chief. Efforts in 1930 to hop up the Chief to keep pace with the newly released and tough Harley VL side-valve Seventy-fours had led to disaster, and Indian dealers were whining loudly. Nothing destroys a weak bottom-end faster than a freshened-up top-end. Indian's 1930-31 customers began proving the truth of that saying, to the dismay of all parties concerned.

It can be argued that this was a major lapse of concentration for Franklin to have let such a 'hand-grenade' Chief go out of the factory doors, without sufficient testing to expose this flaw before customers found out about it the hard way. It is uncharacteristic for a man whose reputation for flawless machine preparation had been second to none since 1903. Either even the best of us can make mistakes, or there were other pressures upon management to get a hotter Chief out into dealer showrooms in undue haste and against his advice. Once the matter had come to a head then Franklin's response, among other changes, was to replace the webbed flywheels, used on Chiefs since 1922, with a solid flywheel like the type used on the Forty-five overhead-valve hill-climb race motors.

The new-look (literally) three-model Indian range was ready for the start of the 1932 sales year. The Chief and the Series 403 Four were immediately embraced as being modern and stylish (see colour photo 36), while retaining all those mechanical traits that Indian customers held dear.

It is never easy to update a motorcycle in a way that makes it better than what was there before, without risk of alienating customers by losing the essential character that had made the model popular in the first place. Just ask Hedstrom fans when Indian switched over to the Powerplus. Just ask the

The 1932 Indian Four, newly 'streamlined' and finally 'integrated' with the Chief and Scout, after the 3rd of six major re-design exercises that occurred between 1927 and 1938. (Indian factory archives)

designers of the Ducati Monster. H-D has faced this problem year after year with the Sportster, and so far has succeeded in the difficult task of making it get better yet stay the same.

With the new Chief and Four, Indian definitely succeeded. Though one has to define success carefully, for Indian sold scarcely more than 200 Fours per year in 1933 and 1934. So we will define success as 'The 1932-on Indian Fours were much loved by those lucky few who were able to buy them'.

On the other hand, history has not treated the new-look 1932 Scout very well. At the time it was released, its main problem was simply that the Scout 101 was a hard act to follow. Fondness for the dearly departed Series 101 clouded popular opinion of the replacement Scout. Both then and in Indian marque writings ever since, the machine that later came to be known as the Standard Scout has been derided as a gutless wonder that combines a Scout's power with a Chief's bulk.

Such is not the case, as a ride on one will clearly demonstrate. Part of the researches for this book (tough, but somebody has to do it)

Charles Franklin, late in life (Photo EMIMA)

involved taking a Standard Scout out for a spin during the Indian Motorcycle Club of Australia's Peter McAliece Memorial Breakfast Run. Though physically the same size as a 'thirties Chief, the difference in dead-weight is clearly apparent. The result is a machine far less intimidating than a Chief, more nifty and a much handier riding package especially in city traffic conditions. The Standard Scout starts so easily, needing no more than a lazy prod of one's boot at the kick start while seated astride and your butt scarcely has to leave the saddle. This completely eliminates any stressful 'What if I stall it at the traffic lights?' feelings that can be part and parcel of the Chief riding experience in confined urban spaces. Sure, the motor needs to be spun freely if you're to make good progress and there's a lot of down-shifting for hills, but that goes for any Scout so if it's a problem for you then get a Chief instead. The main downside of a Standard Scout is that, when you look at one, you really do expect to see a hulking great Chief power-plant in there. What instead greets your eyes is something with generous extra dollops of air layered all around it, making it look like a Chief with a motor that got left in the clothes dryer for far too long.

The Standard Scout is thus a useful motorcycle no matter what anyone says, and there were sufficient customers who appreciated it for it to remain in the range until 1937. As a stop-gap it could be judged a success, which bought the company time until economic conditions improved enough to justify development of a sexier Scout with more appeal to the petrol-head element who missed the Series 101.

The adverse comments about the new Scout must have hit home at the Wigwam, however. At the end of the day, it is the customer who is right. The fact that the Standard Scout is as long, as wide and as tall as a Chief perhaps also pointed to a fresh need for something compact that would not over-awe a first-time motorcycle buyer, which could be easily paddled around the parking lot while they got the hang of being on two wheels. So onto the list of engineering tasks was added the development of new options for an entry-level model of Indian.

There was no chance in 1931 of Indian designing a new motorcycle from the ground-up, however. Times were still way too tough for that, plus it would undo the benefits of the range-integrating work just completed. A bit of a wander through the miles of Wigwam floor area must have revealed that a large back-inventory of Prince components and tooling was still on hand. These readily formed an almost no-cost basis for the rolling chassis of a new Indian lightweight, by providing the forks, wheels, complete power train, most of the frame-lug castings, and all the ancillary items like fenders, toolbox, etc. Virtually the only new item designed for it was an *à la mode* saddle-type gas tank. This rolling ensemble was to be powered by a cute little 30.50 V-twin that itself needed no ground-up design work, for it was essentially a de-bored, de-stroked and slightly-modified Scout motor. One can often run into problems by making an engine bigger, but hardly ever does it hurt to make an engine smaller.

The resulting 'parts bin special' was termed the Scout Pony. It was a marvelous feat of Depression-era design work, for it is an attractive motorcycle that adhered to the American Way of Motorcycling in that it looked right and it sounded right, it met the design brief for an entry-level machine perfectly, yet in terms of cost it was brought into production on the smell of an oily rag. Pricewise it sold for 25% less than a Standard Scout, which was itself 20% less than a Chief. This made it the lowest priced V-twin on the US market. In keeping with the 'no model years' policy of Indian, the Scout Pony (later known as the Junior Scout) officially entered the range as soon as it was ready, which was in or around June of 1932.

The overall result of all these model changes was that the Scout's loss became the Chief's gain. While the new Scout could be derided as possessing the power of a Scout with the weight of a Chief, the flipside is that the Chief could now be pitched as having the power of a Chief allied to the handling of a Scout. Indian advertising certainly did make this pitch, and added that the Chief had now gained 'Scout looks'. For the first time in its model history, the Chief could step out from the shadow of the Scout and take its place in centre stage. It is from 1932 onwards to the end in 1953 (see colour photo 37) that the Chief gained its glamour reputation and developed such strong product recognition in the minds of even the non-motoring public. Sixty years hence in the new millennium, the Chief is the first model most people think about when you say the words 'Indian motorcycle'.

Illness And Death

Charles Franklin was in the thick of all this engineering activity at Indian. He was still the man in charge of design engineering. The design work he performed or coordinated during this 1930-32 period laid the foundation for the new, modern Indians that would see the company out to the end of its days in 1953. The new Chief, Four and Standard Scout frames are his. So are the trademark Indian saddle gas tanks. Slender and shapely in their profile, they make the famous H-D 'fat-bobs' look porky by comparison. He had also contributed elements to the Sport Scout that debuted in 1934. As one of his final acts for the Indian company, he and his colleagues had lashed together the Scout Pony at short notice and very low cost.

This was all done against a personal background of failing health. Photographs of Charles Franklin in factory literature dating from around 1931 onwards show him to be looking rather poorly. His face looks drawn and haggard, and his eyes are sunken. Toward the end of 1931 he asked for a leave of absence to rest and recover his health.

This leave was granted, but the practical effect of it did not initially result in much change of pace. Franklin already had a drawing office set up in his apartment at 71 School Street, from which a steady stream of Indian designs and modifications continued to issue forth. But his health deteriorated to the point where he was incapable of working any further, even from home. He died during the night of 19th October 1932, at the age of 52.

The nature of his illness and death has been mis-reported in previous Indian marque histories. Having obtained a copy of his death certificate, we can now set the record straight. The cause of Franklin's death is given as 'malignant growth of intestines acute myocarditis'. In lay-person's language, this is bowel cancer. Myocarditis is an inflammatory disease of the heart muscle, with a range of possible causes. Very likely it was here a complication of the cancer, or its treatment. In those days, treatment for bowel cancer would have been limited to increasingly massive doses of morphine.

A funeral notice appeared in the *Springfield Republican* of 20th October 1932:

Charles Bayly Franklin of 71 School Street died at his home early this morning. He had been a resident of Springfield for many years and was, prior to August, 1931, employed as Chief Engineer at the Indian Motorcycle Company. He leaves his widow and one daughter, Phyllis Franklin, at home. The funeral will be held at the parlors of the Dickinson-Streeter company.

A subsequent announcement was placed in the *Springfield Sunday Republican* of 23rd October 1932:

The funeral of Charles Bayly Franklin of 71 School Street was held at the parlors of Dickinson-Streeter company yesterday afternoon at 2:00, with an organ prelude at 1:30. Rev. F. Marion Smith officiated and burial was in Oak Grove cemetery. The bearers were F.J. Weschler, T.L. Loose, E.L. Stoughton, G.A. Anderson, J.R. Taylor and M.H. Crandall.

Charles B. Franklin
Chief Engineer

Franklin does not look at all well in this 1931 photo. (EMIMA)

This is an all-star cast of Wigwam staff, past and present. Frank Weschler effectively ran the company from Hendee's departure until the advent of the Wall Street shenanigans. Theron Loose was Production Manager. Taylor and Crandall were draughtsmen from the drawing office of the Design Department. Thomas Callaghan Butler made a transcontinental trip from out west to attend the funeral.

Franklin is buried in Section L - Lot 9814 of Oak Grove cemetery in Springfield. The headstone is extremely simple - one might almost say 'low budget' - with the inscription limited to name, age, and date of death (see colour photo 38). There is no epitaph, and no mention of his loved ones.

Butler recalled years later that he asked Franklin's widow, Nancye, whether he might be able to keep Franklin's work diaries and notebooks, however she refused this request. Butler's comment was that Nancye had a very strong sense of privacy that was impossible for anyone to penetrate. These diaries have apparently vanished without trace, though Franklin's various racing medals and prizes did re-surface much later on and are now a feature of the Indian Motorcycles display at the Lyman and Merrie Wood Museum of Springfield History. A set of hand tools reputed to be Franklin's was offered on eBay some years back, however their provenance is unknown.

According to the Probate Court records, Franklin owned no property and he left around $6,000 to his widow. This is a respectable sum for the Depression era, equivalent to five times the US average annual salary. But this is not so much when one considers that, according to Tommy Butler, Franklin had been earning an average of $6,000 per year for 15 years, and was paying only 10% of his income in rent. His other main outgoings were his daughter's exclusive private education, holidays for Phyllis and Nancye in places like NYC and Atlanta (at the Ritz-Carlton, mind you), and an occasional high-end automobile at about $6,000 per throw.

So what happened to the rest of his money?

Well, there was a Depression going on, and this was all a direct result of the October 1929 Wall Street Crash. A lot of investors lost all their money at this time, and it's easily possible that Franklin was one of them. There were even people who hurled themselves from upper storey windows as a result. For Franklin, the stress of losing his life's savings may even have contributed to his cancer.

This is pure speculation on our part, however. There is now no way of knowing what really went on. Suffice to say that Franklin's death was not a sudden or unexpected one. Maybe he'd already transferred everything he had, except what was immediately needed for his medical bills, over into an account in Nancye's name? There was plenty of time for him to make plans to provide for his family as best he could, after he was gone.

Similarly, there was plenty of time for Nancye and Phyllis to think about what they might want to do next. Neither of the Franklin ladies had ever been in employment, so it comes as a bit of a surprise to learn from the Springfield City Directory for 1933 that Nancye is listed as having removed to New York City. The timing of City Directory collation and publication was such that, in order for the 1933 issue to be amended to suit, they were probably gone from Springfield by the end of 1932. A letter of introduction exists from Phyllis' Springfield dance teacher to Rosina Galli, ballet mistress at the Metropolitan Opera House in New York City, stating that 'she has just recently lost her father and anything you could do for her I would regard as a personal favor'. This letter is dated 24th October 1932, only two days after her father's funeral, so it's clear that the two Franklin ladies had already been planning ahead. By endevouring to make the acquaintance of Rosina Galli, Phyllis was pitching herself at the very highest level of the performing arts in NYC.

Franklin's death was not reported in the quarterly company organ *The Indian News*, however complete runs of this magazine all show that it inexplicably skipped an issue at this time. Franklin's passing may have been regarded as old news by the time publication resumed. Alternatively, perhaps it was company policy to keep this publication fairly upbeat, and not use it to report sobering matters like the passing of one's design engineer.

Phyllis Enid next appears in public records on 26th March 1939, which is when she applied for a Social Security number. There are two curious things about her application. Firstly she has again under-reported her age, this time by eight years compared with the two years she hid from the 1930 US Census enumerators, for she has written her age as 22 instead of 30 and her birthday as 17th September 1916 instead of 1908. Secondly, in the space for Business Name of Present Employer she has entered 'Unemployed'. She was residing, presumably with her mother, Nancye, at 50 West 77th Street NYC.

Judging from some of the very few papers recovered from her NYC apartment after she died in 2007, Phyllis continued to harbour ambitions of a professional career as a classical dancer throughout the 'thirties. It appears that this career plan may not have worked out, or if it had then by now it was fading, so application for a social security number in 1939 could be interpreted as a prelude to obtaining employment in some other sphere of endeavour, such as in commerce. At the same time, this under-reporting of her age perhaps indicates she had not yet given up hope completely of becoming a success on stage? There are few dancers who would not rather be twenty-two years of age than thirty. Phyllis was on first-name terms with some prominent people in classical opera. A

1938 postcard addressed to 'Valerie' Franklin from world-famous mezzo-soprano Carmella Ponselle granted permission to use her name to obtain further auditions at the Metropolitan Opera House.

Phyllis (Valerie) Franklin is a figure as enigmatic as her father. Educated at one of the very best New England private schools, easily the best-looking among her fellow graduands, and reported in the newspapers as taking vacations with her mother in all the very best of holiday destinations, she was clearly on track to fulfil the main expectation of her class and generation which was to marry well. Supposing her intellect was even two-thirds as adequate as her beauty, she could alternatively have gone to college at Vasser and become one of the pioneers among a new age of educated professional women. She did neither, choosing instead to develop her talent and passion for classical dance. This is a similar pattern to that of her father, who in 1910 threw away the expected and respectable options of a tenured career-professional in order to fool around with socially reprehensible motorcycles. The picture which emerges about Phyllis Franklin is that of a determined person who from a young age knew what she wanted from life and was not going to let stuffy convention stand in the way of achieving her ambition. She never married, ultimately worked in the insurance industry in a management level position, and passed away in 2007 at the age of 99.

Franklin's Motorcycling Legacy

Charles Franklin is one of the great unsung heroes of motorcycling history. Franklin's motorcycling deeds are impressive, not least because of the apparently modest and self-effacing way that he went about them. His impact on motorcycle design in the USA was enormous, because he effectively set the agenda of the US industry in production and in racing for the next thirty years or so. His influence can be seen to this day in the products of that Other One of the two factories still in business after World War II and sole survivor from Franklin's times.

Though not among the pioneers, Franklin was part of a second wave of sporting young gentlemen inspired by the likes of Fournier, Jarrott and Edge to take up motorcycling during its formative years. He in turn, by his example in competition, inspired countless others in Britain and Ireland to enter the sport.

When he began in the early 'noughts, the general idea of what constituted a 'motor-cycle' had by no means been finalized. Major components and assemblies eventually taken for granted, like clutches or change-gear transmissions, were either completely lacking or were in a form (like belt drive, or hub gears) that proved to be blind-alleys in motorcycle evolution. By the time Franklin died the motorcycle was fully invented, with the design features and major sub-assemblies that would prevail for the remainder of the 20th Century.

Charles Franklin himself directly contributed to the events that shaped the motorcycle's final form. He was one of the five men who first came up with the very idea of an annual Tourist Trophy race, which subsequently became the main driving force behind motorcycle engineering development. He was a member of the 1911 TT race team whose achievements were one of the final spurs for the wholesale adoption of a free-engine clutch, counter-shaft change-gear transmission, and chain drive in primary and secondary stages, as the industry-standard power-train arrangement in motorcycling.

Franklin's story is the very story of the Indian company itself during its Golden Age. The two tales are intertwined, and they begin and end together. It was in 1910 that Franklin began riding, selling, and race-tuning Indian motorcycles, almost immediately from the moment they evolved from motor bicycles into serious motorcycles. A myth perpetuated mainly by British commentators is that American manufacturers sealed their own doom by failing to come up with fresh ideas, once they'd settled upon the heavyweight V-twin design format. But Franklin ensured that Indian could offer not only twins but also singles and fours, and had capability in side-valve, overhead-valve and even overhead-cam valve actuation formats. It was international trade protectionism and not lack of ideas that best explains why, by the time of his death in 1932, Indian's best days as a commercial venture had passed. Franklin's own final chapter at the Wigwam was to lay the groundwork for a modernized Indian range, after which time the company was merely stumbling along as a business yet the bikes themselves continued to go from strength to strength. These 'streamline' Indians carried the company forward to the post-World War Two period, and nowadays rank among the most highly sought-after of all antique motorcycles.

New management under Ralph Rogers in the late 'forties saw Indian try out a 'wholesome, user-friendly' lightweight motorcycle marketing concept with appeal to middle-America, thereby pre-dating the strategy which brought such success to Honda and other Japanese manufacturers in America during the 'sixties. Let down by detail design flaws in the bikes rather than by the concept itself, this represented a fatal 'near-miss' for Indian. Lightweight motorcycles were not Franklin's personal taste, but he'd have heartily approved of efforts to break through to mass sales in this way. He'd thrown his own energies into similar efforts, like the Light Twin model of 1917-18.

Roger's Indian 'verticals' were a final roll of the dice by Indian, for after this the coffers were empty. Parts still remaining in the factory were used to assemble a few hundred telescopic-forked 'Blackhawk' Chiefs, but these were used up by 1953 so this year and model marks the end of the line for Franklin's Indians as production motorcycles. After this, the only asset left to trade upon was the company's own illustrious name. Controversially this became attached in the 1950s to various motorcycles manufactured in Britain by companies like Brockhouse or Royal Enfield, so they could be marketed in America as 'Indians'. Other similar ploys have been attempted in the decades since, and they continue in the present day, by entities with absolutely no connection whatsoever to the original Indian company. This had been wound-up in the early 'sixties by Joe Berliner without selling the Indian name to anybody, for his intention was to respectfully lay the marque to rest. That these marketing schemes are still thought sufficiently viable to spark long-running and expensive courtroom battles for rights to the trademark, sixty years after production of real Indians ceased, demonstrates the enduring cachet of the Indian name. This is remarkable, and is only possible thanks to the life achievements of men like Hendee, Hedstrom, Gustafson, Weschler, and Franklin.

To put Franklin's contributions toward our pastime of motorcycling into perspective, we must examine his efforts and achievements under not one but *four* disciplines: motorcycle racing competitor; race-engine tuner; racing motorcycle designer; and road motorcycle designer.

Franklin's achievements as a motorcycle racing competitor are by themselves enough to make him a significant historical figure. He was the first big star of Irish national motorcycle competition, and the first Irishman to compete internationally. At one time he ranked alongside the two Collier brothers in the Top Three best of British motorcycle competitors. His race wins and record-breaking successes were sufficiently meritorious to routinely earn him page space in contemporary issues of *The Motor Cycle* or *MotorCycling*, and guaranteed his inclusion in review articles about the top racing cracks of the day. Franklin's competition successes helped to put Indian at the top of motorcycle racing and record breaking in Britain during the pre-WWI era, earning the marque a reputation for speed, reliability and technological sophistication that boosted Indian sales among British motorcyclists despite a stiff selling price.

Franklin's riding style when racing was smooth and conservative, and he rarely fell off. Not for him the balls-out antics and showmanship of a 'Shrimp' Burns or Ray Weishaar. Normally, nice guys come somewhere in the middle. On the other hand, if you ride too much like 'Shrimp' Burns then you either crash, blow up your motor, or kill yourself. Franklin rode with sufficient aggression to be capable of routinely winning 1st places, especially on his old stamping ground of Portmarnock beach or in scratch races around the Brooklands Outer Circuit. Yet he rode in a manner that greatly improved the odds he'd ultimately die of something else, besides a broken neck.

In the Isle of Man TT his record was more mixed but let's face it, in the TT everybody's record is mixed. The TT race is such a lottery that a rider needs to be world-class, and be backed up by machine preparation meticulous beyond the point of paranoia, to be sure of even finishing in the Top Twenty. Franklin's best result was a 2nd place, and all of his TT finishes were in the Top Eight. In chronological order, his TT record from 1908 onwards was 6th, 5th, Retired, 2nd, Retired, 4th, and 8th. These consistent results place him amongst the first rank of TT competitors from any period within the 100 year history of this famous race.

To be a successful motorcycle racing competitor is a career all by itself. Most of the world's top racers in any era just hopped onto a bike and raced - that's all they did and all they had time to do. To be proficient demands commitment to constant practice and to physical fitness, in addition to natural ability, mental strength, and ample courage. There's any number of top racing-motorcycle riders who are worth writing books about, starting with Hailwood or Agostini or Joey Dunlop and working your way through the list.

Then there are the race-engine tuners. They'd take a factory's end product only as a starting point, upon which they'd ply their craft to inject a winning margin of additional mph for a regular stable of rider clients. In Britain between the wars, men who found they were much better at building and modifying engines than at riding them included 'Woolly' Worters and Frances Beart, or in the US there was Al Crocker or Rollie Free or, after the War, Tom Sifton. The task of race-engine building and modification for more speed is a painstaking one, requiring many late nights, endless patience, meticulous technique, a good understanding of engineering principles, and an organized scientific approach toward engine testing and the recording and analysis of results. Again, there are men whose claim to fame was doing only this. Again, the lives of men like Beart and Sifton are worth writing books about.

The smallest and most exclusive group of all is the rider-tuners, that is, those men who not only successfully raced motorcycles but they also successfully tuned the motorcycles they raced. Looking back over the last century to identify the names of the truly outstanding rider-tuners, one quickly finds that the list is a short one. Towering like colossi above the rest are Herbert Le Vack and Eric Fernihough, and 'the rest' are people like George Brough, Victor Horsman, Freddie Dixon, Bill Lacey, Wizard O'Donovan, Ted Baragwanath, and a few others.

To this list, add Charles Franklin.

He tuned his own entries right from the start of his racing career in 1903. He quickly gained a reputation for meticulous, leave nothing to chance preparation. In those days of hit and miss engine manufacture, it was to his skill in preparation that his early racing successes were mainly attributed.

When motor-bicycles became motorcycles and Franklin entered the TT to compete, it was initially on motorcycles of his own design and construction. The TT entry lists would say 'Chater-Lea' beside his name, but that was because he'd bought a bunch of loose Chater-Lea parts. These he hand-assembled around engines ordered especially from JAP. The dubious reputation of British workmanship in those early days meant that Franklin had to immediately tear down each JAP engine he received, and rebuild it to *his* standards.

When his chosen marque of motorcycle became Indian, he again spent much time in the basement of his house taking their engines to bits in order to make them go better. His experiments with Hedstrom era cylinder heads and lumps of braze are said to have come up with the principle of 'squish' at about the same time as, if not before, Harry Ricardo. Franklin spent much time closeted with the Hedstrom eight-valve machines at the Indian Depot in London, and was on-track to get them running at over 100 mph by 1914, until Royal Flying Corps lorries cut up the Brooklands Track too badly for further record attempts.

In 1916 he became a design engineer at the world's biggest motorcycle factory, and his main responsibility was design and development of a range of road machines. Yet Franklin continued to fulfil the function of race-engine tuner to make the Indian stable of race machinery go even faster. He had the assistance of home-grown American tuners like Gustafson Snr and Jnr, but as chief of the

Indian race programme it was Franklin who took primary responsibility for tuning and developing the Indian race bikes to keep them competitive. Franklin deserves special mention for countering the 1919-22 'Wrecking Crew' onslaught of Harley-Davidson racers powered by up to the minute purpose-built race motors. On a limited budget, he did this by race-tuning the only two weapons at his disposal - a side-valve production motor, and an already-outmoded eight-valve design that was a hold-over from an earlier era of racing.

Though he continued in this role of race engine tuner to the very end of his career, the fact he had a whole factory to play with gave Franklin the opportunity to move into another role that all racing buffs dream about but very few achieve - that of racing motorcycle designer. We can partition Franklin's achievements within the Indian racing department into two phases. The first concerns those bikes he developed, and the second concerns those bikes he designed.

The racing motorcycles Franklin developed while working at Indian is the Hedstrom era eight-valve twins and four-valve sloper-singles, and the Gustafson era Powerplus twins and Powerplus sloper singles. The Hedstrom overhead-valve racers were 'developed', in the sense of tuned to go faster, by Franklin both jointly with the two Gustafsons when in the US, and by himself when he was still in Britain. However his work with the Powerplus to create the Daytona went beyond mere tuning. Daytona cylinders are different from production Powerplus ones. They have bigger valves so the pushrods are spaced wider apart, necessitating different crankcases. Although Franklin did not design the Powerplus, this kind of tuning 'development' amounts to major re-design.

The first Indian racer that Franklin designed (from scratch) enters the Indian corporate timeline apparently in 1923 and is a vertical-single - the 1923 Dixon TT bike. This two-camshaft bronze timing cover bottom-end with chain driven magneto was in subsequent years fitted with a host of top-end variations from side-valve to two-valve to four-valve, and even four-valve with twin-carburetors.

The second Franklin-designed racer is the V-twin two-camshaft bronze timing cover bottom-end made famous by the Altoona motor and the two-valve Forty-five overhead hill-climbers of 1926. It first appears in the photographic record at Rhodes Motors of Australia in 1925, fitted with 'handed' V-twin versions of the 1924 four-valve 30.50 single-cylinder heads. The 61 cu in and 80 cu in side-valve hillclimbers of the late 'twenties used this same bottom-end, but with Daytona Powerplus top-ends.

There was a third Franklin-designed racer, but it was still-born. This was the Velocette-inspired overhead-cam 21 cu in single-cylinder racer that never progressed past the prototype stage. It was the other two racer types that actually got raced in anger.

And ... that's it! Despite the high diversity of top-end configurations Franklin used after 1923, the racing singles he designed all used the same bottom-end (the Dixon bike) and the racing V-twins he designed all used the same bottom-end (the Rhodes Special).

So in effect Franklin, in his entire career, only ever designed two race motors that saw use. But they were both extremely versatile, being entered into all main types of racing competition and record breaking. They were fast and successful, ranking in their day among the very fastest motorcycles in the world. Although in technological terms these racers of Franklin's were not ahead of their time, certainly they were perfectly abreast of them.

Very few motorcycle racers, even those who can also tune, ever successfully make the move into the manufacturing side of their chosen sport. To be successful in coming up with a model of motorcycle that has appeal to the man in the street, can gain the confidence of investors to put it into production, and can win sales against competing manufacturers, is a whole different ball-game from the pure pursuit of speed. Each of these two fields requires a completely different set of talents and skills. Anybody who shows ability at both is truly doubly-blessed.

Successful examples of this racing-to-manufacturing career transition are even less common than successful racer-tuners. Of course there's Le Vack who joined JAP, then New Hudson and Motosacoche. George Brough parleyed his speed successes into getting his own little factory, and there was Howard Davies whose HRD concern went rapidly broke with Vincent acquiring the name tooling and patterns in 1928. Road-racer Joe Craig rose to ultimately control Norton's race-shop designs, but he was not let loose anywhere near the production models. Bill Ottoway was similarly hired to add speed to the H-D J-series and to come up with an eight-valve engine, but responsibility for road-bike design remained squarely with engineering control-freak William S Harley.

To this very short list, add the name of Charles Franklin.

As a designer of Indian road machines for everyday use, his trend-setting design elements heavily influenced the US and global motorcycle industries, and were widely imitated. Franklin did not only design some of the fastest motorcycles of his era, he also designed some of the sturdiest, most reliable, stylish, and user-friendly. They were sales hits that saved the Indian factory from going under during the 1920s. They were given names that are iconic to this very day - Indian Scout, and Indian Chief.

The Scout model was innovative in popularizing the concept of a handy-sized middleweight motorcycle at a time when all standard sized motorcycles, even British single cylinder models, were intimidatingly long, tall and heavy. Further, the Scout and Chief embodied a holistic and integrated new approach to motorcycle design which, at the time of their release, was only just beginning to gain ground but is now recognizable as the third main phase of motorcycle industry development - the advent of the 'modern motorcycle'. And thirdly, Franklin maintained the credibility of the side-valve engine format in production road-model motorcycles for years longer than expected by industry insiders, given the contemporary advances in overhead-valve technology.

This third achievement was the result of painstaking and incremental improvements in side-valve engine breathing through exhaustive experimentation in all the standard tuning aspects like valve diameter, lift, duration and over-lap, and most significantly of all in combustion chamber shape. Apart from his very early appreciation of the importance of 'squish', none of Franklin's side-valve work was particularly revolutionary. However its cumulative effect took side-valve motorcycle engine speed development far further forward than anyone else of his era. Many of his ideas were adopted or re-invented by fifties side-valve genius Tom Sifton, and the flat-head V-8 hot-rodders.

For pre-war motorcycle markets the result was an engine type cheaper and easier to manufacture than the overhead-valve types built by the materials and methods then prevailing, with no significant trade-off needing to be made in terms of power output. Add to this the cleanliness and the convenience of lower maintenance enjoyed by owners of a machine where the engine has all its moving parts enclosed, and you have a sales winner. At Indian it was Gustafson Snr who was the innovator in making the switch to side-valve, however it was Franklin who kept it right up there with overhead-valve in terms of performance and he thus guaranteed for side-valve a three-decade longer lease of life as a viable production or racing engine.

The ultimate compliment to Franklin's side-valve engineering was paid by the Other Two of the US Big Three, Excelsior-Henderson and Harley-Davidson. They had been committed to including at least one overhead-valve per cylinder (ioe) since their inception. In racing, both had gone down the overhead-valve and even overhead-cam route, only to be beaten on the tracks of America by Daytona Powerpluses. When H-D sat down to consider major re-designs for modernization of their production engines in the late 1920s, they dropped ioe altogether. Excelsior did the same in the early 1920s with the Excelsior-Henderson Four. Neither did so to follow the British trend into overhead-valve production engines. Rather, it was to follow Franklin into side-valves!

In hindsight this appears to fly in the face of reason, but for the US industry of those times these decisions made sense in terms of providing customers with the best overall balance of power output, durability, ease of maintenance, external cleanliness, and purchase cost. It is thanks to Franklin that we have the Harley VL Seventy-four and U-Model, and the D-Models with their historically-significant descendants the WLA 'Liberator', the KR racing Harleys, and the Servi-car. This is an engineering legacy that stretches to the early 'seventies, and to the present day if you count the Sportster.

British motorcycle manufacturers became the global trend-setters during Franklin's US career. They prided themselves on that fact and in time came to adopt a paternalistic attitude toward the American industry and its products, which in Britain were regarded as 'over-weight, under-powered, and over-here'.

Yet there were British industry engineers who privately much admired the high level of sophistication that the American makers brought to the side-valve engine format, compared to the comparatively crude and undeveloped British 'side-valve sloggers'. This grudging respect is evident in one story related to us by Richard Rosenthal of *The Classic Motor Cycle* about freelance racing Norton engineer Steve Lancefield, who spent some time with H-D in the 1950s and was able to have a good look at the inside of one of their side-valve racers. He wasn't allowed to measure anything or write stuff down but, unbeknown to his hosts, he had a photographic memory. Based upon his observations of this racing Harley, he prepared a heavily worked-on Norton Big 4 side-valve single for his own high speed road use. It is said that, in regular runs from his South London home to places like Southampton or Portsmouth, there was little or nothing got past him.

Paternalism aside, the British would have given their right arms to have come up with the enduring and lucrative 'look' of large American motorcycles, as installed by Constantine on the 'streamline' Excelsior range and quickly picked up by H-D in 1929 and by Franklin for the 1932-onward Indians. It is the American streamline 'look' of rigid-frame V-twins that endures to this day as the ideal in many peoples' minds of what a motorcycle ought to look like. Modern-day British and Japanese efforts to adopt this same 'look' for their own commercial ends, as so-called 'cruisers', always end up looking forced or contrived. Even so, such motorcycles have been steady sellers and have made a lot of money for the industry. As the man in charge of the re-designed 'modern' Indians that went on sale in 1932, Franklin was Indian's representative among the US Big Three who originated the 'streamline' American hard-tail motorcycle format from which cruisers and choppers were later evolved.

Nobody is perfect, and there are a couple of question-marks that hang over Franklin's record as Indian's chief design engineer. It's churlish to turn these question-marks into criticism in the absence of any records to indicate where particular responsibilities lay. If absolutely forced to write on the Franklin report-card 'Could do better', then one area is the amount of engineering resources pumped into the Indian Four. We do not know if that was a result of his own decisions or whether they were made for him by management and he simply oversaw their implementation by Arthur Lemon. It would have been nice if the Ace-to-Indian Four integration 1927-29 and the 1931 Chief-Four range-rationalisation exercises had instead all occurred as a single step completed by 1929. It would have been even nicer if the 1930-31 Chiefs had not been such hand-grenades. If we assume that Franklin would not have willingly allowed things to pan out the way they did, then we can take it that the atmosphere at Indian at this time was not conducive to thinking strategically.

The other significant lapse in concentration, if not by Franklin then by Indian generally, is that they did not capitalize upon the race successes of the overhead-valve Forty-five hill-climb motor to introduce a street-able 61 cu in version with foot-change transmission for sale to the general public.

This could have been achieved by 1928-29, if they hadn't spent so much time fooling with the Four, not to mention shock absorbers, refrigerators, small cars, and outboard engines.

There is a counter-argument that general road conditions in the US were not yet ready for such speedy yet possibly fragile ohv sportsters, whereas an all-enclosed side-valve engine layout suited America just fine. Witness Harley's own decision to adopt side-valve format for all of its V-twins by 1930. Even so, the missed opportunity for Indian to establish a range of overhead-valve, foot-change, saddle-tanked singles and V-twins during the late 1920s under Franklin's guidance is another of the great Indian 'what-ifs' that makes modern-day enthusiasm for the Indian marque such a bitter-sweet experience. Releasing the EL Knucklehead is the one thing H-D did pre-WWII that Indian did not do. It is the one thing that has made all the difference.

We here claim that Franklin is one of the great unsung heroes of motorcycle history. It's not a claim that should be made lightly. What are the truly stand-out feats we can point to in his relatively short life that qualify him for greatness? The next five paragraphs set out our main choices.

Franklin designed an engine type (exemplified by A61-3) which gave Indian the capability to mount an attack upon the outright two-wheeled Land Speed Record in 1925, and came within a hair's breadth of succeeding. In 1920 his development of the Hedstrom eight-valve motor did indeed grab the outright Land Speed Record, and his Daytona Powerplus the 'stock valve' record.

Franklin's 1925 overhead-cam 350cc racer, which we believe was designed for an Isle of Man Junior TT campaign planned for 1926, was the technological equal of anything else available in the world at that time.

By 1927 Franklin had positioned Indian as the only US manufacturer with a comprehensive model range that included a commuting lightweight single, a sporting middleweight V-twin, a work-horse heavyweight V-twin, and a luxury four-cylinder model, with which Indian was poised to do well (and better positioned than either of their US competitors) in any global market that might remain open to them.

During the 1920s Franklin triggered a US motorcycle industry switch to side-valve design, which remained popular and competitive in the US for decades to come.

And Franklin designed the Indian Scout.

These deeds indicate a boldness and confidence by Franklin that his Indian motorcycles need not take anyone's dust, neither in competition nor in street-bike sales. Such boldness was evident from the outset of his career when, scarcely two months after obtaining his first motor bicycle, he set out to claim the Irish End-to-End record.

The competition and record breaking successes in USA, Britain, France, Australia and New Zealand of Franklin-designed Indians racers all show that Franklin was at the forefront of motorcycle design right through the 1920s. Add to this the lasting popularity and influence of his two best road models the Scout and the Chief, and it is evident that Charles Franklin is one of the world's truly great motorcycle designers.

In summary, Charles Bayly Franklin combined the riding skills and sporting qualities required for success in top-level motorcycle racing competition, with the engineering education, intellect and marketing instinct critical for success in motorcycle design and manufacture. This is a rare combination of talents. It makes him a rare individual.

We will finish here with an item from the October-November 1927 issue of *Indian News* published by the Indian Motorcycle Company. Entitled 'Meet the Boys Who Make 'Em', the article profiled Indian company executives and it had this to say about Franklin.

> Charles B Franklin: 'Charlie' is another old stager who needs no introduction to the motorcycle fraternity. He has been associated with motorcycles for over 25 years, and has been actively identified with the Indian organization for fourteen years. 'Charlie' is Chief Engineer in charge of product design and *when we say that he is the man who designed the Indian Scout, that means more to Indian Riders than pages could explain.*(Authors' emphasis)

Any company magazine will naturally be full of hype but, judged from a distance of eighty years, this summary of the man comes across as both factual and profound. For those of us who still feel 'There is magic in the name Indian', it would be difficult to find a finer epitaph for Charles Bayly Franklin 1880-1932 than the words in that last sentence.

Appendix

The Search For Charlie Franklin

Without the internet this research into the life of Charles Franklin would most likely not have happened.

The project started when Liam Diamond in Northern Ireland began to look around for information to back up stories he'd heard from his father and long-time Irish motorcyclists he knew, about a pioneer competitor in Ireland named Charles Franklin. Independently, Tim Pickering in Fiji Islands had followed up his own interest to learn more about the designer of his 1925 Indian Chief motorcycle, by collating articles and book excerpts for a website (see Bibliography p331) as a repository for the very fragmented pieces of published information at that time in existence about Franklin. Liam surfed into this website in January 2007, and left a message on its Guestbook. Discovering a mutual interest, it was decided to try and uncover as much information as possible about the life of Charles Franklin, a man we had both come to regard as one of our motorcycling heroes.

It quickly became obvious that published information about Charles Franklin is very scarce and often inaccurate, so at first our ambitions were modest. Thinking that the trail for any new information about Franklin would by now have long gone cold, the aim was firstly to build a good website dedicated to his memory, and secondly to write a couple of feature articles for publication in the specialist classic motorcycling press, to keep his name alive for a new generation of motorcycle enthusiasts to appreciate.

But after reading through the handful of motorcycle magazine articles already written about Franklin in the last two decades by people like historian Jerry Hatfield, and sifting the information provided in Harry V Sucher's book *The Iron Redskin*, we were able to see the outline of a life story worthy of expansion into a full-length book. A lot more information was going to be needed than we so far had at our disposal, however. We needed new and original material, to avoid producing a work that merely recycled already published information, to resolve apparent contradictions, and to fill the large gaps in knowledge about Franklin.

To address these issues, we decided to find out whether Franklin had any descendants and, if so, whether any 'Franklin papers', memorabilia or keepsakes had been handed down that might assist our project. We also wanted to find out about Franklin's origins, and his social standing within the Ireland of his times.

We began by searching the Ellis Island website, which holds arrival data about many of the millions of immigrants who arrived in America from Britain and Europe. This provided us with details about Charles Franklin's emigration to the United States in November 1916. Harry V Sucher's book *The Iron Redskin* provided us with the name of Franklin's wife, given as Nancy. When this was entered into the search function of this website, it showed that her name was 'Nancye' and she arrived in America in May 1920. A surprise discovery was that Nancye had a young daughter, eleven year old Phyllis Enid Franklin, travelling with her! This was the first time we knew of Charles Franklin having children. None of the previous motorcycle histories had mentioned this, and it raised a possibility of there being living descendants who we now decided to try and trace.

Liam next sought a copy of Franklin's birth and marriage certificates from the Irish public records office in Roscommon. This provided the names of his parents, Lorenzo Clutterbuck Franklin and Annie Honor Wrixon Bayly, and his father's occupation which was stated as 'Shipwright'. Though using the name 'Nancye' when she arrived in the US, Franklin's marriage certificate showed that his wife had married him as 'Annie Wilson Kerr'. Traditionally 'Annie' and 'Nancy' are two different forms of the same name. With this information, the birth certificates of both Nancye and her daughter Phyllis Enid could be obtained.

To learn more about Franklin family origins and descendants we engaged professional genealogist Paul Gorry, whose report revealed other family members like Lorenzo his father, two younger brothers Lorenzo Bruce Franklin Jnr and Rupert Fairfax Franklin, and grandfather Robert Franklin. This Robert Franklin, who died in 1903, was originally from Cahir, in County Tipperary. Charles' father's full name is variously given as Lorenzo Clutterbuck Franklin (for example, in his death notice) and as Lorenzo Bruce Franklin (in the 1901 Census). Possibly he had both as middle names.

Following up the Franklins' connection with Cahir, County Tipperary, Liam made contact with the town librarian Ann Tuohy who effected an introduction to local historian Joe Walsh. He was able to discover that a Robert Franklin Snr from Newtown Emly on the Tipperary/Limerick border came to Cahir in the early 1800's and married the local (Roman Catholic) doctor's daughter. Church of Ireland records of 9th August 1807 show that Robert Franklin (Protestant) of Newtown Emly, married Mary O'Carroll (Roman Catholic) of Cahir, witnessed by her cousin James Doherty Esq. of Kedra and Lieutenant James Ryan of the Cahir Yeomanry. They appeared to have appeased her family and also married in the Catholic church where Franklin is listed as 'heretic'. Notwithstanding Charles Franklin's descent from English plantation families in Ireland, there was also some Celtic Irish blood flowing in his veins!

Robert Snr and Mary built Rosemount House just outside Cahir in the townland of Barnora. This house was demolished in the early 1990's to make way for a new development and all that remains are the entrance gates and stables. Joe Walsh had taken some photos of the old house before the bulldozers moved in.

On the 23rd October 1809, the Franklins baptised their first children, twins Robert Jnr and Ann, and on the 20th September 1812 another child, Margaret. Robert Snr. died in 1830. In 1832, Robert Franklin Jnr. was listed as a Church Warden. On 6th November 1838, Robert Jnr married his neighbour Jane Clutterbuck of Killemly Hall. The wedding took place in St. Pauls Church, Cahir, and was witnessed by Alice and Lorenzo Clutterbuck, Maria Franklin and Richard Hughes. Located in St Pauls Church Cahir are two plaques; 'To memory of Robert & Jane Franklin by their daughter J.C. Fisher 1904', and 'To memory of Lorenzo & Martha Clutterbuck 1919'.

In March 2010 Liam travelled to Cahir, County Tipperary, to meet with Joe Walsh and visit various places of interest connected with the Franklin family. These included the site just outside

'Rosemount House', the Franklin home built in Cahir, Co. Tipperary, in the early 1800s by Charles Franklin's great-grandfather Robert Snr. (Photo Joe Walsh)

the town where Robert Franklin Snr had built 'Rosemount'. There is a new building here now and the owner, Mrs Josephine Casey, was interested to learn for the first time of her home's historical connection. She showed Liam round the back of the house where the old stables still existed in good condition. Liam also went to the Church of Ireland graveyard just outside Cahir, to visit the grave of Charles' grandmother Jane.

Robert Franklin's wife Jane was the daughter of Lorenzo Clutterbuck and Eliza Clutterbuck née Lane. Kirsten Duffield, from the Clutterbuck family on-line website, was able to provide an almost complete family tree of the Clutterbucks in Ireland going back to the middle of the 17th Century. She stated that only one branch of this family had left England to settle in Ireland. Their ancestor Richard Clutterbuck, a 'merchant adventurer' who helped finance Oliver Cromwell's conquest of Ireland after the 1641 Rebellion, obtained thousands of acres in the barony of Middlethird, County Tipperary and at Kilrea, County Derry in 1658. In 1664 Richard presented the Anglican congregation in Kilrea with a silver chalice and paten. This beautiful piece of silverware still exists and is greatly cherished by the present day congregation of Saint Patrick's Church of Ireland in Kilrea. It is known as 'The Clutterbuck Cup.' Richard Clutterbuck died in 1670 aged 71. His son Lawrence became Rector at Kilrea church from 1675 until his death in 1725. Charles Franklin's grandmother Jane Clutterbuck was descended from this line on her father's side.

Jane's mother Eliza's maiden name was Lane, and the certificate for Jane's 1838 marriage to Robert Franklin took care to specifically state that she was the granddaughter of Colonel Lane of

Lanespark, County Tipperary. A websearch of 'Colonel Lane' scored a hit on a message posted on a genealogy website by Beverly Kropp in Australia, seeking information about one of her ancestors called Colonel John Hamilton Lane of Tipperary, Ireland. When contacted, Beverly was kind enough to send a large envelope of material about the Lane family, including a family tree going right back to the middle of the 17th century. It revealed that Charles Franklin's great grandmother Eliza Lane was a direct descendant of the brother of Jane Lane, who had saved the life of Charles, Prince of Wales (later King Charles II) when he was on the run from Parliamentarian forces during the English civil war.

Robert Jnr and Jane Franklin's first child, Lorenzo Clutterbuck Franklin (Charles' father) was born in 1840. A daughter, Mary was born in 1841 and two more daughters, Jane and Eliza, were born in the following years.

To find out more about Charles' mother, Annie Franklin, required some educated guesswork by Liam. Because Charles' brother Robert, (d. 27th December 1879) had been named after his paternal grandfather Robert Franklin, it was likely that Charles' other brother William Bayly Franklin (d. 22nd December 1879) may have been named after his maternal grandfather, hence William Bayly. By the same token Charles' mother, Annie Honor Wrixon Bayly, might have been named after her mother. Sure enough, when 'William Bayly marries Annie Honor Wrixon' was entered into the Google search engine, their names came up! This couple had married in Brinny Church, County Cork on 9th May 1840.

Genealogist Paul Gorry followed this up to find that William Bayly, wife Annie and family had left Ireland to live in England in about 1852. This period was around the time of the famine in Ireland, however there was no evidence that the Baylys moved away because of this. Their daughter, Annie Honnor Wrixon Bayly (spelled Honor in later documentation), Charles' mother, was born in Ireland in 1846. She was nineteen years old when she married twenty-six years old Lorenzo Clutterbuck Franklin in Camberwell, Surrey, England on 6th June 1865. On their marriage certificate Lorenzo's occupation was given as 'clerk'.

A reference to Robert Franklin Jnr was found in the 1881 Slaters Directory under the heading 'Farmers in Cahir'. This was the only time any reference was found to what he may have done for a living, since in vital documents he always stated his occupation as 'gentleman'. Lorenzo is also listed in the 1881 Slaters Directory, and shows that he and a partner had their own company; 'Franklin, Wayt & Co. Shipwrights' at 28 Lower Buckingham Street, Dublin.

After the death of his wife Jane on the 12th January 1891, Robert Franklin Jnr. went to live in Dublin at 8 Appian Way. Charles Franklin and his two younger brothers lived there with him during their teenage years and as young men. The 1901 Census return for 8 Appian Way shows that the head of household was Lorenzo Bruce Franklin (aged 52; iron merchant; widower; born in Dublin). Living him were Lorenzo Bruce Franklin Jnr (19; clerk; not married; born Dublin), Charles Bayly Franklin (20; electric engineer; not married; born Dublin), Rupert Fairfax Franklin (16; scholar; not married; born Dublin), Robert Franklin (92; widower; born Clonmel) and Mary Smyth (25; servant). All the Franklins were stated as of the Church of Ireland.

The death record for Lorenzo C. Franklin shows that he passed away on 13th May 1902 at 8 Appian Way, was a widower aged 62 years, and a merchant. Lorenzo Snr was the last person to be buried in the Franklin family plot at Mount Jerome Cemetery. He had purchased the grant in perpetuity for this plot on 21st April 1887. Six individuals are listed on the grant as buried in the grave; Jane M., William B., Florence A. and Robert (all four children died of scarlatina between December 1879 and October 1880), Lorenzo's wife Annie H.W. (who died in 1898) and Lorenzo himself.

After the death of his son Lorenzo, Robert Jnr moved again to be with his daughter Mary Bailie on her farm at 'Clonaleenaghan House' at Hackballscross, County Louth. Robert Franklin died aged 95 on the 29th December 1903 and was buried in the Kane graveyard, Dundalk.

In summary, Charles Franklin's parents Lorenzo Bruce Clutterbuck Franklin (b. Dublin c1839-40; d. 1902) and Annie Honor Wrixon Bayly (b. County Cork c1846; d.1898) had seven children; Jane Maude (b. c1867; d. 1879), Florence Annie (b. c1871; d. 1880), Robert (b. c1873; d. 1879), William Bayly (b. c1875; d. 1879), Charles Bayly (b. 1st October 1880; d. October 1932), Lorenzo Bruce (b. 31st March 1882; d. April 1937) and Rupert Fairfax (b. 9th March 1885; d. 1956).

Turning now to finding out what became of the Franklins in America, Liam asked his sister, Patricia Buller, a researcher with the BBC in Belfast, for help and was soon put in contact with Margaret Humberston, Head of Archives at the Connecticut Valley Historical Museum (now the Lyman and Merrie Wood Museum of Springfield History). Maggie's own work to prepare a new Indian Motorcycles exhibit based around the recently donated Charlie and Esta Manthos Collection paralleled our own efforts to discover the facts behind Franklin's time at the Indian factory, and this resulted in much useful collaborative work being done.

Tim then contacted Harry V Sucher, author of *The Iron Redskin* and living in retirement in Garden Grove, California. From their initial telephone conversation it soon transpired that the original manuscript for this book had run to some 700 pages, of which only about 300 ended up being published. Dr Sucher is widely acknowledged as the first person to treat American motorcycle history as a serious subject. He'd had the foresight to conduct interviews, either in person or by telephone, with surviving Indian senior-staffers at a time when the Franklin era at Indian was still within living memory. Beginning by meeting and interviewing Frank Weschler in the 1930s when Sucher was himself still a teenager, and ending with regular telephone calls to Tommy Butler in the early seventies and a visit with Helen Hedstrom Carlson, information from these interviews contributed to the writing of *The Iron Redskin*.

Tantalizingly, Tommy Butler had told Sucher that when Franklin died, Butler had asked Nancye if he might be able to gather up and keep Franklin's work diaries and engineering notes, however Nancye had refused.

Already 92 years of age when contacted, Dr Sucher represented the last remaining living link to the Indian factory of Franklin's era. Physically partly incapacitated, which now hindered his ability to write, Dr Sucher nevertheless readily agreed to join us as co-author in a Franklin book project. He offered his own reminiscences and interview information as new and original material toward this project, either imparted over the telephone or as dictated notes laboriously hand-written out for us by his wife Margery. 'Don't ask me what I had for lunch yesterday' he told us, 'but 1928 I can remember as clear as a bell!'

Meanwhile Tim began getting in touch with various contacts among the global network of Indian clubs, such as the Indian Motorcycle Club of Australia, to start pulling together information about the significant Franklin motorcycle models. One result was receipt of photographs of a replica of the Indian motorcycle used to win the 1911 Isle of Man TT race, and the original bike that Freddie Dixon rode in the 1923 TT, taken at a California *concours d'elegance* and kindly contributed by 'RedFred' from San Francisco. There was a very useful two days spent with Indian restorer Mick Atkins in Sydney, and long-distance calls to Lindsay Urquhart in Melbourne, to unravel the design relationships between the various Franklin race bikes. There was also the opportunity to try out some of the different Franklin Indian models under modern road conditions, by participating in the regular road rides and tours organised by the Indian Motorcycle Club of Australia.

Liam followed up a lead provided by Maggie in Springfield that Franklin had attended 'St. Andrews College', St Stephen's Green in Dublin, now located at Blackrock, County Dublin. When contacted, the college found Charles' school record in their archives and they kindly sent us this information.

Liam contacted the Dublin & District Motor Cycle Club, which Franklin had belonged to. Records of their early days are missing, however they suggested we get in touch with Harry Havelin of MCUI who has accumulated much knowledge about Irish motorcycle racing and Isle of Man Tourist Trophy history. Harry has written articles based upon his researches for club newsletters, magazines and souvenir programmes for motorcycle race events. Over twenty years ago he had commenced research specifically on Franklin, after being told by Stanley Woods to find out as much as he could because Franklin was Ireland's first great motorcycle competitor. Harry agreed to contribute to this project the material he had so far gleaned about Charles Franklin. He undertook fresh research, visited and photographed Dublin and Isle of Man locations significant in the Franklin story, and unearthed new material from the National Library in Dublin. It is entirely thanks to Harry's diligence that Part One of this book was able to be written as the first-ever full account of Franklin's early life and career as a racing motorcyclist in Ireland, England and the Continent.

From the outset we decided to locate and contact any descendants of Charles Franklin or his brothers, with the possibility they might have material useful to the biography. Genealogist Richard Doherty in Detroit Michigan agreed to look for decendants of Lorenzo Bruce Franklin who, Ellis Island records revealed, had left Ireland bound for Detroit in 1912. In due course he reported back to say he'd been speaking on the phone with Carol Northern Good, the grand-daughter of Lorenzo and wife Eliza. Carol lives in Indiana, and her aunt Honor Franklin (Charles' niece) had passed to her a bundle of family papers and photos, and a family tree of her grand-mothers' family, the Grahams of Dundalk. In her possession is a photo of the wedding party when Lorenzo and Eliza married in Ireland in 1907, in which Charles Franklin is present. Carol does not possess anything to show there were any links or communications between Lorenzo and Charles after they both came to America. In fact, she'd been completely unaware that her grandfather even had brothers. Mother of five sons and not knowing of any other male Franklins of this line anywhere in the world, Carol Good had given one of her boys the name Franklin just to ensure that the name continued. 'Mathew' Franklin Good is a keen motorcyclist, and owns a Harley. It was a surprise to learn of his family connection to that other great name in American motorcycling, the Indian.

We began searching for any Franklins still in Britain, starting with a clue provided by the Ellis Island arrival information for Lorenzo Franklin Jnr which stated that his last address on leaving Britain had been that of an R Franklin at Bilston, near Wolverhampton in England. British Army war records at this time acquired via ancestry.com turned up the complete Service Record for Lorenzo, who apparently had returned to Britain from Detroit to join the army during WWI. Guessing that a tradition in the Franklin family was to name one son after the father, Liam sent off to the Staffordshire public records office for the birth certificate of any Rupert Franklin born around 1914. About a fortnight later he received a copy of the birth certificate of Rupert Franklin Jnr born in Bilston, Wolverhampton, in April 1915. This certificate confirmed Rupert Fairfax Franklin as the boy's father and his mother as Mary Ann Franklin *née* Thompson.

Another piece in the jigsaw came when we received the Will of Mary Bailie, daughter of Robert and Jane Franklin and thus Charles' aunt. When she died in August 1924, she left her entire 223 acre estate in County Louth, Ireland to Rupert Fairfax Franklin. Charles himself and Rupert's other brother Lorenzo, both by now in the US, received £10 each under this same Will.

To make further headway with tracking down the descendants of Rupert Franklin in England, we engaged the services of Maureen Hunt, a professional researcher in Wolverhampton. The Will of Rupert Franklin Jnr mentioned a daughter, Ann Nesbitt. Liam next put the name of Rupert Franklin into an internet site called 'genesreunited.co.uk' and found that two other people had posted messages requesting information about him. One was a Roger Knights, and the other was Ann Nesbitt! Both were asked if they could help with our project via any old photographs, letters or stories relating to Charles Franklin. Ann Nesbitt confirmed that her grandfather was Rupert Fairfax Franklin who had died in 1956 and that her father was Rupert Jnr. In addition to Rupert Jnr, Rupert Snr and wife Mary had three other sons, Ernest, Robert and George. George the youngest was killed during the battle of Tobruk in North Africa during WWII. Ann also provided the names of her cousins, Andrew Franklin and Angela Davies, who are also grandchildren of Rupert Snr. Roger Knights is related by marriage to the Franklins - Rupert Franklin Jnr was his wife's cousin.

Although finding so many English Franklins seemed promising for our book project, unfortunately it emerged that they knew almost nothing about Charles Franklin. Initially it was thought there might be some letters and photographs in their family archives relating to their Irish background and perhaps some reference to Charles, but after they carried out a search, very little was found. The only photograph we received was a picture of Rupert Jnr taken in the early 1930's. If we thought there was going to be a trunk-full of Franklin 'Letters from America' tucked away somewhere in England, we were to be disappointed.

Following advice from within the Vintage Motor Cycle Club (VMCC) in England we made contact with Rick Howard of Sussex, who as a pioneer- and veteran-era motorcycle and bicycle enthusiast had been able over the years to collect some useful information about the motorcycles and the career of Billy Wells. Rick revealed to us that Billy's son, George Hendee Wells, who is briefly interviewed in a 1995 documentary movie *Old Indians Never Die*, happened to be a friend of his. By way of this introduction, and also facilitated by George's son David Wells in Australia, we were able to get to know (via telephone and email) a terrific gentleman who was only too pleased to share with us his recollections of growing up as the son of England's 'Mr Indian'. Unfortunately, due to a direct hit by one of the Luftwaffe's bombs on his father's house during the London Blitz of WWII, George had to sadly report that there were scarcely any 'Wells papers' left in existence which might otherwise have helped our research. It can safely be assumed that correspondence between the London and Dublin Depots of the Hendee Mfg. Co. organisation in the British Isles would have formed a significant portion of these 'Wells papers', had they still existed. Rick Howard invited Liam and wife Roisin to visit him at home in England to look over his collection of Billy Wells photographs and memorabilia, and he contributed some rare images for publication in this book.

In April 2009, Dr Harry V Sucher passed away. America had now lost its first ever motorcycle historian.

Indian factory photos taken of Charles Franklin late in his career show that he looked unwell during the year before he died, with face very drawn and eyes sunken. We sought to confirm the report in *The Iron Redskin* that Franklin had died of a respiratory ailment such as emphysema, a legacy of his teenage bout with pneumonia. Liam applied to the public records office in Springfield, Massachusetts for his death certificate and a few weeks later received a copy which stated that his death had been caused by 'Malignant Growth of Intestines Acute Myocarditis'. Essentially this is bowel cancer, and a heart condition.

Because we knew from Springfield City Directory information sent to us by Maggie Humberston that Nancye and Phyllis had removed from Springfield to New York City after Charles' death in

1932, we decided to try and trace what had become of them. Did Charles Franklin have any direct descendants? Would one of them still have in their possession his diaries, motorcycle tuning logbooks, old photographs, or any other information directly relevant to our project?

In January 2008 we hired genealogist Margie Ellis of New York and sent her the little information we had in our possession regarding birth dates and a death date we'd found from a Social Security record for Nancye, which showed that she'd passed away in Manhattan on 28th December 1973. We also requested a search for a Valerie Franklin of Manhattan, which a very recent Social Security death record dated September 2007 showed (perhaps coincidentally) had the exact same birth date as Phyllis.

Margie informed us that information about the existence or otherwise of Charles' descendant(s) could be gained by requesting a copy of Nancye's Will. Under New York privacy laws however, this can only be done by next-of-kin. We therefore asked Carol Northern whether, as Charles Franklin's grand-niece, she could make the necessary request. This she did and the Will, when it arrived, showed that Nancye had only a single daughter and that her name was given as Valerie! From this we concluded that, for whatever reason, Phyllis had changed her name to Valerie. Charles Franklin's only daughter had still been living when we'd begun our search for her! It is ironical that only by her death did her existence and whereabouts become revealed to us.

Nancye's Will provided mother and daughter's residential address, which was an apartment in upper eastside Manhattan not far from the Metropolitan Art Museum on Central Park. Margie left letters in the letterboxes of other tenants in the same building, asking for help. After a time she was contacted by one of these neighbours, Steven Harmison, who said he had been a close friend of Valerie Franklin for many years. He confirmed that Valerie had never married or had any children. When we enquired about the possibility of there being any 'Franklin papers' in existence which might assist a biography of Charles Franklin, he responded that when she died he'd been given only a very few hours to locate and retrieve some of Valerie's vital documents before everything was cleared from the apartment for re-letting. He had been holding on to these items in case any next-of-kin ever came to light.

Mr Harmison had known Valerie for the best part of thirty-five years, and was able to provide more background about her. He said that she never talked about her father, or about growing up in Dublin. She got very irate when once during a conversation she was asked if she was from Ireland. She stated in no uncertain terms that she was English! When asked if he thought that perhaps she didn't get on well with her father, he agreed it seemed there had been some kind of rift within the family. He went on to say that Valerie had never married and, because she had lived so long (passing away at 99 years of age), most of her old friends had been long dead. In her later years she associated herself with her church and its ministers and lay people. She started a soup kitchen for the poor in the neighborhood of her place of worship, Saint James Church, Madison Avenue, in New York for which she was highly regarded by the local community.

When asked about Valerie's career, we were told that she was a very clever woman and had worked all her life on Wall Street, ultimately appointed a vice-president of the insurance company she worked for. She once told Mr Harmison that she was the first female to ever become vice-president of any company on Wall Street. This may explain her reluctance to describe herself as Irish. Quite apart from the handicap of being female in a male-dominated profession, in New York City being Irish can in no way be viewed as an asset for a career on Wall Street. In her declining years Valerie developed dementia, and was cared for at the Mary Manning Walsh Home on York Avenue and 72nd Street.

Mr Harmison said that little of any value remained in Valerie's apartment when she died. She had been burgled several times, and at one point a fire had taken hold in an adjoining apartment. In order to bring the fire under control, fire fighters burst through a wall into her apartment. A lot of her property was badly damaged and had to be disposed of.

When Valerie died on 19th September 2007 she was cremated, and he took her ashes and scattered them in a quiet spot near his home in Berkeley Springs, West Virginia. He was not given very much time before the building management sent in a crew to discard everything and re-let Valerie's apartment and, when he did pick out a few items for safe-keeping, he was unaware they might include those of an historical figure. He knew only that he was saving some effects of a long-standing friend and neighbour which might be of interest to her next-of-kin, should there be any.

It turned out he did have a few small items of interest to motorcycle historians. Amongst some photos of Valerie in her younger days, some letters related to her own aspirations as a classical dancer, and Franklin's old wallet with all his various insurance membership cards still inside, there were some photos of Franklin with his buddies, some never before published photos taken of him riding or racing motorcycles, and a technical article about Villiers two-stroke engines. Mr Harmison agreed to forward these items to Carol Northern, the granddaughter of Charles Franklin's brother Lorenzo, and with her permission some of the photos have been included in this book. It appears that nothing in the form of personal notebooks or diaries belonging to Valerie's father have survived.

The main aims of our genealogical research were two-fold. Firstly, we wanted to find out about Franklin's origins and social standing in Ireland. Secondly, we hoped there might be still be in the family a collection of 'Franklin papers' which would shed more light upon his life and his motorcycle career.

We have succeeded in the first aim. But for various reasons that include Franklin's immediate family's indifference to his career in motorcycles, their strong sense of privacy, his extended family's indifference to keeping in touch with each other, Manhattan burglars, FDNY fire fighters, and Hitler's bombs, very little in the way of 'Franklin papers' have come down to us to help better understand the up-close details of his career as a motorcycle competitor or as a motorcycle designer.

Never mind. We gave it our best shot.

Epilogue

Why Any Of This Still Matters

The roar of the exhaust takes on an added crackle as you roll the left-hand throttle further. With this extra surge of power you quickly close the gap. Swinging out into the opposite lane of the rural black-top, a Toyota family saloon bumbling along at a mere 70 mph is easily conquered and left bobbing in the wake of this impressively large motorcycle. Mercifully, at 70-plus the main noise you experience is the rush of wind past your aviator goggles and open-face helmet. The full force of this big vee's thunder is concentrated in a zone about ten feet behind the elegant snail-shell rear fender.

A rolling countryside of vineyards, orchards and sun-browned paddocks streams past as this machine hastens you on toward the eucalypt-covered ranges in the distance. This is Melbourne's Yarra Valley, and today's goal is Black Spur followed by a large English breakfast near the Maroondah Reservoir. The sun is high enough in the sky now to have dispersed both the morning mist and the leaping kangaroos that pose a routine riding hazard for any dawn start in rural Victoria.

Beyond the broad, shapely tear-drop gas tanks, a sweeping set of chromed cow-horn handlebars curve back to put the grips comfortably at hand. Flat foot-boards allow you to shuffle your legs back and get some of your weight onto the balls of your feet, putting you into a slight cafe-racer crouch. This bike had been such a 'bus to manhandle back at the car-park rendezvous, but on the open road it's in its element. With a sprung pan-saddle to ease you gently over the road shocks, and two inches of rear suspension movement to take the sting out of the more serious bumps, you feel supremely comfortable. To Sydney and back? Twelve-hundred-mile round-trip? Not a problem. Balanced against a cushion of wind that takes all strain off your arms, you feel ready to carry on riding forever. At 70 mph the engine is only just getting into its stride.

This is a 1953 Blackhawk Chief, the last of the line. Nothing made after that date is a real Indian. It doesn't matter what anyone says. This is the last Indian to retain design elements bestowed by the model's creator Charles Franklin in 1922. There's even a few component parts still the very same as those of a first-year '22 Chief!

You had given a head start to the older and smaller Indian models in the Club, because a steady 50 mph is more realistic for these early Scouts and Powerpluses. They were now coming into view, a long string of scarlet machines in groups of two or three, trailing a blue haze from their total-loss oiling systems. You'd already smelled them five miles before you saw them, because the distinctive odour of burnt castor oil is persistent in the way it hangs in the air.

The road is climbing steadily now as the foot-hills are approached. This is where a big lazy motor really comes into its own. There's a '36 Sport Scout in front of you, doing well on the flatter sections because those Forty-five motors are rev-happy and can really be spun up when the occasion demands.

On the steeper inclines you can see its rider having to reach for second gear and rev it out, yet even so it's now holding up traffic. Scouts have the advantage around town and in tighter going, because they are more chuckable and much better braked. You'd swapped bikes with a club-mate and tried one earlier that day, so you can now appreciate a Sport Scout's good points. It was infinitely more user-friendly and manageable in terms of ease of starting and low-speed handling. But it felt sooo gutless after stepping off the Blackhawk.

This particular Chief boasts a full 80 cubic inches, with Bonneville cams and some fairing of ports and carburettor internals. With an engine bigger than a Volkswagen Beetle, in higher tune and propelling a lot less weight, you just know that having enough power on tap will simply not be an issue. When you crank that throttle grip, the bike gathers up its skirts and responds eagerly. It simply does not slow down for hills. You romp up them effortlessly, the same as if you were on the flat.

This abundance of power comes in handy right about now, as you become surrounded by the lush greens and browns of virgin eucalypt forest in the Yarra National Park. The road is winding upwards through the woods in a series of loops and hairpin bends. Such a thrill to wind the throttle on and power out of every bend, feeling the bike leap forward. It is surprisingly manoeuvrable and your stance is almost racer-like as you straighten out these twisties. It's the pre-entry braking that needs care, for either brake used by itself provokes an involuntary 'Oh my God!', while both used together are barely adequate. You find it best to get your speed correct before you go in, because applying the front brake half-way round makes the bike want to sit up straight and then you run wide. Still, you are pleasantly surprised at how well the Blackhawk can be flung around through a series of tight bends. It almost feels 'modern'.

The road levels out to a saddle atop the range, and in the lay-by you see a cluster of bright primary colours and gold pin-striping gleaming in the sun. The Club marshalls direct you to turn and go back down off the Spur to the picnic ground. Downhill now, and the engine barely ticks over as you coast to the day's final destination. You're riding one of the fastest machines in the Club, so are not surprised to be one of the first arrivals in the car park by the barbecue area. Rolling to a stop, you let the engine keep on running for half a minute before shutting off. You just love the 'potato-potato-potato' of that deep-sounding engine at idle. You suddenly feel that Wagner's 'Ride of the Valkyries' is not so clichéd after all.

There's a group of modern Harleys already present, and their owners remain poker-faced about the steady stream of scarlet-and-gold now pulling in. It's interesting to observe the studied indifference feigned by some modern-Harley riders when an example of the only motorcycle brand on the planet way cooler than their own suddenly shows up. But hey, the age-old rivalry is all in good fun these days. Owners of equivalent-age antique Harleys are generally welcome at Indian Club runs, so long as they remember their station in life and keep well to the rear of the pack.

The bikes are all parked, saddle-bags are opened, and next thing there is bacon, eggs, sausages and all the trimmings coming off the barbecues, with hot coffee to wash it down. That kookaburra perched on a nearby branch may look cute, but they practice on lizards so you keep one careful eye upon it and the other on the fork-load of bacon you're now raising to your lips. There's good natured banter amongst this group of people, who've known each other since the days when Indians could still be found in derelict barns and purchased for $50. A committee of advisors has formed around one machine as it undergoes some running repairs. Your own gaze keeps straying to the rolling sculpture that has brought you this far today in such effortless speed, comfort and style.

It's time to go. The sun is high in the sky now, and the first car- and bus-loads of day-tripping Melbourne suburbanites are arriving. Soon this picnic area will be awash with nosey rug-rats. You approach the Blackhawk with a determined look in your eye, because getting it started again requires an element of willpower as well as technique. Nowadays one can always kit it out with an electric-starter, as pioneered by Indian in 1914. Your own view is that mastering the starting drill is all part of this bike's mystique. It's still quite warm so won't need any choke, but these are thirsty motors that always want a lot of throttle when starting. Kicking it over while standing astride is not at all ergonomic, owing to the over-hang of generous cylinder finning around the exhaust valve area. Better to leave it leaned-over on its side-stand, get alongside it, then rear up and give it a long swinging kick with plenty of follow-through. To make things worse, now those Harley guys are watching.

It's all cool though, because the second kick does the trick and you roll back the throttle and ignition advance grips until the power strokes can almost be counted over the din of clattery valve gear. At a slow idle the hand-change lever can be used to surprise it into first gear with just the normal amount of 'crunch'. Give it more advance for a faster idle, and you're ready for the off. The engine note scarcely alters as your left foot rocks the clutch up to the friction point and the bike lurches into motion. There's fifty miles of open country roads ahead of you before you again strike Melbourne's northern suburbs. You know you're going to enjoy every single minute of it.

There are other classic bikes that make similar power and maintain similar cruising speeds, often from half of the engine displacement and one-tenth the current purchase price of an Indian Chief. A Triumph Bonneville is a case in point.

You don't care. That case in point is beside the point. It's not what it does. It's how it does it. This Chief is just such a pleasure to ride. It spoils you for riding any other type of motorcycle.

When all else has been said and done, it's the fun of riding-days like this that most brings us to say:-

'Franklin's Indians never die'.

Charles Franklin Bibliography

Clew, J. (1985). *JAP: the Vintage Years*. Haynes Publishing Group.

Drury, N.E. (1980). Motorcycling sixty years ago. *The Official Journal of the Vintage Motorcycle Club*, Issue 227, January 1980, pp. 3-12.

Hartley, P. (1973). *Bikes at Brooklands in the Pioneer Years*. Goose and Sons Ltd.

Hartley, P. (1980). *Brooklands Bikes in the Twenties*. Argus Books Ltd.

Hatfield, J. (1988). Charles Franklin: Indian's unsung hero. *Classic Bike* No. 98, March 1988.

Hatfield, J. (2001). *Indian Scout*. MBI Publishing Company.

Pickering, T. (2006). A connection between Brooklands and motorcycle design in America, (Part One). *The Brooklands Society Gazette*, Vol. 31 No. 4, 2006.

Pickering, T. (2007). A connection between Brooklands and motorcycle design in America, (Part Two). *The Brooklands Society Gazette*, Vol. 32 No. 1, 2007.

Pickering, T and L. Diamond (2007). Charle B. Franklin profile. *The Classic Motorcycle* Vol. 34 No. 9, September 2007.

Sucher, H. (1977). *The Iron Redskin*. Haynes Publishing Group.

Sucher, H. (1994). Charles B. Franklin: Racer and Creator of Classic Indian Motorcycles. *Indian Motorcycle Illustrated*, Autumn 1994.

The life and times of Indian's chief designer Charles B. Franklin http://web.archive.org/web/20080509070525/http://www.geocities.com/charles_b_franklin/

Notes

[1] Birth certificate for Charles Bayly Franklin, Registry, Roscommon
[2] Mount Jerome Cemetery Records, Grave 91 in Section B, Subdivision 362 (No. 7178 Grant in Perpetuity).
[3] 'The Woollen Industry in the Cotswolds.' www.grahamthomas.com, accessed January 2009.
[4] Information about the Clutterbucks in Ireland was provided by Kirsten Duffield, who maintains a website about the Clutterbuck name.
[5] A canton is a portion of a shield on a coat of arms that is smaller than a quarter and which is positioned at the top left of the shield. A 'canton of England' is a representation of the Royal Arms of England upon such a canton. In this case the canton is one of a group of references to the flight from Worcester which comprise the addition of a Crown between the horse's fore hooves, and the motto 'Garde Le Roi' (Guard the King). These additions to the basic coat of arms are rare marks of Royal gratitude, known as 'augmentations of honour' and in this case they are passed from one generation of Lanes to another.
[6] Franklin's connection to the Lanes was established using genealogical information kindly supplied by Lane descendant Beverly Kropp of Brisbane, Australia.
[7] Valuation Office, Dublin.
[8] Land Commission 1930s
[9] Thomas Callaghan Butler, Indian staffer and Franklin contemporary, pers. comm. to H.S.V.
[10] *The Irish Times*, 1st September 1900.
[11] Drury, N.E. (1980). Motorcycling sixty years ago. The Official Journal of the Vintage Motorcycle Club, Issue 227, January 1980, pp. 3-12.
[12] Our thanks go to Jimmy McDermott, retired teacher of Irish history, Belfast, for drafting this political and social summary of Franklin's Ireland for us.
[13] This information about the early FN single-cylinder motorcycles was kindly provided by FN owner and restorer Jacques Maertens of Bruges, Belgium.
[14] Probate 20th February 1904, Robert Franklin.
[15] Bob Montgomery. Sand racing at Portmarnock. *Irish Times* 23rd June 2004.
[16] Mention of 'C.B. Franklin' crops up in several places in Jeff Clew's book *JAP: The Vintage Years* (Haynes).

[17] This information about Rupert Fairfax Franklin in Bilston was provided by Roger Knights.

[18] This biographical information about Billy Wells was kindly provided to us by his son George Hendee Wells, and by Billy Wells historian Rick Howard of the Vintage Motor Cycle Club (VMCC) in England.

[19] The events leading to the establishment of organized motorcycle racing at Brooklands have been researched by Bryan Reynolds and published in his article '100 years of motorcycles at Brooklands' in the *Brooklands Society Gazette* Vol. 33 No. 1, 2008, pp. 16-18.

[20] In a story in the *Boston Globe* of 9th May 1901 about formation of an association of New England cycle track owners, George Hendee, Charles T. Shean and Charles S. Henshaw were named in attendance as representatives of the Springfield track. The first two gentlemen were the track owners. Henshaw was appointed Track Manager for the 1901 season, following the resignation of inaugural manager Jack Prince who moved out West in September 1900 to build and promote other tracks

[21] According to recent research published by Herbert Wagner in *At the Creation: Myth, Reality, and the Origin of the Harley-Davidson Motorcycle, 1901 - 1909* (Wisconsin Historical Society Press), the oft-quoted 1903 date for commencement of H-D production was a marketing department fiction perpetrated from about 1908 onwards to help the Motor Company compete against then industry-leader Indian. Wagner has convincingly demonstrated that the prototype of H-D's first loop-frame single-cylinder model was not completed until late 1904, and actual production for sale of complete Harley-Davidson motorcycles commenced in mid-1905.

[22] See *Boston Globe* 4th December 1905.

[23] The sequence of significant events and dates used for our preceding summary of De Rosier's early competition career are contained in this same biographical and medical-history feature article, which was published in the *Indianapolis Star* of 20th March 1910.

[24] *Oakland Tribune* November 7 1911.

[25] *Bikes at Brooklands in the Pioneer Years* by Peter Hartley, Goose and Son, Ltd.

[26] Evidence of Hedstrom's visit is contained in Peter Hartley's book *Bikes at Brooklands in the Pioneer Years* (Goose and Son, Ltd.) which mentions that Hedstrom visited Brooklands on 27th April to watch Wells' Indians compete in the second B.A.R.C. race meeting of 1910, and verified by US Immigration records which show that Oscar and Julia sailed from Southampton aboard the SS Kronprinz Wilhelm on 13th June 1910 (eighteen days after the TT) bound for New York.

[27] This phrase can be attributed to Frank Westworth, editor of *RealClassic* magazine, who used it in connection with a ride he once took on a 1913 Hedstrom twin.

[28] Our thanks go to Lorenzo Franklin Jnr's grand-daughter Carol Northern for information about this branch of the Franklin family tree.

[29] Thomas Callaghan Butler and Dick Richards, Indian staff and Franklin contemporaries, pers. comm. to HSV, 1972

[30] Discharge Documents, Lorenzo Bruce Franklin, British Army WWI Service and Pension Records, The National Archives. Accessed via www.ancestry.com.

[31] This information about the small-base eight-valve racers, and about Rhodes Motors, is contributed by Lindsay Urquhart of Melbourne, Australia.

[32] http://www.clanmaxwellusa.com/maxcars.htm

[33] See, for example, *The Syracuse Herald*, 20th February 1917

34. 'Poodle-faker' is old British military slang and a put-down of a young officer thought by his peers to be over-attentive to women, preferring their company rather than be 'one of the boys', and thereby turning himself into an imitation of a woman's lapdog.
35. Paleontology being the study of fossilized dinosaur bones to make inferences about their ecology and living habits.
36. Held for years by former Indian dealer Paul Brokaw, this 35mm movie was provided to the AMA Museum in recent times by his son Bill. A five-minute segment has been posted on www.youtube.com under the title 'Hall of Famer Shrimp Burns Goes All Out at 1921 Beverly Hills, Calif., Board Track'.
37. Interestingly, 2011 may bring a rebirth of the side-valve engine in motorcycle competition. European manufacturer Gas-Gas has announced a new water-cooled side-valve design to power an off-road Trials bike. Hugues Brunault, the designer who conceived this 'new' and 'revolutionary' side-valve engine, cites advantages of low centre of gravity and simplicity of valve-train and oiling systems, which saves height and weight compared with upstairs-valves four-strokes yet provides a power delivery broader than two-strokes. Direct your browser to http://www.gasgas.com/4stroke.htm. Franklin would be proud.
38. http://thevintagent.blogspot.com/2010/01/duzmo-levack-tt-replica.html
39. This street had been named Tariff Road circa 1911 at the suggestion of John A Prestwich, in honour of import duties erected by the British government against foreign motorcycles of which Indian was perceived as the main threat.
40. This derives from an analysis carried out by Jerry Hatfield, the results of which appear in his various Indian marque and model histories.
41. http://www.skf.com/portal/skf/home/products?lang=en&maincatalogue=1&newlink=1_2_1
42. The only other published words we've found that clearly and independently reach the same conclusion are in two paragraphs that open a November 1998 *Classic Bike* magazine article written by Jerry Hatfield about the overhead-cam Prince prototype.
43. http://indianmotocycle.webs.com/earlynewspaperarticles.htm, sighted on 21 August 2010.
44. This phrase is attributable to one-time Indian dealer Rollie Free
45. Newspaper clippings about Jim Jones, and the original contract with Indian, are held in the Esta Manthos Indian Motocycle Archives, Lyman and Merrie Wood Museum of Springfield History.
46. This information about Franklin's Roamer comes from the recollections of Thomas Callaghan Butler.
47. To find out more about the 101 Association, direct your web browser to www.101association.com.

Index

Ace motorcycle — 134, 269, 280-282
AJS motorcycle — 174, 196, 200, 205, 213, 220
Alexander, Jimmy — 60, 61, 84, 100, 104
Altoona race motor — 192, 241, 243, 273-274, 282, 314
Anderson, Paul — 243-251
Applebee, Frank — 51, 77, 85, 100, 217
Arpajon, France — 245, 247-248, 250
Auto Cycle Union — 69, 260
Balke, Charles 'Fearless' — 98
Ballycastle — 21, 124
Bauer
  Louis — 280, 283, 285, 287
  Jack — 283-284
Bayly, Annie Honor Wrixon — 5, 320, 322-323
Ball bearings (see Self-aligning ball bearings)
Belt-drive — 20, 49, 72, 76, 78
Bennett, Alec — 220
Bennett, Charlie — 60
Bentley, Walter ('W.O.') — 60
Board-track racing — 16, 47, 53, 55, 97, 153, 154, 182, 187
Bolles, Norman — 287, 301
Booth, Jack — 140, 157, 182,
Bosch magneto — 26, 34, 37, 55, 57
Bridgman, Ernie — 223, 228,
Brooklands — 42, 43, 55, 65, 73, 89, 92, 95, 108, 114, 211, 261
Brough Superior — 160, 219, 231, 249
Burns, Albert 'Shrimp' — 180, 187, 191
Butler, Thomas Callaghan — 116, 131, 134, 142, 149, 161, 169, 189, 232, 263, 308
Cahir, Co. Tipperary — 320-322
Camel, The — 215-219
Canning, Leopold — 10, 19, 29
Carroll, Teddy — 179
Chain-drive — 49-50, 55-56, 72, 76, 78, 88, 126, 150, 166, 168
Chater-Lea Company — 26, 27, 38, 44, 313
Chicago Motordrome — 96
Churchill, Winston — 259
Coil ignition — 4, 10, 34, 44, 49, 55
Clarke, Dudley — 60
Clonaleenaghan House, Co. Louth — 6, 31, 323
Clutch (see Free engine clutch)
Clutterbuck — 5, 320-323
Collier
  Charlie — 16, 24, 33, 38, 44, 57, 61, 73, 81, 86, 90-93, 104, 214, 217
  Harry — 16, 33, 42, 57, 61, 104, 214
Coleman, Percy — 178, 182
Compression ratio — 163, 195, 197, 198, 199-206, 251

Constantine, Arthur — 293
Coupe Internationale race — 24
Cradle frame (see Double-loop full cradle frame)
Creg Willies hill — 43, 45, 61
Crocker, Al — 292, 313
Curtis, Glenn — 53, 77, 182
Davidson, Douglas H. — 214, 218, 219, 222, 225
Davies, Howard R. (HRD) — 106, 220, 228, 279, 315
Demester — 24, 29
Dennis, Ivor — 256
De Rosier, Jake — 53 55, 74 80, 84, 89 92, 96 98, 100, 102
Derkum, Paul 'Dare-devil' — 74, 104, 106
Detachable cylinder head — 241, 242, 254, 274
Detonation (see also Pre-ignition) — 195, 198-201, 204, 207, 251
Devil's Elbow hairpin bend — 45, 61
Dirt-track racing — 153, 156, 178, 240, 254, 261, 272, 276
Dixon, Freddie — 213, 220, 222-225, 230, 241, 263
Double-loop full-cradle frame — 170, 233
Drury, Noel — 7, 18, 25, 33, 40, 43, 44, 56, 62, 64, 68, 69, 106, 225
Dublin — 6, 8
Dublin & District Motor Cycle Club — 42, 57, 101, 115, 119, 120, 139, 324
Dublin Indian Depot — 111, 118, 139
Dunlop, John Boyd — 9, 16
Du Pont, E. Paul — 162, 297, 300
Duzmo motorcycle — 213, 226
Dynamometer — 133, 134, 206, 282
Easter Rising — 9, 115, 118, 143, 210
Ebblewhite, E.V. ('Ebby') — 43, 56, 65, 109, 114
Evans, Guy Lee — 55-61, 68-69, 89
Excelsior motorcycle — 96, 97, 116, 149, 154, 178, 181, 190, 193, 206, 238, 267-269, 281, 293, 302
Excelsior-Henderson Four — 267, 282
Super-X 45 cu.in. — 267, 293, 295,
Fafnir engine — 25
Federation of American Motorcyclists — 53, 97,
F-head (see also Side-valve) — 49, 150, 193
FN motorcycle — 10
Fournier, Henri — 48, 53, 311
Fowler, Rembrandt — 38, 44
Franklin
  Lorenzo Snr — 5-7, 13, 231, 320, 322
  Lorenzo Jnr — 6, 31, 37, 38, 100, 115, 132
  Nancye — 38, 119, 161, 209, 231, 239, 264, 266, 288, 308, 320, 323, 326
  Phyllis Enid ('Valerie') — 43, 119, 161, 209, 231, 239, 264-266, 301, 309-310, 326-327
  Robert Jnr — 5-7, 13, 320-325

Rupert Fairfax	6, 19, 21, 31, 100, 320, 322-325
Fredericks, 'Curley'	189, 192, 273, 277
Free-engine clutch	50, 56, 70, 72, 78, 79, 83, 166, 311
Geiger, Martin	39, 68
Godfrey Cup	217, 219, 224
Godfrey, Oliver	51, 57, 58, 74, 84-88, 100, 104, 106, 109, 112, 115, 201, 217
Godfrey's Ltd motorcycle dealers	100
Gordon Bennett Motor Cup race	11, 16, 17, 25, 30, 37
Great Depression	132, 154, 192, 211, 259, 264, 272, 278, 281, 283, 297, 303, 308, 309
Great 500-Mile Race, The	221, 224
Great Portland Street	50, 51, 75, 100, 151, 217, 252
Greenwich Wheelmen cycle club	47
Gustafson	
Charles Snr.	96, 103, 104, 116, 117, 134, 138, 139, 140, 141, 142, 144, 147, 154, 162, 176, 182, 206, 208, 280
Charles Jnr.	96, 140, 154, 180, 208, 251, 297
Harley Davidson motorcycle	
D-model	172, 269, 273, 295,
Eight-valve racer	156, 157, 180, 182, 188, 190, 191, 192, 206, 254
EL-model Knucklehead	278, 289, 299, 317
J-model	116, 149, 150, 170, 203, 283, 293
'Pea-shooter'	255
Servi-car	304, 316
Sport flat-twin	150, 159, 160, 164, 168, 170, 206, 214, 269
Sportster	238, 269, 305, 316
VL-model	162, 273, 293, 302, 304, 316
U-Model	299, 316
Harley, William S.	149, 187, 239, 315
Hartley, Laurence	203, 206, 216
Harveyson, Reuben	213-216, 220, 223-225
Hastings, T.K. ('Teddy')	46, 50
Harley Davidson Motor Company	49, 52, 117, 150, 155, 158, 162, 180, 191, 217, 237, 238, 253, 260, 264, 303, 315
Hedstrom, Carl Oscar	16, 47-50, 53, 60, 74, 89, 96, 102, 103, 147
Hedstrom & Henshaw tandem pacer	47, 48
Helical gears primary drive	168, 233, 268, 294
Hendee, George M.	16, 40, 46-51, 72, 101, 116, 118, 131, 134
Hendee Mfg. Co. Ltd.	46, 49, 52, 101, 132, 134, 239
Hendee Special motorcycle	102
Henshaw, Charles S.	47-48
Hepburn, Ralph	136, 138, 178, 187, 190, 191, 243, 246
Hill-climb racing	154, 238, 275
Holden, George	116
Horsman, Victor	212, 221, 222, 223, 313
Hosley, Lauren F.	297, 300
Ignition (*see* Coil ignition, Bosch magneto)	
Indian automobile	283-284
Indian factory	72, 133, 263, 297, 300
Indian motorcycle	
Ace	280, 290, 299
Blackhawk Chief	312, 328
Bronze-cover two-camshaft single- cylinder race motor	227, 241, 255, 303, 314
Chief	232-238, 263, 270, 289, 299, 301, 304, 306, 328
'Daytona' Powerplus	183, 186, 188, 191, 221, 240, 273, 314, 317
Dispatch-Tow	303
Eight-valve 'Big-base' racer	96, 98, 108, 155, 156, 195, 214, 215, 216, 218, 224, 242
Eight-valve 'Small-base' racer	140, 141, 149, 182, 187,
Featherweight Model K	115, 135-138, 159
Four	263, 278, 280, 282, 283, 290, 292, 297, 299, 304, 316
Four-cam overhead-valve 45 cu in hill-climb motor	272, 274-276
Light Twin Model O	138, 144-147, 159
Power-plus	117, 134, 135, 140, 141, 144, 147, 148, 149, 150, 151, 163, 176, 179, 188-189, 192, 196, 232, 235
Prince	252-259, 293, 306
Scout	161-176, 236,
Scout Forty-five	269-272
Scout Pony	306
Scout Series 101	289-296, 299
Sport Scout	272, 301, 307, 328
Standard Scout	301, 302, 305,
Vertical-twin	312
Inlet-over-exhaust valves (*see also* Side-valve)	116, 193-195, 197, 202
Isle of Man	
Tourist Trophy (TT) Race	34
1907	37-38
1908	43-45
1909	57-59
1910	60-61
1911	74-88
1912	99-100
1913	104
1914	104-106
1920	196, 213
1921	220
1922	224-225
1923	226-230
International Cup race	
1904	24
1905	25-30
1906	32-33
International Six Days Trial	46
Irish Automobile Club	17, 21, 112
Irish Cyclist & Motorcyclist magazine	10
Irish End-to-End Record	11, 21, 124, 317
Ixion	13, 23, 35, 72, 88, 106, 119, 261
Jarrott, Charles	33, 48, 64, 74
JAP motorcycle engine	25, 26, 32, 33, 45, 62, 219, 224-226, 263
Kerr, Annie Wilson	38, 320
Lancefield, Steve	316
Land Speed Record	12, 182, 250, 317
Lane family	6, 321-322
Lemon, Arthur	134, 281-282, 284, 290, 297
Le Vack, Herbert	108, 115, 160, 182, 212, 213-226, 245, 249-250, 313, 315
Levine, Charles A.	285,
Light Locomotives (Ireland) Bill	12, 17
London Indian Depot	50, 51, 151, 259, 260
Ludlow, Freddy	181, 182, 183, 186, 187

Marion, Indiana, road race	154, 179, 184, 186, 187, 246
Marion frame	179
Marquis de St. Mouzilly de St. Mars	33, 37, 38
Marquis St. Maur	29
Marshall, Jack	38, 44, 57, 194
Matchless motorcycle	16, 24, 33, 38, 42, 44, 57, 73, 78, 84, 90, 93, 100, 217
Maxwell automobile	143,
McKenna Duties	118
McTaggart, W.R.	10, 16, 40, 41
Mecredy, Richard	17
Minerva engine	22, 25, 36, 40, 193
Mizen Head	11, 21, 124
Moorhouse, Arthur	60, 61, 65, 67-69, 80, 84, 85, 95
Montgomery, Bob	21
Motor Car Act 1903	11, 24
Motor Cycle Union of Ireland (M.C.U.I.)	16, 17, 18, 24, 37, 57
Munro, Burt	175
No. 21 Indian racer	75, 78, 80, 89
Norton motorcycle	38, 59, 102, 114, 134, 197, 202, 205, 213, 221, 316
O'Donovan, Dan 'Wizard'	202, 203, 205
Ottaway, William ('Bill')	155, 157, 182, 186, 187
Overhead-cam	179, 196, 206, 257, 259, 311, 314, 315, 317
Overhead-valve	25, 141, 193, 195, 197, 199, 205, 213, 241-242, 251, 253, 255, 257, 269, 272, 277, 315
Page, Valentine	160, 162, 205, 219, 225,
Parsons, Harold	176
Perry, Bob	179, 181
Peugeot	103, 116, 255
Phoenix Park, Dublin	9, 12, 16, 17
Pocket-valve (see also Side-valve)	155, 156, 180, 183, 190, 193, 200
Pool operation	286-287
Portmarnock	17-21, 23, 111-112
Pre-ignition (see also Detonation)	198, 201
Prestwich, John Alfred	25, 44, 62, 224, 225
Prince, Jack	47, 55, 153, 187
Primary drive (see Helical gears primary drive)	
Protectionism	259, 311
Rathmines Electricity Works	7, 20, 70
Reading-Standard motorcycle	116, 140, 149
Redmond, Steve	139
Reliability Trial	10, 17, 19, 24, 46, 138, 153
Rhodes Motors	140, 242, 245, 248, 256, 314
Ricardo, Sir Harry	74, 198, 199, 201, 203-206, 313
Road racing	23, 38, 119, 154, 212, 275, 276
Roamer automobile	288
Rogers, Ralph	312
Rosemount House, Cahir Co. Tipperary	320-321
Rudge motorcycle	104, 197
Saddle tank	144, 278, 279, 293
Schwinn, Ignaz	179, 181, 269, 293, 302
Schulte, Maurice	25, 35, 36, 37
Scott motorcycle	86, 100, 104
Sealy, Oswald	18, 21
Self-aligning ball bearings	227, 241-243
Sellick's Beach, Australia	243, 245, 246, 250
Seymour, Johnny	190, 242, 243, 246, 250, 251
Silver Strand	17, 21, 23
Simms-Bosch magneto	26, 34
Sheldon, James	37, 252
Side-valve	103, 140, 149, 163, 164, 183, 191, 192-207, 214, 220, 226, 27, 241, 248, 249, 254, 269, 272-274, 277, 314-316
Snaefell	25, 37, 56, 62, 77, 83
Speedway racing	145, 243, 260, 261, 263
Springfield Coliseum	16, 47-48
Squish (see also Side-valve)	74, 179, 201-205, 234, 274, 295, 313, 315
St Andrews College	6, 324
Steele, Orie	239, 249, 277
'Streamline'	278, 293, 299, 302, 311, 316
Sunbeam motorcycle	106, 166, 197, 213, 220, 225, 227, 230
Tandem pacer	47-48, 53,
Temple, Claude F.	214, 218, 221, 224, 247
Tetra-ethyl lead	206, 251
Thousand Mile Reliability Trial	46, 50
TT races (see Isle of Man Tourist Trophy)	
Turner, Edward	162, 170
Triumph motorcycle	14, 22, 25, 34-36, 44, 49, 52, 57, 59, 78, 102, 213, 221, 222, 252
Truffault forks	40, 41
Variable gears	37, 50, 72, 77, 78, 88
Velvet Strand	17, 23, 94, 111, 112
Vindec Special motorcycle	38-42, 50
Vondrich, Vaclav	29, 112
Waite, J. Russell	285, 287
Wallace, P.J. 'John'	65, 213, 214
Walker, Gene	179, 180, 182-184, 187, 189-190, 240
Walker, Otto	179-181, 186, 187
Weishaar, Ray	178, 184, 191, 240
Wells	
George Hendee	51, 151, 260, 325
William Huntingdon ('Billy')	38-41, 42, 44, 50-51, 57, 74, 100, 105, 108, 118, 135, 138, 142, 151, 162, 213, 219, 224, 226, 239, 259-263
Weschler, Frank	116, 117, 134, 140, 142, 147, 209, 239, 269, 279-280, 285, 286, 307, 312, 323
Wigwam, The	72, 132-134, 148, 297
Wolters, Joe 'Farmer Boy'	96-98, 155, 181
Wolverton, 'Red'	281
Woods, Stanley	324
Worcester Cycle Manufacturing Co. Ltd.	48
Zenith-JAP motorcycle	219, 225, 226, 231